Alternate Names
of Places

D0902952

ALSO BY ADRIAN ROOM
AND FROM McFARLAND

*African Placenames: Origins and Meanings of the Names
for Natural Features, Towns, Cities, Provinces and Countries,* 2d ed. (2008)

The Pronunciation of Placenames: A Worldwide Dictionary (2007)

*Nicknames of Places: Origins and Meanings of the Alternate and Secondary Names,
Sobriquets, Titles, Epithets and Slogans for 4600 Places Worldwide* (2006)

*Placenames of the World: Origins and Meanings of the Names for 6,600 Countries,
Cities, Territories, Natural Features and Historic Sites,* 2d ed. (2006)

Dictionary of Pseudonyms: 11,000 Assumed Names and Their Origins, 4th ed. (2004)

*Placenames of France: Over 4,000 Towns, Villages,
Natural Features, Regions and Departments* (2004; paperback 2009)

Encyclopedia of Corporate Names Worldwide (2002; paperback 2008)

*A Dictionary of Art Titles: The Origins of the
Names and Titles of 3,000 Works of Art* (2000; paperback 2008)

*A Dictionary of Music Titles: The Origins of the
Names and Titles of 3,500 Musical Compositions* (2000; paperback 2008)

*Literally Entitled: A Dictionary of the Origins of
the Titles of Over 1,300 Major Literary Works
of the Nineteenth and Twentieth Centuries* (1996; paperback 2009)

*Placenames of Russia and the Former Soviet Union:
Origins and Meanings of the Names for Over 2,000
Natural Features, Towns, Regions and Countries* (1996)

*The Naming of Animals: An Appellative Reference to Domestic,
Work and Show Animals Real and Fictional* (1993)

*Corporate Eponymy: A Biographical Dictionary of the
Persons Behind the Names of Major American,
British, European and Asian Businesses* (1992)

Alternate Names of Places

A Worldwide Dictionary

ADRIAN ROOM

McFarland & Company, Inc., Publishers
Jefferson, North Carolina, and London

LIBRARY OF CONGRESS CATALOGUING-IN-PUBLICATION DATA

Room, Adrian.
Alternate names of places : a worldwide dictionary / Adrian Room.
p.   cm.
Includes bibliographical references.

ISBN 978-0-7864-3712-2
softcover : 50# alkaline paper ∞

1. Gazetteers.   I. Title.
G105.R648   2009   910.3 — dc22   2009017992

British Library cataloguing data are available

On the cover: Green hills near Golden Bay, South Island, New Zealand;
globe; both ©2009 Shutterstock

Manufactured in the United States of America

*McFarland & Company, Inc., Publishers
Box 611, Jefferson, North Carolina 28640
www.mcfarlandpub.com*

Contents

Introduction

This new type of geographical dictionary lists the alternate names, current and historical, by which over 7,000 places in the world are or have been known. (The actual number of alternate names is nearer 9,000, since many places have or had more than one such name.)

For the purposes of this record, an alternate name is one that bears or bore an official or at least a semiofficial status, rather than being simply a nickname or a colloquial abbreviation.

An alternate name may be a respelling, as when a name is restored to a correct form from a corrupt original, or it may even be in a completely different language, as when one country is occupied or conquered by another, a fate that historically befell many European states.

Not all name changes are the result of hostilities. Sometimes settlers in virgin territory find it hard to decide on a suitable name for their place of settlement. There are thus places in the United States that have undergone more than one change of name, such as *Glen Ellyn*, Illinois, which finally arrived at its present name after a run of six successive earlier names.

The choice of a new name for a place may be politically motivated, as the hundreds of towns and villages renamed in the former Soviet Union. Here two birds were often killed with one stone, since an undesirable or politically incorrect name could be abolished and replaced with a new politically correct one, which often as not bore no relationship to the earlier name. In some cases, a new name was not even associated with the place in question. Many Soviet places were simply given a generally Communist name, typically with the element *Krasno-*, "red," to reflect the new regime, while others were renamed for Lenin or Stalin without any local connection with these leaders. Some such renamings remain on the map today, almost 20 years after the demise of the Soviet state.

Ideological renaming of this kind was not confined to the USSR, and some towns elsewhere in the Socialist bloc took on new names, such as Hungary's *Dunaújváros*, which for a decade was *Sztálinváros*, or the former East Germany's *Chemnitz*, which for almost forty years was on the map as *Karl-Marx-Stadt*. There were few such renamings in Poland, a country recast with German placenames during World War II, but from 1946 to 1992 the city of *Podgorica* in the former Yugoslavia honored the republic's first president as *Titograd*.

In countries of central and eastern Europe such as these, a new name was often based on a previous name, which was either adapted to the succeeding new language or where possible translated into it. Thus the Slovakian town of *Nové Mesto nad Váhom*, with a name meaning "new town on the Váh," for the river on which it lies, was earlier known by the Hungarian name *Vágújhely* and German name *Waag-Neustadt*, with "new town" translated into the superseding language and the form of the river name accommodated to it.

Many places around the world have roots that go deep into history, with an original name in a now extinct language. Names of biblical origin are often of this type, as are the numerous places in the Roman Empire with Latin names. Such names, marked "Roman" in the present book rather than "Latin," in turn are often of earlier origin, dating back several centuries BC to a defunct language such as ancient Greek or Phoenician. The Roman names of places in France are thus often Gallo-Roman, and based on Gaulish, a Celtic language.

In countries with a colonial heritage there can be a complete change of language, with a native name replaced by a European one, itself in more recent times either reverting to its indigenous original or assuming a new native form. Not many European names remain today on the map of Africa, although English names are still a significant presence in countries such as Australia and New Zealand, despite the prevalence of native names, here respectively Aboriginal and Maori. An analogous situation exists in the United States and Canada, where names of European origin in languages such as English, French, and Spanish remain widespread on the map amongst the numerous Indian names. In South America, and especially Latin America, Spanish and Portuguese names are visibly in evidence today as replacements for historical Indian names. It goes without saying, of course, that not *all* European placenames in countries with a colonial past are substitutions for native names, as a good number of such names are those of newly-founded settlements.

In many countries today more than one language is spoken, so that places officially bear two names. Thus, places in Belgium often bear both French and Flemish names, while places in Ireland are known by an English name and an Irish and places in Wales by an English name and a Welsh. In Belgium, the official form of the name is usually French in the south and Flemish in the north and east, while in Ireland the Irish and English names

exist in tandem, but with English usually being the official form. (Irish equivalents for names in Northern Ireland exist but are generally not official. They are included in the dictionary, however. In this respect, care is needed in differentiating between "northern Ireland," in the Irish Republic, and "Northern Ireland," as part of the United Kingdom.) In Wales, English still mostly predominates, but the Welsh names are invariably used in Welsh-language texts, as in the media and official legislation. Most places in Scotland have equivalent Gaelic names (listed in Edward Dwelly's *Illustrated Gaelic-English Dictionary*) but in regular use retain the English forms of their names. An exception is the Gaelic-speaking Western Isles, where the town of *Stornoway* now officially appears on maps in its Gaelic guise of *Steornabagh*, as do most villages and natural features, including the islands themselves. (Many of these names are not actually Gaelic in origin but Scandinavian, so that the Gaelic form is simply a respelling. *Stornoway* itself is one such.)

In the Basque Country of northern Spain and southwestern France, places are now often known by their Basque names in addition to, or instead of, their respective Spanish or French names. A similar situation applies in Brittany, northwestern France, where Breton names are often bracketed with their French equivalents, while in Catalonia, northeastern Spain, Catalan names are now regularly given pride of place on the map, in acknowledgment of the region's status as an autonomous community. In Switzerland some places have as many as four different forms of name in each of the country's official languages, French, German, Italian, and Romansh, this last being the local language.

For the purposes of this dictionary, alternate current names are often not simply variant spellings but distinctively different. Thus, the name of *La Guajira*, a department of northeastern Colombia, is also spelled *La Goajira* and *La Goagira*, but these are basically one and the same name, not significant alternates. The same goes for names that are essentially a shorter version of an original much longer name. In such cases the present name is exactly the same as the main part of the historical name, so is not a true alternate. Many colonial Spanish and Portuguese names in the Americas began life as an impressive religious dedication, incorporating a saint's name, but today only the basic name or word remains. Such are Argentina's *San Pedro de Jujuy*, now usually *San Pedro*, Uruguay's *Santo Domingo de Soriano*, now *Soriano*, and Brazil's *São Miguel de Jucurutu*, now normally *Jucurutu*. Names of this type are generally absent from the dictionary. But where an earlier lengthy name has now been superseded by a different shorter one, they duly feature. Brazil's *Santo Antônio de Leverger* has a name previously shortened to *Leverger* and before that *Santo Antônio*, but it originated as *Santo Antônio do Rio Abaixo*. Its name has thus changed and is therefore included. Where a well-known name in one of these two languages has an interesting origin, however, it is generally included. A famous example is California's *Los Angeles*, which began life as *El Pueblo de la Reyna de Los Angeles* on a river that the Spanish christened *Porciúncula* in honor of *Nuestra Señora la Reyna de los Angeles de Porciúncula*, "Our Lady the Queen of Angels of the Little Portion." Today the city's name has reduced even further to a colloquial *LA*.

A broad range of places have abandoned a colonial name in favor of an indigenous one, from towns and cities in Africa, such as *Harare*, formerly *Salisbury*, and *Lubumbashi*, formerly *Élisabethville*, to South Pacific islands such as *Fatu Hiva*, formerly *Magdalena Island*, and *Nanumanga*, formerly *Hudson Island*. In such cases, however official and publicly promoted the name change, the old name often continues in general use alongside the new. If the inhabitants of a place, or those familiar with it, have long known it by a particular name which is then replaced by another, a situation is created in which alternate names become current, sometimes for years, and certainly long enough to feature on maps and in gazetteers, even if the old name is regarded as secondary and is printed in parenthesis. Some atlases retain the old name for the physical or geographic map of a region, giving the new name in the political map. Thus, *Philip's Great World Atlas* (see Select Bibliography, p. 255) shows the location of the *New Hebrides* in its physical map of Australia and Oceania, but names the island republic *Vanuatu* in the corresponding political map.

The traditional English spelling of well-known names also persists in general use, even in the media and works of reference. Thus, *The Times Style and Usage Guide*, published in 2003, recommends such spellings as *Dunkirk*, *Gothenburg*, and *Lyons*, as well as the conventionally accepted *Brussels*, *Cologne*, and *Venice*, while the 11th edition of *The Chambers Dictionary*, published as recently as 2008, described the World War I Western Front as a belt of land running from the Belgian coast "through Rheims to Verdun." Not surprisingly, the anomalous situation forms a recurring topic of discussion in the press.

Entries in the dictionary give the current name, location, and description of the place followed by its one or more present or past alternate names, preceded by qualifying words such as "formerly," "conventional," "originally," and in the case of former names by a date, where known, of the relevant name change. Names beginning with a numeral are located alphabetically as if the numeral were spelled out in the language concerned. Thus, *26 Bakinskikh Kommunarov, imeni* is located between *Duzkend* and *Dvigatel'stroy* since the numeral represents Russian *dvadtsat' shest'*, "twenty-six." The same applied to names containing a numeral other than as the first word. Thus, *Pio IX* is located between *Pionersky* and *Piotrków Trybunalski*, since the (Roman) numeral represents Portuguese *nono*, "ninth."

The geographical location of a place is

usually given as a "compass" indication in the country concerned, as "eastern France," "northwestern Turkey," "southern Russia." In extensive English-speaking countries such as the United States, Canada, and Australia, the place is additionally located by state, province, or other administrative region. It should be noted that the "compass" indication is that of the place in the country, rather than that of the administrative region, although the two may coincide. For example, *Cambridge Bay* is in northern Canada in the territory of Nunavut, while *Cape Dorset*, also in Nunavut, is in northeastern Canada. The disparity occurs because Nunavut itself is a large region. Where the named region is smaller, as one of the northeastern states of the USA, the geographical location will tally with that of the place within the country as a whole. Thus *Lackawanna*, in the northeastern state of New York, is in the northeast of the United States, but *San Diego*, in the western state of California, the third-largest state in the country, is more precisely in the southwest of the United States rather than simply in the west of the country.

In cases where places of identical name are located in the same geographical section of a country and are not otherwise distinguished by administrative region, a more exact pin-pointing is given by means of "near" and the name of a local town or city. This typically occurs in Russia, where for example there are two places *Donskoye* in the western part of the country, one near Kaliningrad, the other near Lipetsk. (Administrative regions are not given in non–English-speaking countries, even in extensive lands such as Russia, as these may be of little significance to the general English-speaking reader, who in this particular case would need to "place" the *oblasti* of Kaliningrad and Lipetsk, named for their respective capitals.) It should be observed that former names in eastern Russia identified as Japanese are almost exclusively in the southern half of the Kamchatka peninsula and the

southern Kuril Islands, territory which passed to Japan following the Russo-Japanese War of 1904–05.

Where the name includes a generic term such as "Islands" or "Mt." this is not repeated in the description, so that for example *Bonin Islands* and *McKinley, Mt.* simply have their respective locations ("western Pacific," "Alaska, northwestern United States"). The designations "village," "town," and "city" do not denote official status but define a place in terms of approximate size of population, so that "village" denotes a small community with under 3,000 residents, "town" a larger settlement with up to 20,000 inhabitants, and "city" a center with a population greater than this. Similarly, status titles such as "capital" or "center of government" are not used, although countries that are republics are designated as such.

In the main part of the entry, a date preceded by the word "to" indicates either that an original name was current up to or through that date or else that the name was in use over an unspecified period some time before the stated year. It should be noticed that the dates run *in reverse chronological order*, with the most recent former name given first and the earliest last. Thus *Dearborn*, Michigan, was formerly known as *Dearbornville*; then before that *Pekin*; then before that *Bucklin*; and ultimately, as its original name, *Ten Eyck*. Where a name was current over two separate historical periods, however, the dates run chronologically. Thus, *Beijing* (formerly *Peking*) was known as *Peiping* from 1368 to 1403 and again from 1928 to 1949, and these two periods are given in normal sequence. In a few cases, where a name switches more than once from one language to another, the recurring name is repeated for sake of clarity. Thus, the city of *Cahul* in Moldova, known when in the Soviet Union by the Russian name *Kagul*, bore its present Romanian name from 1919 to 1940, its Russian name before that from 1878 to 1918, its Romanian name before that from 1856 to 1878, and its Russian name before that from 1812 to 1856. The entry thus reads: 1919–1940 Romanian *Cahul*, 1878–1918 Russian *Kagul*, 1868–1878 Romanian *Cahul*, 1812–1856 Russian *Kagul*.

The dates themselves are frequently a significant pointer to historical events, especially in Europe. Thus, 1809 was the year when Sweden ceded Finland to Russia, resulting in wholesale renaming, while the recurring date 1878 marks the Congress of Berlin at the end of the Russo-Turkish War, following an era during which the declining Ottoman Empire fought a series of wars with Poland, Austria, and Russia. That year saw the establishment of Bulgaria as an autonomous principality and the beginning of that country's abandonment of the Turkish placenames that had hitherto existed. The wholesale bulgarization of such names, however, did not take place until 1934, following the installation of Kimon Georgiev as prime minister and the "national restoration" policy of his dictatorial regime.

Dates relating to World War I (1914–18) and World War II (1939–45) usually involve the invasion and occupation of one country by another or, conversely, a peace treaty ending hostilities and establishing a new territorial order. Poland, for example, was occupied by Germany in both world wars and invaded by Soviet armies during the latter. The language names "German," "Polish," and "Russian," among others, appear regularly over this period.

As stated, not all new names were created as a result of war or oppressive hegemony, and in several instances a renaming marked the achievement of autonomy. Greenland, still today an integral part of the Danish realm, changed most of its names from Danish to Greenlandic when the island was granted home rule in 1979, and many of the towns and cities in northeastern South Africa abandoned their Afrikaans or English names in favor of African ones from the 1990s. In northern Canada, English names were largely replaced by Inuit (Eskimo) ones following the creation of the territory of Nunavut in 1999 from the eastern region of the Northwest Territories. In eastern Europe and central Asia new names appeared in most of the former Soviet republics as they celebrated independence in or soon after 1991, the year that brought the collapse of the Soviet Union as a whole.

Placenames in the USSR usually became known to the world in their Russian forms, even where the local language was not even Slavonic. In such cases, the Russian forms are given in round brackets (parentheses). Names in a local language differing from the accepted English form of the name are by contrast given in square brackets. Thus the country called by the English *Latvia* is known to the Latvians as *Latvija* (in square brackets), was known to the Russians when in the Soviet Union as *Latviya* (in round brackets), and when under German rule was named *Lettland* (unbracketed). Former Russian names are mostly given for places in countries speaking a language closely allied to Russian, as particularly Ukraine and Belarus. In these countries there may thus be little difference between the names in the respective languages, and they will require careful distinction.

As a matter of linguistic precision, it should be noted that an apostrophe in a Russian name represents a soft sign, a character (denoting palatalization of the preceding consonant) often omitted in transcription. But in Ukrainian and Belorussian the apostrophe is an integral part of the orthography, and should properly never be omitted. In the present book, the apostrophe thus appears in names in all three languages.

A special situation applies to alternate placenames in China, where names have two forms. The traditional way of romanizing Chinese names is the so-called Wade-Giles system, devised in the mid–19th century by two British scholars, Thomas Wade and Herbert Giles. Distinguished by its use of hyphens and apostrophes, the latter denoting aspiration in consonants, it produced such names as *Hei-lung-chiang*, *Liao-ning*, *Nan-ch'ang*, and *Ch'ing-hai*. This contrasts with the prevalent Pinyin (literally, "spell sound") system, adopted from 1956 and now officially prescribed for English-speaking countries. Examples of Pinyin names with their Wade-Giles equivalents are *Chang-zhi* (*Ch'ang-chih*), *Guiyang* (*Kuei-yang*), *Nan-tong* (*Nan-t'ung*), and *Xiantan* (*Hsiang-t'an*). The name for China itself is *Zhongguo* or *Zhonghua* in Pinyin, *Chung-kuo* or *Chung-hua* in Wade-Giles. The present book uses Pinyin, but for its particular purpose does not treat the two forms of names as alternates. Such pairs could alone make up a gazetteer of their own. This does not mean that Chinese names are altogether excluded, since some have traditional English forms (as *Nanking* for *Nan-jung*) and others, as elsewhere, have historical forms (as *Nanning*, formerly *Yongning*).

Several entries have appended comments. The purpose of such additions is either to provide information regarding the circumstances of a name change or to explain the origin or meaning of a name where this is relevant to such a change. Sometimes an important event such as a battle or treaty has resulted in the historical survival of an earlier name, and in such cases the key facts are provided. The battle of *Eylau* in the Napoleonic Wars was thus waged near the Russian village now known as *Bagrationovsk*, and that of *Königgrätz*, in the Austro-Prussian War, around the Czech town now named *Hradec Králové*.

A key feature of the dictionary is the cross-references. These necessarily outnumber the main entries, since as stated some places have more than one present or past alternate name. Names mentioned in an entry's appended comment are also cross-referenced.

Since language plays a significant role in alternate names, Appendix I, p. 235, lists a selection of names of well-known places in languages other than English, if only because modern atlases, maps, and gazetteers give preference to the local name of a place, rather than its traditional English form. As explained in the preamble to this Appendix, the languages chosen for this purpose belong to different linguistic families.

Appendix II, p. 246, is devoted to a special category of alternate names, as a selection of fictional names of places, meaning not fictional places, but real places known in literature by fictional names. The names of the authors in whose work or works these names appear are also given. In a few noteworthy cases, a place has officially adopted its fictional name, either by a name change or by adding the literary name to its real name. Thus Oliver Goldsmith's "Sweet Auburn! loveliest village of the plain" gave not only the name of the village in Ireland but also the names of several *Auburns* in the United States. In France, the town of *Illiers* added *Combray*, Marcel Proust's name for it, to become *Illiers-Combray*.

The Select Bibliography that closes the dictionary (p. 255) lists works directly related to alternate placenames, from discursive studies to modern and historical gazetteers and atlases.

Stamford, Lincolnshire, England
Summer 2009

THE DICTIONARY

Aabenraa *see* **Åbenrå**

Aachen (city, western Germany) : formerly French *Aix-la-Chapelle*; Roman *Aquae Grani*; alternate Roman *Aquisgranum* (The French name is associated with the treaties of 1668, ending the War of Devolution, and of 1748, ending the War of Succession. In 1818 the city hosted the Conference of the Holy Alliance, or Congress of Aix-la-Chapelle.)

Aalborg *see* **Ålborg**

Aalst (city, west central Belgium) : French *Alost*

Aargau (canton, northern Switzerland) : French *Argovie*

Aarhus *see* **Århus**

Aarlen *see* **Arlon**

Aasiaat (town, western Greenland) : formerly Danish *Egedesminde*

Aat *see* **Ath**

Abakan (town, southern Russia) : 1925–1931 *Khakassk*; to 1925 *Ust'-Abakanskoye*

Abakanskoye *see* **Krasnoturansk**

Abakansko-Zavodskoye *see* **Abaza**

Abakumova *see* **Dzhansugurov**

¹Abay (city, east central Kazakhstan) : to 1961 *Churubay-Nura*

²Abay (town, southern Kazakhstan) : formerly *Abay-Bazar*

Abay *see* **Karaul**

Abaya, Lake (southern Ethiopia) : formerly Italian *Lake Margherita*

Abay-Bazar *see* **²Abay**

Abaza (town, southern Russia) : formerly *Abakansko-Zavodskoye* (The present name is an abbreviated form of the lengthy original, comprising the initial syllables of its two parts.)

Abbatis Villa *see* **¹Abbeville**

Abbazia *see* **Opatija**

¹Abbeville (town, northern France) : Roman *Abbatis Villa*

²Abbeville (town, Louisiana, southern United States) : originally *La Chapelle*

Abbeyleix (town, east central Ireland) : Irish *Mainistir Laoise*

Abdalyar *see* **Lachin**

Abdera *see* **Adra**

Abegweit *see* **Prince Edward Island**

Abellinum *see* **Avellino**

Abemama (atoll, western Kiribati) : formerly *Roger Simpson Island*

Åbenrå (city, southern Denmark) : alternate *Aabenraa*; 1864–1920 German *Apenrade*

Aberafan *see* **Aberavon**

Aberavon (village, southern Wales) : Welsh *Aberafan* (The village is now a district of Port Talbot.)

Aberbrothock *see* **Arbroath**

Abercorn *see* (1) **Mbala**; (2) **Shamva**

Aberdâr *see* **Aberdare**

Aberdare (town, southern Wales) : Welsh *Aberdâr*

Aberdaugleddau *see* **Milford Haven**

Aberdovey (town, western Wales) : Welsh *Aberdyfi*

Aberdyfi *see* **Aberdovey**

Abergavenny (town, southeastern Wales) : Welsh *Y Fenni*; Roman *Gobannium*

Abergwaun *see* **Fishguard**

Aberhonddu *see* **Brecon**

Abermo *see* **Barmouth**

Aberpennar *see* **Mountain Ash**

Abertawe *see* **Swansea**

Aberteifi *see* **Cardigan**

Abilene (town, Kansas, central United States) : to c.1860 *Mud Creek*

Abingdon Island *see* **Pinta, Isla**

Ableman *see* **Rock Springs**

Åbo *see* **Turku**

Abona *see* (1) **Avon**; (2) **Sea Mills**

Abovyan (town, central Armenia) : to 1963 *Elar*

Abrene *see* **Pytalovo**

Abu Simbel (village, southern Egypt) : alternate *Abu Sunbul*

Abu Sunbul *see* **Abu Simbel**

Abyssinia *see* Ethiopia

Acadia (historic territory, eastern North America) : 1604–1713 French *Acadie* (Acadia was centered on Nova Scotia, Canada, but also included New Brunswick, Prince Edward Island, and a coastal area extending as far south as Maine, USA.)

Acadie *see* Acadia

Acate (village, southern Italy) : to *c.*1937 *Biscari*

Accadînlar *see* Dulovo

Accho *see* Acre

Acelum *see* Asolo

Acerra (town, southern Italy) : Roman *Acerrae*

Acerrae *see* Acerra

Achadh an Iúir *see* Virginia

Achadh na Gréine *see* ³Auburn

Achelous (river, central Greece) : alternate ancient Greek *Aspropotamos*

Achkhoy-Martan (village, southwestern Russia) : 1944–*c.*1965 *Novosel'skoye*

Açores *see* Azores

A Coruña *see* La Coruña

Acquackanonk *see* Passaic

Acqui Terme (town, northwestern Italy) : Roman *Aquae Statiellae*

Acraephnium *see* Karditsa

Acre (city, northern Israel) : [Hebrew *'Akko*]; formerly French *St.-Jean d'Acre*; ancient Greek and biblical (New Testament) *Ptolemais*; earlier biblical (Old Testament) *Accho* (The city's name is associated with several historic sieges including the unsuccessful French one of 1799.)

Acunum *see* Montélimar

Adams (town, Massachusetts, northeastern United States) : to 1778 *East Hoosuck*

Adam's Peak (mountain, south central Sri Lanka) : Singhalese *Samanala*

Adana *see* Aden

Ad Dakhla *see* Dakhla

Ad Dawḩah *see* Doha

Ad Dijlah *see* Tigris

Adélie Coast (region, eastern Antarctica) : alternate *Adélie Land*

Adélie Land *see* Adélie Coast

Adelnau *see* Odolanów

Adelphi *see* Arkansas City

Adelsberg *see* Postojna

Aden (city, southern Yemen) : Roman *Adana* (Some biblical scholars have identified the *Eden* of Ezekiel 27:23 with Aden.)

Adernò *see* Adrano

Adîncata *see* Hlyboka

Adıyaman (city, southeastern Turkey) : to 1926 *Hüsnümansur*

Adra (town, southeastern Spain) : Roman *Abdera*

Adramyttium *see* Edremit

Adrano (town, southern Italy) : to 1929 *Adernò*; Roman *Hadranum*

Adria (town, northeastern Italy) : Roman *Atria*

Adria *see* Adriatic Sea

Adrianople *see* Edirne

Adrianopolis *see* Edirne

Adrianoupolis *see* Edirne

Adriatic Sea (southern Europe) : Roman *Adria*; alternate Roman *Mare Adriaticum*

Adygeysk (town, southwestern Russia) : 1976–1992 *Teuchezhsk*

Adzhibakul *see* Qazimāmmād

Aegidia *see* Koper

Aegium *see* Aíyion

Aegyptus *see* Egypt

Aelana *see* Aqaba

Aelia Capitolina *see* Jerusalem

Aemilianum *see* Millau

Aemilian Way *see* Via

Aeminium *see* Coimbra

Aenaria *see* Ischia

Aenona *see* Nin

Aenos *see* Enez

Aeoliae Insulae *see* Lipari Islands

Aeolian Islands *see* Lipari Islands

Aesernia *see* Isernia

Aesis *see* Jesi

Aethalia *see* Elba

Afars and Issas *see* Djibouti

Affreville *see* Khemis Miliana

Afonso Pena *see* Conceição do Almeida

Agadès *see* Agadez

Agadez (city, west central Niger) : formerly French *Agadès*

Agatha *see* Agde

Agawam *see* Ipswich

Agbulakh *see* Tetri-Tskaro

Agde (town, southern France) : ancient Greek *Agatha*

Agedincum *see* Sens

Agen (town, southwestern France) : Roman *Aginnum*

Agincourt (village, northern France) : French *Azincourt* (The English name is associated with the battle of 1415 in which the English won a famous victory over the French.)

Aginnum *see* Agen

Agnetendorf *see* Jagniątków

Agosta *see* ¹Augusta

Agra and Oudh, United Provinces of *see* Uttar Pradesh

Agram *see* Zagreb

Ağrı Dağı *see* Ararat

Agrigento (town, southern Italy) : to 1927 *Girgenti*; Roman *Agrigentum*

Agrigentum *see* **Agrigento**

Agrínion (town, west central Greece) : formerly *Vrakhóri*

Agua Caliente *see* **Palm Springs**

Aguaí (city, southeastern Brazil) : to 1944 *Cascavel*

Agüecha *see* **Ahuachapán**

Agylla *see* **Cerveteri**

Ahaggar (mountains, southern Algeria) : alternate conventional *Hoggar*

Ahfir (town, northeastern Morocco) : to *c.*1959 *Martimprey-du-Kiss*

Ahmadabad (city, northwestern India) : alternate *Ahmedabad*

Ahmadnagar (city, west central India) : alternate *Ahmednagar*

Ahmedabad *see* **Ahmadabad**

Ahmednagar *see* **Ahmadnagar**

Ahuachapán (city, western El Salvador) : formerly *Agüecha*; originally *Güeciapam*

Ahunui (atoll, central French Polynesia) : formerly *Byam Martin Island*

Ahvenanmaa *see* **Åland**

Aigues-Mortes (town, southern France) : Roman *Aquae Mortuae*

Aïn Azel (town, northeastern Algeria) : to *c.*1962 French *Ampère*

Aïn Beïda (town, northeastern Algeria) : to *c.*1962 French *Daoud*

Aïn Beniane (town, northern Algeria) : to *c.*1962 French *Guyotville*

Aïn Berda (town, northeastern Algeria) : to *c.*1962 French *Penthièvre*

Aïn Defla (town, northern Algeria) : to *c.*1962 French *Duperré*

Aïn el Hammam (town, northern Algeria) : to *c.*1962 French *Michelet*

Aïn el Kebira (town, northeastern Algeria) : to *c.*1962 French *Périgotville*

Aïn Makhlouf (town, northeastern Algeria) : to *c.*1962 French *Renier*

Aïn Mokra *see* **Berrahal**

Ainos *see* **Enez**

Aïn Oulmene (town, northeastern Algeria) : to *c.*1962 French *Colbert*

Aintab *see* **Gaziantep**

Aïn Tagourit (village, northern Algeria) : to *c.*1962 French *Bérard*

Aïn Tolba (village, northwestern Algeria) : to *c.*1962 French *De Malherbe*

Aïn Touta (town, northeastern Algeria) : to *c.*1962 French *MacMahon*

Airds *see* **Campbelltown**

Aire-sur-l'Adour (town, southwestern France) : Roman *Vicus Julii*

Aisne (river, northern France) : Roman *Axona*

Aix-en-Provence (city, southeastern France) : Roman *Aquae Sextiae*

Aix-la-Chapelle *see* **Aachen**

Aix-les-Bains (town, eastern France) : Roman *Aquae Gratianae*

Aíyion (city, southwestern Greece) : Roman *Aegium*

Aizkraukle (town, south central Latvia) : 1967–1991 *Stuchka*; to 1967 Russian *imeni Petra Stuchki*

Aizpute (town, western Latvia) : to 1918 German *Hasenpoth*

Ajemler *see* **Aksakovo**

Ajo (town, Arizona, southwestern United States) : originally *Muy Vavi*

Akchi-Karasu *see* **Toktogul**

Akdeniz *see* **Mediterranean Sea**

Akdepe (town, northern Turkmenistan) : formerly Russian *Leninsk*

Akhali Ap'oni (town, northwestern Georgia) : (Russian *Novy Afon*); to 1948 *Psirtskha*

Akhisar (city, western Turkey) : biblical *Thyatira*

Akhisar *see* **Krujë**

Akhmīm (city, east central Egypt) : Roman *Chemmis*, ancient Greek *Panopolis*

Akhta *see* **Hrazdan**

Akhunbabayev (town, eastern Uzbekistan) : to 1975 *Sufikishlak*

Akhuryan (village, northwestern Armenia) : to 1945 *Duzkend*

Akkadınlar *see* **Dulovo**

Akkadünlar *see* **Dulovo**

Akkerman *see* **Bilhorod-Dnistrovs'kyy**

'Akko *see* **Acre**

Akkol' (town, northern Kazakhstan) : formerly Russian *Alekseyevka*

Akku (village, northeastern Kazakhstan) : formerly Russian *Lebyazh'ye*

Ak-Mechet' *see* (1) **Chornomors'ke**; (2) **Kyzylorda**; (3) **Simferopol**

Akmola *see* **Astana**

Akmolinsk *see* **Astana**

Akpalanka *see* **Bela Palanka**

Akra-Leuka *see* **Alicante**

Aksakovo (town, eastern Bulgaria) : to 1934 Turkish *Ajemler*

Aksay (town, northwestern Kazakhstan) : formerly *Kazakhstan* [sic]

Akşehir (town west central Turkey) : ancient Greek *Philomelion*

Ak-Sheikh *see* **Rozdol'ne**

¹Aksu (town, northeastern Kazakhstan) : formerly *Yermak*

²Aksu (town, southern Kazakhstan) : formerly Russian *Belyye Vody*

Aksum (town, northern Ethiopia) : alternate *Axum*; Roman *Axumis*

Aktau (city, western Kazakhstan) : 1964–1991 Russian *Shevchenko*

Aktobe (city, northwestern Kazakhstan) : to 1991 Russian *Aktyubinsk*

Aktogay (town, northeastern Kazakhstan) : formerly Russian *Krasnokutsk*

Aktsyabrski (town, south central Belarus) : (Russian *Oktyabr'sky*); formerly *Karpilovka*

Aktyubinsk *see* **Aktobe**

Akyab *see* **Sittwe**

Alagoa de Baixo *see* **Sertânia**

Alagoa Nova (city, northeastern Brazil) : 1939–1943 *Laranjeiras*

Alagoas *see* **Marechal Deodoro**

Alais *see* **Alès**

Åland (islands, southwestern Finland) : alternate Finnish *Ahvenanmaa* (The Swedish name is more widely used, although the islands have been part of Finland since 1917.)

Alanskoye (village, southwestern Russia) : to 1944 *Psedakh*

Al 'Arabīyah as-Sa'ūdīyah *see* **Saudi Arabia**

Al 'Arīsh (town, northeastern Egypt) : Roman *Rhinocolura*

Alaşehir (city, western Turkey) : ancient Greek *Philadelphia*

Al Ashmunein (village, north central Egypt) : ancient Greek *Hermopolis Magna*

Alaska (state, northwestern United States) : 1799–1867 *Russian America* (The former name, denoting territory held by Russia, applied mainly to Alsaka and the Aleutian Islands but also took in settlements on the Pacific coast as far south as Fort Ross, California.)

Alaska Highway (road, northwestern North America) : formerly *Alcan Highway*

Alatri (town, central Italy) : Roman *Aletrium*

Alauna *see* (1) **Alcester**; (2) **Maryport**

Al-'Ayzarīyah (village, south central West Bank) : biblical *Bethany*

Alba (town, northwestern Italy) : Roman *Alba Pompeia*

Alba *see* (1) **Scotland**; (2) **Warren**

Al Baḥr al-Abyaḍ *see* **Mediterranean Sea**

Al Baḥr al-Aḥmar *see* **Red Sea**

Al Baḥr al-Mutawassiṭ *see* **Mediterranean Sea**

Al Baḥr ar-Rūm *see* **Mediterranean Sea**

Alba Iulia (city, west central Romania) : to 1918 Hungarian *Gyulafehérvár*; to 1867 German *Karlsburg*, earlier German *Weissenburg*; 8th–11th century Slavic *Bălgrad*, Roman *Apulum*

Albania (republic, southern Europe) : [Albanian *Shqipëri*]

¹Albany (city, New York, northeastern United States) : 1652–1664 *Beverwyck*; to 1652 *Fort Orange*

²Albany (town, Western Australia, southwestern Australia) : to 1832 *Frederickstown*

Alba Pompeia *see* **Alba**

Alba Regalis *see* **Székesfehérvár**

Albat *see* **²Kuybysheve**

Albenga (town, northwestern Italy) : Roman *Album Ingaunum*

Albert (town, northern France) : to 1620 *Ancre*

Albert, Lake (central Africa) : 1973–c.1997 *Lake Mobutu Sese Seko*; earlier *Albert Nyanza*

Albert Edward Nyanza *see* **Edward, Lake**

Albert National Park *see* **Virunga National Park**

Albert Nyanza *see* **Albert, Lake**

Albertville *see* **Kalemie**

Albi (town, southern France) : Roman *Albiga*

Albicella *see* **Ávila**

Albiga *see* **Albi**

Albion *see* **Great Britain**

Albion Mines *see* **Stellarton**

Al Bīrah (village, central West Bank) : biblical *Beeroth*

Ålborg (city, northern Denmark) : alternate *Aalborg*; Medieval Latin *Alburgum*

Album Ingaunum *see* **Albenga**

Albuquerque Lins *see* **Lins**

Alburgum *see* **Ålborg**

Alcalá de Henares (city, central Spain) : Roman *Complutum*

Alcan Highway *see* **Alaska Highway**

Alcazarquivir *see* **Ksar el Kebir**

Alcester (town, south central England) : Roman *Alauna*

Alchevsk *see* **Alchevs'k**

Alchevs'k (city, eastern Ukraine) : (Russian *Alchevsk*); 1961–1992 *Komunars'k* (Russian *Kommunarsk*); 1931–1961 *Voroshylovs'k* (Russian *Voroshilovsk*)

Alcira *see* **Alzira**

Alcobaça *see* **Tucuruí**

Aldan (town, eastern Russia) : to 1939 *Nezametny*

Aldborough (village, northern England) : Roman *Isurium Brigantum*

Aldea Grande *see* **Ciénaga**

Alderney (island, Channel Islands, southern United Kingdom) : Roman *Riduna*

Alejandro Selkirk (island, western Juan Fernández, South Pacific) : formerly *Más Afuera*

Aleksandropol' *see* **Gyumri**

Aleksandrovka *see* **Lozno-Oleksandrivka**

¹Aleksandrovo (village, northern Bulgaria) : formerly Turkish *Karakhasan*

²**Aleksandrovo** (village, central Bulgaria) : to 1878 Turkish *Okchelar*

Aleksandrovo *see* **Miladinovci**

Aleksandrovsk (city, western Russia) : 1928–1951 *Aleksandrovsky*; to 1928 *Aleksandrovsky Zavod*

Aleksandrovsk *see* (1) **Belogorsk**; (2) **Polyarny**; (3) **Zaporizhzhya**

Aleksandrovsk-Grushevsky *see* **Shakhty**

Aleksandrovskoye *see* **Kyzyl-Adyr**

Aleksandrovsky *see* (1) **Aleksandrovsk**; (2) **Novosibirsk**

Aleksandrovsky Zavod *see* **Aleksandrovsk**

Aleksandrów Kujawski (town, central Poland) : 1940–1945 German *Alexandrow-Weichsel*

Alekseyevka *see* (1) **Akkol'**; (2) **Terekty**; (3) **Torez**

Alekseyevo-Leonovo *see* **Torez**

Alekseyevo-Orlovka *see* **Shakhtars'k**

Alekseyevsk *see* **Svobodny**

Aleppo (city, northwestern Syria) : [Arabic *Ḥalab*]; ancient Greek *Beroea*

Alès (city, southern France) : to 1926 *Alais*

Alessandria (city, northwestern Italy) : Roman *Civitas Nova*

Aletrium *see* **Alatri**

Alexandretta *see* **İskenderun**

¹**Alexandria** (city, northern Egypt) : [Arabic *Al-Iskandarīyah*] (Alexandria was founded by Alexander the Great, as were the originals of **İskenderun** and **Kandahar**.)

²**Alexandria** (city, Virginia, eastern United States) : to 1749 *Belhaven*

³**Alexandria** (town, Ontario, southeastern Canada) : to 1819 *Priest's Mills*

⁴**Alexandria** (town, southern South Africa) : to 1873 *Olifantshoek*

Alexandria *see* (1) **Arlington**; (2) ³**Jackson**

Alexandria ad Issum *see* **İskenderun**

Alexandria Arachosiorum *see* **Kandahar**

Alexandroúpolis (city, northeastern Greece) : 1913–1919 Bulgarian *Dedeagach*; to 1913 Turkish *Dedeağaç*

Alexandrow-Weichsel *see* **Aleksandrów Kujawski**

Alfatar (town, northeastern Bulgaria) : formerly *General Lazarevo* (The town was in Romania from 1913 to 1940.)

Alfredo Chaves *see* **Veranópolis**

Al Furāt *see* **Euphrates**

Alger *se* **Algiers**

Algeria (republic, northern Africa) : [Arabic *Al-Jazā'ir*]; formerly French *Algérie* (Algeria was occupied by the French in 1830 and gained its independence in 1962.)

Algérie *see* **Algeria**

Algiers (city, northern Algeria) : [Arabic *Al-Jaz-*

ā'ir]; to *c.*1962 French *Alger*; Roman *Icosium* (Algiers was captured by the French in 1830 and became a military and administrative base for their colonies in northern and western Africa. The city was the provisional capital of France in World War II and its French name remains in official use.)

Al Gīzah *see* **Giza**

Al Ḥaḍr (village, northwestern Iraq) : ancient Greek *Hatra*

Al-Hawtah *see* **Laḥij**

Al Hoceima (town, northern Morocco) : to *c.*1958 Spanish *Villa Sanjurjo*

Al Ḥudaydah (city, western Yemen) : conventional *Hodeida*

Alibotush *see* **Gotsev Vrukh**

Ali Boutous *see* **Gotsev Vrukh**

Alicante (city, southeastern Spain) : Roman *Lucentum*; ancient Greek *Akra-Leuka*

Alice Springs (town, Northern Territory, central Australia) : to 1933 *Stuart*

Alinda *see* **Karpuzlu**

Aliquippa (town, Pennsylvania, northeastern United States) : originally *Logstown*

Al-Iskandarīyah *see* ¹**Alexandria**

Al-Ittihad *see* **Madinat ash Sha'b**

Al-Jazā'ir *see* (1) **Algeria**; (2) **Algiers**

Al Khalīl *see* **Hebron**

Al Khums (town, northwestern Libya) : formerly often *Homs*

Al Lādhiqīyah *see* **Latakia**

Allanmyo *see* **Aunglan**

Allenburg *see* ³**Druzhba**

Allenstein *see* **Olsztyn**

Allentown (city, Pennsylvania, northeastern United States) : to 1838 *Northampton*

Alligator *see* **Lake City**

Alma (city, Quebec, eastern Canada) : to 1954 *St.-Joseph-d'Alma*

Alma-Ata *see* **Almaty**

Al Madīnah *see* **Medina**

Al-Maghrib *see* **Morocco**

Al Marj (town, northern Libya) : formerly Italian *Barce*; ancient Greek *Barca*

Almaty (city, southeastern Kazakhstan) : 1921–1991 *Alma-Ata*, to 1921 Russian *Verny*

Al Mawşil *see* **Mosul**

Almenara (city, southeastern Brazil) : to 1944 *Vigia*

Almería (city, southern Spain) : Roman *Portus Magnus*

Almonte (town, Ontario, southeastern Canada) : to 1856 *Sheppard's Fall*

Al Mukhā' *see* **Mocha**

Alost *see* **Aalst**

Alpargatal *see* **Vicente Noble**

Alpesa *see* **Elvas**

Alpes-de-Haute-Provence (department, southeastern France) : to 1970 *Basses-Alpes*

Al Qāhirah *see* **Cairo**

Al-Qaṣrayn (town, west central Tunisia) : English *Kasserine* (The English name is associated with the nearby pass where in 1943 a decisive battle between U.S. and German forces contributed to the collapse of German resistance in northern Africa.)

Al Quds *see* **Jerusalem**

Al-Qusur *see* **Luxor**

Alre *see* **Auray**

Als (island, southern Denmark) : 1864–1920 German *Alsen*

Alsace (region, northeastern France) : 1871–1918, 1940–1944 German *Elsass*; Roman *Alsatia* (*See also* **Lorraine**.)

Alsatia *see* **Alsace**

Alsen *see* **Als**

Alsókubin *see* **Dolný Kubín**

Alsólendva *see* **Lendava**

Altamura (town, southern Italy) : Roman *Lupatia*

Altanbulag (town, northern Mongolia) : to 1921 *Maimachin*

Alta Ripa *see* **Altrip**

Altay (republic, southern Russia) : 1948–1991 *Gorno-Altay*; 1922–1948 *Oyrot*

Altdamm *see* **Dąbie**

Altena *see* ¹**Wilmington**

Altendorf *see* **Spišska Stara Ves**

Altentreptow (town, northwestern Germany) : to 1939 *Treptow*

Altilia (village, central Italy) : Roman *Saepinum*

Altlublau *see* **Stará Ľubovňa**

Alto Parnaíba (town, northeastern Brazil) : to 1944 *Vitória do Alto Parnaíba*

Altrip (village, western Germany) : Roman *Alta Ripa*

Altsandez *see* **Stary Sącz**

Altschmecks *see* **Stary Smokovec**

Altschwanenburg *see* **Gulbene**

Altsohl *see* **Zvolen**

Alturas (town, California, western United States) : to 1874 *Dorris Bridge*

Alūksne (town, northeastern Latvia) : to 1918 German *Marienburg*

Al Urdunn *see* **Jordan**

Álvaro Obregón *see* **Frontera**

Alwand (mountain, western Iran) : ancient Greek *Orontes*

Al Yaman *see* **Yemen**

Alyoshki *see* **Tsyurupyns'k**

Alytus (city, southern Lithuania) : to 1918 Russian *Olita*

Alzira (town, eastern Spain) : alternate *Alcira*; Roman *Saetabicula*

Amamlu *see* **Spitak**

Amandelboom *see* ²**Williston**

Amangeldy (town, north central Kazakhstan) : to 1936 *Batbakkara*

Amapá (town, southern Brazil) : formerly *Montenegro*

Amapari *see* **Ferreira Gomes**

Amarração *see* **Luís Correia**

Amatitlán (town, southeastern Mexico) : to 1938 *Amatlán*

Amatlán *see* **Amatitlán**

Ambacia *see* **Amboise**

Ambaritsa *see* ²**Levski**

Ambianum *see* **Amiens**

Ambleside *see* **Hahndorf**

Ambleston (village, southwestern Wales) : Welsh *Treamlod*

Amboina *see* **Ambon**

Amboise (town, west central France) : Roman *Ambacia*

Ambon (island, eastern Indonesia) : formerly *Amboina* (The city of Ambon on the island had the same former name.)

Amboy *see* **Perth Amboy**

Ambracia *see* **Arta**

Ambridge (town, Pennsylvania, northeastern United States) : to 1906 *Economy* (Remains of the former village, a German communal group, are preserved as *Old Economy*.)

Ambrizete *see* **N'zeto**

Ambrolauri (town, northern Georgia) : to mid-1930s *Yenukidze*

Ambroz *see* **Plasencis**

Amelia (town, southern Italy) : Roman *Ameria*

Amélie-les-Bains-Palada (town, southern France) : to 1840 *Arles-les-Bains*

Ameria *see* **Amelia**

America *see* **United States**

Americana (city, southeastern Brazil) : to 1938 *Villa Americana*

Amherst (town, Nova Scotia, eastern Canada) : to 1759 *La Planche*

Amherst *see* **Kyaikkami**

Amichow *see* **Kaiyuan**

Amida *see* **Diyarbakır**

Amiens (city, northern France) : Roman *Ambianum*; Celtic *Samarobriva*

Amisia *see* **Ems**

Amissa *see* **Omiš**

Amisus *see* **Samsun**

Amman (city, northwestern Jordan) : ancient Greek *Philadelphia*; biblical *Rabbah*; alternate biblical *Rabbath-Ammon* (The city was not the biblical Philadelphia, which lies beneath the modern town of Alaşehir, western Turkey.)

Ammanford (town, southern Wales) : Welsh *Rhydaman*

Ammokhostos *see* **Famagusta**

Amnéville (town, northeastern France) : 1870–1918, 1939–1944 German *Stahlheim*

Amoea *see* **Portalegre**

Amoy *see* **Xiamen**

Ampère *see* **Aïn Azel**

Ampezzo (village, northeastern Italy) : to 1918 German *Hayden*

Amrit (village, western Syria) : ancient Greek *Marathus*

[1]Amsterdam (city, New York, northeastern United States) : to 1804 *Veedersburg*

[2]Amsterdam (town, northeastern South Africa) : to 1882 *Roburnia*

Amu Darya (river, central Asia) : ancient Greek *Oxus*

Amursk (city, eastern Russia) : to 1958 *Padali*

Amvrosiyevka *see* **Amvrosiyivka**

Amvrosiyivka (town, eastern Ukraine) : (Russian *Amvrosiyevka*); to 1944 *Donets'ko-Amvrosiyivka* (Russian *Donetsko-Amvrosiyevka*)

Anaconda (town, Montana, northwestern United States) : to 1888 *Copperopolis*

Anadolu *see* **Anatolia**

Anadyr' (town, eastern Russia) : to 1923 *Novo-Mariinsk*

Anagastum *see* **Nikšić**

Anagni (town, central Italy) : Roman *Anagnia*

Anagnia *see* **Anagni**

Analândia (town, southeastern Brazil) : to 1944 *Anápolis*

Anan'evo (village, northeastern Kyrgyzstan) : to 1942 *Sazanovka*

Anantnag (town, northern India) : formerly *Islamabad*

Anápolis *see* (1) **Analândia**; (2) **Simão Dias**

Anatolia (region, western Asia) : [Turkish *Anadolu*]; traditional *Asia Minor* (Anatolia corresponds to modern Asian Turkey, amounting to about 97 percent of the country's area.)

An Baile Meánach *see* **Ballymena**

An Bhlarna *see* **Blarney**

An Cabhán *see* **Cavan**

An Caisleán Nua *see* **[3]Newcastle**

Ancaster (village, east central England) : Roman *Causennis* (The Roman name, often cited as *Causennae*, may have really been that of a fort at Sapperton, 7 miles to the southeast.)

An Charraig Dhubh *see* **Blackrock**

An Chathair *see* **Caher**

Anchialus *see* **Pomoriye**

Anchieta *see* **Piatã**

An Chorr Chríochach *see* **Cookstown**

An Clár *see* **Clare**

An Clochán *see* **Clifden**

An Clochán Liath *see* **Dungloe**

An Cóbh *see* **Cobh**

An Coireán *see* **Waterville**

An Comar *see* **Comber**

Ancre *see* **Albert**

Ancyra *see* **Ankara**

An Daingean *see* (1) **Daingean**; (2) **Dingle**

Andalaly *see* **Nozhay-Yurt**

Andalucía *see* **[1]Andalusia**

[1]Andalusia (region, southern Spain) : [Spanish *Andalucía*]

[2]Andalusia (town, Alabama, southeastern United States) : to 1846 *New Site*

Andalusia *see* **Jan Kempdorp**

Andemattunnum *see* **Langres**

Anderitum *see* **Pevensey**

Andernach (city, western Germany) : Roman *Antunnacum*

Andes *see* **Virgilio**

Andijon (city, eastern Uzbekistan) : (Russian *Andizhan*)

Andirá (city, southern Brazil) : to 1944 *Ingá*

Andizhan *see* **Andijon**

Andorra (principality, southwestern Europe) : [French *Andorre*] (The official language of Andorra is Catalan, but Spanish and French are also spoken.)

Andorra-la-Vella (town, west central Andorra) : [French *Andorre-la-Vieille*; Spanish *Andorra-la-Vieja*]

Andorra-la-Vieja *see* **Andorra-la-Vella**

Andorre *see* **Andorra**

Andorre-la-Vieille *see* **Andorra-la-Vella**

Andover Forge *see* **Stanhope**

Andreyev *see* **Jędrzejów**

Andreyevka *see* **Kabanbay**

Andreyevsk *see* **Tezebazar**

Andreyevskoye *see* **Dneprovskoye**

Andrichau *see* **Andrychów**

An Droim Mór *see* **Dromore**

Andropov *see* **Rybinsk**

Andrychów (town, southern Poland) : 1940–1945 German *Andrichau*

Anenii Noi (town, eastern Moldova) : formerly Russian *Novyye Aneny*

Anericiacum *see* **Annecy**

Angaco Norte (town, western Argentina) : formerly *Kilómetro 924*

Angerapp *see* **Ozyorsk**

Angerburg *see* **Węgorzewo**

Angers (city, western France) : Roman *Juliomagus*

Anglesey (island, northwestern Wales) : Welsh

Môn; Roman *Mona* (The Roman name is said to mean "mountain," specifically referring to **Holyhead** Mountain on the island.)

Anglo-Egyptian Sudan *see* **Sudan**

Angoche (town, eastern Mozambique) : to 1976 Portuguese *António Enes*

Angola (country, southwestern Africa) : to 1914 *Portuguese West Africa* (Although the name became officially recognized in 1914, Angola did not achieve independence until 1975.)

Angora *see* **Ankara**

Angostura *see* **Ciudad Bolívar**

Angoulême (city, western France) : Roman *Ecolisma*

Angra Pequena *see* **Lüderitz**

Angrezabad *see* **English Bazar**

Angus (administrative district, eastern Scotland) : to 1928 *Forfarshire*

An Iarmhí *see* **Westmeath**

Anicium *see* **Le Puy**

Aniene (river, central Italy) : Roman *Anio*

Anio *see* **Aniene**

Aniva (town, eastern Russia) : 1905–1945 Japanese *Rutaka*

Anjouan *see* **Nzwani**

Ankara (city, west central Turkey) : formerly conventional English *Angora*; Roman *Ancyra*

Ankhialo *see* **Pomoriye**

An Longfort *see* **Longford**

An Lorgain *see* **Lurgan**

An Mhí *see* **Meath**

An Muileann gCearr *see* **Mullingar**

Annaba (city, northeastern Algeria) : to *c*.1962 French *Bône*; Roman *Hippo Regius*

Annapolis (city, Maryland, northeastern United States) : to 1695 *Anne Arundel Town*; originally *Providence* (Annapolis is the seat of *Anne Arundel County*, preserving the earlier name.)

Annapolis Royal (town, Nova Scotia, eastern Canada) : to 1713 *Port Royal*

An Nás *see* **Naas**

An Nāṣirah *see* **Nazareth**

Anne Arundel Town *see* **Annapolis**

Annecy (city, eastern France) : Medieval Latin *Anericiacum*

Annenfeld *see* **Şämkir**

Annian Way *see* **Via**

An Níl *see* **Nile**

Annobón (island, southwestern Equatorial Guinea) : 1973–1979 *Pagalu*

An Ómaigh *see* **Omagh**

Anqing (city, eastern China) : 1911–1949 *Hwaining*

An Ráth *see* **Ráth Luirc**

An Sciobairín *see* **Skibbereen**

Ansedonia (village, western Italy) : Roman *Cosa*

Ansloga *see* **Oslo**

An Sráidbhaile *see* **Stradbally**

An Srath Bán *see* **Strabane**

Anstrude *see* **Bierry-les-Belles-Fontaines**

Antakya (city, southern Turkey) : biblical *Antioch*; Roman *Antiochia* (There are two biblical Antiochs. This one, in the Roman province of Syria, was the starting point of Paul's journey to Rome. The other, also visited by Paul, was in the Roman province of Galatia, or as Acts 13:14 has it, "Antioch in Pisidia," in modern southwestern Turkey. Both were named for the Syrian emperor Antiochus, father of Seleucus I, but the Antioch that is now Antakya was the largest and most important of all the 16 cities that took his name. A third was *Antiochia Margiana*, otherwise **Merv** in present-day Turkmenistan, while a fourth, *Antiochia Persis*, may have been modern **Būshehr**, in southwestern Iran.)

Antalya (city, southwestern Turkey) : biblical *Attalia*; ancient Greek *Attaleia*

Antananarivo (city, east central Madagascar) : formerly French *Tananarive*

An tAonach *see* **Nenagh**

Antarctic *see* **Antarctica**

Antarctica (continent surrounding South Pole) : alternate popular *Antarctic*

Antarctic Ocean (southern parts of Pacific, Atlantic, and Indian oceans) : alternate *Southern Ocean*

Antarctic Peninsula (northwestern Antarctica) : 1938–1964 (UK) *Graham Land*, (U.S.) *Graham Peninsula* or *Palmer Peninsula*; Spanish *Tierra de O'Higgins* (*Graham Land* is now used for the northern part of the peninsula, and *Palmer Land* for the southern part.)

An Teampall Mór *see* **Templemore**

Antequera (city, southern Spain) : Roman *Antiquaria*; alternate Roman *Anticaria*

Antibes (town, southeastern France) : ancient Greek *Antipolis*

Antibos *see* **Štip**

Anticaria *see* **Antequera**

Anticosti (island, Quebec, eastern Canada) : formerly French *Assomption*

An tInbhear Mór *see* **Arklow**

Antioch *see* (1) **Antakya**; (2) **Būshehr**; (3) **Merv**

Antiochia *see* **Antakya**

Antiochia Margiana *see* **Merv**

Antipatria *see* **Berat**

Antipolis *see* **Antibes**

Antipyrgos *see* **Tobruk**

Antiquaria *see* **Antequera**

Antium *see* **Anzio**

An tIúr *see* Newry

Antivari *see* Bar

Antivestaeum Promontorium *see* Land's End

An t-Òb *see* Leverburgh

António Enes *see* Angoche

Antono-Kodintsevo *see* Kominternivs'ke

Antonove-Kodyntseve *see* Kominternivs'ke

Antopal' (town, southwestern Belarus) : (Russian *Antopol'*); 1919–1939 Polish *Antopol*

Antopol' *see* Antopal'

Antratsit *see* Antratsyt

Antratsyt (city, eastern Ukraine) : (Russian *Antratsit*); to 1962 *Bokovo-Antratsyt* (Russian *Bokovo-Antratsit*)

Antrea *see* Kamennogorsk

Antrim (town, central Northern Ireland) : Irish *Aontroim*

Antsiranana (city, northern Madagascar) : to 1977 Portuguese and Spanish *Diégo-Suarez*

Antsohimbondrona (village, northern Madagascar) : formerly French *Port St.-Louis*

Antunnacum *see* Andernach

Antwerp (city, northern Belgium) : [Flemish *Antwerpen*; French *Anvers*]

Antwerpen *see* Antwerp

An Uaimh *see* Navan

Anvers *see* Antwerp

Anyang (city, east central China) : to 1913 *Zhangde*

Anzaldo (town, central Bolivia) : to 1900s *Paredón*

Anzio (town, western Italy) : Roman *Antium*

Aontroim *see* Antrim

Aorangi *see* Cook, Mt.

Aosta (town, northwestern Italy) : Roman *Augusta Praetoria*

Aotea *see* Great Barrier Island

Aotearoa *see* New Zealand

Apalachicola (town, Florida, southeastern United States) : to 1831 *West Point*

Aparecida *see* Bertolínia

Apennines (mountains, central Italy) : [Italian *Appennini*]

Apenrade *see* Åbenrå

Aphrodisias *see* Geyre

Apizaco (city, east central Mexico) : formerly *Barrón Escandón*

Apollonia *see* Sozopol

Appennini *see* Apennines

Appian Way *see* Via

Appleton (city, Wisconsin, north central United States) : originally *Grand Chute*

Aprel'sk (town, eastern Russia) : to 1925 *Nadezhdinsky Priisk*

Aprutium *see* Abruzzi

Apt (town, southeastern France) : Roman *Apta Julia*

Apta Julia *see* Apt

Apuania *see* Massa-Carrara

Apulia *see* Puglia

Apulum *see* Alba Iulia

Aqaba (town, southwestern Jordan) : Roman *Aelana*; biblical *Ezion-geber*; alternate biblical *Elath* (The biblical names are now often regarded as those of two distinct places.)

Aqmola *see* Astana

Aq Qaleh (town, northeastern Iran) : to 1980 *Pahlavi Dezh*

Aquae Arnemetiae *see* Buxton

Aquae Augustae *see* Dax

Aquae Calidae *see* (1) Bagnols-les-Bains; (2) ¹Bath; (3) Vichy

Aquae Calidae Pisanorum *see* San Giuliano Terme

Aquae Flaviae *see* Chaves

Aquae Grani *see* Aachen

Aquae Gratianae *see* Aix-les-Bains

Aquae Helveticae *see* ²Baden

Aquae Mattiacae *see* Wiesbaden

Aquae Mortuae *see* Aigues-Mortes

Aquae Originis *see* Orense

Aquae Pannoniae *see* ¹Baden

Aquae Sextiae *see* Aix-en-Provence

Aquae Statiellae *see* Acqui Terme

Aquae Sulis *see* ¹Bath

Aquae Tarbellicae *see* Dax

Aquidneck *see* Rhode Island

Aquincum *see* Budapest

Aquino (town, south central Italy) : Roman *Aquinum*

Aquinum *see* Aquino

Aquisgranum *see* Aachen

Aquitaine (region, southwestern France) : Roman *Aquitania*

Aquitania *see* Aquitaine

Arabestan *see* Khuzestan

Arabian Desert *see* Eastern Desert

Arabian Gulf *see* Persian Gulf

Araçá *see* Mari

Araçoiaba da Serra (town, southeastern Brazil) : to 1944 *Campo Largo*

Aracoma *see* Logan

Aracruz (city, southeastern Brazil) : to 1944 *Santa Cruz*

Arae Flaviae *see* Rottweil

Aragon (region, northeastern Spain) : [Spanish *Aragón*]

Aragón *see* Aragon

Araguaçu *see* Paraguaçu Paulista

Araguari (city, eastern Brazil) : formerly *Freguesia do Brejo Alegre*

Araguatins (city, north central Brazil) : to 1944 Portuguese *São Vicente*

Ara Jovis *see* **Aranjuez**

Arāk (city, west central Iran) : to mid–1930s *Sultanabad*

Arakan *see* **Rakhine**

Aranjuez (town, central Spain) : Roman *Ara Jovis*

Aranyoszmarót *see* **Zlaté Moravce**

Araquari (town, southern Brazil) : to 1944 *Parati*

Ararat (mountain, eastern Turkey) : Turkish *Ağrı Dağı* (The English and biblical name relates to the Assyrian kingdom of *Urartu*, around Lake Van.)

Araripina (city, northeastern Brazil) : to 1944 Portuguese *São Gonçalo dos Campos*

Aras (river, eastern Turkey) : ancient Greek *Araxas* (The river, which for about half its course forms the border between Armenia and Azerbaijan to the north and Turkey and Iran to the south, was confused by the historian Herodotus with the *Oxus* or **Amu Darya**.)

Arausio *see* ¹**Orange**

Araxas *see* **Aras**

Arbe *see* **Rab**

Arbeia *see* **South Shields**

Arberth *see* **Narberth**

Arbon (town, northeastern Switzerland) : Roman *Arbor Felix*

Arborea (village, western Sardinia, Italy) : *c.1935–c.1944 Mussolinia di Sardegna*; to *c.1935 Villaggio Mussolini*

Arbor Felix *see* **Arbon**

Arbroath (town, eastern Scotland) : formerly *Aberbrothock* (The town's name means "mouth of the *Brothock*" and the river here is still known by this name. The old name was popularized by Robert Southey's 1802 ballad "The Inchcape Rock." *See also* **Bell Rock**.)

Archangel *see* **Arkhangel'sk**

Arcobriga *see* **Arcos de la Frontera**

Arcos de la Frontera (town, southwestern Spain) : Roman *Arcobriga*

Arcoverde (city, northeastern Brazil) : to 1944 Portuguese *Rio Branco*

Arctic Bay (village, Nunavut, northern Canada) : alternate Inuit *Ikpiarjuk*

Arctic Red River *see* **Tsiigehtchic**

Ardennes (wooded plateau, southwestern Belgium/northeastern France) : Roman *Arduenna Silva*

Ardino (town, southern Bulgaria) : to 1878 Turkish *Egridere*

Ard Mhic Nasca *see* **Holywood**

Arduenna Silva *see* **Ardennes**

Area *see* **Mundelein**

Areia *see* **Ubaíra**

Arekhawsk (town, northeastern Belarus) : (Russian *Orekhovsk*); to 1946 Russian *Orekhi-Vydritsa*

Arelate *see* **Arles**

Arenacum *see* **Arnhem**

Arensburg *see* **Kuressaare**

Arezzo (city, north central Italy) : Roman *Arretium*

Argenta *see* **North Little Rock**

Argentia (village, Newfoundland and Labrador, eastern Canada) : formerly *Little Placentia*

Argentina (republic, southern South America) : officially *Argentine Republic*; colloquially *the Argentine*

Argentine, the *see* **Argentina**

Argentine Republic *see* **Argentina**

Argentoratum *see* **Strasbourg**

Argovie *see* **Aargau**

Argyrokastron *see* **Gjirokastër**

Århus (city, eastern Denmark) : alternate *Aarhus*

Ariccia (town, central Italy) : Roman *Aricia*

Aricia *see* **Ariccia**

Ariconium *see* **Weston under Penyard**

Arīḥā *see* **Jericho**

Ariminum *see* **Rimini**

Arizona City *see* **Yuma**

Arkadelphia (town, Arkansas, south central United States) : to 1838 *Blakelytown*

Arkadioúpolis *see* **Lüleburgaz**

Arkansas City (town, Kansas, central United States) : to 1872 *Creswell*, earlier *Adelphi*; originally *Walnut City*

Arkhangelo-Pashiysky Zavod *see* **Pashiya**

Arkhangel'sk (city, northwestern Russia) : English conventional *Archangel*; to 1613 Russian *Novyye Kholmogory* (The English name became familiar in World War II as that of the port receiving convoys of lend-lease goods from Britain and the USA.)

Arklow (town, eastern Ireland) : Irish *An tInbhear Mór*

Arles (city, southeastern France) : Roman *Arelate*

Arles-les-Bains *see* **Amélie-les-Bains-Palada**

¹**Arlington** (county, Virginia, eastern United States) : to 1920 *Alexandria*; originally *Bellehaven*

²**Arlington** (town, Massachusetts, northeastern United States) : 1807–1867 *West Cambridge*; to 1807 *Menotomy*

Arlington Heights (town, Illinois, north central United States) : to 1874 *Dunton*

Arlon (town, southeastern Belgium) : Flemish *Aarlen*; Roman *Orolaunum*

Arman *see* **Kardam**

Armavir (city, western Armenia) : 1938–1992

Oktemberyan; to 1938 *Sardarabad* (The city should not be confused with the town of the same name in southwestern Russia, although both are named for the historic capital of Urartu, the ancient kingdom that became Armenia.)

Armenia (republic, western Asia) : [Armenian *Hayasdan*] (This Armenia should not be confused with the much larger ancient country of the name, now occupied by modern Armenia, Turkey, and Iran and commonly identified with the biblical *Minni*.)

Armenierstadt *see* **Gherla**

Armenopolis *see* **Gherla**

Armorica *see* **Brittany**

Arnheim *see* **Arnhem**

Arnhem (city, eastern Netherlands) : 1939–1945 German *Arnheim*; Roman *Arenacum*

Arnissa (village, northeastern Greece) : to 1913 Turkish *Ostrovo*

Arnswalde *see* **Choszczno**

Arorae (island, west central Kiribati) : formerly *Hurd Island*

Arpino (town, central Italy) : Roman *Arpinum*

Arpinum *see* **Arpino**

Arrabona *see* **Győr**

Ar Raqqah (town, northern Syria) : ancient Greek *Nicephorium*

Arras (city, northern France) : Roman *Nemetacum Atrebatum*; Celtic *Nemetocenna*

Arretium *see* **Arezzo**

Arriaca *see* **Guadalajara**

Ar Riyāḍ *see* **Riyadh**

Arroyo de la Luz (town, western Spain) : to *c*.1940 *Arroyo del Puerco*

Arroyo del Puerco *see* **Arroyo de la Luz**

Arsenaria *see* **Arzew**

Arsen'yev (town, eastern Russia) : to 1952 *Semyonovka*

Arshaly (town, north central Kazakhstan) : formerly Russian *Vishnyovka* (This Arshaly, near the capital, Astana, should not be confused with the settlement of the same name in the east of the country, south of Semey.)

Arsinoë *see* **El Faiyum**

Arta (town, northwestern Greece) : to 1912 Turkish *Narda*; ancient Greek *Ambracia*

Artashat (town, southern Armenia) : to 1945 *Kamarlu*

Artemove (town, eastern Ukraine) : (Russian *Artyomovo*); to 1921 *Nelipivs'kyy Khutir* (Russian *Nelepovsky Khutor*)

Artemivs'k (city, eastern Ukraine) : (Russian *Artyomovsk*); to 1923 *Bakhmut*

Artesia (town, New Mexico, southwestern United States) : to 1905 *Stegman*

Arti (town, west central Russia) : to 1929 *Artinsky Zavod*

Artigas (city, northwestern Uruguay) : to 1930s Spanish *San Eugenio*

Artigas *see* **Río Branco**

Artinsky Zavod *see* **Arti**

Artur de Paiva *see* **Matala**

Artyomovo *see* **Artemove**

Artyomovsk (town, eastern Russia) : to 1939 *Ol'khovsky*

Artyomovsk *see* **Artemivs'k**

Artyomovsky (town, west central Russia) : to 1938 *Yegorshino*

Aruanã (town, central Brazil) : to 1944 Portuguese *Leopoldina*

Arun (river, southern England) : formerly *Tarrant*; Roman *Trisantona*

Arunachal Pradesh (state, northeastern India) : 1954–1972 *North East Frontier Agency*

Arundel *see* **Kennebunkport**

Arviat (village, Nunavut, north central Canada) : to 1989 *Eskimo Point*

Arys *see* **Orzysz**

Arzew (town, northwestern Algeria) : Roman *Arsenaria*

Aš (town, western Czech Republic) : to 1918, 1938–1945 German *Asch*

¹Asaka (city, eastern Uzbekistan) : formerly Russian *Leninsk*; 1935–1937 *Assake*; 1934–1935 Russian *Zelensk;* to 1934 *Assake*

²Asaka (city, central Japan) : to 1932 *Hizaori*

Asba Littoria *see* **Asebe Tefere**

Asbest (town, west central Russia) : to 1933 *Kudel'ka*

Asbestos Hill *see* **Purtuniq**

Ascension Island *see* **Pohnpei**

Asch *see* **Aš**

Ascoli Piceno (town, central Italy) : Roman *Asculum Picenum*

Ascoli Satriano (town, southeastern Italy) : Roman *Asculum Apulum*

Asculum Apulum *see* **Ascoli Satriano**

Asculum Picenum *see* **Ascoli Piceno**

Asebe Tefere (town, east central Ethiopia) : 1936–1941 Italian *Asba Littoria*

Asenovgrad (town, southern Bulgaria) : to 1934 *Stanimaka*

Asfeld (village, northeastern France) : 1671–1728 *Avaux-la-Ville*; to 1671 *Écry*

Aşgabat (city, southern Turkmenistan) : (Russian *Ashkhabad*); 1919–1927 Russian *Poltoratsk*

Ashdod (city, southwestern Israel) : Roman *Azotus*

Asheville (city, North Carolina, eastern United States) : to 1797 *Morristown*

Ashkelon *see* **Ashqelon**

Ashkhabad *see* **Aşgabat**

Ashland (city, Kentucky, east central United States) : to 1854 *Poage's Settlement*

Ashley Center *see* **Vernal**

Ashmyany (town, northwestern Belarus) : (Russian *Oshmyany*); 1921–1945 Polish *Oszmiana*

Ashots'k' (village, northwestern Armenia) : formerly *Gukasyan*

Ashqelon (city, southwestern Israel) : biblical *Ashkelon*

Ashraf *see* **Behshahr**

Ash Shām *see* (1) **Damascus**; (2) **Syria**

Ash Shāriqah (emirate, United Arab Emirates) : conventional *Sharjah*

Asht *see* **Shaidan**

Ashur *see* **Qal'at Sharqāt**

Asia Minor *see* **Anatolia**

Asisium *see* **Assisi**

Asloga *see* **Oslo**

Asmara (city, northern Eritrea) : alternate *Asmera*

Asmera *see* **Asmara**

Asolo (town, northeastern Italy) : Roman *Acelum*

Aspadana *see* **Eşfahān**

Asparukhovo (village, eastern Bulgaria) : to 1934 *Chenge*

Aspinwall *see* **Colón**

Aspropotamos *see* **Achelous**

Assab (former administrative region, southeastern Eritrea) : 1936–1941 Italian *Dancalia Meridionale*

Assake *see* ¹**Asaka**

Assiniboia (town, Saskatchewan, southern Canada) : to 1913 *Leeville*

Assisi (town, central Italy) : Roman *Asisium*

Assling *see* **Jesenice**

Assomption *see* **Anticosti**

As Sūdān *see* **Sudan**

Assur *see* **Qal'at Sharqāt**

As Suways *see* **Suez**

Asta Colonia *see* **Asti**

Astacus *see* **İzmit**

Astana (city, north central Kazakhstan) : 1994–1998 *Aqmola*; 1961–1994 Russian *Tselinograd*; 1832–1961 Russian *Akmolinsk*; earlier *Akmola*

Asta Pompeia *see* **Asti**

Astapovo *see* **Lev Tolstoy**

Asterabad *see* **Gorgān**

Asti (city, northwestern Italy) : Roman *Asta Pompeia*; alternate Roman *Asta Colonia*

Astorga (town, northwestern Spain) : Roman *Asturica Augusta*

Astrakhan'-Bazar *see* **Cälilabad**

Astrida *see* **Butare**

Asturica Augusta *see* **Astorga**

Aswan (city, southeastern Egypt) : ancient Greek *Syene*

Asyut (city, east central Egypt) : ancient Greek *Lycopolis*

Atakent (village, southern Kazakhstan) : formerly Russian *Il'ich*

Atamyrat (town, southeastern Turkmenistan) : formerly *Kerki*

Atella di Caserta (town, southern Italy) : 1927–1945 *Atella di Napoli*

Atella di Napoli *see* **Atella di Caserta**

Aternum *see* **Pescara**

Ateste *see* **Este**

Ath (town, southwestern Belgium) : Flemish *Aat*

Athenae *see* ¹**Athens**

Athenry (town, western Ireland) : Irish *Baile Átha an Rí*

¹**Athens** (city, eastern Greece) : [modern Greek *Athínai*]; Roman *Athenae*

²**Athens** (village, Ontario, southeastern Canada) : formerly *Farmersville*

Athens *see* **Oshkosh**

Athínai *see* ¹**Athens**

Athlone (town, central Ireland) : Irish *Baile Átha Luain*

Athol (town, Massachusetts, northeastern United States) : to 1762 *Pequoiag*

Athy (town, east central Ireland) : Irish *Baile Átha Í*

Atig (town, west central Russia) : to 1929 *Atigsky Zavod*

Atigsky Zavod *see* **Atig**

Atlanta (city, Georgia, southeastern United States) : 1843–1845 *Marthasville*; to 1843 *Terminus*

Atlixco (city, south central Mexico) : originally *Villa de Carrión*

Atria *see* **Adria**

Attaleia *see* **Antalya**

Attalia *see* **Antalya**

Attinianum *see* **Vodnjan**

Attock (district, central Pakistan) : to 1978 *Campbellpur*

Atwood (village, Ontario, southeastern Canada) : to 1883 *Newry Station*

Atyrau (city, western Kazakhstan) : to 1992 Russian *Gur'yev*

Aubigny *see* **Lévis**

¹**Auburn** (city, New York, northeastern United States) : originally *Hardenberg's Corners*

²**Auburn** (city, Washington, northwestern United States) : to 1893 *Slaughter*

³**Auburn** (village, east central Ireland) : Irish *Achadh na Gréine*; formerly *Lissoy* (The village is said to be the original of Oliver Goldsmith's "Sweet Auburn! loveliest village of the plain,"

in his 1770 poem *The Deserted Village*, as the writer spent his childhood here. The literary description prompted the name's adoption elsewhere, as for the two above.)

Auch (city, southwestern France) : Roman *Augusta Auscorum*; earlier Roman *Elimberrum*

Audenarde *see* **Oudenaarde**

Auderghem (town, central Belgium) : Flemish *Oudergem*

Auerbakhovsky Rudnik *see* **Rudnichny**

Auezov (town, eastern Kazakhstan) : to 1967 *Bakyrchik*

Aufidus *see* **Ofanto**

Augsburg (city, southern Germany) : Roman *Augusta Vindelicorum*

Augst (village, northern Switzerland) : Roman *Augusta Raurica*

¹**Augusta** (city, southern Italy) : alternate *Agosta*

²**Augusta** (city, Maine, northeastern United States) : to 1797 *Harrington*; earlier *Fort Western*; originally *Cushnoc*

Augusta *see* **London**

Augusta Auscorum *see* **Auch**

Augusta Nemetum *see* **Speyer**

Augusta Praetoria *see* **Aosta**

Augusta Raurica *see* **Augst**

Augusta Suessionum *see* **Soissons**

Augusta Taurinorum *see* **Turin**

Augusta Trajana *see* **Stara Zagora**

Augusta Treverorum *see* **Trier**

Augusta Vangionum *see* **Worms**

Augusta Vindelicorum *see* **Augsburg**

Augustobona *see* **Troyes**

Augusto Cardosa *see* **Metangula**

Augustodunum *see* **Autun**

Augustodurum *see* **Bayeux**

Augustonemetum *see* **Clermont**

Augustoritum *see* **Limoges**

Augustów (town, northeastern Poland) : to 1919 Russian *Avgustov*

Aujuittuq *see* **Grise Fiord**

Aulenbach *see* **Kalinovka**

Aulie-Ata *see* **Taraz**

Auliyekol' (town, northern Kazakhstan) : formerly Russian *Semiozyornoye*

Aulon *see* **Vlorë**

Aulowönen *see* **Kalinovka**

Aumale *see* **Sour el Ghozlane**

Aunglan (town, central Myanmar) : formerly *Allanmyo*

Aunus *see* **Olonets**

Aupaluk (village, Quebec, eastern Canada) : formerly *Hopes Advance Bay*

Aurangabad (city, western India) : formerly *Khadki*

Auray (town, northwestern France) : [Breton *Alre*]

Aurelia Aquensis *see* **Baden-Baden**

Aurelianum *see* **Orléans**

Aurelian Way *see* **Via**

Aurinx *see* **Jaén**

Aurisina (village, northeastern Italy) : to 1918 German *Nabresina*

¹**Aurora** (city, Colorado, west central United States) : to 1907 *Fletcher*

²**Aurora** (city, Illinois, north central United States) : originally *McCarty's Mills*

³**Aurora** (town, Ontario, southeastern Canada) : to 1854 *Mitchell's Corners*

Ausa *see* **Vich**

Auschwitz *see* **Oświęcim**

Auspitz *see* **Hustopeče**

Aussig *see* **Ústí nad Labem**

Aust-Agder (county, southern Norway) : to 1919 *Nedenes*

Austerlitz *see* **Slavkov u Brna**

Austin (city, Texas, southern United States) : to 1839 *Waterloo*

Australia (country, Oceania) : to 1817 *New Holland* (A former alternate name for the land was *New South Wales*, later limited in area to that of the present southeastern state.)

Australian Capital Territory (territory, southeastern Australia) : to 1938 *Federal Capital Territory*

Austria (republic, central Europe) : [German *Österreich*]

Austria-Hungary (former monarchy, central Europe) : [German *Österreich-Ungarn*] (The "dual monarchy" was formed in 1867 but collapsed in 1918 at the end of World War I.)

Autesiodorum *see* **Auxerre**

Autricum *see* **Chartres**

Autun (town, east central France) : Roman *Augustodunum*

Auxerre (town, central France) : Roman *Autesiodorum*

Auximum *see* **Osimo**

Auyuittuq National Park (Nunavut, northeastern Canada) : to 1975 *Baffin Island National Park*

Avaricum *see* **Bourges**

Avaux-la-Ville *see* **Asfeld**

Avellaneda (city, east central Argentina) : to 1904 Spanish *Barracas al Sur*

Avellino (town, southern Italy) : Roman *Abellinum*

Avenches (town, western Switzerland) : Roman *Aventicum*

Avennio *see* **Avignon**

Aventicum *see* **Avenches**

Avgustov *see* **Augustów**

Avignon (city, southeastern France) : Roman *Avennio*

Ávila (city, central Spain) : Roman *Albicella*
Avliköy *see* Zhivkovo
Avlonya *see* Vlorë
Avon (river, southwestern England) : Roman *Abona* (The Roman name was given to a number of *Avon* rivers in southern England, including the one on which **Sea Mills** stands.)
Avratalan *see* Koprivshtitsa
Axona *see* Aisne
Axum *see* Aksum
Axumis *see* Aksum
Ayacucho (city, south central Peru) : to 1825 *Huamanga*
Ayagoz (town, eastern Kazakhstan) : to 1939 Russian *Sergiopol'*
Aydın (city, southwestern Turkey) : formerly *Güzelhisar*
Ayers Rock (monolith, Northern Territory, central Australia) : Aboriginal *Uluru*
[1]Aylmer (town, Quebec, southeastern Canada) : to 1847 *Symnes Landing*
[2]Aylmer (town, Ontario, southeastern Canada) : formerly *Troy*
Ayodhya (city, northern India) : formerly *Oudh*
Ayteke Bi (town, southern Kazakhstan) : formerly *Zhangaqazaly*; earlier Russian *Novokazalinsk*
Ayutinsky (town, southwestern Russia) : formerly *Vlasovo-Ayuta*
Ayutla *see* Ciudad Tecúm Umán
Ayvalık (town, northwestern Turkey) : ancient Greek *Heraclea*
Azania *see* South Africa
Azerbaijan (republic, central Asia) : ancient Greek *Media Atropotene* (The Greek name locates the territory in the part of ancient Media that was named after Atropates.)
Azincourt *see* Agincourt
Azores (island group, North Atlantic) : [Portuguese *Açores*]
Azotus *see* Ashdod
Azov, Sea of (southeastern Ukraine/southwestern Russia) : Roman *Maeotis Palus*
Azovs'ke (town, southern Ukraine) : (Russian *Azovskoye*); to 1945 *Kolay*
Azovskoye *see* Azovs'ke
Azurduy (town, south central Bolivia) : to 1900s *Pomabamba*
Aẕ Ẕahrān *see* Dhahran
Baalbek (town, eastern Lebanon) : ancient Greek *Heliopolis*
Baarle-Hertog (town, northern Belgium) : French *Baer-le-Duc* (The town is a Belgian exclave in the Netherlands.)
Babadaykhan (town, southern Turkmenistan) : formerly *Kirovsk*

Babcock's Grove *see* Glen Ellyn
Babaeski (town, northwestern Turkey) : 1920–1992 modern Greek *Eleutherai*
Babelsberg (city district, eastern Germany) : to 1938 *Nowawes* (Babelsberg was united with Neubabelsburg in 1938 and incorporated into Potsdam in the early 1940s.)
Babimost (town, western Poland) : 1793–1807, 1815–1945 German *Bomst*
Bābol (city, northern Iran) : to 1930 *Bārfurush*
Bābol Sar (town, northern Iran) : to 1930s *Meshed-e Sar*
Baborów (town, southern Poland) : to 1945 German *Bauerwitz*
Babruysk (city, central Belarus) : (Russian *Bobruysk*); to 1918 Russian *Bobruysk*
[1]Babushkin (city, western Russia) : to 1938 *Losinoostrovskaya* (Babushkin became part of Moscow in 1960.)
[2]Babushkin (town, southern Russia) : to 1941 *Mysovsk*
Babushkina, imeni (village, western Russia) : to c.1940 *Ledengskoye*
Bačka Palanka (town, northwestern Serbia) : to 1918, 1941–1944 Hungarian *Palánka*
Bačka Topola (town, northern Serbia) : to 1918, 1941–1944 Hungarian *Topolya*
Back River (Nunavut, northern Canada) : alternate *Great Fish River*
Bactra *see* Balkh
Badajoz (city, southwestern Spain) : Roman *Pax Augusta*
Badalona (town, northeastern Spain) : Roman *Baetulo*
Bad Altheide *see* Polanica Zdrój
Bad Düben (town, east central Germany) : to 1948 *Düben*
[1]Baden (town, northeastern Austria) : Roman *Aquae Pannoniae*
[2]Baden (town, northern Switzerland) : Roman *Aquae Helveticae*
Baden-Baden (city, southwestern Germany) : Roman *Aurelia Aquensis*
Bad Flinsberg *see* Świeradów Zdrój
Bad Königsdorf *see* Jastrzębie Zdrój
Bad Kudowa *see* Kudowa Zdrój
Bad Landeck *see* Lądek Zdrój
Bad Polzin *see* Połczyn Zdrój
Bad Reinerz *see* Duszniki Zdrój
Bad Salzbrunn *see* Szczawno Zdrój
Bad Schönfliess in Neumark *see* Trzcińsko Zdrój
Bad Segeberg (town, northwestern Germany) : to 1924 *Segeberg*
Bad Warmbrunn *see* Cieplice Śląskie Zdrój
Bae Colwyn *see* Colwyn Bay

Baer-le-Duc *see* Baarle-Hertog
Baeterrae *see* Béziers
Baetis *see* Guadalquivir
Baetulo *see* Badalona
Baffin Island (Nunavut, northern Canada) : formerly *Baffin Land*
Baffin Island National Park *see* Auyuittuq National Park
Baffin Land *see* Baffin Island
Bagachka *see* Velyka Bahachka
Bagenalstown *see* Muine Bheag
Bagh a Chaisteil *see* Castlebay
Baghdat'i (town, western Georgia) : 1940–1991 Russian *Mayakovsky*
Baghramyan (village, western Armenia) : formerly *Norakert*
Bagni della Porretta *see* Porretta Terme
Bagni San Giuliano *see* San Giuliano Terme
Bagnols-les-Bains (village, southern France) : Roman *Aquae Calidae*
Bagrationovsk (town, western Russia) : to 1946 German *Preussisch-Eylau* (The German name gave that of the 1807 battle of *Eylau* in the Napoleonic Wars, an indecisive encounter between the allied Russians and Prussians and the French. The town's current name derives from the Russian general Pyotr Bagration, who was present at the battle.)
Bahachka *see* Velyka Bahachka
Bahia *see* Salvador
Bahía Blanca (city, eastern Argentina) : to 1895 *Nueva Buenos Aires*
Baḥr al-Abyaḍ *see* White Nile
Baḥr al-Azraq *see* Blue Nile
Baḥr Lūt *see* Dead Sea
Baia Mare (town, northwestern Romania) : to 1918, 1940–1945 Hungarian *Nagybánya*
Baile Ailein *see* Balallan
Baile an Chaisil *see* ²Ballycastle
Baile an Mhóta *see* Ballymote
Baile an Róba *see* Ballinrobe
Baile Átha an Rí *see* Athenry
Baile Átha Cliath *see* Dublin
Baile Átha Í *see* Athy
Baile Átha Luain *see* Athlone
Baile Átha Troim *see* Trim
Baile Chaisleáin *see* ¹Ballycastle
Baile Chathail *see* Charlestown
Baile Coimín *see* Blessington
Baile Locha Riach *see* Loughrea
Baile Mhic Andáin *see* Thomastown
Baile Mhistéala *see* Mitchelstown
Baile Monaidh *see* Ballymoney
Baile na Lorgan *see* Castleblayney
Baile Nua na hArda *see* Newtownards
Baile Riobaird *see* Robertstown

Baile Shlaine *see* Slane
Baile Uí Fhiacháin *see* ³Newport
Baile Uí Mhatháin *see* Ballymahon
Bailieborough (town, northern Ireland) : Irish *Coill an Chollaigh*
Bailundo (town, west central Angola) : 1930s–1970s *Vila Teixeira da Silva*
Bailundo *see* Luau
Baixo Mearim *see* Vitória do Mearim
Bajada de Santa Fe *see* Paraná
Bajocasses *see* Bayeux
Bakal (town, west central Russia) : to 1928 *Bakalsky Zavod*
Bakalsky Zavod *see* Bakal
Bakar (village, western Croatia) : 1941–1944 Italian *Buccari*
Baker (town, North Dakota, northwestern United States) : to 1908 *Lorraine*
Baker *see* Baker City
Baker City (town, Oregon, western United States) : to 1989 *Baker*
Baker Lake (village, Nunavut, northern Canada) : alternate Inuit *Qamanittuaq*
Bakhmut *see* Artemivs'k
Bakhtaran *see* Kermanshah
Bakwanga *see* Mbuji-Mayi
Bakyrchik *see* Auezov
Bala (town, northern Wales) : Welsh *Y Bala* (*Bala Lake*, on which the town stands, is known in Welsh as *Llyn Tegid*.)
Balallan (village, Western Isles, northwestern Scotland) : Gaelic *Baile Ailein*
Balanda *see* Kalininsk
Balázsfalva *see* Blaj
Balbunar *see* Kubrat
Balchik (town, northeastern Bulgaria) : 1913–1940 Romanian *Balcic*; ancient Greek *Dionysopolis*
Balcic *see* Balchik
Balclutha (town, southern New Zealand) : formerly *Clutha Ferry*
Baldenburg *see* Biały Bór
Baldy, Mt. *see* San Antonio, Mt.
Bâle *see* Basel
Bâle-Ville *see* Basel-Stadt
Balfour (town, northeastern South Africa) : to 1905 *McHattiesburg*
Bălgrad *see* Alba Iulia
Bali Efendi *see* Knyazhevo
Balıhisar (village, central Turkey) : ancient Greek and Roman *Pessinus*
Balkan Mountains (central Bulgaria) : [Bulgarian *Stara Planina*]; Roman *Haemus*
Balkansky Priisk *see* Balkany
Balkany (town, west central Russia) : to 1929 *Balkansky Priisk*

Balkh (town, north central Afghanistan) : ancient Greek *Bactra*

Balkhash (city, eastern Kazakhstan) : to 1936 *Bertys*

Balkis (village, southern Turkey) : ancient Greek *Zeugma* (The Greek name, meaning "junction," referred to the twin colonies that stood either side of the Euphrates here.)

Balla Balla *see* **Mbalabala**

Ballina (town, western Ireland) : Irish *Béal an Átha*

Ballinasloe (town, western Ireland) : Irish *Béal Átha na Sluaighe*

Ballinrobe (town, western Ireland) : Irish *Baile na Róba*

¹**Ballycastle** (town, northern Northern Ireland) : Irish *Baile Chaisleáin*

²**Ballycastle** (village, northwestern Ireland) : Irish *Baile an Chaisil*

Ballydesmond (town, southeastern Ireland) : to 1938 *Kingwilliamstown*

Ballymahon (town, north central Ireland) : Irish *Baile Uí Mhatháin*

Ballymena (town, north central Northern Ireland) : Irish *An Baile Meánach*

Ballymoney (town, northern Northern Ireland) : Irish *Baile Monaidh*

Ballymote (town, northwestern Ireland) : Irish *Baile an Mhóta*

Ballyshannon (town, northwestern Ireland) : Irish *Béal Átha Seanaidh*

Balombo (town, western Angola) : 1920s–*c.*1979 Portuguese *Norton de Matos*

Balpyk Bi (town, southeastern Kazakhstan) : formerly Russian *Kirovsky*

Balsas (city, northeastern Brazil) : to 1944 *Santo Antônio de Balsas*

Bălţi (town, north central Moldova) : (Russian *Bel'tsy*); to 1918 Russian *Bel'tsy*

Baltic Port *see* **Paldiski**

Baltinglass (town, western Ireland) : Irish *Bealach Conglais*

Baltisch-Port *see* **Paldiski**

Baltiysk (town, western Russia) : to 1945 German *Pillau*

Baltiysky port *see* **Paldiski**

Baltser *see* ²**Krasnoarmeysk**

Balykchy (town, northern Kyrgyzstan) : 1989–1992 *Issyk-Kul'*; to 1989 Russian *Rybach'ye*

Banaba (island, western Kiribati) : alternate *Ocean Island*

Banatski Karlovac (village, northern Serbia) : formerly *Rankovićevo*; to 1947 *Karlovac*

Banbridge (town, south central Northern Ireland) : Irish *Droichead na Banna*

Bancroft (village, Ontario, southeastern Canada) : to 1878 *York River*

Bancroft *see* **Chililabombwe**

Bandar-e Abbas (city, southern Iran) : to 1622 English *Gombroon*

Bandar-e Anzali (city, northwestern Iran) : to 1980 *Bandar-e Pahlavi*

Bandar-e Būshehr *see* **Būshehr**

Bandar-e Emām Khomeinī (city, southwestern Iran) : to 1979 *Bandar-e Shahpur*

Bandar-e Pahlavi *see* **Bandar-e Abzali**

Bandar-e Shah *see* **Bandar-e Torkeman**

Bandar-e Shahpur *see* **Bandar-e Emām Khomeinī**

Bandar-e Torkeman (town, northern Iran) : to 1979 *Bandar-e Shah*

Bandar Maharani *see* **Muar**

Bandar Seri Begawan (city, northern Brunei) : to 1970 *Brunei Town*

Bandon (town, southern Ireland) : Irish *Droichead na Bandan*

Bandundu (city, western Democratic Republic of the Congo) : to 1966 French *Banningville*

Banghāzī (city, northern Libya) : conventional *Benghazi*; ancient Greek *Berenice*; earlier ancient Greek *Hesperides*; alternate ancient Greek *Euhesperides*

Bangkok (city, central Thailand) : locally *Krung Thep* (The city's local name, traditionally translated "city of angels," represents the first part of a famously lengthy full name.)

Bangladesh (republic, southern Asia) : 1947–1971 *East Pakistan*; to 1947 *East Bengal*

¹**Bangor** (town, eastern Northern Ireland) : Irish *Beannchar*

²**Bangor** (city, Maine, northeastern United States) : 1787–1791 *Sunbury*; to 1787 *Kenduskeag Plantation*

Bangor is-coed *see* **Bangor-on-Dee**

Bangor-on-Dee (village, northeastern Wales) : Welsh *Bangor is-coed*

Banias (village, southwestern Syria) : Roman and biblical *Caesarea Philippi*; ancient Greek *Paneas*

Banivs'ke *see* **Slov'yanohirs'k**

Banjul (city, western Gambia) : to 1973 *Bathurst*

Bankä (town, southeastern Azerbaijan) : 1939–*c.*1940 Russian *imeni Kirova*; to 1939 *imeni Narimanova*

Banki *see* ¹**Krasnogorsk**

Bannack City *see* **Idaho City**

Bannau Brycheiniog *see* **Brecon Beacons**

Banningville *see* **Bandundu**

Bannovalium *see* **Horncastle**

Bannovsky *see* **Slov'yanohirs'k**

Bannu (town, north central Pakistan) : 1869–1903 *Edwardesabad*; to 1869 *Dalipnagar*

Banská Bystrica (town, central Slovakia) : to 1918 Hungarian *Besztercebánya*; to 1867 German *Neusohl*

Banská Štiavnica (town, southern Slovakia) : to 1918 Hungarian *Selmecbánya*; to 1867 German *Schemnitz*

Bantry (town, southwestern Ireland) : Irish *Beanntraí*

Banzart *see* **Bizerta**

Banzyville *see* **Mobayi-Mbongo**

Bar (town, southwestern Montenegro) : formerly Italian *Antivari*

Barabbas *see* **Barvas**

Baran (town, eastern Belarus) : *c.*1918–1920s Russian *Krasny Oktyabr'*

Baranavichy (city, western Belarus) : (Russian *Baranovichi*); 1919–1939 Polish *Baranowicze*; to 1918 Russian *Baranovichi*

Baranchinsky (town, west central Russia) : to 1928 *Baranchinsky Zavod*

Baranchinsky Zavod *see* **Baranchinsky**

Baranovichi *see* **Baranavichy**

Baranowicze *see* **Baranavichy**

Barão de Cocais (city, southeastern Brazil) : to 1944 *Morro Grande*

Barbuda (island, eastern West Indies) : formerly *Dulcina*

Barbudo *see* **El Banco**

Barca *see* **Al Marj**

Barce *see* **Al Marj**

Barcelona (city, northeastern Spain) : formerly *Barcinona*; Roman *Barcino* (The full title of the Roman port city was *Colonia Julia Augusta Paterna Barcino*.)

Barcino *see* **Barcelona**

Barcinona *see* **Barcelona**

Barczewo (town, northeastern Poland) : to 1945 German *Wartenburg*

Bardejov (town, northeastern Slovakia) : to 1918 Hungarian *Bártfa*; to 1867 German *Bartfeld*

Bardo (town, southwestern Poland) : to 1945 German *Wartha*

Bardsey (island, western Wales) : Welsh *Ynys Enlli*

Bardstown (town, Kentucky, east central United States) : originally *Salem*

Bārfurush *see* **Bābol**

Bar Harbor (town, Maine, northeastern United States) : to 1918 *Eden*

Bari (city, southeastern Italy) : Roman *Barium*

Barium *see* **Bari**

Bar-le-Duc (town, northeastern France) : Medieval Latin *Castrum Barrum*

Barlinek (town, northwestern Poland) : to 1945 German *Berlinchen*

Barmen-Elberfeld *see* **Wuppertal**

Barmouth (town, western Wales) : Welsh *Abermo*; alternate Welsh *Y Bermo*

Bärn *see* **MoravskýBeroun**

Barnsdall (town, Oklahoma, south central United States) : to 1921 *Bigheart*

Baroda *see* **Vadodara**

Barotseland *see* **Western**

Barra (island, Western Isles, northwestern Scotland) : Gaelic *Barraigh*

Barra Bonita *see* **Ibaiti**

Barracas al Sur *see* **Avellaneda**

Barraigh *see* **Barra**

Barre (town, Vermont, northeastern United States) : originally *Wildersburgh*

Barretts Cross *see* **Kensington**

Barrón Escandón *see* **Apizaco**

Barry (town, southern Wales) : Welsh *Y Barri*

Barstow (city, California, western United States) : to 1886 *Waterman Junction*; originally *Fishpond*

Bartang (village, southeastern Tajikistan) : to *c.*1935 *Siponzh*

Bartenstein *see* **Bartoszyce**

Bártfa *see* **Bardejov**

Bartfeld *see* **Bardejov**

Bartholomew Island *see* **Malo**

Bartolo *see* **Betanzos**

Bartoszyce (town, northeastern Poland) : to 1945 German *Bartenstein*

Barvas (village, Western Isles, northwestern Scotland) : Gaelic *Barabhas*

Bärwalde *see* **Barwice**

Barwice (town, northwestern Poland) : to 1945 German *Bärwalde*

Baryshnikovo *see* **[1]Krasnogorskoye**

Basarabeasca (town, southern Moldova) : (Russian *Bessarabka*); formerly Russian *Romanovka*

Basargechar *see* **Vardenis**

Basel (city, northern Switzerland) : conventional English *Basle*; French *Bâle*; Italian *Basilea*; Roman *Basilea*; earlier Roman *Robur* (English generally uses the German form of the name, although older French *Basle* was long current and the spelling *Basil* also existed. The city is capital of, and virtually coextensive with, the demicanton of **Basel-Stadt**.)

Basel-Landschaft (demicanton, northern Switzerland) : French *Bâle-Campagne* (The demicanton was formed in 1833 by the division of **Basel** canton into two half-cantons.)

Basel-Stadt (demicanton, northern Switzerland) : French *Bâle-Ville* (The demicanton was formed in 1833 by the division of **Basel** canton into two half-cantons.)

Bashanta *see* **Gorodovikovsk**

Bashkicheti *see* **Dmanisi**

Bashkiria *see* **Bashkortostan**

Bashkortostan (republic, western Russia) : to 1991 *Bashkiria*

Bashtanka (town, southern Ukraine) : to *c.*1930 *Poltavka*

Basil *see* **Basel**

Basilea *see* **Basel**

Basilicata (region, southern Italy) : Roman *Lucania*

Basle *see* **Basel**

[1]Basque Country (region, northern Spain) : [Spanish *País Vasco*; Basque *Euskadi*] (The Roman region of *Vasconia* gave the Spanish name of this region as well as that of **Gascony**, France, and ultimately the word *Basque* itself. *Cp.* [2]**Basque Country**.)

[2]Basque Country (region, southwestern France) : [French *Pays Basque*] (Unlike Spain's [1]**Basque Country**, which is both a historical region and an autonomous community, the French region is cultural only.)

Basses-Alpes *see* **Alpes-de-Haute-Provence**

Basses-Pyrénées *see* **Pyrénées-Atlantiques**

Bassett-town *see* [2]**Washington**

Bassopiano Orientale *see* **Massawa**

Bastenaken *see* **Bastogne**

Basti *see* **Baza**

Bastogne (town, southeastern Belgium) : Flemish *Bastenaken*

Basutoland *see* **Lesotho**

Batalhão *see* **Taperoá**

Batalpashinsk *see* **Cherkessk**

Batalpashinskaya *see* **Cherkessk**

Batavia *see* **Jakarta**

Batbakkara *see* **Amangeldy**

[1]Bath (city, southwestern England) : Medieval Latin *Bathonia*; Roman *Aquae Sulis*; alternate Roman *Aquae Calidae*

[2]Bath (village, Ontario, southeastern Canada) : to 1812 *Ernestown*

Bath *see* **Berkeley Springs**

Bathonia *see* [1]**Bath**

Bathurst (town, New Brunswick, eastern Canada) : to 1826 *St. Peters*; originally *Nepisiguit*

Bathurst *see* **Banjul**

Bathurst Inlet (village, Nunavut, northern Canada) : alternate Inuit *Qingaq*

Batken (town, western Kyrgyzstan) : to 1945 *Batken-Buzhum*

Batken-Buzhum *see* **Batken**

Batna (city, northeastern Algeria) : to 1849 French *Nouvelle-Lambèse*

Bat'ovany *see* **Partizánske**

Bat Yam (city, west central Israel) : to 1936 *Bayit veGan*

Baudens *see* **Belarbi**

Baudouinville *see* **Moba**

Bauerwitz *see* **Baborów**

Bauman *see* **Shofirkon**

Baumanabad *see* **Panj**

Bausk *see* **Bauska**

Bauska (town, southern Latvia) : to 1918 Russian *Bausk*

Bauyrzhan Momyshuly (town, southern Kazakhstan) : formerly Russian *Burnoye*

Bauzanum *see* **Bolzano**

Bavaria (state, southern Germany) : [German *Bayern*]

Baxt (town, eastern Uzbekistan) : to 1963 Russian *Velikoalekseyevsky*

Bayan Tumen *see* **Choybalsan**

Bayern *see* **Bavaria**

Bayeux (town, northwestern France) : Roman *Augustodurum*; Celtic *Bajocasses*

Bayganin (village, west central Kazakhstan) : formerly *Karaulkeldy*

Bayhead (village, Western Isles, northwestern Scotland) : Gaelic *Ceann a Bhaigh*

Bayit veGan *see* **Bat Yam**

Baykadam *see* **Saudakent**

Baykonur *see* **Baykonyr**

Baykonyr (town, south central Kazakhstan) : (Russian *Baykonur*); formerly Russian *Leninsk* (The town is the site of the Soviet space-launch complex, which for purposes of disinformation borrowed the name of another Baykonyr, 220 miles to the northeast, near Zhezkazgan.)

Bayley's Reward *see* **Coolgardie**

Baymak (town, west central Russia) : to 1944 *Baymak-Tanalykovo*

Baymak-Tanalykovo *see* **Baymak**

[1]Bayonne (town, southwestern France) : Roman *Lapurdum*

[2]Bayonne (city, New Jersey, northeastern United States) : to 1869 *Konstable Hoeck*

Bayrak *see* **Kalinins'k**

Bayram-Ali *see* **Bayramaly**

Bayramaly (city, southeastern Turkmenistan) : formerly *Bayram-Ali*

Bayrūt *see* **Beirut**

Bayt Laḥm *see* **Bethlehem**

Baza (city, southern Spain) : Roman *Basti*

Bazarcik *see* **Dobrich**

Bazargic *see* **Dobrich**

Bazin *see* **Pezinok**

Beaconsfield (town, Victoria, southeastern Australia) : to 1879 *Brandy Creek*

Bealach Conglais *see* **Baltinglass**

Béal an Átha *see* **Ballina**

Béal an Mhuirthead *see* **Belmullet**

Béal Átha na Muice *see* Swinford
Béal Átha na Sluaighe *see* Ballinasloe
Béal Átha Seanaidh *see* Ballyshannon
Béal Feirste *see* Belfast
Béal na mBuillí *see* Strokestown
Béal Tairbirt *see* Belturbet
Beannchar *see* ¹Bangor
Beanntraí *see* Bantry
Beaucaire (town, southern France) : Medieval
    Latin *Belli Quadrum*; Roman *Ugernum*
Beaufort (village, southeastern Wales) : Welsh
    Cendl
Beaufort *see* Montmorency-Beaufort
Beaumaris (town, northwestern Wales) : Welsh
    Biwmares
Beaumont (city, Texas, southern United States) :
    to 1835 *Tevis Bluff*
Beaune (town, east central France) : Roman *Belna*
Beauvais (town, northern France) : Roman
    Bellovacum; earlier Roman *Caesaromagus*
Beaver River *see* Beaverton
Beaverton (village, Ontario, southeastern Can-
    ada) : to 1928 *Beaver River*
Bečej (town, northern Serbia) : to 1918, 1941–
    1944 Hungarian *Óbecse* (The town was also
    known as *Stari Bečej*, "Old Bečej," matching
    the former Hungarian name.)
Béchar (town, western Algeria) : to *c.*1962
    French *Colomb-Béchar*
Bechuanaland *see* Botswana
Bécs *see* Vienna
Beda Littoria *see* Sidi Rafa
Bedeau *see* Ras el Ma
Bedford (town, Quebec, southeastern Canada) :
    formerly *Stanbridge Falls*
Bedloe's Island *see* Liberty Island
Bednodem'yanovsk (town, western Russia) : to
    1925 *Spassk*
Będzin (town, southeastern Poland) : 1940–1945
    German *Bendsburg*; to 1915 Russian *Bendin*
Beekmanton *see* Sleepy Hollow
Beeroth *see* Al Bīrah
Beersheba (town, southern Israel) : [Hebrew
    Be'er Sheva'; Arabic *Bīr as-Saba'*]
Be'er Sheva' *see* Beersheba
Beeson's Town *see* Uniontown
Beeton (village, Ontario, southeastern Canada) :
    to 1878 *Clarksville*
Begovat *see* Bekobod
Behshahr (town, northern Iran) : to mid–1930s
    Ashraf
Bei-alan *see* Smirnenski
Beijing (city, northeastern China) : formerly
    conventional *Peking*; 1368–1403, 1928–1949
    Peiping; 13th century *Khanbalik* (conventional
    Cambaluc); earlier *Yen*

Beinn na Faoghla *see* Benbecula
Beirut (city, western Lebanon) : [Arabic *Bayrūt*];
    formerly French *Beyrouth*; Roman *Berytus*
    (The city was captured by the French in 1918
    in a campaign against Turkey.)
Beit Guvrin (kibbutz, western Israel) : ancient
    Greek *Eleutheropolis*
Beitsch *see* Biecz
Beja (city, southern Portugal) : Roman *Pax Julia*
Béja (town, northern Tunisia) : Roman *Vacca*
Bejaïa (city, northeastern Algeria) : to *c.*1962
    French *Bougie*; Roman *Saldae*
Bekabad *see* Bekobod
Bek-Budi *see* Qarshi
Bekobod (city, eastern Uzbekistan) : (Russian
    Bekabad); to 1964 *Begovat*
Bela Aliança *see* Rio do Sul
Bela-Bela (town, northern South Africa) :
    1920–2002 *Warmbad* (alternate English
    Warmbaths); to 1920 *Hartingsburg*
Bela Crkva (town, eastern Serbia) : to 1918 Hun-
    garian *Fehértemplom*; to 1867 German *Weiss-
    kirchen*
Bela Palanka (town, southeastern Serbia) : to
    1878 Turkish *Akpalanka*
Bělá pod Bezdězem (town, western Czech Re-
    public) : to 1918, 1939–1945 German *Weiss-
    wasser*
Belarbi (village, northwestern Algeria) : to *c.*1962
    French *Baudens*
Belarus (republic, eastern Europe) : to 1991 *Be-
    lorussia* [Russian *Belorossiya*]; earlier English
    traditional *White Russia*
Bela Slatina *see* Byala Slatina
Belavezha *see* Białowieża
Bela Vista *see* Echaporã
Belaya Kalitva (city, western Russia) : to 1941
    Ust'-Belokalitvenskaya
Belaya Padleskaya *see* Biała Podlaska
Belaya Podlyashskaya *see* Biała Podlaska
Belaya Tserkov' *see* Bila Tserkva
Belém (city, northern Brazil) : alternate *Pará*
Belém *see* Palmeirais
Belerium *see* Land's End
Belfast (city, eastern Northern Ireland) : Irish
    Béal Feirste
Belfast *see* Port Fairy
Belgard *see* Białogard
Belgian Congo *see* Congo, Democratic Re-
    public of the
België *see* Belgium
Belgique *see* Belgium
Belgium (kingdom, northwestern Europe) :
    [Flemish *België*; French *Belgique*]; to 1830
    Spanish Netherlands
Belgoray *see* Biłgoraj

Belgorod *see* **Bilhorod-Dnistrovs'kyy**

Belgorod-Dnestrovsky *see* **Bilhorod-Dnistrovs'kyy**

Belgrade (city, central Serbia) : [Serbo-Croat *Beograd*]; Roman *Singidunum*

Belhaven *see* ²**Alexandria**

Beligrad *see* **Berat**

Belingwe *see* **Mberengwa**

Belinsky (town, southwestern Russia) : to 1948 *Chembar*

Belize (country, northeastern Central America) : 1840–1971 *British Honduras*

Bella Unión (city, northwestern Uruguay) : to 1930s *Santa Rosa*

Bella Vista (town, southern Mexico) : to 1934 *San Pedro Remate*

Belle-Anse (town, southern Haiti) : formerly *Saltrou*

Belle Glade (town, Florida, southeastern United States) : to 1921 *Hillsborough Canal Settlement*

Bellehaven *see* **Arlington**

Belleville (city, Ontario, southeastern Canada) : to 1816 *Meyers' Creek*

Bellingham (city, Washington, northwestern United States) : to 1903 *Whatcom* (The city was formed when Whatcom merged with three other communities.)

Bellingshausen Island *see* **Motu One**

Belli Quadrum *see* **Beaucaire**

Bellovacum *see* **Beauvais**

Bell Rock (island, eastern Scotland) : alternate *Inchcape Rock* (The alternate name was popularized by Robert Southey's 1802 ballad "The Inchcape Rock." *See also* **Arbroath**.)

Belluno (city, northeastern Italy) : Roman *Bellunum*

Bellunum *see* **Belluno**

Belmeken *see* **Kolarov**

Belmonte *see* **Kuito**

Belmullet (town, western Ireland) : Irish *Béal an Mhuirthead*

Belna *see* **Beaune**

Belogorsk (city, eastern Russia) : 1935–1957 *Kuybyshevka-Vostochnaya*; 1931–1935 *Krasnopartizansk*; 1926–1931 *Aleksandrovsk*; 1860–1926 *Bochkarevo*

Belogorsk *see* **Bilohirs'k**

Belogor'ye *see* **Bilohirya**

Belo Horizonte (city, eastern Brazil) : to 1901 *Cidade de Minas*

Belokamensk *see* **Inkerman**

Belolutsk *see* **Biloluts'k**

Belolutskaya *see* **Biloluts'k**

Belomorsk (town, northwestern Russia) : to 1938 *Soroka*

Belorossiya *see* **Belarus**

Belorussia *see* **Belarus**

Beloretsk (town, west central Russia) : to 1923 *Beloretsky Zavod*

Beloretsky Zavod *see* **Beloretsk**

Beloshchel'ye *see* **Nar'yan-Mar**

Belostok *see* **Białystok**

Belotsarsk *see* **Kyzyl**

Belovár *see* **Bjelovar**

Belovezha *see* **Białowieża**

Belovo *see* **Zemen**

Belovodsk *see* **Bilovods'k**

Belovodskoye *see* **Bilovods'k**

Belsk *see* **Bielsk Podlaski**

Bel'tsy *see* **Bălţi**

Belturbet (town, northern Ireland) : Irish *Béal Tairbirt*

Bely Bychek *see* **Chagoda**

Bely Klyuch *see* **Krasny Klyuch**

Belyye Kresty *see* **Sazonovo**

Belyye Vody *see* ²**Aksu**

Beman's Corners *see* **Newmarket**

Benacus *see* **Garda**

Benares *see* **Varanasi**

Benbecula (island, Western Isles, northwestern Scotland) : Gaelic *Beinn na Faoghla*

Bend (city, Oregon, western United States) : originally *Farewell Bend*

Bender *see* **Tighina**

Bendery *see* **Tighina**

Bendigo (city, Victoria, southeastern Australia) : to 1891 *Sandhurst*

Bendin *see* **Będzin**

Bendix *see* **Teterborough**

Bendsburg *see* **Będzin**

Beneditinos (town, northeastern Brazil) : to 1944 *São Benedito*

Benefactor *see* ¹**San Juan**

Beneschau *see* (1) **Benešov**; (2) **Dolní Benešov**

Benešov (town, central Czech Republic) : to 1918, 1939–1945 German *Beneschau*

Benevento (city, southern Italy) : Roman *Beneventum*; earlier Roman *Maleventum*

Beneventum *see* **Benevento**

Benghazi *see* **Banghāzī**

Benin (country, western Africa) : to 1975 *Dahomey*

Bennachie (upland area, northeastern Scotland) : Roman *Graupius Mons* (The Roman name has been spuriously connected with the *Grampian* mountains in this part of Scotland.)

Ben Slimane (town, northwestern Morocco) : formerly French *Boulhaut*

Bentinck *see* ³**Durham**

Benton Harbor (town, Michigan, north central United States) : originally *Brunson Harbor*

Bentschen *see* **Zbąszyń**

Beograd *see* **Belgrade**

Berane (town, eastern Montenegro) : 1949–1992 *Ivangrad*

Bérard *see* **Aïn Tagourit**

Berat (town, south central Albania) : Medieval Slavonic *Beligrad*; ancient Greek *Antipatria*

Beraun *see* **Beroun**

Berdichev *see* **Berdychiv**

Berdyansk *see* **Berdyans'k**

Berdyans'k (city, southeastern Ukraine) : (Russian *Berdyansk*); 1939–1958 *Osypenko* (Russian *Osipenko*)

Berdychiv (city, west central Ukraine) : (Russian *Berdichev*); to 1918 Russian *Berdichev*

Berea *see* **Véroia**

Beregovo *see* **Berehove**

Beregovoy (village, eastern Russia) : formerly *Kharino*

Beregszász *see* **Berehove**

Berehove (city, western Ukraine) : (Russian *Beregovo*); 1944–1945 Czech *Berehovo*; 1938–1945 Hungarian *Beregszász*; 1919–1938 Czech *Berehovo*; to 1918 German *Sächsisch-Bereg*

Berehovo *see* **Berehove**

Berenice *see* **Banghāzī**

Berenicia *see* **Préveza**

Berent *see* **Kościerzyna**

Bereza Kartuska *see* **Byaroza**

Berezanka (town, southern Ukraine) : to *c.*1960 *Tylyhulo-Berezanka* (Russian *Tiligulo-Berezanka*)

Berezhany (town, western Ukraine) : 1919–1939 Polish *Brzeżany*

Bereznik (town, northwestern Russia) : to 1962 *Semyonovskoye*

Berezniki (town, western Russia) : to 1933 *Usol'ye-Solikamskoye*

Bergama (town, western Turkey) : Roman *Pergamum*; ancient Greek *Pergamon*

Bergamo (city, northern Italy) : Roman *Bergomum*

Bergen (city, southwestern Norway) : originally *Bjørgvin*

Bergen *see* **Mons**

Bergen Iron Works *see* [1]**Lakewood**

Bergomum *see* **Bergamo**

Bergreichenstein *see* **Kašperské Hory**

Bergstadt *see* **Lešnica**

Bergytown *see* **Hespeler**

Berkeley Springs (town, West Virginia, east central United States) : formerly (and still officially) *Bath*

Berkovets *see* **Kotsyubyns'ke**

Berkovets' *see* **Kotsyubyns'ke**

Berlengas *see* **Valença do Piauí**

[1]**Berlin** (town, Connecticut, northeastern United States) : to 1785 *Kensington*

[2]**Berlin** (town, New Hampshire, northeastern United States) : to 1821 *Maynesborough*

Berlin *see* **Kitchener**

Berlinchen *see* **Barlinek**

Bermuda (island group, northwestern Atlantic) : formerly English *Somers Islands*

Bern (city, west central Switzerland) : French *Berne*; Italian *Berna* (English generally prefers the German form of the name, although the French form is sometimes used alternately.)

Berna *see* **Bern**

Bernardsville (town, New Jersey, northeastern United States) : to 1840 *Vealtown*

Berne *see* **Bern**

Bernolákovo (town, southwestern Slovakia) : to 1918, 1938–1945 Hungarian *Cseklész*

Bernstadt *see* **Bierutów**

Bernstein *see* **Pełczyce**

Beroea *see* **Aleppo**

Beroun (town, western Czech Republic) : to 1918, 1938–1945 German *Beraun*

Berrahal (village, northeastern Algeria) : formerly *Aïn Mokra*

Berriam *see* **Kewanee**

Bertolínia (town, northeastern Brazil) : to 1944 *Aparacida*

Bertys *see* **Balkhash**

Beruniy (town, western Uzbekistan) : to 1958 *Shabbaz*

Berwyn *see* **Gene Autry**

Beryoza *see* **Byaroza**

Berytus *see* **Beirut**

Besançon (city, eastern France) : Roman *Vesontio*

Beshariq (town, western Uzbekistan) : *c.*1940–1983 Russian *Kirovo*; 1937–*c.*1940 Russian *imeni Kirova*

Bessarabka *see* **Basarabeasca**

Beszterce *see* **Bistriţa**

Besztercebánya *see* **Banská Bystrica**

Betanzos (town, southeastern Bolivia) : to 1900s *Bartolo*

Bethany *see* **Al-'Ayzarīyah**

Bethlehem (city, south central West Bank) : [Arabic *Bayt Laḥm*]

Beth-shemesh *see* **Heliopolis**

Bet She'an (town, northeastern Israel) : ancient Greek *Scythopolis*

Bettendorf (city, Iowa, north central United States) : to 1902 *Lilienthal*

Beuthen *see* **Bytom**

Beuvray, Mont (mountain, east central France) : Roman *Bibracte* (The Roman name was that of a hill fort here, the original capital of the Aedui, a Celtic people, who later moved to *Augustodunum*, modern **Autun**.)

Beverly *see* **Beverly Hills**

Beverly Hills (city, California, western United States) : 1906–1914 *Beverly*; to 1906 *Rancho Rodeo de las Aguas*

Beverwyck *see* ¹**Albany**

Bewcastle (hamlet, northern England) : Roman *Fanum Cocidi* (The assignment of the Roman name to this particular location is tentative but made on plausible grounds.)

Beyläqan (town, southern Azerbaijan) : to 1989 Russian *Zhdanovsk*

Beyrouth *see* **Beirut**

Beyuk-Vedi *see* **Vedi**

Bezdružice (village, western Czech Republic) : to 1918, 1939–1945 German *Weseritz*

Bezhitsa (town, western Russia) : 1936–1943 *Ordzhonikidzegrad* (The town was incorporated into the city of Bryansk in 1956.)

Béziers (city, southern France) : Roman *Baeterrae*

Bezmer (village, southeastern Bulgaria) : to 1934 Turkish *Khamzoren*

Bhadgaon (town, central Nepal) : formerly *Bhaktapur*

Bhaktapur *see* **Bhadgaon**

Bhārat *see* **India**

Bhatner *see* **Hanumangarh**

Bhutan (kingdom, southeastern Asia) : local (Tibetan) *Druk-Yul* (The local name gave the country's English byname "Land of the Dragon.")

Biafra, Bight of (western Africa) : alternate *Bight of Bonny*

Biała (town, southwestern Poland) : to 1945 German *Zülz*

Biała Piska (town, northeastern Poland) : 1938–1945 German *Bialla*; to 1938 German *Gehlenburg*

Biała Podlaska (town, eastern Poland) : 1939–1941 Belarussian *Belaya Padleskaya*; to 1918 Russian *Belaya Podlyashskaya*

Bialla *see* **Biała Piska**

Białogard (town, northwestern Poland) : to 1945 German *Belgard*

Białowieża (village, eastern Poland) : 1939–1941 Belarussian *Belavezha*; to 1915 Russian *Belovezha*

Biały Bór (town, northwestern Poland) : to 1945 German *Baldenburg*

Biały Kamień (town, southwestern Poland) : to 1945 German *Weiss-stein*

Białystok *see* **Białystok**

Białystok (city, northeastern Poland) : 1941–1944 German *Bialystok*; 1939–1941 Russian *Belostok*; 1795–1807 German *Bialystok*

Biarritz (town, southwestern France) : [Basque *Miarritze*]

Bibala (town, southwestern Angola) : to *c.*1979 Portuguese *Vila Arriaga*

Bibracte *see* **Beuvray, Mont**

Bibrka (town, western Ukraine) : (Russian *Bobrka*); to 1939 Polish *Bóbrka*

Biddeford *see* **Saco**

Biecz (town, southeastern Poland) : to 1945 German *Beitsch*

Biel (city, northwestern Switzerland) : French *Bienne*

Bielau *see* **Pilawa**

Bielawa (town, southwestern Poland) : to 1945 German *Langenbielau*

Bielitz *see* **Bielsko**

Bielsko (town, southern Poland) : to 1919, 1939–1945 German *Bielitz* (In 1950 Bielsko united with *Biała* to form the city of *Bielsko-Biała*.)

Bielsk Podlaski (town, northeastern Poland) : 1807–1915 Russian *Belsk*

Bienne *see* **Biel**

Bierry-les-Belles-Fontaines (village, north central France) : 1738–1882 *Anstrude*

Bierutów (town, southwestern Poland) : to 1945 German *Bernstadt*

Big Boiling Springs *see* **Russellville**

Big Bull Falls *see* **Wausau**

Big Glades *see* **Wise**

Bigheart *see* **Barnsdall**

Bight of Biafra *see* **Biafra, Bight of**

Big Lick *see* **Roanoke**

Big St. Joseph Station *see* **South Bend**

Bihać (town, western Bosnia-Herzegovina) : to 1878 Turkish *Bihkeh*

Bihkeh *see* **Bihać**

Bikini (atoll, central Marshall Islands) : formerly *Eschscholtz Island*

Biläsuvar (town, southeastern Azerbaijan) : formerly Russian *Pushkino*

Bila Tserkva (town, northern Ukraine) : (Russian *Belaya Tserkov'*); to 1918 Russian *Belaya Tserkov'*; to 1155 Russian *Yur'yev*

Bileća (town, southern Bosnia-Herzegovina) : to 1878 Turkish *Bilek*

Bilek *see* **Bileća**

Biłhoraj (town, eastern Poland) : to 1915 Russian *Belgoray*

Bilhorod-Dnistrovs'kyy (city, southern Ukraine) : (Russian *Belgorod-Dnestrovsky*); 1940–1944 Russian *Belgorod*; 1918–1940 Romanian *Cetatea Albă*; 1812–1918 Russian *Belgorod*; 1484–1812 Turkish *Akkerman*; ancient Greek *Tyras*

Bilimbay (town, west central Russia) : to 1929 *Bilimbayevsky Zavod*

Bilimbayevsky Zavod *see* **Bilibay**

Bilin *see* **Bílina**

Bílina (town, northwestern Czech Republic) : to 1918, 1938–1945 German *Bilin*
Billings *see* **Monett**
Bilohirs'k (town, southern Ukraine) : (Russian *Belogorsk*); to 1944 *Karasubazar*
Bilohirya (town, west central Ukraine) : (Russian *Belogor'ye*); to 1946 *Lyakhivtsi* (Russian *Lyakhovtsy*)
Bilokam'yans'k *see* **Inkerman**
Biloluts'k (town, eastern Ukraine) : (Russian *Belolutsk*); to 1927 *Biloluts'ka* (Russian *Belolutskaya*)
Biloluts'ka *see* **Biloluts'k**
Bílovec (town, eastern Czech Republic) : to 1918, 1938–1945 German *Wagstadt*
Bilovods'k (town, eastern Ukraine) : (Russian *Belovodsk*); to 1937 *Bilovods'ke* (Russian *Belovodskoye*)
Bilovods'ke *see* **Bilovods'k**
Bindloe Island *see* **Marchena, Isla**
Binghamton (city, New York, northeastern United States) : originally *Chenango Point*
Binn Éadair *see* **Howth**
Biograd na Moru (town, southern Croatia) : to 1918 Italian *Zaravecchia*
Bioko (island, northwestern Equatorial Guinea) 1973–1979 *Macías Nguema Biyogo*; 1494–1973 *Fernando Po*; earlier Portuguese *Formosa*
Biorra *see* **Birr**
Bipontium *see* **Zweibrücken**
Birgu *see* **Vittoriosa**
Birkat Qārūn (lake, northern Egypt) : ancient Greek *Lake Moeris* (The present lake is smaller in size than the original, whose ancient Egyptian name means "big lake.")
Bir Mogreïn (town, northern Mauritania) : to *c.*1958 French *Fort-Trinquet*
Birnbaum *see* **Międzychód**
Birobidzhan (city, southeastern Russia) : to 1928 *Tikhon'kaya*
Birr (town, central Ireland) : Irish *Biorra*; formerly English *Parsonstown*
Bīr as-Saba' *see* **Beersheba**
Biruintsa *see* **Ştefan Vodă**
Biryuch *see* ¹**Krasnogvardeyskoye**
Biryusinsk (town, eastern Russia) : to 1987 *Suyetikha*
Biržai (town, northern Lithuania) : (Russian *Birzhay*); to 1918 Russian *Birzhi*
Birzhay *see* **Biržai**
Birzhi *see* **Biržai**
Birzula *see* **Kotovs'k**
Bisanthe *see* **Tekirdağ**
Biscari *see* **Acate**
Biscay, Bay of (western France/northern Spain) : French *Golfe de Gascogne*; Spanish *Golfo de*

Vizcaya; Roman *Mare Cantabricum* (English prefers to name the bay for the Spanish province of **Vizcaya**; French for the French province of **Gascony**. The Roman name relates to the modern Spanish province of **Cantabria**. Geographers point out that the English name generally covers a larger stretch of water than the French or Spanish.)
Bischoflack *see* **Škofja Loka**
Bischofsburg *see* **Biskupice**
Bischofstal *see* **Ujazd**
Bischofstein *see* **Bisztynek**
Bischofteinitz *see* **Horšovský Týn**
Bisert (town, west central Russia) : to 1942 *Bisertsky Zavod*
Bisertsky Zavod *see* **Bisert**
Bishkek (city, northern Kyrgyzstan) : 1926–1991 Russian *Frunze*; 1862–1926 Russian *Pishpek*
Bishopston (village, southern Wales) : Welsh *Llandeilo Ferwallt*
Biskupice (town, southeastern Poland) : to 1945 German *Bischofsburg*
Biskupiec (town, northeastern Poland) : to 1945 German *Bischofswerder*
Bismarck (city, North Dakota, northern United States) : to 1873 *Camp Hancock*; earlier *Camp Greeley*; originally *Crossing on the Missouri*
Bismarckburg *see* **Kasanga**
Bistriţa (city, north central Romania) : 1940–1944 Hungarian *Beszterce*; to 1867 German *Bistritz*
Bistritz *see* **Bistriţa**
Bisztynek (town, northeastern Poland) : to 1945 German *Bischofstein*
Bitola (city, southern Macedonia) : to 1913 Turkish *Monastir*
Bitonto (town, southeastern Italy) : Roman *Butuntum*
Bitterne (village, southern England) : Roman *Clausentum* (The Roman name has also been applied to the village of Wickham, 6 miles to the west, but the coastal site, with its historic naval base, is the traditional one. Bitterne is now a suburb of Southampton.)
Bituricum *see* **Bourges**
Biwmares *see* **Beaumaris**
Biyuk-Onlar *see* **Oktyabrs'ke**
Bizerta (city, northern Tunisia) : alternate *Banzart*; Roman *Hippo Zarytus*, earlier Roman *Hippo Diarrhytus*
Bjelovar (town, central Croatia) : to 1918 Hungarian *Belovár*
Bjørgvin *see* **Bergen**
Björkö *see* ²**Primorsk**
Björneborg *see* **Pori**

Blachownia (town, southern Poland) : to 1945 German *Blechhammer*

Black Forest (wooded region, western Germany) : [German *Schwarzwald*]

Black Mountain (southern Wales) : Welsh *Y Mynydd Du* (The range lies to the west of the **Black Mountains**, which partly extend into England.)

Black Mountains (southeastern Wales) : Welsh *Mynydd Du* (The Welsh name translates as "Black Mountain," and a plural equivalent, *Y Mynyddoedd Duon*, is sometimes found.)

Black River (southwestern China/northern Vietnam) : Vietnamese *Song Da*; Chinese *Hei Chiang*

Black River *see* **Lorain**

Blackrock (town, eastern Ireland) : Irish *An Charraig Dhubh*

Black Sea (southern Europe) : former alternate English *Euxine Sea*; Roman *Pontus Euxinus*

Blackwell's Island *see* **Roosevelt Island**

Blackwood (town, southern Wales) : Welsh *Coed-duon*

Blaenavon (town, southeastern Wales) : Welsh *Blaenafon*; formerly often English *Blenavon*

Blaendulais *see* **Seven Sisters**

Blagoevgrad (town, southwestern Bulgaria) : to 1950 *Gorna Dzhumaya*; to 1913 Turkish *Cuma*

Blagoveshchensk (town, west central Russia) : to 1942 *Blagoveshchensky Zavod*

Blagoveshchensky Zavod *see* **Blagoveshchensk**

Blaj (town, central Romania) : to 1918 Hungarian *Balázsfalva*; to 1867 German *Blasendorf*

Blakang Mati *see* **Sentosa**

Blakelytown *see* **Arkadelphia**

Blaketown *see* **Greymouth**

Blanco *see* **Luperón**

Blarney (village, southern Ireland) : Irish *An Bhlarna*

Blasendorf *see* **Blaj**

Blatna *see* **Blatná**

Blatná (town, southwestern Czech Republic) : to 1918, 1939–1945 German *Blatna*

Blechhammer *see* **Blachownia**

Bled (town, northwestern Slovenia) : to 1918, 1941–1945 German *Veldes*

Blenavon *see* **Blaenavon**

¹Blenheim (village, southern Germany) : German *Blindheim* (The English name is famed for the battle of 1704 in which the English and Austrians defeated the French and Bavarians in the War of the Spanish Succession. Germans usually know the battle as *Höchstadt*.)

²Blenheim (town, Ontario, southeastern Canada) : formerly *Rondeau*

Blessington (town, eastern Ireland) : Irish *Baile Coimín*

Blestium *see* **Monmouth**

Blindheim *see* **¹Blenheim**

Bloemfontein (city, south central South Africa) : [Sotho *Mangaung*]

Bloom *see* **Chicago Heights**

¹Bloomfield (town, Connecticut, northeastern United States) : to 1835 *Wintonbury*

²Bloomfield (town, New Jersey, northeastern United States) : to 1796 *Wardsesson*

Blooming Grove *see* **Bloomington**

Bloomington (city, Illinois, north central United States) : to 1831 *Blooming Grove*; originally *Keg Grove*

Bloomington *see* **Muscatine**

Bloomsburg (town, Pennsylvania, northeastern United States) : to 1870 *Eyertown*

Bluefields *see* **Zelaya**

Blue Nile (river, southern Sudan) : [Arabic *Baḥr al-Azraq*]

Bluff (town, southern New Zealand) : formerly *Port Macquarie*

Bluffs *see* **¹Quincy**

Blumenau *see* **Stettler**

Blyukherovo *see* **²Leninskoye**

Boa Esperança (town, southeastern Brazil) : to 1940 *Dores da Boa Esperança*

Boa Esperança *see* (1) **Boa Esperança do Sul**; (2) **Esperantina**

Boa Esperança do Sul (town, southeastern Brazil) : to 1944 *Boa Esperança*

Boat Yard *see* **Kingsport**

Boa Vista *see* (1) **Erechim**; (2) **Tocantinópolis**

Bobolice (town, northwestern Poland) : to 1945 German *Bublitz*

Bobriki *see* **Novomoskovsk**

Bobrka *see* **Bibrka**

Bóbrka *see* **Bibrka**

Bobruysk *see* **Babruysk**

Bocâina (town, southeastern Brazil) : to 1938 *São João da Bocâina*

Bocaiúva *see* (1) **Bocaiúva do Sul**; (2) **Macatuba**

Bocaiúva do Sul (town, southern Brazil) : 1944–1948 *Imbuial*; to 1944 *Bocaiúva*

Bochkarevo *see* **Belogorsk**

Bod *see* **Tibet**

Bodenbach *see* **Podmokly**

Bodensee *see* **Constance, Lake**

Bodincomagus *see* **Casale Monferrato**

Bodrum (town, southwestern Turkey) : ancient Greek *Halicarnassus*

Bogatynia (town, southwestern Poland) : to 1945 German *Reichenau*

Boghari *see* **Ksar el Boukhari**

Bogodukhovka *see* **Chkalovo**

Bogomdarovanny *see* **Kommunar**

Bogomolstroy *see* **Krasnoural'sk**

Bogor (city, southern Indonesia) : to 1945 Dutch *Buitenzorg*

Bogorodsk *see* (1) **Kamskoye Ust'ye**; (2) **Noginsk**

Bogorodskoye *see* [1]**Leninskoye**

Bogoslovsk *see* **Karpinsk**

Bogotá (city, central Colombia) : formerly Spanish (and still official) *Santa Fé de Bogotá*; earlier *Santa Fé de Bacatá*

Bogoyavlensk *see* [1]**Zhovtneve**

Bogoyavlenskoye *see* [1]**Pervomaysky**

Bogumin *see* **Bohumín**

Boguszów (town, southwestern Poland) : to 1945 German *Gottesberg*

Bo Hai (gulf, eastern China) : alternate *Gulf of Chihli*

Bohemia (historic kingdom, central Europe) : [German *Böhmen*; Czech *Čechy*] (Bohemia now occupies the west and center of the Czech Republic, **Moravia** the eastern part.)

Bohemian Forest (southeastern Germany/southwestern Czech Republic) : [German *Böhmerwald*; Czech *Český Les*]

Böhmen *see* **Bohemia**

Böhmerwald *see* **Bohemian Forest**

Böhmisch-Brod *see* **Český Brod**

Böhmisch-Kamnitz *see* **Česká Kamenice**

Böhmisch-Krumau *see* **Český Krumov**

Böhmisch-Leipa *see* **Česká Lípa**

Böhmisch-Skalitz *see* **Česká Skalice**

Böhmisch-Trübau *see* **Česká Třebová**

Bohoyavlens'ke *see* [1]**Zhovtneve**

Bohumín (town, eastern Czech Republic) : 1939–1945 German *Oderberg*; 1918–1919, 1938–1939 Polish *Bogumin*; to 1918 German *Oderberg*

Boiling Springs *see* **Rutherford**

Bois-le-Duc *see* **'s-Hertogenbosch**

Boissevain (village, Manitoba, central Canada) : to 1886 *Cherry Creek*

Bojodurum *see* **Passau**

Bokovo-Antratsit *see* **Antratsyt**

Bokovo-Antratsyt *see* **Antratsyt**

Boldumsaz (town, northern Turkmenistan) : formerly *Kalinin*; to 1936 *Porsy*

Bolesławiec (town, southwestern Poland) : to 1945 German *Bunzlau*

Boleszkowice (town, northwestern Poland) : to 1945 German *Fürstenfelde*

Bolgar (town, western Russia) : 1935–1991 *Kuybyshev*; 1926–1935 *Spassk-Tatarsky*; to 1926 *Spassk*

Bolívar, Cerro (mountain, eastern Venezuela) : to 1948 *La Parida*

Bolivia (republic, west central South America) : to 1825 *Upper Peru*

Bolkenhain *see* **Bolków**

Bolków (town, southwestern Poland) : to 1945 German *Bolkenhain*

Bolnisi (town, southern Georgia) : 1936–1943 *Lyuksemburgi*; 1921–1936 *Lyuksemburg*; to 1921 *Yekaterinofeld*

Bologhine (town, northern Algeria) : to *c.*1962 French *St.-Eugène* (The town is now a suburb of Algiers.)

Bologna (city, northern Italy) : Roman *Bononia*; Etruscan *Felsina*

Bolsena (town, central Italy) : Roman *Volsinii*

Bol'shakovo (village, western Russia) : 1938–1945 German *Kreuzingen*; to 1938 German *Gross-Skaisgirren*

Bol'shaya Garmanda *see* **Evensk**

Bol'shaya Martynovka (village, western Russia) : to *c.*1944 *Martynovka*

Bol'shaya Seydemenukha *see* **Kalinins'ke**

Bolshevik *see* **Sveta Anastasiya**

Bol'shevo (town, western Russia) : 1928–mid-1950s *Stalinsky*

Bol'shiye Arabuzy *see* [4]**Pervomayskoye**

Bol'shiye Soli *see* **Nekrasovskoye**

Bol'shoy Kosheley *see* [2]**Komsomol'skoye**

Bol'shoy Tokmak *see* **Tokmak**

Bol'shoy Yanisol' *see* **Velyka Novosilka**

Bolton *see* **Stonefort**

Bolzano (town, northern Italy) : to 1918 German *Bozen*; Roman *Bauzanum*

Bombay *see* **Mumbai**

Bombon, Lake *see* **Taal, Lake**

Bom Jardim (city, southeastern Brazil) : 1944–1948 *Vergel*

Bom Jardim *see* **Bom Jardim de Minas**

Bom Jardim de Minas (town, southeastern Brazil) : to 1944 *Bom Jardim*

Bomst *see* **Babimost**

Bonaparte *see* **Réunion**

Bondyuzhsky *see* **Mendeleyevsk**

Bône *see* **Annaba**

Bonfim *see* (1) **Senhor do Bonfim**; (2) **Silvânia**

Bonin Islands (western Pacific) : Japanese *Ogasawara-gunto* (The islands belong to Japan but were under United States administration from 1945 to 1968.)

Bonna (city, western Germany) : Roman *Bonna*

Bonna *see* **Bonn**

Bonny, Bight of *see* **Biafra, Bight of**

Bononia *see* (1) **Bologna**; (2) **Boulogne**; (3) **Vidin**

Bonvilston (village, southeastern Wales) : Welsh *Tresimwn*

Boone (town, Iowa, north central United States) : to 1871 *Montana*
Boothia Felix *see* **Boothia Peninsula**
Boothia Peninsula (Nunavut, northern Canada) : formerly *Boothia Felix*
Borbetomagus *see* **Worms**
Borchalo *see* **Marneuli**
Borcovicium *see* **Housesteads**
Borda do Campo *see* **São Bernardo do Campo**
Bordeaux (city, southeastern France) : Roman *Burdigala*
Borden (village, Prince Edward Island, eastern Canada) : to 1916 *Carleton Point*
Bordentown (town, New Jersey, northeastern United States) : originally *Farnsworth's Landing*
Borders *see* **Scottish Borders**
Bordj el Kiffan (town, northern Algeria) : to *c*.1962 French *Fort-de-l'Eau*
Bordj Omar Driss (town, east central Algeria) : to *c*.1962 French *Fort-Flatters*
Borgå *see* **Porvoo**
Borgh *see* **Borve**
Borgo San Donnino *see* **Fidenza**
Borgonovo *see* **Sušak**
Borgotaro *see* **Borgo Val di Taro**
Borgo Val di Taro (town, north central Italy) : to *c*.1930 *Borgotaro*
Borgworm *see* **Waremme**
Borinquén *see* **Puerto Rico**
Borislav *see* **Boryslav**
Borisoglebsk *see* **Daugavpils**
Borisoglebskiye Slobody *see* **Borisoglebsky**
Borisoglebsky (town, western Russia) : to 1962 *Borisoglebskiye Slobody*
Borisovgrad *see* **Pŭrvomay**
Borjas Blancas (town, northeastern Spain) : Catalan *Les Borges Blanques*
Borjom *see* **Borjomi**
Borjomi (city, central Georgia) : to 1936 *Borjom*
Borovsk (town, west central Russia) : to 1949 *Ust'-Borovaya* (The town is now part of the city of Solikamsk.)
Borshchev *see* **Borshchiv**
Borshchiv (town, southwestern Ukraine) : (Russian *Borshchev*); to 1939 Polish *Borszczów*
Borszczów *see* **Borshchiv**
Bor u České Lípy *see* **Nový Bor**
Borve (village, Western Isles, northwestern Scotland) : Gaelic *Borgh* (The Gaelic name is that of villages in the Isle of Lewis and on Barra. A third Borve in Harris has the Gaelic name *Na Buirgh*. The name itself is of Scandinavian origin and means simply "fort.")
Boryslav (city, western Ukraine) : (Russian *Borislav*); to 1939 Polish *Borysław*
Borysław *see* **Boryslav**

Borysthenes *see* **Dnieper**
Bosanski Brod (town, northern Bosnia-Herzegovina) : to 1878 Turkish *Brod*
Bosanski Novi (town, northwestern Bosnia-Herzegovina) : to 1878 Turkish *Novi*
Boscawen Island *see* **Niuatoputopu**
Boshnyakovo (town, eastern Russia) : 1905–1945 Japanese *Nishi-shakutan*
Bösing *see* **Pezinok**
Boskovice (town, eastern Czech Republic) : to 1918, 1939–1945 German *Boskowitz*
Boskowitz *see* **Boskovice**
Bosna i Hercegovina *see* **Bosnia-Herzegovina**
Bosna-Saray *see* **Sarajevo**
Bosnia-Herzegovina (republic, southeastern Europe) : [Serbo-Croat *Bosna i Hercegovina*]
Bosphorus *see* **Bosporus**
Bosporus (strait, northwestern Turkey) : alternate *Bosphorus* (The spelling of the alternate name is irregular, as the origin is in Greek *-poros*, "passage," not *-phoros*, "bearing." This Bosporus, connecting the Black Sea with the Sea of Marmara, was known in full as *Bosporus Thracius*, "Thracian Bosporus," as distinct from the *Bosporus Cimmerius*, "Cimmerian Bosporus," now *Kerch Strait*, between the Black Sea and the Sea of Azov.)
Bosquet *see* **Hadjadj**
Bossier City (city, Louisiana, southern United States) : originally *Cane's Landing*
Boston *see* **Manhattan**
Botevgrad (city, western Bulgaria) : to 1934 *Orkhaniye*; to 1878 Turkish *Orhanie*
Botev Peak (central Bulgaria) : to 1950 Turkish *Yumrukchal*; earlier *Ferdinandov Vrukh*
Botswana (republic, southern Africa) : to 1966 *Bechuanaland*
Bottle Hill *see* **Madison**
Boufatis (village, northwestern Algeria) : to *c*.1962 French *St.-Louis*
Bougaa (village, northern Algeria) : to *c*.1962 French *Lafayette*
Bougie *see* **Bejaia**
Boulder Dam *see* **Hoover Dam**
Boulhaut *see* **Ben Slimane**
Boulogne (city, northern France) : Roman *Bononia*; earlier Roman *Gesoriacum* (The city's full name is *Boulogne-sur-Mer*, as distinct from *Boulogne-Billancourt*, a suburb of Paris.)
Bountiful (city, Utah, western United States) : to 1855 *Sessions' Settlement*
Bourbon *see* **Réunion**
Bourbontown *see* ²**Paris**
Bourbon-Vendée *see* **La Roche-sur-Yon**
Bourges (city, central France) : Roman *Avaricum*
Bourg-Léopold *see* **Leopoldsburg**

Bourg-Madame (village, southern France) : to 1815 *La Guingette*

Bourgogne *see* **Burgundy**

Bourg Royal *see* **Charlesbourg**

Bourne (town, Massachusetts, northeastern United States) : to 1884 *Monument*

Bous (town, southwestern Germany) : 1936–1945 *Buss*

Bovec (village, northwestern Slovenia) : 1919–1947 Italian *Plezzo*; to 1918 German *Flitsch*

Bovium *see* **Cowbridge**

Bowditch Island *see* **Tokelau**

Bowes (town, northeastern England) : Roman *Lavatris*

Box Elder *see* **Brigham City**

Boykovo (village, eastern Russia) : 1905–1945 Japanese *Kataoka*

Boyle (town, north central Ireland) : Irish *Mainistir na Búille*

Boyoma Falls (north central Democratic Republic of the Congo) : to 1972 *Stanley Falls*

Bozcaada (island, western Turkey) : ancient Greek *Tenedos*

Boz Dağ (mountain, western Turkey) : ancient Greek *Tmolus*

Bozeman (city, northwestern United States) : originally *Missouri*

Bozen *see* **Bolzano**

Bozhedarivka *see* **Shchors'k**

Bozhedarovka *see* **Shchors'k**

Bozhidar *see* (1) **Kaolinovo**; (2) **Rozino**

Boží Dar (village, northwestern Czech Republic) : to 1918, 1939–1945 German *Gottesgab*

Bracara Augusta *see* **Braga**

Bradford (town, Pennsylvania, northeastern United States) : to 1873 *Littleton*

Braga (city, northwestern Portugal) : Roman *Bracara Augusta*

Bragança (town, northeastern Portugal) : traditional English *Braganza*; Roman *Brigantia* (The English spelling is associated with the royal house that ruled Portugal from 1640 to 1910 and also Brazil, as a Portuguese colony, from 1822 to 1889.)

Bragança *see* **Bragança Paulista**

Bragança Paulista (city, southeastern Brazil) : to 1944 *Bragança*

Braganza *see* **Bragança**

Bragg's Spur *see* **West Memphis**

Brăila (city, southeastern Romania) : to 1829 Turkish *İbrail*

Braine-l'Alleud (town, central Belgium) : Flemish *Eigenbrakel*

Braine-le-Château (town, central Belgium) : Flemish *Kasteelbrakel*

Braine-le-Comte (town, south central Belgium) : Flemish *'s-Gravenbrakel*

Braintree (town, Massachusetts, northeastern United States) : to 1640 *Monoticut*

Brancaster (village, eastern England) : Roman *Branodunum*

Brandeis an der Elbe *see* **Brandýs nad Labem**

Brandy Creek *see* **Beaconsfield**

Brandýs nad Labem (town, north central Czech Republic) : to 1918, 1939–1945 German *Brandeis an der Elbe* (In 1960 Brandýs nad Labem joined with neighboring Stará Boleslav to form the twin town Brandýs nad Labem-Stará Boleslav.)

Braniewo (town, northeastern Poland) : to 1945 German *Braunsberg*

Branodunum *see* **Brancaster**

Branogenium *see* **Leintwardine**

Brańsk (town, northeastern Poland) : 1807–1915, 1939–1941 Russian *Bryansk*

Brantovka *see* ⁵**Oktyabr'sky**

Brashear City *see* **Morgan City**

Brasil *see* **Brazil**

Braslav *see* **Braslaw**

Braslaw (town, northern Belarus) : (Russian *Braslav*); 1919–1939 Polish *Brasław*

Brasław *see* **Braslaw**

Braşov (city, central Romania) : 1950–1960 *Stalin* or *Oraşul Stalin*; 1867–1918 Hungarian *Brassó*, to 1867 German *Kronstadt* (The German name should not lead to confusion with the Russian town of **Kronshtadt**. In the former alternate name, Romanian *Oraşul* means "city," giving an equivalent to Russian *Stalingrad*, now **Volgograd**.)

Brassó *see* **Braşov**

Brasstown Bald (mountain, Georgia, southeastern United States) : formerly *Mt. Enotah*

Bratan (mountain, central Bulgaria) : 1950–1969 *Morozov*; to 1950 *Golyam Bratan*

Bratislava (city, southwestern Slovakia) : to 1918 Hungarian *Pozsony*; to 1867 German *Pressburg*

Brattleboro (town, Vermont, northeastern United States) : to 1753 *Fort Dummer*

Brätz *see* **Brojce**

Braunau *see* **Broumov**

Braunsberg *see* **Braniewo**

Braunschweig (city, northern Germany) : conventional English *Brunswick* (The English name primarily applied to the former duchy.)

Bravoniacum *see* **Kirkby Thore**

Bray (town, eastern Ireland) : Irish *Bré*

Brazil (republic, east central South America) : [Portuguese *Brasil*]

Bré *see* **Bray**

Breage *see* **Vermilion**

Brecknock *see* **Brecon**

Břeclav (city, southern Czech Republic) : to 1918, 1938–1945 German *Lundenburg*

Brecon (town, southeastern Wales) : alternate dated *Brecknock*; Welsh *Aberhonddu* (The alternate name was more commonly current for the former county and subsequent unitary authority, abolished in 1996, and remains in use for the town's Brecknock Museum.)

Brecon Beacons (mountains, southeastern Wales) : Welsh *Bannau Brycheiniog* (The mountains take their name from the former county of *Breconshire*, of which **Brecon** was the county town.)

Bregenz (town, western Austria) : Roman *Brigantium*

Breisach (town, southwestern Germany) : Roman *Mons Brisiacus*; earlier Roman *Brisiacum*

Breitenstein *see* ²**Ul'yanovo**

Breizh *see* **Brittany**

Brejo da Madre de Deus (city, northeastern Brazil) : 1939–1948 *Madre de Deus*

Brelsford *see* **Coffs Harbour**

Bremenhaven *see* **Bremerhaven**

Bremenium *see* ²**Rochester**

Bremerhaven (city, northern Germany) : English formerly often *Bremenhaven*; 1939–1947 *Wesermünde* (Founded in 1827, the city was absorbed in 1939 by Wesermünde, itself formed in 1924 from the merger of two other towns. In 1947 the combined municipality reverted to the original name, meaning "port for *Bremen*.")

Bremersdorp *see* **Manzini**

Bremetenacum Veteranorum *see* **Ribchester**

Brenner *see* **Brennero**

Brennero (village, northern Italy) : to 1919 German *Brenner*

Brescia (city, northern Italy) : Roman *Brixia*

Breslau *see* **Wrocław**

Bressanone (town, northern Italy) : to 1919 German *Brixen*

Brest (city, southwestern Belarus) : 1921–1939 Polish *Brześć nad Bugiem*; to 1921 Russian *Brest-Litovsk* (The Russian name is familiar from the treaty of 1918 between Germany and Russia and from its use in World War II, when Brest was in German hands.)

Brest-Litovsk *see* **Brest**

Bretagne *see* **Brittany**

Brewster, Cape (eastern Greenland) : [Greenlandic *Kangikajik*]

Brezhnev *see* **Naberezhnyye Chelny**

Brežice (town, southern Slovenia) : to 1918, 1941–1945 German *Rann*

Brezno (town, central Slovakia) : to 1918 Hungarian *Breznobánya*; to 1867 German *Bries*

Breznobánya *see* **Brezno**

Briançon (town, southeastern France) : Roman *Brigantium*

Bricksburg *see* ¹**Lakewood**

Brickton *see* **Park Ridge**

Bridgend (town, southern Wales) : Welsh *Pen-y-Bont ar Ogwr*

Bridgeport (city, Connecticut, northeastern United States) : to 1800 *Stratfield*; originally *Newfield*

Bridgeton (city, New Jersey, northeastern United States) : formerly *Bridgetown*; originally *Cohansey Bridge*

¹**Bridgetown** (town, southwestern Barbados) : formerly *St. Michael's Town*; originally *Indian Bridge*

²**Bridgetown** (village, Nova Scotia, eastern Canada) : to 1824 *Hicks Ferry*

Bridgetown *see* (1) **Bridgeton**; (2) **Mount Holly**

Bridgewater (town, Massachusetts, northeastern United States) : originally *Titicut*

Bridlington *see* ²**Burlington**

Brieg *see* **Brzeg**

Bries *see* **Brezno**

Briesen *see* **Wąbrzeźno**

Brigantia *see* **Bragança**

Brigantinus Lacus *see* **Constance, Lake**

Brigantium *see* (1) **Bregenz**; (2) **Briançon**; (3) **La Coruña**

Brigetio *see* **Szőny**

Brigham City (town, Utah, west central United States) : to 1856 *Box Elder*

Brighthelmstone *see* **Brighton**

Brighton (city, southern England) : formerly *Brighthelmstone*

Brindisi (city, southeastern Italy) : Roman *Brundisium*

Brisbane (city, Queensland, eastern Australia) : to 1834 *Edenglassie*

Brisiacum *see* **Breisach**

Bristol (city, Connecticut, northeastern United States) : formerly *New Cambridge*

Bristol *see* ²**Dover**

Bristol Channel (southeastern Wales/southwestern England) : alternate *Severn Sea*; Welsh *Môr Hafren* (The Welsh name has the same meaning as the alternate English name.)

Britain *see* (1) **Great Britain**; (2) **United Kingdom**

Britannia *see* **Great Britain**

British Central Africa Protectorate *see* **Malawi**

British Columbia (province, western Canada) : 1849–1858 *New Caledonia*

British East Africa *see* **Kenya**
British Guiana *see* **Guyana**
British Honduras *see* **Belize**
British North America *see* **Canada**
Briton Ferry (town, southern Wales) : Welsh
  Llansawel
Brittany (region, northwestern France) : [French
  Bretagne; Breton *Breizh*]; Roman *Armorica*
  (The eastern part of the Roman region became
  Normandy, but the Celtic name gave Breton
  Armor for its coastal regions, as against *Argoat*,
  the hinterland. The name is present today in
  the department of **Côtes-d'Armor**.)
Briva Curretia *see* **Brive-la-Gaillarde**
Briva Isarae *see* **Pontoise**
Brive *see* **Brive-la-Gaillarde**
Brive-la-Gaillarde (town, south central France) :
  formerly *Brive*; Roman *Briva Curretia*
Brixen *see* **Bressanone**
Brixia *see* **Brescia**
Brno (city, southeastern Czech Republic) : to
  1918, 1939–1945 German *Brünn*
Bro *see* **Kristinehamn**
Broads, The (region of lakes, eastern England) :
  alternate *Norfolk Broads*
Brocavum *see* **Brougham**
Brochów (town, southwestern Poland) : to 1945
  German *Brockau*
Brock *see* **Sunderland**
Brockau *see* **Brochów**
Brockton (city, Massachusetts, northeastern
  United States) : to 1874 *North Bridgewater*
Brockville (town, Ontario, southeastern
  Canada) : formerly *Elizabethtown*
Brod (town, central Macedonia) : to *c.*1945 *Južni
  Brod*
Brod *see* (1) **Bosanski Brod**; (2) **Slavonski
  Brod**
Brodnica (town, north central Poland) : 1772–
  1807, 1815–1919, 1939–1945 German *Strasburg
  in Westpreussen*
Brojce (town, northwestern Poland) : to 1945
  German *Brätz*
Broken Hill (city, New South Wales, southeast-
  ern Australia) : Aboriginal *Willyama*
Broken Hill *see* **Kabwe**
Bromberg *see* **Bydgoszcz**
Bromont (village, Quebec, eastern Canada) : to
  1966 *West Shefford*
Bronkhorstspruit (town, northeastern South
  Africa) : to 1935 *Erasmus*
Bronson *see* **Kalamazoo**
Brookfield (town, Illinois, north central United
  States) : to 1905 *Grossdale*
Brookline (town, Massachusetts, northeastern
  United States) : to 1705 *Muddy River*

Brooks Islands *see* **Midway Islands**
Brossard (city, Quebec, southeastern Canada) :
  to 1958 *Brosseau Station* (The city is now a
  suburb of Montreal.)
Brosseau Station *see* **Brossard**
Brotas *see* **Brotas de Macaúbas**
Brotas de Macaúbas (town, eastern Brazil) : to
  1944 *Brotas*
Brotherstown *see* **Rockwood**
¹Brough (village, east central England, near
  Newark-on-Trent) : Roman *Crococalana*
²Brough (village, central England, near Hather-
  sage) : Roman *Navio*
³Brough (village, eastern England, near Hull) :
  Roman *Petuaria*
⁴Brough (village, northwestern England, near
  Kirkby Stephen) : Roman *Verteris* (The name
  Brough, pronounced "Bruff," derives from Old
  English *burh*, "fortified place," referring to the
  Roman fort in each of these four places.)
Brougham (hamlet, northwestern England) :
  Roman *Brocavum*
Broughton (village, northeastern Wales) : Welsh
  Brychdyn
Broughton *see* **Effingham**
Broughton Island *see* **Qikiqtarjuaq**
Broumov (town, northern Czech Republic) : to
  1918, 1938–1945 German *Braunau*
Brownsville *see* **Ogden**
Brownville *see* **Phenix City**
Bruges (city, northwestern Belgium) : Flemish
  Brugge (English generally uses the French form
  of the name, although the city is in the Flem-
  ish-speaking half of the country.)
Bruges-sur-Mer *see* **Zeebrugge**
Brugge *see* **Bruges**
Brundisium *see* **Brindisi**
Bruneck *see* **Brunico**
Brunei Town *see* **Bandar Seri Begawan**
Brunico (town, northern Italy) : to 1918 German
  Bruneck
Brünn *see* **Brno**
Brunson Harbor *see* **Benton Harbor**
Brunswick (town, Maine, northeastern United
  States) : to 1717 *Pejepscot*
Brunswick *see* **Braunschweig**
Bruntál (town, eastern Czech Republic) : to
  1918, 1938–1945 German *Freudenthal*
Brusa *see* **Bursa**
Bruselas *see* **Puntarenas**
Brussel *see* **Brussels**
Brussels (city, central Belgium) : [Flemish
  Brussel; French *Bruxelles*] (The city, officially
  bilingual, is geographically in the Flemish-
  speaking half of Belgium although the major-
  ity of the population speak French.)

Bruttium *see* Calabria
Brüx *see* Most
Bruxelles *see* Brussels
Bryansk *see* Brańsk
Bryantsivs'kyy Rudnyk *see* Soledar
Bryantsovsky Rudnik *see* Soledar
Brychdyn *see* Broughton
Brynbuga *see* Usk
Bryson (village, Quebec, southeastern Canada) : to 1873 *Havelock*; earlier *Hargreaves*
Brzeg (town, southwestern Poland) : to 1945 German *Brieg*; Roman *Civitas Altae Ripae*
Brześć nad Bugiem *see* Brest
Brzeżany *see* Berezhany
Brzeziny (town, central Poland) : 1940–1945 German *Löwenstadt*
Buayan *see* General Santos
Bublitz *see* Bobolice
Buccari *see* Bakar
Buccino (village, southern Italy) : Roman *Volcei*
Buchanan (town, western Liberia) : formerly *Grand Bassa*
Bucharest (city, southern Romania) : [Romanian *Bucureşti*]
Buckhorn *see* ¹Hastings
Buckley (town, northeastern Wales) : Welsh *Bwcle*
Bucklin *see* Dearborn
Buck's Bridge *see* ²Hanover
Buck's Crossing *see* ²Hanover
Bucureşti *see* Bucharest
Budapest (city, north central Hungary) : Roman *Aquincum* (The Roman name originally applied to *Buda*, on the right bank of the Danube, which in 1872 joined with *Pest*, on the left bank, to form the present city.)
Bud'onnivka *see* Novoazovs'k
Budua *see* Budva
Budva (town, southern Montenegro) : to 1918 Italian *Budua*
Budweis *see* České Budějovice
Budwitz *see* Moravské Budějovice
Budyonnovka *see* Novoazovs'k
Budyonnovsk (city, southwestern Russia) : 1957–1973 *Prikumsk*; 1935–1957 *Budyonnovsk*; 1920–1935 *Prikumsk*; to 1920 *Svyatoy Krest*
Budyonnoye *see* ¹Krasnogvardeyskoye
Budyonny *see* Chat-Bazar
Buena Vista *see* De Kalb
Buenos Aires (province, eastern Argentina) : 1946–1955 *Eva Perón* (The province does not include the national capital, Buenos Aires, which was not renamed.)
Buffalo (city, New York, northeastern United States) : to 1816 *New Amsterdam* (The city's present name was in popular use from the first.)

Builth Wells (town, south central Wales) : Welsh *Llanfair-ym-Muallt* (English *Builth* is an anglicized form of Welsh *Buallt*, here in its mutated form *Muallt*.)
Buitenzorg *see* Bogor
Bujumbura (city, western Burundi) : to 1962 *Usumbura*
Bukavu (town, eastern Democratic Republic of the Congo) : 1927–1952 *Costermansville*
Bukitinggi (city, western Indonesia) : formerly *Fort de Kock*
Bulatselivka *see* ¹Shevchenkove
Bulatselovka *see* ¹Shevchenkove
Bulembu (town, northwestern Swaziland) : to 1976 *Havelock*
Bŭlgarevo (town, eastern Bulgaria) : to 1934 Turkish *Urumyenikoy*
Bulgaria (republic, southeastern Europe) : [Bulgarian *Bŭlgariya*]
Bŭlgariya *see* Bulgaria
Bulung'ur (town, eastern Uzbekistan) : formerly Russian *Krasnogvardeysk*; to 1930s *Rostovtsevo*
Bunclody (town, southeastern Ireland) : Irish *Bun Clóidí*; to 1950 English *Newtownbarry*
Bun Clóidí *see* Bunclody
Buncrana (town, northwestern Ireland) : Irish *Bun Cranncha*
Bun Cranncha *see* Buncrana
Bun Dobhrain *see* Bundoran
Bundoran (town, northwestern Ireland) : Irish *Bun Dobhrain*
Bunge Rudnik *see* Yunokomunarivs'k
Bunge Rudnyk *see* Yunokomunarivs'k
Bunzlau *see* Bolesławiec
Burbank *see* Moorhead
Burdigala *see* Bordeaux
Bureya-Pristan' *see* Novobureysky
Bur Gavo (village, southeastern Somalia) : to *c*.1926 *Port Durnford*
Burgh Castle (village, eastern England) : Roman *Gariannum* (The Roman name was long cited in the form *Gariannonum*.)
Burgundy (region, central France) : [French *Bourgogne*]
Burkina Faso (republic, western Africa) : to 1984 *Upper Volta*
¹Burlington (city, North Carolina, eastern United States) : to 1887 *Company Shops*
²Burlington (town, New Jersey, northeastern United States) : formerly *Bridlington*; originally *New Beverly*
Burlington Bay *see* ²Hamilton
Burma *see* Myanmar
Burnie (town, Tasmania, southeastern Australia) : originally *Emu Bay Settlement*
Burnoye *see* Bauyrzhan Momyshuly

Burrium *see* Usk

Burry Port (town, southern Wales) : Welsh *Porth Tywyn*

Bursa (city, northwestern Turkey) : formerly *Brusa*; Roman *Prusia ad Olympum*

Burundi (republic, east central Africa) : to 1966 *Urundi*

Burwick *see* Woodbridge

Busch *see* Elk City

Būshehr (city, southwestern Iran) : alternate *Bandar-e Būshehr*; conventional *Bushir* (The original city here may have been named *Antioch*, as was Antakya.)

Bushir *see* Būshehr

Buss *see* Bous

Butare (town, southern Rwanda) : to 1962 *Astrida*

Butler (town, Wisconsin, northern United States) : to 1930 *New Butler*

Bütow *see* Bytów

Butterworth (town, southeastern South Africa) : 1976–1994 *Gcuwa*

Buttevant (town, southwestern Ireland) : Irish *Cill na Mallach*

Butuntum *see* Bitonto

Butysh *see* Kama

Buxentum *see* Policastro Bussentino

Buxton (town, central England) : Roman *Aquae Arnemetiae*

Buynaksk (town, southwestern Russia) : to 1922 *Temir-Khan-Shura*

Bwcle *see* Buckley

Byala Slatina (town, northern Bulgaria) : to *c.*1945 *Bela Slatina*

Byam Martin Island *see* Ahunui

Byaroza (town, southwestern Belarus) : (Russian *Beryoza*); 1919–1939 Polish *Bereza Kartuska*

Byblos *see* Jubayl

Byczyna (town, southern Poland) : to 1945 German *Pitschen*

Bydgoszcz (city, north central Poland) : 1772–1807, 1815–1919, 1939–1945 German *Bromberg*

Byorksky *see* Krasnoostrovsky

Byron Island *see* Nikunau

Bystrovka *see* Kemin

Bystrzyca (river, southwestern Poland) : to 1945 German *Weistritz*

Bystrzyca Kłodzka (town, southwestern Poland) : to 1945 German *Habelschwerdt*

Bytča (town, northwestern Slovakia) : to 1918 Hungarian *Nagybittse*

Bytom (city, southwestern Poland) : to 1945 German *Beuthen*

Bytów (town, northern Poland) : to 1945 German *Bütow*

Bytown *see* ¹Ottawa

Byzantium *see* Istanbul

Caa-Catí *see* General Paz

Caála (town, west central Angola) : 1930–*c.*1975 Portuguese *Vila Robert Williams*

Cabaret (town, central Haiti) : formerly *Duvalierville*

Cabellio *see* Cavaillon

Cabillonum *see* Chalon-sur-Saône

Cabo Fisterra *see* Finisterre, Cape

Cabo Verde *see* Cape Verde

Cabo Yubi *see* Tarfaya

Cabra (town, southern Spain) : Roman *Igabrum*

Cabrália *see* Cabrália Paulista

Cabrália Paulista (town, southeastern Brazil) : 1944–1948 *Pirajaí*; to 1944 *Cabrália*

Cacaguatique *see* Ciudad Barrios

Caçapava *see* Caçapava do Sul

Caçapava do Sul (city, southern Brazil) : to 1944 *Caçapava*

Cáceres (city, western Brazil) : to 1939 *São Luiz de Cáceres*

Cacheira do Sul (city, southern Brazil) : to 1944 *Cachoeira*

Cachoeira *see* (1) Cachoeira do Sul; (2) Cachoeira Paulista; (3) Solonópole

Cachoeira Paulista (city, southeastern Brazil) : 1944–1948 *Valparaíba*; to 1944 *Cachoeira*

Cachoeiras *see* Cachoeiras de Macacu

Cachoeiras de Macacu (city, southeastern Brazil) : to 1943 *Cachoeiras*

Cacongo (town, northwestern Angola) : to *c.*1975 Portuguese *Guilherme Capelo*

Čadca (town, northwestern Slovakia) : to 1918 Hungarian *Csaca*

Cadillac (town, Michigan, northern United States) : to 1877 *Clam Lake*

Cadiz *see* Cádiz

Cádiz (city, southwestern Spain) : English conventional *Cadiz*; Roman *Gades*; Phoenician *Gadir*

Cadoxton (village, southern Wales) : Welsh *Tregatwg* (The village is now a district of Barry.)

Cadoxton-juxta-Neath (village, southern Wales) : Welsh *Llangatwg Nedd* (The additions to the respective names distinguish the village from Cadoxton by locating it near Neath.)

Cadurcum *see* Cahors

Cadwell's Corners *see* Deerfield

Caene *see* Qena

Caerdydd *see* Cardiff

Caere *see* Cerveteri

Caerffili *see* Caerphilly

Caerfyrddin *see* Carmarthen

Caergybi *see* Holyhead

Caerhun (village, northern Wales) : Roman *Canovium* (The Roman fort based its name on that of the *Conwy* River here, which itself gave the name of the nearby town of **Conwy**.)

Caerleon (town, southeastern Wales) : Welsh *Caerllion-ar-Wysg*, Roman *Isca* (The Roman name is that of the river here, itself giving the modern name of **Usk**. The *-leon* and *-llion* of the respective names derive from the fuller Roman name *Isca Legionum*, the latter word meaning "of the legions." An alternate Roman fuller form was *Isca Silurum*.)

Caerllion-ar-Wysg *see* **Caerleon**

Caernarfon (town, northwestern Wales) : traditional English *Carnarvon*; Roman *Segontium* (The traditional form of the name is preserved in an aristocratic title and in placenames in the former British colonies, as Australia and South Africa.)

Caerphilly (town, southeastern Wales) : Welsh *Caerffili*

Caerwent (village, southeastern Wales) : Roman *Venta Silurum*

Caesaraugusta *see* **Saragossa**

Caesarea (ancient city, western Israel) : Hebrew *Horbat Qesari*; Roman *Caesarea Maritima*; alternate Roman *Caesarea Palaestina*; originally Greek *Strato's Tower* (The Hebrew name means "ruins of *Caesarea*," referring to the biblical city built by Herod the Great. Nearby is the modern settlement of *Kessaria*, named for it. The additions to the Roman names distinguished the city from *Caesarea Philippi*, now **Banias**.)

Caesarea *see* (1) **Cherchell**; (2) **Jersey**; (3) **Qisarya**

Caesarea Cappadociae *see* **Kayseri**

Caesarea Maritima *see* **Caesarea**

Caesarea Mazaca *see* **Kayseri**

Caesarea Palaestinae *see* **Caesarea**

Caesarea Philippi *see* **Banias**

Caesarobriga *see* **Talavera de la Reina**

Caesarodunum *see* **Tours**

Caesaromagus *see* (1) **Beauvais**; (2) **Chelmsford**

Caesena *see* **Cesena**

Cagliari (city, southern Sardinia, Italy) : Roman *Caralis*

Caher (town, south central Ireland) : Irish *An Chathair*

Cahersiveen (town, southwestern Ireland) : Irish *Cathair Saidhbhín*

Cahors (city, south central France) : Roman *Cadurcum*; earlier Roman *Divona*

Cahul (city, southern Moldova) : (Russian *Kagul*); 1919–1940 Romanian *Cahul*; 1878–1918 Russian *Kagul*; 1856–1878 Romanian *Cahul*; 1812–1856 Russian *Kagul*

Caia (town, central Mozambique) : 1954–1981 Portuguese *Vila Fontes*

Caiapônia (town, central Brazil) : to 1944 Spanish *Rio Bonito*

Caieta *see* **Gaeta**

Cairlinn *see* **Carlingford**

Cairo (city, northern Egypt) : [Arabic *Al Qāhirah*; alternate Arabic *Miṣr*] (The alternate Arabic name is also that of **Egypt**.)

Caiseal *see* **Cashel**

Caisleán an Bharraigh *see* **Castlebar**

Caistor St. Edmund (village, eastern England) : Roman *Venta Icenorum*

Caiuás *see* **Rio Brilhante**

Čakovec (town, northern Croatia) : to 1918, 1941–1944 Hungarian *Csáktornya*

Calabria (region, southern Italy) : Roman *Bruttium*

Calae *see* **Chelles**

Calagurris *see* **Calahorra**

Calah *see* **Nimrud**

Calahorra (town, northern Spain) : Roman *Calagurris*

Calanais *see* **Callanish**

Calandula (town, northern Angola) : to *c.*1975 Portuguese *Duque de Bragança*

Calauria *see* **Póros**

Calcaria *see* **Tadcaster**

Calcutta *see* **Kolkata**

Caldas (town, southeastern Brazil) : 1940–1948 *Parreiras*

Caldey (island, southwestern Wales) : Welsh *Ynys Bŷr*

Caledonia *see* **Scotland**

Caledonia Australis *see* **Gippsland**

Cales *see* **Calvi**

Calgary (city, Alberta, southwestern Canada) : originally *Fort Brisebois*

Calhoun (town, Georgia, southeastern United States) : to 1850 *Oothcaloga*

Calicut *see* **Kozhikode**

Calidonia *see* **Scotland**

Cälilabad (town, southeastern Azerbaijan) : (Russian *Dzhalilabad*); to 1967 Russian *Astrakhan'-Bazar*

Callanish (village, Western Isles, northwestern Scotland) : Gaelic *Calanais*

Calleva Atrebatum *see* **Silchester**

Callipolis *see* **Gallipoli**

Čalovo *see* **Veľký Meder**

Calumet (village, Michigan, north central United States) : to 1929 *Red Jacket*

Calumet City (city, Illinois, north central United States) : to 1924 *West Hammond* (The city is a suburb of Chicago.)

Calvary (hill, central Israel) : ancient Greek *Gol-*

gotha (The Bible has both English and Greek names, respectively of Latin and Aramaic origin, for the site of Jesus' crucifixion.)

Calvi (village, southwestern Italy) : Roman *Cales*

Camacupa (town, central Angola) : to 1891 Portuguese *Vila General Machado*

Camagüey (city, eastern Cuba) : to 1903 *Puerto Príncipe*, earlier *Santa María del Puerto del Príncipe* (The city was founded at the site of the present coastal town of Nuevitas but was later moved inland to its present location.)

Camanongue (town, north central Angola) : to *c.*1975 Portuguese *Vila Bugaço*

Camaquã (city, southern Brazil) : to 1939 Portuguese *São João de Camaquã*

Camaracum *see* **Cambrai**

Camaratuba *see* **São Joaquim do Monte**

Camarazal *see* **Mulungu**

Cambaluc *see* **Beijing**

Cambé (city, southern Brazil) : to 1944 *Nova Dantzig*

Camberiacum *see* **Chambéry**

Cambirela *see* **Santo Amaro da Imperatriz**

Cambodia (republic, southeastern Asia) : 1976–1989 *Kampuchea*; 1970–1976 *Khmer Republic*

Cambodunum *see* (1) **Kempten**; (2) **Leeds**

Camboglanna *see* **Castlesteads**

Cambrai (city, northern France) : Roman *Camaracum*

Cambria *see* **Wales**

¹**Cambridge** (city, eastern England) : Medieval Latin *Cantabrigia*; Roman *Duroliponte*

²**Cambridge** (city, Massachusetts, northeastern United States) : to 1638 *New Towne*

Cambridge Bay (village, Nunavut, northern Canada) : alternate Inuit *Ikaluktutiak*

Cambridge Farms *see* **Lexington**

Cambundi-Catembo (town, north central Angola) : to *c.*1975 Portuguese *Nova Gaia*

¹**Camden** (town, New South Wales, southeastern Australia) : formerly *Camden Park*; to 1805 *Cowpastures*

²**Camden** (town, Arkansas, south central United States) : to 1844 *Écore à Fabre*

³**Camden** (town, South Carolina, southeastern United States) : to 1768 *Pine Tree Hill*

Camden Park *see* ¹**Camden**

Camerino (town, central Italy) : Roman *Camerinum*

Camerinum *see* **Camerino**

Cameron Bay *see* **Echo Bay**

Cameroon (republic, western Africa) : formerly English *the Cameroons* (The former name referred to the German protectorate of *Kamerun*. After World War I it was divided into British and French administrative zones and in 1960

the French trust territory of *Cameroun* gained its independence.)

Cameroons, the *see* **Cameroon**

Cameroun *see* **Cameroon**

Cammin-in-Pommern *see* **Kamień Pomorski**

Campagna di Roma (region, west central Italy) : Roman *Campania* (The Roman region was closely tied to **Rome**, whereas the modern region of *Campania* lies further south and is centered on **Naples**.)

Campania *see* (1) **Campagna di Roma**; (2) **Champagne**

Camp-Bataille *see* **Souk el Arba de l'Oued Beth**

Campbell (town, Ohio, north central United States) : to 1926 *East Youngstown*

Campbellpur *see* (1) **Attock**; (2) **Hasan Abdal**

Campbellton (town, New Brunswick, eastern Canada) : to 1833 *Martin's Point*

Campbelltown (city, New South Wales, southeastern Australia) : to 1820 *Airds*

Camp Eagle Pass *see* **Eagle Pass**

Campestre *see* **São José do Campestre**

Camp Greeley *see* **Bismarck**

Camp Hancock *see* **Bismarck**

Campina Grande (city, northeastern Brazil) : to 1864 *Porta do Sertão*

Campinas (city, southeastern Brazil) : formerly *Nossa Senhora da Conceição de Campinas de Matto Grosso*

Campine *see* **Kempenland**

Campo Belo *see* **Itatiaia**

Campo Florido (town, southeastern Brazil) : to 1944 Portuguese *Campo Formoso*

Campoformido (village, northeastern Italy) : formerly *Campo Formio* (The former name remains in historical use for the 1797 treaty between France and Austria ending the first phase of the Napoleonic Wars.)

Campo Formio *see* **Campoformido**

Campo Formoso *see* (1) **Campo Florido**; (2) **Orizona**

Campo Largo *see* **Araçoiaba da Serra**

Campo Quijano (town, northwestern Argentina) : to 1930s *Kilómetro 1172*

Campos *see* **Tobias Barreto**

Camptown *see* **Irvington**

Camulodunum *see* **Colchester**

Canaan *see* **Palestine**

Canada (country, North America) : to 1763 *New France* (The former name, representing French *Nouvelle-France*, is sometimes applied to the territory now occupied by Canada. Properly, it denotes only the lands held or claimed by the French crown.)

Canada East *see* **Quebec**

Canada West *see* **Ontario**

Çanakkale (city, northwestern Turkey) : formerly *Kale i-Sultanye*

Canaveral, Cape (Florida, southeastern United States) : 1963–1973 *Cape Kennedy*

Cancello (village, southern Italy) : Roman *Suessula*

Canchungo (town, western Guinea-Bissau) : formerly Portuguese *Teixeira Pinto*

Candia *see* (1) **Crete**; (2) **Iráklion**

Canea (city, northern Crete, Greece) : to 1912 Turkish *Hanya*; ancient Greek *Cydonia*

Canelones (city, southern Uruguay) : formerly *Guadalupe*

Cane's Landing *see* **Bossier City**

Cangamba (town, south central Angola) : to *c.*1975 Portuguese *Vila de Aljustrel*

Cangó *see* **General Artigas**

Caniçado *see* **Guijá**

Çankırı (city, north central Turkey) : Roman *Germanicopolis*; earlier Roman *Gangra*

Canonium *see* **Kelvedon**

Canosa di Puglia (town, southeastern Italy) : Roman *Canusium*

Canóvanas *see* **Loíza**

Canovium *see* **Caerhun**

Cantabria (province, northern Spain) : formerly *Santander*

Cantabrigia *see* ¹**Cambridge**

Canterbury (city, southeastern England) : Ecclesiastical Latin *Cantuaria*; Roman *Durovernum*

Canterbury *see* ¹**Christchurch**

Cantium *see* ¹**Kent**

¹**Canton** (city, southeastern China) : Chinese *Guangzhou* (The English name represents Chinese *Kwangtung*, the name of the province of which Guangzhou is the capital.)

²**Canton** (town, Massachusetts, northeastern United States) : to 1797 *Punkapoag*

³**Canton** (town, South Dakota, north central United States) : to 1867 *Commerce City*

Cantuaria *see* **Canterbury**

Canusium *see* **Canosa di Puglia**

Cap-de-la-Madeleine (city, Quebec, southeastern Canada) : originally *Cap-des-Trois-Rivières*

Cap-de-Lévy *see* **Lauzon**

Cap-des-Trois-Rivières *see* **Cap-de-la-Madeleine**

Cape : for names of capes *see* the next word, as **Colville, Cape**

Cape Breton Island (Nova Scotia, eastern Canada) : formerly French *Île Royale* (The island takes its present name from its eastern cape.)

Cape Colony *see* **Cape Province**

Cape Dorset (village, Nunavut, northeastern Canada) : alternate Inuit *Kingnait*

Cape Island *see* **Cape May**

Capela (town, northeastern Brazil) : 1944–1948 Portuguese *Conceição do Paraíba*

Capelle-au-Bois *see* **Kapelle-op-den-Bos**

Capellen-lez-Anvers *see* **Kapellen**

Cape May (town, New Jersey, northeastern United States) : to 1869 *Cape Island*

Cape of Good Hope *see* **Good Hope, Cape of**

Cape Palmas *see* **Harper**

Cape Province (former province, southern South Africa) : to 1910 *Cape Colony* (The province ceased to exist in 1994 when it was divided into the three provinces *Eastern Cape*, *Northern Cape*, and *Western Cape*. See also **Good Hope, Cape of**.)

Cape Town (city, southwestern South Africa) : Afrikaans *Kapstad*

Cape Verde (island republic, North Atlantic) : [Portuguese *Cabo Verde*]

Cape York Peninsula (Queensland, northeastern Australia) : to 1770 *Carpentaria Land*

Capivari *see* **Silva Jardim**

Capiz *see* **Roxas**

Capodistria *see* **Koper**

Caporetto *see* **Kobarid**

Cappoquin (town, southern Ireland) : Irish *Ceapach Choinn*

Capreae *see* **Capri**

Caprese Michelangelo (village, central Italy) : formerly *Caprese* (The village added the name of the famous Renaissance artist Michelangelo, who was born here in 1475.)

Capri (island, western Italy) : Roman *Capreae*

Capsa *see* **Gafsa**

Capua (town, southern Italy) : Roman *Casilinum* (The town took its present name from the nearby Roman city of *Capua*, now the village of **Santa Maria di Capua Vetere**, whose inhabitants settled here in A.D. 656 after fleeing the Saracens.).

Capua *see* **Santa Maria di Capua Vetere**

Caraguatay *see* **Cordillera**

Caralis *see* **Cagliari**

Caransebeş (town, western Romania) : to 1918 Hungarian *Karánsebes*

Caraza *see* **Santiváñez**

Carbonia *see* ²**Ottawa**

Carcaso *see* **Carcassonne**

Carcassonne (city, southern France) : Roman *Carcaso*

Carcross (village, Yukon Territory, northwestern Canada) : to 1905 *Caribou Crossing*

Cardiff (city, southeastern Wales) : Welsh *Caerdydd*

Cardigan (town, western Wales) : Welsh *Aberteifi* (The town's English name is a corrupt form of

that of **Ceredigion**, the county in which it
lies.)

Carei (town, northwestern Romania) : to 1918,
1940–1944 Hungarian *Nagykároly*; to 1867
German *Grosskarol*

Caribou (town, Maine, northeastern United
States) : to 1877 *Lyndon Village*

Caribou Crossing *see* **Carcross**

Caribrod *see* ³**Dimitrovgrad**

Carignan (village, northeastern France) : to 1662
Ivoy

Carinthia (region, southern Austria) : [German
Kärnten]

Caririaçu (city, northeastern Brazil) : to 1944
Portuguese *São Pedro do Cariry*

Carlabhagh *see* **Carloway**

Carleton (village, Quebec, eastern Canada) :
originally *Tracadigetche*

Carleton Point *see* **Borden**

Carlingford (town, northeastern Ireland) : Irish
Cairlinn

Carlisle (city, northwestern England) : Roman
Luguvalium

Carlopago *see* **Karlobag**

Carlos Reyles (town, central Uruguay) : to
*c.*1945 *Molles*

Carlovitz *see* **Sremski Karlovci**

Carlow (town, eastern Ireland) : Irish *Ceatharlach*

Carloway (village, Western Isles, northwestern
Scotland) : Gaelic *Carlabhagh*

Carlsbad (city, New Mexico, southwestern
United States) : to 1899 *Eddy*

Carlsbad *see* **Karlovy Vary**

Carmarthen (town, southwestern Wales) : Welsh
Caerfyrddin; Roman *Moridunum*; alternate
Roman *Maridunum* (The alternate Roman
name, though meaning "fort by the sea," does
not derive from Latin *mare*, "sea," but from a
related Celtic source that gave Welsh *môr*. The
second part of the Welsh name, in its basic
form *-myrddin*, gave the name of the Arthurian wizard *Merlin*, whose name today appears
in that of **Merlin's Bridge**.)

Carmo *see* (1) **Carmona**; (2) **Carmópolis**

Carmona (town, southern Spain) : Roman
Carmo

Carmópolis (town, northeastern Brazil) : to 1944
Carmo

Carnarvon (town, southwestern South Africa) :
to 1874 *Harmsfontein*

Carnarvon *see* **Caernarfon**

Carnium *see* **Kranj**

Carnotum *see* **Chartres**

Carolina (town, northeastern Puerto Rico) :
originally *Trujillo Bajo*

Carpentaria Land *see* **Cape York Peninsula**

Carpentoracte *see* **Carpentras**

Carpentras (town, southeastern France) : Roman
Carpentoracte

Carradoc *see* **Mount Brydges**

Carraig Fhearghasa *see* **Carrickfergus**

Carraig Mhachaire Rois *see* **Carrickmacross**

Carraig na Siúire *see* **Carrick-on-Suir**

Carrhae *see* **Haran**

Carrickfergus (town, eastern Northern Ireland) :
Irish *Carraig Fhearghasa*

Carrickmacross (town, northeastern Ireland) :
Irish *Carraig Machaire Rois*

Carrick-on-Shannon (town, northwestern Ireland) : Irish *Cora Droma Rúisc*

Carrick-on-Suir (town, southern Ireland) : Irish
Carraig na Siúire

Carriden (village, southern Scotland) : Roman
Velunia

Carrollton (town, Georgia, southeastern United
States) : to 1829 *Troupsville*

Carseoli *see* **Carsoli**

Carsoli (town, central Italy) : Roman *Carseoli*

Carson City (city, Nevada, western United
States) : originally *Eagle Station*

Carstensz, Mt. *see* **Jaya, Mt.**

Cartagena (city, southeastern Spain) : Roman
Carthago Nova

Carthage (historic city, northern Tunisia) :
Roman *Carthago*

Carthago *see* **Carthage**

Carthago Nova *see* **Cartagena**

Casablanca (city, western Morocco) : alternate
Arabic *Dar el Beida*; formerly French *Maison
Blanche*; earlier Portuguese *Casa Branca* (A
fuller form of the Arabic name is *ad-Dār al-
Bayḍā'.* The French colonial name was also
that of **Dar el Beida**.)

Casa Branca *see* **Casablanca**

Cas-blaidd *see* **Wolf's Castle**

Cascavel *see* **Aguaí**

Casco *see* **Portland**

Cas-gwent *see* **Chepstow**

Cashel (town, south central Ireland) : Irish
Caiseal

Casilinum *see* **Capua**

Casim *see* **General Toshevo**

Casinum *see* **Cassino**

Čáslav (city, central Czech Republic) : to 1918,
1939–1945 German *Tschaslau*

Casllwchwr *see* **Loughor**

Cas-mael *see* **Puncheston**

Casnewydd-ar-Wysg *see* ¹**Newport**

Caspian Sea (eastern Europe/western Asia) :
Roman *Caspium Mare*; alternate Roman *Hyrcanum Mare* (The alternate name of the great

salt lake, bordered in Europe by Russia and in Asia by Azerbaijan, Iran, Turkmenistan, and Kazakhstan, derives from *Hyrcania*, the Roman name of the former province of northern Iran now known as **Gorgān**.)

Caspium Mare *see* **Caspian Sea**

Cassaigne *see* **Sidi Ali**

Cassian Way *see* **Via**

Cassino (town, central Italy) : to 1871 *San Germano*; Roman *Casinum*

Cassiterides *see* **Scilly, Isles of**

Casteggio (village, northern Italy) : Roman *Clastidium*

Castel Giubileo (village, western Italy) : Roman *Fidenae*

Castellammare (village, southern Italy) : Roman *Velia*; ancient Greek *Elea*

Castellammare di Stabia (town, southern Italy) : Roman *Stabiae*

Castell-nedd *see* **Neath**

Castell-newydd *see* ²**Newcastle**

Castellnewydd Emlyn *see* **Newcastle Emlyn**

Castell-paen *see* **Painscastle**

Castellum Tingitanum *see* **Ech Chélif**

Castelnuovo *see* **Herceg-Novi**

Castelo *see* (1) **Castelo do Piauí**; (2) **Manuel Urbano**

Castelo do Piauí (town, northeastern Brazil) : 1944–1948 Portuguese *Marvão*; to 1944 Portuguese *Castelo*

Castelrosso *see* **Kastellorizon**

Castile (region, central Spain) : [Spanish *Castilla*]

Castilla *see* **Castile**

Castlebar (town, western Ireland) : Irish *Caisleán an Bharraigh*

Castlebay (town, Western Isles, northwestern Scotland) : Gaelic *Bagh a Chaisteil*

Castleblayney (town, northern Ireland) : Irish *Baile na Lorgan*

Castleford (town, northern England) : Roman *Lagentium*

Castle Mountain (Alberta, western Canada) : 1946–1979 *Mt. Eisenhower*

Castlerea (town, north central Ireland) : Irish *Caisleán Riabhach*

Castlereagh *see* **Penrith**

Castlesteads (village, northwestern England) : Roman *Camboglanna*

Castra Albiensium *see* **Castres**

Castra Batava *see* **Passau**

Castra Exploratorum *see* **Netherby**

Castra Regina *see* **Regensburg**

Castres (city, southern France) : Roman *Castra Albiensium*

Castrogiovanni *see* **Enna**

Castrum Barrum *see* **Bar-le-Duc**

Castrum Deutonis *see* **Duisburg**

Castrum Helenae *see* **Elne**

Castrum Hennae *see* **Enna**

Castrum Novum *see* **Santa Marinella**

Castua *see* **Kastav**

Cas-wis *see* **Wiston**

Catabola (town, central Angola) : to *c*.1979 Portuguese *Nova Sintra*

Catalonia (region, northeastern Spain) : [Spanish *Cataluña*; Catalan *Catalunya*]

Cataluña *see* **Catalonia**

Catalunya *see* **Catalonia**

Catamarca (city, northwestern Argentina) : originally *Londres*

Catana *see* **Catania**

Catandica (town, western Mozambique) : 1915–1976 Portuguese *Vila Gouveia*

Catanduva (city, southeastern Brazil) : originally *Vila Adolfo*

Catania (city, southern Italy) : Roman *Catana*

Cataractonium *see* **Catterick Bridge**

Catfish's Camp *see* ²**Washington**

Cathair na Mart *see* **Westport**

Cathair Saidhbhín *see* **Cahersiveen**

Cathay *see* **China**

Catonsville (town, Maryland, northeastern United States) : to *c*.1800 *Johnnycake* (The town is now a suburb of Baltimore.)

Cattaro *see* **Kotor**

Catterick Bridge (village, northern England) : Roman *Cataractonium* (The village took its present name from the Roman name, which is traditionally derived from Latin *cataracta*, "waterfall," referring to the nearby rapids (cataract) on the Swale River. But as in many cases the Roman name is of Celtic origin, and almost certainly means "battle ramparts.")

Caucaia (city, northeastern Brazil) : to 1944 *Soure*

Caucasus (mountains, southeastern Europe/southwestern Asia) : [Russian *Kavkaz*]

Caunus *see* **Dalyan**

Causennis *see* **Ancaster**

Cavaillon (town, southeastern France) : Roman *Cabellio*

Cavan (town, northern Ireland) : Irish *An Cabhán*

Cavazuccherina *see* **Iesolo**

Caviúna *see* **Rolândia**

Cawnpore *see* **Kanpur**

Caxias (city, northeastern Brazil) : formerly *São José das Aldeias Altas*

Caxias *see* **Duque de Caxias**

Cayenne (city, northeastern French Guiana) : to 1777 *La Ravardière*

Cayo *see* **San Ignacio**

Ceanannus Mór *see* Kells

Ceann a Bhaigh *see* Bayhead

Ceapach Choinn *see* Cappoquin

Ceará *see* Fortaleza

Ceatharlach *see* Carlow

Čechy *see* Bohemia

Cedar Hall *see* Val-Brillant

Cedar Rapids (city, Iowa, north central United States) : to 1849 *Rapids City*

Cedynia (town, northwestern Poland) : to 1945 German *Zehden*

Cefalù (town, southern Italy) : Roman *Cephalaedium*

Cegidfa *see* Guilsfield

Cei Connah *see* Connah's Quay

Ceinewydd *see* New Quay

Celaenae *see* Dinar

Celbridge (town, eastern Ireland) : Irish *Cill Droichid*

Celebes *see* Sulawesi

Celje (city, northeastern Slovenia) : to 1918, 1941–1945 German *Cilli*

Cenchrea *see* Kechries

Cenchreae *see* Kechries

Cendl *see* Beaufort

Centerville *see* Centralia

Central African Empire *see* Central African Republic

Central African Republic (republic, central Africa) : 1976–1979 *Central African Empire*; to 1958 *Ubangi-Shari*

Central Arctic *see* Kitikmeot

Centralia (town, Washington, northwestern United States) : to 1891 *Centerville*

Central Provinces and Berar *see* Madhya Pradesh

Centreville *see* Vernon

Centum Cellae *see* Civitavecchia

Centurion (town, northeastern South Africa) : to 1995 *Verwoerdburg*

Centuripae *see* Centuripe

Centuripe (town, southern Italy) : Roman *Centuripae*

Cephalaedium *see* Cefalù

Cerasus *see* Giresun

Ceredigion (county, western Wales) : to 1974 *Cardiganshire* (In the year stated the former county became a unitary authority but in 1996 regained county status. The town of **Cardigan** has a corrupt form of the name, originally that of an early kingdom.)

Cernăuţi *see* Chernivtsi

Cerro (Spanish, "mountain") : for names beginning thus, *see* the next word, as **Bolívar, Cerro**

Cerveteri (town, western Italy) : Roman *Caere*; ancient Greek *Agylla*

Cesena (town, northern Italy) : Roman *Caesena*

Cēsis (town, northern Latvia) : to 1918 German *Wenden*

Česká Kamenice (town, northern Czech Republic) : to 1918, 1939–1945 German *Böhmisch-Kamnitz*

Česká Lípa (city, northwestern Czech Republic) : to 1918, 1938–1945 German *Böhmisch-Leipa*

Česká Republika *see* Czech Republic

Česká Skalice (town, northeastern Czech Republic) : to 1918, 1939–1945 German *Böhmisch-Skalitz*

Česká Třebová (town, north central Czech Republic) : to 1918, 1938–1945 German *Böhmisch-Trübau*

České Budějovice (city, southwestern Czech Republic) : to 1918, 1939–1945 German *Budweis*

České Velenice (town, southern Czech Republic) : 1938–1945 German *Gmünd* (The German name applied both to the present Czech town and, as now, to the Austrian town south of it across the Lainsitz River. The railroad station at the Czech town was already named Gmünd as early as 1919.)

Československo *see* Czechoslovakia

Český Brod (town, west central Czech Republic) : to 1918, 1939–1945 German *Böhmisch-Brod*

Český Krumlov (town, southwestern Czech Republic) : 1938–1945 German *Krumau an der Moldau*; to 1918 German *Böhmisch-Krumau*

Český Les *see* Bohemian Forest

Český Těšín (town, eastern Czech Republic) : 1939–1945 German *Teschen*; 1938–1939 Polish *Cieszyn Zachodni*; to 1918 German *Teschen* (See comments for **Cieszyn** below.)

Cetatea Albă *see* Bilhorod-Dnistrovs'kyy

Cette *see* Sète

Ceyhan (river, southern Turkey) : Roman *Pyramus*

Ceylanpınar (village, southeastern Turkey) : to c.1945 *Resülayn*

Ceylon *see* Sri Lanka

Ceynowa *see* Kuźnica

Chachapoyas (town, northern Peru) : originally *San Juan de la Frontera de los Chachapoyas*

Chaco (province, northeastern Argentina) : 1950–1955 *Presidente Juán Perón*

Chad *see* ⁸Oktyabr'sky

Chadwick's Bay *see* ²Dunkirk

Chagoda (town, western Russia) : to 1932 *Bely Bychek*

Chajaya *see* General Ramón Gonzáles

Chalakazaki *see* Kyzyl-Asker

Chalcedon *see* Kadıköy

Châlons-en-Champagne (town, northeastern

France) : to 1995 *Châlons-sur-Marne*; Roman *Durocatalaunum*

Châlons-sur-Marne *see* **Châlons-en-Champagne**

Chalon-sur-Saône (city, east central France) : Roman *Cabillonum*

Chambarak (town, northeastern Armenia) : formerly Russian *Krasnosel'sk*

Chambéry (city, southeastern France) : Medieval Latin *Camberiacum*

Champagne (region, northeastern France) : Roman *Campania* (The Roman name has remained unaltered for the modern region of *Campania*, southern Italy.)

Champion *see* **Painesville**

Chanda *see* **Chandrapur**

Chandrapur (city, western India) : formerly *Chanda*

Chang *see* **Yangtze**

Chang'an (town, central China) : to 1942 *Wangkü*

Changchun (city, northeastern China) : 1932–1945 *Xinjing*

Changning (town, southwestern China) : to 1935 *Yutian*

Changshun (town, southern China) : to 1942 *Changzhai*

Changzhai *see* **Changshun**

Changzhou (city, eastern China) : 1912–1949 *Wutsin*

Channel Islands *see* **Santa Barbara Islands**

Chanzy *see* **Sidi Ali Ben Youb**

Chao Phraya (river, northern Thailand) : traditional English *Maenam* (The English name is a short form of the full name *Mae Nam Chao Phraya*, in which Thai *Mae Nam* is "river.")

Chapayev (town, northwestern Kazakhstan) : 1939–1971 *Chapayevo*; to 1939 *Lbishchensk*

Chapayevo *see* **Chapayev**

Chapayevsk (city, western Russia) : 1919–1929 *Trotsk*; to 1919 *Ivashchenkovo*

Chapin *see* **Edinburg**

Chaplygin (town, western Russia) : to 1958 *Ranenburg*; formerly *Slobodskoye*

Charazani *see* **Villa General Pérez**

Chardzhou *see* **Türkmenabat**

Chardzhuy *see* **Türkmenabat**

Charente-Inférieure *see* **Charente-Maritime**

Charente-Maritime (department, western France) : to 1941 *Charente-Inférieure*

Ch'arents'avan (city, west central Armenia) : to 1967 *Lusavan*

Charlesbourg (city, Quebec, eastern Canada) : originally *Bourg Royal*

Charles City *see* ¹**Charleston**

Charles Island *see* **Santa María**

¹**Charleston** (city, South Carolina, southeastern United States) : 1722–1783 *Charles City*; originally *Charles Towne*

²**Charleston** (city, West Virginia, east central United States) : to 1819 *Charles Town*

Charlestown (town, western Ireland) : Irish *Baile Chathail*

Charlestown *see* **Lorain**

Charles Town *see* (1) ²**Charleston**; (2) **Wellsburg**

Charles Towne *see* ¹**Charleston**

Charlesville *see* **Djokupunda**

Charleville *see* **Ráth Luirc**

Charlotte-Amalie (town, western U.S. Virgin Islands) : 1921–1936 *St. Thomas*

Charlottenburg (town, eastern Germany) : originally *Lietzenburg* (The town became a district of Berlin in 1920.)

Charlottetown (city, Prince Edward Island, eastern Canada) : to 1763 *Port la Joie*

Chartres (city, north central France) : Roman *Carnotum*; earlier Roman *Autricum*

Chat-Bazar (village, northwestern Kyrgyzstan) : 1937–1991 Russian *Budyonny*

Châteaudun-du-Rhumel *see* **Chelghoum el Aïd**

Châteauroux (town, central France) : 1789–1792 *Indreville*

Château-Salins (village, northeastern France) : 1940–1944 German *Salzburgen*

Chatham *see* ²**East Hampton**

Chatham Island *see* ²**San Cristóbal**

Châtillon-Coligny (village, north central France) : formerly *Châtillon-sur-Loing*

Châtillon-sur-Loing *see* **Châtillon-Coligny**

Chattahoochee (town, Florida, southeastern United States) : to 1941 *River Junction*

Chattanooga (city, Tennessee, east central United States) : to 1838 *Ross's Landing*

Chauncey *see* **West Lafayette**

Chaves (city, northern Portugal) : Roman *Aquae Flaviae*

Cheb (city, western Czech Republic) : to 1918, 1938–1945 German *Eger*

Chebanka *see* ²**Chornomors'ke**

Cheboygan (town, Michigan, northern United States) : formerly *Inverness*; originally *Duncan*

Chedabucto *see* **Guysborough**

Chegutu (town, northeastern Zimbabwe) : to 1984 *Hartley*

Chehalis *see* **Grays Harbor**

Cheju (island, southern South Korea) : formerly *Quelpart*

Chekalin (town, western Russia) : to 1944 *Likhvin*

¹**Chekhov** (town, eastern Russia) : 1905–1945 Japanese *Noda*

[2]**Chekhov** (city, western Russia) : to 1954 *Lopasnya*

Chelghoum el Aïd (town, northeastern Algeria) : to *c*.1962 French *Châteaudun-du-Rhumel*

Chelles (town, northern France) : Roman *Calae*

Chełm (city, eastern Poland) : to 1915 Russian *Kholm*

Chełmno (town, north central Poland) : 1939–1945 German *Kulm*; 1772–1807, 1815–1919 German *Culm*

Chelmsford (city, southeastern England) : Roman *Caesaromagus*

Chelmsford Dam *see* **Ntshingwayo Dam**

Chełmsko Śląskie (town, southwestern Poland) : to 1945 German *Schömberg*

Chełmża (town, north central Poland) : 1939–1945 German *Kulmsee*; 1772–1807, 1815–1919 German *Culmsee*

Chelny *see* **Naberezhnyye Chelny**

Chembar *see* **Belinsky**

Chemmis *see* **Akhmīm**

Chemnitz (city, eastern Germany) : 1953–1990 *Karl-Marx-Stadt*

Chenango Point *see* **Binghamton**

Chengde (city, northeastern China) : conventional *Jehol*

Chenge *see* **Asparukhovo**

Chennai (city, southeastern India) : to 1996 *Madras*

Chepstow (town, southeastern Wales) : Welsh *Cas-gwent*

Cherchell (town, northern Algeria) : Roman *Caesarea*

Cherente *see* **Miracema do Norte**

Cherkas'ke *see* **Zymohir'ya**

Cherkasskoye *see* **Zymohir'ya**

Cherkessk (city, southwestern Russia) : 1937–1939 *Yezhovo-Cherkessk*; 1930–1937 *Sulimov*; 1880–1930 *Batalpashinsk*; to 1880 *Batalpashinskaya*

Chernenko *see* (1) **Sharypovo**; (2) **Şoldăneşti**

Chernivtsi (city, southwestern Ukraine) : (Russian *Chernovtsy*); 1919–1940 Romanian *Cernăuţi*; to 1918 German *Czernowitz*

Chernomorskoye *see* [1,2]**Chornomors'ke**

Chernorech'ye (town, southwestern Russia) : to 1940 *Novyye Aldy* (The town is now incorporated into the city of Grozny)

Chernovtsy *see* **Chernivtsi**

Chernyakhovsk (city, western Russia) : to 1946 German *Insterburg*

Chernyayevo *see* **Yangiyer**

Chernyshevskoye (town, western Russia) : to 1938 German *Eydtkuhnen*

Cherry Creek *see* **Boissevain**

Cherry Hill (town, New Jersey, northeastern

United States) : to 1961 *Delaware* (The town is now a suburb of Philadelphia.)

Chersky (town, eastern Russia) : to *c*.1960 *Nizhniye Kresty*

Chersonesus *see* **Crimea**

Chersonesus Aurea *see* **Malay Peninsula.**

Cherven' *see* **Chyerven'**

[1]**Chervone** (town, northern Ukraine) : (Russian *Chervonoye*); to 1957 *Yesman*

[2]**Chervone** (town, west central Ukraine) : (Russian *Chervonoye*); to *c*.1935 Russian *Krasnoye*

Chervonoarmeysk *see* (1) **Chervonoarmiys'k**; (2) **Radyvyliv**

Chervonoarmeyskoye *see* **Vily'nyans'k**

Chervonoarmiys'k (town, northern Ukraine) : (Russian *Chervonoarmeysk*); to 1935 *Pulyny* (Russian *Pulin*)

Chervonoarmiys'k *see* **Radyvyliv**

Chervonoarmiys'ke *see* **Vil'nyans'k**

Chervonograd *see* **Chervonohrad**

Chervonogrigorovka *see* **Chervonohryhorivka**

Chervonogvardeyskoye *see* **Chervonogvardiys'ke**

Chervonogvardiys'ke (town, eastern Ukraine) : (Russian *Chervonogvardeyskoye*); to 1965 *Krynychans'kyy* (Russian *Krinichansky*) (In this name and those below the Russian equivalent does not translate Ukrainian *Chervono-* but transliterates it. The proper Russian equivalent would be as **Krasnogvardeyskoye**.)

Chervonohrad (city, western Ukraine) : (Russian *Chervonograd*); to 1939, 1944–1953 Polish *Krystynopol* (Ukrainian *Krystynopil'*; Russian *Kristinopol'*)

Chervonohryhorivka (town, southeastern Ukraine) : (Russian *Chervonogrigorovka*); to 1939 Russian *Krasnogrigor'yevka*

Chervonoye *see* [1,2]**Chervone**

Chervonozavods'ke (town, east central Ukraine) : (Russian *Chervonozavodskoye*); to *c*.1961 *Stalinka*

Chervonozavodskoye *see* **Chervonozavods'ke**

Chervonyy Prapor *see* **Rubizhne**

Cheshnegir *see* **Sadovo**

Chesnokovka *see* **Novoaltaysk**

[1]**Chester** (city, northwestern England) : Roman *Deva* (The Roman name is that of the **Dee** River, on which Chester stands.)

[2]**Chester** (city, Pennsylvania, northeastern United States) : to 1681 *Upland*

Chesterfield Inlet (village, Nunavut, north central Canada) : alternate Inuit *Igluligaarjuk*

Chester-le-Street (town, northeastern England) : Roman *Concangis*

Chesterton (village, east central England) : Roman *Durobrivae* (This Chesterton, near Peterborough, should not be confused with the one that is now a district of Cambridge.)

Chetumal (city, eastern Mexico) : originally *Payo Obispo*

Ch'ew Bahir (lake, southwestern Ethiopia) : formerly *Lake Stefanie*

Chiange (town, southwestern Angola) : to *c*.1975 Portuguese *Vila de Almoster*

Chiari (town, northern Italy) : Roman *Clarium*

Chibia (town, southwestern Angola) : 1935–1980 Portuguese *João de Almeida*

Chibizovka *see* **Zherdevka**

Chibyu *see* **Ukhta**

Chicacole *see* **Srikakulam**

Chicago Heights (city, Illinois, north central United States) : 1849–1901 *Bloom*; originally *Thorn Grove* (The city is a southern suburb of Chicago.)

Chichester (city, southern England) : Roman *Noviomagus* (The Roman name also had the fuller form *Noviomagus Regnorum*.)

Chicualacuala (town, western Mozambique) : to 1981 *Malvérnia*

Chieti (city, central Italy) : Roman *Teate*

Chiflik *see* **Lovnidol**

Chihli *see* **Hopeh**

Chihli, Gulf of *see* **Bo Hai**

Childsburgh *see* **Hillsborough**

Chilia-Nouăb *see* **Kiliya**

Chililabombwe (town, northern Zambia) : to 1964 *Bancroft*

Chililaya *see* **Puerto Pérez**

Chilly *see* **Chilly-Mazarin**

Chilly-Mazarin (town, northern France) : to 1812 *Chilly*

Chilumba (town, northern Malawi) : to 1966 *Deep Bay*

Chimanimani (town, eastern Zimbabwe) : 1980–1982 *Mandidzuzure*; to 1980 *Melsetter*

Chimkent *see* **Shymkent**

Chimoio (city, south central Mozambique) : 1916–1975 *Vila Pery*

China (republic, eastern and central Asia) : [Chinese *Zhonghua*]; formerly English *Cathay* (The English name, related to *Kitay*, the Russian name of China, is preserved in commercial use for the Cathay Pacific airline, based in Hong Kong.)

Chinese Turkestan *see* **Xinjiang Uygur**

Chinhoyi (town, north central Zimbabwe) : to 1980 *Sinoya*

Chinnai *see* ²**Krasnogorsk**

Chinnereth, Sea of *see* **Galilee, Sea of**

Chinomiji *see* **Tyatino**

Chioggia (town, northern Italy) : Roman *Fossa Clodia*

Chipata (town, southeastern Zambia) : to 1964 *Fort Jameson*

Chipinga *see* **Chipinge**

Chipinge (town, eastern Zimbabwe) : to 1980 *Chipinga*

Chipuriro *see* **Guruve**

Chirchiq (town, eastern Uzbekistan) : 1932–1934 Russian *Komsomol'sky*; to 1932 Russian *Kirgiz-Kulak*

Chirk (town, northern Wales) : Welsh *Y Waun*

Chisasibi (village, Quebec, eastern Canada) : formerly *Fort George*

Chishima-retto *see* **Kuril Islands**

Chişinău (city, central Moldova) : (Russian *Kishinyov*); 1919–1940 Romanian *Chişinău*; 1812–1918 Russian *Kishinyov*

Chistyakovo *see* **Torez**

Chitato (town, northeastern Angola) : to *c*.1975 Portuguese *Portugália*

Chitipa (town, northern Malawi) : to 1966 *Fort Hill*

Chittaranjan (town, northeastern India) : to 1966 *Mihidjan*

Chiusi (town, central Italy) : Roman *Clusium*

Chivhu (town, central Zimbabwe) : to 1980 *Enkeldoorn*

Chizhev *see* **Czyżew**

Chkalov (island, eastern Russia) : to 1936 *Udd*

Chkalov *see* **Orenburg**

Chkalove (village, southeastern Ukraine) : (Russian *Chkalovo*); to 1939 *Novomykolayivka* (Russian *Novonikolayevka*)

Chkalovo (town, northern Kazakhstan) : to 1939 *Bogodukhovka*

Chkalovo *see* **Chkalove**

Chkalovsk (town, western Russia) : 1927–1937 *Vasilyovo*; to 1927 *Vasilyova Sloboda*

¹**Chkalovskoye** (village, western Russia) : to 1939 *Shikhirdany*

²**Chkalovskoye** (village, southeastern Russia) : to 1939 *Zenkovka*

Chlumec (town, northwestern Czech Republic) : to 1918, 1938–1945 German *Kulm*

Chobienia (town, southwestern Poland) : to 1945 German *Köben an der Oder*

Chocianów (town, southwestern Poland) : to 1945 German *Kotzenau*

Chociwel (town, northwestern Poland) : to 1945 German *Freienwalde*

Chodau *see* **Chodov**

Chodov (town, western Czech Republic) : to 1918, 1938–1945 German *Chodau*

Chodzież (town, western Poland) : 1793–1807, 1815–1918, 1939–1945 German *Kolmar*

Chojna (town, northwestern Poland) : to 1945 German *Königsberg*

Chojnice (town, north central Poland) : to 1918, 1939–1945 German *Konitz*

Chojnów (town, southwestern Poland) : to 1945 German *Hoynau*

Chókwé (town, southern Mozambique) : 1971–1980 Portuguese *Trigo de Morais*; 1963–1971 Portuguese *Vila Trigo de Moraes*; 1960–1964 Portuguese *Vila Alferes Chamusca*; to 1960 *Guijá*

Choloma (town, northwestern Honduras) : to early 1930s Spanish *El Paraíso*

Chomolungma *see* **Everest, Mt.**

Chomutov (city, northwestern Czech Republic) : to 1918, 1938–1945 German *Komotau*

Chong-Ak-Dzhol *see* **Jangy-Jol**

Chongqing (city, south central China) : traditionally *Chungking*

Chop (town, western Ukraine) : 1944–1945 Czech *Čop*; 1938–1944 Hungarian *Csap*; 1919–1938 Czech *Čop*; to 1918 Hungarian *Csap*

¹Chornomors'ke (town, southern Ukraine, near Yevpatoriya) : (Russian *Chernomorskoye*); to 1944 *Ak-Mechet'*

²Chornomors'ke (town, southern Ukraine, near Odessa) : (Russian *Chernomorskoye*); 1945–1988 *Gvardiys'ke* (Russian *Gvardeyskoye*); to 1945 *Chebanka*

Chortkiv (town, southwestern Ukraine) : (Russian *Chortkov*); to 1939 Polish *Czortków*

Chortkov *see* **Chortkiv**

Chorzów (city, southern Poland) : formerly *Królewska Huta*; to 1921, 1939–1945 German *Königshütte* (The city passed from Germany to Poland in 1921 and gained its current name in 1934 on the union of Królewska Huta with three other villages.)

Chosŏn *see* **Korea**

Choszczno (town, northwestern Poland) : to 1945 German *Arnswalde*

Chotěboř (town, central Czech Republic) : to 1918, 1938–1945 German *Chotieborsch*

Chotieborsch *see* **Chotěboř**

Choybalsan (city, eastern Mongolia) : 1931–1946 *Bayan Tumen*; to 1931 *San Beise*

Christburg *see* **Dzierzgoń**

¹Christchurch (city, southeastern New Zealand) : originally *Canterbury*

²Christchurch (village, southeastern Wales) : *Eglwys y Drindod* (The village is now a district of the city of Newport.)

Christiania *see* **Oslo**

Christiansville *see* **Kingsport**

Christieville *see* **Iberville**

Christmas Island *see* **Kiritimati**

Chrysopolis *see* **Üsküdar**

Chrzanów (town, southern Poland) : 1940–1945 German *Krenau*

Chubarivka *see* **Polohy**

Chubarovka *see* **Polohy**

Chuchelná (village, eastern Czech Republic) : to 1919, 1938–1945 German *Kutelna*

Chudskoye *see* **Peipus, Lake**

Chungking *see* **Chongqing**

Chuquisaca *see* **Sucre**

Chur (town, eastern Switzerland) : French *Coire*; Italian *Coira*; Roman *Curia Rhaetorum*

Churchill (river, Newfoundland and Labrador, eastern Canada) : to 1965 *Hamilton* (The river should not be confused with the much longer river of the same name in Manitoba.)

Churchill Falls (Newfoundland and Labrador, eastern Canada) : to 1965 *Grand Falls* (The falls, in Labrador, should be distinguished from the falls for which the town of *Grand Falls*, Newfoundland, is named.)

Churchville *see* **Sweetsburg**

Churubay-Nura *see* **¹Abay**

Chusetown *see* **Seymour**

Chusovoy (town, western Russia) : to 1933 *Chusovskoy Zavod*

Chusovskoy Zavod *see* **Chusovoy**

Chust *see* **Khust**

Chuuk (islands, central Micronesia) : formerly *Truk*

Chwitffordd *see* **Whitford**

Chyerven' (town, central Belarus) : (Russian *Cherven'*); to 1924 Russian *Igumen*

Chyorny Rynok *see* **Kochubey**

Chystyakove *see* **Torez**

Chythri *see* **Kythrea**

Chyzhew *see* **Czyżew**

Ciarraí *see* **¹Kerry**

Cidade de Minas *see* **Belo Horizonte**

Ciechanów (town, north central Poland) : 1940–1945 German *Zichenau*

Ciechocinek (town, north central Poland) : 1939–1945 German *Hermannsbad*

Ciénaga (city, northern Colombia) : originally *Aldea Grande*

Cienfuegos (city, central Cuba) : originally *Fernandina de Jagua* (The city was renamed following the destruction of the original settlement in a storm in 1825.)

Cieplice Śląskie Zdrój (town, southwestern Poland) : to 1945 German *Bad Warmbrunn* (The town is now part of the city of **Jelenia Góra**.)

Čierne (town, northwestern Slovakia) : 1938–1939 Polish *Czarne Beskidzkie*

Cieszyn (city, southern Poland) : to 1918, 1939–1945 German *Teschen* (Cieszyn lies on the border with the Czech Republic, facing **Český Těšín** across the Olza River, and originally formed a single entity with it. In 1920 the city was divided into two towns, that on the Polish side being known to the Czechs as *Polský Těšín*. In 1938 the two were reunited under Polish rule. The German name thus relates to the whole city, which in 1945 was returned to Poland. From 1938 to 1939 the railroad station in Český Těšín bore the Polish name *Cieszyn Zachodni*, "Western Cieszyn.")

Cieszyn Zachodni *see* **Český Těšín**

Cilgeti *see* **Kilgetty**

Cill Airne *see* **Killarney**

Cill Chainnigh *see* **Kilkenny**

Cill Chaoi *see* **Kilkee**

Cill Chaoil *see* **Kilkeel**

Cill Dalua *see* **Killaloe**

Cill Droichid *see* **Celbridge**

Cilli *see* **Celje**

Cill Mhantáin *see* **Wicklow**

Cill Mocheallóg *see* **Kilmallock**

Cill na Mallach *see* **Buttevant**

Cill Rois *see* **Kilrush**

Cîmpulung (town, south central Romania) : to 1918 German *Kimpolung*

Cincinnati (city, Ohio, east central United States) : to 1790 *Losantiville*

Cinco de Outubro *see* **Xá-Muteba**

Cintra *see* **Sintra**

Cionn tSáile *see* **Kinsale**

Cirencester (town, west central England) : Roman *Corinium*

Cirò (town, southern Italy) : ancient Greek *Crimissa*

Cirta *see* **Constantine**

Cistercium *see* **Cîteaux**

Cîteaux (village, eastern France) : Roman *Cistercium*

Citlaltépetl (volcano, east central Mexico) : alternate *Orizaba*

City of Kansas *see* ¹**Kansas City**

Ciudad Altamirano (town, southwestern Mexico) : to 1936 *Pungarabato*

Ciudad Arce (rown, west central El Salvador) : to c.1948 *El Chilamatal*

Ciudad Barrios (town, eastern El Salvador) : to 1913 *Cacaguatique*

Ciudad Bolívar (city, eastern Venezuela) : to 1846 *Angostura* (The full form of the original name was *San Tomás de la Nueva Guayana de la Angostura*.)

Ciudad Colón (town, central Costa Rica) : formerly *Pacaca*

Ciudad Darío (town, west central Nicaragua) : formerly *Metapa*

Ciudad de las Casas *see* **San Cristóbal de las Casas**

Ciudad del Este (city, eastern Paraguay) : to 1989 *Puerto Presidente Stroessner*; earlier *Puerto Flor de Lis*

Ciudad de San Cristóbal *see* **San Cristóbal de las Casas**

Ciudad Guayana (city, eastern Venezuela) : formerly *Santo Tomé de Guayana*

Ciudad Guzmán (city, southwestern Mexico) : formerly *Zapotlán el Grande*

Ciudad Hidalgo (city, west central Mexico) : formerly *Villa Hidalgo*

Ciudad Ixtepec (city, southern Mexico) : formerly *San Jerónimo Ixtepec*

Ciudad Juárez (city, northern Mexico) : to 1888 *El Paso del Norte* (The city, on the Rio Grande opposite El Paso, United States, originally included settlements on both sides of the river but these were split by the 1848 Treaty of Guadalupe Hidalgo and the Mexican town was renamed 40 years later. For the treaty town's name, *see* **Gustavo A. Madero**.)

Ciudad Madero (city, northeastern Mexico) : to 1930 *Villa de Cecilia*

Ciudad Mante (city, northeastern Mexico) : formerly *Villa Juárez*

Ciudad Mendoza (city, eastern Mexico) : formerly *Santa Rosa*

Ciudad Porfirio Díaz *see* **Piedras Negras**

Ciudad Real de Chiapa *see* **San Cristóbal de las Casas**

Ciudad Sandino (town, northwestern Nicaragua) : formerly *El Jícaro*

Ciudad Tecúm Umán (town, southwestern Guatemala) : formerly *Ayutla*

Ciudad Trujillo *see* **Santo Domingo**

Ciudad Venustiano Carranza (town, western Mexico) : formerly *San Gabriel*

Cividale del Friuli (town, northeastern Italy) : Roman *Forum Julii*

Civita Castellana (town, central Italy) : Roman *Falerii Novi*; earlier Roman *Falerii Veteres*

Civitas Altae Ripae *see* **Brzeg**

Civitas Ebroicorum *see* **Évreux**

Civitas Nemetum *see* **Speyer**

Civitas Nova *see* **Alessandria**

Civitas Tricassium *see* **Troyes**

Civitavecchia (town, western Italy) : Roman *Trajani Portus*; earlier Roman *Centum Cellae*

Clairfontaine *see* **El Aouinet**

Clam Lake *see* **Cadillac**

Clare (county, western Ireland) : Irish *An Clár*

Clarium *see* **Chiari**

Clark's City *see* **Livingston**

Clarksdale (town, Mississippi, southeastern United States) : originally *Clarksville*

Clarksville *see* (1) **Beeton**; (2) **Clarksdale**

Clastidium *see* **Casteggio**

Clausentum *see* **Bitterne**

Clawdd Offa *see* **Offa's Dyke**

Clazomenae *see* **Klazumen**

Cleaveland *see* **Cleveland**

Clementsport (village, Nova Scotia, eastern Canada) : to 1851 *Moose River*

Clermont (town, south central France) : Roman *Augustonemetum* (In 1630 Clermont united with neighboring Montferrand to form the city of *Clermont-Ferrand*.)

Cleveland (city, Ohio, northeastern United States) : to 1832 *Cleaveland*

Cleves *see* **Kleve**

Clifden (town, western Ireland) : Irish *An Clochán*

Clifton *see* **Niagara Falls**

Clinton (town, Ontario, southeastern Canada) : to 1844 *The Corners*

Clodian Way *see* **Via**

Cloich na Coillte *see* **Clonakilty**

Clonakilty (town, southwestern Ireland) : Irish *Cloich na Coillte*

Clones (town, northern Ireland) : Irish *Cluain Eois*

Clonmacnoise (village, central Ireland) : Irish *Cluain Mhic Nóis*

Clonmel (town, southern Ireland) : Irish *Cluain Meala*

Cluain Cearbán *see* **Louisburgh**

Cluain Eois *see* **Clones**

Cluainín *see* **Manorhamilton**

Cluain Meala *see* **Clonmel**

Cluain Mhic Nóis *see* **Clonmacnoise**

Cluj (town, northwestern Romania) : to 1918, 1940–1945 Hungarian *Kolozsvár*; to 1867 German *Klausenburg* (Cluj united with neighboring Napoca in the mid–1970s to form the city of *Cluj-Napoca*.)

Clunia *see* **Feldkirch**

Clusium *see* **Chiusi**

Clutha (river, southern New Zealand) : Maori *Matau*; formerly *Molyneux*

Clutha Ferry *see* **Balclutha**

Clyde *see* **Wairoa**

Clyde River (village, Nunavut, northeastern Canada) : alternate Inuit *Kangiqtugaapik*

Coalbanks *see* **Lethbridge**

Coal Harbour *see* **Wesleyville**

Coatzacoalcos (city, east central Mexico) : formerly Spanish *Puerto México*

Cóbh (town, southwestern Ireland) : Irish *An Cóbh*; 1849–1922 English *Queenstown*

Coblenz *see* **Koblenz**

Coca (town, eastern Ecuador) : formerly Spanish *Puerto Francisco de Orellana*

Cochabamba (city, central Bolivia) : to 1786 Spanish *Villa de Oropeza*

Cochato *see* **Randolph**

Coco (river, northern Nicaragua) : formerly Spanish *Segovia*

Cocos Islands (eastern Indian Ocean) : formerly *Keeling Islands*

Coed-duon *see* **Blackwood**

Coelho Neto (city, northeastern Brazil) : to 1939 *Curralinho*

Coffs Harbour (town, New South Wales, eastern Australia) : to 1861 *Brelsford*

Cognac (town, southwestern France) : Roman *Comniacum*

Cohansey Bridge *see* **Bridgeton**

Coill an Chollaigh *see* **Bailieborough**

Coimbra (city, west central Portugal) : Roman *Aeminium*

Coira *see* **Chur**

Coire *see* **Chur**

Colbert *see* **Aïn Oulmene**

Colchester (city, southeastern England) : Roman *Camulodunum*

Çölemerik *see* **Hakkâri**

Coleraine (town, northern Northern Ireland) : Irish *Cúil Raithin*

Coligny (town, north central South Africa) : to c.1918 *Treurfontein*

Colinas (city, northeastern Brazil) : to 1944 *Picos*

College Park (city, Georgia, southeastern United States) : to 1895 *Manchester*

Collegeville *see* **East Lansing**

Colleville-Montgomery (village, northwestern France) : to 1946 *Colleville-sur-Orne*

Colleville-sur-Orne *see* **Colleville-Montgomery**

Colliston *see* **Gowanbank**

Cologne (city, western Germany) : [German *Köln*]; Roman *Colonia Agrippinensis*. (The Roman city, with full title *Colonia Claudia Ara Agrippinensium*, was founded by the emperor Claudius and named in honor of his wife, Julia Agrippina.)

Colomb-Béchar *see* **Béchar**

Colón (city, north central Panama) : to 1890 *Aspinwall*

Colonia (city, southwestern Uruguay) : originally *Colônia do Sacramento* (The city's full Spanish name is *Colonia del Sacramento*, translating the original Portuguese.)

Colonia Agrippinensis *see* **Cologne**

Colonia del Sacramento *see* **Colonia**

Colônia do Sacramento *see* **Colonia**

Colonia Julia Fanestris *see* **Fano**

Colonia Leopoldina (town, northeastern Brazil) : to 1944 *Leopoldina*

Colonia Mineira *see* **Siqueira Campos**
Colonias *see* **Pando**
Colomb-Béchar *see* **Béchar**
Colorado City *see* **Yuma**
Colorado Springs (city, Colorado, west central United States) : originally *Fountain Colony*
[1]**Columbia** (city, Missouri, central United States) : to 1821 *Smithton*
[2]**Columbia** (town, Pennsylvania, northeastern United States) : to 1790 *Wright's Ferry* (The name was changed when the town was under consideration as a possible U.S. capital.)
[1]**Columbus** (city, Indiana, north central United States) : originally *Tiptona*
[2]**Columbus** (city, Mississippi, southern United States) : to 1821 *Possum Town*
Colville, Cape (northern New Zealand) : Maori *Moehau*
Colville Town *see* **Nanaimo**
Colwyn Bay (town, northern Wales) : Welsh *Bae Colwyn*
Comacchio (town, northern Italy) : Roman *Comacium*
Comacium *see* **Comacchio**
Comandante Arbues *see* **Mirandópolis**
Comayagua (city, west central Honduras) : originally *Valladolid de Santa María de Comayagua*
Comber (town, eastern Northern Ireland) : Irish *An Comar*
Comitán (city, southeastern Mexico) : formerly *Comitán de las Flores* (The city's present full name is *Comitán de Domínguez*.)
Comitán de Dominguez *see* **Comitán**
Comitán de las Flores *see* **Comitán**
Commencement City *see* **Tacoma**
Commerce *see* **Nauvoo**
Commerce City *see* [3]**Canton**
Communism Peak *see* **Ismoili Somoni, Peak**
Comniacum *see* **Cognac**
Como (city, northern Italy) : Roman *Comum*
Company Shops *see* [1]**Burlington**
Compendium *see* **Compiègne**
Compiègne (town, northern France) : Roman *Compendium*
Complutum *see* **Alcalá de Henares**
Comum *see* **Como**
Comunanza (village, central Italy) : *c.*1937–1945 *Comunanza del Littorio*
Comunanza del Littorio *see* **Comunanza**
Conca *see* **Cuenca**
Concangis *see* **Chester-le-Street**
Conceição de Macabu (town, southeastern Brazil) : to 1943 *Macabu*
Conceição do Almeida (town, eastern Brazil) : to 1944 Portuguese *Afonso Pena*
Conceição do Paraíba *see* **Capela**

[1]**Concord** (city, California, western United States) : to 1869 *Todos Santos*
[2]**Concord** (town, Massachusetts, northeastern United States) : originally *Musketaquid*
[3]**Concord** (city, New Hampshire, northeastern United States) : to 1765 *Penacook Plantation*
Condate *see* (1) **Northwich**; (2) **Rennes**; (3) **St.-Claude**
Condé-Smendou *see* **Zighoud Youcef**
Condivincum *see* **Nantes**
Conemaugh *see* **Johnstown**
Confluentes *see* **Koblenz**
Congo (river, west central Africa) : alternate *Zaire* or *Zaïre* (The name *Zaire* is preferred in Angola, and *Zaïre* in the Democratic Republic of the Congo, whose former name it gave.)
Congo, Democratic Republic of the (central Africa) : 1971–1997 *Zaïre*; 1965–1971 *Congo (Kinshasa)*; 1960–1965 *Congo (Léopoldville)*; 1908–1960 *Belgian Congo*; 1885–1908 *Congo Free State*
Congo, Republic of the (western Africa) : 1960–1970 *Congo (Brazzaville)*; 1958–1960 *Congo Autonomous Republic*; 1883–1958 *Middle Congo* (If the name *Congo* alone is used, it is this country that is usually meant.)
Congo Autonomous Republic *see* **Congo, Republic of the**
Congo (Brazzaville) *see* **Congo, Republic of the**
Congo Free State *see* **Congo, Democratic Republic of the**
Congo (Kinshasa) *see* **Congo, Democratic Republic of the**
Congo (Léopoldville) *see* **Congo, Democratic Republic of the**
Congonhas (city, southeastern Brazil) : to 1948 *Congonhas do Campo*
Congonhas do Campo *see* **Congonhas**
Connacht (region, western Ireland) : traditional English *Connaught* (The traditional form of the name became familiar as a ducal title and hence from its use as a fashionable street or commercial name, as London's Connaught Square and Connaught hotel.)
Connah's Quay (town, northeastern Wales) : Welsh *Cei Connah*
Connaught *see* **Connacht**
Connecticut Farms *see* [1]**Union**
Conquista *see* **Vitória da Conquista**
Conselheiro Lafaiete (city, southeastern Brazil) : formerly *Lueluz*
Consentia *see* **Cosenza**
Constance *see* **Konstanz**
Constance, Lake (northeastern

Switzerland/southwestern Germany) : [German *Bodensee*]; Roman *Brigantinus Lacus*

Constanţa (city, southeastern Romania) : to 1878 Turkish *Küstenja*; Roman *Constantiana*; ancient Greek *Tomi*

Constantia *see* (1) **Coutances**, (2) **Konstanz**

Constantiana *see* **Constanţa**

Constantine (city, northeastern Algeria) : [Arabic *Qusanṭīnah*]; Roman *Cirta*

Constantinople *see* **Istanbul**

Constant's Warehouse *see* **Suffolk**

Conway *see* **Conwy**

Conwy (town, northern Wales) : formerly English *Conway*

Cook, Mt. (southwestern New Zealand) : Maori *Aorangi*

Cookstown (town, central Northern Ireland) : Irish *An Chorr Chríochach*

Coolgardie (town, Western Australia, southwestern Australia) : formerly *Fly Flat*; earlier *Bayley's Reward*; originally *Gnaralbine*

Coolidge, Mt. (South Dakota, north central United States) : to 1927 *Sheep Mountain*

Coos Bay (town, Oregon, northwestern United States) : to 1944 *Marshfield*

Čop *see* **Chop**

Copenhagen (city, eastern Denmark) : [Danish *København*]

Copperbelt (province, northern Zambia) : to 1969 *Western* (The province was renamed when the earlier name was reassigned to Barotseland in western Zambia.)

Copper City *see* **Valdez**

Coppermine *see* **Kugluktuk**

Copperopolis *see* **Anaconda**

Coptos *see* **Qift**

Coquilhatville *see* (1) **Équateur**; (2) **Mbandaka**

Cora *see* **Cori**

Cora Droma Rúisc *see* **Carrick-on-Shannon**

Coral Harbour (village, Nunavut, northern Canada) : alternate Inuit *Salliq*

Corbeil (town, northern France) : Roman *Corbilium* (In 1951 Corbeil was united with neighboring Essonnes to form the town of *Corbeil-Essonnes*.)

Corbilium *see* **Corbeil**

Corbinton *see* **Hillsborough**

Corbridge (town, northeastern England) : Roman *Corstopitum* (Although traditionally applied to the town, the Roman name is almost certainly corrupt, and was probably closer to *Coriosopitum*. Moreover, it properly applied to the nearby site now named *Corchester*, not to the town itself.)

Corcaigh *see* **Cork**

Corcyra *see* **Corfu**

Cordeiro *see* **Cordeirópolis**

Cordeirópolis (town, southeastern Brazil) : to 1944 *Cordeiro*

Cordillera (department, central Paraguay) : to 1944 *Caraguatay*

Córdoba (city, southern Spain) : traditional English *Cordova*; Roman *Corduba*

Cordova *see* **Córdoba**

Corduba *see* **Córdoba**

Coreaú (town, northeastern Brazil) : to 1944 *Palma*

Corfu (island, western Greece) : [modern Greek *Kérkira*]; Roman *Corcyra* (The island gained its present Italian name when a Venetian possession from 1386 to 1797.)

Cori (town, south central Italy) : Roman *Cora*

Corinium *see* **Cirencester**

¹Corinth (city, southeastern Greece) : [modern Greek *Kórinthos*]

²Corinth (town, Mississippi, southeastern United States) : to 1857 *Cross City*

Coriosopitum *see* **Corbridge**

Corito *see* **Cortona**

Cork (city, southern Ireland) : Irish *Corcaigh*

Corneille *see* **Merouana**

Corneto *see* **Tarquinia**

Cornouaille (region, northwestern France) : [Breton *Kernev-veur*]

¹Cornwall (county, southwestern England) : Cornish *Kernow*

²Cornwall (city, Ontario, southeastern Canada) : to 1797 *New Johnston*

Coro (city, northwestern Venezuela) : originally *Santa Ana de Coriana*

Corona (city, California, southwestern United States) : to 1896 *South Riverside*

Coronium *see* **La Coruña**

Corrientes (city, northeastern Argentina) : originally *San Juan de Vera de las Siete Corrientes*

Corse *see* **Corsica**

Corsica (island, northwestern Mediterranean) : [French *Corse*]

Corstopitum *see* **Corbridge**

Cortazar (city, north central Mexico) : to 1857 *San José de los Amoles*

Cortona (city, central Italy) : Roman *Corito*

Cortracum *see* **Kortrijk**

Corumbá *see* **Corumbá de Goiás**

Corumbá de Goiás (town, central Brazil) : to 1944 *Corumbá*

Corumbalina (town, central Brazil) : to 1933 Portuguese *Santa Cruz*

Corunna *see* **La Coruña**

Corupá (town, southern Brazil) : to 1944 *Hansa*

Corvallis (city, Oregon, northwestern United States) : to 1853 *Marysville*

Corvallis *see* Norwalk

Coryel's Ferry *see* (1) Lambertville; (2) New Hope

Cosa *see* Ansedonia

Cosedia *see* Coutances

Cosel *see* Koźle

Cosenza (city, southern Italy) : Roman *Consentia*

Costa de Monte Grande *see* San Isidro

Costa Mesa (city, California, western United States) : to 1921 *Harper*

Costermansville *see* Bukavu

Côte d'Ivoire *see* Ivory Coast

Côte-Notre-Dame-de-Liesse *see* Côte-St.-Luc

Côte-St.-Luc (city, Quebec, southeastern Canada) : formerly *Côte-Notre-Dame-de-Liesse* (The city is now a suburb of Montreal.)

Côtes-d'Armor (department, northwestern France) : to 1990 *Côtes-du-Nord*

Côtes-du-Nord *see* Côtes-d'Armor

Coţman *see* Kitsman'

Cotopaxi (province, north central Ecuador) : to 1939 Spanish *León*

Cotrone *see* Crotone

Cottage City *see* Oak Bluffs

Cottage Hill *see* Elmhurst

Courtrai *see* Kortrijk

Coutances (town, northwestern France) : Roman *Constantia*; earlier Celtic *Cosedia*

Covilhã (city, east central Portugal) : Roman *Silia Hermia*

Cowansville (town, Quebec, southeastern Canada) : to 1876 *Nelsonville*

Cowbridge (town, southern Wales) : Welsh *Y Bont-faen*; Roman *Bovium*

Cow Commons *see* Somerville

Cowford *see* ¹Jacksonville

Cowpastures *see* ¹Camden

Coxim (city, western Brazil) : 1939–1948 *Herculânia*

Cracow *see* Kraków

Crane Creek *see* Melbourne

Craneville *see* Cranford

Cranford (town, New Jersey, northeastern United States) : to 1871 *Craneville*

Crayford (town, southeastern England) : Roman *Noviomagus*

Crescent City *see* Greymouth

Creswell *see* Arkansas City

Crete (island, southern Greece) : [modern Greek *Kríti*]; Roman *Candia*

Crickhowell (village, southeastern Wales) : Welsh *Crucywel*

Crimea (peninsula, southern Ukraine) : [Ukrainian and Russian *Krym*]; formerly *Taurida* (Russian *Tavrida*); ancient Greek *Chersonesus* (The Greek name, meaning literally "dry is-

land," applied to a number of peninsulas in Europe. This one was known to the Romans as *Chersonesus Taurica*, "Tauric Chersonese," as distinct from the *Chersonesus Thracia*, "Thracian Chersonese," or Gallipoli Peninsula. The city of Kherson in the southwestern Crimea has a name of the same origin. *See also* Malay Peninsula.)

Crimissa *see* Cirò

Cristina *see* Cristinápolis

Cristinápolis (town, northeastern Brazil) : to 1944 *Cristina*

Crna Gora *see* ¹Montenegro

Croatia (republic, southeastern Europe) : [Serbo-Croat *Hrvatska*]

Crococalana *see* ¹Brough

Crocodilopolis *see* El Faiyum

Crook's Rapids *see* ²Hastings

Cross City *see* ²Corinth

Crossen *see* (1) Krosno; (2) Krosno Odrzańskie

Crossing on the Missouri *see* Bismarck

Cross Plains *see* Dalton

Cross River (state, southeastern Nigeria) : to 1976 *South-Eastern*

Crossroads *see* New Market

Crotona *see* Crotone

Crotone (town, southern Italy) : to 1928 *Cotrone*; Roman *Crotona*

Crucywel *see* Crickhowell

Cruzeiro *see* Joaçaba

Cruzeiro do Sul *see* Joaçaba

Csaca *see* Čadca

Csáktornya *see* Čakovec

Csap *see* Chop

Cseklész *see* Bernolákovo

Csikszereda *see* Miercurea Ciuc

Csorba *see* Štrba

Cuamba (city, northwestern Mozambique) : 1942–1975, Portuguese *Nova Freixo*

Cuando (river, southeastern Angola/southwestern Zambia) : alternate *Kwando* (The river is known by the Portuguese name *Cuando* in Angola and as *Kwando* in Zambia, for part of its course forming the border between the two countries. *Cp.* Cuango.)

Cuango (river, northern Angola/western Democratic Republic of the Congo) : alternate *Kwango* (The river is known by the Portuguese name *Cuango* in Angola and as *Kwango* in the Democratic Republic of the Congo, for part of its course forming the border between the two countries. *Cp.* Cuando.)

Cuatreros *see* General Daniel Cerri

Cuatro de Junio *see* La Toma

Cubujuquí *see* Heredia

Cúcuta (city, northeastern Colombia) : to 1793 *San José de Guasimal* (The city's full name is *San José de Cúcuta*)

Cuenca (city, east central Spain) : Roman *Conca*

Cuevas del Almanzora (town, southeastern Spain) : formerly *Cuevas de Vera*

Cuevas de Vera *see* Cuevas del Almanzora

Cuicul *see* Djemila

Cúil an tSúdaire *see* Portarlington

Cúil Raithin *see* Coleraine

Culebra *see* Dewey

Culebra Cut *see* Gaillard Cut

Culm *see* Chełmno

Culmsee *see* Chełmża

Cuma *see* Blagoevgrad

Cumaná (city, northeastern Venezuela) : originally *Nueva Córdoba*

Cumbe *see* Euclides da Cunha

Cumberland (city, Maryland, northeastern United States) : to 1763 *Will's Creek*

Cunetio *see* Mildenhall

Cupcina (village, northern Moldova) : formerly Russian *Kalininsk*

Ćuprija (town, east central Serbia) : to 1830 Turkish *Köprü*

Curador *see* Presidente Dutra

Curia Rhaetorum *see* Chur

Curicó (city, central Chile) : originally *San José de Buena Vista de Curicó*

Curralinho *see* Coelho Neto

Curt-Bunar *see* Tervel

Curzola *see* Korčula

Cushnoc *see* ²Augusta

Cuyo *see* Puerto Princesa

Cwmbran (town, southeastern Wales) : Welsh *Cwmbrân*

Cwmbrân *see* Cwmbran

Cwm Ogwr *see* Ogmore Vale

Cybinka (town, western Poland) : to 1945 German *Ziebingen*

Cyclades (islands, southeastern Greece) : [modern Greek *Kikládhes*]

Cydonia *see* Canea

Cydweli *see* Kidwelly

Cymru *see* Wales

Cyprus (island republic, eastern Mediterranean) : [modern Greek *Kypros*; Turkish *Kibris*] (The southern two-thirds of Cyprus are occupied by Greece, the original and still internationally recognized government of the island. The northern third is occupied by Turkey, who in 1983 unilaterally proclaimed it the *Turkish Republic of Northern Cyprus*.)

Cyrene *see* Shaḥḥāt

Cyropolis *see* Khujand

Czaplinek (town, northwestern Poland) : to 1945 German *Tempelburg*

Czarna Woda (town, northern Poland) : to 1918, 1939–1945 German *Schwarzwasser*

Czarne (town, northwestern Poland) : to 1945 German *Hammerstein*

Czarne Beskidzkie *see* Čierne

Czarnikau *see* Czarnków

Czarnków (town, western Poland) : 1939–1945 German *Scharnikau*; 1793–1919 German *Czarnikau*

Czechoslavakia (former republic, central Europe) : [Czech *Československo*] (In 1993 the country was divided into the present Czech Republic and Slovakia.)

Czech Republic (republic, central Europe) : [Czech *Česká Republika*] (The country was formed in 1993 from the western part of Czechoslovakia, the eastern part becoming Slovakia.)

Czernina (town, western Poland) : 1937–1945 German *Lesten*; to 1937 German *Tschirnau*

Czernowitz *see* Chernivtsi

Częstochowa (city, southern Poland) : 1939–1945 German *Tschenstochau*

Człopa (town, northwestern Poland) : to 1945 German *Schloppe*

Człuchów (town, northwestern Poland) : to 1945 German *Schlochau*

Czortków *see* Chortkiv

Czyżew (town, eastern Poland) : 1939–1941 Belarussian *Chyzhew*; to 1915 Russian *Chizhev* (The town is now formally known as *Czyżew-Osada*.)

Daber *see* Dobra

Dąbie (city district, northwestern Poland) : to 1945 German *Altdamm* (Dąbie was incorporated into what is now Szczecin in 1939.)

Dąbromierz (village, southwestern Poland) : to 1945 German *Hohenfriedeberg*

Dąbrowa Górnicza (city, southwestern Poland) : 1939–1945 German *Dombrowa*; to 1915 Russian *Dombrova*

Dąbrowno (town, northeastern Poland) : to 1945 German *Gilgenburg*

Dacca *see* Dhaka

Dachnoye (village, eastern Russia) : 1905–1945 Japanese *Shimba*

Dačice (town, southern Czech Republic) : to 1918, 1939–1945 German *Datschitz*

Dagon *see* Yangôn

Dahomey *see* Benin

Daingean (village, east central Ireland) : Irish *An Daingean*; to 1920 *Philipstown*

Dairbhre *see* ³Valencia

Dairen *see* Dalian

Dairyland *see* **La Palma**

Dajabón (province, northwestern Dominican Republic) : to 1961 Spanish *Libertador*

Dakhla (town, western Western Sahara) : alternate *Ad Dakhla*; to 1976 Spanish *Villa Cisneros*

Dalarna (region, west central Sweden) : formerly *Dalecarlia*

Dalby (town, Queensland, eastern Australia) : to 1854 *Myall Creek Station*

Dalecarlia *see* **Dalarna**

Dalence *see* **Teniente Bullaín**

¹Dali (city, southern China) : to 1980s *Xiaguan* (The city's present name is that of its former prefecture.)

²Dali (village, central Cyprus) : Roman *Idalium*; ancient Greek *Idalion*

Dalian (city, eastern China) : 1945–1955 Russian *Dal'ny*; 1905–1945 Japanese *Dairen*; 1898–1905 Russian *Dal'ny* (The city subsequently merged with **Lüshun**, combining the first part of each name to become *Lüda*.)

Dalipnagar *see* **Bannu**

Dalle *see* **Yirga Alem**

Dalmacija *see* **Dalmatia**

Dalmatia (region, southern Croatia) : [Serbo-Croat *Dalmacija*]

Dal'negorsk (city, eastern Russia) : to 1972 *Tetyukhe*

Dal'nerechensk (city, eastern Russia) : to 1973 *Iman*

Dal'ny *see* **Dalian**

Dalton (city, Georgia, southeastern United States) : originally *Cross Plains*

Dalyan (village, southwestern Turkey) : ancient Greek *Caunus*

Damanhur (city, northern Egypt) : Roman *Hermopolis Parva*

Damascus (city, southwestern Syria) : [Arabic *Dimashq*; alternate Arabic *Ash Shām*] (The city's alternate Arabic name, meaning "the north," is identical to that of **Syria**.)

Damietta (city, northern Egypt) : [Arabic *Dumyāṭ*]

Da Nang (city, central Vietnam) : French colonial *Tourane*

Danastris *see* **Dniester**

Danby *see* **Glen Ellyn**

Dancalia Meridionale *see* **Assab**

Dangriga (town, central Belize) : formerly *Stann Creek*

Danish West Indies *see* **Virgin Islands of the United States**

Danmark *see* **Denmark**

Dansalan *see* **Marawi**

Danube (river, central Europe) : [Bulgarian *Dunav*; German *Donau*; Hungarian *Duna*; Romanian *Dunărea*; Russian *Dunay*]; Roman *Danubius* (The Romans were in awe of the Danube. In his *Panegyricus* Pliny writes: *Magnum est, imperator auguste, magnum est stare in Danubii ripa*, "It is a great thing, O noble emperor, great, to stand on the banks of the Danube.")

Danubius *see* **Danube**

Danum *see* **Doncaster**

Danvers (town, Massachusetts, northeastern United States) : to 1775 *Salem Village*

Danzig *see* **Gdańsk**

Daoud *see* **Aïn Beïda**

Dapsang *see* **K2**

Dara Dere *see* **Zlatograd**

Darasun *see* **Vershino-Darasunsky**

Dardanelles (strait, northwestern Turkey) : traditional English *Hellespont* (The classical name, associated in legend with the Greek lovers Hero and Leander, is historically famed from the crossing of the strait by the Persian king Xerxes in 480 B.C. in his invasion of Greece and that of Alexander the Great in 334 B.C. in his expedition against Persia.)

Dardania *see* **Kosovo**

Dar el Beida (town, northern Algeria) : to *c.*1962 French *Maison Blanche* (The French colonial name was also that of **Casablanca**.)

Dar el Beida *see* **Casablanca**

Darıdere *see* **Zlatograd**

Darien (town, Georgia, southeastern United States) : originally *New Inverness*

Darkau *see* **Darkov**

Darkehmen *see* **Ozyorsk**

Darkov (village, eastern Czech Republic) : 1939–1945 German *Darkau*; 1938–1939 Polish *Darków*; to 1918 German *Darkau*

Darków *see* **Darkov**

Darłowo (town, northwestern Poland) : to 1945 German *Rügenwalde*

Darwin (city, Northern Territory, northern Australia) : to 1911 *Palmerston*

Dashev *see* **Dashiv**

Dashiv (village, central Ukraine) : (Russian *Dashev*); to *c.*1930 *Staryy Dashiv* (Russian *Stary Dashev*)

Dashkesan *see* **Daşkäsän**

Dashtobod (town, eastern Uzbekistan) : formerly Russian *Ul'yanovo*; to 1974 Russian *Obruchevo*

Daşkäsän (town, western Azerbaijan) : (Russian *Dashkesan*); to 1948 Russian *Verkhny Dashkesan*

Daşoguz (city, northern Turkmenistan) : to 1994 Russian *Tashauz*

Datschitz *see* **Dačice**

Dauba *see* **Dubá**

Daugavgriva *see* **Daugavgrīva**

Daugavgrīva (town, northern Latvia) : (Russian *Daugavgriva*); 1917–1918, 1940–1944 German *Dünamünde*; to 1917 Russian *Ust'-Dvinsk*

Daugavpils (city, southeastern Latvia) : 1941–1944 German *Dünaburg*; 1893–1920 Russian *Dvinsk*; 1656–1667, Russian *Borisoglebsk*; to 1656 German *Dünaburg*

Daulatabad (village, western India) : to 1327 *Devagiri*

Dauphin Island (Alabama, southeastern United States) : to 1708 *Massacre Island*

David-Gorodok *see* **Davyd Haradok**

Davos (town, eastern Switzerland) : Romansh *Tavau*

Davyd-Haradok (town, southern Belarus) : (Russian *David-Gorodok*); 1919–1939 Polish *Dawidgródek*; to 1919 Russian *David-Gorodok*

Dawidgródek *see* **Davyd-Haradok**

Dawley *see* **Telford**

Dawson (village, Yukon Territory, northwestern Canada) : formerly *Dawson City*

Dawson City *see* **Dawson**

Dax (town, southwestern France) : Roman *Aquae Augustae*; earlier Roman *Aquae Tarbellicae*

Dayton (town, Tennessee, southeastern United States) : to 1895 *Smith's Crossroads*

Dead Sea (eastern West Bank/western Jordan) : [Arabic *Baḥr Lūt*]; alternate biblical *Salt Sea*; Roman *Mare Mortuum*

Dearborn (city, Michigan, northeastern United States) : 1833–1893 *Dearbornville*; previously *Pekin*; earlier *Bucklin*; originally *Ten Eyck*

Dearbornville *see* **Dearborn**

Death Valley (California, western United States) : locally *Tomesha* (The great depression, now a national park, received its English name in 1849 from goldseekers attempting to cross it.)

Debar (town, western Macedonia) : to 1913 Turkish *Dibra*; Roman *Deborus*

Dębica (town, southeastern Poland) : 1939–1945 German *Dembica*

Dęblin (town, eastern Poland) : 1940–1945 German *Demblin*; to 1915 Russian *Ivangorod*

Dębno (town, northwestern Poland) : to 1945 German *Neudamm*

Deborus *see* **Debar**

Debrecen (city, eastern Hungary) : to 1867 German *Debreczin*

Debreczin *see* **Debrecen**

Debrzno (town, northwestern Poland) : to 1945 German *Preussisch-Friedland*

De Cantillon *see* **North Little Rock**

Děčín (city, northern Czech Republic) : to 1918, 1938–1945 German *Tetschen*

Dedeağaç *see* **Alexandroúpolis**

Dedeagach *see* **Alexandroúpolis**

Dedford *see* **East Greenwich**

Dedovsk (town, western Russia) : 1925–1940 *Dedovsky*; to 1925 *Guchkovo*

Dedovsky *see* **Dedovsk**

Dee (river, northeastern Wales/northwestern England) : Welsh *Dyfrdwy*; Roman *Deva* (The Roman name gave that of the city of **Chester**, which stands on the river.)

Deep Bay *see* **Chilumba**

Deep Hollow *see* **Scranton**

Deep River (town, Connecticut, northeastern United States) : to 1947 *Saybrook*

Deer Creek *see* **Roseburg**

Deerfield (town, Illinois, central United States) : originally *Cadwell's Corners*

Deer Lodge (town, Montana, northwestern United States) : originally *La Barge*

Değirmenlik *see* **Kythrea**

Dehqonobod (village, southern Uzbekistan) : (Russian *Dekhkanabad*); to *c.*1935 *Tengi-Kharam*

Deichow *see* **Dychów**

Dej (city, northwestern Romania) : to 1918, 1940–1944 Hungarian *Dés*

De Kalb (city, Illinois, central United States) : to 1856 *Buena Vista*

Dekhkanabad *see* **Dehqonobod**

De Laage Prairie *see* **South Holland**

Delatyn *see* **Delyatyn**

Delaware *see* **Cherry Hill**

Delémont (town, northwestern Switzerland) : German *Delsberg*

Delhi (city, northern India) : alternate official *New Delhi*; alternate popular *Old Delhi*; local alternate *Shahjahanabad* (Delhi is really two cities in one. The local name refers to Shah Jahan, who built the seventh city of Delhi in 1638. Construction of *New Delhi*, just south of Old Delhi, began in 1912, and the capital was moved there from the older city in 1931.)

Délįne (village, Northwest Territories, northwestern Canada) : to 1999 *Fort Franklin*

Delray *see* **Delray Beach**

Delray Beach (city, Florida, southeastern United States) : to 1923 *Delray*

Del Rio (city, Texas, southern United States) : to 1833 *San Felipe del Rio*

Delsberg *see* **Delémont**

Delvinë (town, southern Albania) : 1919–1921 modern Greek *Delvinon*

Delvinon *see* **Delvinë**

Delyatin *see* **Delyatyn**

Delyatyn (town, southwestern Ukraine) : (Russian *Delyatin*); to 1939 Polish *Delatyn*

De Malherbe *see* **Aïn Tolba**
Dembica *see* **Dębica**
Demblin *see* **Dęblin**
Demersville *see* **Victoriaville**
Demidov (town, western Russia) : to 1918 *Porech'ye*
Demirhisar *see* **Sidirókastro**
Dem'yanovka *see* **Uzynkol'**
Denali *see* **McKinley, Mt.**
Denali National Park and Preserve (Alaska, northwestern United States) : to 1980 *Mt. McKinley National Park*
Denbigh (town, northern Wales) : Welsh *Dinbych*
Den Bosch *see* **'s-Hertogenbosch**
Dendera (village, eastern Egypt) : ancient Greek *Tentyra*
Dendermonde (town, northern Belgium) : French *Termonde*
Den Haag *see* **Hague, The**
Denia (city, eastern Spain) : Roman *Dianium*
Deniliquin (town, New South Wales, southeastern Australia) : to 1850 *Sandhills*
Deninoo Kue *see* **Fort Resolution**
Denisovka (town, northern Kazakhstan) : formerly *Ordzhonikidze*
Denmark (kingdom, northwestern Europe) : [Danish *Danmark*]
Denver (city, Colorado, west central United States) : to 1858 *St. Charles*
Denwood *see* **Wainwright**
Deodoro *see* **Piraquara**
De Panne (town, western Belgium) : French *La Panne*
Derbeshka *see* **Derbeshkinsky**
Derbeshkinsky (town, western Russia) : to 1940 *Derbeshka*
Derbinskoye *see* **Tymovskoye**
¹Derby (city, north central England) : Roman *Derventio* (The Roman name is either that of the **Derwent** River here or of the Roman fort at Little Chester, north of the city center.)
²Derby (town, Kansas, central United States) : to 1930 *El Paso*
Derry *see* **Londonderry**
Derryfield *see* ²**Manchester**
Dertona *see* **Tortona**
Dervent *see* **Klisura**
Derventio *see* (1) ¹**Derby**; (2) **Derwent**; (3) **Malton**; (4) **Papcastle**
Derwent (river, northern England) : Roman *Derventio* (There are several *Derwent* rivers in England, as those at ¹**Derby**, **Malton**, and **Papcastle**, but not all had the Roman name.)
Dés *see* **Dej**
Descartes (town, west central France) :

1802–1967 *La Haye-Descartes*; to 1802 *La Haye-en-Touraine* (The town first added then wholly adopted the name of the philosopher René Descartes, who was born here.)
Deschnaer Kuppe *see* **Velká Deštná**
Deseret *see* **Utah**
Desiderii Fanum *see* **St.-Dizier**
Des Plaines (city, Illinois, north central United States) : to 1869 *Rand*
Desterro *see* **Florianópolis**
Dětmarovice (town, eastern Czech Republic) : 1939–1945 German *Dittmarsdorf*; 1918–1919, 1938–1939 Polish *Dziećmorowice*; to 1918 German *Dittmarsdorf*
Détrie *see* **Sidi Lahssen**
Detroit (city, Michigan, northeastern United States) : originally French *Fort-Pontchartrain-du-Détroit*
Detskoye Selo *see* **Pushkin**
Deutsch-Brod *see* **Havlíčkův Brod**
Deutschendorf *see* **Poprad**
Deutsch-Eylau *see* **Iława**
Deutsch-Gabel *see* **Jablonné v Podještědí**
Deutsch-Krawarn *see* **Kravaře**
Deutsch-Krone *see* **Wałcz**
Deutschland *see* **Germany**
Deutsch-Proben *see* **Nitrianske Pravno**
Deux-Ponts *see* **Zweibrücken**
Deux-Rivières *see* **St.-Stanislas**
Deva (city, west central Romania) : to 1918 Hungarian *Déva*
Deva *see* (1) ¹**Chester**; (2) **Dee**
Déva *see* **Deva**
Devagiri *see* **Daulatabad**
Devana *see* **Kintore**
Dévén *see* ²**Devín**
¹Devin (town, southwestern Bulgaria) : to 1934 *Dovlen*
²Devín (town, southwestern Slovakia) : 1938–1945 German *Theben*; to 1918 Hungarian *Dévén*; to 1867 German *Theben* (Devín is now a district of Bratislava.)
Devona *see* **Kintore**
Devonport (town, southwestern England) : to 1824 *Plymouth Dock* (The town is now a district of Plymouth.)
Dewdney *see* **Okotoks**
Dewey (town, eastern Puerto Rico) : to *c.*1940 *Culebra*
Dhahran (town, eastern Saudia Arabia) : [Arabic *Aẓ Ẓahrān*]
Dhaka (city, central Bangladesh) : formerly conventional *Dacca*
Diamantina (city, southeastern Brazil) : formerly *Tejuco*
Dianium *see* **Denia**

Dibio *see* Dijon

Dibra *see* Debar

Dicaearchia *see* Pozzuoli

Didymoteichon (town, northeastern Greece) :
1915–1919 Bulgarian *Dimotika*; to 1915 Turkish
Dimetoka

Diedenhofen *see* Thionville

Diefurt *see* Żnin

Diégo-Suarez *see* Antsiranana

Dieppe (town, New Brunswick, eastern Canada)
: to 1946 *Leger Corner*

Dievenow *see* Dziwnów

Diez y Ocho de Julio (village, southeastern
Uruguay) : to 1909 *San Miguel*

Dignano d'Istria *see* Vodnjan

Dijon (city, eastern France) : Roman *Divio*; alternate Roman *Dibio*

Dikaia (town, northeastern Greece) : 1915–1919
Bulgarian *Kadükoy*; to 1913 Turkish *Kadıköy*

Diksmuide (town, western Belgium) : French
Dixmude

Dillon (town, Montana, northwestern United
States) : to 1881 *Terminus*

Dimashq *see* Damascus

Dimetoka *see* Didymoteichon

Dimitrov *see* Dymytrov

¹Dimitrovgrad (city, southern Bulgaria) : to 1947
Rakovski (The city was built in 1947 and incorporated three villages, the largest of which
was Rakovski.)

²Dimitrovgrad (city, western Russia) : to 1972
Melekess

³Dimitrovgrad (town, southeastern Serbia) : to
1950 *Caribrod* (The town was in Bulgaria from
1913 to 1919.)

Dimitrovo *see* Pernik

Dimotika *see* Didymoteichon

Dinbych *see* Denbigh

Dinbych-y-pysgod *see* Tenby

Dingle (town, southwestern Ireland) : Irish *An
Daingean*

Diomede Islands (eastern Russia/northwestern
United States) : alternate Russian *Gvozdev Islands* (*Big Diomede*, which belongs to Russia, is
alternately known as *Ratmanov Island*.)

Dionysopolis *see* Balchik

Dioscurias *see* Sokhumi

Diospolis *see* Thebes

Dirizhabl'stroy *see* Dolgoprudny

Dirschau *see* Tczew

Disko *see* ¹Qeqertarsuaq

Dittmarsdorf *see* Dětmarovice

Divinópolis (city, southeastern Brazil) : to 1912
Espírito Santo da Itapecerica

Divio *see* Dijon

Divnogorsk (city, eastern Russia) : to 1963 *Skit*

Divodurum *see* Metz

Divona *see* Cahors

Dixmude *see* Diksmuide

Diyarbakır (city, southeastern Turkey) : Roman
Amida

Djailolo *see* Halmahera

Djakovica (town, western Kosovo) : to 1913
Turkish *Yakova*

Djanet (town, northeastern Algeria) : to *c.*1962
French *Fort-Charlet*

Djemila (town, central Algeria) : Roman *Cuicul*

Djeneral Hanri *see* Gorče Petrov

Djevdjelija *see* Gevgelija

Djibouti (republic, eastern Africa) : 1967–
1977 *Afars and Issas*; 1888–1967 *French Somaliland*

Djokupunda (town, south central Democratic
Republic of the Congo) : to 1972 French
Charlesville

Dmanisi (town, southern Georgia) : to 1947
Bashkicheti

Dmitriyevskoye *see* Talas

Dmitrovsk *see* Dmitrovsk-Orlovsky

Dmitrovsk-Orlovsky (town, western Russia) : to
1929 *Dmitrovsk*

Dnepr *see* Dnieper

Dneprodzerzhinsk *see* Dniprodzerzhyns'k

Dnepropetrovsk *see* Dnipropetrovs'k

Dneprovskoye (village, western Russia) : to
*c.*1960 *Andreyevskoye*

Dnestr *see* Dniester

Dnieper (river, western Russia) : [Russian
Dnepr]; ancient Greek *Borysthenes*

Dniester (river, western Ukraine) : [Ukrainian
Dnistro]; (Russian *Dnestr*); Roman *Danastris*;
ancient Greek *Tyras*

Dniprodzerzhyns'k (city, east central Ukraine) :
(Russian *Dneprodzerzhinsk*); to 1936 *Kamyan-
s'ke* (Russian *Kamenskoye*)

Dnipropetrovs'k (city, south central Ukraine) :
(Russian *Dnepropetrovsk*); 1802–1926 *Katery-
noslav* (Russian *Yekaterinoslav*); 1796–1802
Novorossiysk; to 1796 *Katerynoslav* (Russian
Yekaterinoslav)

Dnistro *see* Dniester

Dobbiaco (town, northern Italy) : to 1919 German *Toblach*

Dobele (town, west central Latvia) : to 1918 Russian *Doblen*

Doberai (peninsula, eastern Indonesia) : to 1963
Dutch *Vogelkop*

Dobiegniew (town, western Poland) : to 1945
German *Woldenberg*

Doblen *see* Dobele

Dobra (town, northwestern Poland) : to 1945
German *Daber*

Dobřany (town, western Czech Republic) : to 1918, 1939–1945 German *Wiesengrund*

Dobre Miasto (town, northeastern Poland) : to 1945 German *Guttstadt*

Dobrich (town, northeastern Bulgaria) : 1949–1991 *Tolbukhin*; 1940–1949 *Dobrich*; 1913–1940 Romanian *Bazargic*; 1878–1913 *Dobrich*; to 1878 Turkish *Bazarcik*

Dobrinka (village, western Russia) : to *c.*1940 *Nizhnyaya Dobrinka*

Dobrna (village, western Slovenia) : to 1918 German *Neuhaus*

Dobrodzień (town, southern Poland) : to 1945 German *Guttentag*

Dobromil' *see* Dobromyl'

Dobromyl' (town, western Ukraine) : (Russian *Dobromil'*); to 1939 Polish *Dobromil*

Dobropillya (town, eastern Ukraine) : (Russian *Dobropol'ye*); 1941–1946 Russian *Krasnoarmeysky Rudnik*; *c.*1935–1941 *Rot-Front*; *c.*1918–*c.*1935 *Val'dgeym*; to *c.*1918 Russian *Svyatogorovsky Rudnik* (The city's German-influenced history gave the names *Rot-Front*, "Red Front," and *Val'dgeym*, a transliteration of *Waldheim*.)

Dobropol'ye *see* Dobropillya

Dobrovol'sk (town, western Russia) : 1938–1945 German *Schlossberg*; to 1938 German *Pillkallen*

Dobroye (village, eastern Russia) : 1905–1945 Japanese *Naibo*

Dobruška (town, north central Czech Republic) : to 1918, 1929–1945 German *Gutenfeld*

Dobrzany (town, northwestern Poland) : to 1945 German *Jacobshagen*

Doc Penfro *see* Pembroke Dock

Doctor Petru Groza *see* Ştei

Doha (city, eastern Qatar) : [Arabic *Ad Dawḥah*]

Doire *see* Londonderry

Dojran (village, southeastern Macedonia) : to 1913 Turkish *Doyran*

Dokshitsy *see* Dokshytsy

Dokshukino *see* Nartkala

Dokshytsy (town, northern Belarus) : (Russian *Dokshitsy*); 1919–1939 Polish *Dokszyce*

Dokszyce *see* Dokshytsy

Doktor Yosifovo (village, northwestern Bulgaria) : to 1950 *Vŭlkova Slatina*

Dokuchayevka *see* Karamendy

Dokuchayevsk *see* Dokuchayevs'k

Dokuchayevs'k (city, eastern Ukraine) : (Russian *Dokuchayevsk*); to 1954 *Olenivs'ki Kar'yery* (Russian *Yelenovskiye Kar'yery*)

Dolban *see* Liman

Dolgellau (town, western Wales) : formerly conventional *Dolgelley*

Dolgelley *see* Dolgellau

Dolgoprudny (city, western Russia) : 1935–1938 *Dirizhabl'stroy*

Dolina *see* Dolyna

Dolinsk (town, eastern Russia) : 1905–1945 Japanese *Ochiai*

Dolinskaya *see* Dolyns'ka

Dolinskoye *see* Dolyns'ke

Dolisie *see* Loubomo

Dolní Benešov (town, eastern Czech Republic) : to 1919, 1938–1945 German *Beneschau*

Dolni Chiflik (town, eastern Bulgaria) : to 1989 *Georgi Traykov*

Dolný Kubín (town, northern Slovakia) : to 1918 Hungarian *Alsókubin*

Dolyna (town, western Ukraine) : (Russian *Dolina*); to 1939 Polish *Dolina*

Dolyns'ka (town, central Ukraine) : (Russian *Dolinskaya*); mid–1920s, 1940–1944 *Shevchenkove* (Russian *Shevchenkovo*)

Dolyns'ke (village, southern Ukraine) : (Russian *Dolinskoye*); to 1945 *Valegotsulovo*

Dolzhikovo-Orlovskoye *see* Sverdlovs'k

Domažlice (town, western Czech Republic) : to 1918, 1939–1945 German *Taus*

Dombarovka *see* Dombarovsky

Dombarovsky (town, southwestern Russia) : to 1939 *Dombarovka*

Dombasle *see* El Hachem

Dombrowa *see* Dąbrowa Górnicza

Dominican Republic (central West Indies) : formerly *Santo Domingo* (The former name, now that of the republic's capital, was originally applied to the whole island of **Hispaniola** of which the Dominican Republic now occupies the eastern two thirds.)

Dominion (town, Nova Scotia, eastern Canada) : to 1906 *Dominion No. 1* (The numeric name referred to a local mine shaft.)

Dominion City (village, Manitoba, southern Canada) : to 1878 *Roseau* (The name was changed to avoid confusion with *Roseau*, Minnesota, USA, and *Rosseau*, Ontario.)

Dominion No. 1 *see* Dominion

Domitian Way *see* Via

Domman-Asfal'tovy Zavod *see* [1]Leninsky

Domnau *see* Domnovo

Domnovo (village, western Russia) : to 1945 German *Domnau*

Don (river, southwestern Russia) : ancient Greek and Roman *Tanais* (The classical name was also that of a city at the river's estuary. *See* **Nedvigovka**.)

Donau *see* Danube

Doncaster (city, north central England) : Roman *Danum*

Donegal (town, northwestern Ireland) : Irish *Dún na nGall*

Donetsk (town, southwestern Russia) : to 1955 *Gundorovka*

Donetsk *see* Donets'k

Donets'k (city, eastern Ukraine) : (Russian *Donetsk*); 1924–1961 *Stalino*; to 1924 *Yuzivka* (Russian *Yuzovka*)

Donetsko-Amvrosiyevka *see* Amvrosiyivka

Donets'ko-Amvrosiyivka *see* Amvrosiyivka

Dongbei *see* Manchuria

Dong Kinh *see* Hanoi

[1]Donskoye (village, western Russia, near Kaliningrad) : to 1945 German *Grossdirschkeim*

[2]Donskoye (village, western Russia, near Lipetsk) : 1930s–*c*.1965 *Vodop'yanovo*; to 1930s *Patriarsheye*

Doornik *see* Tournai

Dorchester (town, southern England) : Roman *Durnovaria*

Dordogne (river, southwestern France) : Roman *Duranius*

Dores da Boa Esperança *see* Boa Esperança

Doristhal *see* Razino

Dorna Watra *see* Vatra Dornei

Dorpat *see* Tartu

Dorris Bridge *see* Alturas

Dosmahlen *see* [1]Pushkino

Dostyk (village, eastern Kazakhstan) : formerly Russian *Druzhba*

Dothan (city, Alabama, southeastern United States) : to 1911 *Dothen*; originally *Poplar Head*

Dothen *see* Dothan

Double Springs *see* Gadsden

Douglas (town, Wyoming, western United States) : originally *Tent Town*

Douro (river, northern Spain/northern Portugal) : alternate Spanish *Duero*; Roman *Durius*

Dovbysh (town, west central Ukraine) : to 1944 *Markhlevsk* (From 1925 to the 1930s the region here was organized as a Polish district, with the town known as *Marchlewsk*.)

[1]Dover (town, southeastern England) : Roman *Dubris*

[2]Dover (city, New Hampshire, northeastern United States) : originally *Bristol*

Dover, Strait of (southeastern England/northern France) : French *Pas de Calais* (The French name gave that of a department in northern France. *Cp.* English Channel.)

Dovey (river, western Wales) : Welsh *Dyfi* (The English form of the name gave that of Aberdovey.)

Dovlen *see* [1]Devin

Dovzhykove-Orlovs'ke *see* Sverdlovs'k

Downpatrick (town, southeastern Northern Ireland) : Irish *Dún Pádraig*

Doyran *see* Dojran

Draa Ben Khedda (town, northern Algeria) : to *c*.1962 French *Mirabeau*

Draa Esmar (village, northern Algeria) : to *c*.1962 French *Lodi*

Drable *see* José Enrique Rodó

Dragomirovo *see* [2]Proletarsk

Drahichyn (town, southwestern Belarus) : (Russian *Drogichin*); 1919–1939 Polish *Drohiczyn*; to 1918 Russian *Drogichin*

Dramburg *see* Drawsko Pomorskie

Drauburg *see* Dravograd

Dravograd (town, northeastern Slovenia) : to 1918, 1941–1945 German *Drauburg*

Drawno (town, northwestern Poland) : to 1945 German *Neuwedell*

Drawsko Pomorskie (town, northwestern Poland) : to 1945 German *Dramburg*

Drenewydd Gelli-farch *see* Shirenewton

Drepanum *see* Trapani

Dresser (village, Wisconsin, northern United States) : to 1940 *Dresser Junction*

Dresser Junction *see* Dresser

Dreux (town, north central France) : Roman *Drocae*; Celtic *Durocassis*

Drezdenko (town, western Poland) : to 1945 German *Driesen*

Driesen *see* Drezdenko

Drissa *see* Vyerkhnyadzvinsk

Drocae *see* Dreux

Drogheda (town, northeastern Ireland) : Irish *Droichead Átha*

Drogichin *see* Drahichyn

Drogobych *see* Drohobych

Drohiczyn *see* Drahichyn

Drohobych (city, western Ukraine) : (Russian *Drogobych*); to 1939 Polish *Drohobycz*

Drohobycz *see* Drohobych

Droichead Átha *see* Drogheda

Droichead na Bandan *see* Bandon

Droichead na Banna *see* Banbridge

Droichead Nua (town, eastern Ireland) : formerly (and still alternate) *Newbridge*

Droim Seanbho *see* Drumshanbo

Droitwich (town, west central England) : Roman *Salinae*. (The Roman name referred to the saltworks here, as it did at Middlewich.)

Dromore (town, east central Northern Ireland) : Irish *An Droim Mór*

Drossen *see* Ośno Lubuskie

Drug *see* Durg

Druk-Yul *see* Bhutan

Drumshanbo (town, northern Ireland) : Irish *Droim Seanbho*

Druskenniki *see* Druskininkai
Druskienniki *see* Druskininkai
Druskininkai (town, southern Lithuania) :
1919–1939 Polish *Druskienniki*; to 1918 Russian
Druskenniki
¹Druzhba (town, northern Ukraine) : to 1962
Khutir-Mykhaylivs'kyy (Russian *Khutor-
Mikhaylovsky*) (The town was formed on the
merger of Khutir-Mykhaylivs'kyy with two
other settlements.)
²Druzhba (town, western Ukraine) : to 1957 *Ze-
lena*
³Druzhba (village, western Russia) : to 1945
German *Allenburg*
Druzhba *see* (1) Dostyk; (2) Sveti Konstantin
Druzhkivka (city, eastern Ukraine) : (Russian
Druzhkovka); to 1938 *Havrylivs'kyy Zavod*
(Russian *Gavrilovsky Zavod*)
Druzhkovka *see* Druzhkivka
Dry Diggings *see* Placerville
Duarte, Pico (mountain, central Dominican Re-
public) : 1936–1961 *Monte Trujillo*
Dubá (town, northern Czech Republic) : to 1918,
1939–1945 German *Dauba*
Düben *see* Bad Düben
Dubh Linn *see* Dublin
Dublin (city, eastern Ireland) : local Irish *Dubh
Linn*; alternate (official) Irish *Baile Átha
Cliath*; Roman *Eblana* (The Roman name first
appeared in the writings of the 2d-century
A.D. geographer Ptolemy and although lacking
an initial *D* is basically identical with the mod-
ern name.)
Dubris *see* ¹Dover
Dubrovnik (town, southern Croatia) : to 1918
Italian *Ragusa*
Duchcov (town, northwestern Czech Republic) :
to 1918, 1938–1945 German *Dux*
Duck Creek Cross Roads *see* Smyrna
Duero *see* Douro
Duisburg (city, western Germany) : 1929–1934
Duisburg-Hamborn; Roman *Castrum Deutonis*
Duisburg-Hamborn *see* Duisburg
Duke of Clarence Island *see* Nukunonu
Dukhovsky *see* Guliston
Dulcigno *see* Ulcinj
Dulcina *see* Barbuda
Dŭlgopol (town, eastern Bulgaria) : formerly
Novo Selo; to 1878 Turkish *Yeni Derbent*
Dulovo (town, northeastern Bulgaria) : formerly
Akkadŭnlar; 1913–1940 Romanian *Accadînlar*;
to 1878 Turkish *Akkadınlar*
Dumbarton *see* Dunbarton
Dumnonium Promontorium *see* Lizard, The
Dumontville *see* St.-Jerôme
Dumyāṭ *see* Damietta

Duna *see* Danube
Dünaburg *see* Daugavpils
Dunajská Streda (town, southwestern Slovakia)
: to 1918, 1938–1945 Hungarian *Dunaszerdahely*
Dünamünde *see* Daugavgriva
Dunărea *see* Danube
Dunaszerdahely *see* Dunajská Streda
Dunaújváros (city, west central Hungary) :
1951–1961 *Sztálinváros*
Dunav *see* Danube
Dunay *see* Danube
Dunbarton (former county, west central Scot-
land) : formerly *Dumbarton* (The county, also
known as *Dunbartonshire*, originally had a
name identical to that of its administrative
center, the town of *Dumbarton*. The spelling
of the county name with *n* instead of *m* was
then adopted to avoid confusion between the
two.)
Duncan *see* Cheboygan
Dundalk (town, northeastern Ireland) : Irish
Dún Dealgan
Dún Dealgan *see* Dundalk
Dunedin (city, southeastern New Zealand) :
originally *New Edinburgh*
Dunedin *see* Edinburgh
Dungannon (town, southern Northern Ireland) :
Irish *Dún Geanainn*
Dún Garbhán *see* Dungarvan
Dungarvan (town, southern Ireland) : Irish *Dún
Garbhán*
Dún Geanainn *see* Dungannon
Dungloe (town, northwestern Ireland) : Irish *An
Clochán Liath*
Dunkerque *see* ¹Dunkirk
¹Dunkirk (city, northern France) : [French
Dunkerque] (The English form of the name,
although long current, gained particular favor
following the evacuation of British troops
from France against the odds in 1940, a feat
which gave the patriotic phrase "Dunkirk
spirit" for a gallant effort.)
²Dunkirk (town, New York, northeastern United
States) : originally *Chadwick's Bay*
Dún Laoghaire (town, eastern Ireland) : 1821–
1921 English *Kingstown*; earlier *Dunleary*
Dunleary *see* Dún Laoghaire
Dún na nGall *see* Donegal
Dunnet Head (promontory, northeastern Scot-
land) : Roman *Tarvedunum*
Dún Pádraig *see* Downpatrick
Dunstable (town, southeastern England) :
Roman *Durocobrivis*
Dunstable *see* Nashua
Dunton *see* Arlington Heights

DuPage Center *see* Glen Ellyn
Duperré *see* Aïn Defla
Düpnice *see* Dupnitsa
Dupnitsa (city, western Bulgaria) : 1952–1990
    Stanke Dimitrov; 1949–1952 *Marek*; to 1949
    Stupnitsa; to 1878 Turkish *Düpnice* (*Marek* was
    the *nom de guerre* of the Bulgarian Communist
    leader Georgi Dimitrov, who gave the name of
    [1]Dimitrovgrad.)
Düppel *see* Dybbøl
Duque de Bragança *see* Calandula
Duque de Caxias (city, southeastern Brazil) :
    1931–1943 *Caxias*; to 1931 *Meriti Station* (The
    city is is now a suburb of Rio de Janeiro.)
Duranius *see* Dordogne
Durazzo *see* Durrës
Durban (city, eastern South Africa) : [Zulu
    eThekwini]; 1835–1854 *D'Urban*; to 1835 *Port
    Natal*
D'Urban *see* Durban
Düren (city, western Germany) : Romann *Mar-
    codurum*
Durg (town, east central India) : formerly *Drug*
[1]Durham (city, North Carolina, eastern United
    States) : formerly *Durhamville*
[2]Durham (town, New Hampshire, northeastern
    United States) : to 1732 *Oyster River*
[3]Durham (town, Ontario, southeastern Canada)
    : to 1866 *Bentinck*
Durhamville *see* [1]Durham
Durius *see* Douro
Durlas *see* Thurles
Durnovaria *see* Dorchester
Durobrivae *see* (1) Chesterton; (2) [1]Rochester
Durocassis *see* Dreux
Durocatalaunum *see* Châlons-en-Champagne
Durocobrivis *see* Dunstable
Durocortorum *see* Reims
Duroliponte *see* [1]Cambridge
Durostorum *see* Silistra
Durovernum *see* Canterbury
Durovigutum *see* Godmanchester
Durrës (city, western Albania) : 1939–1943 Ital-
    ian *Durazzo*; Roman *Dyrrhachium*; ancient
    Greek *Epidamnus* (The Roman name was orig-
    inally that of the headland here on which the
    Greek city arose.)
D'Urville Island (central New Zealand) : Maori
    Rangitoto
Dushanbe (city, southwestern Tajikistan) :
    1929–1961 *Stalinabad*; to 1929 *Dyushambe*
Dushet *see* Dusheti
Dusheti (town, east central Georgia) : to 1936
    Dushet
Dŭstí (town, southwestern Tajikistan) : formerly
    Pyandzh

Duszniki Zdrój (town, southwestern Poland) :
    to 1945 German *Bad Reinerz*
Dutch East Indies *see* Indonesia
Dutch Guiana *see* Surinam
Dutch New Guinea *see* Irian Jaya
Dutch West Indies *see* Netherlands Antilles
Duvalierville *see* Cabaret
Duvno *see* Tomislavgrad
Dux *see* Duchcov
Duzdab *see* Zāhedān
Duzkend *see* Akhuryan
26 Bakinskikh Kommunarov, imeni *see*
    Neftçala
Dvigatel'stroy *see* Kaspiysk
Dvinsk *see* Daugavpils
Dvŭr Králové nad Labem (city, northern Czech
    Republic) : to 1918, 1938–1945 German *Kön   ig-
    inhof an der Elbe*
Dybbøl (town, southern Denmark) : 1850–1920
    German *Düppel*
Dychów (village, western Poland) : to 1945 Ger-
    man *Deichow*
Dyffryn Taf *see* Merthyr Vale
Dyfi *see* Dovey
Dyfrdwy *see* Dee
Dyme *see* Kato Achaia
Dymytrov (city, eastern Ukraine) : (Russian
    Dimitrov); 1957–1972 *Novoekonomichne* (Rus-
    sian *Novoekonomicheskoye*); 1937–1957 *Novyy
    Donbas* (Russian *Novy Donbass*)
Dyrrhachium *see* Durrës
Dysna (town, northern Belarus) : 1919–1939 Pol-
    ish *Dzisna*
Dyushambe *see* Dushanbe
Dzagidzor *see* Tumanyan
Dzaudzhikau *see* Vladikavkaz
Dzerzhinsk (city, western Russia) : formerly
    Rastyapino (The city was formed in 1930 on
    the amalgamation of Rastyapino with two
    other communities.)
Dzerzhinsk *see* (1) [1,2]Dzerzhyns'k;
    (2) Dzyarzhynsk
Dzerzhinskogo, imeni *see* Nar'yan-Mar
Dzerzhinskoye (village, eastern Russia) : for-
    merly *Rozhdestvenskoye*
Dzerzhinsky (city, western Russia) : to 1938
    Trudovaya Kommuna imeni Dzerzhinskogo
Dzerzhinsky *see* Sorsk
[1]Dzerzhyns'k (city, eastern Ukraine) : (Russian
    Dzerzhinsk); to 1938 *Shcherbynivka* (Russian
    Shcherbinovka)
[2]Dzerzhyns'k ((town, west central Ukraine) :
    (Russian *Dzerzhinsk*); to 1933 *Romanov*
Dzhalal-ogly *see* Stepanavan
Dzhalilabad *see* Cälilabad
Dzhambul *see* Taraz

Dzhansugurov (town, eastern Kazakhstan) : formerly *Abakumova*

Dzharkent *see* Zharkent

Dzhirgalantu *see* Hovd

Dzhugeli *see* Zestap'oni

Dzhumaya *see* Blagoevgrad

Działdowo (town, northern Poland) : to 1919, 1939–1945 German *Soldau*

Dziećmorowice *see* Dětmarovice

Dzierzgoń (town, northern Poland) : to 1945 German *Christburg*

Dzierżoniów (town, southwestern Poland) : to 1945 German *Reichenbach*

Dzisna *see* Dysna

Dziwnów (town, northwestern Poland) : to 1945 German *Dievenow*

Dzurchi *see* Pervomays'ke

Dzyarzhynsk (city, central Belarus) : (Russian *Dzerzhinsk*); to c.1935 *Kaydanovo*

Éadan Doire *see* Edenderry

Eagle Nest (village, New Mexico, southwestern United States) : to 1935 *Therma*

Eagle Pass (city, Texas, southern United States) : formerly *Camp Eagle Pass*; originally *El Paso de Aquila*

Eagle Rock *see* Idaho Falls

Eagle Station *see* Carson City

Earlston (town, southeastern Scotland) : formerly *Ercildoune* (The original name became an alternate byname of the 13th-century Scottish poet Thomas the Rhymer.)

Earp's Corner *see* Fairfax

East Bengal *see* Bangladesh

East Chelmsford *see* Lowell

East Detroit *see* Eastpointe

Easter Island (eastern Pacific) : alternate native *Rapa Nui*

Eastern Transvaal *see* Mpumalanga

East Gary *see* Lake Station

East Greenwich (town, Rhode Island, northeastern United States) : 1686–1689 *Dedford*

East Hamburg *see* Orchard Park

¹East Hampton (town, New York, northeastern United States) : originally *Maidstone* (The town is one of the fashionable Long Island resorts that make up the *Hamptons*.)

²East Hampton (town, Connecticut, northeastern United States) : to 1915 *Chatham*

East Haven (town, Connecticut, northeastern United States) : to 1707 *Iron Works Village*

East Hoosuck *see* Adams

East Indies *see* Indonesia

East Lansing (city, Michigan, north central United States) : to 1907 *Collegeville*

East Livermore *see* Livermore Falls

East Liverpool (city, Ohio, north central United States) : to 1834 *Fawcettstown*; originally *St. Clair*

East London (city, southeastern South Africa) : originally *Port Rex*

East Maitland *see* Maitland

East Moline (city, Illinois, north central United States) : originally *Port Byron Junction*

East Pakistan *see* Bangladesh

Eastpointe (town, Michigan, northern United States) : 1929–1992 *East Detroit*; to 1929 *Halfway Village*

Eastport (town, Maine, northeastern United States) : to 1798 *Moose Island* (The earlier name remains for the island on which the town lies.)

East Providence (city, Rhode Island, northeastern United States) : to 1862 *West Seekonk*

East River *see* Wallingford

East Rockport *see* ²Lakewood

East St. Louis (city, Illinois, north central United States) : to 1861 *Illinoistown*

East Thomaston *see* Rockland

East Timor (republic, eastern Malay Archipelago) : 1975–1999 *Timor Timur*; to 1975 Portuguese *Timor*

Eastview *see* ²Vanier

East Windsor (town, Ontario, southeastern Canada) : to 1929 *Ford City* (East Windsor merged with the city of Windsor in 1935.)

East Youngstown *see* Campbell

Ebbw Vale (town, southeastern Wales) : Welsh *Glynebwy*

Ebchester (village, northeastern England) : Roman *Vindomora*

Ebenrode *see* Nesterov

Eberswalde (town, northeastern Germany) : formerly *Neustadt* (The earlier name, meaning simply "new town," was gradually superseded by the present one. In 1970 the town merged with neighboring Finow to form the city of *Eberswalde-Finow*.)

Eblana *see* Dublin

Ebora *see* Évora

Eboracum *see* ¹York

Eborakon *see* ¹York

Ebro (river, northeastern Spain) : Roman *Iberus*

Ebudae *see* Hebrides

Eburodunum *see* (1) Embrun; (2) Yverdon

Ebytown *see* Kitchener

Ecbatana *see* Hamadan

Echaot'l Koe *see* Fort Liard

Echaporã (town, southeastern Brazil) : to 1944 Portuguese *Bela Vista*

Ech Chélif (town, northern Algeria) : 1964–1981 *El Asnam*; to 1964 French *Orléansville*; Roman *Castellum Tingitanum*

Echmiadzin *see* **Ejmiatsin**

Echo Bay (village, Northwest Territories, northern Canada) : formerly *Port Radium*; to 1937 *Cameron Bay* (The mines here, yielding pitchblende ore from which radium was extracted, closed in 1960.)

Eckengraf *see* **Viesīte**

Ecolisma *see* **Angoulême**

Economy *see* **Ambridge**

Écore à Fabre *see* ²**Camden**

Ecorse (town, Michigan, north central United States) : originally *Grandport*

Écry *see* **Asfeld**

Eddy *see* **Carlsbad**

Eden *see* (1) **Aden**; (2) **Bar Harbor**

Edenburg *see* **Knox**

Edenderry (town, east central Ireland) : Irish *Éadan Doire*

Edenglassie *see* **Brisbane**

Edessa (town, northeastern Greece) : to 1913 Turkish *Vodena*

Edessa *see* **Şanlıurfa**

Edgartown (town, Massachusetts, northeastern United States) : originally *Nunnepog*

Edgeworthstown (town, north central Ireland) : Irish *Meathas Troim*; formerly alternate *Mostrim*

Edinburg (city, Texas, southern United States) : to 1911 *Chapin*

Edinburgh (city, southeastern Scotland) : historical and literary *Dunedin* (The historical name, properly Gaelic *Dun Eideann*, gave that of **Dunedin**, New Zealand.)

Edingen *see* **Enghien**

Edirne (city, western Turkey) : formerly English *Adrianople*; 1930–1922 modern Greek *Adrianoupolis*; to 1913 Bulgarian *Odrin*; Roman *Adrianopolis* (The former English name is that of a battle of A.D. 378 in which the Roman emperor Valens fell to the Visigoths.)

Edison (city, New Jersey, northeastern United States) : to 1954 *Raritan*

Edith Cavell, Mt. (Alberta, southwestern Canada) : to 1916 *Montagne de la Grande Traverse*

Edith Ronne Land *see* **Ronne Ice Shelf**

Edmundston (town, New Brunswick, eastern Canada) : to 1848 *Petit-Sault*

Edo *see* **Tokyo**

Edremit (town, northwestern Turkey) : Roman *Adramyttium*

Edson (town, Alberta, west central Canada) : to 1911 *Heatherwood*

Edward, Lake (east central Africa) : 1973–1979 *Lake Idi Amin Dada*; to 1908 *Albert Edward Nyanza*

Edwardesabad *see* **Bannu**

Eesti *see* **Estonia**

Éfaté (island, central Vanuatu) : formerly *Sandwich Island*

Effingham (town, Illinois, north central United States) : to 1859 *Broughton*

Egedesminde *see* **Aasiaat**

Eger (town, northern Hungary) : to 1867 German *Erlau*

Eger *see* **Cheb**

Eglwys y Drindod *see* ²**Christchurch**

Egmont, Mt. (northwestern New Zealand) : Maori *Taranaki* (The Maori name is official for the region and former province here.)

Eğribos *see* **Khalkís**

Egridere *see* **Ardino**

Eğripalanka *see* **Kriva Palanka**

Egypt (republic, northeastern Africa) : [Arabic *Mişr*]; Roman *Aegyptus* (In 1958 Egypt formed a union with Syria as the *United Arab Republic*. Syria left in 1961 but the name continued for Egypt alone until 1971. The Arabic name is also that of **Cairo**.)

Ehrenforst *see* **Sławięcice**

Eibenschitz *see* **Ivančice**

Eigenbrakel *see* **Braine-l'Alleud**

Eighty Mile Beach (coastal region, Western Australia, northwestern Australia) : to 1946 *Ninety Mile Beach* (The region, actually about 85 miles in length, was renamed to avoid confusion with Ninety Mile Beach in Victoria, southeastern Australia.)

Eilean Leodhais *see* **Isle of Lewis**

Eilean Siar *see* **Western Isles**

Eimeo *see* **Moorea**

Einsiedeln (town, east central Switzerland) : French *Notre-Dame-des-Ermites*

Éire *see* **Ireland**

Eisenbrod *see* **Železný Brod**

Eisenburg *see* **Vasvár**

Eisenhower, Mt. (New Hampshire, northeastern United States) : formerly *Mt. Pleasant*

Eisenhower, Mt. *see* **Castle Mountain**

Eisenstadt (town, eastern Austria) : to 1920 Hungarian *Kismarton*

Eisenstein *see* **Železná Ruda**

Eišiškės (town, southern Lithuania) : (Russian *Eyshishkes*); 1921–1939 Polish *Ejszyszki*

Ejmiatsin (city, western Armenia) : (Russian *Echmiadzin*); to 1945 *Vagarshapat*

Ejszyszki *see* **Eišiškės**

Ekeli *see* **Zahirabad**

El Aouinet (village, northeastern Algeria) : to c.1962 French *Clairfontaine*

Elar *see* **Abovyan**

El Araïche *see* **Larache**

El Asnam *see* **Ech Chélif**

Elath *see* **Aqaba**

Elba (island, western Italy) : Roman *Ilva*; ancient Greek *Aethalia*

El Banco (city, northern Colombia) : formerly *Nuestra Señora de la Candelaria de El Banco*; 1544–1749 *Tamalameque*; earlier *Barbudo*; originally *Sompallón*

El Bayadh (town, northwestern Algeria) : to *c.*1962 French *Géryville*

Elbing *see* **Elbląg**

Elbląg (city, northern Poland) : 1772–1945 German *Elbing*

Elbogen *see* **Loket**

Elbow *see* **Portland**

El Cerrito (city, California, western United States) : originally *Rust*

Elche (city, southeastern Spain) : Roman *Ilici*

El Chilamatal *see* **Ciudad Arce**

El Chorro *see* **General Enrique Mosconi**

El Djem (town, northeastern Tunisia) : Roman *Thysdrus*

Eldorado (city, southeastern Brazil) : to 1948 *Xiririca*

Eldorado *see* **New Denver**

Elea *see* **Castellammare**

Eleftheroupolis (town, northeastern Greece) : formerly Bulgarian *Pravishta*

Elektrogorsk (city, western Russia) : to 1946 *Elektroperedacha*

Elektroperedacha *see* **Elektrogorsk**

Elektrostal' (city, western Russia) : to 1938 *Zatish'ye*

Elektrougli (town, western Russia) : to 1935 *Kudinovo*

Elektrovoz *see* **Stupino**

El Eulma (town, northeastern Algeria) : to *c.*1962 French *St.-Arnaud*

Eleutherai *see* **Babaeski**

Eleutheropolis *see* **Beit Guvrin**

El Fahs (town, north central Tunisia) : formerly French *Pont-du-Fahs*

El Ferrol (city, northwestern Spain) : 1939–1982 *El Ferrol del Caudillo*

El Ferrol del Caudillo *see* **El Ferrol**

Elgin *see* **Niagara Falls**

El Hachem (town, northwestern Algeria) : to *c.*1962 French *Dombasle*

El Harrach (town, northern Algeria) : to *c.*1962 French *Maison-Carrée* (El Harrach is now a suburb of Algiers.)

Elimberrum *see* **Auch**

Elin Pelin (town, western Bulgaria) : to 1950 *Novoseltsi*

Eliocroca *see* **Lorca**

Élisabethville *see* (1) **Katanga**; (2) **Lubumbashi**

Elista (city, western Russia) : 1944–1957 *Stepnoy*

Elizabeth (city, New Jersey, northeastern United States) : to 1740 *Elizabethtown*

Elizabeth City (town, North Carolina, eastern United States) : originally *Redding*

Elizabethtown *see* (1) **Brockville**; (2) **Elizabeth**; (3) **Hagerstown**; (4) **Hopkinsville**

Elizabeth Town *see* **New Norfolk**

Elizabethville *see* **Moundsville**

El Jadida (city, western Morocco) : to 1821 *Mazagan*

El Jícaro *see* **Ciudad Sandino**

El Jovero *see* **Miches**

Ełk (town, northeastern Poland) : to 1945 German *Lyck*

El Kala (town, northeastern Algeria) : to *c.*1962 French *La Calle*

Elk City (town, Oklahoma, south central United States) : originally *Busch*

Elkhovo (town, southeastern Bulgaria) : to 1878 Turkish *Kızılagaç*

Elkton (town, Maryland, northeastern United States) : to 1787 *Head of Elk*; originally *Friendship*

Ellás *see* **Greece**

Ellensburg (town, Washington, northwestern United States) : originally *Robber's Roost*

Ellice Islands *see* **Tuvalu**

Elliotdale (town, southeastern South Africa) : locally *Xhora*

Ellis Island (New York, northeastern United States) : originally *Oyster Island*

Elmhurst (city, Illinois, north central United States) : to 1869 *Cottage Hill* (The town is now a suburb of Chicago.)

Elmina (town, southern Ghana) : formerly Portuguese *São Jorge da Mina*

Elmira (city, New York, northeastern United States) : to 1828 *Newtown*

Elne (town, southern France) : Roman *Castrum Helenae*; earlier Roman *Illiberis*

El Paraíso *see* **Choloma**

El Paso (city, Texas, southern United States) : originally *El Paso del Norte*

El Paso *see* ²**Derby**

El Paso del Norte *see* (1) **El Paso**; (2) **Juárez**

El Progreso (town, east central Guatemala) : to *c.*1920 *Guastatoya*

El Pueblito (town, central Mexico) : 1946–1989 Spanish *Villa Corregidora*

El Pueblo *see* **Los Angeles**

El Pueblo de la Reyna de Los Angeles *see* **Los Angeles**

El Salvador (republic, western Central America) : alternate dated *Salvador* (The alternate name risks confusion with *San Salvador*, the country's capital, whose own name is in turn sometimes mistaken for that of the country.)

Elsass *see* **Alsace**

Elsene *see* **Ixelles**

Elsinore (town, eastern Denmark) : Danish *Helsingør* (The traditional English name has remained current largely thanks to Shakespeare's use of it as the setting of *Hamlet*.)

Elvas (town, east central Portugal) : Roman *Alpesa*

Elvershagen *see* **Łagiewniki**

Ely (town, Minnesota, northern United States) : originally *Florence*

El Zapallar *see* **General José de San Martín**

Embarcadero *see* **Redwood City**

Embrun (town, southeastern France) : Roman *Eburodunum*

Emerita Augusta *see* **Mérida**

Emesa *see* **Homs**

Emilia *see* **Emilia-Romagna**

Emilia-Romagna (region, north central Italy) : to 1948 *Emilia*

Emirli *see* **Orestiada**

Emmahaven *see* **Telukbayur**

Emmitsburg (town, Maryland, northeastern United States) : to *c*.1786 *Poplar Fields*

Emona *see* **Ljubljana**

Emporion *see* **Empùries**

Empingham Reservoir *see* **Rutland Water**

Empùries (village, notheastern Spain) : ancient Greek *Emporion*

Ems (river, northwestern Germany) : Roman *Amisia*

Emu Bay Settlement *see* **Burnie**

Encarnación (city, southeastern Paraguay) : formerly *Itapúa*

Encina *see* **Uvalde**

Encinal *see* **Sunnyvale**

Encruzilhada *see* **Encruzilhada do Sul**

Encruzilhada do Sul (city, southern Brazil) : to 1944 *Encruzilhada*

Enderby (town, British Columbia, southwestern Canada) : to 1887 *Lambly's Landing*

Energetichesky *see* **Otegen Batyr**

Enez (town, southwestern Turkey) : 1920–1922 modern Greek *Ainos*; ancient Greek *Aenos*

Engel's (city, western Russia) : 1914–1931 *Pokrovsk*; to 1914 *Pokrovka* (The city, named in honor of the German socialist philosopher and founder of Communism Friedrich Engels, was the capital of the former Volga German Autonomous Soviet Socialist Republic.)

Engerau *see* **Petrźalka**

Enghien (town, west central Belgium) : Flemish *Edingen*

Enghien *see* **Montmorency**

England *see* **United Kingdom**

English Bazar (city, northeastern India) : alternate *Angrezabad*

English Channel (southern England/northern France) : French *La Manche* (The French name gave that of a department in northern France. *Cp.* **Dover, Strait of.**)

Engyum *see* **Gangi**

Enham Alamein (village, southern England) : to 1945 *Knights Enham*

Enkeldoorn *see* **Chivhu**

Enna (city, southern Italy) : to 1927 *Castrogiovanni*; Roman *Castrum Hennae*

Ennis (town, western Ireland) : Irish *Inis*

Enniscorthy (town, southeastern Ireland) : Irish *Inis Córthaidh*

Enniskillen (town, southwestern Northern Ireland) : Irish *Inis Ceithleann*; traditional English *Inniskilling* (The traditional spelling is associated with the Royal Inniskilling Fusiliers, the British army regiment raised in 1689 to defend the town.)

Ennistimon (town, western Ireland) : Irish *Inis Díomáin*

Enotah, Mt. *see* **Brasstown Bald**

Enso *see* **Svetogorsk**

Entre Rios *see* (1) **Malema**; (2) **Ribeirão Prêto**; (3) **Rio Brilhante**; (4) **Três Rios**

Eochaill *see* **Youghal**

Eoforwic *see* ¹**York**

Eolie Islands *see* **Lipari Islands**

Eperjes *see* **Prešov**

Épernay (town, northeastern France) : Roman *Sparnacum*

Epidamnus *see* **Durrës**

Epiphania *see* **Hama**

Epitácio Pessoa *see* **Pedro Avelino**

Eporedia *see* **Ivrea**

Équateur (province, northwestern Democratic Republic of the Congo) : 1935–1947 French *Coquilhatville*

Equatoria (former province, southern Sudan) : to 1936 *Mongalla*

Equatorial Guinea (republic, western Africa) : to 1968 *Spanish Guinea*

Erasmus *see* **Bronkhorstspruit**

Erastivka *see* **Vyshneve**

Erastovka *see* **Vyshneve**

Ercildoune *see* **Earlston**

Ercolano (town, southern Italy) : formerly *Resina*; Roman *Herculaneum*

Erdély *see* **Transylvania**

Erechim (city, southern Brazil) : 1939–1944 Portuguese *José Bonifácio*; to 1939 Portuguese *Boa Vista*

Erechim *see* **Getúlio Vargas**

¹**Ereğli** (town, northwestern Turkey) : ancient Greek *Heraclea Pontica*

²**Ereğli** (town, south central Turkey) : ancient Greek *Heraclea Cybistra*

Eretz Yisra'el *see* **Palestine**

Erice (town, southern Italy) : to 1934 *Monte San Giuliano*

Eridanus *see* **Po**

Erikdere *see* **Kallithea**

Erin *see* **Ireland**

Erivan *see* **Yerevan**

Erlau *see* **Eger**

Ernestown *see* ²**Bath**

Er Rachidia (city, east central Morocco) : to 1979 *Ksar es Souk*

Erseka *see* **Ersekë**

Ersekë (town, southern Albania) : 1919–1921 modern Greek *Erseka*

Érsekújvár *see* **Nové Zámky**

Erzgebirge (mountain range, central Europe) : dated English *Ore Mountains*

Erzsébetfalva *see* **Pesterzsébet**

Escaut *see* **Scheldt**

Eschenbach *see* **Wolframs-Eschenbach**

Eschscholtz Island *see* **Bikini**

Esenguly (town, western Turkmenistan) : formerly *Gasan-Kuli*

Eşfahān (city, west central Iran) : traditional *Isfahan*, alternate traditional *Ispahan*; Roman *Aspadana*

Esigodini (town, southwestern Zimbabwe) : to 1982 *Essexvale*

Eskice *see* **Xánthi**

Eskicumaa *see* **Tŭrgovishte**

Eski Dzhumaya *see* **Tŭrgovishte**

Eskifoça *see* **Foça**

Eskihisar (village, southwestern Turkey) : ancient Greek *Stratonicea*

Eskimo Point *see* **Arviat**

Eski Stambul *see* **Veliki Preslav**

Eskizağra *see* **Stara Zagora**

Eslāmābād-e Gharb : (city, western Iran) : to 1982 *Shāhābād*

Esopus *see* ¹**Kingston**

España *see* **Spain**

Española *see* **Hispaniola**

Esperantina (city, northeastern Brazil) : to 1944 Portuguese *Boa Esperança*

Espírito Santo *see* **Indiaroba**

Espírito Santo da Itapecerica *see* **Divinópolis**

Essaouira (city, western Morocco) : to 1959 *Mogador*

Esseg *see* **Osijek**

Essexvale *see* **Esigodini**

Este (town, northern Italy) : Roman *Ateste*

Esthonia *see* **Estonia**

Estonia (republic, northeastern Europe) : [Estonian *Eesti*]; alternate English dated *Esthonia*

Estremadura *see* **Extremadura**

Esutoru *see* **Uglegorsk**

Esztergom (town, northern Hungary) : to 1867 German *Gran*; Roman *Strigonium*

Étampes (town, northern France) : Low Latin *Stampae*

eThekwini *see* **Durban**

Ethiopia (republic, northeastern Africa) : formerly usually *Abyssinia* (The former name was introduced by the Portuguese in the 16th century, adopted from an Arabic original.)

Etna (volcano, southern Italy) : [Sicilian *Mongibello*]; Roman *Aetna*

Euboea (island, east central Greece) : Medieval Italian *Negroponte*

Euclides da Cunha (city, eastern Brazil) : to 1939 *Cumbe*

Eugenópolis (city, southeastern Brazil) : to 1944 Portuguese *São Manuel*

Eugubium *see* **Gubbio**

Euhesperides *see* **Banghāzī**

Eulau *see* **Jílové**

Eupen (town, eastern Belgium) : French *Néau*

Euphrates (river, southeastern Syria/central Iraq) : [Arabic *Al Furāt*]

Eurymedon *see* **Köprü**

Eusebeia *see* **Kayseri**

Euskadi *see* ¹**Basque Country**

Euxine Sea *see* **Black Sea**

Evan *see* **Penrith**

Evanston (city, Illinois, north central United States) : formerly *Ridgeville*; to 1850 *Grosse Pointe*

Eva Perón *see* (1) **Buenos Aires**; (2) **La Pampa**; (3) **La Plata**

Evensk (town, eastern Russia) : to 1951 *Bol'shaya Garmanda*

Everest, Mt. (northeastern Nepal/southern Tibet) : alternate Tibetan *Chomolungma*

Everett (city, Massachusetts, northeastern United States) : to 1870 *South Malden*

Évora (city, south central Portugal) : Roman *Liberalitas Julia*; ealier Roman *Ebora*

Évreux (city, northwestern France) : Roman *Mediolanum*; alternate Roman *Civitas Ebroicorum*

Exeter (city, southwestern England) : Roman *Isca Dumnoniorum*

Extremadura (region, west central Spain) : alternate *Estremadura*

Eydtkuhnen *see* **Chernyshevskoye**

Eyertown *see* **Bloomsburg**

Eyshishkes *see* **Eišiškės**

Ezhva (town, western Russia) : formerly *Sloboda* (Ezhva is now a suburb of Syktyvkar.)

Ezion-geber *see* Aqaba
Faenza (city, northern Italy) : Roman *Faventia*
Faeroe Islands (North Atlantic) : [Danish *Færøerne*; Faroese *Føroyar*]
Færøerne *see* Faeroe Islands
Faesulae *see* Fiesole
Făgăraş (city, central Romania) : to 1918 Hungarian *Fogaras*; to 1867 German *Fogarasch*
Fairbanks *see* Presque Isle
Fairfax (town, Virginia, eastern United States) : 1805–1859 *Providence*; originally *Earp's Corner*
Fairfield *see* ¹Hamilton
Fairmont (town, West Virginia, east central United States) : to 1843 *Middletown*
Fairmount *see* West Orange
Fairport *see* Horseheads
Fairview *see* McCook
Faisalabad (city, northeastern Pakistan) : to 1979 *Lyallpur*
Fakaofo (atoll, southern Tokelau, South Pacific) : formerly *Bowditch Island*
Fakel (town, western Russia) : to *c.*1960 *Sergiyevsky*
Falerii Novi *see* Civita Castellana
Falerii Veteres *see* Civita Castellana
Falkenau *see* Sokolov
Falkenberg *see* (1) Niemodlin; (2) Złocieniec
Falkland Islands (South Atlantic) : alternate Spanish *Islas Malvinas* (Administered as a British crown colony, the islands have long been claimed by Spanish-speaking Argentina.)
Falknov *see* Sokolov
Fallriver *see* Fall River
Fall River (city, Massachusetts, northeastern United States) : to 1831 *Troy*; originally *Fallriver*
Falls Station *see* Kisangani
Falmouth *see* Portland
Fama Augusta *see* Famagusta
Famagusta (town, eastern Cyprus) : [Turkish *Gazimağusa*]; Roman *Fama Augusta*; ancient Greek *Ammokhostos* (The town's Turkish name evolved from the Roman name prefixed by Turkish *gazi*, "war veteran," while the Roman name evolved from the Greek.)
Fanning Island *see* Tabuaeran
Fano (town, central Italy) : Roman *Colonia Julia Fanestris*; earlier Roman *Fanum Fortunae*
Fanum Cocidi *see* Bewcastle
Fanum Fortunae *see* Fano
Farewell, Cape (southern Greenland) : [Danish *Kap Farvel*; Greenlandic *Nunap Isua*]
Farewell Bend *see* Bend
Farg'ona (city, eastern Uzbekistan) : (Russian *Fergana*); 1907–1924 Russian *Skobelev*; to 1907 Russian *Novy Margelan*

Farmersville *see* ²Athens
Farnsworth's Landing *see* Bordentown
Farroupilha (city, southern Brazil) : to 1934 Portuguese *Nova Vicenza*
Fārs (province, southwestern Iran) : Roman *Persis* (Fārs is more or less identical with the ancient province of *Pars*, the nucleus of the Persian empire. *See* Iran.)
Farvel, Kap *see* Farewell, Cape
Farwell *see* Revelstoke
Fasano (town, southeastern Italy) : ancient Greek *Gnathia*
Fashoda *see* Kodok
Fatu Hiva (island, northern French Polynesia) : formerly *Magdalena Island*
Faventia *see* Faenza
Fawcettstown *see* East Liverpool
Faya (town, northern Chad) : formerly French *Largeau*
Fayetteville (city, Arkansas, south central United States) : to 1829 *Washington Court House*
Faylakah (island, eastern Kuwait) : ancient Greek *Icaros*
Fdérik (town, northwestern Mauritania) : formerly French *Fort-Gouraud*
Fécamp (town, northern France) : Roman *Fiscannum*
Fedala *see* Mohammedia
Federal Capital Territory *see* Australian Capital Territory
Federal Republic of Yugoslavia *see* Yugoslavia
Fehértemplom *see* Bela Crkva
Feira *see* Luangwa
Feled *see* Jesenské
Felipe Carrillo Puerto (town, southeastern Mexico) : to 1935 *Santa Cruz de Bravo*
Fellin *see* Viljandi
Felshtin *see* ²Gvardiys'ke
Felsina *see* Bologna
Felsőőr *see* Oberwart
Feltre (town, northern Italy) : Roman *Feltria*
Feltria *see* Feltre
Fénérive *see* Fenoarivo
Fenoarivo (town, northeastern Madagascar) : formerly French *Fénérive*
Feodosiya (town, southern Ukraine) : to 1783 Italian *Kaffa*; ancient Greek *Theodosia*
Ferdinand *see* Montana
Ferdinandovo *see* Pŭrvenets
Ferdinandov Vrukh *see* Botev Peak
Ferdows (town, northeastern Iran) : to 1920s *Tun*
Ferentino (town, central Italy) : Roman *Ferentinum*
Ferentinum *see* Ferentino
Fergana *see* Farg'ona

Fermo (town, eastern Italy) : Roman *Firmum Picenum*

Fermoy (town, southern Ireland) : Irish *Mainistir Fhear Maí*

Fernandina (island, western Galápagos Islands, Ecuador) : formerly *Narborough Island*

Fernandina de Jagua *see* **Cienfuegos**

Fernando Po *see* **Bioko**

Ferney *see* **Ferney-Voltaire**

Ferney-Voltaire (town, eastern France) : to 1881 *Ferney* (The name of the writer Voltaire, who lived in the town and died here, was first added during the Revolution of 1789–92.)

Ferrara (city, northern Italy) : Roman *Forum Alieni*

Ferreira Gomes (town, northern Brazil) : 1939–1943 *Amapari*

Ferro *see* **Hierro**

Ferryside (village, southwestern Wales) : Welsh *Glan-y-Fferi*

Ferryville *see* **Menzel Bourguiba**

Festenberg *see* **Twardogóra**

Festiniog *see* **Ffestiniog**

Fethülislâm *see* **Kladovo**

Fezzan (region, southwestern Libya) : Roman *Phazania*

Ffestiniog (town, northern Wales) : formerly conventional *Festiniog* (The spelling with one *f* was long current for the *Festiniog* Railway, a narrow-gauge railroad running from Blaenau Ffestiniog, north of Ffestiniog, to **Porthmadog**.)

Fforest Clud *see* **Radnor Forest**

Ffynnon Taf *see* **Taff's Well**

Fidenae *see* **Castel Giubileo**

Fidentia *see* **Fidenza**

Fidenza (town, northern Italy) : to 1927 *Borgo San Donnino*; Roman *Fidentia*

Fiesole (town, north central Italy) : Roman *Faesulae*

Figueira *see* **Governador Valadares**

Filaştīn *see* **Palestine**

Filehne *see* **Wieleń**

Filibe *see* **Plovdiv**

Filipea de Nossa Senhora das Neves *see* **João Pessoa**

Fillmore *see* **Plano**

Filurina *see* **Florina**

Finistère (department, northwestern France) : [Breton *Penn-ar-Bed*] (The name of the department refers to the peninsula here, known traditionally in English as *Finisterre*, from Latin *finis terrae*, "end of the earth," itself a translation of the Breton name.)

Finisterre *see* **Finistère**

Finisterre, Cape (northwestern Spain) : [Galician *Cabo Fisterra*]; Roman *Nerium Promontorium* (The cape's name is an exact counterpart of the French **Finistère**.)

Finland (republic, northern Europe) : [Finnish *Suomi*]

Firchau *see* **Wierzchowo**

Firenze *see* ¹**Florence**

Firmum Picenum *see* **Fermo**

Firusbey *see* **Uroševac**

Fiscannum *see* **Fécamp**

Fischhausen *see* ¹**Primorsk**

Fishguard (town, southwestern Wales) : Welsh *Abergwaun*

Fishpond *see* **Barstow**

Fisterra, Cabo *see* **Finisterre, Cape**

Fitchburg (city, Massachusetts, northeastern United States) : originally *Turkey Hills*

Fiume *see* **Rijeka**

Fizuli *see* **Füzuli**

Flaminian Way *see* **Via**

Flanders (region, northern France/western Belgium/southwestern Netherlands) : French *Flandre*; Flemish *Vlaanderen* (The name of the historical county survives in the adjacent Belgian provinces of East Flanders and West Flanders, Flemish *Oost-Vlaanderen* and *West-Vlaanderen*.)

Flandre *see* **Flanders**

Flatholm (island, southeastern Wales) : Welsh *Ynys Echni*

Flatow *see* **Złotów**

Flensborg *see* **Flensburg**

Flensburg (city, northern Germany) : 1460–1864 Danish *Flensborg*

Fletcher *see* ¹**Aurora**

Flevo Lacus *see* **IJsselmeer**

Flint (town, northeastern Wales) : Welsh *Y Fflint*

Flitsch *see* **Bovec**

Florânia (town, northeastern Brazil) : to 1944 *Flores*

¹**Florence** (city, central Italy) : [Italian *Firenze*]; Roman *Florentia*

²**Florence** (city, South Carolina, southeastern United States) : to *c*.1859 *Wilds*

Florence *see* **Ely**

Florentia *see* ¹**Florence**

Flores *see* (1) **Florânia**; (2) **Timon**

Florianópolis (city, southern Brazil) : to 1893 Portuguese *Desterro*

Florina (town, north central Greece) : to 1913 Turkish *Filurina*

Florissant (city, Missouri, central United States) : to 1939 *St. Ferdinand*

Flushing *see* **Vlissingen**

Fly Flat *see* **Coolgardie**

Foça (village, western Turkey) : alternate

Eskifoça; ancient Greek *Phocaea* (*Eskifoça*, "old Foça," distinguishes the place from *Yenifoça*, "new Foça," founded in 1421.)

Fogaras *see* **Făgăraş**

Fogarasch *see* **Făgăraş**

Fokino (town, western Russia) : to 1964 *Tsementny*

Foligno (town, central Italy) : Roman *Fulginium*

Fondi (town, south central Italy) : Roman *Fundi*

Fondouk *see* **Khemis el Khechna**

Fontarabia *see* **Fuenterrabía**

Foochow *see* **Fuzhou**

Ford City *see* **East Windsor**

Forest (town, central Belgium) : Flemish *Vorst* (The town is now suburb of Brussels.)

Forest Park (village, Illinois, north central United States) : to 1907 *Harlem* (The village is now a residential suburb of Chicago.)

Forfarshire *see* **Angus**

Forks of Tar River *see* [1]**Washington**

Forlì (city, northern Italy) : Roman *Forum Livii*

Former Yugoslav Republic of Macedonia *see* **Macedonia**

Formia (town, south central Italy) : formerly *Mola di Gaeta*; Roman *Formiae*

Formiae *see* **Formia**

Formosa *see* (1) **Bioko**; (2) **Ilhabela**; (3) **Taiwan**

Føroyar *see* **Faeroe Islands**

Forst *see* **Zasieki**

Fort-Aleksandrovsky *see* **Fort-Shevchenko**

Fortaleza (city, northeastern Brazil) : formerly *Fortaleza Nova de Bragança*; to 1823 *Villa do Forte da Assumpção*

Fortaleza *see* **Pedra Azul**

Fortaleza Nova de Bragança *see* **Fortaleza**

Fort-Archambault *see* **Sarh**

Fort-Bayard *see* **Zhanjiang**

Fort Benton (town, Montana, northwestern United States) : to 1850 *Fort Lewis*

Fort Brisebois *see* **Calgary**

Fort Camosun *see* [2]**Victoria**

Fort-Carnot *see* **Ikongo**

Fort Carillon *see* **Ticonderoga**

Fort-Charles *see* **Waskaganish**

Fort-Charlet *see* **Djanet**

Fort Chimo *see* **Kuujjuaq**

Fort Christina *see* [1]**Wilmington**

Fort Clark *see* **Peoria**

Fort Cornwallis *see* **George Town**

Fort-Crampel *see* **Kaga Bandoro**

Fort Crook *see* **Offutt Air Force Base**

Fort-Dauphin *see* **Tôlanaro**

Fort-de-France (city, western Martinique) : originally *Fort-Royal*

Fort de Kock *see* **Bukitinggi**

Fort-de-l'Eau *see* **Bordj el Kiffan**

Fort-de-Polignac *see* **Illizi**

Fort Dummer *see* **Brattleboro**

Fort Duquesne *see* **Pittsburgh**

Fortezza (village, northern Italy) : to 1918 German *Franzenfeste*

Fort-Flatters *see* **Bordj Omar Driss**

Fort-Foureau *see* **Kousséri**

Fort Frances (town, Ontario, southern Canada) : to 1830 *Fort St. Pierre*

Fort Franklin *see* **Déline**

Fort Garry *see* **Winnipeg**

Fort George *see* (1) **Chisasibi**; (2) **Prince George**

Fort Good Hope (village, Northwest Territories, northwestern Canada) : alternate Inuit *Radili Ko*

Fort-Gouraud *see* **Fdérik**

Fort Hall *see* **Murang'a**

Fort Hertz *see* **Putao**

Fort Hill *see* **Chitipa**

Fort Jameson *see* **Chipata**

Fort Johnston *see* **Mangoche**

Fort-Lamy *see* **N'Djamena**

Fort-Laperrine *see* **Tamanrasset**

Fort Lewis *see* **Fort Benton**

Fort Liard (village, Northwest Territories, west central Canada) : alternate Inuit *Echaot'l Koe*

Fort Macleod (town, Alberta, southwestern Canada) : to 1952 *Macleod*

Fort McMurray (city, Alberta, central Canada) : to 1875 *Fort of the Forks*

Fort McPherson (village, Northwest Territories, northwestern Canada) : alternate Inuit *Teet'lit Zhen*

Fort Manning *see* **Mchinji**

Fort Maurepas *see* **Ocean Springs**

Fort Miami *see* **St. Joseph**

Fort Miro *see* [1]**Monroe**

Fort Nashborough *see* **Nashville**

Fort-National *see* **L'Arbaa Naït Irathen**

Fort Norman *see* **Tulita**

Fort of the Forks *see* (1) **Fort McMurray**; (2) **Fort Simpson**

Fort Orange *see* [1]**Albany**

Fort Pitt *see* **Pittsburgh**

Fort-Pontchartrain-du-Détroit *see* **Detroit**

Fort Providence (village, Northwest Territories, north central Canada) : alternate Inuit *Zhahti Koe*

Fort Resolution (village, Northwest Territories, central Canada) : alternate Inuit *Deninoo Kue*

Fort Rosalie *see* **Natchez**

Fort Rosebery *see* **Mansa**

Fort-Rousset *see* **Owando**

Fort-Royal *see* **Fort-de-France**

Fort-Rupert *see* Waskaganish
Fort-St.-Jacques *see* Waskaganish
Fort St. Jean Baptiste *see* Natchitoches
Fort St. Pierre *see* Fort Frances
Fort Salisbury *see* Harare
Fort Sandeman *see* Zhob
Fort-Shevchenko (town, southwestern Kaza-khstan) : 1857–1939 Russian *Fort-Aleksan-drovsky*; to 1857 Russian *Novopetrovskoye* (The town was briefly renamed *Fort Uritskogo* in the 1920s.)
Fort Simpson (village, Northwest Territories, northwestern Canada) : alternate Inuit *Liidli Kue*; to 1821 *Fort of the Forks*
Fort Smith (town, Northwest Territories, central Canada) : alternate Inuit *Thebacha*
Fort Thomas (town, Kentucky, east central United States) : to 1867 *Highlands* (The town is now a residential suburb of Cincinnati.)
Fort-Trinquet *see* Bir Mogreïn
Fort Tyson *see* Quartzsite
Fort Uritskogo *see* Fort-Shevchenko
Fort Utah *see* Provo
Fort Victoria *see* (1) Masvingo; (2) [2]Victoria
Fort Walton *see* Fort Walton Beach
Fort Walton Beach (city, Florida, southeastern United States) : to 1953 *Fort Walton*
Fort Western *see* [2]Augusta
Forum Alieni *see* Ferrara
Forum Julii *see* (1) Cividale del Friuli; (2) Fréjus
Forum Livii *see* Forlì
Fossa Clodia *see* Chioggia
Foucauld *see* Souk Jemaâ Oulad Abbou
Fountain Colony *see* Colorado Springs
Fourth Creek *see* Statesville
Fraidorf *see* Novoselivs'ke
France (republic, western Europe) : formerly *Gaul*; Roman *Gallia* (The historical name is now generally applied to France, although it originally denoted a wider region, extending over modern France and Belgium, with parts of Germany and the Netherlands, and at one time also part of northern Italy.)
Franciade *see* St.-Denis
Francisco Morazán (department, south central Honduras) : to 1943 *Tegucigalpa*
Franconia (region, south central Germany) : [German *Franken*]
Franken *see* Franconia
Frankenstein *see* Ząbkowice Śląskie
Frankfort *see* Frankfurt
Frankfurt (city, west central Germany) : for-merly traditional English *Frankfort* (The for-mer spelling was current both for this city, in full *Frankfurt am Main*, and its namesake in

eastern Germany, in full *Frankfurt an der Oder*.)
Franklin Mills *see* [2]Kent
Franklinville *see* Valdosta
Františkovy Lázně (town, western Czech Republic) : to 1918, 1938–1945 German *Franzensbad*
Franzenfeste *see* Fortezza
Franzensbad *see* Františkovy Lázně
Fraserburg Road *see* Leeu-Gamka
Fraserville *see* Rivière-du-Loup
Frauenburg *see* (1) Frombork; (2) Saldus
Frauenstadt *see* Wadowice
Fraustadt *see* Wschowa
Frederickstown *see* [2]Albany
Fredericktown *see* [2]Winchester
Frederikshåb *see* Paamiut
Frederiksnagar *see* Serampore
Frederikstad *see* João Pessoa
Fredrikshald *see* Halden
Fredrikshamn *see* Hamina
Freeport *see* Wayne
Free State (province, east central South Africa) : 1854–1900, 1910–1995 *Orange Free State*
Freguesia de Nossa Senhora da Aparecida *see* Lorena
Freguesia de Santo Antônio de Guaratinguetá *see* Guaratinguetá
Freguesia do Brejo Alegre *see* Araguari
Freiberg *see* Příbor
Freiburg *see* Fribourg
Freiburg in Schlesien *see* Świebodzice
Freienwalde *see* Chociwel
Frei Paulo (town, northeastern Brazil) : to 1944 *São Paulo*
Freistadt *see* (1) Fryštát; (2) Hlohovec
Freiwaldau *see* Jeseník
Freixo (village, north central Portugal) : Roman *Longobriga* (This Freixo must be distinguished from the village of the same name northwest of Braga and from *Freixo de Espada á Cinta*, to the east.)
Fréjus (town, southeastern France) : Roman *Forum Julii*
French Guiana (department, northeastern South America) : [French *Guyane Française*]
French Guinea *see* Guinea
French Somaliland *see* Djibouti
French Sudan *see* Mali
Frenchtown *see* [2]Monroe
Freudenthal *see* Bruntál
Freystadt *see* (1) Kisielice; (2) Kożuchów
Fribourg (town, western Switzerland) : German *Freiburg*; Italian *Friburgo*
Friburgo *see* Fribourg
Friedau *see* Ormož

Friedeberg *see* Strzelce Krajeńskie
Friedeck-Friedberg *see* Frýdek-Místek
Friedenfeld *see* [1]Komsomol'skoye
Friedland *see* (1) Frýdlant; (2) Mieroszów; (3) Pravdinsk
Friedrichshain (town, eastern Germany) : 1930s–1945 *Horst Wessel Stadt* (Friedrichshain is now a district of Berlin.)
Friedrichstadt *see* Jaunjelgava
Friedrich-Wilhelmshafen *see* Madang
Friendly Islands *see* Tonga
Friendship *see* Elkton
Frisches Haff *see* Vistula Lagoon
Friuli *see* Udine
Frobisher Bay *see* Iqaluit
Frohenbruck an der Lainsitz *see* Veselí nad Lužnicí
Frombork (town, northern Poland) : to 1918, 1938–1945 German *Frauenburg*
Fronteiras (city, northeastern Brazil) : to 1944 *Socorro*
Frontera (town, southeastern Mexico) : formerly *Álvaro Obregón*
Frosinone (town, central Italy) : Roman *Frusino*
[1]Frunze (town, western Kyrgyzstan) : to 1940 *Kadamshay*
[2]Frunze (town, eastern Ukraine) : 1910–1930 *Sentyanivka* (Russian *Sentyanovka*); to 1910 *Novoselivka* (Russian *Novosyolovka*)
Frunze *see* Bishkek
Frunzens'ke (town, southern Ukraine) (Russian *Frunzenskoye*); to 1944 *Partenit*
Frunzenskoye *see* (1) Frunzens'ke; (2) Pülgön
Frunzensky *see* Frunzens'kyy
Frunzens'kyy (town, east central Ukraine) : (Russian *Frunzensky*); to *c*.1935 *Kam'yanka* (Russian *Kamenka*) (The town is now a suburb of Dnipropetrovs'k.)
Frunzivka (town, southwestern Ukraine) : (Russian *Frunzovka*); to 1926 *Zakharivka* (Russian *Zakharovka*)
Frunzovka *see* Frunzivka
Frusino *see* Frosinone
Frýdek-Místek (city, eastern Czech Republic) : 1939–1945 German *Friedeck-Friedberg* (The twin towns of Frýdek, in Silesia, and Místek, in Moravia, were united as a single city in 1960. Místek was known as *Friedberg* to 1918.)
Frýdlant (town, northern Czech Republic) : to 1918, 1938–1945 German *Friedland*
Fryštát (town, eastern Czech Republic) : 1939–1945 German *Freistadt*; 1918–1919, 1938–1939 Polish *Frysztat*; to 1918 German *Freistadt* (The town is now part of Karviná.)
Frysztat *see* Fryštát
Frývaldov *see* Jeseník

Fuenterrabia (city, northwestern Spain) : Basque *Hondarribia*; formerly English *Fontarabia*
Fuerte Constitucional *see* Mercedes
Fukuyama *see* Matsumae
Fulginium *see* Foligno
Fulton (town, Missouri, central United States) : originally *Volney*
Fundi *see* Fondi
Fünfkirchen *see* Pécs
Furmanov (city, western Russia) : to 1941 *Sereda*
Furmanovka *see* Moyynkum
Furmanovo *see* Zhalpaktal
Furneaux Island *see* Marutea North
Furnes *see* Veurne
Fürstenfelde *see* Boleszkowice
Furukamappu *see* Yuzhno-Kuril'sk
Fusine in Valromana (village, northern Italy) : to 1918 German *Weissenfels*
Fuzhou (city, southeastern China) : conventional English *Foochow*
Füzuli (town, southern Azerbaijan) : (Russian *Fizuli*); to 1959 Russian *Karyagino*
Gaberones *see* Gabarone
Gabès (town, southeastern Tunisia) : Roman *Tacape*
Gablonz an der Neisse *see* Jablonec nad Nisou
Gaborone (city, southeastern Botswana) : to 1969 *Gaberones*
Gabrova *see* Gabrovo
Gabrovo (city, north central Bulgaria) : to 1878 Turkish *Gabrova*
Gabú (town, northwestern Guinea-Bissau) : formerly Portuguese *Nova Lamego*
Gades *see* Cádiz
Gadir *see* Cádiz
Gadsden (city, Alabama, southeastern United States) : originally *Double Springs*
Gaeta (town, western Italy) : Roman *Caieta*
Gafsa (town, west central Tunisia) : Roman *Capsa*
Gafurov *see* Ghafurov
[1]Gagarin (town, western Russia) : to 1968 *Gzhatsk*
[2]Gagarin (town, eastern Uzbekistan) : to 1974 *Yerzhar*
Gago Coutinho *see* Lumbala N'guimbo
Gaillard Cut (section of Panama Canal, central Panama) : to 1913 *Culebra Cut*
Gaillimh *see* Galway
Galanta (town, northwestern Slovakia) : to 1918, 1938–1945 Hungarian *Galánta*
Galánta *see* Galanta
Galaţi (city, southeastern Romania) : 1939–1945 German *Galatz*
Galatz *see* Galaţi
Galgóc *see* Hlohovec

Galich *see* Halych

¹Galicia (historical region, east central Europe) : 1919–1939 Polish *Halicz* (The former Austrian crown land was the scene of much fighting in World War I.)

²Galicia (historical region, northwestern Spain) : Roman *Gallaecia*

Galilee, Sea of (lake, northern Israel) : alternate biblical *Lake of Gennesaret* or *Sea of Chinnereth* or *Sea of Tiberias*

Gallaecia *see* ²Galicia

Galle (city, southern Sri Lanka) : formerly *Point de Galle*

Gallia *see* France

Gallipoli (town, northwestern Turkey) : Turkish *Gelibolu*; ancient Greek *Callipolis* (The English name has been in common use since World War I, when the peninsula here was the scene of determined Turkish resistance to Allied forces. This Gallipoli should not be confused with the town of the same name in southeastern Italy, also anciently known as *Callipolis*. Modern references to the Turkish town mostly use the Turkish name.)

Galt (city, Ontario, southeastern Canada) : to 1827 *Shade's Mills* (In 1973 Galt merged with Hespeler and Preston to form the new city of Cambridge.)

Galway (town, western Ireland) : Irish *Gaillimh*

Gameti *see* Rae Lakes

Gamlakarleby *see* Kokkola

Gäncä (city, western Azerbaijan) : (Russian *Gyandzha*); 1935–1989 Russian *Kirovabad*; 1918–1935 Russian *Gyandzha*; 1804–1918 Russian *Yelizavetpol'*

Gancheshty *see* Hînceşti

Gand *see* Ghent

Ganda (town, western Angola) : to 1980 *Vila Mariano Machado*

Gangi (town, southern Italy) : Roman *Engyum*

Gangra *see* Çankırı

Ganko *see* Hanko

Gant'iadi (town, northwestern Georgia) : to 1948 Russian *Pilenkovo*

Ganxian *see* Ganzhou

Ganzhou (city, southeastern China) : 1911–1949 *Ganxian*

Gap (town, southeastern France) : Roman *Vapincum*

Gára Kritsim *see* Stamboliyski

Garda (town, northern Italy) : Roman *Benacus*

Gardabani (town, southern Georgia) : to 1947 *Karayazy*

Gardner Island *see* Nikumaroro

Gargždai (town, western Lithuania) : to 1917 *Gordž*

Gariannum *see* Burgh Castle

Garmo, Mt. *see* Ismoili Somoni, Peak

Garonne (river, southwestern France) : Roman *Garumna*

Garray (village, north central Spain) : Roman *Numantia*

Garrison Reservoir *see* Sakakawea, Lake

Garumna *see* Garonne

Gasan-Kuli *see* Esenguly

Gascony (historic region, southwestern France) : Roman *Vasconia*

Gassen *see* Jasień

Gastello (town, eastern Russia) : 1905–1945 Japanese *Nairo*

Gasten *see* Gostynin

Gatchina (city, western Russia) : 1929–1944 *Krasnogvardeysk*; 1923–1929 *Trotsk*

Gatooma *see* Kadoma

Gaul *see* France

Gauteng (province, northeastern South Africa) : April–December 1994 *Pretoria-Witwatersrand-Vaal*

Gavarr (town, central Armenia) : formerly *Kamo*; to 1959 *Nor-Bayazet*

Gavren *see* Milkovitsa

Gavrilovka *see* Taldykorgan

Gavrilovsky Zavod *see* Druzhkivka

Gaya *see* Kyjov

Gaza (city, northern Gaza Strip) : [Arabic *Ghazzah*]

Gaziantep (city, south central Turkey) : to 1922 *Aintab*; earlier *Hamtap* (The city's name represents the earlier name prefixed by Turkish *gazi*, "war veteran," as for **Famagusta**.)

Gazimağusa *see* Famagusta

Gcuwa *see* Butterworth

Gdańsk (city, northern Poland) : 1793–1945 German *Danzig* (During the period 1920 to 1939, when Danzig, for the second time, had the status of a free city, the Polish name was in use for the railroad station and by the postal authorities. The German name still has resonance from the period of World War II, which was precipitated by Poland's refusal to accede to Hitler's demand in 1939 that Danzig be given to Germany.)

Gdingen *see* Gdynia

Gdyel (village, northwestern Algeria) : to c.1962 French *St.-Cloud*

Gdynia (city, northern Poland) : 1940–1945 German *Gotenhafen*; to 1919 German *Gdingen*

Gebal *see* Jubayl

Gebel Musa *see* Sinai, Mt.

Gediz (river, western Turkey) : ancient Greek *Hermus*

Gegechkori *see* Martvili

Gehlenburg *see* Biała Piska

Geiersberg *see* Letohrad

Gela (city, southern Italy) : to 1927 *Terranova di Sicilia*

Geldenaken *see* Jodoigne

Gelderland (province, eastern Netherlands) : formerly English *Guelderland* (The English spelling was probably popularly associated with the *guilder*, a former Dutch coin.)

Gelibolu *see* Gallipoli

Gelnica (town, east central Slovakia) : to 1918 Hungarian *Gölnicbánya*; to 1867 German *Göllnitz*

Gembloers *see* Gembloux

Gembloux (town, central Belgium) : French *Gembloers*

Genabum *see* Orléans

Genaro Codina (town, central Mexico) : formerly *San Jose de la Isla*

Genck *see* Genk

Gene Autry (village, Oklahoma, south central United States) : to 1942 *Berwyn*

General Alvarado *see* Miramar

General Artigas (town, southeastern Paraguay) : formerly *Cangó*

General Câmara (town, southern Brazil) : to 1938 *Santo Amaro*

General Daniel Cerri (town, eastern Argentina) : formerly *Cuatreros*

General Enrique Martínez (town, east central Uruguay) : to early 1930s *La Charqueada*

General Enrique Mosconi (village, northern Argentina) : formerly *El Chorro*

General Freire *see* Muxaluando

General Grant National Park *see* Kings Canyon National Park

Generalissimul Suvorov (village, east central Romania) : formerly *Plăineşti*

General José de San Martín (town, northern Argentina) : formerly *El Zapallar*

General Lazarevo *see* Alfatar

General Paz (village, northeastern Argentina) : formerly *Caa-Catí*

General Ramón Gonzáles (town, western Bolivia) : formerly *Chajaya*

General San Martín (town, central Argentina) : formerly *Villa Alba* (The town, southeast of General Acha, should not be confused with the cities of the same name respectively northwest of Buenos Aires and in northeastern Argentina.)

General Santos (city, southern Philippines) : to 1954 *Buayan*

General Simón Bolívar (town, northern Mexico) : formerly *San Bartolo*

General Toshevo (town, northeastern Bulgaria) : 1913–1940 Romanian *Casim*

General Trías (town, northern Mexico) : formerly *Santa Isabel*

General Uriburu *see* Zárate

General Vargas (town, southern Brazil) : to 1944 *São Vicente*

Geneva (city, southwestern Switzerland) : [French *Genève*; German *Genf*; Italian *Ginevra*]

Geneva, Lake (southwestern Switzerland/eastern France) : French *Lac Léman*; Roman *Lacus Lemanus*

Genève *see* Geneva

Genf *see* Geneva

Genk (city, northeastern Belgium) : formerly *Genck*

Gennesaret, Lake of *see* Galilee, Sea of

Genoa (city, northwestern Italy) : [Italian *Genova*]; Roman *Genua*

Genova *see* Genoa

Gent *see* Ghent

Genua *see* Genoa

George *see* ³Georgetown

Georgenswalde *see* Otradnoye

Georges Clemenceau *see* Stidia

¹Georgetown (city, northeastern Guyana) : 1784–1812 Dutch *Stabroek*

²Georgetown (town, Kentucky, east central United States) : to 1790 *McClelland's Station*

³Georgetown (town, Washington, DC, northeastern United States) : to 1789 *George* (Georgetown is one of the District of Columbia's original three towns.)

Georgetown *see* Janjanbureh

George Town (city, western Malaysia) : occasionally *Penang*; formerly usually *Pinang*; originally *Fort Cornwallis* (The name *Pinang* remains current for the island on which the city lies and for the state of which it is the capital.)

Georgia (republic, southwestern Asia) : [Georgian *Sak'art'velo*]; Roman *Iberia* (The Roman name should not be confused with that of modern *Iberia*, the European peninsula occupied by Spain and Portugal.)

Georgi Damyanovo (village, northwestern Bulgaria) : to 1950 *Lopusha*

Georgi Dimitrov *see* Koprinka

Georgi Traykov *see* Dolni Chiflik

Georgiu-Dezh *see* Liski

Georgiye-Osetinskoye *see* Nazran'

Georgsmarienhütte (city, northwestern Germany) : to 1856 *Malbergen* (The city grew from the *Georgs-Marien-Bergwerks- und Hüttenverein*, the iron and steel works set up in

1856 in the municipality of Malbergen, which itself became part of the future city in 1937.)

Geraardsbergen (town, west central Belgium) : French *Grammont*

Gerace (village, southern Italy) : ancient Greek *Locri Epizephyrii*

Geraldton *see* **Innisfail**

Gerdauen *see* ²**Zheleznodorozhny**

Gerlachovka *see* **Gerlachovský Peak**

Gerlachovský Peak (northern Slovakia) : early 1950s *Stalin Peak*; to 1949 *Gerlachovka*

German Flats *see* **Ilion**

Germania *see* **Germany**

Germanicopolis *see* **Çankırı**

German Ocean *see* **North Sea**

German South West Africa *see* **Namibia**

Germany (republic, western Europe) : [German *Deutschland*]; Roman *Germania* (The Roman name applied to territory east of the Rhine and north of the Danube that only approximately corresponds to the present country. It was never part of the Roman empire. *Germania* was also the name of the megacity planned by Adolf Hitler to replace Berlin.)

Gernika-Lumo *see* **Guernica**

Gerona (city, northeastern Spain) : Catalan *Girona*; Roman *Gerunda*

Geroyskoye (village, western Russia) : to 1945 German *Gertlauken*

Gertlauken *see* **Geroyskoye**

Gertsa *see* **Hertsa**

Gerunda *see* **Gerona**

Geryusy *see* **Goris**

Géryville *see* **El Bayadh**

Gesoriacum *see* **Boulogne**

Gettysburg (town, Pennsylvania, northeastern United States) : to 1800 *Gettystown*

Gettystown *see* **Gettysburg**

Getúlio Vargas (city, southern Brazil) : to 1934 *Erechim*

Gevaram (kibbutz, southwestern Israel) : formerly *Kibbutz Mahar*

Gevgeli *see* **Gevgelija**

Gevgelija (town, southeastern Macedonia) : 1913–1941 Serbian *Djevdjelija*; to 1913 Turkish *Gevgeli*

Geyre (village, southwestern Turkey) : ancient Greek *Aphrodisias*

Gha'em Shahr (city, northern Iran) : to 1980 *Shahi*

Ghafurov (town, northern Tajikistan) : (Russian *Gafurov*); 1953–1978 *Sovetobod* (Russian *Sovetabad*); to 1953 *Ispisar*

Ghana (republic, western Africa) : to 1957 *Gold Coast*

Ghar al-Milh (town, northern Tunisia) : formerly *Porto Farina*

Ghazaouet (town, northwestern Algeria) : to *c*.1962 French *Nemours*

Ghazzah *see* **Gaza**

Ghent (city, northwestern Belgium) : [Flemish *Gent*; French *Gand*]

Gheorge Gheorgiu-Dej *see* **Oneşti**

Gheorgeni (town, east central Romania) : to 1918, 1940–1944 Hungarian *Gyergyószentmiklós*

Gherla (town, northern Romania) : 1940–1945 Hungarian *Szamosújvár*; to 1867 German *Armenierstadt*; Roman *Armenopolis*

Ghistelles *see* **Gistel**

Ghriss (town, northwestern Algeria) : to *c*.1962 French *Thiersville*

Giannitsa (town, northern Greece) : to 1913 Turkish *Yenice*

Giant Mountains *see* **Riesengebirge**

Gibson's Pasture *see* **Lancaster**

Gila Bend (town, Arizona, southwestern United States) : originally *Santos Apóstoles San Simón y Judas*

Gilan *see* **Gnjilane**

Gilbert Islands *see* **Kiribati**

Gilgenburg *see* **Dąbrowno**

Ginevra *see* **Geneva**

G.I. Petrovskogo, imeni *see* **Horodyshche**

Gippsland (region, Victoria, southeastern Australia) : to 1840 *Caledonia Australis*

Girált *see* **Giraltovce**

Giraltovce (town, eastern Slovakia) : to 1918 Hungarian *Girált*

Girard *see* **Woodland Hills**

Girardot (city, central Colombia) : originally *Pastor Montero*

Giresun (city, northeastern Turkey) : Roman *Cerasus*; earlier *Pharnacia*

Girgenti *see* **Agrigento**

Girne *see* **Kyrenia**

Girona *see* **Gerona**

Gisborne (city, northeastern New Zealand) : Maori *Turanga* (The earlier name was changed to avoid confusion with the town of *Tauranga* to the northwest.)

Gistel (town, western Belgium) : French *Ghistelles*

Gitschin *see* **Jičín**

Giurgiu (city, southern Romania) : originally Italian *San Giorgio*

Giza (city, northern Egypt) : [Arabic *Al Gīzah*]

Giżycko (town, northeastern Poland) : to 1945 German *Lötzen*

Gjirokastër (town, southern Albania) : 1919–1921 modern Greek *Argyrokastron*

Gjoa Haven (village, Nunavut, northern Canada) : alternate Inuit *Uqsustuq*

Gladville *see* **Wise**

Glamorgan (region, southern Wales) : Welsh
Morgannwg (In 1974 the county of *Glamorganshire* was divided into the three counties
Mid Glamorgan, *South Glamorgan*, and *West Glamorgan*. These were abolished in 1996 but
the name remains current for the present
county of **Vale of Glamorgan**.)

Glannoventa see Ravenglass

Glan-y-Fferi see Ferryside

Glaris see Glarus

Glarona see Glarus

Glarus (town, east central Switzerland) : French
Glaris; Italian *Glarona*

Glasbury (village, eastern Wales) : Welsh *Y Clas-ar-Wy*

Glasgow see [1]Scarborough

Glasgow Junction see Park City

Glatz see Kłodzko

Gleann Dá Loch see Glendalough

Głębokie see Hlybokaye

Gleiwitz see Gliwice

Glendalough (wooded valley, eastern Ireland) :
Irish *Gleann Dá Loch*

Glen Ellyn (village, Illinois, north central United
States) : 1882–1889 *Prospect Park*; 1851–1882
Danby; 1849–1851 *Newton's Station*; 1835–1849
Stacy's Corners; 1834–1835 *DuPage Center*; to
1834 *Babcock's Grove* (The name changes mark
the village's seven stages of development from
the year of its founding in 1833.)

Glens Falls (town, New York, northeastern
United States) : to 1788 *Wing's Falls*

Glenview (village, Illinois, north central United
States) : to 1895 *Oak Glen*; formerly *Hutchings*;
earlier *The Grove*; originally *South Northfield*
(The village is now a suburb of Chicago.)

Glevum see Gloucester

Gliwice (city, southwestern Poland) : to 1945
German *Gleiwitz*

Glogau see Głogów

Głogów (city, southwestern Poland) : to 1945
German *Glogau*

Głogówek (town, southern Poland) : to 1945
German *Oberglogau*

Gloucester (city, west central England) : Roman
Glevum

Gloversville (town, New York, northeastern
United States) : to 1832 *Kingsboro*

Głubczyce (town, southwestern Poland) : to
1945 German *Leobschütz*

Glubokaya see Hlyboka

Glubokoye see Hlybokaye

Głuchołazy (town, southern Poland) : to 1945
German *Ziegenhals*

Glynebwy see Ebbw Vale

Gmünd see České Velenice

Gnadenburg see Vinogradnoye

Gnadenflyur see [1]Pervomayskoye

Gnaralbine see Coolgardie

Gnathia see Fasano

Gnesen see Gniezno

Gniezno (town, west central Poland) : 1793–
1807, 1815–1919, 1939–1945 German *Gnesen*

Gnjilane (village, eastern Kosovo) : to 1913 Turkish *Gilan*

Gobannium see Abergavenny

Gobi (desert, central Asia) : alternate Chinese
Shamo

Godhavn see [2]Qeqertarsuaq

Göding see Hodonín

Godmanchester (town, eastern England) :
Roman *Durovigutum*

Godthåb see Nuuk

Godwin Austen, Mt. see K2

Godwinville see Ridgewood

Goedgegun see Nhlangano

Gökçeada (island, western Turkey) : to 1973
Imroz; ancient Greek *Imbros*

Gokpala see Mikhaylovo

Golaya Snova see Golosnovka

Goldap see Gołdap

Gołdap (town, northeastern Poland) : to 1945
German *Goldap*

Goldberg see Złotoryja

Gold Coast see Ghana

Golden Khersonese see Malay Peninsula

Goldingen see Kuldīga

Goleniów (town, northwestern Poland) : to 1945
German *Gollnow*

Golfe de Gascogne see Biscay, Bay of

Golfe du Lion see Lion, Golfe du

Golfo de Vizcaya see Biscay, Bay of

Golgotha see Calvary

Goliad (town, Texas, southern United States) : to
1829 *Nuestra Señora del Espíritu Santo Zuñiga*

Göllnitz see Gelnica

Gollnow see Goleniów

Gölnicbánya see Gelnica

Golodnaya Step' see Guliston

Golosnovka (village, western Russia) : to c.1938
Golaya Snova

Golovnina (village, eastern Russia) : 1905–1945
Japanese *Tomari*

Golubovka see Komisarivka

Golubovsky Rudnik see [1]Kirovs'k

Golyama Kutlovitsa see Montana

Golyam Bratan see Bratan

Goly Karamysh see [2]Krasnoarmeysk

Golyshi see Vetluzhsky

Golyshmanovo (town, southern Russia) : to
1948 *Katyshka*

Gombroon see Bandar Abbas

Good Hope, Cape of (southwestern South Africa) : originally *Cape of Storms* (The cape is said to have been first named, as Portuguese *Cabo Tormentoso*, by its discoverer in 1488, Bartholomeu Dias. The present name, Portuguese *Cabo da Boa Esperança*, is generally stated to have been given soon after by John II of Portugal, but may really have been given by Dias himself. *See also* **Cape Province**.)

Gopher Creek *see* **Virden**

Góra (town, western Poland) : to 1945 German *Guhrau*

Goranboy (town, west central Azerbaijan) : formerly Russian *Shaumyanovsk*; to 1938 Russian *Nizhny Agdzhakend*

Górče Petrov (town, northern Macedonia) : 1913–1941 Serbian *Djeneral Hanri*

Gordion *see* **Yassıhüyük**

Gordium *see* **Yassıhüyük**

Gordž *see* **Gargždai**

Gorey (town, southeastern Ireland) : Irish *Guaire*

Gorgān (city, northern Iran) : to 1930s *Asterabad* (The modern name is also that of the former province here known to the Romans as *Hyrcania*.)

Gorgeana *see* [2]**York**

Gorinets *see* **Horyniec**

Goris (city, southwestern Armenia) : to 1924 *Geryusy*

Göritz *see* **Górzyca**

Gorizia (city, northeastern Italy) : to 1919 German *Görz* (In 1947 Yugoslavia gained the northern part of the town and named it **Nova Gorica**, "new Gorizia." In World War I the town was the scene of an Italian victory over Austrian forces in 1916.)

Görkau *see* **Jirkov**

Gor'ky *see* **Nizhny Novgorod**

Gor'ky-Pavlovy *see* **Kaminsky**

Görlitz-Moys *see* **Zgorzelec**

Gorlovka *see* **Horlivka**

Gorna Dzhumaya *see* **Blagoevgrad**

Gornja Radgona (town, northeastern Slovenia) : 1941–1944 German *Ober-Radkersburg* (Gornja Radgona lies on the Mura River opposite the Austrian town of Bad Radkersburg.)

Gorno-Altay *see* **Altay**

Gorno-Altaysk (city, southern Russia) : 1932–1948 *Oyrot-Tura*; to 1932 *Ulala*

Gorno Derekoi *see* **Momchilovtsi**

[1]**Gornozavodsk** (town, eastern Russia) : 1905–1945 Japanese *Naihoro*

[2]**Gornozavodsk** (town, west central Russia) : to 1965 *Novopashiysky*

Gorny (village, southeastern Russia) : to 1965 *Solnechny*

Gornyak (town, southern Russia) : to 1946 *Zolotushino*

Gornyak *see* **Hirnyk**

Gorodenka *see* **Horodenka**

Gorodishche *see* (1) **Horodyshche**; (2) **Marhanets'**

Gorodishche-Shevchenkovskoye *see* **Horodyshche**

Gorodok *see* (1) **Horodok**; (2) **Zakamensk**

Gorodovikovsk (town, southwestern Russia) : to 1971 *Bashanta*

Gorokhov *see* **Horokhiv**

Gorongosa (village, central Mozambique) : to 1980 Portuguese *Vila Paiva de Andrada*

Górowo Iławeckie (town, northeastern Poland) : to 1945 German *Landsberg*

Gorsko-Ivanovskoye *see* **Hirs'ke**

Gorskoye *see* **Hirs'ke**

Goryacheistochnenskaya (village, southwestern Russia) : to *c.*1940 *Goryachevodsk* (The health resort's name was changed from general "hot water" to specific "hot springs.")

Goryachevodsk *see* **Goryacheistochnenskaya**

Görz *see* **Gorizia**

Gorzów Wielkopolski (city, western Poland) : to 1945 German *Landsberg an der Warthe*

Górzyca (town, western Poland) : to 1945 German *Göritz*

Goskopi *see* **Kopeysk**

Gospić (town, western Croatia) : to 1867 German *Gospich*

Gospich *see* **Gospić**

Gostingen *see* **Gostyń**

Gostinopolye *see* **Volkhov**

Gostyn *see* **Gostyń**

Gostyń (town, western Poland) : 1939–1945 German *Gostingen*; 1793–1807, 1815–1919 German *Gostyn*

Gostynin (town, central Poland) : 1940–1945 German *Gasten*

Göteborg (city, southwestern Sweden) : traditional English *Gothenburg*

Gotenhafen *see* **Gdynia**

Gotera *see* **San Francisco Gotera**

Gothenburg *see* **Göteborg**

Gotnya *see* [1]**Proletarsky**

Gotse Delchev (town, southwestern Bulgaria) : to 1950 *Nevrokop*

Gotsev Vrukh (mountain, southwestern Bulgaria) : to 1953 *Alibotush* (The peak is on the border with Greece, where it is known as *Ali Boutous*.)

Gottesberg *see* **Boguszów**

Gottesgab *see* **Boží Dar**

Gottschee *see* **Kočevje**

Gottwaldov *see* **Zlín**

Gotval'd *see* **Zmiyiv**

Governador Valadares (city, southeastern Brazil) : to 1939 *Figueira*

Gowanbank (village, eastern Scotland) : formerly *Colliston* (The village was presumably renamed to avoid confusion with *Collieston*, north of Aberdeen.)

Gower (peninsula, southern Wales) : Welsh *Gŵyr*

Gower Road *see* **Gowerton**

Gowerton (town, southern Wales) : Welsh *Tregŵyr*; to 1886 *Gower Road*

Gracias *see* **Lempira**

Gräfenberg *see* **Lázně Jeseník**

Graham Land *see* **Antarctic Peninsula**

Graham Peninsula *see* **Antarctic Peninsula**

Grama *see* **São Sebastião da Grama**

Grammont *see* **Geraardsbergen**

Gran *see* **Esztergom**

Gran Canaria (island, central Canary Islands, Spain) : traditional English *Grand Canary*

Grand Bassa *see* **Buchanan**

Grand-Brûlé *see* **Laterrière**

Grand Canary *see* **Gran Canaria**

Grand Chute *see* **Appleton**

Grande Comore *see* **Njazidja**

Grande Prairie *see* **²Grand Forks**

Grand Falls *see* **Churchill Falls**

¹Grand Forks (city, North Dakota, northern United States) : originally *Les Grandes Fourches*

²Grand Forks (town, British Columbia, southwestern Canada) : to 1897 *Grande Prairie*

Grandport *see* **Ecorse**

Grand Rapids *see* **Wisconsin Rapid**

Granite Creek *see* **Mareeba**

Granville *see* **Vancouver**

Graslitz *see* **Kraslice**

Grassholm (island, southwestern Wales) : Welsh *Gwales*

Grassy Mountain *see* **Oglethorpe, Mt.**

Gråsten (town, southern Denmark) : formerly German *Gravenstein*

Gratianopolis *see* **Grenoble**

Gratz *see* **Graz**

Grätz *see* **Grodzisk Wielkopolski**

Graubünden (canton, eastern Switzerland) : French *Grisons*; Italian *Grigioni*

Graudenz *see* **Grudziądz**

Graupius Mons *see* **Bennachie**

Grave Creek *see* **Moundsville**

Gravelly Bay *see* **Port Colborne**

Gravenstein *see* **Gråsten**

Grays Harbor (county, Washington, northwestern United States) : to 1915 *Chehalis*

Graz (city, southeastern Austria) : formerly *Gratz*

Great Barrier Island (northeastern New Zealand) : Maori *Aotea*

Great Britain (kingdom, western Europe) : alternate colloquial *Britain*; Roman *Britannia*; earlier *Albion* (Roman *Britannia* strictly applied to modern England, Wales, and Scotland south of the Antonine Wall, which extended from the Forth River in the east to the Clyde in the west. Great Britain is itself the largest and main part of the **United Kingdom**. The colloquial name is associated with the 1940 Battle of Britain between German and British air forces, intended by Hitler as a preliminary to his planned invasion of Britain.)

Greater St. Lucia Wetlands Park *see* **iSimangaliso Wetlands Park**

Great Falls *see* **Somersworth**

Great Fish River *see* **Back River**

Great Grimsby *see* **Grimsby**

Great Haystack *see* **Lafayette, Mt.**

Great Salt Lake City *see* **Salt Lake City**

Great Whale River *see* **Kuujjuarapik**

Great Yarmouth *see* **Yarmouth**

Grebyonka *see* **Hrebinka**

Grebyonkovsky *see* **Hrebinka**

Greece (republic, southern Europe) : [modern Greek *Ellás*]; ancient Greek *Hellas*

Greeley (city, Colorado, west central United States) : originally *Union Colony*

Green Bay (city, Wisconsin, northern United States) : originally *La Baye*

Greenbriar *see* **Parma**

Greenfield (village, northeastern Wales) : Welsh *Maes-glas*

Greenland (island, northeastern North America) : [Danish *Grønland*; Greenlandic *Kalaallit Nunaat*]

Green's Bluff *see* **³Orange**

Green's Shore *see* **Summerside**

¹Greenville (city, North Carolina, eastern United States) : to 1786 *Martinsborough*

²Greenville (city, South Carolina, southeastern United States) : to 1821 *Pleasantburg*

Greenwood (town, Mississippi, southeastern United States) : to 1844 *Williams Landing*

Greifenberg *see* **Gryfice**

Greifenhagen *see* **Gryfino**

Greiffenberg *see* **Gryfów Śląski**

Grelibre *see* **Grenoble**

Grenoble (city, southeastern France) : 1793 *Grelibre*; Roman *Gratianopolis* (The Revolutionary name replaced an aristocratic *noble* with an egalitarian *libre*, "free.")

Grenville Island *see* **Rotuma**

Gresffordd *see* **Gresford**

Gresford (town, northeastern Wales) : Welsh *Gresffordd*

Gretna (town, Louisiana, southern United
   States) : to 1913 *Mechanicsham*
Greyerz *see* Gruyères
Greymouth (town, western New Zealand) : for-
   merly *Greytown*; earlier *Blaketown*, originally
   Crescent City
Greystones (town, eastern Ireland) : Irish *Na
   Clocha Liatha*
Greytown *see* Greymouth
Griffintown *see* Smithville
Grigioni *see* Graubünden
Grimm *see* Kamensky
Grimsby (town, eastern England) : from 1979
   officially *Great Grimsby* (The formal name dis-
   tinguishes the town from the nearby village of
   Little Grimsby.)
Grimshader (village, Western Isles, northwestern
   Scotland) : Gaelic *Griomaisiader*
Griomaisiader *see* Grimshader
Grise Fiord (village, Nunavut, northern Canada)
   : alternate Inuit *Aujuittuq*
Grishino *see* Krasnoarmiys'k
Grisons *see* Graubünden
Grobin *see* Grobiņa
Grobiņa (town, western Latvia) : (Russian
   Grobinya); to 1918 Russian *Grobin*
Grobinya *see* Grobiņa
Gródek Jagielloński *see* Horodok
Grodekovo *see* Pogranichny
Grodisk *see* Grodzisk Mazowiecki
Grodków (town, southwestern Poland) : to 1945
   German *Grottkau*
Grodno *see* Hrodna
Grodzisk Mazowiecki (town, east central
   Poland) : to 1915 Russian *Grodisk*
Grodzisk Wielkopolski (town, western Poland)
   : to 1945 German *Grätz*
Grønland *see* Greenland
Grosmont (village, eastern Wales) : Welsh *Y
   Grysmwnt*
Gross-Bitesch *see* Velká Bíteš
Grossdale *see* Brookfield
Grossdirschkeim *see* ¹Donskoye
Grossendorf bei Putzig *see* Wielka Wieś
Grosse Pointe *see* Evanston
Grosse Pointe Woods (town, Michigan, north-
   ern United States) : to 1939 *Lochmoor* (The
   town, one of five named Grosse Pointe, is now
   a residential suburb of Detroit.)
Grosshammer *see* Velké Hamry
Grossheidekrug *see* ¹Vzmor'ye
Grosskanischa *see* Nagykanizsa
Gross-Karlowitz *see* Velké Karlovice
Grosskarol *see* Carei
Gross-Lindenau *see* Ozyorki
Gross-Meseritsch *see* Velké Meziříčí

Gross-Müllen *see* Mielno
Gross-Opatowitz *see* Velké Opatovice
Gross-Pawlowitz *see* Velké Pavlovice
Gross-Popowitz *see* Velké Popovice
Gross-Priesen *see* Velké Březno
Gross-Salze *see* Wielicka
Gross-Schönau *see* Velký Šenov
Gross-Skaisgirren *see* Bolshakovo
Gross-Steffelsdorf *see* Rimavská Sobota
Gross-Strehlitz *see* Strzelce
Gross-Ullersdorf *see* Velké Losiny
Grosswardein *see* Oradea
Gross-Wartenberg *see* Syców
Grosulovo *see* Velyka Mykhaylivka
Grottau an der Niesse *see* Hrádek nad Nisou
Grottkau *see* Grodków
Grover *see* Tiltonsville
Groves (town, Texas, southern United States) :
   originally *Pecan Grove*
Grovesend (village, southern Wales) : Welsh
   Pengelli
Grozdyovo (village, eastern Bulgaria) : 1934–
   1950 *Rakovets*; to 1878 Turkish *Köprüköy*
Grubeshov *see* Hrubieszów
Grudovo *see* Sredets
Grudziądz (city, north central Poland) : 1772–
   1919, 1939–1945 German *Graudenz*
Grukhi *see* Novovyatsk
Grumbkowfelde *see* Pravdino
Grumbkowkeiten *see* Pravdino
Grumento Nova (village, southern Italy) :
   Roman *Grumentum*
Grumentum *see* Grumento Nova
Grunau *see* Jeżów
Grünberg *see* Zielona Góra
Grünfelde *see* Stębark
Grünheide *see* Kaluzhskoye
Grunwald *see* Stębark
Grushka *see* ¹Ul'yanovka
Grüssau *see* Krzeszów
Gruyères (town, western Switzerland) : German
   Greyerz
Gruzitsino *see* Krasny Profintern
Gryfice (town, northwestern Poland) : to 1945
   German *Greifenberg*
Gryfino (town, northwestern Poland) : to 1945
   German *Greifenhagen*
Gryfów Śląski (town, southwestern Poland) : to
   1945 German *Greiffenberg*
Guachalla (town, western Bolivia) : to *c.*1945 *Il-
   abaya*
Guaçuí (city, southeastern Brazil) : to 1944 Por-
   tuguese *Siqueiro Campos*
Guadalajara (city, central Spain) : Roman *Arri-
   aca*
Guadalupe *see* Canelones

Guadalupe Hidalgo *see* **Gustavo A. Madero**

Guaíba (city, southern Brazil) : to *c.*1925 Portuguese *Pedras Brancas*

Guaire *see* **Gorey**

Guanahani *see* ¹**San Salvador**

Guangzhou *see* ¹**Canton**

Guantánamo (city, eastern Cuba) : to 1843 *Santa Catalina del Saltadero del Guaso*

Guapó (town, east central Brazil) : to 1944 Portuguese *Ribeirão*

Guaporé *see* ¹**Rondônia**

Guarani *see* **Pacajus**

Guaratinguetá (city, southeastern Brazil) : originally *Freguesia de Santo Antônio de Guaratinguetá*

Guaraúna (town, southern Brazil) : to 1944 Portuguese *Valinhos*

Guarulhos (city, southeastern Brazil) : originally *Nossa Senhora da Conceição dos Guarulhos*

Guastatoya *see* **El Progreso**

Guayama (town, southeastern Puerto Rico) : originally *San Antonio de Padua de Guayama*

Guayaquil (city, southwestern Ecuador) : originally *Santiago de Guayaquil*

Gubadag (town, northern Turkmenistan) : formerly Russian *Tel'mansk*; to 1938 *Taza-Kala*

Gubbio (town, central Italy) : Medieval Latin *Eugubium*; Roman *Iguvium*

Guben (city, eastern Germany) : 1961–1990 *Wilhelm-Pieck-Stadt*

Gubin (town, western Poland) : to 1945 German *Guben* (The town was originally part of the German city of **Guben**, but came under Polish administration when East Germany was divided along the Oder River in 1945.)

Gubkin (town, western Russia) : to 1939 *Korobkovo*

Guchkovo *see* **Dedovsk**

Güeciapam *see* **Ahuachapán**

Guelderland *see* **Gelderland**

Guened *see* **Vannes**

Guernica (town, northern Spain) : Basque *Gernika-Lumo* (The Basque name is the equivalent of Spanish *Guernica y Luno*, "Guernica and Luno," the latter being the surrounding district with which the original town was united as a municipality in 1882.)

Guernsey (island, Channel Islands, southern United Kingdom) : Roman *Sarnia* (The Roman name has also been assigned to the smaller island of *Herm*, east of Guernsey.)

Gugark' (village, western Armenia) : formerly *Megrut*

Guhrau *see* **Góra**

Guijá (town, southern Mozambique) : 1964–1980 Portuguese *Vila Alferes Chamusca*; to 1964 Portuguese *Caniçado*

Guijá *see* **Chókwé**

Guilford (town, Connecticut, northeastern United States) : to 1643 *Menunketuck*

Guilherme Capelo *see* **Cacongo**

Guilsfield (village, eastern Wales) : Welsh *Cegidfa*

Guinea (republic, western Africa) : to 1958 *French Guinea*

Guinea-Bissau (republic, western Africa) : to 1973 *Portuguese Guinea*

Guiratinga (town, western Brazil) : 1939–1943 Portuguese *Lajeado*; to 1939 Portuguese *Santa Rita do Araguaia*

Gukasyan *see* **Ashots'k'**

Gulbahor (town, northeastern Uzbekistan) : to 1977 *Kirda*

Gulbene (town, northeastern Latvia) : to 1918 German *Schwanenburg* (Under German rule, the town was properly *Altschwanenburg*, "Old Schwanenburg," as against the village of *Neuschwanenburg*, "New Schwanenburg," now *Jaungulbene*, 10 miles to the southwest.)

Gulcha-Guzar *see* **Gülchö**

Gülchö (town, southern Kyrgyzstan) : to 1938 *Gulcha-Guzar*

Gulf, The *see* **Persian Gulf**

Gulf of Chihli *see* **Bo Hai**

Gulf of Lions *see* **Lion, Golfe du**

Gulistan *see* **Guliston**

Guliston (city, east central Uzbekistan) : (Russian *Gulistan*); *c.*1905–1961 *Mirzachul* (Russian *Golodnaya Step'*); to *c.*1905 Russian *Dukhovsky*

Gumbinnen *see* **Gusev**

Gumpolds *see* **Humpolec**

Gum Pond *see* **Tupelo**

Gum Springs *see* **Shawnee**

Gümülcine *see* **Komotiní**

Gundorovka *see* **Donetsk**

Güns *see* **Kőszeg**

Gurkfeld *see* **Krško**

Gurkovo (town, southeastern Bulgaria) : to 1878 Turkish *Gyavur Kuyusu*

Guruve (town, northern Zimbabwe) : 1980–1982 *Chipuriro*; to 1980 *Sipolilo* (The two former names are really one and the same.)

Gur'yev *see* **Atyrau**

Gur'yevsk (town, western Russia) : to 1945 German *Neuhausen*

Gusev (city, western Russia) : to 1945 German *Gumbinnen*

Gusevka *see* **Novosibirsk**

Gusinoozersk (city, eastern Russia) : to 1953 *Shakhty*

Güssing (town, eastern Austria) : to 1919 Hungarian *Németújvár*

Gustavo A. Madero (city, central Mexico) : to 1931 *Guadalupe Hidalgo* (The city, now a part of Mexico City, gave its name to the 1848 Treaty of Guadalupe Hidalgo, ending the Mexican War.)

Gusyatin *see* **Husyatyn**

Gúta *see* **Kolárovo**

Gutenfeld *see* **Dobruška**

Guttentag *see* **Dobrodzień**

Guttstadt *see* **Dobre Miasto**

Guyana (republic, northern South America) : to 1966 *British Guiana*

Guyane Française *see* **French Guiana**

Guyotville *see* **Aïn Benian**

Guysborough (village, Nova Scotia, eastern Canada) : to 1901 *Chedabucto*

Güzelhisar *see* **Aydın**

Gvardeysk (town, western Russia) : to 1945 German *Tapiau*

Gvardeyskoye *see* (1) [2]**Chornomors'ke**; (2) [1,2]**Hvardiys'ke**

Gvozdev Islands *see* **Diomede Islands**

Gwales *see* **Grassholm**

Gwelo *see* **Gweru**

Gwenfô *see* **Wenvoe**

Gweru (city, southwestern Zimbabwe) : to 1982 *Gwelo*

Gwy *see* **Wye**

Gŵyr *see* **Gower**

Gyachrypsh (village, northwestern Georgia) : 1944–1992 *Leselidze*; to 1944 Russian *Yermolovsk*

Gyanafalva *see* **Jennersdorf**

Gyandzha *see* **Gäncä**

G.Ya. Sedova, imeni *see* **Syedove**

Gyavur Kuyusu *see* **Gurkovo**

Gyergyőszentmiklós *see* **Gheorgeni**

Győr (city, northwestern Hungary) : to 1867 German *Raab*; Roman *Arrabona*

Győrszentmárton *see* **Pannonhalma**

Gyulafehérvár *see* **Alba Iulia**

Gyumri (city, northwestern Armenia) : 1924–1990 Russian *Leninakan*; 1840–1924 Russian *Aleksandropol'*; to 1840 *Kumayri* (The earliest name, from which the present name evolved in a corrected form, remains current for the city's historical center.)

Gyumyurdzhina *see* **Komotiní**

Gzhatsk *see* [1]**Gagarin**

Haapsalu (town, western Estonia) : to 1918 German *Hapsal*

Habelschwerdt *see* **Bystrzyca Kłodzka**

Habitancum *see* **Risingham**

Hacieles *see* **Pŭrvomay**

Hackensack (city, New Jersey, northeastern United States) : to 1921 *New Barbadoes*

Hadersleben *see* **Haderslev**

Haderslev (city, southwestern Denmark) : 1864–1920 German *Hadersleben*

Hadjadj (village, northwestern Algeria) : to *c*.1962 French *Bosquet*

Hadjout (town, northern Algeria) : to *c*.1962 French *Marengo*

Hadranum *see* **Adrano**

Hadrumetum *see* **Sousse**

Haemus *see* **Balkan Mountains**

Hafren *see* **Severn**

Hagerstown (city, Maryland, northeastern United States) : to 1814 *Elizabethtown*

Hagioi Saranta *see* **Saranda**

Hague, The (city, southwestern Netherlands) : [Dutch *'s-Gravenhage*] (The formal Dutch name has a shorter common form *Den Haag*.)

Hahndorf (town, South Australia, southern Australia) : 1918–1935 *Ambleside*

Hailar (city, northeastern China) : 1910–1947 *Hulun*

Hainaut (province, southwestern Belgium) : Flemish *Henegouwen*

Haindorf *see* **Hejnice**

Hainspach *see* **Lipová**

Haiti (republic, central West Indies) : to 1802 French *St.-Domingue* (*See also* **Hispaniola**.)

Hakkâri (city, southeastern Turkey) : formerly *Çölemerik*

Hal *see* **Halle**

Ḥalab *see* **Aleppo**

Halbstadt *see* **Meziměstí**

Halden (town, southeastern Norway) : 1665–1928 Swedish *Fredrikshald*

Halfmoon Bay *see* **Oban**

Halfway Village *see* **Eastpointe**

Halicarnassus *see* **Bodrum**

Halicz *see* (1) [1]**Galicia**; (2) **Halych**

Hall Beach (village, Nunavut, northern Canada) : alternate Inuit *Sanirajak*

Halle (town, central Belgium) : French *Hal*

Hallerowo *see* **Wielka Wieś**

Hallowell *see* [1]**Picton**

Halmahera (island, northeastern Indonesia) : formerly *Djailolo*

Halq el Oued (town, northern Tunisia) : formerly French *La Goulette*

Halych (town, western Ukraine) : (Russian *Galich*); 1919–1939 Polish *Halicz*

Halys *see* **Kızılırmak**

Hama (city, western Syria) : ancient Greek *Epiphania*

Hamadan (city, western Iran) : ancient Greek *Ecbatana*

Hamadia (town, northern Algeria) : to *c*.1962 French *Victor Hugo*

Hämeenlinna (city, southern Finland) : to 1809 Swedish *Tavastehus*

Hamelin *see* Hameln

Hameln (city, north central Germany) : traditional English *Hamelin*

Hamıdabad *see* Isparta

[1]Hamilton (city, Ohio, north central United States) : originally *Fairfield* (In 1986 the city added an exclamation point to its name as *Hamilton!* in a bid to draw attention to itself, although the addition was not widely or even officially adopted.)

[2]Hamilton (city, Ontario, southeastern Canada) : to 1815 *Burlington Bay*

Hamilton *see* Churchill

Hamina (town, southeastern Finland) : to 1809 Swedish *Fredrikshamn*

Hammerstein *see* Czarne

Hammond (city, Indiana, north central United States) : to 1873 *State Line*; originally *Hohman*

Hamônia *see* Ibirama

Hampden *see* Murchison

Hampton *see* Ruth

Hamtap *see* Gaziantep

Hamza (town, northeastern Uzbekistan) : (Russian *Khamza*); 1963–1974 Russian *imeni Khamzy Khakimzade*; *c.*1929–1963 Russian *Vannovsky*; to *c.*1929 *Shakhimardan*

Hanan's Bluff *see* Yazoo City

Handlová (town, west central Slovakia) : formerly Hungarian *Nyitrabánya*

Hangö *see* Hanko

Hangtown *see* Placerville

Hanko (town, southwestern Finland) : to 1809 Swedish *Hangö* (The Soviet naval base leased from Finland here in 1940 after the Russo-Finnish War was named *Ganko*.)

Hannover *see* [1]Hanover

Hannuit *see* Hannut

Hannut (town, east central Belgium) : French *Hannuit*

Hanoi (city, northern Vietnam) : 1428–1787 Chinese *Dong Kinh*; alternate French *Tonquin*, English *Tonkin* or *Tongking* (From 1883 to 1945, during the French colonial period, the European form of the Chinese name was applied to the entire region around the city.)

[1]Hanover (city, northern Germany) : [German *Hannover*] (The English spelling has historical resonance from the British royal house of Hanover, which provided six monarchs over the 18th and 19th centuries, from George I to Victoria.)

[2]Hanover (town, Ontario, southeastern Canada) : formerly *Buck's Bridge*; originally *Buck's Crossing.*

Hansa *see* Corupá

Hanumangarh (city, northwestern India) : to 1805 *Bhatner*

Hanya *see* Canea

Hapsal *see* Haapsalu

Haran (village, southeastern Turkey) : Roman *Carrhae*

Harare (city, north central Zimbabwe) : 1897–1982 *Salisbury*; originally *Fort Salisbury*

Harbin (city, northeastern Russia) : 1932–1945 Japanese *Pinkiang*

Hardenberg's Corners *see* [1]Auburn

Hardscrabble *see* Streator

Hargreaves *see* Bryson

Haridwar (city, northern India) : originally *Kapila*

Harlem *see* Forest Park

Harmanli *see* Kharmanli

Harmonie *see* New Harmony

Harmsfontein *see* Carnarvon

Harper (town, southeastern Liberia) : to 1857 *Cape Palmas*

Harper *see* Costa Mesa

Harrington *see* [2]Augusta

Harris *see* Isle of Lewis

Harrisburg (city, Pennsylvania, northeastern United States) : formerly *Louisbourg*; to 1785 *Harris' Ferry*

Harris' Corner *see* Winter Haven

Harris' Ferry *see* Harrisburg

Harrison *see* Scranton

Harrodsburg (town, Kentucky, east central United States) : formerly *Oldtown*; originally *Harrodstown*

Harrodstown *see* Harrodsburg

Hartingsburg *see* Bela-Bela

Hartley *see* Chegutu

Harvey (city, Illinois, north central United States) : originally *South Lawn*

Hasan Abdal (town, northern Pakistan) : formerly *Campbellpur*

Hasei Nameche (village, northwestern Algeria) : to *c.*1962 French *Rivoli*

Haselberg *see* Krasnoznamensk

Hasenpoth *see* Aizpute

Hasköy *see* Khaskovo

[1]Hastings (town, Minnesota, northern United States) : originally *Buckhorn*

[2]Hastings (village, Ontario, southeastern Canada) : to 1847 *Crook's Rapids*

Hatra *see* Al Ḥaḍr

Hatzfeld *see* Jimbolia

Haussonvillers *see* Naciria

Haut-Congo *see* Orientale

Hauturu *see* Little Barrier Island

Haut-Zaïre *see* Orientale

Havana (city, western Cuba) : [Spanish *La Habana*]

Havelock *see* (1) **Bryson**; (2) **Bulembu**

Haverfordwest (town, southwestern Wales) : Welsh *Hwlffordd*

Havířov (city, eastern Czech Republic) : 1939–1945 German *Schlesisch-Schumbarg*; 1938–1939 Polish *Szumbark Śląski*; to 1918 German *Schlesisch-Schumbarg*

Havlíčkův Brod (city, central Czech Republic) : to 1918, 1939–1945 German *Deutsch-Brod* (The Czech name *Německý Brod*, "German ford," was formerly also current as a translation of the German.)

Havre-St.-Pierre (village, Quebec, eastern Canada) : to 1930 *St.-Pierre-de-la-Pointe-aux-Esquimaux*

Havrylivs'kyy Zavod *see* **Druzhkivka**

Hawaii (island state of United States, central Pacific) : formerly *Sandwich Islands*

Hawarden (town, northeastern Wales) : Welsh *Penarlâg*

Hayasdan *see* **Armenia**

Hayden *see* **Ampezzo**

Hayden's Ferry *see* **Tempe**

Haynesville *see* **Johnson City**

Hay-on-Wye (town, eastern Wales) : Welsh *Y Gelli Gandryll*

Hayrabolu (town, northwestern Turkey) : 1920–1922 modern Greek *Khairepolis*

Hay River (town, Northwest Territories, central Canada) : alternate Inuit *Xatl'o Dehe*

Head of Elk *see* **Elkton**

Heatherwood *see* **Edson**

Heaton's Furnace *see* **Niles**

Hebrides (island group, northwestern Scotland) : Roman *Hebudae* (The Roman name was applied to the Inner Hebrides, and did not include the Outer Hebrides or **Western Isles**.)

Hebron (town, southern West Bank) : [Arabic *Al Khalīl*], biblical *Kiriath-Arba* (The name Kiriath-Arba predates the better-known biblical name Hebron.)

Hebudae *see* **Hebrides**

Heerwegen *see* **Polkowice**

Hefei (city, eastern China) : to 1912 *Luzhou*

Hegyeshalom (village, northwestern Hungary) : to 1867 German *Strass-Sommerein*

Hei Chiang *see* **Black River**

Heidekrug *see* **Šilutė**

Heiligenbeil *see* **Mamonovo**

Heilsberg *see* **Lidzbark Warmiński**

Heinrichswalde *see* **Slavsk**

Heisternest *see* **Jastarnia**

Hejnice (town, northern Czech Republic) : to 1918, 1939–1945 German *Haindorf*

Hel (village, northern Poland) : 1772–1919, 1939–1945 German *Hela*

Hela *see* **Hel**

Helena (town, Arkansas, south central United States) : to 1821 *St. Francis*; originally *Monticello*

Helgoland *see* **Heligoland**

Heligoland (island, eastern North Sea) : German *Helgoland* (The English name has a historic legacy. The island was seized by the British in 1807, ceded to Germany in 1890, attacked by the Allies as a German naval stronghold in World War II, and after the war used as a bombing range by the Royal Air Force until 1952, when it was returned to Germany.)

Heliopolis (ancient city, northern Egypt) : biblical *On*; alternate biblical *Beth-shemesh*

Heliopolis *see* **Baalbek**

Hellas *see* **Greece**

Hellespont *see* **Dardanelles**

Hellgate *see* **Missoula**

Helsingfors *see* **Helsinki**

Helsingør *see* **Elsinore**

Helsinki (city, southern Finland) : to 1809 Swedish *Helsingfors* (The Swedish name was originally that of the city founded in 1550 north of the present city, which arose in 1640. The name prevailed until 1917, when Finland gained independence from Russia.)

Helvetia *see* **Switzerland**

Hendy-gwyn *see* **Whitland**

Henegouwen *see* **Hainaut**

Henkenhagen *see* **Ustronie Morskie**

Heraclea *see* (1) **Ayvalık**; (2) **Policoro**

Heraclea Cybistra *see* ²**Ereğli**

Heraclea Pontica *see* ¹**Ereğli**

Heracleum *see* **Iráklion**

Heraklion *see* **Iráklion**

Herbertshöhe *see* **Kokopo**

Hercegfalva *see* **Mezőfalva**

Herceg-Novi (town, southwestern Montenegro) : to 1918 Italian *Castelnuovo*

Herch-la-Ville *see* **Herk-de-Stad**

Herculândia (town, southeastern Brazil) : to 1944 *Herculânia*

Herculaneum *see* **Ercolano**

Herculânia *see* (1) **Coxim**; (2) **Herculândia**

Herdonia *see* **Ordona**

Heredia (town, central Costa Rica) : formerly *Villavieja*; originally *Cubujuquí*

Heretaunga *see* **Hutt**

Héristal *see* **Herstal**

Herk-de-Stad (town, east central Belgium) : French *Herch-la-Ville*

Herm *see* **Guernsey**

Hermannsbad *see* **Ciechocinek**

Hermannstadt *see* **Sibiu**
Hermanus (town, southwestern South Africa) : to 1904 *Hermanuspietersfontein*
Hermanuspietersfontein *see* **Hermanus**
Hermon, Mt. (ridge, southern Lebanon) : Arabic *Jabal ash-Shaykh* (The ridge is mentioned several times in the Bible, where it is also called *Senir* or *Sirion*, and the three names may have originally been those of the mountain cluster's three main peaks.)
Hermopolis Magna *see* **Al Ashmunein**
Hermopolis Parva *see* **Damanhur**
Hermsdorf *see* **Sobięcin**
Hermus *see* **Gediz**
Hernandarias (town, eastern Paraguay) : formerly *Tacurupucú*
Heroica Ciudad de Tlaxiaco *see* **Tlaxiaco**
Heroica Matamoros *see* **Matamoros**
Heroica Puebla de Zaragoza *see* **Puebla**
Herriott's Falls *see* **Lakefield**
Herrnstadt *see* **Wąsosz**
Herstal (town, eastern Belgium) : French *Héristal*
Herţa *see* **Hertsa**
Hertsa (town, western Ukraine) : (Russian *Gertsa*); to 1940 Romanian *Herţa*
Hervey Island *see* ¹**Manuae**
Hesperides *see* **Banghāzī**
Hespeler (town, Ontario, southeastern Canada) : to 1858 *Bergytown* (In 1973 Hespeler combined with two other towns, **Galt** and Preston, to form the new city of Cambridge.)
Hesse (state, central Germany) : [German *Hessen*]
Hessen *see* **Hesse**
Heydebreck *see* **Kędzierzyn-Koźle**
Hezargrad *see* **Razgrad**
Hibernia *see* **Ireland**
Hickory *see* ¹**Warren**
Hicks Ferry *see* ²**Bridgetown**
Hidalgo del Parral (city, north central Mexico) : formerly *Parral*
Hiddekel *see* **Tigris**
Hierapolis *see* **Pamukkale**
Hierosolyma *see* **Jerusalem**
Hierro (island, western Canary Islands, Spain) : formerly *Ferro*
Higashi-naibuchi *see* **Uglezavodsk**
Highlands *see* **Fort Thomas**
Hillsboro *see* **Hillsborough**
Hillsborough (town, North Carolina, eastern United States) : 1766–1965 *Hillsboro*; 1759–1766 *Childsburgh*; earlier *Corbinton*; originally *Orange*
Hillsborough Canal Settlement *see* **Belle Glade**

Himarë (town, southern Albania) : 1919–1921 modern Greek *Kheimarra*
Hînceşti (town, south central Moldova) : formerly Russian *Kotovsk*; 1940–1965 Russian *Kotovskoye*; to 1940 *Gancheshty*
Hindenburg *see* **Zabrze**
H.I. Petrovs'koho, imeny *see* **Horodyshche**
Hippo Diarrhytus *see* **Bizerta**
Hipponium *see* **Vibo Valentia**
Hippo Regius *see* **Annaba**
Hippo Zarytus *see* **Bizerta**
Hirnyk (town, eastern Ukraine) : (Russian *Gornyak*); to 1958 *Sotshorodok* (Russian *Sotsgorodok*)
Hirochi *see* **Pravda**
Hirschberg *see* **Jelenia Góra**
Hirs'ke (town, eastern Ukraine) : (Russian *Gorskoye*); to c.1940 *Hirs'ko-Ivanivs'ke* (Russian *Gorsko-Ivanovskoye*)
Hirs'ko-Ivanivs'ke *see* **Hirs'ke**
Hispalis *see* **Seville**
Hispania *see* **Spain**
Hispaniola (island, central West Indies) : formerly Spanish *Española* (The French name *St.-Domingue*, now usually associated with **Haiti**, which occupies the western third of Hispaniola, was sometimes also applied to the entire island, of which the eastern two thirds are now occupied by the **Dominican Republic**, with capital **Santo Domingo**.)
Histonium *see* **Vasto**
Hizaori *see* ²**Asaka**
Hlohovec (town, western Slovakia) : to 1918 Hungarian *Galgóc*; to 1867 German *Freistadt*
Hlučín (town, eastern Czech Republic) : to 1919, 1938–1945 German *Hultschin*
Hlyboka (town, southwestern Ukraine) : (Russian *Glubokaya*); 1919–1940 Romanian *Adîncata*
Hlybokaye (town, northern Belarus) : (Russian *Glubokoye*); 1919–1939 Polish *Głębokie*
Hnúšť'a (town, south central Slovakia) : to 1918 Hungarian *Likér*
Ho Chi Minh City (city, southern Vietnam) : to 1976 *Saigon* (The old name continues to have local and popular currency, if only from the 1989 musical *Miss Saigon*.)
Hochstadt *see* **Vysoké nad Jizerou**
Hodeida *see* **Al Ḥudaydah**
Hodonín (town, eastern Czech Republic) : to 1918, 1939–1945 German *Göding*
Hoei *see* **Huy**
Hoek van Holland *see* **Hook of Holland**
Hofmeyr (town, southern South Africa) : to 1911 *Maraisburg*
Hoggar *see* **Ahaggar**

Hog Heaven *see* ²Moscow
Hog Island *see* Paradise Island
Hohenbruck *see* Třebechovice pod Orebem
Hohenelbe *see* Vrchlabí
Hohenfriedeberg *see* Dąbromerz
Hohenfurth *see* Vyšší Brod
Hohenmauth *see* Vysoké Mýto
Hohensalza *see* Inowrocław
Hohensalzburg *see* Lunino
Hohenstadt *see* Zábřeh
Hohenstein *see* (1) Olsztynek; (2) Pszczółki
Hohhot (city, northern China) : alternate *Huhe-hot*; to 1954 *Kweisui* (The earlier name combined those of the formerly adjacent cities *Kuei-hua* and *Suiyuan*.)
Hohman *see* Hammond
Hokkaido (island, northern Japan) : to 1869 *Yezo*
Holcomb *see* Mundelein
Holešov (town, eastern Czech Republic) : to 1918, 1939–1945 German *Holleschau*
Holman (village, Northwest Territories, northern Canada) : alternate Inuit *Uluqsaqtuua*
Holland *see* Netherlands
Hollandia *see* Jayapura
Holleschau *see* Holešov
Holmgard *see* Veliky Novgorod
Holsteinsborg *see* Sisimiut
Holt City *see* Lake Louise
Holubivka *see* Komisarivka
Holubivs'kyy Rudnyk *see* ¹Kirovs'k
Holy Cross, Mount of the (peak, Colorado, west central United States) : 1929–1950 *Holy Cross National Monument*
Holy Cross National Monument *see* Holy Cross, Mount of the
Holyhead (town, northwestern Wales) : Welsh *Caergybi*
Holy Island (northwestern Wales) : Welsh *Ynys Gybi*
Holy Island *see* Lindisfarne
Holywell (town, northeastern Wales) : Welsh *Treffynnon*
Holywood (town, eastern Northern Ireland) : Irish *Ard Mhic Nasca*
Homonna *see* Humenné
Homs (city, west central Syria) : Roman *Emesa*
Homs *see* Al Khums
Hondarribia *see* Fuenterrabía
Honey Creek *see* West Allis
Hong *see* Red River
Hong Kong (special administrative zone, southeastern China) : Chinese *Xianggang* (The current name, a corruption of the Chinese, became established over the period 1898–1997, when the territory was leased to Britain.)
Honto *see* Nevel'sk

Hook of Holland (cape, southwestern Netherlands) : [Dutch *Hoek van Holland*] (The cape is named not for the country of *Holland*, meaning the **Netherlands**, but for its western, low-lying part, now divided into the provinces of North Holland and South Holland, Dutch *Noord-Holland* and *Zuid-Holland*.)
Hoover Dam (Colorado River, Arizona/Nevada, western United States) : to 1947 *Boulder Dam*
Hope (village, northeastern Wales) : *Yr Hôb*
Hopeh (province, northeastern China) : to 1911 *Chihli*
Hopes Advance Bay *see* Aupaluk
Hopewell *see* ²Paris
Hopkinsville (city, Kentucky, east central United States) : to 1797 *Elizabethtown*
Hopkinsville *see* Kirksville
Horbat Qesari *see* Caesarea
Horeb, Mt. *see* Sinai, Mt.
Horgos *see* Horgoš
Horgoš (village, northern Serbia) : to 1918, 1941–1944 Hungarian *Horgos*
Hořice (town, northern Czech Republic) : to 1918, 1939–1945 German *Horschitz*
Horlivka (city, eastern Ukraine) : (Russian *Gorlovka*)
Horncastle (town, eastern England) : Roman *Bannovalium* (A case has been made for locating the named Roman settlement at the modern town of Caistor, 25 miles to the north, but the identification given here is generally preferred, if only because Celtic *Banno-* means "horn.")
Hornell (town, New York, northeastern United States) : to 1820 *Upper Canisteo*
Horní Dvořiště (village, southwestern Czech Republic) : to 1918, 1938–1945 German *Oberhaid*
Horochów *see* Horokhiv
Horodenka (town, western Ukraine) : (Russian *Gorodenka*); to 1939 Polish *Horodenko*
Horodok (town, western Ukraine) : (Russian *Gorodok*); to 1939 Polish *Gródek Jagielloński*
Horodyshche (town, central Ukraine) : (Russian *Gorodishche*); 1933–1944 *imeny H.I. Petrovs'koho* (Russian *imeni G.I. Petrovskogo*); 1929–1933 *Horodyshche-Shevchenkivs'ke* (Russian *Gorodishche-Shevchenkovskoye*)
Horodyschche *see* Marhanets'
Horodyschche-Shevchenkivs'ke *see* Horodyshche
Horokhiv (town, western Ukraine) : (Russian *Gorokhov*); 1919–1939 Polish *Horochów*
Hořovice (town, west central Czech Republic) : to 1918, 1939–1945 German *Horschowitz*
Horschitz *see* Hořice

Horschowitz *see* Hořovice

Horseheads (town, New York, northeastern United States) : to 1840s *Fairport*

Horšovský Týn (town, western Czech Republic) : to 1918, 1938–1945 German *Bischofteinitz*

Horst Wessel Stadt *see* Friedrichshain

Horton Corner *see* Kentville

Horyniec (village, southeastern Poland) : 1939–1941 Russian *Gorinets*

Hot Springs *see* Truth or Consequences

Hotval'd *see* Zmiyiv

Hotzenplotz *see* Osoblaha

Housesteads (historic site, northeastern England) : Roman *Vercovicium* (The name of the Roman fort here on Hadrian's Wall was long cited as *Borcovicium*.)

Hovd (town, western Mongolia) : formerly *Dzhirgalantu* (The former name became an official alternate name in 1928.)

Howth (town, eastern Ireland) : Irish *Binn Éadair* (Howth is now a suburb of Dublin.)

Hoynau *see* Chojnów

Hradec Králové (town, northwestern Czech Republic) : to 1918, 1939–1945 German *Königgrätz* (The German name is associated with the nearby site of the battle of 1866 in which the Prussians decisively defeated the Austrians during the Austro-Prussian War.)

Hrádek nad Nisou (town, northern Czech Republic) : to 1918, 1939–1945 German *Grottau an der Niesse*

¹Hranice (town, eastern Czech Republic) : to 1918, 1939–1945 German *Mährisch-Weisskirchen*

²Hranice (town, western Czech Republic) : to 1918, 1938–1945 German *Rossbach* (This Rossbach should not be confused with the village of the same name in eastern Germany that was the scene of a Prussian victory over the French and Austrians in 1757 during the Seven Years' War.)

Hrazdan (town, central Armenia) : (Russian *Razdan*); to 1959 *Akhta*

Hrebinka (town, north central Ukraine) : (Russian *Grebyonka*); to 1959 *Hrebinkivs'kyy* (Russian *Grebyonkovsky*)

Hrebinkivs'kyy *see* Hrebinka

Hrodna (city, western Belarus) : (Russian *Grodno*); 1919–1939 Polish *Grodno*; to 1918 Russian *Grodno*

Hrosulove *see* Velyka Mykhaylivka

Hrubieszów (town, eastern Poland) : to 1915 Russian *Grubeshov*

Hrushka *see* ¹Ul'yanovka

Hrvatska *see* Croatia

Hryshyne *see* Krasnoarmiys'k

Hsia-men *see* Xiamen

Huaicho *see* Puerto Acosta

Huamanga *see* Ayacucho

Huambo (city, west central Angola) : 1928–1975 Portuguese *Nova Lisboa*

Huancavelica (town, central Peru) : originally *Vila Rica de Oropesa*

Huang Hai *see* Yellow Sea

Huang He *see* Huango Ho

Huang Ho (river, north central and eastern China) : alternate *Hwang He*; traditional English *Yellow River* (The Pinyin form of the name, *Huang He*, is usually preferred on maps. The river flows through the Bo Hai into the Yellow Sea.)

Huangyuan (town, northwestern China) : to 1912 *Tangar*

Huánuco (city, central Peru) : originally *León de los Caballeros de Huánuco*

Hudson Island *see* Nanumanga

Hueneme *see* Port Hueneme

Huesca (city, northeastern Spain) : Roman *Osca*

Huhehot *see* Hohhot

Huicheng *see* Shexian

¹Hull (city, northeastern England) : alternate (official) *Kingston upon Hull*

²Hull (city, Quebec, southeastern Canada) : to 1875 *Wrightstown*

Hull Island *see* Orona

Hultschin *see* Hlučín

Hulun *see* Hailar

Humenné (town, eastern Slovakia) : to 1918 Hungarian *Homonna*

Hummelstadt *see* Lewin Kłodski

Hummock Hill *see* Whyalla

Humphrey Island *see* Manihiki

Humphreyville *see* Seymour

Humpolec (town, south central Czech Republic) : to 1918, 1939–1945 German *Gumpolds*

Hunedoara (city, west central Romania) : to 1918 Hungarian *Vajdahunyad*

Hunericopolis *see* Sousse

Hungary (republic, central Europe) : [Hungarian *Magyarország*; German *Ungarn*] (The German name became historically associated with the monarchy of **Austria-Hungary**.)

Hungerburg *see* Narva-Jõesuu

Huntersville *see* North Little Rock

Huntington Beach (city, California, southwestern United States) : 1901–1904 *Pacific City*; to 1901 *Shell Beach*

Huntington Park (city, California, southwestern United States) : to 1904 *La Park* (The city is a residential suburb of Los Angeles.)

Huntly (town, northern New Zealand) : Maori *Rahuipukeko*

Huntsville (city, Alabama, south central United States) : to 1811 *Twickenham*

Hurbanovo (town, southern Slovakia) : to 1948 *Stará Ďala*; to 1918, 1939–1945 Hungarian *Ógyalla* (Both of the earlier names mean "Old Ďala.")

Hurd Island *see* Arorae

Huron *see* Point Edward

Husiatyn *see* Husyatyn

Hüsnümansur *see* Adıyaman

Hustopeče (town, southeastern Czech Republic) : to 1918, 1938–1945 German *Auspitz*

Husyatyn (town, western Ukraine) : (Russian *Gusyatin*); to 1939 Polish *Husiatyn*

Huszt *see* Khust

Hutchings *see* Glenview

Hutt (river, central New Zealand) : Maori *Heretaunga*

Huy (town, eastern Belgium) : Flemish *Hoei*

Hvar (town, southern Croatia) : to 1918 Italian *Lesina* (The town is on the island of the same name, known to the ancient Greeks as *Pharos*.)

¹Hvardiys'ke (town, southern Ukraine) : (Russian *Gvardeyskoye*); to 1944 *Sarabuz*

²Hvardiys'ke (village, western Ukraine) : (Russian *Gvardeyskoye*); to 1946 *Felshtin*

Hvardiys'ke *see* Chornomors'ke

Hviezdoslavov (village, southwestern Slovakia) : to 1918, 1938–1945 Hungarian *Uszor*

Hwaining *see* Anqing

Hwange (town, western Zimbabwe) : to 1982 *Wankie*

Hwang Hai *see* Yellow Sea

Hwang Ho *see* Huang Ho

Hwlffordd *see* Haverfordwest

H.Ya. Syedova, imeny *see* Syedove

Hydaspes *see* Jhelum

Hydruntum *see* Otranto

Hyrcania *see* Gorgān

Hyrcanum Mare *see* Caspian Sea

Ialoveni (town, central Moldova) : (Russian *Yaloven'*); formerly Russian *Kutuzov*

Iaşi (city, northeastern Romania) : formerly German *Jassy* (The town received its German name when it became a customs post in the late 14th or early 15th century.)

Ibaiti (city, southern Brazil) : to 1944 *Barra Bonita*

Ibatuba *see* Soledade de Minas

Iberia *see* (1) Georgia; (2) Spain

Iberus *see* Ebro

Iberville (town, Quebec, southeastern Canada) : to 1854 *Christieville*

Ibiapinópolis *see* Soledade

Ibiraçu (town, southeastern Brazil) : to 1944 Portuguese *Pau Gigante*

Ibirama (town, southeastern Brazil) : to 1944 Portuguese *Hamônia*

Ibirarema (town, southeastern Brazil) : to 1944 Portuguese *Pau d'Alho*

Ibiúna (city, southeastern Brazil) : to 1944 Portuguese *Una*

Iboti *see* Neves Paulista

İbrail *see* Brăila

Içana (town, northwestern Brazil) : to 1944 Portuguese *São Felipe*

Icaros *see* Faylakah

Icaturama *see* Santa Rosa do Viterbo

Iceland (island republic, North Atlantic) : [Icelandic *Ísland*]

Ichki-Grammatikovo *see* Sovyets'kyy

Iconium *see* Konya

Icosium *see* Algiers

Idaho City (village, Idaho, northwestern United States) : originally *Bannack City*

Idaho Falls (city, Idaho, northwestern United States) : to 1890 *Eagle Rock*

Idalion *see* ²Dali

Idalium *see* ²Dali

Idi Amin Dada, Lake *see* Edward, Lake

Idria *see* Idria

Idrija (town, western Slovenia) : 1919–1947 Italian *Idria*

Ieper *see* Ypres

Iesolo (town, northern Italy) : to *c*.1930 *Cavazuccherina*

Iferten *see* Yverdon

Igabrum *see* Cabra

Iglau *see* Jihlava

Igló *see* Spišská Nová Ves

Igluligaarjuk *see* Chesterfield Inlet

Iguaçu *see* (1) Itaetê; (2) Laranjeiras do Sul

Iguaratinga *see* São Francisco do Maranhão

Iguatama (town, southeastern Brazil) : to 1944 Portuguese *Pôrto Real*

Igumen *see* Chyerven'

Iguvium *see* Gubbio

İhtiman *see* Ikhtiman

IJsselmeer (lake, northwestern Netherlands) : formerly *Zuider Zee*; Roman *Flevo Lacus*

Ikaahuk *see* Sachs Harbour

Ikaluktutiak *see* Cambridge Bay

Ikhtiman (town, west central Bulgaria) : to 1878 Turkish *İhtiman*

Ikongo (town, southeastern Madagascar) : formerly French *Fort-Carnot*

Ikpiarjuk *see* Arctic Bay

Ikramovo *see* Juma

Ilabaya *see* Guachalla

Ilava (town, western Slovakia) : to 1918 Hungarian *Illava*

Iława (town, northern Poland) : to 1945 German *Deutsch-Eylau*

Ilchester (village, southern England) : Roman *Lindinis*

Ilebo (town, southwestern Democratic Republic of the Congo) : to 1972 French *Port-Francqui*

Île de France *see* Mauritius

Ilek (village, southwestern Russia) : to 1914 *Iletsky Gorodok*

Ilerda *see* Lérida

Île Royale *see* Cape Breton Island

Île St.-Jean *see* Prince Edward Island

Ilet *see* Krasnogorsky

Iletsk *see* Sol'-Iletsk

Iletskaya Zashchita *see* Sol'-Iletsk

Iletsky Gorodok *see* Ilek

Ilhabela (town, southeastern Brazil) : to 1944 Portuguese *Formosa*; originally Portuguese *Villa Bella*

Ili *see* Kapchagay

Il'ich *see* Atakent

Il'ichyovsk *see* Şärur

Ilici *see* Elche

Il'insky (town, eastern Russia) : 1905–1945 Japanese *Kushunnai*

Ilion (town, New York, northeastern United States) : to 1852 *Remington's Corners*; earlier *Morgan's Landing*; originally *German Flats*

Ilion *see* ˈTroy

Ilirska Bistrica (town, southwestern Slovenia) : 1941–1945 German *Windisch-Feistritz*; 1919–1947 Italian *Villa del Nevoso*; to 1918 German *Windisch-Feistritz* (The town was part of Italy over the period 1919 to 1947.)

Ilium *see* ˈTroy

Iliysk *see* Kapchagay

Ilkenau *see* Olkusz

Ilkley (town, northern England) : Roman *Olicana* (The Roman name is popularly associated with the town but may in fact, and in a better form *Olenacum*, have been that of the Roman fort at *Elslack*, some 12 miles to the west. *See also* Wharfe.)

Illava *see* Ilava

Illiberis *see* Elne

Illiers *see* Illiers-Combray

Illiers-Combray (town, north central France) : to 1970 *Illiers* (The addition to the town's name is the fictional name assigned to it by the writer Marcel Proust, who although born elsewhere spent many of his childhood holidays here. He may have based the name on the nearby village of *Combres*, although there is a real *Combray* in northwestern France.)

Illinoistown *see* East St. Louis

Illizi (town, eastern Algeria) : to *c*.1962 French *Fort-de-Polignac*

Illukst *see* Ilūkste

Ilmenau *see* (1) Jordanów; (2) Limanowa

Ilston (village, southern Wales) : Welsh *Llanilltud Gŵyr*

Ilūkste (town, southeastern Latvia) : to 1918 Russian *Illukst*

Ilulissat (town, western Greenland) : to 1985 Danish *Jakobshavn*

Ilva *see* Elba

Iman *see* Dalnerechensk

Imbros *see* Gökçeada

Imbuial *see* Bocaiúva do Sul

imeni (Russian, "named after") : for names starting thus, *see* the next word, as Kirova, imeni

imeny (Ukrainian, "named after") : for names starting thus, *see* the next word, as Sverdlova, imeny

Imperatorskaya Gavan' *see* Sovetskaya Gavan'

Imperia (province, northwestern Italy) : to 1923 *Porto Maurizio* (The province is named for its capital, the city of Imperia, formed in 1923 from the union of Porto Maurizio with various villages.)

Imroz *see* Gökçeada

In *see* Smidovich

Inchcape Rock *see* Bell Rock

Indefatigable Island *see* Santa Cruz

India (republic, southern Asia) : [Hindi *Bhārat*] (When India achieved independence in 1947 it was thought that the new republic would adopt its native name, but Prime Minister Nehru demanded that his country retain its long-familiar name.)

Indiana Colony *see* Pasadena

Indian Bridge *see* ˈBridgetown

Indian Head *see* Nashua

Indiaroba (town, northeastern Brazil) : to 1944 Portuguese *Espírito Santo*

Indigreat *see* Portland

Indonesia (republic, southeastern Asia) : alternate *East Indies*; to 1949 *Dutch East Indies* (The alternate name is also more widely applied to India, Indochina, and the Malay Archipelago, of which last Indonesia is the chief constituent part.)

Indrapura Peak *see* Kerinci, Mt.

Indreville *see* Châteauroux

İnebahti *see* Návkatos

Ingá *see* Andirá

Ingichka (town, eastern Uzbekistan) : formerly Russian *Rudnik-Ingichka*

Inian's Ferry *see* New Brunswick

Inis *see* Ennis

Inis Córthaidh *see* Enniscorthy

Inis Díomáin *see* Ennistimon

Inkerman (town, southern Ukraine) : 1976–1991 *Bilokam'yans'k* (Russian *Belokamensk*) (When the village of Inkerman was raised to town status in 1976 its name was retained for the railroad station. The name went down in history as the scene of the 1854 Crimean War battle in which the British and French gained victory over the Russians.)

Inkermann *see* Oued Rhiou

Inland Sea (southwestern Japan) : [Japanese *Seto-naikai*]

Inner Mongolia *see* Mongolia

Innichen *see* San Candido

Innisfail (town, Queensland, northeastern Australia) : to 1911 *Geraldton*

Inniskilling *see* Enniskillen

Innokent'yevskaya *see* ²Lenino

Inowrocław (city, north central Poland) : 1904–1919, 1939–1945 German *Hohensalza*

Insterburg *see* Chernyakhovsk

Insula *see* Lille

Interamna Lirenas *see* Pignataro Interamna

Interamna Nahars *see* Terni

Interamnium *see* Teramo

Interamnium Flavium *see* Ponferrada

Inukjuak (village, Quebec, eastern Canada) : formerly *Port Harrison*

Invercargill (city, southern New Zealand) : to 1857 *Kelly's Point*

Invermein *see* Scone

Inverness *see* Cheboygan

Ioannina (city, northwestern Greece) : to 1913 Turkish *Yanya*

Iolcus *see* Volos

Ionio (village, southeastern Italy) : Roman *Manduria* (The Italian name is now primarily that of the *Ionian* Sea.)

Ipatovo (town, southwestern Russia) : to 1930s *Vinodel'noye*

İpek *see* Peć

Ipiaú (city, eastern Brazil) : to 1944 Portuguese *Rio Novo*

Ipswich (town, Massachusetts, northeastern United States) : to 1634 *Agawam*

Iqaluit (town, Nunavut, northern Canada) : to 1987 *Frobisher Bay*

Iráklion (city, northern Crete, Greece) : conventional *Heraklion*; to 1912 Turkish *Kandiye*; Medieval Italian *Candia*; Roman *Heracleum* (The city is the capital of Crete.)

Iran (republic, southwestern Asia) : to 1935 *Persia*

Irapiranga *see* Itaporanga d'Ajuda

Irbitsky Zavod *see* Krasnogvardeysky

Ireland (republic, western Europe) : 1937–1949 Irish *Éire*; 1922–1937 English *Irish Free State*; Roman *Hibernia* (The Roman name was for the whole island of Ireland, which in 1920 was divided into northern and southern parts, as the present Northern Ireland, part of the UK, and republic of Ireland. The Irish name still has some official use, as in postal addresses, although the Post Office prefers "Republic of Ireland" for this purpose.)

Irian Barat *see* Papua

Irian Jaya *see* Papua

Irian Jaya Barat *see* West Papua

Irish Free State *see* Ireland

Iriston (village, southwestern Russia) : to 1941 *Tulatovo*

Irmine *see* Teplohirs'k

Irmino *see* Teplohirs'k

Irminsky Rudnik *see* Teplohirs'k

Irmins'kyy Rudnyk *see* Teplohirs'k

Iron Works Village *see* East Haven

Iruña *see* Pamplona

Irvington (town, New Jersey, northeastern United States) : to 1852 *Camptown*

Is (town, west central Russia) : to 1933 *Sverdlovsky Priisk*

Isaacson *see* Nogales

Isady *see* Semibratovo

Isayevo-Dedovo *see* ²Oktyabr'skoye

Isca *see* (1) Caerleon; (2) Usk

Isca Dumnoniorum *see* Exeter

Isca Legionum *see* Caerleon

Isca Silurum *see* Caerleon

Ischia (island, southern Italy) : Roman *Aenaria*; ancient Greek *Pithecusae*

Ise (city, southeastern Japan) : to 1956 *Uji-yamada*

Isernia (town, south central Italy) : Roman *Aesernia*

Isfahan *see* Eşfahān

Ishanovo *see* Pioner

iSimangaliso Wetland Park (southeastern South Africa) : to 2007 *Greater St. Lucia Wetland Park* (Many nature reserves in this part of South Africa now have Zulu names. This one, a World Heritage Site of more than 1,000 square miles, was renamed both to cast off its colonial name and to avoid confusion with the Caribbean island of *St. Lucia*.)

Isiro (town, northeastern Democratic Republic of the Congo) : formerly *Paulis*

Isis *see* ¹Thames

İskenderun (city, southern Turkey) : traditional English *Alexandretta*; formerly English *Skanderoon* (The city takes its name from the nearby Roman city of *Alexandria ad Issum*, founded by Alexander the Great, whose own name is preserved in that of **Alexandria**.)

İşkodra *see* **Shkodër**

Iskra (village, south central Bulgaria) : to 1950 *Popovo*; to 1906 Turkish *Karadzhilar*

Isla (Spanish, "island") : for names starting thus, *see* the next word, as **Pinta, Isla**

Isla de la Juventud *see* **Juventud, Isla de la**

Isla de León *see* ²**San Fernando**

Isla de Pinos *see* **Juventud, Isla de la**

Islamabad *see* **Anantnag**

Islam-Terek *see* ³**Kirovs'ke**

Ísland *see* **Iceland**

Island Flats *see* **Kingsport**

Islas Malvinas *see* **Falkland Islands**

Isle Mascareigne *see* **Réunion**

Isle of Lewis (Western Isles, northwestern Scotland) : Gaelic *Eilean Leodhais* (The name *Lewis* is also applied to the larger, northern part of the island, as distinct from *Harris*, the smaller, southern part, joined to it by an isthmus at **Tarbert**.)

Isle of Pines *see* **Juventud, Isla de la**

Isle of Thanet *see* **Thanet, Isle of**

Isle of Wight *see* **Wight, Isle of**

Isle of Youth *see* **Juventud, Isla de la**

İslimie *see* **Sliven**

Ismail *see* **Izmayil**

Ismeli *see* ⁴**Oktyabr'skoye**

Ismoili Somoni, Peak (northeastern Tajikistan) : 1952–1998 *Communism Peak*; 1932–1952 *Stalin Peak*; 1928–1932 *Mt. Garmo*

Isola Farnese (village, western Italy) : Roman *Veii*

Ispahan *see* **Eşfahān**

Isparta (city, western Turkey) : formerly *Hamıdabad*

Isperikh (town, northeastern Bulgaria) : to 1934 Turkish *Kemanlar*

Ispica (town, southern Italy) : to 1935 *Spaccaforno*

Ispisar *see* **Ghafurov**

Israel (republic, southwestern Asia) : [Hebrew *Yisra'el*; Arabic *Isrā'īl*] (The present republic adopted the ancient biblical name in 1948, when it was established in the former British mandate of **Palestine**. A possible new name *Zion* was considered at the time, as an alternate name for the biblical land.)

Isrā'īl *see* **Israel**

Issyk-Kul' *see* **Balykchy**

Istanbul (city, northwestern Turkey) : [Turkish *İstanbul*]; alternate English literary *Stamboul*; 330–1930 *Constantinople*; to 330 ancient Greek *Byzantium* (The city was chosen by Constantine the Great as the capital of his Byzantine Empire and retained his name for 1600 years.)

İstanbul *see* **Istanbul**

İştip *see* **Štip**

Istra (town, western Russia) : to 1930 *Voskresensk*

İstrumca *see* **Strumica**

Isurium Brigantum *see* **Aldborough**

Itabaiana (city, northeastern Brazil) : 1944–1948 *Tabaiana*

Itabira (city, southeastern Brazil) : 1944–1948 Portuguese *Presidente Vargas*

Itaetê (town, eastern Brazil) : to 1944 *Iguaçu*

Itaguatins (town, north central Brazil) : to 1944 Portuguese *Santo Antônio da Cachoeira*

Itajahy do Sul *see* **Rio do Sul**

Italia *see* **Italy**

Italica *see* **Santiponce**

Italy (republic, southern Europe) : [Italian *Italia*]

Itamorotinga *see* **Serra Branca**

Itapagé (city, northeastern Brazil) : to 1944 Portuguese *São Francisco*

Itaparica *see* **Petrolândia**

Itapecerica *see* **Itapecerica da Serra**

Itapecerica da Serra (city, southeastern Brazil) : to 1944 *Itapecerica*

Itapetininga (city, southeastern Brazil) : formerly *Nossa Senhora dos Prazeres de Itapetininga*

Itapira *see* **Ubaitaba**

Itaporanga (town, northeastern Brazil) : to 1939, 1944–1948 Portuguese *Misericórdia*

Itaporanga *see* **Itaporanga d'Ajuda**

Itaporanga d'Ajuda (town, northeastern Brazil) : 1944–1948 *Irapiranga*; to 1944 *Itaporanga*

Itapúa *see* **Encarnación**

Itatiaia (town, southeastern Brazil) : to 1943 Portuguese *Campo Belo*

Itatupá (town, northern Brazil) : to 1943 Portuguese *Sacramento*

Itebej (village, northern Serbia) : to 1947 *Srpski Itebej*

Ittoqqortoormiit (village, eastern Greenland) : formerly Danish *Scoresbysund*

Ituberá (town, eastern Brazil) : to 1944 Portuguese *Santarém*

Itumbiara (city, east central Brazil) : to 1944 Portuguese *Santa Rita do Paranaíba*

Iúna (town, southeastern Brazil) : to 1944 Portuguese *Rio Pardo*

Ivanava (town, southwestern Belarus) : (Russian *Ivanovo*); to 1945 *Yanaw* (Russian *Yanov*)

Ivančice (town, southern Czech Republic) : to 1918, 1939–1945 German *Eibenschitz*

Ivangorod *see* **Dęblin**

Ivangrad *see* **Berane**

Ivanishchi (town, western Russia) : early 1920s–1942 *Ukrepleniye Kommunizma*

Ivanivka (town, southern Ukraine) : (Russian *Ivanovka*); 1858–1946 *Yanivka* (Russian *Yanovka*); to 1858 *Malobaranivka* (Russian *Malobaranovka*)

Ivano-Frankivs'k (city, western Ukraine) : (Russian *Ivano-Frankovsk*); 1945–1962 Ukrainian *Stanislav*; 1941–1945 German *Stanislau*; 1939–1941 Ukrainian *Stanislav*; 1919–1939 Polish *Stanisławów*; 1772–1919 German *Stanislau*; 1662–1772 Polish *Stanisławów*; to 1662 Ukrainian *Stanislaviv*

Ivano-Frankove (town, western Ukraine) : (Russian *Ivano-Frankovo*); to 1945 *Yaniv* (Russian *Yanov*)

Ivano-Frankovo *see* **Ivano-Frankove**

Ivano-Frankovsk *see* **Ivano-Frankivs'k**

Ivanopil' (town, west central Ukraine) : (Russian *Ivanopol'*); to 1946 *Yanushpil'* (Russian *Yanushpol'*)

Ivanopol' *see* **Ivanopil'**

Ivanovka *see* **Ivanivka**

Ivanovo (city, western Russia) : 1871–1932 *Ivanovo-Voznesensk* (The former name arose when the original village of Ivanovo merged with neighboring Voznesenskaya.)

Ivanovo *see* **Ivanava**

Ivanovo-Voznesensk *see* **Ivanovo**

Ivanovskoye *see* **Smychka**

Ivanski (village, eastern Bulgaria) : 1878–1950 *Zlokuchen*; to 1878 Turkish *Köprüköy*

Ivanteyevka (city, western Russia) : 1928–1938 *Ivanteyevsky*

Ivanteyevsky *see* **Ivanteyevka**

Ivashchenkovo *see* **Chapayevsk**

Ivaylovgrad (town, southeastern Bulgaria) : to 1934 Turkish *Ortaköy*

Ivory Coast (republic, western Africa) : alternate French *Côte d'Ivoire* (The French name was declared the official protocol name in 1986.)

Ivoy *see* **Carignan**

Ivrea (town, northwestern Italy) : Roman *Eporedia*

Ixelles (town, central Belgium) : Flemish *Elsene* (The town is now a suburb of Brussels.)

Izhevsk (city, western Russia) : 1984–1987 *Ustinov*; to 1917 *Izhevsky Zavod*

Izhevsky Zavod *see* **Izhevsk**

Izhma *see* **Sosnogorsk**

Izluchistaya *see* ³**Zhovtneve**

Izmail *see* **Izmayil**

Izmayil (city, southwestern Ukraine) : (Russian *Izmail*); 1856–1878, 1919–1940 Romanian *Ismail*

İzmir (city, western Turkey) : ancient Greek and biblical *Smyrna*

İzmit (city, northwestern Turkey) : ancient Greek *Nicomedia*; earlier *Astacus*

İznik (village, northwestern Turkey) : ancient Greek *Nicaea* (The Greek name is best known as that of a 13th-century empire and its capital. The Christian creed known as the *Nicene* Creed is based on the results of the ecumenical council held in the town in A.D. 325. A second council was held in 767.)

Izobil'no-Tishchenskoye *see* **Izobil'ny**

Izobil'noye *see* **Izobil'ny**

Izobil'ny (city, southwestern Russia) : mid–1930s–1965 *Izobil'noye*; to mid–1930s *Izobil'no-Tishchenskoye*

İzvornik *see* **Zvornik**

Izyaslavl' *see* **Zaslawye**

Jääski *see* **Lesogorsky**

Jabal ash-Shaykh *see* **Hermon, Mt.**

Jabalpur (city, central India) : formerly *Jubbulpore*

Jablonec nad Nisou (city, northern Czech Republic) : to 1918, 1938–1945 German *Gablonz an der Neisse*

Jablonka *see* **Jabłonka**

Jabłonka (town, southern Poland) : 1939–1945 Slovakian *Jablonka*

Jablonné v Podještědí (town, central Czech Republic) : to 1918, 1938–1945 German *Deutsch-Gabel*

Jablunkau *see* **Jablunkov**

Jablunkov (town, eastern Czech Republic) : to 1918, 1938–1945 German *Jablunkau*

Jaboatão *see* **Japoatã**

Jacarézinho *see* **Ourinhos**

Jáchymov (town, northwestern Czech Republic) : to 1918, 1938–1945 German *Sankt Joachimsthal* (The German name had the adjectival form *Joachimsthaler*, the latter half of which gave the English word *dollar*, from the coins minted here.)

¹**Jackson** (city, Michigan, north central United States) : to 1833 *Jacksonopolis*; originally *Jacksonburgh*

²**Jackson** (city, Mississippi, southern United States) : to 1822 *Le Fleur's Bluff*

³**Jackson** (city, Tennessee, east central United States) : to 1822 *Alexandria*

Jacksonburgh *see* ¹**Jackson**

Jacksonopolis *see* ¹**Jackson**

¹**Jacksonville** (city, Florida, southeastern United States) : to 1822 *Cowford*

²**Jacksonville** (city, North Carolina, eastern United States) : to 1842 *Onslow Courthouse*; originally *Wantland's Ferry*

Jacksonville *see* **Old Hickory**

Jacobshagen *see* **Dobrzany**

Jacob's Well see ¹Marion
Jacuí see Sobradinho
Jadera see Zadar
Jadotville see Likasi
Jaén (city, southern Spain) : Roman *Aurinx*
Jaffa (city, western Israel) : [Hebrew *Yafo*]; biblical *Joppa* (In 1950 the city was incorporated into Tel Aviv to become *Tel Aviv-Yafo*.)
Jägerndorf see Krnov
Jagniątków (village, southwestern Poland) : to 1945 German *Agnetendorf*
Jagodina (city, south central Serbia) : 1946–1992 *Svetozarevo*
Jaguari see Jaguariúna
Jaguariúna (town, southeastern Brazil) : to 1944 *Jaguari*
Jaguaruana (town, southeastern Brazil) : to 1944 Portuguese *União*
Jakarta (city, southwestern Indonesia) : to 1949 Dutch *Batavia*
Jakobshavn see Ilulissat
Jakobstad see Pietarsaari
Jakobstadt see Yēkabpils
Jamaica Square see South Floral Park
James Island see ²San Salvador
Jangy-Jol (village, western Kyrgyzstan) : to 1942 *Chong-Ak-Dzhol*
Janichen see Svoboda
Janjanbureh (town, central Gambia) : to 1995 *Georgetown*
Jan Kempdorp (town, central South Africa) : to 1953 *Andalusia*
Janské Lázně (village, northern Czech Republic) : to 1918, 1939–1945 German *Johannisbad*
Japan (island state, western Pacific) : [Japanese *Nihon*]
Japoatã (town, northeastern Brazil) : to 1944 *Jaboatão*
Jaraguá see Jaraguá do Sul
Jaraguá do Sul (city, southern Brazil) : to 1944 *Jaraguá*
Jarboesville see Lexington Park
Jarocin (town, western Poland) : 1793–1807, 1815–1919, 1939–1945 German *Jarotschin*
Jaroměř (town, north central Czech Republic) : to 1918, 1939–1945 German *Jermer*
Jaroslau see Jarosław
Jarosław (city, southeastern Poland) : 1772–1919, 1939–1944 German *Jaroslau*
Jarotschin see Jarocin
Jaryczów Nowy see Novyy Yarychiv
Jaša Tomić (town, northeastern Serbia) : to 1918 Hungarian *Modos*
Jasień (town, western Poland) : to 1945 German *Gassen*
Jasiňa see Yasinya

Jasło (town, southeastern Poland) : 1940–1945 German *Jessel*
Jassy see Iaşi
Jastrow see Jastrowie
Jastrowie (town, northwestern Poland) : to 1945 German *Jastrow*
Jastarnia (village, northern Poland) : 1772–1919, 1939–1945 German *Heisternest*
Jastrzębie Zdrój (town, southwestern Poland) : to 1945 German *Bad Königsdorf*
Jatobá see Petrolândia
Jauer see Jawor
Jaungulbene see Gulbene
Jaunjelgava (town, south central Latvia) : to 1918 German *Friedrichstadt* (The town, with name meaning "New Jelgava," lies 50 miles east of Jelgava.)
Jaunlatgale see Pytalovo
Javorina (village, northern Slovakia) : 1938–1939 Polish *Jaworzyna*
Jawor (town, southwestern Poland) : to 1945 German *Jauer*
Jaworów see Yavoriv
Jaworzina Śląska (town, southwestern Poland) : to 1945 German *Königszelt*
Jaworzyna see Javorina
Jaxartes see Syrdar'ya
Jaya, Mt. (eastern Indonesia) : formerly *Mt. Sukarno*; earlier *Mt. Carstensz*
Jayapura (city, northeastern Indonesia) : 1963–1969 *Sukarnapura*; earlier Dutch *Hollandia*
Jayhun see Amu Darya
Jędrzejów (town, south central Poland) : to 1915 Russian *Andreyev*
Jefferson see (1) Martins Ferry; (2) Watkins Glen
Jehol see Chengde
Jēkabpils (town, south central Latvia) : (Russian *Yekabpils*); to 1918 German *Jakobstadt*
Jelenia Góra (city, southwestern Poland) : to 1945 German *Hirschberg*
Jelgava (city, central Latvia) : (Russian *Yelgava*); 1941–1944 German *Mitau*; to 1917 Russian *Mitava*
Jelly's Corner see ¹Shelburne
Jengish Chokusu see Pobeda Peak
Jennersdorf (town, eastern Austria) : to 1918 Hungarian *Gyanafalva*
Jerez de Badajoz see Jerez de los Caballeros
Jerez de los Caballeros (town, western Spain) : originally *Jerez de Badajoz*
Jericho (town, eastern West Bank) : [Arabic *Arīḥā*]; originally *Tell es Sultan*
Jermer see Jaroměř
Jernigan see Orlando

Jersey (island, Channel Islands, southern United Kingdom) : Roman *Caesarea* (The Roman name has also been assigned to the much smaller island of *Sark*, north of Jersey.)

Jersey City (city, New Jersey, northeastern United States) : to 1820 *Paulus Hook*

Jersey Homesteads *see* ¹Roosevelt

Jerusalem (city, central Israel) : [Hebrew *Yerushalayim*; Arabic *Al Quds*]; alternate biblical *Salem* or *Zion*; ancient Greek and Latin *Hierosolyma* (Jerusalem was refounded in the 2d century A.D. by the Roman emperor Hadrian under the name *Aelia Capitolina*. *See also* Palestine.)

Jesenice (town, northwestern Slovenia) : to 1918, 1941–1945 German *Assling*

Jeseník (town, northeastern Czech Republic) : formerly *Frývaldov*; to 1918, 1938–1945 German *Freiwaldau*

Jesenské (town, southern Slovakia) : to 1918, 1938–1945 Hungarian *Feled*

Jesi (town, east central Italy) : Roman *Aesis*

Jessel *see* Jasło

Jesselton *see* Kota Kinabalu

Jewie *see* Vievis

Jeziorany (town, northeastern Poland) : to 1945 German *Seeburg*

Jeżów (town, central Poland) : to 1945 German *Grunau*

Jezupol *see* ¹Zhovten'

Jhelum (river, northern India/northeastern Pakistan) : ancient Greek *Hydaspes*

Ji'an (city, southeastern China) : to 1914 *Luling*

Jiangning *see* Nanjing

Jičín (town, northern Czech Republic) : to 1918, 1939–1945 German *Gitschin*

Jihlava (city, western Czech Republic) : to 1918, 1939–1945 German *Iglau*

Jilemnice (town, northern Czech Republic) : to 1918, 1939–1945 German *Starkenbach*

Jílové (town, northern Czech Republic) : to 1918, 1939–1945 German *Eulau*

Jimbolia (town, western Romania) : to 1918 Hungarian *Zsombolya*; to 1867 German *Hatzfeld*

Jim Thorpe (town, Pennsylvania, northeastern United States) : to 1954 *Mauch Chunk*

Jimtown *see* Miami

Jindřichův Hradec (town, southern Czech Republic) : to 1918, 1939–1945 German *Neuhaus*

Jinmen *see* Quemoy

Jirkov (town, northwestern Czech Republic) : to 1918, 1939–1945 German *Görkau*

Joaçaba (city, southern Brazil) : 1939–1943 *Cruzeiro*; c.1928–1938 *Cruzeiro do Sul*; earlier *Limeira*

João de Almeida *see* Chibia

João Pessoa (city, northeastern Brazil) : to 1930 *Paraíba*; 17th century *Frederikstad*; originally *Filipea de Nossa Senhora das Neves*

João Pessoa *see* (1) Mimoso do Sul; (2) Pôrto

Joaquín V. González (town, northwestern Argentina) : formerly *Kilómetro 1082*

Jodoigne (town, east central Belgium) : Flemish *Geldenaken*

Johannes *see* Sovetsky

Johannisbad *see* Janské Lázně

Johannisburg *see* Pisz

Johnnycake *see* Catonsville

Johnson City (town, Tennessee, eastern United States) : 1859–1861 *Haynesville*; to 1859 *Johnson's Depot*

Johnson's Depot *see* Johnson City

Johnstown (city, Pennsylvania, northeastern United States) : to 1834 *Conemaugh*

Joigny (town, north central France) : Roman *Joviniacum*

Jomboy (town, eastern Uzbekistan) : to 1977 *Khoshdala*

Joppa *see* Jaffa

Jordan (kingdom, southwestern Asia) : [Arabic *Al Urdunn*]; 1921–1949 *Transjordan*

Jordânia (town, southeastern Brazil) : to 1944 *Palestina*

Jordanów (town, southern Poland) : 1939–1945 German *Ilmenau*

Jórvik *see* ¹York

José Batlle y Ordoñez (town, southeastern Uruguay) : to 1907 *Nico Pérez* (The former name remains in use for the part of the town that extends west into the department of Florida.)

José Bonifácio *see* Erechim

José de Freitas (town, northeastern Brazil) : to 1939 *Livramento*

José Enrique Rodó (town, southwestern Uruguay) : to 1924 *Drable* (The former name is still in use for the town's railroad station.)

Josephinenhütte *see* Szklarska Poręba

Joviniacum *see* Joigny

Juan Lazaze (town, southwestern Uruguay) : to 1909 *Sauce* (The town's port is still sometimes referred to by the former name as *Puerto Sauce* or *Puerto del Sauce*.)

Juàzeiro *see* Juàzeiro do Norte

Juàzeiro do Norte (city, northeastern Brazil) : to 1944 *Juàzeiro*

Jubayl (village, western Lebanon) : ancient Greek *Byblos*; biblical *Gebal* (The historic city exported *papyrus* to Egypt and its Greek name actually gave this word, hence also English *paper* and, via Greek *biblion*, "book," *Bible* and other *biblio-* words, as *bibliography*.)

Jubbulpore *see* **Jabalpur**

Jucás (town, northeastern Brazil) : to 1944 Portuguese *São Mateus*

Judaea (historical region, southern Palestine) : biblical *Judah* (The historical name, of Graeco-Roman origin and alternately spelled *Judea*, is also biblical. In the 2d century A.D. the Roman emperor Hadrian expelled all Jews from the province and renamed it *Syria Palaestina*. *See* **Palestine**.)

Judah *see* **Judaea**

Judea *see* **Judaea**

Juiz de Fora (city, southeastern Brazil) : formerly *Paraibuna*

Julia Joza *see* **Tarifa**

Juliana Top *see* **Mandala, Mt.**

Julianehåb *see* **Qaqortoq**

Julian Way *see* **Via**

Julia Traducta *see* **Tarifa**

Juliobona *see* **Lillebonne**

Juliomagus *see* **Angers**

Juma (town, eastern Uzbekistan) : 1930s *Ikramovo*

Jundiaí (city, southeastern Brazil) : formerly *Vila Formosa de Nossa Senhora do Destêrro de Jundiaí*

Jungbunzlau *see* **Mladá Boleslav**

Jungwoschitz *see* **Mladá Vožice**

Juqueri *see* **Mairiporã**

Juripiranga (town, northeastern Brazil) : to 1944 Portuguese *Serrinha*

Jurupa *see* **Riverside**

Justinianopolis *see* (1) **Kırşehir**; (2) **Sousse**

Justinopolis *see* **Koper**

Jutland (peninsula, continental Denmark/northern Germany) : [Danish *Jylland*; German *Jütland*] (The name is usually applied only to continental Denmark, although the territory actually extends south to the Eider River, which separates Schleswig from Holstein in northern Germany.)

Jütland *see* **Jutland**

Juvavum *see* **Salzburg**

Juventino Rosas (town, central Mexico) : to 1938 *Santa Cruz de Galeana*

Juventud, Isla de la (island, western Cuba) : to 1978 *Isla de Pinos* (The island is also known by the corresponding English former and present names *Isle of Pines* and *Isle of Youth*.)

Južni Brod *see* **Brod**

Jylland *see* **Jutland**

K2 (mountain, northeastern Pakistan) : alternate English *Mt. Godwin Austen*; locally *Dapsang*

Kaaden *see* **Kadaň**

Kaapstad *see* **Cape Town**

Kabalega Falls (northwestern Uganda) : to 1972 *Murchison Falls*

Kabanbay (village, eastern Kazakhstan) : formerly Russian *Andreyevka*

Kaban'ye *see* **Krasnorichens'ke**

Kabwe (city, central Zambia) : to 1965 *Broken Hill*

Kačanik (town, southern Kosovo) : to 1913 Turkish *Orhanie*

Kadamshay *see* ¹**Frunze**

Kadaň (town, northwestern Czech Republic) : to 1918, 1938–1945 German *Kaaden*

Kadıköy (town, northwestern Turkey) : ancient Greek *Chalcedon*

Kadıköy *see* **Dikaia**

Kadiyevka *see* **Stakhanov**

Kadiyivka *see* **Stakhanov**

Kadnitsy *see* **Leninskaya Sloboda**

Kadoma (town, central Zimbabwe) : to 1980 *Gatooma*

Kadŭkoy *see* **Dikaia**

Kaffa *see* **Feodosiya**

Kafiristan *see* **Nuristan**

Kaga Bandoro (town, central Central African Republic) : formerly French *Fort-Crampel*

Kagan *see* **Kogon**

Kaganovich *see* (1) **Novokashirsk**; (2) **Polis'ke**; (3) **Sokuluk**; (4) **Tovarkovsky**

Kaganovichabad *see* **Kolkhozobod**

Kaganovichi Pervyye *see* **Polis'ke**

Kagera (region, northwestern Tanzania) : formerly *Ziwa Magharibi*; formerly alternate *West Lake*

Kagul *see* **Cahul**

Kahlberg *see* **Krynica Morska**

Kaiba-to *see* **Moneron**

Kainda *see* **Kayyngdy**

Kaiser Wilhelm Canal *see* **Kiel Canal**

Kaišiadorys (town, south central Lithuania) : (Russian *Kayshyadoris*); to 1918 Russian *Koshedary*

Kaiyuan (city, southern China) : to 1931 *Amichow*

Käkisalmi *see* **Priozyorsk**

Kakumabetsu *see* **Shelekhovo**

Kalaallit Nunaat *see* **Greenland**

Kalabak *see* **Radomir**

Kalachevsky Rudnik *see* **Lenina, imeny**

Kalachevs'kyy Rudnyk *see* **Lenina, imeny**

Kalamazoo (city, Michigan, north central United States) : to 1836 *Bronson*

Kalata *see* **Kirovgrad**

Kalatinsky Zavod *see* **Kirovgrad**

Kalay-Lyabiob *see* **Tojikobod**

Kalay-Mirzabay *see* **Kalininobod**

Kalay-Valmar *see* Rushon

Kale i-Sultane *see* Çanakkale

Kalemie (city, eastern Democratic Republic of the Congo) : 1915–1966 French *Albertville*

Kalevala (town, northwestern Russia) : to 1963 Finnish *Uhtua* (Russian *Ukhta*)

Kalgan *see* Zhangjiakou

Kalinin (village, southwestern Tajikistan) : formerly Russian *Voroshilovabad*

Kalinin *see* (1) Boldumsaz; (2) Tver'

Kalininabad *see* Kalininobod

Kalinindorf *see* Kalinins'ke

Kaliningrad (city, western Russia) : to 1946 German *Königsberg*

Kaliningrad *see* Korolyov

Kalinino (village, western Russia) : to 1939 *Norusovo*

Kalinino *see* Tashir

Kalininobod (village, southwestern Tajikistan) : (Russian *Kalininabad*); to c.1935 *Kalay-Mirzabay*

Kalininsk (town, southwestern Russia) : to 1962 *Balanda*

Kalininsk *see* (1) Cupcina; (2) Kalinins'k

Kalinins'k (town, eastern Ukraine) : (Russian *Kalininsk*); to c.1935 *Bayrak*

Kalininskaya (village, southwestern Russia) : to c.1960 *Popovichskaya*

Kalinins'ke (town, southern Ukraine) : (Russian *Kalininskoye*); 1927–1944 *Kalinindorf*; to 1927 *Velyka Seydemynukha* (Russian *Bol'shaya Seydemenukha*)

Kalininskoye *see* Kalinins'ke

Kalininsky *see* Korolyov

Kalinovka (village, western Russia) : 1938–1945 German *Aulenbach*; to 1938 German *Aulowönen*

Kalisch *see* Kalisz

Kalisz (city, west central Poland) : 1793–1807, 1940–1945 German *Kalisch*

Kalisz Pomorski (town, northwestern Poland) : to 1945 German *Kallies*

Kalkandelen *see* Tetovo

Kalkfontein-Sud *see* Karasburg

Kallies *see* Kalisz Pomorski

Kallithea (town, east central Greece) : to 1913 Turkish *Erikdere* (Kallithea is now a suburb of Athens.)

Kalmytsky Bazar *see* Privolzhsky

Kaloyanovo (village, west central Bulgaria) : to 1934 *Seldzhikovo*

Kaluzhskoye (village, western Russia) : to 1945 German *Grünheide*

Kama (town, western Russia) : to 1966 *Butysh*

Kamarlu *see* Artashat

Kamenets *see* Kamyanets

Kamenets-Podol'sky *see* (1) Kam'yanets-Podil's'kyy; (2) [2]Khmel'nyts'kyy

Kamenice nad Lipou (town, southern Czech Republic) : to 1918, 1938–1945 German *Kamnitz an der Linde*

Kamenický Šenov (town, northern Czech Republic) : to 1918, 1939–1945 German *Steinschönau*

Kamenitsa *see* Velingrad

Kamenka *see* (1) Frunzens'kyy; (2) Kam'yanka

Kamenka-Bugskaya *see* Kam'yanka-Buz'ka

Kamenka-Dneprovskaya *see* Kam'yanka-Dniprovs'ka

Kamenka-na-Dnepre *see* Kam'yanka-Dniprovs'ka

Kamenka-Shevchenkovskaya *see* Kam'yanka

Kamen'-Kashirsky *see* Kamin'-Kashyrs'kyy

Kamenka-Strumilovskaya *see* Kam'yanka-Buz'ka

Kamennogorsk (town, northwestern Russia) : to 1948 Finnish *Antrea*

Kamenno-Millerovo *see* [1]Kam'yane

Kamennoye *see* [1,2]Kam'yane

Kamenny Khutor *see* [2]Kam'yane

Kamensk *see* Kamensk-Ural'sky

Kamenskaya *see* Kamensk-Shakhtinsky

Kamenskoye (village, northeastern Russia) : formerly *Ust'-Penzhino*

Kamenskoye *see* Dniprodzerzhyns'k

Kamensk-Shakhtinsky (town, southwestern Russia) : to 1927 *Kamenskaya*

Kamensk-Ural'sky (town, west central Russia) : 1935–1940 *Kamensk*; to 1935 *Kamensky*

Kamensky (town, southwestern Russia) : to 1941 *Grimm* (The town's earlier German name is due to its location in the former Volga German Autonomous Soviet Socialist Republic.)

Kamensky *see* Kamensk-Ural'sky

Kamenz *see* Kamieniec Ząbkowicki

Kamieniec Litewski *see* Kamyanets

Kamieniec Ząbkowicki (town, southwestern Poland) : to 1945 German *Kamenz*

Kamień Koszyrski *see* Kamin'-Kashyrs'kyy

Kamienna Góra (town, southwestern Poland) : to 1945 German *Landeshut*

Kamień Pomorski (town, northwestern Poland) : to 1945 German *Cammin-in-Pommern*

Kamin'-Kashyrs'kyy (town, northwestern Ukraine) : (Russian *Kamen'-Kashirsky*); 1919–1939 Polish *Kamień Koszyrski*

Kaminsky (town, western Russia) : to 1947 *Gor'ky-Pavlovy*

Kamionka Strumiłowa *see* Kam'yanka-Buz'ka

Kami-shikuka *see* Leonidovo

Kamnik (town, northern Slovenia) : to 1918, 1941–1944 German *Stein*

Kamnitz an der Linde *see* **Kamenice nad Lipou**

Kamo *see* **Gavarr**

Kampuchea *see* **Cambodia**

Kamskoye Ust'ye (town, western Russia) : to *c.*1928 *Bogorodsk*

[1]**Kam'yane** (town, eastern Ukraine) : (Russian *Kamennoye*); formerly *Kam'yanno-Millerove* (Russian *Kamenno-Millerovo*)

[2]**Kamy'ane** (town, southeastern Ukraine) : (Russian *Kamennoye*); 1945–1957 *Kam'yanyy Khutir* (Russian *Kamenny Khutor*); to 1945 *Yantsivs'kyy Kar'yer* (Russian *Yantsovsky Kar'yer*)

Kamyanets (town, southwestern Belarus) : (Russian *Kamenets*); 1919–1939 Polish *Kamieniec Litewski*

Kam'yanets-Podil's'kyy (city, southwestern Ukraine) : (Russian *Kamenets-Podol'sky*)

Kam'yanets-Podil's'kyy *see* [2]**Khmel'nyts'kyy**

Kam'yanka (town, central Ukraine) : (Russian *Kamenka*); 1930–1944 *Kam'yanka-Shevchenkivs'ka* (Russian *Kamenka-Shevchenkovskaya*)

Kam'yanka *see* **Frunzens'kyy**

Kam'yanka-Buz'ka (town, western Ukraine) : (Russian *Kamenka-Bugskaya*); to 1939 Polish *Kamionka Strumiłowa* (Russian *Kamenka-Strumilovskaya*)

Kam'yanka-Dniprovs'ka (town, southeastern Ukraine) : (Russian *Kamenka-Dneprovskaya*); formerly *Kam'yanka-na-Dnipri* (Russian *Kamenka-na-Dnepre*); to 1920 *Mala Znam'yanka* (Russian *Malaya Znamenka*)

Kam'yanka-na-Dnipri *see* **Kam'yanka-Dniprovs'ka**

Kam'yanka-Shevchenkivs'ka *see* **Kam'yanka**

Kam'yanno-Millerove *see* [1]**Kam'yane**

Kamyans'ke *see* **Dniprodzerzhyns'k**

Kam'yanyy Khutir *see* [2]**Kam'yane**

Kananga (city, south central Democratic Republic of the Congo) : to 1972 *Luluabourg*

Kanash (city, western Russia) : to 1920 *Shikhrany*

Kandahar (city, south central Afghanistan) : Roman *Alexandria Arachosiorum* (The city was founded by Alexander the Great, whose name is preserved in that of **Alexandria**.)

Kandiye *see* **Iráklion**

Kandyagash (town, west central Kazakhstan) : formerly Russian *Oktyabr'sk*

Kangding (city, central China) : to 1913 *Tatsienlu*

Kangikajik *see* **Brewster, Cape**

Kangiqcliniq *see* **Rankin Inlet**

Kangiqsualujjuaq (village, Quebec, eastern Canada) : formerly *Port-Nouveau-Québec*

Kangiqsujuaq (village, Quebec, eastern Canada) : formerly *Wakeham*

Kangiqtugaapik *see* **Clyde River**

Kangirsuk (village, Quebec, eastern Canada) : formerly *Payne*

KaNgwane *see* **Swaziland**

Kanjiža (village, northern Serbia) : to 1918, 1941–1944 Hungarian *Magyarkanizsa*

Kanpur (city, northern India) : English traditional *Cawnpore*

Kansas *see* [1]**Kansas City**

[1]**Kansas City** (city, Missouri, central United States) : 1853–1889 *City of Kansas*; 1839–1853 *Town of Kansas*; 1850–1853 *Kansas*; to 1850 *Westport Landing* (The added words distinguished the city from the territory, now state, of *Kansas*.)

[2]**Kansas City** (city, Kansas, central United States) : to 1886 *Wyandotte* (The present city was formed by the amalgamation of eight towns, the earliest of which was Wyandotte.)

Kanth *see* **Kąty Wrocławskie**

Kanukov *see* **Privolzhsky**

Kaolinovo (town, northeastern Bulgaria) : to 1950 *Bozhidar*; earlier *Shumnu Bokhchalar*

Kapchagay (town, southeastern Kazakhstan) : *c.*1969–*c.*1971 *Ili*; to *c.*1969 *Iliysk*

Kapellen (town, northern Belgium) : French *Capellen-lez-Anvers* (The French suffix, meaning "near **Antwerp**," distinguishes the town from **Kapelle-op-den-Bos**.)

Kapelle-op-den-Bos (town, central Belgium) : French *Capelle-au-Bois*

Kap Farvel *see* **Farewell, Cape**

Kapila *see* **Haridwar**

Kapitan Andreevo (village, southeastern Bulgaria) : to 1934 Turkish *Viranteke*

Kaplice (town, southern Czech Republic) : to 1918, 1938–1945 German *Kaplitz*

Kaplitz *see* **Kaplice**

Kapsukas *see* **Marijampolė**

Kapuskasing (town, Ontario, southern Canada) : to 1917 *MacPherson*

Karaağaç *see* [1]**Levski**

Karabagish *see* **Xonobod**

Karabalyk (town, northern Kazakhstan) : formerly Russian *Komsomolets*

Karabunar *see* **Sredets**

Karachayevsk (town, southwestern Russia) : 1944–1957 *Klukhori*; to 1944 *Mikoyan-Shakhar*

Kara-Darya *see* **Payshanba**

Karadzhilar *see* **Iskra**

Karaferya *see* **Véroia**

Karafuto *see* **Sakhalin**

Karakalli *see* **Özalp**

Karakhasan *see* [1]**Aleksandrovo**

Karaklis *see* **Vanadzor**

Karakol (city, eastern Kyrgyzstan) : 1889–1921, 1939–1991 Russian *Przheval'sk*

Karakubbud *see* ¹Komsomol's'ke
Karakubstroy *see* ¹Komsomol's'ke
Karamendy (village, northern Kazakhstan) : formerly Russian *Dokuchayevka*
Karánsebes *see* Caransebeş
Karansky Kamenny Kar'yer *see* Myrne
Karans'kyy Kam'yanyy Kar'yer *see* Myrne
Karasburg (town, southern Namibia) : to 1939 *Kalkfontein-Sud*
Karasubazar *see* Bilohirs'k
Karatova *see* Kratovo
Karaul (village, eastern Kazakhstan) : formerly *Abay*
Karaulkeldy *see* Bayganin
Karayazy *see* Gardabani
Kardam (village, northeastern Bulgaria) : 1913–1940 Romanian *Arman*
Kardeljevo *see* Ploče
Karditsa (town, central Greece) : ancient Greek *Acraephnium*
Karen *see* Kayin
Karenni *see* Kayah
Karfreit *see* Kobarid
Kargalinskoye (village, northwestern Kazakhstan) : formerly *Zhilyanka*
Kargowa (town, western Poland) : to 1945 German *Unruhstadt*
Karhumäki *see* Medvezh'yegorsk
Karkeln *see* Mysovka
Karkonosze *see* Riesengebirge
Karla Libknekhta, imeni (town, western Russia) : to 1930 *Pensky Sakharny Zavod*
Karla Libknekhta, imeni *see* (1) Pokrovs'ke; (2) Shyrokolanivka; (3) Soledar
Karla Libknekhta, imeny *see* (1) Pokrovs'ke; (2) Shyrokolanivka
Karla Marksa, imeni *see* Karlo-Marksove
Karla Marksa, imeny *see* Karlo-Marksove
Karlburg *see* Rusovce
Karl-Marx-Stadt *see* Chemnitz
Karlobag (village, western Croatia) : to 1918 Italian *Carlopago*
Karlo-Libknekhtivs'k *see* Soledar
Karlo-Libknekhtovsk *see* Soledar
Karlo-Marksove (town, eastern Ukraine) : (Russian *Karlo-Marksovo*); 1924–1965 *imeny Karla Marksa* (Russian *imeni Karla Marksa*); to 1924 *Sofiyivs'kyy Rudnyk* (Russian *Sofiyevsky Rudnik*); originally *Sofiyivka* (Russian *Sofiyevka*)
Karlo-Marksovo *see* Karlo-Marksove
Karlovac (city, central Croatia) : to 1867 German *Karlstadt*
Karlovac *see* Banatski Karlovac
Karlovo (town, central Bulgaria) : 1953–1962 *Levskigrad*

Karlovy Vary (city, northwestern Czech Republic) : to 1918, 1938–1945 German *Karlsbad*
Karlowitz *see* Sremski Karlovci
Karlsbad *see* Karlovy Vary
Karlsburg *see* Alba Iulia
Karlstad (city, south central Sweden) : to 1584 *Tingvalla*
Karlstadt *see* Karlovac
Karlstein *see* Karlštejn
Karlštejn (village, west central Czech Republic) : to 1918, 1939–1945 German *Karlstein*
Karnataka (state, southwestern India) : to 1973 *Mysore*
Karnobat (town, eastern Bulgaria) : 1953–1962 *Polyanovgrad*
Kärnten *see* Carinthia
Karpacz (town, southwestern Poland) : to 1945 German *Krummhübel*
Karpathos (island, southeastern Greece) : 1306–1540, 1912–1947 Italian *Scarpanto*
Karpilovka *see* Aktsyabrski
Karpinsk (town, western Russia) : *c.*1935–1941 *Ugol'ny*; originally *Bogoslovsk*
Karpuzlu (village, western Turkey) : ancient Greek *Alinda*
Kārsava (town, eastern Latvia) : to 1917 Russian *Korsovka*
Karthaus *see* Kartuzy
Kartonnaya Fabrika *see* M.I. Kalinina, imeni
Kartsa *see* ¹Oktyabr'skoye
Kartuzy (town, northern Poland) : 1772–1807, 1815–1919, 1939–1945 German *Karthaus*
Karviná (city, eastern Czech Republic) : 1939–1945 German *Karwin*; 1918–1919, 1938–1939 Polish *Karwina*; to 1918 German *Karwin*
Karwin *see* Karviná
Karwina *see* Karviná
Karyagino *see* Füzuli
Kasanga (town, southwestern Tanzania) : formerly German *Bismarckburg*
Kaschau *see* Košice
Kasevo *see* Neftekamsk
Kashgar *see* Kash
Kashi (city, western China) : conventional English *Kashgar*
Kashirinskoye *see* ²Oktyabr'skoye
Kashiwabara *see* Severo-Kuril'sk
Kashkatau (town, southwestern Russia) : 1944–1990 *Sovetskoye*
Kashlaköy *see* Zimnitsa
Käsmark *see* Kežmarok
Kašperské Hory (town, southwestern Czech Republic) : to 1918, 1939–1945 German *Bergreichenstein*
Kaspiysk (town, southwestern Russia) : 1936–1947 *Dvigatel'stroy*

Kaspiysky *see* **Lagan'**

Kassa *see* **Košice**

Kasserine *see* **Al-Qaṣrayn**

Kastav (village, western Croatia) : 1920–1944 Italian *Castua*

Kasteelbrakel *see* **Braine-le-Château**

Kastellorizon (island, southeastern Greece) : alternate Turkish *Megisti*; 1932–1947 Italian *Castelrosso* (The island is claimed by Turkey and its Turkish name is primary on many maps.)

Katanga (province, southeastern Democratic Republic of the Congo) : 1972–1997 *Shaba*; 1947–1972 *Katanga*; 1935–1947 French *Élisabethville*; to 1935 *Katanga* (In 1960 Katanga proclaimed itself a republic in the former Congo but its secession was ended in 1963.)

Kataoka *see* **Boykovo**

Katerynoslav *see* **Dnipropetrovs'k**

Katharinenstadt *see* **Marks**

Kato Achaia (town, western Greece) : ancient Greek *Dyme*

Katoomba (town, New South Wales, southeastern Australia) : originally *The Crushers*

Katowice (city, southern Poland) : 1953–1958 *Stalinogród;* to 1921, 1939–1945 German *Kattowitz*

Katscher *see* **Kietrz**

Kattowitz *see* **Katowice**

Katyk *see* **Shakhtars'k**

Katyshka *see* **Golyshmanovo**

Kąty Wrocławskie (town, southwestern Poland) : to 1945 German *Kanth*

Kaufman Peak *see* **Lenin Peak**

Kaukehmen *see* **Yasnoye**

Kaunas (city, central Lithuania) : 1795–1918 Russian *Kovno* (The Russian name is associated with the 1915 siege by German troops which ended in the capture of the town.)

Kaunchi *see* **Yangiyul**

Kaupangr *see* **Trondheim**

Kavadar *see* **Kavadarci**

Kavadarci (village, north central Macedonia) : 1913–1941 Serbian *Kavadar*

Kavaklı *see* **Topolovgrad**

Kavaklii *see* **Topolovgrad**

Kavala *see* **Kaválla**

Kaválla (city, northeastern Greece) : to 1913 Turkish *Kavala*

Kavkaz *see* **Caucasus**

Kawakami *see* **Sinegorsk**

Kaya (state, eastern Myanmar) : to 1952 *Karenni*

Kaydanovo *see* **Dyarzhynsk**

Kayin (state, eastern Myanmar) : formerly *Karen*

Kaylar *see* **Ptolemaïs**

Kayseri (city, central Turkey) : Roman *Caesarea Cappadociae*; alternate Roman *Caesarea Mazaca*; ancient Greek *Eusebeia*

Kayshyadoris *see* **Kaišiadorys**

Kayyngdy (town, northern Kyrgyzstan) : (Russian *Kainda*); *c.*1945–1957 Russian *Molotovsk*

Kazakhstan *see* **Aksay**

Kazan *see* **Kotel**

Kazgorodok *see* **Korgalzhyn**

Kazi-Magomed *see* **Qazimāmmād**

Kazincbarcika (city, northeastern Hungary) : to 1948 *Sajókazinc*

Kazinka (village, western Russia) : formerly *Novaya Zhizn'*

Kazygurt (village, southern Kazakhstan) : formerly Russian *Leninskoye*

Kechries (village, southeastern Greece) : biblical *Cenchrea*; ancient Greek *Cenchreae* (Paul sailed from this eastern port of ¹**Corinth** on his second missionary journey.)

Kėdainiai (town, central Lithuania) : to 1918 Russian *Keydany*

Kędzierzyn *see* **Kędzierzyn-Koźle**

Kędzierzyn-Koźle (town, southern Poland) : to 1945 German *Heydebreck*; to 1934 *Kędzierzyn*

Keeler's Mills *see* **Norwood**

Keeling Islands *see* **Cocos Islands**

Keflavík Field (airfield, southwestern Iceland) : to 1946 *Meeks Field* (The present international airport evolved from the U.S. Army air base built here in World War II.)

Keg Grove *see* **Bloomington**

Kegulta *see* **Sadovoye**

Kékő *see* **Modrý Kameň**

Kellogg (town, Idaho, northwestern United States) : to 1894 *Milo*

Kellomäki *see* **Komarovo**

Kells (town, northeastern Ireland) : Irish *Ceanannus Mór* (The English name predominates thanks to the Irish national treasure known as the *Book of Kells*, an illuminated gospel book originally in the monastery here but now in the library of Trinity College, Dublin.)

Kelly's Point *see* **Invercargill**

Kel'tsy *see* **Kielce**

Kelvedon (village, southeastern England) : Roman *Canonium*

Kemanlar *see* **Isperikh**

Kemer (village, northwestern Turkey) : Roman *Parium*; ancient Greek *Parion*

Kemerovo (city, southern Russia) : to 1932 *Shcheglovsk*

Kemin (town, northern Kyrgyzstan) : formerly Russian *Bystrovka*

Kempen *see* **Kępno**

Kempenland (region, northern Belgium) : French *Campine*

Kemper *see* **Quimper**

Kempten (city, southern Germany) : Roman *Cambodunum*

Kenduskeag Plantation *see* **²Bangor**

Kenitra (city, northwestern Morocco) : 1932–1958 French *Port-Lyautey*

Kenmare (town, southwestern Ireland) : Irish *Neidín*

Kennebunkport (town, Maine, northeastern United States) : 1717–1821 *Arundel* (Local author Kenneth Roberts used the town's former name as the title and setting of his 1930 novel about Maine, the first of a series.)

Kennedy, Cape *see* **Canaveral, Cape**

Kenora (town, Ontario, southern Canada) : to 1905 *Rat Portage* (The last two letters of the town's present name preserve the first two of its earlier name.)

Kenosha (city, Wisconsin, north central United States) : to 1850 *Southport*; originally *Pike Creek*

Kensington (village, Prince Edward Island, eastern Canada) : to early 1870s *Barretts Cross*

Kensington *see* **¹Berlin**

¹Kent (county, southeastern England) : Roman *Cantium* (The Roman name applied to the peninsula here, between the Thames estuary and the Strait of Dover.)

²Kent (city, Ohio, north central United States) : to 1867 *Franklin Mills*; originally *Riedsburg*

Kentville (town, Nova Scotia, eastern Canada) : to 1826 *Horton Corner*

Kenya (republic, eastern Africa) : to 1920 *British East Africa*

Kępno (town, southwestern Poland) : 1793–1807, 1815–1919, 1939–1945 German *Kempen*

Kerbi *see* **Poliny Osipenko, imeni**

Kerch (city, southern Ukraine) : ancient Greek *Panticapaeum* (The *Kerch Strait*, connecting the Sea of Azov with the Black Sea, was known to the Romans as the *Bosporus Cimmerius*, as distinct from the *Bosporus Thracius*, connecting the Black Sea with the Sea of Marmara. The name **Bosporus** alone usually refers to the latter.)

Kerensk *see* **Vadinsk**

Kerinci, Mt. (western Indonesia) : to 1963 *Indrapura Peak*

Kerki *see* **Atamyrat**

Kérkira *see* **Corfu**

Kermanshah (city, western Iran) : formerly (and now also alternate) *Bakhtaran*

Kermine *see* **Navoiy**

Kernev-veur *see* **Cornouaille**

Kernow *see* **¹Cornwall**

¹Kerry (county, southwestern Ireland) : Irish *Ciarraí*

²Kerry (village, eastern Wales) : Welsh *Llanfihangel-yng-Ngheri*

Keşan (town, northwestern Turkey) : 1920–1922 modern Greek *Kesani*

Kesani *see* **Keşan**

Keshishkend *see* **Yeghegnadzor**

Kesmárk *see* **Kežmarok**

Kessaria *see* **Caesarea**

Ketchenery (town, southwestern Russia) : formerly *Sovetskoye*

Kętrzyn (city, northern Poland) : to 1945 German *Rastenburg*

Kettering (city, Ohio, north central United States) : to 1952 *Van Buren*

Kettle Creek Village *see* **St. Thomas**

Kęty (town, southern Poland) : 1940–1945 German *Liebenwerde*

Kewanee (town, Illinois, north central United States) : originally *Berriam*

Kexholm *see* **Priozyorsk**

Keydany *see* **Kėdainiai**

Kežmarok (town, northern Slovakia) : to 1918 Hungarian *Kesmárk*; to 1867 German *Käsmark*

Khabnoye *see* **Polis'ke**

Khadki *see* **Aurangabad**

Khadzhi-Dimitrovo (town, northern Bulgaria) : formerly *Saryar*

Khadzhi-Eles *see* **Pŭrvomay**

Khainboaz *see* **Republic Pass**

Khairepolis *see* **Hayrabolu**

Khakassk *see* **Abakan**

Khakkulabad *see* **²Naryn**

Khakurate *see* **Takhtamukay**

Khalkís (city, central Greece) : to 1830 Turkish *Eğribos*

Khal'mer-Sede *see* **Tazovsky**

Khalturin *see* **Orlov**

Khamza *see* **Hamza**

Khamzoren *see* **Bezmer**

Khamzy Khakimzade, imeni *see* **Hamza**

Khanabad *see* **Xonobod**

Khanbalik *see* **Beijing**

Khankendy *see* **Xankändi**

Khanty-Mansiysk (city, central Russia) : to 1940 *Ostyako-Vogul'sk* (Both names are ethnic in origin, from the *Khanty*, formerly the *Ostyak*, and the *Mansi*, formerly the *Vogul*.)

Kharagauli (town, west central Georgia) : 1949–1991 Russian *Ordzhonikidze*

Kharino *see* **Beregovoy**

Kharkiv (city, northeastern Ukraine) : (Russian *Khar'kov*); to 1918 Russian *Khar'kov*

Khar'kov *see* **Kharkiv**

Kharmanli (town, southern Bulgaria) : to 1878 Turkish *Harmanli*

Khaskovo (city, southern Bulgaria) : to 1878 Turkish *Hasköy*

Khatsapetivka *see* **Vuhlehirs'k**

Khatsapetovka *see* **Vuhlehirs'k**

Khavast *see* **Xovos**

Khebda (village, southwestern Russia) : formerly *Sovetskoye*

Kheimarra *see* **Himarë**

Khem-Beldyr *see* **Kyzyl**

Khemis el Khechna (town, northern Algeria) : to *c.*1962 French *Fondouk*

Khemis Miliana (town, northern Algeria) : to *c.*1962 French *Affreville*

Kherson (city, southern Ukraine) : ancient Greek *Chersonesus* (The Greek name, which gave the modern one, properly applied to the **Crimea**, in which the city is located.)

Khibinogorsk *see* ¹**Kirovsk**

Khíos (town, eastern Greece) : to 1812 Turkish *Sakız* (The town lies on the island of the same name.)

Khlebarovo *see* **Tsar Kaloyan**

Khlynov *see* **Vyatka**

Khmel'nitsky *see* ¹,²**Khmel'nyts'kyy**

¹**Khmel'nyts'kyy** (city, west central Ukraine) : (Russian *Khmel'nitsky*); to 1954 *Proskuriv* (Polish *Proskurów*, Russian *Proskurov*); to 1780 *Ploskyriv* (Polish *Ploskirów*; Russian *Ploskirov*)

²**Khmel'nyts'kyy** (administrative region, western Ukraine) : (Russian *Khmel'nitsky*); to 1954 *Kam'yanets-Podil's'kyy* (Russian *Kamenets-Podol'sky*)

Khmer Republic *see* **Cambodia**

Khobda (village, northwestern Kazakhstan) : formerly Russian *Novoalekseyevka*

Khodzhaakhrar *see* **Ulugbek**

Khodzhaarif *see* **Shofirkon**

Khodzhent *see* **Khujand**

Kholm *see* **Chełm**

Kholmsk (town, eastern Russia) : 1905–1945 Japanese *Maoka*

Khoni (town, western Georgia) : 1936–1991 *Tsulukidze*

Khorixas (town, northwestern Namibia) : to 1974 *Welwitschia*

Khorramshahr (city, southwestern Iran) : to 1924 *Mohammerah*

Khortitsa *see* **Verkhnya Khortytsya**

Khortytsya *see* **Verkhnya Khortytsya**

Khoshdala *see* **Jomboy**

Khovrino *see* **Krasnooktyabr'sky**

Khrapunovo *see* **Vorovskogo, imeni**

Khrisoupolis (town, northeastern Greece) : to 1912 Turkish *Sarışaban*

Khrushchov *see* **Svitlovods'k**

Khrushchyov *see* **Svitlovods'k**

Khujand (city, northwestern Tajikistan) : (Russian *Khodzhent*); 1936–1991 *Leninobod* (Russian *Leninabad*); to 1936 Russian *Khodzhent*; ancient Greek *Cyropolis*

Khust (town, western Ukraine) : 1939–1945 Hungarian *Huszt*; 1919–1945 Czech *Chust*; to 1918 Hungarian *Huszt*

Khutir-Mykhaylivs'kyy *see* ¹**Druzhba**

Khutor-Mikhaylovsky *see* ¹**Druzhba**

Khuzestan (region, southwestern Iran) : formerly *Arabestan*; ancient Greek *Susiana* (The name *Arabestan* remains current in Arab countries.)

Kianly *see* **Tarta**

Kibbutz Mahar *see* **Gevaram**

Kibris *see* **Cyprus**

Kidwelly (town, southern Wales) : Welsh *Cydweli*

Kiel Canal (north central Germany) : alternate German *Nord-Ostsee Kanal*; formerly *Kaiser Wilhelm Canal*

Kielce (city, southeastern Poland) : to 1915 Russian *Kel'tsy*

Kietrz (town, southern Poland) : to 1945 German *Katscher*

Kiev (city, north central Ukraine) : [Ukrainian *Kyiv*]; (Russian *Kiyev*) to 1918 Russian *Kiyev*

Kikinda (city, northern Serbia) : to *c.*1947 *Velika Kikinda*; to 1918 Hungarian *Nagykikinda*

Kikládhes *see* **Cyclades**

Kikvidze (town, western Russia) : to 1936 *Preobrazhenskaya*

Kilbourn *see* **Wisconsin Dells**

Kildare (town, east central Ireland) : Irish *Cill Dara*

Kilgetty (village, southwestern Wales) : Welsh *Cilgeti*

Kiliya (town, southwestern Ukraine) : 1919–1940 Romanian *Chilia-Nouă* (Kilya is on the river of the same name, here forming the border with Romania. The Romanian name means "new Kiliya," as against *Chilia-Veche*, "old Kilya," on the Romanian side of the river.)

Kilkee (town, western Ireland) : Irish *Cill Chaoi*

Kilkeel (town, southeastern Northern Ireland) : Irish *Cill Chaoil*

Kilkenny (town, southeastern Ireland) : Irish *Cill Chainnigh*

Kilkis (town, northeastern Greece) : to 1913 Turkish *Kükü*

Killaloe (town, western Ireland) : Irish *Cill Dalua*

Killarney (town, southwestern Ireland) : Irish *Cill Airne*

Killiniq (village, Quebec, northeastern Canada) : formerly *Port Burwell*

Killybegs (town, northwestern Ireland) : Irish *Na Cealla Beaga*

Kilmallock (town, southwestern Ireland) : Irish *Cill Mocheallóg*

Kilómetro 924 *see* **Angaco Norte**

Kilómetro 1082 *see* **Joaquín V. González**

Kilómetro 1172 *see* **Campo Quijano**

Kilrush (town, western Ireland) : Irish *Cill Rois*

Kim (town, northern Tajikistan) : to 1929 Russian *Santo* (The oil-producing town's former name represents a Russian acronym meaning "Central Asian Oil Trading Organization.")

Kimberley (town, British Columbia, southwestern Canada) : to 1896 *Mark Creek Crossing*

Kimch'aek (city, eastern North Korea) : to 1952 *Song jin*

Kimmirut *see* **Lake Harbour**

Kimovsk (city, western Russia) : to 1948 *Mikhaylovka*

Kimpolung *see* **Cîmpulung**

Kincardine (town, Ontario, southeastern Canada) : to 1858 *Penetangore*

Kincraig *see* **Naracoorte**

King Country (region, northwestern New Zealand) : Maori *Rohe Potae*

Kingdom of Serbs, Croats, and Slovenes *see* **Yugoslavia**

King George V National Park *see* **Taman Negara National Park**

Kingisepp (city, western Russia) : to 1922 *Yamburg*

Kingisepp *see* **Kuressaare**

Kingnait *see* **Cape Dorset**

Kingsboro *see* **Gloversville**

Kings Canyon National Park (California, western United States) : to 1940 *General Grant National Park*

King's County *see* **Offaly**

King's Ferry *see* **Queensferry**

King's Lynn (town, eastern England) : to 1537 (and current local) *Lynn*; formerly *Lynn Regis*

King's Mill Station *see* **Kingsport**

Kingsport (city, Tennessee, east central United States) : formerly *King's Port*; earlier *King's Mill Station*; originally *Island Flats* (Other names to 1774 were *Boat Yard* and *Christiansville*.)

King's Port *see* **Kingsport**

¹Kingston (city, New York, northeastern United States) : 1661–1669 *Wiltwyck*; to 1661 *Esopus*

²Kingston (village, Rhode Island, northeastern United States) : to 1885 *Little Rest*

Kingston *see* (1) **Kinston**; (2) **West Lafayette**

Kingston upon Hull *see* **¹Hull**

Kingstown *see* **Dún Laoghaire**

Kingsville *see* **Thetford Mines**

Kingwilliamstown *see* **Ballydesmond**

Kinsale (town, southern Ireland) : Irish *Cionn tSáile*

Kinshasa (city, western Democratic Republic of the Congo) : to 1966 French *Léopoldville*

Kinston (city, North Carolina, eastern United States) : to 1784 *Kingston*

Kintore (village, northeastern Scotland) : Roman *Devona* (The Roman name, especially in the form *Devana*, has also been applied to the city of Aberdeen, 12 miles to the southeast. The name is properly that of the *Don* River, on which both Kintore and Aberdeen stand.)

Királyhelmec *see* **Kráľovský Chlmec**

Kirawsk (town, east central Belarus) : (Russian *Kirovsk*); to c.1940 *Staritsy*

Kırcalı *see* **Kŭrdzhali**

Kirchdrauf *see* **Spišské Podhradie**

Kirchholm *see* **Salaspils**

Kirda *see* **Gulbahor**

Kirghizia *see* **Kyrgyzstan**

Kirgiz-Kulak *see* **Chirchiq**

Kiriath-Arba *see* **Hebron**

Kiribati (island republic, southwestern Pacific) : to 1979 *Gilbert Islands* (The republic takes its name from the islands now in its western part but formerly in the British *Gilbert and Ellice Islands* colony. The latter islands subsequently became the republic of **Tuvalu**.)

Kirillovka *see* **²Shevchenkove**

Kirillovo (village, eastern Russia) : 1905–1945 Japanese *Uryu*

Kiritimati (island, eastern Kiribati) : formerly *Christmas Island* (*Kiritimati* represents a local pronunciation of the original English name.)

Kirkby Thore (village, northwestern England) : Roman *Bravoniacum*

Kırk-Kilise *see* **Kırklareli**

Kırklareli (city, northwestern Turkey) : formerly *Kırk-Kilise*; 1920–1922 modern Greek *Saranta Ekklēsiai*; 1912–1913 Bulgarian *Lozengrad*

Kirksville (town, Missouri, central United States) : originally *Hopkinsville*

Kirmasti *see* **Mustafakemalpaşa**

Kirov (city, western Russia) : to 1936 *Pesochnya*

Kirov *see* **Vyatka**

Kirova, imeni *see* (1) **Bankä**; (2) **Beshariq**; (3) **Kirove**; (4) **²Kirovs'k**

Kirova, imeny *see* (1) **Kirove**; (2) **²Kirovs'k**

Kirovabad *see* (1) **Gäncä**; (2) **Panj**

Kirovakan *see* **Vanadzor**

Kirove (town, eastern Ukraine) : (Russian *Kirovo*); 1938–1965 *imeny Kirova* (Russian *imeny Kirova*); to 1938 *Syevernyy Rudnyk* (Russian *Severny Rudnik*)

Kirove *see* **Kirovohrad**

Kirovgrad (city, western Russia) : 1928–1935 *Kalata*; to 1928 *Kalatinsky Zavod*

Kirovo (village, west central Russia) : to 1939 *Voskresenskoye*

Kirovo *see* (1) **Beshariq**; (2) **Kirove**;(3) **Kirovohrad**

Kirovograd *see* **Kirovohrad**

Kirovohrad (city, south central Ukraine) : (Russian *Kirovograd*); 1934–1939 *Kirove* (Russian *Kirovo*); 1924–1934 *Zinov'yevs'k* (Russian *Zinov'yevsk*); to 1924 *Yelyzavethrad* (Russian *Yelizavetgrad*)

[1]**Kirovsk** (town, northwestern Russia) : to 1934 *Khibinogorsk*

[2]**Kirovsk** (town, western Russia) : to 1953 *Nevdubstroy*

Kirovsk *see* (1) **Babadaykhan**; (2) **Kirawsk**; (3) [1,2]**Kirovs'k**

[1]**Kirovs'k** (city, eastern Ukraine, near Stakhanov) : (Russian *Kirovsk*); to 1944 *Holubivs'kyy Rudnyk* (Russian *Golubovsky Rudnik*)

[2]**Kirovs'k** (town, eastern Ukraine, near Krasnyy Lyman) : (Russian *Kirovsk*); 1941–1965 *imeny Kirova* (Russian *imeni Kirova*); to 1941 *Popivka* (Russian *Popovka*)

[1]**Kirovs'ke** (city, eastern Ukraine, near Yenakiyeve) : (Russian *Kirovskoye*) to 1956 *Nova Khrestivka* (Russian *Novaya Krestovka*)

[2]**Kirovs'ke** (town, eastern Ukraine, near Dnipropetrovs'k) : (Russian *Kirovskoye*); to 1938 *Obukhivka* (Russian *Obukhovka*)

[3]**Kirovs'ke** (town, southern Ukraine) : (Russian *Kirovskoye*); to 1944 *Islam-Terek*

Kirovskoye *see* (1) [1,2,3]**Kirovs'ke**; (2) **Kyzyl-Adyr**

[1]**Kirovsky** (town, southwestern Russia) : to 1934 *Nikitinskiye Promysly*

[2]**Kirovsky** (town, eastern Russia) : to 1939 *Uspenka*

Kirovsky *see* **Balpyk Bi**

Kisangani (city, northwestern Democratic Republic of the Congo) : to 1966 *Stanleyville*; originally *Falls Station*

Kishinyov *see* **Chişinău**

Kishkenekol' (town, northern Kazakhstan) : formerly *Kzyltu*

Kisielice (town, northeastern Poland) : to 1919, 1939–1945 German *Freystadt*

Kismarton *see* **Eisenstadt**

Kisszeben *see* **Sabinov**

Kisumu (town, western Kenya) : formerly *Port Florence*

Kiszucaújhely *see* **Kysucké Nové Mesto**

Kita-kozawa *see* **Tel'novsky**

Kitchener (city, Ontario, southern Canada) : 1824–1916 *Berlin*; earlier *Ebytown*; originally *Sand Hill*

Kitikmeot (region, Northwest Territories, northern Canada) : to 1982 *Central Arctic*

Kitsman' (town, western Ukraine) : 1919–1940 Romanian *Coţman*; to 1918 German *Kotzmann*

Kittery (town, Maine, northeastern United States) : originally *Piscataqua Plantation*

Kivertsi (town, northwestern Ukraine) : (Russian *Kivertsy*); 1919–1939 Polish *Kiwerce*

Kivertsy *see* **Kivertsi**

Kiwerce *see* **Kivertsi**

Kiyev *see* **Kiev**

Kızılağaç *see* **Elkhovo**

Kızılırmak (river, north central Turkey) : ancient Greek *Halys* (The ancient name means "salt river," the modern name "red river.")

Kladovo (village, eastern Serbia) : to 1878 Turkish *Fethülislâm*

Klaipėda (city, eastern Lithuania) : to 1945 German *Memel* (The Lithuanian and German names were both in use over the period 1923–1939. The German name is a corrupt form of that of the *Neman* River, at the mouth of which the city lies.)

Klamath Falls (town, Oregon, northwestern United States) : to 1893 *Linkville*

Klatovy (town, southwestern Czech Republic) : to 1918, 1939–1945 German *Klattau*

Klattau *see* **Klatovy**

Klausberg *see* **Mikulczyce**

Klausenburg *see* **Cluj**

Klazumen (village, southwestern Turkey) : ancient Greek *Clazomenae* (The original Greek city was on the mainland, but was then moved to a nearby island for fear of an attack.)

Kléber *see* **Sidi Ben Yekba**

Klein Boetsap *see* **Reivilo**

Klein-Schlattern *see* **Zlatna**

Kleve (city, western Germany) : formerly English *Cleves* (The English name is historically familiar from Anne of *Cleves*, fourth wife of Henry VIII.)

Klimentina *see* **Trud**

Klisura (town, central Bulgaria) : to 1878 Turkish *Dervent*

Kljajićevo (village, northern Serbia) : to 1948 *Krnjaja*

Kłodnica (town, southern Poland) : to 1945 German *Klodnitz*

Klodnitz *see* **Kłodnica**

Kłodzko (city, southwestern Poland) : to 1945 German *Glatz*

Kluczbork (town, southern Poland) : to 1945 German *Kreuzburg*

Klukhori *see* **Karachayevsk**

Klyuchevsk (town, western Russia) : to 1933
Tyoply Klyuch
Klyuchinsky *see* Krasnomaysky
Knelston (village, southern Wales) : Welsh *Llan-y-Tair-Mair*
Knighton (town, eastern Wales) : Welsh *Trefyclo*
Knights Enham *see* Enham Alamein
Knob Lake *see* Schefferville
Knock (village, western Ireland) : Irish *An Cnoc*
Knox (town, Pennsylvania, northeastern United States) : to 1933 *Edenburg*
Knoxville (city, Tennessee, east central United States) : to 1791 *White's Fort*
Knyaginin *see* Knyaginino
Knyaginino (town, western Russia) : to 1926
Knyaginin
Knyaginya Nadezhda *see* Nova Nadezhda
Knyazheva Polyana *see* Smirnenski
Knyazhevo (town, western Bulgaria) : to 1878
Turkish *Bali Efendi* (The town is now a suburb of Sofia.)
Knyaz Simeonovo *see* Obedinenie
Koartac *see* Quaqtaq
Kobarid (village, northwestern Slovenia) : 1919–1947 Italian *Caporetto*; to 1918 German *Karfreit*
Kobbelbude *see* Svetly
Köben an der Oder *see* Chobienia
København *see* Copenhagen
Koblenz (city, western Germany) : Roman *Confluentes*
Kobryn (city, southwestern Belarus) : 1919–1939
Polish *Kobryń*
Kobryń *see* Kobryn
Koçana *see* Kočani
Kočane *see* Kočani
Kočani (village, east central Macedonia) : 1913–1941 Serbian *Kočane*; to 1913 Turkish *Koçana*
Kočevje (town, southern Slovenia) : to 1918 German *Gottschee*
Kochina *see* Profesor Ishirkovo
Kochubey (town, southwestern Russia) : to *c.*1960 *Chyorny Rynok*
Kochubeyevskoye (village, southwestern Russia) : formerly *Ol'ginskoye*
Kodok (town, southeastern Sudan) : to 1905
Fashoda (The historical name is associated with the 1898 "Fashoda Incident" which brought Britain and France to the brink of war. The Anglo-French entente formed in 1904 prompted the British to change the name to efface the memory of the incident.)
Kofarnihon (city, western Tajikistan) : 1936–1992 *Orjonikidzeobod* (Russian *Ordzhonikidzeabad*); to 1936 *Yangi-Bazar*
Kogon (city, southern Uzbekistan) : (Russian *Kagan*); to *c.*1935 Russian *Novaya Bukhara*

Kohlfurt *see* Węgliniec
Koivisto *see* ²Primorsk
Kokankishlak *see* Paxtaobod
Kokenhausen *see* Koknese
Kokkola (town, western Finland) : formerly Swedish *Gamlakarleby* (The Swedish name means "old *Karleby*," and almost half of the town's inhabitants are Swedish-speaking.)
Koknese (village, south central Latvia) : to 1917 German *Kokenhausen*
Kokopo (town, central Papua New Guinea) : formerly German *Herbertshöhe*
Kolarov (mountain, western Bulgaria) : to 1949
Belmeken
Kolarovgrad *see* Shumen
Kolárovo (town, western Slovakia) : to 1918, 1938–1945 Hungarian *Gúta*
Kolay *see* Azovs'ke
Kolberg *see* Kołobrzeg
Kol'chugino *see* Leninsk-Kuznetsky
Kolin *see* Kolín
Kolín (town, north central Czech Republic) : to 1918, 1939–1945 German *Kolin*
Kolkata (city, northeastern India) : conventional English *Calcutta* (The English name is associated with the Black Hole of Calcutta, the small room in which many English were imprisoned by the nawab of Bengal in 1756, as well as with the Calcutta Cup, awarded from 1878 to the winner of an annual rugby match between England and Scotland.)
Kolkhozabad *see* (1) Kolkhozobod (2) Vose
Kolkhozobod (town, southwestern Tajikistan) : (Russian *Kolkhozabad*); to 1950s Russian *Kaganovichabad*
Kolkhozobod *see* Vose
Kolmar *see* Chodzież
Köln *see* Cologne
Koło (town, central Poland) : 1940–1945 German *Warthbrücken*
Kołobrzeg (city, northwestern Poland) : to 1945 German *Kolberg*
Kolomea *see* Kolomyya
Kołomyja *see* Kolomyya
Kolomyya (city, western Ukraine) : to 1939 Polish *Kołomyja*; earlier German *Kolomea*
Kolosjoki *see* Nikel'
Kolozsvár *see* Cluj
Komárno (city, southwestern Slovakia) : to 1867 German *Komorn* (Komárno, on the north bank of the Danube, is a twin city of **Komárom**, on the south bank.)
Komárom (city, northwestern Hungary) : to 1867 German *Komorn* (Komárom, on the south bank of the Danube, is a twin city of **Komárno**, on the north bank.)

Komarovo (town, western Russia) : to 1948 Finnish *Kellomäki*

Komavangard *see* Sobinka

Komintern *see* (1) Marhanets'; (2) Novo-shakhtinsk

Kominternivs'ke (town, southern Ukraine) : (Russian *Kominternovskoye*); to 1933 *Antonove-Kodyntseve* (Russian *Antono-Kodintsevo*)

Kominternovskoye *see* Kominternivs'ke

Komisarivka (town, eastern Ukraine) : (Russian *Komissarovka*); to 1917 *Holubivka* (Russian *Golubovka*)

Komissarovka *see* Komisarivka

Kommunar (town, southern Russia) : to 1932 *Bogomdarovanny*

Kommunarsk *see* Alchevs'k

Komorn *see* (1) Komárno, (2) Komárom

Komotau *see* Chomutov

Komotiní (town, northeastern Greece) : 1913–1919 Bulgarian *Gyumyurdzhina*; to 1913 Turkish *Gümülcine*

Kompong Som *see* Sihanoukville

Komsomolabad *see* Komsomolobod

Komsomolets *see* Karabalyk

Komsomolobod (village, central Tajikistan) : (Russian *Komsomolabad*); to c.1935 *Pombachi*

Komsomol'sk (village, western Russia) : to 1945 German *Löwenhagen*

[1]Komsomol's'ke (town, eastern Ukraine) : (Russian *Komsomol'skoye*); to 1949 *Karakubbud* (Russian *Karakubstroy*)

[2]Komsomol's'ke (village, west central Ukraine) : (Russian *Komsomol'skoye*); to c.1935 *Makhnivka* (Russian *Makhnovka*)

[1]Komsomol'skoye (village, southwestern Russia) : to 1941 German *Friedenfeld* (The town's earlier German name is due to its location in the former Volga German Autonomous Soviet Socialist Republic.)

[2]Komsomol'skoye (village, western Russia) : to 1939 *Bol'shoy Kosheley*

Komsomol'skoye *see* [1,2]Komsomol's'ke

[1]Komsomol'sky (village, southwestern Russia) : formerly *Krasny Kamyshanik*

[2]Komsomol'sky (village, western Russia) : formerly *Zavodskoy*

Komsomol'sky *see* (1) Chirchiq; (2) Komsomol's'kyy; (3) Yugorsk

Komsomol's'kyy (town, eastern Ukraine) : (Russian *Komsomol'sky*); to 1943 *Tsentrosoyuz*

Komunars'k *see* Alchevs'k

Konakovo (town, western Russia) : to 1930 *Kuznetsovo*

Kondinskoye (town, western Russia) : formerly *Nakhrachi*

Kondinskoye *see* [3]Oktyabr'skoye

Königgratz *see* Hradec Králové

Königinhof an der Elbe *see* Dvůr Králové nad Labem

Königliche Weinberge *see* Královské Vino-hrady

Königsberg *see* (1) Chojna; (2) Kaliningrad

Königshütte *see* Chorzów

Königszelt *see* Jaworzina Śląska

Konitz *see* Chojnice

Konopischt *see* Konopiště

Konopiště (village, central Czech Republic) : to 1918, 1939–1945 German *Konopischt*

Konradshof *see* Skawina

Konstable Hoeck *see* [2]Bayonne

Konstadt *see* Wołczyn

Konstantinograd *see* Krasnohrad

Konstantinovka *see* (1) Kostyantynivka; (2) Yuzhnoukrayins'k

Konstanz (city, southwestern Germany) : traditional English (and still current French) *Constance*; Roman *Constantia* (*see also* Constance, Lake)

Konuma *see* [2]Novoaleksandrovsk

Konya (city, southwestern Turkey) : Roman *Iconium*

Konyrat (town, east central Kazakhstan) : formerly Russian *Kounradsky*

Koper (town, southwestern Slovenia) : 1919–1954 Italian *Capodistria*; Roman *Justinopolis*; earlier Roman *Aegidia* (From 1947 to 1954, when it passed to Yugoslavia, Koper was in Zone B of the Free Territory of Trieste.)

Kopeysk (city, southwestern Russia) : 1928–1933 *Kopi*; to 1928 *Goskopi*; originally *Ugol'nyye Kopi*

Kopi *see* Kopeysk

Kopreinitz *see* Koprivnica

Koprinka (reservoir, central Bulgaria) : to c.1989 *Georgi Dimitrov*

Koprivnica (town, central Croatia) : to 1867 German *Kopreinitz*

Kopřivnice (city, eastern Czech Republic) : formerly German *Nesselsdorf*

Koprivshtitsa (town, west central Bulgaria) : to 1878 Turkish *Avratalan*

Köprü (river, southern Turkey) : ancient Greek *Eurymedon*

Köprü *see* Ćuprija

Köprüköy *see* (1) Grozdyovo; (2) Ivanski

Köprülü *see* Veles

Kopychintsy *see* Kopychyntsi

Kopychyntsi (town, west central Ukraine) : (Russian *Kopychintsy*); to 1939 Polish *Kopyczyńce*

Kopyczyńce *see* Kopychyntsi

Korcë (city, southeastern Albania) : 1919–1921 modern Greek *Korytsa*

Korčula (town, southern Croatia) : 1941–1943 Italian *Curzola*

Korday (town, southeastern Kazakhstan) : formerly *Georgiyevka* (The town, near the border with Kyrgyzstan, should not be confused with the village of *Kurday*, 30 miles to the northeast.)

Korea (country, eastern Asia) : [Korean *Chosŏn* or *Taehan*] (The Korean names belong respectively to the republics of *North Korea* and *South Korea*.)

Korenica *see* Titova Korenica

Korenovsk (city, southwestern Russia) : 1961 *Korenovskaya*

Korenovskaya *see* Korenovsk

Korets' (town, northwestern Ukraine) : 1919–1939 Polish *Korzec*

Korgalzhyn (town, north central Kazakhstan) : formerly Russian *Kurgal'dzhinsky*; to 1937 Russian *Kazgorodok*

Kórinthos *see* ¹Corinth

Körmöcbánya *see* Kremnica

Kornevo (village, western Russia) : to 1945 German *Zinten*

Korobkovo *see* Gubkin

Korolyov (city, western Russia) : 1938–1996 *Kaliningrad*; 1928–1938 *Kalininsky*; earlier *Podlipki* (The city is now a suburb of Moscow. Its former name should not lead to confusion with Kaliningrad, in the western exclave of this name.)

Körömező *see* Yasinya

Koromo *see* Toyota

Korovino *see* Solntsevo

Korpona *see* Krupina

Korsakov (city, eastern Russia) : 1905–1945 Japanese *Otomari*; to 1905 *Korsakovsky*

Korsakovsky *see* Korsakov

Korsovka *see* Kārsava

Korsun' *see* Korsun'-Shevchenkivs'kyy

Korsun'-Shevchenkivs'kyy (city, north central Ukraine) : (Russian *Korsun'-Shevchenkovsky*); to 1944 *Korsun'* (Russian *Korsun'*)

Korsun'-Shevchenkovsky *see* Korsun'-Shevchenkivs'kyy

Kortrijk (city, northwestern Belgium) : French *Courtrai*; Roman *Cortracum* (Although the town is in the Flemish-speaking half of Belgium, English speakers often refer to it by its French name, itself historically associated with the 1302 Battle of the Golden Spurs, in which the Flemish defeated the French.)

Koryakovsky Forpost *see* Pavlodar

Korytsa *see* Korcë

Korzec *see* Korets'

Kosava (town, southwestern Belarus) : (Russian *Kossovo*); 1919–1939 Polish *Kosów*

Koschmin *see* Koźmin

Kościan (town, west central Poland) : 1793–1807, 1815–1919, 1939–1935 German *Kosten*

Kościerzyna (town, northern Poland) : 1772–1919, 1939–1945 German *Berent*

Koshedary *see* Kaišiadorys

Koshu-Kavak *see* Krumovgrad

Košice (city, southeastern Slovakia) : to 1918, 1938–1945 Hungarian *Kassa*; to 1867 German *Kaschau*

Kosiorovo *see* Stanychno-Luhans'ke

Kosiv (town, western Ukraine) : (Russian *Kosov*); 1919–1939 Polish *Kosów*

Köslin *see* Koszalin

Kosmet *see* Kosovo

Kosov *see* Kosiv

Kosovo (republic, southeastern Europe) : 1946–1971 Serbian *Kosovo-Metohija*; alternate former *Kosmet*; Roman *Dardania* (*Kosmet* is a short form of the longer Serbian name.)

Kosovo-Metohija *see* Kosovo

Kosovska Mitrovica (town, north central Kosovo) : formerly *Titova Mitrovica*; to 1913 Turkish *Mitroviça* (The first word of the name distinguishes the town from Sremska Mitrovica in Serbia.)

Kosów *see* Kosiv

Kosseir *see* Quseir

Kossovo *see* Kosava

Kossów *see* Kosava

Kosta-Khetagurovo *see* Nazran'

Kosten *see* Kościan

Köstendil *see* Kyustendil

Kostolac (town, eastern Serbia) : Roman *Viminacium*

Kostopil' (city, northwestern Ukraine) : (Russian *Kostopol'*); 1919–1939 Polish *Kostopol*

Kostopol' *see* Kostopil'

Kostrzyn (town, western Poland) : to 1945 German *Küstrin*

Kostyantynivka (town, eastern Ukraine) : (Russian *Konstantinovka*)

Kostyantynivka *see* Yuzhnoukrayins'k

Kostyantynohrad *see* Krasnohrad

Kosyorove *see* Stanychno-Luhans'ke

Koszalin (city, northwestern Poland) : to 1945 German *Köslin*

Kőszeg (town, western Hungary) : to 1867 German *Güns*

Kotabaru *see* Zhezdy

Kota Kinabalu (city, northeastern Malaysia) : to 1968 *Jesselton*

Kotel (town, east central Bulgaria) : to 1878 Turkish *Kazan*

¹Kotel'nikovo (town, southwestern Russia) : to 1929 *Kotel'nikovskaya*

²**Kotel'nikovo** (village, western Russia) : to 1949 *Salyuzi*

Kotel'nikovskaya *see* ¹**Kotel'nikovo**

Kotor (town, southwestern Montenegro) : 1941–1943 Italian *Cattaro*

Kotovsk (town, western Russia) : 1930–1940 *Krasny Boyevik*

Kotovsk *see* (1) **Hînceşti**; (2) **Kotovs'k**

Kotovs'k (city, southwestern Ukraine) : (Russian *Kotovsk*); to 1935 *Birzula*

Kotovskoye *see* **Hînceşti**

Kotsmann *see* **Kitsman'**

Kotsyubinskoye *see* **Kotsyubyns'ke**

Kotsyubyns'ke (town, north central Ukraine) : (Russian *Kotsyubinskoye*); to 1941 *Berkovets'* (Russian *Berkovets*) (Kotsyubyns'ke is now a suburb of Kiev.)

Kotzenau *see* **Chocianów**

Kounradsky *see* **Konyrat**

Kousséri (city, northern Cameroon) : formerly French *Fort-Foureau*

Kovel' (city, central Ukraine) : 1919–1939 Polish *Kowel*

Kovno *see* **Kaunas**

Kowary (town, southwestern Poland) : formerly *Krzyżatka*; to 1945 German *Schmiedeberg*

Kowel *see* **Kovel'**

Koza *see* **Okinawa**

Kozhikode (city, southwestern India) : dated English *Calicut* (The city was long in British hands, and its English name was probably influenced by *Calcutta*, now **Kolkata**.)

Koźle (town, southern Poland) : to 1945 German *Cosel*

Kozlikha *see* **Sitniki**

Kozlov *see* **Michurinsk**

Kozludzha *see* **Suvorovo**

Koźmin (town, west central Poland) : 1793–1807, 1815–1919, 1939–1945 German *Koschmin*

Kożuchów (town, western Poland) : to 1945 German *Freystadt*

Kozyol *see* **Mykhaylo-Kotsyubyns'ke**

Krainburg *see* **Kranj**

Krakau *see* **Kraków**

Kraków (city, southern Poland) : conventional English *Cracow*; 1795–1818, 1940–1945 German *Krakau*

Kraljevica (town, western Croatia) : to 1867 Italian *Porto Rè*

Kraljevina Serba, Hrvata i Slovenaca *see* **Yugoslavia**

Kraljevo (city, south central Serbia) : 1949–mid–1960s *Rankovićevo*

Kralovan *see* **Kral'ovany**

Kral'ovany (village, northern Slovakia) : to 1918 Hungarian *Kralován*

Kralovice (town, west central Czech Republic) : to 1918, 1939–1945 German *Kralowitz*

Královské Vinohrady (village, west central Czech Republic) : to 1918 German *Königliche Weinberge* (The village was incorporated into Prague in 1919 as district *Praha XII.*)

Kráľovský Chlmec (town, southeastern Slovakia) : to 1918, 1938–1944 Hungarian *Királyhelmec*

Kralowitz *see* **Kralovice**

Kralup an der Moldau *see* **Kralupy nad Vltavou**

Kralupy nad Vltavou (town, north central Czech Republic) : to 1918, 1939–1945 German *Kralup an der Moldau*

Kranj (city, northern Slovenia) : to 1918, 1941–1944 German *Krainburg*; Roman *Carnium*

Kranjska Gora (village, northwestern Slovenia) : to 1918 German *Kronau*

Kranz *see* **Zelenogradsk**

Krapkowice (town, southwestern Poland) : to 1945 German *Krappitz*

Krappitz *see* **Krapkowice**

Kraskino (town, eastern Russia) : formerly *Novokiyevskoye*

Krāslava (town, southeastern Latvia) : to 1918 Russian *Kreslavka*

Kraslice (town, northwestern Czech Republic) : to 1918, 1939–1945 German *Graslitz*

Krasnaya Gora *see* ¹**Krasnogorsk**

Krasnaya Sloboda *see* **Krasnoslobodsk**

Krasni Okny (town, southern Ukraine) : (Russian *Krasnyye Okny*); to 1919 *Okny*

¹**Krasnoarmeysk** (town, western Russia, near Moscow) : 1928–1947 *Krasnoarmeysky*; to 1928 *Voznesenskaya Manufaktura* (The earliest name was that of a textile factory, originally renamed *fabrika imeni Krasnoy Armii i Flota*, "factory named for the Red Army and Navy.")

²**Krasnoarmeysk** (town, western Russia, near Saratov) : 1926–1942 *Bal'tser*; to 1926 *Goly Karamysh* (The name *Bal'tser*, first given by German settlers in the form *Balzer* at the end of the 18th century, existed in parallel with *Goly Karamysh* until 1926, when it became the sole name.)

³**Krasnoarmeysk** (town, southwestern Russia) : to 1920 *Sarepta* (The town, now a suburb of Volgograd, evolved its former name from the biblical name *Zarephath*. See **Tsrifin**.)

Krasnoarmeysk *see* (1) **Krasnoarmiys'k**; (2) **Tayynsha**

Krasnoarmeyskaya *see* **Poltavskaya**

Krasnoarmeyskoye (village, western Russia) : to 1939 *Peredniye Traki*

Krasnoarmeyskoye *see* (1) **Krasnoarmiys'k**; (2) **Urus-Martan**; (3) **Vil'nyans'k**

Krasnoarmeysky *see* [1]**Krasnoarmeysk**

Krasnoarmeysky Rudnik *see* **Dobropillya**

Krasnoarmiys'k (city, eastern Ukraine) : (Russian *Krasnoarmeysk*); 1938–1964 *Krasnoarmiys'ke* (Russian *Krasnoarmeyskoye*); 1934–1938 *Postysheve* (Russian *Postyshevo*); to 1934 *Hryshyne* (Russian *Grishino*)

Krasnoarmiys'ke *see* **Krasnoarmiys'k**

Krasnodar (city, southwestern Russia) : to 1920 *Yekaterinodar*

Krasnodon (city, eastern Ukraine) : to 1938 *Sorokyne* (Russian *Sorokino*)

Krasnogorovka *see* **Krasnohorivka**

[1]**Krasnogorsk** (city, western Russia) : to 1932 *Optikogorsk*; formerly *Krasnaya Gora*; originally *Banki* (The settlement of Krasnaya Gora arose when an optical factory was moved to Banki in 1927. The two were then united as Optikogorsk.)

[2]**Krasnogorsk** (town, eastern Russia) : 1905–1945 Japanese *Chinnai*

[1]**Krasnogorskoye** (village, western Russia) : to 1938 *Baryshnikovo*

[2]**Krasnogorskoye** (village, southern Russia) : formerly *Staraya Barda*

Krasnogorsky (town, western Russia) : to 1938 *Ilet*

Krasnogorsky Rudnik *see* **Krasnohorivka**

Krasnograd *see* **Krasnohrad**

Krasnogrigor'yevka *see* **Chervonohryhorivka**

Krasnogvardeysk *see* (1) **Bulung'ur**; (2) **Gatchina**

[1]**Krasnogvardeyskoye** (town, western Russia) : early 1920s–1960s *Budyonnoye*; to early 1930s *Biryuch*

[2]**Krasnogvardeyskoye** (village, southwestern Russia, near Krasnodar) : formerly *Nikolayevskoye*

[3]**Krasnogvardeyskoye** (village, southwestern Russia, near Stavropol') : formerly *Yevdokimovskoye*

Krasnogvardeyskoye *see* **Krasnohvardiys'ke**

Krasnogvardeysky (town, west central Russia) : to 1938 *Irbitsky Zavod*

Krasnohirs'kyy Rudnyk *see* **Krasnohorivka**

Krasnohorivka (town, eastern Ukraine) : (Russian *Krasnogorovka*); formerly *Krasnohirs'kyy Rudnyk* (Russian *Krasnogorsky Rudnik*)

Krasnohrad (town, northeastern Ukraine) : (Russian *Krasnograd*); to 1922 *Kostyantynohrad* (Russian *Konstantinograd*)

Krasnohvardiys'ke (town, southern Ukraine) : (Russian *Krasnogvardeyskoye*); to 1945 *Kurman-Kemelchi*

Krasnokokshaysk *see* **Yoshkar-Ola**

Krasnokutsk *see* **Aktogay**

Krasnomaysky (town, western Russia) : to 1940 *Klyuchinsky*

Krasnooktyabr'sky (town, western Russia) : to 1928 *Khovrino* (The town is now part of Moscow.)

Krasnooktyabr'sky *see* **Shopokov**

Krasnoostrovsky (village, western Russia) : 1940–1948 *Byorksky* (The previous name is a Russian adjectival form of the former Finnish name *Björko*.)

Krasnopartizansk *see* **Belogorsk**

Krasnorechenskoye *see* **Krasnorichens'ke**

Krasnorichens'ke (town, eastern Ukraine) : (Russian *Krasnorechenskoye*); formerly *Kaban'ye*

Krasnosel'sk *see* **Chambarak**

Krasnoslobodsk (town, southwestern Russia) : to 1955 *Krasnaya Sloboda*

Krasnoturansk (town, southern Russia) : formerly *Abakanskoye*

Krasnotur'insk (town, west central Russia) : to 1944 *Tur'inskiye Rudniki*

Krasnoural'sk (town, western Russia) : 1929–1932 *Uralmedstroy*; to 1929 *Bogomolstroy*

Krasnoural'sky Rudnik *see* **Novoasbest**

Krasnovodsk *see* **Turkmenbashi**

Krasnoyarsk (city, east central Russia) : originally *Krasny Yar*

Krasnoye *see* [2]**Chervone**

Krasnoye Ekho (town, western Russia) : to 1925 *Novogordino*

Krasnoye Selo (town, western Russia) : formerly *Krasny* (The former village was incorporated into Leningrad in 1973.)

Krasnoye Znamya *see* **Rubizhne**

Krasnozavodsk (town, western Russia) : to 1940 *Zagorsky*

Krasnoznamensk (town, western Russian) : 1938–1945 German *Haselberg*; to 1938 German *Lasdehnen*

Krasnoznamenskoye *see* **Yegindykol'**

Krasny *see* (1) **Krasnoye Selo**; (2) **Mozhga**

Krasny Bor (village, western Russia) : formerly *P'yany Bor*

Krasny Boyevik *see* **Kotovsk**

Krasny Kamyshanik *see* [1]**Komsomol'sky**

Krasny Klyuch (town, southwestern Russia) : formerly *Bely Klyuch*

Krasny Liman *see* **Krasnyy Lyman**

Krasny Luch *see* **Krasnyy Luch**

Krasny Mayak (town, western Russia) : to 1925 *Yakunchikov*

Krasny Oktyabr' (village, western Russia, near Kirzhach) : to 1919 *Voznesensky*

Krasny Oktyabr' *see* **Baran**

Krasny Profintern (town, western Russia) : c.1926–1945 *Gruzitsino*; to c.1926 *Ponizovkino*

Krasny Steklovar (town, western Russia) : to 1939 *Kuzhery*

Krasny Sulin (city, southwestern Russia) : to 1926 *Sulin*

Krasny Tekstil'shchik (town, southwestern Russia) : to 1929 *Saratovskaya Manufaktura*

Krasny Ural *see* Uralets

Krasny Yar *see* Krasnoyarsk

Krasnyye Okny *see* Krasni Okny

Krasnyy Luch (city, eastern Ukraine) : (Russian *Krasny Luch*); to 1926 *Kryndachivka* (Russian *Krindachyovka*)

Krasnyy Lyman (city, eastern Ukraine) : (Russian *Krasny Liman*); to 1938 *Lyman* (Russian *Liman*)

Kratovo (village, northern Macedonia) : to 1913 Turkish *Karatova*

Kratske *see* Podchinny

Kravaře (town, eastern Czech Republic) : to 1919, 1938–1945 German *Deutsch-Krawarn*

Kremenets *see* Kremenets'

Kremenets' (city, western Ukraine) : 1919–1939 Polish *Krzemieniec*; to 1918 Russian *Kremenets*

Kremges *see* Svitlovods'k

Kremhes *see* Svitlovods'k

Kremnica (town, central Slovakia) : to 1918 Hungarian *Körmöcbánya*; to 1867 German *Kremnitz*

Kremnitz *see* Kremnica

Kremsier *see* Kroměříž

Krenau *see* Chrzanów

Kreslavka *see* Krāslava

Kressendorf *see* Krzeszowice

Kreuz *see* (1) Križevci; (2) Krzyż

Kreuzberg *see* Slavskoye

Kreuzburg *see* (1) Kluczbork; (2) Krustpils

Kreuzingen *see* Bolshakovo

Krindachyovka *see* Krasny Luch

Krinichansky *see* Chervonogvardiys'ke

Kristiania *see* Oslo

Kristiinankaupunki (town, western Finland) : formerly Swedish *Kristinestad* (The town is generally known by its Swedish name and its inhabitants are largely Swedish-speaking.)

Kristinehamn (town, west central Sweden) : to 1642 *Bro*

Kristinestad *see* Kristiinankaupunki

Kristinopol' *see* Chervonohrad

Kritsim *see* Stamboliyski

Kriva Palanka (village, northern Macedonia) : to 1913 Turkish *Eğripalanka*

Krivaya Kosa *see* Syedove

Krivoy Rog *see* Kryvyy Rih

Križevci (town, central Croatia) : to 1867 German *Kreuz*

Krk (town, northwestern Croatia) : to 1918, 1941–1943 Italian *Veglia* (The town lies on the island of the same name.)

Krkonoše *see* Riesengebirge

Krn (mountain, northwestern Slovenia) : 1919–1947 Italian *Nero*

Krnjaja *see* Kljajićevo

Krnov (town, northeastern Czech Republic) : to 1918, 1938–1939 German *Jägerndorf*

Królewska Huta *see* Chorzów

Kroměříž (town, eastern Czech Republic) : to 1867, 1939–1945 German *Kremsier*

Kronau *see* Kranjska Gora

Kronshlot *see* Kronshtadt

Kronshtadt (town, western Russia) : to 1723 *Kronshlot* (The former name is a Russian transliterated form of Swedish *Kronslott*, "crown castle." The present name represents German *Kronstadt*, "crown city," as formerly for **Braşov**, Romania.)

Kronstadt *see* Braşov

[1]Kropotkin (town, southwestern Russia) : to 1921 *Romanovsky Khutor*

[2]Kropotkin (town, southern Russia) : to 1930 *Tikhono-Zadonsky*

Krosno (town, southeastern Poland) : 1940–1945 German *Crossen*

Krosno Odrzańskie (town, western Poland) : to 1945 German *Crossen*

Krotoschin *see* Krotoszyn

Krotoszyn (town, west central Poland) : 1793–1807, 1815–1919, 1939–1945 German *Krotoschin*

Krško (town, southern Slovenia) : to 1918 German *Gurkfeld*

Kruglyakov *see* [7]Oktyabr'sky

Krujë (town, north central Albania) : to 1912 Turkish *Akhisar*

Krumau an der Moldau *see* Český Krumlov

Krummhübel *see* Karpacz

Krumovgrad (town, southern Bulgaria) : to 1934 Turkish *Koshu-Kavak*

Krumovo (village, south central Bulgaria) : to 1893 Turkish *Pasha Makhala*

Krung Thep *see* Bangkok

Krupina (town, southern Slovakia) : to 1918 Hungarian *Korpona*

Krustpils (town, central Latvia) : to 1918 German *Kreuzburg*

Krylovkskaya (village, southwestern Russia) : formerly *Yekaterinovskaya*

Krym *see* Crimea

Krymsk (town, southwestern Russia) : formerly *Krymskaya*

Krymskaya *see* Krymsk

Kryndachivka *see* Krasnyy Luch

Krynica Morska (village, northern Poland) : to 1945 German *Kahlberg*

Krynychans'kyy *see* Chervonogvardiys'ke
Krystynopil' *see* Chervonohrad
Krystynopol *see* Chervonohrad
Kryva Kosa *see* Syedove
Kryvyy Rih (city, eastern Ukraine) : (Russian *Krivoy Rog*)
Krzemieniec *see* Kremenets'
Krzeszów (town, southeastern Poland) : to 1945 German *Grüssau*
Krzeszowice (town, southern Poland) : 1940–1945 German *Kressendorf*
Krzyż (town, west central Poland) : 1793–1807, 1815–1945 German *Kreuz*
Krzyżatka *see* Kowary
Ksar Chellala (town, northern Algeria) : to c.1962 French *Reibell*
Ksar el Boukhari (town, northern Algeria) : to c.1962 French *Boghari*
Ksar el Kebir (city, northern Morocco) : conventional English *Alcazarquivir* (The English name is a Spanish corruption of the Arabic original.)
Ksar es Souk *see* Er Rachidia
Książ Wielkopolski (town, western Poland) : 1793–1807, 1815–1919, 1939–1945 German *Xions*
Kuala Sepetang (town, western Malaysia) : formerly *Port Weld*
Kubrat (town, northeastern Bulgaria) : to 1878 Turkish *Balbunar*
Kuckerneese *see* Yasnoye
Kuçovë (town, south central Albania) : 1950–1991 *Qyteti Stalin* (Albanian *qytet* means "city," and the former name corresponds to both Romanian *Oraşul Stalin*, now **Braşov**, and Russian *Stalingrad*, now **Volgograd**.)
Kudelka *see* Asbest
Kudinovo *see* Elektrougli
Kudirkos Naumiestis (town, southwestern Lithuania) : to 1918 German *Neustadt-Schirwindt*; earlier *Vladislavovas* (The town lies on the Russian border across the Sheshupe River from **Kutuzovo**, sharing its former German name, with Lithuanian *Naumiestis* corresponding to German *Neustadt*, "new town.")
Kudowa Zdrój (town, southwestern Poland) : to 1945 German *Bad Kudowa*
Kugaaruk (village, Nunavut, northern Canada) : to 1999 *Pelly Bay*
Kugluktuk (village, Nunavut, northern Canada) : to 1999 *Coppermine*
Kuito (town, central Angola) : to 1976 Portuguese *Silva Porto*; earlier *Belmonte*
Kukarka *see* ²Sovetsk
Kukkus *see* Privolzhskoye
Kukshik *see* ²Pervomaysky

Küküş *see* Kilkis
Kulan (village, southern Kazakhstan) : formerly Russian *Lugovoye* (The new name avoids confusion with the town of *Lugovoy*, a few miles to the northeast.)
Kuldiga *see* Kuldīga
Kuldīga (town, western Latvia) : (Russian *Kuldiga*); to 1918 German *Goldingen*
Kuleli-Burgas *see* Pithion
Küleliburgaz *see* Pithion
Kulm *see* (1) Chełmno; (2) Chlumec
Kulmsee *see* Chełmża
Kumanova *see* Kumanovo
Kumanovo (city, northern Macedonia) : to 1913 Turkish *Kumanova*
Kumayri *see* Gyumri
Kunersdorf *see* Kunowice
Kungrad *see* Qunghirot
Kunming (city, southwestern China) : to 1912 *Yunnanfu*
Kunowice (village, western Poland) : to 1945 German *Kunersdorf*
Kuokkala *see* Repino
Kuolayarvi (village, northwestern Russia) : 1937–1940 *Salla* (In 1940 the original Finnish village of Salla was ceded to the USSR and its population resettled in the village of *Kursu*, 30 miles to the southwest, which was then renamed **Salla**.)
Kurakhivdres *see* Kurakhove
Kurakhivdresbud *see* Kurakhove
Kurakhove (town, eastern Ukraine) : (Russian *Kurakhovo*); 1943–1956 *Kurakhivdres*; earlier *Kurakhivdresbud* (Russian *Kurakhovstroy*)
Kurakhovo *see* Kurakhove
Kurakhovstroy *see* Kurakhove
Kŭrdzhali (town, southern Bulgaria) : to 1878, 1885–1913 Turkish *Kırcalı*
Kuressaare (town, western Estonia) : 1952–1988 *Kingisepp*; to 1918 German *Arensburg*
Kurgal'dzhinsky *see* Korgalzhyn
Kurganinsk (town, southwestern Russia) : to 1961 *Kurgannaya stanitsa*
Kurgannaya stanitsa *see* Kurganinsk
Kurganovka (town, southern Russia) : to 1944 *Zaboyshchik* (The town is now a suburb of Beryozovsky.)
Kuril Islands (eastern Russia) : 1875–1945 Japanese *Chishima-retto*
Kuril'sk (town, eastern Russia) : 1905–1945 Japanese *Shana*
Kurman-Kemelchi *see* Krasnohvardiys'ke
Kursu *see* Salla
Kurtbunar *see* Tervel
Kuryk (town, southwestern Kazakhstan) : formerly *Yeraliyev*

Kushnarenkovo (village, western Russia) : to 1930s *Topornino*

Kushunnai *see* **Il'insky**

Kussen *see* **Vesnovo**

Küstenja *see* **Constanţa**

Küstrin *see* **Kostrzyn**

Kus'ye-Aleksandrovsky (town, western Russia) : to 1946 *Kus'ye-Aleksandrovsky Zavod*

Kus'ye-Aleksandrovsky Zavod *see* **Kus'ye-Aleksandrovsky**

Kutelna *see* **Chuchelná**

Kutná Hora (city, central Czech Republic) : to 1918, 1939–1945 German *Kuttenberg*

Kuttenberg *see* **Kutná Hora**

Kutuzov *see* **Ialoveni**

Kutuzovo (village, western Russia) : to 1945 German *Schirwindt* (The former town lies on the Lithuanian border across the Sheshupe River from **Kudirkos-Naumiestis**, sharing its former German name.)

Kuujjuaq (village, Quebec, eastern Canada) : formerly *Fort Chimo*

Kuujjuarapik (village, Quebec, eastern Canada) : alternate Cree *Whapmagoostui*; formerly *Poste-de-la-Baleine*; to 1965 *Great Whale River*

Kuvango (town, south central Angola) : formerly Portuguese *Vila da Ponte*

Kuybyshev *see* (1) **Bolgar**; (2) **Samara**

Kuybysheva, imeni *see* **Rishtan**

[1]**Kuybysheve** (town, southeastern Ukraine) : (Russian *Kuybyshevo*); to 1926 *Tsarekostyantynivka* (Russian *Tsarekonstantinovka*)

[2]**Kuybysheve** (town, southern Ukraine) : (Russian *Kuybyshevo*); to 1944 *Albat*

Kuybyshevka-Vostochnaya *see* **Belogorsk**

Kuybyshevo *see* (1) [1,2]**Kuybysheve**; (2) **Rishtan**

Kuzhery *see* **Krasny Steklovar**

Kuznetsk (city, western Russia) : to 1780 *Naryshkino*

Kuznetsk-Sibirsky *see* **Novokuznetsk**

Kuznetsovo *see* **Konakovo**

Kuźnica (village, northeastern Poland) : 1772–1919, 1939–1945 German *Ceynowa*

Kvirily *see* **Zestafoni**

Kwando *see* **Cuando**

Kwango *see* **Cuango**

KwaZulu-Natal (province, eastern South Africa) : to 1994 *Natal*

Kweisui *see* **Hohhot**

Kwekwe (city, central Zimbabwe) : to 1980 *Que Que*

Kwidzyn (town, northern Poland) : to 1919, 1939–1945 German *Marienwerder*

Kyaikkami (town, southern Myanmar) : formerly *Amherst*

Kyakhta (city, southern Russia) : to 1935 *Troits-kosavsk* (The city was formed by combining the town of Troitskosavsk with the village of *Kyakhta*, taking the latter's name.)

Kyiv *see* **Kiev**

Kyjov (town, southeastern Czech Republic) : to 1918, 1939–1945 German *Gaya*

Kyŏmip'o *see* **Songnim**

Kypros *see* **Cyprus**

Kyrenia (town, northern Northern Cyprus) : Turkish *Girne* (Kyrenia should not be confused with *Cyrene*, northern Africa.)

Kyrgyzstan (republic, west central Asia) : to 1991 *Kirghizia*

Kyrylivka *see* [2]**Shevchenkove**

Kyšperk *see* **Letohrad**

Kysucké Nové Mesto (town, northwestern Slovakia) : to 1918 Hungarian *Kiszucaújhely*

Kythrea (town, northern Cyprus) : Turkish *Degirmenlik*; ancient Greek *Chythri*

Kyupriya *see* **Primorsko**

Kyustendil (city, southwestern Bulgaria) : to 1878 Turkish *Köstendil*

Kyzyl (city, southeastern Russia) : 1918–1926 *Khem-Beldyr*; to 1918 *Belotsarsk*

Kyzyl-Adyr (town, northwestern Kyrgyzstan) : formerly Russian *Kirovskoye*; to 1937 Russian *Aleksandrovskoye*

Kyzyl-Asker (village, northern Kyrgyzstan) : to 1944 *Chalakazaki* (The village is now a suburb of Bishkek.)

Kyzyl-Burun *see* **Siyäzän**

Kyzylorda (city, south central Kazakhstan) : 1925–1991 *Kzyl-Orda*; 1917–1925 *Ak-Mechet'*; 1853–1917 Russian *Perovsk*; to 1853 *Ak-Mechet'*

Kyzyl-Suu (village, eastern Kyrgyzstan) : formerly *Pokrovka*

Kzyl-Mazar *see* **Sovet**

Kzyl-Orda *see* **Kyzylorda**

Kzyltu *see* **Kishkenekol'**

Labacum *see* **Ljubljana**

Laband *see* **Łabędy**

La Barge *see* **Deer Lodge**

La Baye *see* **Green Bay**

Labdah (historic site, northwestern Libya) : Roman *Leptis Magna*

Łabędy (town, southern Poland) : to 1945 German *Laband* (The town is now part of Gliwice.)

Labes *see* **Łobez**

Labiau *see* **Polessk**

Labicanan Way *see* **Via**

Labinsk (city, southwestern Russia) : to 1947 *Labinskaya*

Labinskaya *see* **Labinsk**

Labuan (town, eastern Malaysia) : formerly *Vic-*

toria (The town lies on the island of the same name.)

La Calle *see* **El Kala**

Lacasaigh *see* **Laxay**

Lacasdal *see* **Laxdale**

Laccadive, Minicoy, and Amindivi Islands *see* **Lakshadweep**

Lac des Quatre Cantons *see* **Lucerne, Lake**

Lacedaemon *see* **Sparta**

La Chapelle *see* ²**Abbeville**

La Charqueada *see* **General Enrique Martínez**

Lachin (town, southern Azerbaijan) : to 1926 *Abdalyar*

Lachine *see* **La Salle**

Lackawanna (city, New York, northeastern United States) : to 1909 *Limestone Hill*

Lac La Martre *see* **Wha Ti**

Lacobriga *see* **Lagos**

La Concepción *see* **Riaba**

Laconia (town, New Hampshire, northeastern United States) : formerly *Meredith Bridge*

La Coruña (city, northwestern Spain) : [Galician *A Coruña*]; traditional English *Corunna*; Medieval Latin *Coronium*; Roman *Brigantium*. (The traditional name is associated with the English victory over the French in 1809 during the Peninsular War.)

Lactodurum *see* **Towcester**

Lacus Lemanus *see* **Geneva, Lake**

Lądek Zdrój (town, southwestern Poland) : to 1945 German *Bad Landeck*

Ladrones Islands *see* **Mariana Islands**

Ladushkin (town, western Russia) : to 1945 German *Ludwigsort*

La Estrelleta (province, western Dominican Republic) : to 1965 *San Rafael*

Lafayette (city, Louisiana, southern United States) : to 1884 *Vermilionville*

Lafayette *see* **Bougaa**

Lafayette, Mt. (New Hampshire, northeastern United States) : to 1825 *Great Haystack*

Lagan' (town, southwestern Russia) : 1944–1991 *Kaspiysky*

Lagentium *see* **Castleford**

Laggan *see* **Lake Louise**

Łagiewniki (town, southwestern Poland) : to 1945 German *Elvershagen*

Lago dei Quattro Cantoni *see* **Lucerne, Lake**

Lago di Patria (village, south central Italy) : Roman *Liternum*

Lagos (city, southern Portugal) : Roman *Lacobriga*

La Goulette *see* **Halq el Oued**

La Granja *see* **San Ildefonso**

La Guadeloupe (village, Quebec, southeastern Canada) : to 1949 *St.-Évariste Station*

La Guingette *see* **Bourg-Madame**

La Habana *see* **Havana**

La Haye-Descartes *see* **Descartes**

La Haye-en-Touraine *see* **Descartes**

Laḥij (town, southwestern Yemen) : in 1960s *Al-Hawtah*

Lähn *see* **Wleń**

Laibach *see* **Ljubljana**

Lajeado *see* **Guiratinga**

La Junta (town, Colorado, west central United States) : originally *Otero*

Lake (or **Lake of**) : for names beginning thus, *see* next word, as **Constance, Lake**

Lake City (town, Florida, southeastern United States) : to 1859 *Alligator*

Lakefield (village, Ontario, southeastern Canada) : to 1874 *Herriott's Falls*

Lake Harbour (village, Nunavut, northeastern Canada) : alternate Inuit *Kimmirut*

Lakehead *see* **Thunder Bay**

Lake Louise (village, Alberta, southwestern Canada) : to 1914 *Laggan*; originally *Holt City*

Lake's Crossing *see* **Reno**

Lake Station (town, Indiana, north central United States) : formerly *East Gary*

Lakeview *see* **Winter Park**

¹**Lakewood** (town, New Jersey, northeastern United States) : formerly *Bricksburg*; previously *Bergen Iron Works*; earlier *Washington's Furnace*; originally *Three Partners' Mill*

²**Lakewood** (city, Ohio, north central United States) : 1871–1889 *East Rockport*; to 1871 *Rockport*

Lakhdaria (town, northern Algeria) : to *c.*1962 French *Palestro*

Lakinsk (town, western Russia) : to 1969 *Lakinsky*

Lakinsky *see* **Lakinsk**

Lakshadweep (union territory, southwestern India) : to 1973 *Laccadive, Minicoy and Aminidivi Islands* (The first of the multiple names, in an improved form, gave the present name.)

La Laguna *see* **Padilla**

La Manche *see* **English Channel**

Lambaesis *see* **Tazoult-Lambèse**

Lambertville (town, New Jersey, northeastern United States) : originally *Coryel's Ferry* (The town lies across the Delaware River from **New Hope**, and the original ferry plied between the two.)

Lambly's Landing *see* **Enderby**

Lamía (city, central Greece) : to 1830 Turkish *Zeytun*

Lamoricière *see* **Ouled Mimoun**

La Motte-Montfort *see* **La Motte-Servolex**

La Motte-Servolex (town, eastern France) : to
1802 *La Motte-Montfort*

Lampedusa (island, central Mediterranean) : ancient Greek *Lopadusa*

Lampeter (town, west central Wales) : Welsh
Llanbedr Pont Steffan

Lamphey (village, southwestern Wales) : Welsh
Llandyfái

Lamta (historic site, eastern Tunisia) : Roman
Leptis Minor

Lancaster (city, Pennsylvania, northeastern
United States) : originally *Gibson's Pasture*

Lancaster *see* ³Lincoln

Lanchester (town, northeastern England) :
Roman *Longovicium*

Łańcut (town, southeastern Poland) : 1940–1945
German *Landshut*

Landeck *see* Lędyczek

Landeshut *see* Kamienna Góra

Landsberg *see* Górowo Iławeckie

Landsberg an der Warthe *see* Gorzów
Wielkopolski

Land's End (peninsula, southwestern England) :
Roman *Antivestaeum Promontorium*; earlier
Roman *Belerium*

Landshut *see* Łańcut

Landskron *see* Lanškroun

Landwarów *see* Lentvaris

Langenbielau *see* Bielawa

Langfuhr *see* Wrzeszcz

Langres (town, east central France) : Roman
Andemattunnum

Langtry (village, Texas, southern United States) :
formerly *Vinegaroon*

Lansing (city, Michigan, north central United
States) : to 1848 *Michigan*

Lanškroun (town, east central Czech Republic) :
to 1918, 1938–1945 German *Landskron*

Lanuvio (village, central Italy) : Roman *Lanuvium*

Lanuvium *see* Lanuvio

Laodicea ad Mare *see* Latakia

Laoighis *see* Laois

Laois (county, central Ireland) : alternate
Laoighis; formerly *Leix*; 1557–1920 English
Queen's County

Laon (town, northern France) : Roman *Lugdunum*

La Palma (town, California, southwestern
United States) : to 1965 *Dairyland*

La Pampa (province, central Argentina) :
1952–1955 *Eva Perón*

La Panne *see* De Panne

La Parida *see* Bolívar, Cerro

La Park *see* Huntington Park

La Paz (city, western Colombia) : formerly *La
Paz de Ayacucho*; to 1825 *Nuestra Señora de la
Paz*

La Paz de Ayacucho *see* La Paz

La Piedad Cavadas (city, northwestern Mexico)
: to 1871 *Zula la Vieja*

La Planche *see* Amherst

Lapland (region, northern Europe) : [Swedish
Lappland; Finnish *Lappi*; Russian *Laplandiya*]
(English generally prefers the Norwegian form
of the name. The region extends over northern
Scandinavia and the Kola Peninsula in northwestern Russia.)

Laplandiya *see* Lapland

La Plata (province, eastern Argentina) : 1946–
1955 *Eva Perón*

La Plata *see* Sucre

Lappeenranta (city, southeastern Finland) : formerly Swedish *Villmanstrand*

Lappi *see* Lapland

Lappland *see* Lapland

Laptevo *see* Yasnogorsk

Laptev Sea (northeastern Russia) : to 1913 *Nordenskjöld Sea*

Lapu-Lapu (city, central Philippines) : formerly
Opon

Lapurdum *see* ¹Bayonne

Larache (city, northwestern Morocco) : Arabic *El
Araïche*; Roman *Lixus* (The Spanish corruption
of the Arabic name persists in general use.)

Laranjal *see* Laranjal Paulista

Laranjal Paulista (city, southeastern Brazil) : to
1944 *Laranjal*

Laranjeiras *see* (1) Alagoa Nova; (2) Laranjeiras do Sul

Laranjeiras do Sul (city, southern Brazil) : 1944–
1948 *Iguaçu*; to 1944 *Laranjeiras*

La Ravardière *see* Cayenne

L'Arbaa Naït Irathen (town, northern Algeria) :
to *c.*1962 French *Fort-National*

Largeau *see* Faya

Larino (town, south central Italy) : Roman *Larinum*

Larinsky *see* Never

Larinum *see* Larino

La Rioja (autonomous region, northern Spain) :
to 1980 *Logroño*

Lárissa (city, northern Greece) : to 1881 Turkish
Yenişehir

Larne (town, northeastern Northern Ireland) :
Irish *Latharna*

La Rochelle (city, western France) : Medieval
Latin *Rupella*

La Roche-sur-Yon (town, western France) :
1848–1870 *Napoléon-Vendée*, 1814–1848 *Bourbon-Vendée*, 1804–1814 *Napoléon-Vendée*

La Salle (city, Quebec, southeastern Canada) : to
1912 *Lachine*; originally *St. Sulpice* (The city,
now a southern suburb of Montreal, received

its current name when a group of inhabitants moved to the site of the present western suburb of *Lachine* and took that name with them, allowing the original Lachine to become incorporated as a city.)

Lasdehnen *see* **Krasnoznamensk**

Laško (village, east central Slovenia) : to 1918 German *Tüffer*

Las Mulatas *see* **San Blas Islands**

Las Peñas *see* **Puerto Vallarta**

Las Rosas (town, southern Mexico) : to 1934 *Pinola*

Latakia (city, western Syria) : [Arabic *Al Lādhiqīyah*]; Roman *Laodicea ad Mare* (This is not the biblical Laodicea, which was Roman *Laodicea ad Lycum* near modern Denizli in western Turkey.)

Laterrière (town, Quebec, eastern Canada) : originally *Grand-Brûlé*

Latharna *see* **Larne**

Latina (city and province, south central Italy) : to 1947 *Littoria*

Latinum *see* **Meaux**

Latin Way *see* **Via**

Latium *see* **Lazio**

La Toma (town, west central Argentina) : formerly *Cuatro de Junio*

La Tranche *see* ²**Thames**

La Trinitaria (town, southern Mexico) : to 1934 *Zapaluta*

Latvia (republic, northwestern Europe) : [Latvian *Latvija*]; (Russian *Latviya*); 1941–1944 German *Lettland*. (None of these names should be confused with those of neighboring **Lithuania**.)

Latvija *see* **Latvia**

Lauban *see* **Lubań**

Lauenburg *see* **Lębork**

Laugharne (village, southwestern Wales) : Welsh *Talacharn*

Lauis *see* **Lugano**

Laun *see* **Louny**

Launceston (city, Tasmania, southeastern Australia) : originally *Patersonia*

Laurahütte *see* **Siemianowice Śląskie**

Laurana *see* **Lovran**

Lauriacum *see* **Lorsch**

Lausanne (city, western Switzerland) : Italian *Losanna*; Roman *Lausodunum*

Lausitz *see* **Lusatia**

Lausodunum *see* **Lausanne**

Lautenburg *see* **Lidzbark**

Lauzon (town, Quebec, southeastern Canada) : to 1867 *Cap-de-Lévy* (In 1989 the town merged with **Lévis** to form the city of *Lévis-Lauzon*.)

Lavarande *see* **Sidi Lakdar**

Lavatris *see* **Bowes**

Lavinium *see* **Pratica di Mare**

Lavras *see* **Lavras da Mangabeira**

Lavras da Mangabeira (city, northeastern Brazil) : to 1944 *Lavras*

Lawnsville *see* **Logan**

Lawrence (town, southern New Zealand) : formerly *Tuapeka*

Laxay (village, Western Isles, northwestern Scotland) : Gaelic *Lacasaigh*

Laxdale (village, Western Isles, northwestern Scotland) : Gaelic *Lacasdal*

Lazio (region, central Italy) : Roman *Latium* (The Roman name of this district around Rome gave that of the *Latin* language, first spoken here.)

Lázně Jeseník (village, western Czech Republic) : to 1918, 1938–1945 German *Gräfenberg*

Lazovsk *see* **Sîngerei**

Lbishchensk *see* **Chapayev**

Leaf Bay *see* **Tasiujaq**

Leba *see* **Łeba**

Łeba (town, northern Poland) : to 1945 German *Leba*

¹**Lebanon** (republic, southwestern Asia) : [Arabic *Lubnān*]

²**Lebanon** (city, Pennsylvania, northeastern United States) : originally *Steitztown*

Lębork (city, northern Poland) : to 1945 German *Lauenburg*

Lebyazh'ye *see* **Akku**

Lecce (city, southeastern Italy) : Roman *Lupiae*

Le Center (town, Minnesota, northern United States) : to 1931 *Le Sueur Center*

Łęczyca (town, central Poland) : 1940–1945 German *Lentschütz*; to 1915 Russian *Lenchitsa*

Ledeč nad Sázavou (town, central Czech Republic) : to 1918, 1939–1945 German *Ledetsch an der Saaz*

Ledengskoye *see* **Babushkina, imeni**

Ledetsch an der Saaz *see* **Ledeč nad Sázavou**

Ledo Salinarius *see* **Lons-le-Saunier**

Ledra *see* **Nicosia**

Lędyczek (town, northwestern Poland) : to 1945 German *Landeck*

Leeds (city, northern England) : Roman *Cambodunum* (The Roman name was that of an as yet unlocated Roman fort. Given the meaning of the name, itself of Celtic origin, as "fort at a bend," it may have been at the confluence of the Sheepscar Beck with the Aire River.)

Leeu-Gamka (town, southern South Africa) : formerly *Fraserburg Road*

Leeville *see* **Assiniboia**

Lefkoşa *see* **Nicosia**

Le Fleur's Bluff *see* ²Jackson

Leger Corner *see* Dieppe

Leghorn *see* Livorno

Legnano (city, northern Italy) : Roman *Leunanium*

Legnica (city, southwestern Poland) : to 1945 German *Liegnitz* (The German name is associated with the 1760 Prussian defeat of the Austrians during the Seven Years' War.)

Legnickie Pole (village, southwestern Poland) : to 1945 German *Wahlstatt*

Legohli *see* Norman Wells

Le Havre (city, northern France) : originally *Le Havre-de-Grâce* (The English knew the port as *Newhaven* for a time following its founding in 1517.)

Le Havre-de-Grâce *see* Le Havre

Leicester (city, central England) : Roman *Ratae Corieltauvorum*

Leiden (city, western Netherlands) : English *Leyden*; Roman *Lugdunum* (The Roman name also appears in the expanded form *Lugdunum Batavorum*. The English spelling is traditionally associated with the 1574 siege of the city during the Netherlands War of Independence, in which the Dutch were attacked by Walloon and German troops.)

Léim an Bhradáin *see* Leixlip

Léim an Mhadaidh *see* Limavady

Leintwardine (village, western England) : Roman *Branogenium*

Leipe *see* Lipno

Leitir Ceannain *see* Letterkenny

Leitmeritz *see* Litoměřice

Leitomishl *see* Litomyšl

Leitrim (county, northwestern Ireland) : Irish *Liatroim*

Leix *see* Laois

Leixlip (village, eastern Ireland) : Irish *Léim an Bhradáin*

Le Kef (town, northern Tunisia) : Roman *Sicca Veneria*

Leksura *see* Lentekhi

Lemberg (village, Saskatchewan, southern Canada) : to 1905 *Sifton*

Lemberg *see* L'viv

Lemeshensky *see* Orgtrud

Lempira (department, western Honduras) : to 1943 *Gracias*

Lemsal *see* Limbaži

Lenchitsa *see* Łęczyca

Lençóis *see* Lençóis Paulista

Lençóis Paulista (city, southeastern Brazil) : 1944–1948 *Ubirama*; to 1944 *Lençóis*

Lendava (town, northeastern Slovenia) : to 1918, 1941–1944 Hungarian *Alsólendva*

Lengwethen *see* Lunino

Lenin (town, western Tajikistan) : formerly *Leninsky*; c.1960–1970 *imeni Sardarova Karakhana*; to c.1960 *Koktash*

Lenina, imeni *see* Lenina, imeny

Lenina, imeny (town, south central Ukraine) : (Russian *imeni Lenina*); to c.1926 *Kalachevs'kyy Rudnyk* (Russian *Kalachevsky Rudnik*) (The town is now a suburb of Kryvyyh Rih.)

Leninabad *see* (1) Khujand; (2) Qanliko'l

Leninakan *see* Gyumri

Lenine (town, southern Ukraine) : (Russian *Lenino*); to 1957 *Sim Kolodyaziv* (Russian *Sem' Kolodezey*)

Leningrad (town, southwestern Tajikistan) : formerly Russian *Leningradsky*; to 1973 *Mŭ'minobod* (Russian *Muminabad*)

Leningrad *see* St. Petersburg

Leningradskaya (village, southwestern Russia) : to 1930s *Umanskaya*

Leningradsky *see* Leningrad

¹Lenino (town, western Russia) : formerly *Tsaritsyno* (The town is now incorporated into Moscow.)

²Lenino (town, southern Russia) : to 1930s *Innokent'yevskaya* (The town is now part of the city of Irkutsk.)

Lenino *see* (1) Lenine; (2) Leninsk-Kuznetsky

Leninobod *see* (1) Khujand; (2) Qanliko'l

Leninogorsk (town, western Russia) : to 1955 *Novaya Pis'myanka*

Leninogorsk *see* Ridder

Lenin Peak (mountain, southern Kyrgyzstan/ northern Tajikistan) : to 1928 *Kaufman Peak*

Leninsk (town, southwestern Russia) : to 1919 *Prishib*

Leninsk *see* (1) Akdepe; (2) ¹Asaka; (3) Baykonyr; (4) Taldom

Leninskaya Sloboda (town, western Russia) : to 1935 *Kadnitsy*

Leninsk-Kuznetsky (city, southern Russia) : 1922–1925 *Lenino*; to 1922 *Kol'chugino*

Leninskoe (village, southern Kyrgyzstan) : to 1937 Russian *Pokrovka*

¹Leninskoye (town, western Russia) : 1917– c.1940 *Shabalino*; to 1917 *Bogorodskoye*

²Leninskoye (town, eastern Russia) : formerly *Mikhaylovo-Semyonovskoye*; to 1939 *Blyukherovo*

Leninskoye *see* (1) Kazygurt; (2) Uzynkol'

Leninsk-Turkmensky *see* Türkmenabat

¹Leninsky (town, western Russia, near Tula) : to 1935 *Domman-Asfal'tovy Zavod*

²Leninsky (town, western Russia, near Koz'-modem'yansk) : to 1941 *Marino*

Leninsky *see* Lenin

Lenínváros *see* (1) **Pesterzsébet**; (2) **Tiszaújváros**

Lenox (town, Massachusetts, northeastern United States) : to 1767 *Yokuntown*

Lens (town, northern France) : Roman *Lentium*

Lensk (city, eastern Russia) : to 1963 *Mukhtuya*

Lentekhi (town, northwestern Georgia) : to 1938 *Leksura*

Lentia *see* **Linz**

Lentini (town, southern Italy) : ancient Greek *Leontini*

Lentium *see* **Lens**

Lentschütz *see* **Łęczyca**

Lentvaris (town, southeastern Lithuania) : 1919–1939 Polish *Landwarów*; to 1918 Russian *Lyandvarovo*

Leobschütz *see* **Głubczyce**

Leodocia *see* **Red Bluff**

León *see* **Cotopaxi**

León de los Caballeros de Huánuco *see* **Huánuco**

Leonidovo (town, eastern Russia) : 1905–1945 Japanese *Kami-shikuka*

Leontini *see* **Lentini**

Leopold, Lake *see* **Mai-Ndombe, Lake**

Leopoldina *see* (1) **Aruanã**; (2) **Colonia Leopoldina**; (3) **Parnamirim**

Leopoldov (town, western Slovakia) : to 1918 Hungarian *Lipótvár*; to 1867 German *Leopoldstadt*

Leopoldsburg (town, northeastern Belgium) : French *Bourg-Léopold*

Leopoldstadt *see* **Leopoldov**

Léopoldville *see* **Kinshasa**

Leopolis *see* **L'viv**

Lepanto *see* **Návpaktos**

Le Port (town, northwestern Réunion) : formerly *Port-des-Galets*

Leptis Magna *see* **Labdah**

Leptis Minor *see* **Lamta**

Le Puy (city, south central France) : Medieval Latin *Podium*

Lérida (city, northeastern Spain) : Catalan *Lleida*; Roman *Ilerda*

Lermontov (town, southwestern Russia) : to 1956 *Lermontovsky*

Lermontovsky *see* **Lermontov**

Les Borges Blanques *see* **Borjas Blancas**

Lesbos (island, eastern Greece) : alternate *Mytilene* (The alternate name is in regular use for the island's chief town, often in its Greek form *Mitilíni*.)

Leschnitz *see* **Lešnica**

Leselidze *see* **Gyachrypsh**

Les Grandes Fourches *see* ¹**Grand Forks**

Leskhimstroy *see* **Syeverodonets'k**

Leskovac (city, southeastern Serbia) : to 1878 Turkish *Leskovaç*

Leskovaç *see* **Leskovac**

Leslau *see* **Włocławek**

Lešnica (town, southern Poland) : 1937–1945 German *Bergstadt*; to 1937 German *Leschnitz*

Lesnoy *see* **Umba**

Lesogorsk (town, eastern Russia) : 1905–1945 Japanese *Nayoshi*

Lesogorsky (town, northwestern Russia) : 1940–1948 *Yaski*; to 1940 Finnish *Jääski* (The town passed from Finland to the USSR in 1940 but was not renamed until 1948.)

Lesotho (kingdom, southern Africa) : to 1966 *Basutoland*

Lesovka *see* **Ukrains'k**

Lesozavodsky *see* **Novovyatsk**

Les Petites Côtes *see* **St. Charles**

Lessen *see* **Lessines**

Lessine (town, west central Belgium) : Flemish *Lessen*

Lesten *see* **Czernina**

Les Trembles *see* **Sidi Hamadouche**

Le Sueur Center *see* **Le Center**

Leszno (city, west central Poland) : 1793–1807, 1815–1919, 1939–1945 German *Lissa*

Lethbridge (city, Alberta, southwestern Canada) : to 1885 *Coalbanks*

Letocetum *see* **Wall**

Letohrad (town, north central Czech Republic) : to 1950 *Kyšperk*; to 1918, 1939–1945 German *Geiersberg*

Letterkenny (town, northwestern Ireland) : Irish *Leitir Ceanainn*

Letterston (village, southwestern Wales) : Welsh *Treletert*

Letzeburg *see* ²**Luxembourg**

Leubus *see* **Lubiąż**

Leucarum *see* **Loughor**

Leunanium *see* **Legnano**

Leutensdorf *see* **Litvínov**

Leuthen *see* **Lutynia**

Leutschau *see* **Levoča**

Leuven *see* **Louvain**

Léva *see* **Levice**

Leverburgh (village, Western Isles, northwestern Scotland) : Gaelic *An t-Òb*; to 1918 *Obbe*

Leverger *see* **Santo Antônio do Leverger**

Leverville *see* **Lusanga**

Levice (town, southern Slovakia) : to 1918, 1938–1958 Hungarian *Léva*; to 1867 German *Lewentz*

Le Vieux Village *see* **Sainte Genevieve**

Lévis (town, Quebec, southeastern Canada) : to 1861 *Aubigny* (In 1989 the town merged with **Lauzon** to form the city of *Lévis-Lauzon*.)

Levittown *see* **Willingboro**

Levkás (town, western Greece) : formerly Italian *Santa Maura* (The town is on the island of the same name.)

Levkosía *see* **Nicosia**

Levoča (town, north central Slovakia) : to 1918 Hungarian *Lőcse*; to 1867 German *Leutschau*

¹**Levski** (town, northern Bulgaria) : to 1897 Turkish *Karaağaç*

²**Levski** (mountain, north central Bulgaria) : to 1942 *Ambaritsa*

Levskigrad *see* **Karlovo**

Lev Tolstoy (town, western Russia) : to 1927 *Astapovo*

Lewentz *see* **Levice**

Lewes (town, Delaware, northeastern United States) : to *c*.1685 *Zwaanendael*

Lewin Brzeski (town, southwestern Poland) : to 1945 German *Löwen*

Lewin Kłodski (town, southwestern Poland) : to 1945 German *Hummelstadt*

Lewis *see* **Isle of Lewis**

Lexington (town, Massachusetts, northeastern United States) : to 1713 *Cambridge Farms*

Lexington Park (town, Maryland, northeastern United States) : to 1950 *Jarboesville*

Leyden *see* **Leiden**

Liakoura (mountain, central Greece) : formerly *Parnassus*

Liatroim *see* **Leitrim**

Libau *see* **Liepāja**

Libava *see* **Liepāja**

Liberalitas Julia *see* **Évora**

Liberec (city, northern Czech Republic) : to 1918, 1938–1945 German *Reichenberg*

Libertador *see* **Dajabón**

Liberty Island (New York, northeastern United States) : to 1956 *Bedloe's Island*

Lībīyah *see* **Libya**

Liburnum *see* **Livorno**

Libya (republic, northern Africa) : [Arabic *Lībīyah*]

Licata (town, southern Italy) : ancient Greek *Phintias*

Lichinga (town, northwestern Mozambique) : to 1982 *Vila Cabral*

Lidzbark (town, north central Poland) : 1772– 1919, 1939–1945 German *Lautenburg* (The full name *Lidzbark Wielkopolski* distinguished the town from **Lidzbark Warmiński**.)

Lidzbark Warmiński (town, northern Poland) : 1772–1945 German *Heilsberg*

Liebau *see* **Lubawka**

Liebenau bei Schwiebus *see* **Lubrza**

Liebenfelde *see* **Zales'ye**

Liebenthal *see* **Lubomierz**

Liebenwerde *see* **Kęty**

Liège (city, eastern Belgium) : Flemish *Luik*; formerly German *Lüttich* (English always uses the French name, formerly spelled *Liége*, with an acute accent, and in official use in Belgian French until 1946. The city was part of France from 1792 to 1815, part of the Netherlands from 1815 to 1830, and under German occupation in both world wars.)

Liége *see* **Liège**

Liegnitz *see* **Legnica**

Liepāja (city, western Latvia) : (Russian *Liepaya*); 1941–1945 German *Libau*; to 1918 Russian *Libava*

Liepaya *see* **Liepāja**

Lier (town, northern Belgium) : French *Lierre*

Lierre *see* **Lier**

Lietuva *see* **Lithuania**

Lietzenburg *see* **Charlottenburg**

Lievenhof *see* **Līvāni**

Lifudzin *see* **Rudny**

Liger *see* **Loire**

Ligovo *see* **Uritsk**

Liidli Kue *see* **Fort Simpson**

Likasi (city, southeastern Democratic Republic of the Congo) : to 1966 French *Jadotville*

Likér *see* **Hnúšť'a**

Likhachyovo *see* **Pervomays'kyy**

Likhovskoy (town, western Russia) : to 1930 *Likhaya*

Likhvin *see* **Chekalin**

Lilienthal *see* **Bettendorf**

Lille (city, northern France) : formerly *L'Isle*; earlier Flemish *Rijssel*; Medieval Latin *Insula*

Lillebonne (town, northern France) : Roman *Juliobona*

Lilybaeum *see* **Marsala**

Liman (town, southwestern Russia) : to 1944 *Dolban*

Liman *see* **Krasnyy Lyman**

Limanowa (town, southern Poland) : 1940–1945 German *Ilmenau*

Limavady (town, northern Northern Ireland) : Irish *Léim an Mhadaidh*

Limbazhi *see* **Limbaži**

Limbaži (town, northern Latvia) : (Russian *Limbazhi*); to 1918 German *Lemsal*

Limbe (town, southwestern Cameroon) : to 1982 *Victoria*

Limbourg *see* **Limburg**

Limburg (province, northeastern Belgium) : French *Limbourg*

Limeira (city, southeastern Brazil) : formerly *Nossa Senhora das Dores de Tatuibi*

Limeira *see* **Joaçaba**

Limerick (town, southwestern Ireland) : Irish *Luimneach*

Limestone *see* **Maysville**

Limestone Hill *see* **Lackawanna**

Limìn Vathéos *see* **Samos**

Limoeiro *see* (1) **Limoeiro do Anadia**; (2) **Limoeiro do Norte**

Limoeiro do Anadia (city, northeastern Brazil) : to 1944 *Limoeiro*

Limoeiro do Norte (city, northeastern Brazil) : to 1944 *Limoeiro*

Limoges (city, west central France) : Roman *Augustoritum*

Limonum *see* **Poitiers**

Limpopo (province, northern South Africa) : 1995–2002 *Northern*; 1993–1995 *Northern Transvaal*

Linares (city, central Chile) : 1794–1875 *San Ambrosio de Linares*; to 1794 *San Javier de Bella Isla*

[1]**Lincoln** (city, eastern England) : Roman *Lindum*

[2]**Lincoln** (town, Illinois, north central United States) : to 1853 *Postville*

[3]**Lincoln** (city, Nebraska, central United States) : to 1867 *Lancaster*

Lincolnwood (village, Illinois, north central United States) : to 1935 *Tessville* (The village is now a residential suburb of Chicago.)

Lindiacum *see* **Lintgen**

Lindinis *see* **Ilchester**

Lindisfarne (island, northeastern England) : alternate *Holy Island*

Lindsay (town, Ontario, southeastern Canada) : originally *Purdy's Mills*

Lindum *see* [1]**Lincoln**

Linkville *see* **Klamath Falls**

Linlithgowshire *see* **West Lothian**

Lins (city, southeastern Brazil) : formerly *Albuquerque Lins*; originally *Santo Antônio do Campestre*

Lintgen (town, south central Luxembourg) : Roman *Lindiacum*

Linz (city, northern Austria) : Roman *Lentia*

Lion, Golfe du (sea inlet, southern France) : dated English *Gulf of Lions*; Roman *Sinus Gallicus*

Lions, Gulf of *see* **Lion, Golfe du**

Lios Dúin Bhearna *see* **Lisdoonvarna**

Lios Mór *see* **Lismore**

Lios na gCearrbhach *see* **Lisburn**

Lios Tuathail *see* **Listowel**

Lipari Islands (southern Italy) : English traditional *Aeolian Islands*; Italian *Isole Eolie* or *Isole Lipari*; Roman *Aeoliae Insulae* (*Lipari* is the largest island of the group.)

Lipiany (town, northwestern Poland) : to 1945 German *Lippehne*

Lipno (town, central Poland) : 1940–1945 German *Leipe*

Lipótvár *see* **Leopoldov**

Lipová (village, northern Czech Republic) : to 1945 German *Hainspach*

Lippehne *see* **Lipiany**

Liptószentmiklós *see* **Liptovský Mikuláš**

Liptovský Mikuláš (city, northern Slovakia) : to 1952 *Liptovský Svätý Mikuláš*; to 1918 Hungarian *Liptószentmiklós*

Liptovský Svätý Mikuláš *see* **Liptovský Mikuláš**

Lisboa *see* **Lisbon**

Lisbon (city, western Portugal) : [Portuguese *Lisboa*]; Roman *Olisipo*

Lisburn (town, eastern Northern Ireland) : Irish *Lios na gCearrbhach*

Lisdoonvarna (town, western Ireland) : Irish *Lios Dúin Bhearna*

Lisichansk *see* **Lysychans'k**

Lisieux (city, northwestern France) : Roman *Noviomagus*

Lisivka *see* **Ukrains'k**

Liski (city, western Russia) : 1965–1991 *Georgiu-Dezh*; 1943–1965 *Liski*; 1928–1943 *Svoboda* (The city first took its present name on absorbing the village of *Liski* in 1943.)

L'Isle *see* **Lille**

Lismore (town, southern Ireland) : Irish *Lios Mór*

Lissa *see* (1) **Leszno**; (2) **Vis**

Lissoy *see* [3]**Auburn**

Listowel (town, southwestern Ireland) : Irish *Lios Tuathail*

Litauen *see* **Lithuania**

Liternum *see* **Lago di Patria**

Lithuania (republic, northwestern Europe) : [Lithuanian *Lietuva*]; (Russian *Litva*); 1941–1944 German *Litauen*. (None of these names should be confused with those of neighboring **Latvia**.)

Litoměřice (town, northern Czech Republic) : to 1918, 1938–1945 German *Leitmeritz*

Litomyšl (town, east central Czech Republic) : to 1918, 1939–1945 German *Leitomischl*

Litovel (town, eastern Czech Republic) : to 1918, 1939–1945 German *Littau*

Littau *see* **Litovel**

Little Barrier Island (northeastern New Zealand) : Maori *Hauturu*

Littleborough (village, east central England) : Roman *Segelocum*

Little Fort *see* **Waukegan**

Little Muddy *see* [1]**Williston**

Little Placentia *see* Argentia
Little Rest *see* ²Kingston
Little Russia *see* Ukraine
Little Thames *see* ¹Stratford
Littleton *see* Bradford
Littoria *see* Latina
Litva *see* Lithuania
Litvino *see* Sosnovoborsk
Litvínov (city, northwestern Czech Republic) : to 1918, 1938–1945 German *Leutensdorf* (The present city was formed in *c.*1948 from the union of *Horní Litvínov* and *Dolní Litvínov*, formerly German *Ober-Leutensdorf* and *Nieder-Leutensdorf.*)
Litzmannstadt *see* Łódź
Līvāni (town, southeastern Latvia) : to 1917 German *Lievenhof*
Livermore Falls (town, Maine, northeastern United States) : to 1930 *East Livermore*
Liverpool (town, Nova Scotia, eastern Canada) : to 1759 *Port Senior*; earlier *Port Rossignol*; originally *Ogumkiqueok*
Livingston (town, Montana, northwestern United States) : originally *Clark's City*
Livingstone *see* Maramba
Livland *see* Livonia
Livonia (region, Estonia/Latvia) : [German *Livland*]
Livorno (city, northwestern Italy) : traditional English *Leghorn*; Roman *Liburnum*
Livramento *see* (1) José de Freitas; (2) Livramento do Brumado; (3) Nossa Senhora do Livramento
Livramento do Brumado (city, eastern Brazil) : to 1944 *Livramento*
Lixus *see* Larache
Lizard, The (peninsula, southwestern England) : Roman *Dumnonium Promontorium*; earlier Roman *Ocrinum Promontorium*
Ljubljana (city, central Slovenia) : 1941–1944 Italian *Lubiana*; to 1918 German *Laibach*; Medieval Latin *Labacum*; Roman *Emona*
Ljutomer (town, northeastern Slovenia) : to 1918, 1941–1945 German *Luttenberg*
Llanandras *see* Presteigne
Llanbedr Gwynlł̂wg *see* Peterstone Wentloog
Llanbedr Pont Staffan *see* Lampeter
Llanbedr-y-fro *see* Peterston-super-Ely
Llanddewi Nant Hodni *see* Llanthony
Llanddunwyd *see* Welsh St. Donats
Llandeilo Ferwallt *see* Bishopston
Llandovery (town, southern Wales) : Welsh *Llanymddyfri*
Llandrillo-yn-Rhos *see* Rhos-on-Sea
Llandudoch *see* St. Dogmaels
Llandyfái *see* Lamphey

Llanelli (town, northern Wales) : formerly often *Llanelly*
Llanelly *see* Llanelli
Llanelwy *see* St. Asaph
Llanerch Banna *see* Penley
Llaneurgain *see* Northop
Llanfair-ym-Muallt *see* Builth Wells
Llanfihangel Troddi *see* Mitchel Troy
Llanfihangel-yng-Ngheri *see* ²Kerry
Llanfihangel-y-Pwll *see* Michaelston-le-Pit
Llangatwg Nedd *see* Cadoxton-juxta-Neath
Llanilltud Faerdref *see* Llantwit Fardre
Llanilltud Fawr *see* Llantwit Major
Llanilltud Gŵyr *see* Ilston
Llansanffraid-ar-Ogwr *see* St. Brides Minor
Llansanffraid-yn-Elfael *see* Llansantfraed-in-Elwell
Llansantffraed-in-Elwell (village, east central Wales) : Welsh *Llansanffraid-yn-Elfael*
Llansawel *see* Briton Ferry
Llanthony (village, southeastern Wales) : Welsh *Llanddewi Nant Hodni*
Llantwit Fardre (village, southern Wales) : Welsh *Llanilltud Faerdref*
Llantwit Major (town, southern Wales) : Welsh *Llanilltud Fawr*
Llanymddyfri *see* Llandovery
Llan-y-Tair-Mair *see* Knelston
Lleida *see* Lérida
Lleyn (peninsula, northwestern Wales) : Welsh *Llŷn*
Llŷn *see* Lleyn
Llyn Tegid *see* Bala
L.M. Kaganovicha, imeni *see* Popasna
Löbau (town, eastern Germany) : formerly Sorbian (Wendish) *Lubij*
Löbau *see* Lubawa
Loben *see* Lubliniec
Łobez (town, northwestern Poland) : to 1945 German *Labes*
Lobivka *see* Yasenivs'kyy
Lobovka *see* Yasenivs'kyy
Lobva (town, west central Russia) : to 1928 *Lobinsky Zavod*
Lobvinsky Zavod *see* Lobva
Locarno (town, southern Switzerland) : German *Luggarus*
Loch Baghasdail *see* Lochboisdale
Lochboisdale (village, Western Isles, northwestern Scotland) : Gaelic *Loch Baghasdail*
Loch Garman *see* Wexford
Lochmaddy (village, Western Isles, northwestern Scotland) : Gaelic *Loch nam Madach*
Lochmoor *see* Grosse Pointe Woods
Loch nam Madach *see* Lochmaddy
Locri Epizephyrii *see* Gerace

Lőcse *see* **Levoča**

Lod (city, central Israel) : biblical *Lydda*

Lodi (city, California, western United States) : to 1873 *Mokelumne Station*

Lodi *see* **Draa Esmar**

Lodz *see* **Łódź**

Łódź (city, central Poland) : 1940–1945 German *Litzmannstadt*; 1939–1940 German *Lodz*; to 1915 Russian *Lodz'*

Lodz' *see* **Łódź**

Lofça *see* **Lovech**

Logan (town, West Virginia, east central United States) : 1852–1907 *Aracoma*; to 1852 *Lawnsville*

Logan, Mt. (Yukon Territory, northwestern Canada) : formerly *Mt. Pierre E. Trudeau* (On the death in 2000 of Canadian premier Pierre E. Trudeau, it was proposed to rename Canada's highest mountain for him. The name proved controversial, however, and in 2006 was instead assigned to an unnamed peak in the Cariboo Mountains, British Columbia.)

Logstown *see* **Aliquippa**

Loire (river, central and western France) : Roman *Liger*

Loire-Atlantique (department, western France) : to 1957 *Loire-Inférieure*

Loire-Inférieure *see* **Loire-Atlantique**

Loíza (town, northeastern Puerto Rico) : formerly *Canóvanas*

Loket (town, western Czech Republic) : to 1918, 1938–1945 German *Elbogen*

Lombardia *see* **Lombardy**

Lombardy (region, north central Italy) : [Italian *Lombardia*]

Lomonosov (town, western Russia) : to 1948 German *Oranienbaum*

Lomza *see* **Łomża**

Łomża (town, northeastern Poland) : 1941–1945 German *Lomza*; 1939–1941 Belarussian *Lomzha*; to 1915 Russian *Lomzha*; 1795–1807 German *Lomza*

Lomzha *see* **Łomża**

Londinium *see* **London**

London (city, southeastern England) : Roman *Londinium* (London was also known by the honorific Roman title *Augusta*. It is not known when the title was conferred but it may have been on the occasion of the visit of the emperor Constantius I in A.D. 306. The original Roman settlement was established in *c.* A.D. 50.)

Londonderry (city, northern Northern Ireland) : Irish *Doire*; to 1613 (and still alternate) English *Derry* (*Londonderry*, the official name, is preferred by Protestants and Unionists, the latter supporting the union of Northern Ireland with Great Britain as part of the United Kingdom, while *Derry*, without the *London* prefix, is favored by Catholics and Nationalists or Republicans.)

Londres *see* **Catamarca**

Long Beach (city, California, southwestern United States) : to 1888 *Willmore City*

Longford (town, north central Ireland) : Irish *An Longfort*

Longobriga *see* **Freixo**

Longovicium *see* **Lanchester**

Lons-le-Saunier (town, eastern France) : Roman *Ledo Salinarius*

Lopadusa *see* **Lampedusa**

Lopasnya *see* ²**Chekhov**

Lopatino *see* **Volzhsk**

López de Filippis *see* **Mariscal Estigarribia**

Lopusha *see* **Georgi Damyanovo**

Lorain (city, Ohio, north central United States) : 1836–1874 *Charlestown*; to 1836 *Black River*

Lorca (town, southeastern Spain) : Roman *Eliocroca*

Lord Hood Island *see* **Marutea South**

Lorena (city, southeastern Brazil) : to 1782 *Pôrto de Guaipacaré*; originally *Freguesia de Nossa Senhora da Aparecida*

Lorient (city, western France) : formerly *L'Orient*

L'Orient *see* **Lorient**

Lorraine (region, northeastern France) : formerly German *Lothringen*; Roman *Lotharingia* (In 1871 the northeastern quarter of the former province of Lorraine was ceded to Germany and united with **Alsace** as French *Alsace-Lorraine*, German *Elsass-Lothringen*. The territory returned to France in 1919 but was again held by Germany from 1940 to 1944. Lorraine is now a department of northeastern France.)

Lorraine *see* **Baker**

Lorsch (town, central Germany) : Roman *Lauriacum*

Los Angeles (city, California, southwestern United States) : to 1850 formally *El Pueblo de la Reyna de Los Angeles* (The formal name is often confused with that of the river here, now known by the same name as that of the city but originally called the *Porciúncula* in honor of *Nuestra Señora la Reyna de los Angeles de Porciúncula*, "Our Lady the Queen of Angels of Porciúncula." This last word, meaning "Little Portion," is the title of a chapel near Assisi, Italy. In early years the city was long informally known as simply *El Pueblo*.)

Losanna *see* **Lausanne**

Losantiville *see* **Cincinnati**

Losinoostrovskaya *see* ¹**Babushkin**

Losino-Petrovsky (town, western Russia) : to 1928 *Petrovskaya Sloboda*
Loslau *see* Wodzisław Śląski
Los Llanos *see* Santa Rosa de Copán
Los Llanos de Santa Rosa *see* Santa Rosa de Copán
Losonc *see* Lučenec
Lotharingia *see* Lorraine
Lötzen *see* Giżycko
Loubomo (town, southwestern Congo) : to 1975 *Dolisie*
Loughor (town, southern Wales) : Welsh *Casllwchwr*; Roman *Leucarum*
Loughrea (town, western Ireland) : Irish *Baile Locha Riach*
Louisbourg (town, Nova Scotia, southeastern Canada) : to 1966 *Louisburg*
Louisbourg *see* Harrisburg
Louisburg *see* Louisbourg
Louisburgh (town, western Ireland) : Irish *Cluain Cearbán*
Louis-Gentil *see* Youssoufia
Louis Trichardt *see* Makhado
Louisville *see* Ottumwa
Louny (city, northwestern Czech Republic) : to 1918, 1938–1945 German *Laun*
Lourenço Marques *see* Maputo
Louth (village, northeastern Ireland) : Irish *Lú*
Louvain (city, central Belgium) : Flemish *Leuven* (The city is in the Flemish-speaking part of Belgium but its cultural fame has given its French name preference among English speakers. The Catholic University of Louvain is divided into two distinct bodies: the *Katholieke Universiteit te Leuven*, in Louvain itself, where the language of instruction is Flemish, and the *Université Catholique de Louvain*, in the new town of *Louvain-la-Neuve*, some 15 miles to the southwest, where the language is French.)
Lovech (city, northern Bulgaria) : to 1918 Turkish *Lofça*
Lovich *see* Łowicz
Lovnidol (village, north central Bulgaria) : formerly *Chiflik*
Lovran (town, western Croatia) : 1919–1947 Italian *Laurana*
Lowell (city, Massachusetts, northeastern United States) : to 1826 *East Chelmsford*
Löwen *see* Lewin Brzeski
Löwenberg *see* Lwówek Śląski
Löwenhagen *see* Komsomol'sk
Löwenstadt *see* Brzeziny
Löwentin *see* Niegocin, Lake
Lower Canada *see* Quebec
Lower Ferry *see* Queensferry
Lower King's Ferry *see* Queensferry

Łowicz (town, central Poland) : 1940–1945 German *Lowitsch*; to 1915 Russian *Lovich*; 1793–1807 German *Lowitsch*
Lowitsch *see* Łowicz
Lozengrad *see* Kırklareli
Lozno-Aleksandrovka *see* Lozno-Oleksandrivka
Lozno-Oleksandrivka (town, eastern Ukraine) : (Russian *Lozno-Aleksandrovka*); to mid–1930s *Oleksandrivka* (Russian *Aleksandrovka*)
Lú *see* Louth
Luanda (city, northern Angola) : formerly Portuguese *São Paulo de Luanda*
Luangwa (town, southeastern Zambia) : formerly Portuguese *Feira*
Luau (town, west central Angola) : 1930s–*c*.1976 Portuguese *Vila Teixeira de Souza*
Luba (town, northwestern Equatorial Guinea) : formerly Spanish *San Carlos*
Lubaczów (town, southeastern Poland) : 1939–1941 Ukrainian *Lyubachiv* (Russian *Lyubachev*)
Lubań (city, southwestern Poland) : to 1945 German *Lauban*
Lubango (city, southwestern Angola) : to 1975 Portuguese *Sá da Bandeira*
Lubawa (town, northern Poland) : 1772–1807, 1815–1919, 1939–1945 German *Löbau*
Lubawka (town, southwestern Poland) : to 1945 German *Liebau*
Lübben (town, eastern Germany) : formerly Wendish (Sorbian) *Lubin*
Lüben *see* Lubin
Lubiana *see* Ljubljana
Lubiąż (village, southwestern Poland) : to 1945 German *Leubus*
Lubij *see* Löbau
Lubin (town, southwestern Poland) : to 1945 German *Lüben*
Lubin *see* Lübben
Lubliniec (town, southern Poland) : 1939–1945 German *Loben*; to 1921 German *Lublinitz*
Lublinitz *see* Lubliniec
Lubnān *see* ¹Lebanon
Lubomierz (town, southwestern Poland) : to 1945 German *Liebenthal*
Luboml *see* Lyuboml'
Lubrza (town, western Poland) : to 1945 German *Liebenau bei Schwiebus*
Lubsko (town, western Poland) : to 1945 German *Sommerfeld*
Lubumbashi (city, southeastern Democratic Republic of the Congo) : to 1966 French *Élisabethville*
Luca *see* Lucca
Lucania *see* Basilicata
Lucca (city, north central Italy) : Roman *Luca*

Lučenec (town, southern Slovakia) : to 1918, 1938–1945 Hungarian *Losonc*

Lucentum *see* **Alicante**

Lucera (town, southeastern Italy) : Roman *Luceria*

Luceria *see* **Lucera**

Lucerna *see* **Lucerne**

Lucerne (city, central Switzerland) : German *Luzern*; Italian *Lucerna* (English invariably prefers the French form of the city's name.)

Lucerne, Lake (central Switzerland) : [French *Lac des Quatre Cantons*; German *Vierwaldstätter See*; Italian *Lago dei Quattro Cantoni*] (The continental languages name the lake for the four Forest Cantons that surround it. Three of these, Schwyz, Uri, and Unterwalden, formed the original alliance of 1291 from which modern Switzerland evolved. English names the lake for **Lucerne**, which joined the alliance in 1332.)

Łuck *see* **Luts'k**

Lucus Augusti *see* **Lugo**

Lüda *see* **Dalian**

Ludchurch (village, southwestern Wales) : Welsh *Yr Eglwys Lwyd*

Lüderitz (town, southwestern Namibia) : formerly Portuguese *Angra Pequena*

Ludington (town, Michigan, north central United States) : to 1871 *Marquette*

Luditz *see* **Žlutice**

Ludlow (town, Massachusetts, northeastern United States) : to 1775 *Stony Hill*

Ludwigshafen (city, southwestern Germany) : to 1843 *Rheinschanze*

Ludwigsort *see* **Ladushkin**

Ludza (town, eastern Latvia) : to 1918 Russian *Lyutsin*

Lueluz *see* **Conselheiro Lafaiete**

Lugano (town, southern Switzerland) : German *Lauis* (The town, on the lake of the same name, should not be confused with **Locarno**, further north on Lake Maggiore.)

Lugansk *see* (1) **Luhans'k**; (2) **Stanychno-Luhans'ke**

Lugdunum *see* (1) **Laon**; (2) **Leiden**; (3) **Lyon**

Lugdunum Batavorum *see* **Leiden**

Lugdunum Convenarum *see* **St.-Bertrand-de-Comminges**

Luggarus *see* **Locarno**

Lugo (town, northwestern Spain) : Roman *Lucus Augusti*

Lugoj (city, western Romania) : to 1918 Hungarian *Lugos*; to 1867 German *Lugosch*

Lugos *see* **Lugoj**

Lugosch *see* **Lugoj**

Lugovaya Proleyka *see* ³**Primorsk**

Lugovoye *see* **Kulan**

Luguvalium *see* **Carlisle**

Luhans'k (city, eastern Ukraine) : (Russian *Lugansk*); 1970–1990 *Voroshylovhrad* (Russian *Voroshilovgrad*); 1958–1970 *Luhans'k* (Russian *Lugansk*); 1935–1958 *Voroshylovhrad* (Russian *Voroshilovgrad*)

Luhans'k *see* **Stanychno-Luhans'ke**

Luik *see* **Liège**

Luimneach *see* **Limerick**

Luís Correia (city, northeastern Brazil) : to 1939 Portuguese *Amarração*

Lukiv (town, northwestern Ukraine) : (Russian *Lukov*); to 1946 *Matseyiv* (Russian *Matseyevo*)

Lukov *see* **Lukiv**

Lüleburgaz (town, northwestern Turkey) : 1920–1922 modern Greek *Arkadioúpolis*; to 1913 Bulgarian *Lyule-Burgas*

Luling *see* **Ji'an**

Luluabourg *see* **Kananga**

Lumbala N'guimbo (town, southeastern Angola) : to 1975 Portuguese *Gago Coutinho*

Lumby (village, British Columbia, southwestern Canada) : to 1894 *White Valley*

Lundenburg *see* **Břeclav**

Luninets (town, southern Belarus) : 1919–1939 Polish *Łuniniec*

Łuniniec *see* **Luninets**

Lunino (village, western Russia) : 1938–1945 German *Hohensalzburg*; to 1938 German *Lengwethen*

Lun'yevka (town, west central Russia) : to *c*.1928 *Lun'yevskiye Kopi*

Lun'yevskiye Kopi *see* **Lun'yevka**

Lupatia *see* **Altamura**

Luperón (town, northern Dominican Republic) : to 1927 *Blanco*

Lupiae *see* **Lecce**

Lupilichi (town, northwestern Mozambique) : to 1980 Portuguese *Olivença*

Lurgan (town, east central Northern Ireland) : Irish *An Lorgain*

Lusanga (town, southwestern Democratic Republic of the Congo) : to 1972 French *Leverville*

Lusatia (region, eastern Germany) : [German *Lausitz*]

Lusavan *see* **Ch'arents'avan**

Lüshun (city, northeastern China) : traditional English *Port Arthur*; 1905–1945 Japanese *Ryojun* (The English name is associated with the Japanese victory over the Russians here in 1905 during the Russo-Japanese War.)

Lusitania *see* **Portugal**

Lü-ta *see* **Dalian**

Lutetia *see* ¹**Paris**

Łutselk'e (village, Northwest Territories, central Canada) : to 1999 *Snowdrift*

Lutsk *see* Luts'k

Luts'k (city, northwestern Ukraine) : (Russian *Lutsk*); 1919–1939 Polish *Łuck* (The Russian name is historically associated with the fighting between Austrian and Russian forces in and around the fortified town during World War I.)

Luttenberg *see* Ljutomer

Lüttich *see* Liège

Lutynia (village, southwestern Poland) : to 1945 German *Leuthen* (The German name is associated with the Prussian defeat of Austria in 1757 during the Seven Years' War.)

¹Luxembourg (grand duchy, western Europe) : German *Luxemburg* (The German spelling of the name is sometimes used to avoid undue French emphasis.)

²Luxembourg (city, south central Luxembourg) : [Luxemburgian *Letzeburg*]

Luxemburg *see* ¹Luxembourg

Luxor (town, northern Egypt) : [Arabic *Al-Qusur*]

Luzern *see* Lucerne

Lǔzhene *see* Malchika

Luzhou *see* Hefei

Luziânia (city, central Brazil) : to 1944 *Santa Luzia*

Luzilândia (city, northeastern Brazil) : to 1944 Portuguese *Pôrto Alegre*

L'viv (city, western Ukraine) : (Russian *L'vov*); 1941–1944 German *Lemberg*; 1919–1941 Polish *Lwów*; to 1918 German *Lemberg*; Medieval Latin *Leopolis* (The German name was prominent for the scene of fighting between Austrian and Russian forces in World War I.)

L'vov *see* L'viv

Lwów *see* L'viv

Lwówek (town, western Poland) : to 1945 German *Neustadt bei Pinne*

Lwówek Śląski (town, western Poland) : to 1945 German *Löwenberg*

Lyakhivtsi *see* Bilohirya

Lyakhovtsy *see* Bilohirya

Lyallpur *see* Faisalabad

Lyandvarovo *see* Lentvaris

Lychidnos *see* Ohrid

Lyck *see* Ełk

Lycopolis *see* Asyut

Lydda *see* Lod

Lykhachive *see* Pervomays'kyy

Lyman *see* Krasnyy Lyman

Lympne (village, southeastern England) : Roman *Portus Lemanis*

Lynchville *see* ²Rome

Lyndon Village *see* Caribou

Lynn (town, Massachusetts, northeastern United States) : to 1637 *Saugus*

Lynn *see* King's Lynn

Lynn Regis *see* King's Lynn

Lyon (city, southeastern France) : conventional English *Lyons*; Roman *Lugdunum* (A more classical form of the Roman name is *Lugudunum*, recorded for an unlocated site in England, perhaps in the north of the country. The French city's full formal Roman title was *Colonia Copia Claudia Augusta Lugdunum*.)

Lyons *see* Lyon

Lysa Hora *see* Shevchenko

Lysaya Gora *see* Shevchenko

Lysychans'k (city, eastern Ukraine) : (Russian *Lisichansk*)

Lyttelton (town, southeastern New Zealand) : to 1858 *Port Cooper*

Lyubachev *see* Lubaczów

Lyubachiv *see* Lubachów

Lyubinsky (town, southern Russia) : to 1947 *Novolyubino*

Lyuboml' (town, northwestern Ukraine) : 1919–1939 Polish *Luboml*

Lyudvipol' *see* Sosnove

Lyudvypil' *see* Sosnove

Lyuksemburg *see* (1) Bolnisi; (2) Rozivka

Lyuksemburgi *see* Bolnisi

Lyule-Burgas *see* Lüleburgaz

Lyutsin *see* Ludza

Maarianhamina (town, southwestern Finland) : to 1809 Swedish *Mariehamn* (The town is in Åland, where the predominance of Swedish means that its Swedish name is preferred.)

Maas *see* Meuse

Maastricht (town, southeastern Netherlands) : Roman *Trajectum ad Mosam* (The Roman name locates the town at a crossing of the Meuse, just as Utrecht arose by a ford over the Rhine.)

Macabu *see* Conceição de Macabu

Macaloge (town, northwestern Mozambique) : to 1976 *Miranda*

Macapá *see* Peri Mirim

Macarsca *see* Makarska

Macassar *see* Ujung Pandang

Macatuba (town, southeastern Brazil) : to 1944 *Bocaiúva*

Macaubal (town, southeastern Brazil) : to 1944 *Macaúbas*

Macaúbas *see* Macaubal

McCarty's Mills *see* ²Aurora

McClelland's Station *see* ²Georgetown

McCook (town, Nebraska, central United States) : originally *Fairview*

McDonald's Bridge *see* **Oneonta**

Macedonia (republic, southern Europe) : [Macedonian *Makedonija*] (When Macedonia seceded from Yugoslavia in 1992, neighboring Greece objected to its name, claiming it exclusively for its northern region. Macedonia accordingly joined the United Nations in 1993 as the *Former Yugoslav Republic of Macedonia,* a name acceptable to Greece. The first two words were later dropped, giving *Republic of Macedonia* as a name of continuing concern to Greece. The matter was addressed by the World Council of Hellenes Abroad in a full-page ad headed "What's in a Name?" in the London *Times* of April 2, 2008.*)

Maceriae *see* **Mézières**

Macguire's Punt *see* **Shepparton**

Machaire Fíolta *see* **Magherafelt**

McHattiesburg *see* **Balfour**

Machigonne *see* **Portland**

Macías Nguema Biyogo *see* **Bioko**

Mackeim *see* **Maków Mazowiecki**

Mackensen *see* **Orlyak**

McKinley, Mt. (Alaska, northwestern United States) : alternate (Koyukon) *Denali* (In 1975 the Alaska legislature officially adopted the name *Denali* for the mountain and a bill was introduced to Congress on the matter in 1977. See James Kari, "The Tenada-Denali-Mount McKinley Controversy," in *Names*, Vol. 84, No. 3, September 1986, pp. 347–351.)

Macleod *see* **Fort Macleod**

McLoughlin, Mt. (Oregon, northwestern United States) : formerly *Mt. Pitt*

MacMahon *see* **Aïn Touta**

Macomb (city, Illinois, north central United States) : to 1830 *Washington*

Macon (city, Georgia, southeastern United States) : to 1823 *Newtown*

Mâcon (city, east central France) : Roman *Matisco*

Macoraba *see* **Mecca**

MacPherson *see* **Kapuskasing**

Macroom (town, southwestern Ireland) : Irish *Maigh Chromtha*

Madagascar (island republic, western Indian Ocean) : 1960–1975 *Malagasy Republic*

Madang (town, north central Papua New Guinea) : originally German *Friedrich-Wilhelmshafen*

Madauros *see* **M'daourouch**

Madhya Pradesh (state, central India) : to 1947 *Central Provinces and Berar*

Madinat ash Sha'b (town, southwestern Yemen) : to 1967 *al-Ittihad*

Madison (town, New Jersey, northeastern United States) : to 1834 *Bottle Hill*

Madison *see* ³**Orange**

Madona (town, east central Latvia) : formerly German *Modohn*

Madras *see* (1) **Chennai**; (2) **Tamil Nadu**

Madre de Deus *see* **Brejo da Madre de Deus**

Maeander *see* **Menderes**

Maenam *see* **Chao Phraya**

Maenorbŷr *see* **Manorbier**

Maeotis Palus *see* **Azov, Sea of**

Maerun *see* **Marshfield**

Maes-glas *see* **Greenfield**

Maesyfed *see* **New Radnor**

Mafeking *see* **Mafikeng**

Mafikeng (town, northern South Africa) : to 1980 *Mafeking* (The former spelling became widely known from a famous Boer War siege here. The announcement of the town's relief by British troops on May 17, 1900 brought

*The following is a transcript of the text:

Why is the Macedonian question so delicate and complex? *The term "Macedonia" is not exclusively related to a specific state. Rather, it has always been used to delineate a wider geographical area, approximately 51 percent of which is part of Greece, 37 percent is in the Former Yugoslav Republic of Macedonia, 11 percent in Bulgaria and 1 percent in Albania. The choice of one state alone to monopolize the name "Macedonia"—the largest part of which lies outside its borders—neither reflects geographical and political reality, nor contributes to stability in the Balkans.*

Why does Greece oppose the name "Republic of Macedonia"? *"Republic of Macedonia," or just "Macedonia," fails to solve the problem, as it does not distinguish the new country from the Northern Greek region of Macedonia, or from the parts of the wider Macedonia, which are also in Bulgaria and Albania. Furthermore, it is associated with the argument for the unification of "Greater Macedonia"—a policy conceived by Stalin and Tito and pursued by the leadership in FYROM to the present day. The name is therefore linked with an ongoing policy that foresees territorial claims to a part of Greek teritory, that has had a Greek identity for more than three millennia, and is associated with immense pain and suffering by the peoples in the region.*

Why does Greece favor a compound name? *Greece unlike FYROM has made great strides to try and resolve the name issue under U.N. auspices and has gone more than half-way to find a solution. It has sat at the negotiating table since 1995 and has shown willingness to consider a compound name such as "North Macedonia," which includes the term "Macedonia" but attaches an adjective to it to distinguish it from the Greek province with the same name. This is sensible, reasonable and fair for both sides. A win–win situation.*

Why is it time to end the debate? *Today, the conditions for achieving a breakthrough are better than ever. Greece is the single largest investor in the Former Yugoslav Republic of Macedonia (FYROM). Athens supports FYROM's bids for NATO and EU membership, but this crucial issue must be resolved first. Alliances and partnerships can only be fostered among countries if there is good will, mutual trust and good neighbourly relations.*

scenes of riotous revelry in London and resulted in the temporary coining of the verb
maffick to mean "to celebrate joyously.")

Magallanes *see* **Punta Arenas**

Magdalena Island *see* **Fatu Hiva**

Magherafelt (town, central Northern Ireland) :
Irish *Machaire Fíolta*

Maghnia (town, northwestern Algeria) : to
*c.*1962 French *Marnia*

Magnesia *see* **Manisa**

Magnus Portus *see* ¹**Portsmouth**

Maguntan-hama *see* **Pugachyovo**

Magyarkanizsa *see* **Kanjiža**

Magyarország *see* **Hungary**

Magyaróvár (former town, northwestern Hungary) : to 1867 German *Ungarisch-Altenburg*
(In 1945 the town combined with **Moson** to
form the city of *Mosonmagyaróvár*.)

Mahabad (town, northwestern Iran) : to 1930s
Saujbulagh

Mahilyow (city, eastern Belarus) : (Russian
Mogilyov); to 1918 Russian *Mogilyov*

Mahón (town, eastern Balearic Islands, Spain) :
traditional English *Port Mahon*; Roman *Portus
Magonis*

Mährisch-Budwitz *see* **Moravské Budějovice**

Mährisch-Kromau *see* **Moravský Krumlov**

Mährisch-Ostrau *see* **Ostrava**

Mährisch-Schönberg *see* **Šumperk**

Mährisch-Trübau *see* **Moravská Třebová**

Mährisch-Weisskirchen *see* ¹**Hranice**

Mahto *see* **Pierre**

Maidstone *see* ¹**East Hampton**

Maigh Chromtha *see* **Macroom**

Maighean Rátha *see* **Mountrath**

Maigh Eo *see* **Mayo**

Maigh Nuad *see* **Maynooth**

Maimachin *see* **Altanbulag**

Main Camp *see* **West Wyalong**

Mai-Ndombe, Lake (western Democratic Republic of the Congo) : to 1973 *Lake Leopold*

Mainistir Fhear Maí *see* **Fermoy**

Mainistir Laoise *see* **Abbeyleix**

Mainistir na Búille *see* **Boyle**

Mainistir na Corann *see* **Midleton**

Mainland (island, Orkney Islands, northern
Scotland) : alternate literary *Pomona*

Mainz (city, western Germany) : 1792–1793,
1797–1816, 1918–1930 French *Mayence*; Roman
Mogontiacum (The French name was long the
usual form in English.)

Mairiporã (city, southeastern Brazil) : to 1948
Juqueri

Maison Blanche *see* (1) **Casablanca**; (2) **Dar el
Beida**

Maison-Carrée *see* **El Harrach**

Maisons-Laffitte (town, northern France) : formerly *Maisons-sur-Seine*. (The town, which
added the name of a French banker in the 19th
century, is now a Paris suburb.)

Maisons-sur-Seine *see* **Maisons-Laffitte**

Maitland (city, New South Wales, southeastern
Australia) : originally *Wallis Plains* (The city
was formed in 1944 when the two towns of
East Maitland, earlier *Maitland* and originally
Wallis Plains, and *West Maitland*, originally
Molly Morgan's Plains, combined with nearby
Morpeth.)

Majorca (island, central Balearic Islands, western
Mediterranean) : [Spanish *Mallorca*]

Major Isidoro (town, northeastern Brazil) : to
1944 *Sertãozinho*

Makanza (town, northwestern Democratic Republic of the Congo) : to 1972 French *Nouvelle
Anvers*

Makarov (town, eastern Russia) : 1905–1945
Japanese *Shiritoru*

Makarska (town, southern Croatia) : to 1918
Italian *Macarsca*

Makedonija *see* **Macedonia**

Makeyevka *see* **Makiyivka**

Makhachkala (city, southwestern Russia) : 1857–
1922 *Petrovsk-Port*; to 1857 *Petrovskoye*

Makhado (town, northeastern South Africa) : to
2003 *Louis Trichardt*

Makharadze *see* **Ozurget'i**

Makhlata *see* **Pelovo**

Makhmuzlii *see* **Todor Ikonomovo**

Makhnivka *see* ²**Komsomol's'ke**

Makhnovka *see* ²**Komsomol's'ke**

Makhsudabad *see* **Murshidabad**

Makinka *see* **Makinsk**

Makinsk (city, northern Kazakhstan) : to 1944
Makinka

Makiyivka (city, southeastern Ukraine) : (Russian *Makeyevka*); 1920–1931 *Dmytriyevs'k* (Russian *Dmitriyevsk*)

Makkah *see* **Mecca**

Makov *see* **Maków Mazowiecki**

Maków Mazowiecki (town, east central Poland)
: 1940–1945 German *Mackeim*; to 1915 Russian
Makov

Mala *see* **Mallow**

Malabo (town, northwestern Equatorial Guinea)
: to 1973 Spanish *Santa Isabel*

Malaca *see* **Málaga**

Malacka *see* **Malacky**

Malacky (town, western Slovakia) : to 1918 Hungarian *Malacka*

Maladzyechna (town, west central Belarus) :
(Russian *Molodechno*); 1919–1939 Polish
Mołodeczno; to 1918 Russian *Molodechno*

Málaga (city, northern Spain) : Roman *Malaca*

Malagasy Republic *see* **Madagascar**

Malahide (town, eastern Ireland) : Irish *Mullach Íde*

Malatya (city, east central Turkey) : ancient Greek *Melitene*

Malawi (republic, southeastern Africa) : to 1964 *Nyasaland*

Malawi, Lake (southeastern Africa) : alternate *Lake Nyasa*

Malaya *see* **Malaysia**

Malaya Znamenka *see* **Kam'yanka-Dniprovs'ka**

Malay Peninsula (southeastern Asia) : Roman *Chersonesus Aurea* (The Roman name translates as *Golden Chersonese*, as which the peninsula was at one time known to English speakers. *Chersonesus* is a name of Greek origin applied to various European peninsulas, one of the best known being the **Crimea**.)

Malaysia (independent country, southeastern Asia) : to 1963 *Malaya* (The former federation of *Malaya*, comprising nine states on the Malay peninsula, became independent in 1957 and in 1963 combined with three other states to form the federation of *Malaysia*.)

Mala Znam'yanka *see* **Kam'yanka-Dniprovs'ka**

Malbergen *see* **Georgsmarienhütte**

Malbork (city, northern Poland) : 1772–1945 German *Marienburg*

Malchika (village, northern Bulgaria) : to 1950 *Lŭzhene*

Malebo Pool (southwestern Democratic Republic of the Congo) : to 1972 *Stanley Pool*

Malema (town, north central Mozambique) : 1921–1980 Portuguese *Entre Rios*

Maleventum *see* **Benevento**

Mali (republic, western Africa) : 1958–1960 *Sudanese Republic*; 1920–1958 *French Sudan*

Malines *see* **Mechlin**

Malinovoye Ozero (town, southern Russia) : formerly *Mikhaylovsky*

Malko Tărnovo (town, southeastern Bulgaria) : to 1913 Turkish *Tırnova*

Malles Venosta (village, northern Italy) : to 1919 German *Mals*

Mallorca *see* **Majorca**

Mallow (town, southwestern Ireland) : Irish *Mala*

Mallwen *see* **Mayskoye**

Mallwischken *see* **Mayskoye**

Malo (island, north central Vanuatu) : formerly *Bartholomew Island*

Malobaranivka *see* **Ivanivka**

Malobaranovka *see* **Ivanivka**

Malokuril'skoye (village, eastern Russia) : 1905–1945 Japanese *Shakotan*

Malpaís *see* **San Nicolás de Buenos Aires**

Mals *see* **Malles Venosta**

Malta (island republic, central Mediterranean) : Roman and biblical *Melita*

Malton (town, northern England) : Roman *Derventio* (The Roman name was that of the **Derwent** River here.)

Małuowice (village, southwestern Poland) : to 1945 German *Mollwitz*

Malvérnia *see* **Chicualacuala**

Malvinas, Islas *see* **Falkland Islands**

Maly Taymyr (island, northern Russia) : to *c*.1918 *Tsarevicha Alekseya*

Mamonovo (town, western Russia) : to 1945 German *Heiligenbeil*

Mamucium *see* ¹**Manchester**

Man, Isle of (Irish Sea, British Isles) : Roman *Monapia* (The Roman name, which may originally have been *Manavia*, derives from a root meaning simply "mountain," as for **Anglesey**, but here referring to the island's central mountain of Snaefell.)

Manáos *see* **Manaus**

Manaus (city, northwestern Brazil) : 1850–1939 *Manáos*; formerly *Villa da Barra*; originally *São José do Rio Negrinho*

Manavia *see* **Man, Isle of**

Mancetter (village, central England) : Roman *Manduessedum*

¹**Manchester** (city, northwestern England) : Roman *Mamucium* (The Roman name was long misspelled *Mancunium*, giving "Mancunian" as the adjectival form of the city's name.)

²**Manchester** (city, New Hampshire, northeastern United States) : 1751–1810 *Derryfield*; earlier *Tyngstown*; originally *Old Harry's Town*

Manchester *see* (1) **College Park**; (2) **Virden**; (3) **Yazoo City**

Manchukuo *see* **Manchuria**

Manchuria (historical region, northeastern China) : alternate Chinese *Dongbei*; 1932–1945 *Manchukuo*

Mandala, Mt. (eastern Indonesia) : formerly *Juliana Top*

Mandidzuzure *see* **Chimanimani**

Manduessedum *see* **Mancetter**

Manduria *see* **Ionio**

Mangaung *see* **Bloemfontein**

Mangoche (town, southern Malawi) : to 1964 *Fort Johnston*

Manguaba *see* ¹**Pilar**

Mangush *see* **Pershotravneve**

Manhattan (city, Kansas, central United States) : to 1856 *Boston*

Manhattan *see* **New York**

Manhush *see* **Pershotravneve**

Manica (town, western Mozambique) : to 1976 Portuguese *Vila Pery*

Manihiki (atoll, northern Cook Islands) : formerly *Humphrey Island*

Maniitsoq (village, southwestern Greenland) : formerly Danish *Sukkertoppen*

Manisa (city, western Turkey) : ancient Greek *Magnesia*

Manitou (village, Manitoba, central Canada) : to 1881 *Manitou City*

Manitou City *see* **Manitou**

Manorbier (village, southwestern Wales) : Welsh *Maenorbŷr*

Manorhamilton (town, northwestern Ireland) : Irish *Cluainín*

Manra (island, central Kiribati) : formerly *Sydney Island*

Mansa (town, northern Zambia) : to 1964 *Fort Rosebery*

Mansfield (town, Connecticut, northeastern United States) : to 1702 *Ponde Town*

Mantes-Gassicourt *see* **Mantes-la-Jolie**

Mantes-la-Jolie (city, northern France) : formerly *Mantes-Gassicourt*; Medieval Latin *Medanta*

Mantova *see* **Mantua**

Mantua (city, northern Italy) : [Italian *Mantova*] (English has preserved the Roman name of the city.)

¹Manuae (atoll, southeastern Cook Islands) : formerly *Hervey Island*

²Manuae (atoll, northwestern French Polynesia) : formerly *Scilly Island*

Manuel Urbano (town, western Brazil) : to 1944 Portuguese *Castelo*

Manyame, Lake (north central Zimbabwe) : formerly *Lake Robertson*

Manzini (city, central Swaziland) : to 1960 *Bremersdorp*

Manzovka *see* **Sibirtsevo**

Mao (city, northwestern Dominican Republic) : to 1959 *Valverde*

Maoka *see* **Kholmsk**

Maputo (city, southern Mozambique) : to 1976 Portuguese *Lourenço Marques*

Maracaibo (city, northwestern Venezuela) : originally *Nueva Zamora*

Maraisburg *see* **Hofmeyr**

Marakanda *see* **Samarkand**

Máramarossziget *see* **Sighetu-Marmaţiei**

Maramba (city, southern Zambia) : alternate *Livingstone*

Marandellas *see* **Marondera**

Marathus *see* **Amrit**

Marawi (city, southern Philippines) : formerly *Dansalan*

Marburg *see* **Maribor**

Marchand *see* **Rommani**

Marche (region, central Italy) : traditional English *The Marches* (The English name for a border country is found elsewhere, as the *Welsh Marches* between England and Wales.)

Marchena, Isla (island, northern Galápagos Islands, Ecuador) : formerly *Bindloe Island*

Marches, The *see* **Marche**

Marchlewsk *see* **Dovbysh**

Marcodurum *see* **Düren**

Mare Adriaticum *see* **Adriatic Sea**

Mare Cantabricum *see* **Biscay, Bay of**

Marechal Deodoro (city, northeastern Brazil) : to 1939 *Alagoas*

Marechal Floriano *see* **Piranhas**

Mareeba (town, Queensland, northeastern Australia) : originally *Granite Creek*

Mare Germanicum *see* **North Sea**

Mare Internum *see* **Mediterranean Sea**

Marek *see* **Dupnitsa**

Mare Mortuum *see* **Dead Sea**

Marengo *see* **Hadjout**

Mare Nostrum *see* **Mediterranean Sea**

Mare Rubrum *see* **Red Sea**

Marganets *see* (1) **Marhanets'**; (2) **Zhezdy**

Margecany (town, east central Slovakia) : to 1918 Hungarian *Margitfalu*

Marggrabowa *see* **Olecko**

Margherita, Lake *see* **Abaya, Lake**

Margitfalu *see* **Margecany**

Marhanets' (city, southeastern Ukraine) : (Russian *Marganets*); c.1926–1938 *Komintern*; to c.1926 *Horodyshche* (Russian *Gorodishche*)

Mari (town, northeastern Brazil) : to 1944 *Araçá*

Mariana (city, southeastern Brazil) : formerly *Vila de Albuquerque*

Mariana Islands (western Pacific) : to 1668 *Ladrones Islands*

Mariánské Lázně (town, western Czech Republic) : to 1918, 1938–1945 German *Marienbad*

Maria Pereira *see* **Mombaça**

Maria Rast *see* **Ruše**

Maria-Theresiopel *see* **Subotica**

Mari Autonomous Soviet Socialist Republic *see* **Mari El**

Maribor (city, northern Slovenia) : to 1945 German *Marburg*

Maridunum *see* **Carmarthen**

Mariehamn *see* **Maarianhamina**

Mari El (republic, western Russia) : to 1992 *Mari Autonomous Soviet Socialist Republic* (The second word of the present name is Mari *el*, "land.")

Marienbad *see* Mariánské Lázně
Marienburg *see* (1) Alūksne; (2) Malbork
Marienhausen *see* Viļaka
Marienhof *see* Nikitovka
Mariental *see* ¹Sovetskoye
Marienwerder *see* Kwidzyn
Marignano *see* Melegnano
Mariinskoye *see* Mar'yevka
Mariinsk Water System *see* Volga-Baltic Waterway
Marijampolė (city, southern Lithuania) : (Russian *Mariyampole*) 1955–1989 *Kapsukas*
Marino *see* ²Leninsky
¹Marion (city, Ohio, north central United States) : to 1822 *Jacob's Well*
²Marion (town, Alabama, southeastern United States) : originally *Muckle Ridge*
Mariscal Estigarribia (town, northern Paraguay) : to 1945 *López de Filippis*
Maritsa *see* (1) Ognyanovo; (2) Simeonovgrad
Mariupol' (city, southeastern Ukraine) : 1948–1989 Russian *Zhdanov*
Mariyampole *see* Marijampolė
Mark Creek Crossing *see* Kimberley
Markhlevsk *see* Dovbysh
Märkisch Friedland *see* Mirosławiec
Markovo (town, western Russia) : to 1940 *Markovo-Sbornoye*
Markovo-Sbornoye *see* Markovo
Marks (city, western Russia) : 1920–1941 *Marksshtadt*; to 1920 *Yekaterinenshtadt* (The former names are Russian forms of the respective German names *Marxstadt*, "Marx city," and *Katharinenstadt*, "Catherine city." The region here was settled in the 18th century by Germans invited by decree of Catherine the Great and from 1924 to 1941, in the USSR, was organized as the Volga German Autonomous Soviet Socialist Republic, with capital at Engel's, 30 miles down the Volga River.)
Marksshtadt *see* Marks
Marmara, Sea of (northwestern Turkey) : ancient Greek *Propontis* (The sea's Greek name means "before the sea," as it lies on the route to the Black Sea via the Bosporus.)
Marmaroschsiget *see* Sighetu-Marmaţiei
Marne (river, northeastern France) : Roman *Matrona*
Marneuli (city, southern Georgia) : to 1947 *Borchalo*
Marnia *see* Maghnia
Maroc *see* Morocco
Marondera (city, east central Zimbabwe) : to 1982 *Marandellas*
Marosvásárhely *see* Târgu Mureş

Marquês de Valença (city, southeastern Brazil) : to 1943 Portuguese *Valença*
Marquette (town, Michigan, north central United States) : originally *Worcester*
Marquette *see* Ludington
Marracuene (town, southern Mozambique) : to 1975 Portuguese *Vila Luísa*
Marruás *see* Pôrto
Marsala (town, southern Italy) : Roman *Lilybaeum*
Marsa Matruh (town, northwestern Egypt) : Roman *Paraetonium*
Marseille (city, southern France) : conventional English *Marseilles*, Roman *Massilia*; ancient Greek *Massalia* (The *r* in the French name is said to have entered by association with the Roman god *Mars*.)
Marseilles *see* Marseille
Marshfield (village, southeastern Wales) : Welsh *Maerun*
Marshfield *see* Coos Bay
Marthasville *see* Atlanta
Martil (town, northwestern Morocco) : formerly Spanish *Río Martín*
Martimprey-du-Kiss *see* Ahfir
Martin (city, northwestern Slovakia) : formerly *Turčiansky Svätý Martin*; to 1918 Hungarian *Turócszentmárton*
Martinsborough *see* ¹Greenville
Martins Ferry (town, Ohio, north central United States) : formerly *Martinsville*; originally *Jefferson*
Martin's Point *see* Campbellton
Martinsville *see* Martins Ferry
Martvili (town, western Georgia) : 1939–1991 *Gegechkori*
Martynovka *see* Bol'shaya Martynovka
Martyropolis *see* Silvan
Marutea North (atoll, central French Polynesia) : formerly *Furneaux Island*
Marutea South (atoll, southeastern French Polynesia) : formerly *Lord Hood Island*
Marvão *see* Castelo do Piauí
Marxwalde *see* Neuhardenberg
Mary (city, southeastern Turkmenistan) : to 1937 Russian *Merv* (The present city was founded in 1884 and took its name from the ancient city of *Merv*, 19 miles to the east.)
Maryborough (town, Victoria, southeastern Australia) : originally *Simson's Ranges*
Maryborough *see* Port Laoise
Mar'yevka (village, northern Kazakhstan) : to 1939 Russian *Mariinskoye*
Mar'yino *see* Pristen'
Maryport (town, northwestern England) : Roman *Alauna* (The Roman fort stood at the

mouth of the *Ellen* River here and was named for it.)

Marystown (town, Newfoundland and Labrador, eastern Canada) : formerly *Mortier Bay*

Marysville *see* **Corvallis**

Más Afuera *see* **Alejandro Selkirk**

Más a Tierra *see* **Robinson Crusoe**

Mason City (city, Iowa, north central United States) : formerly *Masonic Grove*; earlier *Shibboleth*

Masonic Grove *see* **Mason City**

Massa-Carrar (province, central Italy) : *c.*1938–1945 *Apuania*

Massacre Island *see* **Dauphin Island**

Massalia *see* **Marseille**

Massawa (former administrative region, central and southeastern Eritrea) : to 1941 Italian *Bassopiano Orientale*

Massilia *see* **Marseille**

Massow *see* **Maszewo**

Masuren *see* **Masuria**

Masuria (region, northeastern Poland) : [Polish *Mazury*]; formerly German *Masuren*

Masvingo (town, south central Zimbabwe) : 1980–1982 *Nyanda*; to 1980 *Fort Victoria*

Maszewo (town, northwestern Poland) : to 1945 German *Massow*

Mata Grande (city, northeastern Brazil) : to 1939 Portuguese *Paulo Affonso*

Matala (town, southwestern Angola) : formerly Portuguese *Artur de Paiva*

Matamoros (city, northeastern Mexico) : alternate *Heroica Matamoros*; to 1851 *San Juan de los Esteros*

Matau *see* **Clutha**

Mataúna *see* **Palmeiras de Goiás**

Matisco *see* **Mâcon**

Matões *see* **Parnarama**

Matrona *see* **Marne**

Matrosovo (village, western Russia) : to 1945 German *Uggehnen*

Matseyevo *see* **Lukiv**

Matseyiv *see* **Lukiv**

Matsumae (town, northern Japan) : to 1930s *Fukuyama*

Matterhorn (mountain, northwestern Italy/southern Switzerland) : French *Mont Cervin*; Italian *Monte Cervino* (English prefers the German name.)

Mattersburg (town, eastern Austria) : to 1924 *Mattersdorf*; to 1919 Hungarian *Nagymárton*

Mattersdorf *see* **Mattersburg**

Mauch Chunk *see* **Jim Thorpe**

Maura Gefura *see* **Uzunköprü**

Mauretania *see* **Mautitania**

Mauritania (republic, western Africa) : formerly French *Mauritanie* (The name is also an alternate spelling for *Mauretania*, the ancient region of northern Africa that was the location of the Roman provinces of *Mauretania Caesariensis* and *Mauretania Tingitana*.)

Mauritanie *see* **Mauritania**

Mauritius (island state, eastern Indian Ocean) : 1721–1810 *Île de France*

Mauritius, Cape *see* **Zhelaniya, Cape**

Mauritzstad *see* **Recife**

Mavromati (village, southern Greece) : ancient Greek *Messene*

Mawlamyine (city, southeastern Myanmar) : conventional *Moulmein*

Maxambamba *see* **Nova Iguaçu**

Mayagüez (city, western Puerto Rico) : originally *Nuestra Señora de la Candelaria de Mayagüez*

Mayakovsky *see* **Baghdat'i**

Mayence *see* **Mainz**

Maynesborough *see* ²**Berlin**

Maynooth (town, eastern Ireland) : Irish *Maigh Nuad*

Mayo (county, northwestern Ireland) : Irish *Maigh Eo*

Mayskoye (village, western Russia) : 1938–1945 German *Mallwen*; to 1938 German *Mallwischken*

Maysville (town, Kentucky, east central United States) : originally *Limestone*

Mazagan *see* **El Jadida**

Mažeikiai (city, northwestern Lithuania) : to 1918 Russian *Murav'yovo*

Mazovetsk *see* **Wysokie Mazowieckie**

Mazsalaca (town, northern Latvia) : to 1917 German *Salisburg*

Mazury *see* **Masuria**

Mazyr (town, southeastern Belarus) : (Russian *Mozyr'*); 1919–1939 Polish *Mozyrz*; to 1918 Russian *Mozyr'*

Mbala (town, northeastern Zambia) : to 1968 *Abercorn*

Mbalabala (town, southwestern Zimbabwe) : to 1982 *Balla Balla*

Mbandaka (town, western Democratic Republic of the Congo) : to 1966 French *Coquilhatville*

Mbanza-Congo (town, northwestern Angola) : to 1980 *São Salvador do Congo*

Mbanza-Ngungu (town, western Democratic Republic of the Congo) : to 1966 French *Thysville*

Mberengwa (town, southern Zimbabwe) : to 1982 *Belingwe*

¹**Mbini** (river, eastern Equatorial Guinea) : formerly Spanish *Río Benito*

²**Mbini** (region, eastern Equatorial Guinea) : alternate Spanish *Río Muni*

Mbuji-Mayi (city, south central Democratic Republic of the Congo) : to 1966 *Bakwanga*

Mchinji (town, western Malawi) : to *c.*1966 *Fort Manning*

M'daourouch (village, northeastern Algeria) : ancient Greek *Madauros*

Meath (county, eastern Ireland) : Irish *An Mhí*

Meathas Troim *see* **Edgeworthstown**

Meaux (city, northern France) : Roman *Latinum*

Mecca (city, western Saudi Arabia) : [Arabic *Makkah*]; ancient Greek *Macoraba*

Mechanics Grove *see* **Mundelein**

Mechanicsham *see* **Gretna**

Mechelen *see* **Mechlin**

Mechlin (city, northern Belgium) : [Flemish *Mechelen*; French *Malines*]

Mechtal *see* **Miechowice**

Mecklenburg *see* **Shepherdstown**

Medanta *see* **Mantes-la-Jolie**

Medeia *see* **Midye**

Medgyes *see* **Mediaş**

Media Atropatene *see* **Azerbaijan**

Mediaş (city, central Romania) : to 1918 Hungarian *Medgyes*; to 1867 German *Mediasch*

Mediasch *see* **Mediaş**

Medina (city, western Saudi Arabia) : [Arabic *Al Madīnah*]; formerly Arabic *Yathrib* (The Arabic name, meaning simply "the city," is a short form of *Madīnat an-Nabiy*, "city of the prophet," to which the name was changed following the arrival of Muhammad here in A.D. 622 in flight from **Mecca**.)

Mediolanum *see* (1) **Évreux**; (2) **Milan**; (3) ¹**Whitchurch**

Mediolanum Santonum *see* **Saintes**

Mediomatricum *see* **Metz**

Mediterranean Sea (between Europe, Asia, and Africa) : Roman *Mare Internum*; alternate Roman *Mare Nostrum* (The sea borders Arabic-speaking countries in Asia and Africa and its Arabic names include *Al Baḥr al-Abyaḍ*, "the white sea," *Al Baḥr al-Mutawassiṭ*, "the middle sea," and *Al Baḥr ar-Rūm*, "the sea of Rome." In Turkey, to the northeast, the sea is known as *Akdeniz*, "white sea," like the Arabs.)

Medma *see* **Rosarno**

Mednogorsk (city, southwestern Russia) : to 1939 *Medny*

Medny *see* **Mednogorsk**

Medvezh'ya Gora *see* **Medvezh'yegorsk**

Medvezh'yegorsk (town, northwestern Russia) : to 1938 *Medvezh'ya Gora*; formerly Finnish *Karhumäki*

Medvode (town, central Slovenia) : to 1918 German *Zwischenwässern*

Medzilaborce (town, eastern Slovakia) : to 1918 Hungarian *Mezőlaborc*

Meeks Field *see* **Keflavík Field**

Meftah (town, northern Algeria) : to *c.*1962 French *Rivet*

Megisti *see* **Kastellorizon**

Megrut *see* **Gugark'**

Mehlauken *see* **Zales'ye**

Mehomie *see* **Razlog**

Meirionnydd *see* **Merioneth**

Meklong *see* **Samut Songkhram**

Melbourne (city, Florida, southeastern United States) : originally *Crane Creek*

Melegnano (town, northern Italy) : formerly *Marignano*

Melekess *see* ²**Dimitrovgrad**

Melenik *see* **Melnik**

Melfort (town, Saskatchewan, south central Canada) : to 1904 *Stoney Creek*

Melilla (city, northern Morocco) : formerly Arabic *Russ Adir* (The city has been a Spanish possession since 1497.)

Melita *see* **Malta**

Melitene *see* **Malatya**

Melitopol' (town, southern Ukraine) : to 1841 *Novooleksandrivka* (Russian *Novo-Aleksandrovka*)

Melnik (city, southwestern Bulgaria) : to 1913 Turkish *Melenik*

Melnik *see* **Mělník**

Mělník (town, northwestern Czech Republic) : to 1918, 1938–1945 German *Melnik*

Melodunum *see* **Melun**

Melsetter *see* **Chimanimani**

Melun (town, northern France) : Roman *Melodunum*

Melville Island (Northern Territory, northern Australia) : Aboriginal *Yermalner*

Memel *see* **Klaipėda**

Memmate *see* **Mende**

Memphis (historic city, northern Egypt) : biblical *Noph* (The ancient city is now partly covered by the modern village of *Mit Rahina*.)

Menai Bridge (town, northwestern Wales) : Welsh *Porthaethwy*

Menai Strait (northwestern Wales) : Welsh *Y Fenai*

Menapia *see* **St. David's**

Mende (town, southern France) : Roman *Memmate*

Mendeleyevsk (town, western Russia) : to 1967 *Bondyuzhsky*

¹**Menderes** (river, western Turkey) : ancient Greek *Maeander* (The river, also known as *Büyükmenderes*, "Great Menderes," for distinction from ²**Menderes**, was famous in ancient

legend for its wanderings and its Greek name gave English *meander*.)

²**Menderes** (river, northwestern Turkey) : ancient Greek *Scamander* (The river is also known as *Küçükmenderes*, "Little Menderes," for distinction from ¹**Menderes**.)

Menen (town, southwestern Belgium) : French *Menin*

Ménerville *see* **Thenia**

Menevia *see* **St. David's**

Menin *see* **Menen**

Menongue (town, south central Angola) : to 1975 Portuguese *Serpa Pinto*

Menorca *see* **Minorca**

Menotomy *see* ²**Arlington**

Mentana (town, western Italy) : Roman *Nomentum*

Menton (town, southeastern France) : formerly Italian *Mentone*

Mentone *see* **Menton**

Menunketuck *see* **Guilford**

Menzel Bourguiba (town, northern Tunisia) : to 1963 French *Ferryville*

Meran *see* **Merano**

Merano (town, northern Italy) : to 1918 German *Meran*

Mercedes (city, west central Argentina) : to 1861 *Fuerte Constitucional*

Meredith Bridge *see* **Laconia**

Merény *see* **Vondrišel**

Mérida (town, southwestern Spain) : Roman *Emerita Augusta*

Merioneth (county, western Wales) : Welsh *Meirionnydd* (The county was abolished in 1974 and the Welsh name alone is now that of an administrative district.)

Meriti Station *see* **Duque de Caxias**

Merlin's Bridge (village, southwestern Wales) : Welsh *Pont Myrddin* (The village is now essentially a suburb of Haverfordwest. The apparent name of the Arthurian wizard *Merlin* is a corruption of *Mary Magdalen*, to whom a former chapel here was dedicated.)

Merlo (city, eastern Argentina) : originally *Villa de San Antonio del Camino* (The city is now a suburb of Buenos Aires.)

Merouana (town, northeastern Algeria) : to *c.*1962 French *Corneille*

Merrittsville *see* **Welland**

Merry Mount *see* ²**Quincy**

Merthyr Tudful *see* **Merthyr Tydfil**

Merthyr Tydfil (town, southern Wales) : Welsh *Merthyr Tudful*

Merthyr Vale (village, southern Wales) : Welsh *Dyffryn Taf*; alternate Welsh *Ynysowen*.

Merv (historic city, southeastern Turkmenistan) :

Roman *Antiochia Margiana* (The ancient city gave the original name of the modern city of **Mary**.)

Mesembria *see* **Nesebŭr**

Meseritz *see* **Międzyrzecz**

Meshed-e Sar *see* **Bābol Sar**

Mesolóngion (town, west central Greece) : to 1830 Turkish *Misolongi*

Messana *see* **Messina**

Messene *see* **Mavromati**

Messina (city, southern Italy) : ancient Greek *Messana*; originally ancient Greek *Zancle*

Mestia (village, northwestern Georgia) : to *c.*1955 *Seti*

Metangula (village, northwestern Mozambique) : to 1980 Portuguese *Augusto Cardosa*

Metapa *see* **Ciudad Darío**

Metapontion *see* **Metapontum**

Metapontum (ancient city, southern Italy) : ancient Greek *Metapontion*

Metlika (village, southern Slovenia) : to 1918 German *Möttling*

Metz (city, northeastern France) : Roman *Mediomatricum*; earlier Roman *Divodurum*

Meuse (river, western Europe) : Dutch *Maas*; Roman *Mosa* (English speakers prefer the French form of the river's name. The Dutch form is found in the name of **Maastricht**.)

Meyers' Creek *see* **Belleville**

Mexico (republic, southern North America) : [Spanish *México*]

México *see* (1) **Mexico**; (2) **Mexico City**

Mexico City (city, south central Mexico) : [Spanish *México*]; to 16th century Nahuatl *Tenochtitlán*

Mezhdurechensk (city, southern Russia) : to 1955 *Ol'zheras*

Mezhdurech'ye *see* **Shali**

Mézières (town, northeastern France) : Roman *Maceriae* (In 1966 Mézières amalgamated with neighboring Charleville to form the city of Charleville-Mézières.)

Meziměstí (town, northeastern Czech Republic) : to 1918, 1939–1945 German *Halbstadt*

Mezőfalva (town, west central Hungary) : to 1951 *Hercegfalva*

Mezőlaborc *see* **Medzilaborce**

Mezőszilas (town, west central Hungary) : to 1942 *Szilasbalhás*

M'fumbiro *see* **Virunga**

Miadzioł *see* **Myadzel**

Miami (town, Oklahoma, south central United States) : to 1890 *Jimtown*

Miami Beach (city, Florida, southeastern United States) : to 1916 *Ocean Beach*

Miamisport *see* **Peru**

Miarritze *see* Biarritz

Miastko (town, northwestern Poland) : to 1945 German *Rummelsburg*

Miava *see* Myjava

Michaelston-le-Pit (village, southeastern Wales) : Welsh *Llanfihangel-y-Pwll*

Michalovce (town, eastern Slovakia) : to 1918 Hungarian *Nagymihály*

Michelet *see* Aïn el Hammam

Miches (town, eastern Dominican Republic) : to 1936 Spanish *El Jovero*

Michigan *see* Lansing

Michurin *see* Tsarevo

Michurinsk (city, western Russia) : to 1932 *Kozlov*

Middle Congo *see* Congo, Republic of the

Middle East (countries of southwestern Asia/northwestern Africa) : to 1940s *Near East*

Middle Island *see* South Island

Middle Plantation *see* Williamsburg

Middletown (village, eastern Wales) : Welsh *Treberfedd*

Middletown *see* Fairmont

Middlewich (town, northwestern England) : Roman *Salinae* (The Roman name referred to the saltworks here, as it did at Droitwich.)

Midilli *see* Mytilene

Midiya *see* Midye

Midleton (town, southern Ireland) : Irish *Mainistir na Corann*

Midway *see* Rockford

Midway Islands (central Pacific) : to 1967 *Brooks Islands*

Midye (village, northwestern Turkey) : 1920–1922 modern Greek *Medeia*; to 1913 Bulgarian *Midiya*

Miechowice (town, southern Poland) : to 1945 German *Mechtal*

Międzybórz (town, southwestern Poland) : to 1945 German *Neumittelwalde*

Międzychód (town, western Poland) : to 1945 German *Birnbaum*

Międzylesie (town, southwestern Poland) : to 1945 German *Mittelwalde*

Międzyrzecz (town, western Poland) : to 1945 German *Meseritz*

Międzyzdroje (town, northwestern Poland) : to 1945 German *Misdroy*

Mielau *see* Mława

Mielno (village, northern Poland) : to 1945 German *Gross-Möllen*

Miercurea-Ciuc (city, east central Romania) : to 1918, 1940–1944 Hungarian *Csikszereda*

Mieroszów (town, southwestern Poland) : to 1945 German *Friedland*

Miess *see* Stříbro

Mihidjan *see* Chittaranjan

M.I. Kalinina, imeni (town, western Russia) : to 1938 *Kartonnaya Fabrika*

Mikashevichi (town, southern Belarus) : 1919–1939 Polish *Mikaszewicze*

Mikaszewicze *see* Mikashevichi

Mikha Tskhakaya *see* Senaki

Mikhaylo-Kotsyubinskoye *see* Mykhaylo-Kotsyubyns'ke

Mikhaylovgrad *see* Montana

Mikhaylovka *see* (1) Kimovsk; (2) Sarykemer

Mikhaylovo (village, south central Bulgaria) : formerly *Gokpala*

Mikhaylovo *see* Zhelyu Voivoda

Mikhaylovo-Semyonovskoye *see* ²Leninskoye

Mikhaylovsk (town, west central Russia) : to 1942 *Mikhaylovsky Zavod*

Mikhaylovskoye *see* Shpakovskoye

Mikhaylovsky *see* Malinovoye Ozero

Mikhaylovsky Zavod *see* Mikhaylovsk

Mikkeli (city, southeastern Finland) : to 1918 Russian *Sankt-Mikhel*; to 1809 Swedish *Sankt Michel*

Mikołajów *see* ²Mykolayiv

Mikoyan *see* Yeghegnadzor

Mikoyana, imeni *see* ¹Oktyabr'sky

Mikoyanovka *see* ²Oktyabr'sky

Mikoyan-Shakhar *see* Karachayevsk

Mikulczyce (town, southern Poland) : 1935–1945 German *Klausberg*; to 1935 German *Mikultschütz*

Mikulińce *see* Mykulynci

Mikulintsy *see* Mykulynci

Mikulov (town, southeastern Czech Republic) : to 1918, 1938–1945 German *Nikolsburg*

Mikultschütz *see* Mikulczyce

Miladinovci (town, north central Macedonia) : 1913–1914 Serbian *Aleksandrovo*

Milan (city, northern Italy) : [Italian *Milano*]; Roman *Mediolanum*

Milano *see* Milan

Milazzo (town, southern Italy) : Roman *Mylae*

Mildenhall (village, southern England) : Roman *Cunetio* (This Mildenhall, near Marlborough, should not be confused with the village of the same name near Newmarket in eastern England, despite the latter's fame for the hoard of Roman silver found there.)

Milevsko (town, west central Czech Republic) : to 1918, 1939–1945 German *Mühlhausen*

Milford Haven (town, southwestern Wales) : Welsh *Aberdaugleddau*

Mili (atoll, southeastern Marshall Islands) : formerly *Mulgrave Islands*

Milicz (town, southwestern Poland) : to 1945 German *Militsch*

Militsch *see* Milicz

Milkovitsa (town, northern Bulgaria) : formerly *Gavren*

Millau (town, southern France) : Roman *Aemilianum*

Milltown *see* Milton

Milo *see* Kellogg

Milton (town, southern New Zealand) : formerly *Milltown* (The perception of the name as literary led to the naming of the town's streets for poets.)

Milverton (village, Ontario, southeastern Canada) : to 1871 *West's Corner*

Mimidanum *see* Minden

Mimoso do Sul (city, southeastern Brazil) : to 1944 *João Pessoa*

Minami-nayoshi *see* Shebunino

Minatitlán (city, south central Mexico) : originally *Paso de la Fabrica*

Mindelo (city, northwestern Cape Verde) : alternate *Porto Grande*

Minden (city, northwestern Germany) : Roman *Mimidanum*

Mineiros *see* Mineiros do Tietê

Mineiros do Tietê (town, southeastern Brazil) : to 1944 *Mineiros*

Minera (village, northeastern Wales) : Welsh *Mwynglawdd*

Minnedosa (town, Manitoba, southern Canada) : to 1880 *Tanner's Crossing*

Minni *see* Armenia

Minorca (island, eastern Balearic Islands, western Mediterranean) : [Spanish *Menorca*]

Mińsk Mazowiecki (town, east central Poland) : to 1915 Russian *Novominsk*

Min'yar (town, southwestern Russia) : to *c.*1928 *Min'yarsky Zavod*

Min'yarsky Zavod *see* Min'yar

Mirabeau *see* Draa Ben Khedda

Mirabel (city, Quebec, southeastern Canada) : to 1973 *Ste.-Scholastique*

Miracatus (town, southeastern Brazil) : to 1944 *Prainha*

Miracema *see* Miracema do Norte

Miracema do Norte (city, north central Brazil) : 1944–1948 *Cherente*; to 1944 *Miracema*

Miramar (town, eastern Argentina) : formerly Spanish *General Alvarado*

Miranda *see* Macaloge

Mirandópolis (city, southeastern Brazil) : to 1944 Portuguese *Comandante Arbues*

Mir-Bashir *see* Tärtär

Mirnoye *see* Myrne

Mirosławiec (town, northwestern Poland) : to 1945 German *Märkisch Friedland*

Mirsk (town, southwestern Poland) : to 1945 German *Friedeberg* (For a time after 1945 the town took the Polish name *Spokojna Góra*, "peaceful mountain," translating the German.)

Mirzachul *see* Guliston

Mirzoyan *see* Taraz

Misamis *see* Ozamiz

Misdroy *see* Międzyzdroje

Misericórdia *see* Itaporanga

Misivri *see* Nesebŭr

Miskin (village, southern Wales) : Welsh *Meisgyn*

Misolongi *see* Mesolóngion

Mişr *see* (1) Cairo; (2) Egypt

Mission (village, British Columbia, southwestern Canada) : 1922–1973 *Mission City*; to 1922 *Mission Junction*; originally *St. Mary's Mission*

Mission City *see* Mission

Mission Junction *see* Mission

Missoula (city, Montana, northwestern United States) : originally *Hellgate*

Missouri *see* Bozeman

Místek *see* Frýdek-Místek

Mitau *see* Jelgava

Mitava *see* Jelgava

Mitchell Island *see* Nukulaelae

Mitchell's Corners *see* ³Aurora

Mitchelstown (town, south central Ireland) : Irish *Baile Mhistéala*

Mitchel Troy (village, southeastern Wales) : Welsh *Llanfihangel Troddi*

Mitilíni *see* Mytilene

Mitizirovo *see* Vasil Levski

Mit Rahina *see* Memphis

Mitroviça *see* Kosovo Mitrovica

Mitrowitz *see* Sremska Mitrovica

Mittelwalde *see* Międzylesie

Mitterburg *see* Pazin

Mittimatalik *see* Pond Inlet

Mladá Boleslav (town, northern Czech Republic) : to 1918, 1938–1945 German *Jungbunzlau*

Mladá Vožice (town, central Czech Republic) : to 1918, 1939–1945 German *Jungwoschitz*

Mława (town, north central Poland) : 1940–1945 German *Mielau*

Mnichovo Hradiště (town, northern Czech Republic) : to 1918, 1939–1945 German *Münchengrätz*

Moehau *see* Colville, Cape

Moeris, Lake *see* Birkat Qārūn

Moba (town, southeastern Democratic Republic of the Congo) : formerly French *Baudouinville*

Mobayi-Mbongo (town, northwestern Democratic Republic of the Congo) : to 1972 French *Banzyville*

Mobilong *see* Murray Bridge

Mobutu Sese Seko, Lake *see* Albert, Lake

Moçambique *see* Mozambique

Moçâmedes *see* **Namibe**

Mocha (city, southwestern Yemen) : [Arabic *Al Mūkha*]

Modena (town, western Italy) : Roman *Mutina*

Modern *see* **Modra**

Modica (town, southern Italy) : ancient Greek *Motyca*

Modicia *see* **Monza**

Modimolle (town, northeastern South Africa) : to 2002 *Nylstroom*

Modlin (town, east central Poland) : to 1915 Russian *Novogeorgiyevsk* (The town is now part of the city of Nowy Dwór Mazowiecki.)

Modohn *see* **Madona**

Modor *see* **Modra**

Modos *see* **Jaša Tomić**

Modra (town, western Slovakia) : to 1918 Hungarian *Modor*; to 1867 German *Modern*

Modrý Kameň (town, southern Slovakia) : to 1918 Hungarian *Kékő*

Moeskroen *see* **Mouscron**

Mogador *see* **Essaouira**

Mogilyov *see* **Mahilyow**

Mogilyov Podol'sky *see* **Mohyliv Podil's'kyy**

Mogontiacum *see* **Mainz**

Mohammadia (town, northwestern Algeria) : to *c.*1962 French *Perrégaux*

Mohammedia (town, western Morocco) : to 1960 *Fedala*

Mohammerah *see* **Khorramshahr**

Mohrin *see* **Moryń**

Mohrungen *see* **Morąg**

Mohyliv Podil's'kyy (town, western Ukraine) : (Russian *Mogilyov Podol'sky*)

Mokelumne Station *see* **Lodi**

Mokopane (town, northeastern South Africa) : to 2002 *Potgietersrus*

Moksobomyo *see* **Shwebo**

Mokvin *see* **Mokvyn**

Mokvyn (town, western Ukraine) : (Russian *Mokvin*); formerly *Pershotravneve* (Russian *Pershotravnevoye*) (The former Russian name does not translate the Ukrainian, which corresponds to Russian **Pervomayskoye**, but simple transliterates it.)

Mola di Gaeta *see* **Formia**

Mold (town, northeastern Wales) : Welsh *Yr Wyddgrug*

Moldau *see* (1) **Moldava nad Bodvou**; (2) **Moldova**; (3) **Vltava**

Moldautein *see* **Týn nad Vltavou**

Moldava nad Bodvou (town, southeastern Slovakia) : to 1918, 1938–1945 Hungarian *Szepsi*; to 1867 German *Moldau*

Moldavia *see* **Moldova**

Moldova (republic, southeastern Europe) : to 1991 English *Moldavia*; to 1918 German *Moldau*

Molenbeek-St.-Jean (town, central Belgium) : Flemish *Sint-Jans-Molenbeek* (The town is now a suburb of Brussels.)

Molles *see* **Carlos Reyles**

Mollwitz *see* **Małujowice**

Molly Morgan Plains *see* **Maitland**

Molodechno *see* **Maladzyechna**

Mołodeczno *see* **Maladzyechna**

Molotov *see* **Perm'**

Molotova, imeni *see* **Uchkuprik**

Molotovabad *see* **Uch-Korgon**

Molotovo *see* **Uchkuprik**

Molotovsk *see* (1) **Kayyngdy**; (2) **Nolinsk**; (3) **Severodvinsk**

Molvitino *see* **Susanino**

Molyneux *see* **Clutha**

Mombaça (city, northeastern Brazil) : to 1944 Portuguese *Maria Pereira*

Momchilgrad (town, southern Bulgaria) : to 1934 Turkish *Mŭstanli*

Momchilovtsi (village, southern Bulgaria) : to 1934 *Gorno Derekoi* (The first part of the earlier name is Bulgarian, the second part Turkish.)

Môn *see* **Anglesey**

Mona *see* **Anglesey**

Monaghan (town, northern Ireland) : Irish *Muineachán*

Monapia *see* **Man, Isle of**

Monastir (town, northeastern Tunisia) : Roman *Ruspina*

Monastir *see* **Bitola**

Mönchengladbach (city, western Germany) : 1951–1960 *Mönchen-Gladbach*; to 1951 *München-Gladbach* (The earlier name was altered to avoid confusion with **Munich**.)

Mönchen-Gladbach *see* **Mönchengladbach**

Moncton (city, New Brunswick, eastern Canada) : to 1855 *The Bend*

Moneron (island, eastern Russia) : 1905–1945 Japanese *Kaiba-to*

Monett (town, Missouri, central United States) : to 1877 *Plymouth*; originally *Billings*

Monfestino in Serra Mazzoni *see* **Serramazzoni**

Mongalla *see* **Equatoria**

Mongibello *see* **Etna**

Mongolia (republic, east central Asia) : to 1921 *Outer Mongolia* (The earlier name arose by contrast with *Inner Mongolia*, or *Nei Mongol*, now an autonomous region of northern China, but formerly the southern part of the more extensive historic region of Mongolia.)

Monmouth (town, southeastern Wales) : Welsh

Trefynwy; Roman *Blestium* (The original county of *Monmouthshire*, Welsh *Sir Fynwy*, was abolished in 1974 but restored in 1996.)

Monod *see* **Sidi Allal Bahraoui**

Monoticut *see* **Braintree**

¹Monroe (city, Louisiana, southern United States) : to 1819 *Fort Miro*

²Monroe (city, Michigan, north central United States) : to 1817 *Frenchtown*

Monroeville (town, Pennsylvania, northeastern United States) : to 1951 *Patton Township*

Mons (town, southwestern Belgium) : Flemish *Bergen*

Monsanto *see* **Monte Santo de Minas**

Mons Brisiacus *see* **Breisach**

Monschau (town, western Germany) : to 1918 *Montjoie*

Montagnac *see* **Remchi**

Montagne de la Grande Traverse *see* **Edith Cavell, Mt.**

Montagu Island *see* **Nguna**

Montaigu *see* **Scherpenheuvel**

Montana (city, northwestern Bulgaria) : 1945–1990 *Mikhaylovgrad*; 1891–1945 *Ferdinand*; earlier *Golyama Kutlovitsa*; Roman *Montanensia*

Montana *see* **Boone**

Montanensia *see* **Montana**

Mont Cervin *see* **Matterhorn**

Monte Alegre *see* **Timbiras**

Monte Azul (city, southeastern Brazil) : to 1939 *Tremedal*

Monte Azul *see* **Monte Azul Paulista**

Monte Azul do Turvo *see* **Monte Azul Paulista**

Monte Azul Paulista (town, southeastern Brazil) : 1944–1948 *Monte Azul do Turvo*; to 1944 *Monte Azul*

Monte Cervino *see* **Matterhorn**

Monteleone di Calabria *see* **Vibo Valentia**

Montellum Aymardi *see* **Montélimar**

¹Montenegro (republic, southeastern Europe) : [Serbo-Croat *Crna Gora*]

²Montenegro (city, southern Brazil) : to 1930s Portuguese *São João de Montenegro*

Montenegro *see* **Amapá**

Monte Nevoso *see* **Snežnik**

Montenotte *see* **Sidi Akacha**

Monte Perdido *see* **Perdido, Monte**

Monterey *see* **Monterrey**

Montería (city, northwestern Colombia) : originally *San Jerónimo de Buenavista*

Monterrey (city, northern Mexico) : traditional English *Monterey* (The English spelling is preserved in the name of *Monterey*, California, United States.)

Monte San Giuliano *see* **Erice**

Monte Santo de Minas (town, southeastern Brazil) : 1944–1948 *Monsanto*

Montezuma *see* **Winona**

Montgolfier *see* **Rahouia**

Montgomery (town, eastern Wales) : Welsh *Trefaldwyn*

Montgomery *see* **Sahiwal**

Montgomery Court House *see* **Rockville**

Monticello *see* **Helena**

Montjoie *see* **Monschau**

Montmorency (town, northern France) : 1689–1789 *Enghien* (The town took its former name from the dukes of **Enghien** in Belgium.)

Montmorency-Beaufort (village, north central France) : to 1689 *Beaufort* (In the year stated the village added the name of **Montmorency** when that town was renamed, retaining it when the town regained its original name in 1789.)

Montpelier *see* **Montpellier**

Montpellier (city, southern France) : traditional English *Montpelier* (The English spelling is preserved in the name of *Montpelier*, California, United States.)

Mont Perdu *see* **Perdido, Monte**

Montreal (city, Quebec, southeastern Canada) : officially French *Montréal*; to 1724 French *Ville-Marie-de-Montréal*

Montréal *see* **Montreal**

Monument *see* **Bourne**

Monza (city, northern Italy) : Roman *Modicia*

Moodyville *see* **North Vancouver**

Mookgophong (town, northeastern South Africa) : to 2002 *Naboomspruit*

Moorea (island, west central French Polynesia) : formerly *Eimeo*

Moore's Bluff *see* **Selma**

Moorhead (city, Minnesota, north central United States) : originally *Burbank*

Moose Island *see* **Eastport**

Moose River *see* **Clementsport**

Moquegua (city, southern Peru) : originally *Villa de Santa Catalina del Guadalcázar del Valle de Moquegua*

Morąg (town, northeastern Poland) : to 1945 German *Mohrungen*

Morava *see* **Moravia**

Moravia (region, eastern Czech Republic) : [Czech *Morava*]

Moravská Ostrava *see* **Ostrava**

Moravská Třebová (town, eastern Czech Republic) : to 1918, 1938–1945 German *Mährisch-Trübau*

Moravské Budějovice (town, southern Czech Republic) : 1929–1945 German *Mährisch-Budwitz*; to 1918 German *Budwitz*

Moravský Beroun (town, eastern Czech Republic) : to 1918, 1938–1945 German *Bärn*

Moravský Krumlov (town, southern Czech Republic) : to 1918, 1939–1945 German *Mährisch-Kromau*

Mordovskaya Bokla *see* [2]Sovetskoye

Morea *see* Peloponnese

Morelia (city, west central Mexico) : originally *Valladolid*

Morgan City (town, Louisiana, southern United States) : to 1876 *Brashear City*

Morgannwg *see* Glamorgan

Morgan's Landing *see* Ilion

Morganstown (village, southern Wales) : Welsh *Treforgan*; alternate Welsh *Pentre-poeth*

Morgenroth *see* Ruda Śląska

Môr Hafren *see* Bristol Channel

Moridunum *see* Carmarthen

Morocco (kingdom, northwestern Africa) : [Arabic *Al-Maghrib*]; formerly French *Maroc* (Most of present Morocco was known as *French Morocco* from 1912 to 1956, when the country gained its independence.)

Morón (city, east central Argentina) : 1930–1943 *Seis de Septiembre*

Morozov *see* Bratan

Morris (village, Manitoba, southern Canada) : formerly *Scratching River*

Morriston (village, southern Wales) : Welsh *Treforys* (The village is now a district of Swansea.)

Morristown (town, New Jersey, northeastern United States) : to 1740 *West Hanover*

Morristown *see* Asheville

Morro Grande *see* Barão de Cocais

Mortier Bay *see* Marystown

Moryń (town, northwestern Poland) : to 1945 German *Mohrin*

Mosa *see* Meuse

Mościska *see* Mostyska

[1]Moscow (city, western Russia) : [Russian *Moskva*]

[2]Moscow (town, Idaho, northwestern United States) : to 1876 *Hog Heaven*

Mosel *see* Moselle

Mosella *see* Moselle

Moselle (river, northeastern France/western Germany) : German *Mosel*, Roman *Mosella*

Moses Lake (town, Washington, northwestern United States) : to 1938 *Neppel*

Mosi-oa-Tunya *see* Victoria Falls

Moskovsky *see* Shahrihon

Moskva *see* [1]Moscow

Moson (town, northwestern Hungary) : to 1867 German *Wieselburg* (In 1945 the town combined with Magyaróvár to form the city of *Mosonmagyaróvár*.)

Mosonmagyaróvár *see* (1) Magyaróvár; (2) Moson

Mossoró (city, northeastern Brazil) : originally *Santa Luiza de Mossoró*

Most (city, northwestern Czech Republic) : to 1918, 1938–1945 German *Brüx*

Mostrim *see* Edgeworthstown

Mostyska (town, western Ukraine) : to 1939 Polish *Mościska*

Mosty Wielkie *see* Velyki Mosty

Mosul (city, northern Iraq) : [Arabic *Al Mawşil*]

Motodomari *see* Vostochny

Möttling *see* Metlika

Motu One (atoll, western French Polynesia) : formerly *Bellingshausen Island*

Motyca *see* Modica

Moulmein *see* Mawlamyine

Mound City *see* Moundsville

Moundsville (town, West Virginia, east central United States) : to 1865 *Mound City* (In the year stated the town merged with the nearby settlement of *Grave Creek*, renamed *Elizabethville* in 1798.)

Mount (or Mount of or Mount of the) : for names beginning thus, *see* the next word, as McKinley, Mt. or Olives, Mount of or Holy Cross, Mount of the

Mountain Ash (town, southern Wales) : Welsh *Aberpennar*

Mountain Home (town, Idaho, northwestern United States) : originally *Rattlesnake Station*

Mount Brydges (village, Ontario, southeastern Canada) : to 1856 *Carradoc*

Mount Holly (town, New Jersey, northeastern United States) : formerly *Bridgetown*; originally *Northampton*

Mt. McKinley National Park *see* Denali National Park and Preserve

Mount Marie *see* Pine Bluff

Mount Pleasant *see* Richmond Hill

Mountrath (town, central Ireland) : Irish *Maighean Rátha*

Mount Shasta (town, California, western United States) : to 1925 *Sisson*

Mount Wollaston *see* [2]Quincy

Mouscron (town, western Belgium) : Flemish *Moeskroen*

Moylgrove (village, southwestern Wales) : Welsh *Trewyddel*

Moyobamba (city, north central Peru) : originally *Santiago de los Valles de Moyobamba*

Moyynkum (town, southern Kyrgyzstan) : formerly Russian *Furmanovka*

Mozambique (republic, southeastern Africa) : [Portuguese *Moçambique*]; formerly *Portuguese East Africa* (The present name was current for some time before the country achieved independence in 1975. The Portuguese name is now generally on the map for *Moçambique*, the seaport town in the northeast of the country and its capital until 1907.)

Mozhga (city, western Russia) : *c*.1920–1926 *Krasny*; to *c*.1920 *Syuginsky* (The city was formed in 1926 on incorporating nearby Syuginsky Zavod.)

Mozirje (village, northern Slovenia) : to 1918 German *Prassburg*

Mozyr' *see* **Mazyr**

Mozyrz *see* **Mazyr**

Mpumalanga (province, northeastern South Africa) : 1994–1995 *Eastern Transvaal*

Mrągowo (town, northeastern Poland) : to 1945 German *Sensburg*

Mrewa *see* **Murewa**

Mrkonjić-Grad (town, central Bosnia-Herzegovina) : to 1930s *Varcar Vakuf*

Mstislavl' *see* **Mstislaw**

Mstislaw (town, eastern Belarus) : (Russian *Mstislavl'*); to 1918 Russian *Mstislavl'*

Muar (city, southwestern Malaysia) : formerly *Bandar Maharani*

Muckle Ridge *see* [2]**Marion**

Muconda (town, northeastern Angola) : formerly Portuguese *Nova Chaves*

Mud Creek *see* **Abilene**

Muddy River *see* **Brookline**

Mud River *see* **Paisley**

Mud Town *see* **Watts**

Mühlbach *see* **Sebeş**

Mühlhausen *see* **Milevsko**

Muineachán *see* **Monaghan**

Muine Bheag (town, eastern Ireland) : alternate *Bagenalstown*

Mukačevo *see* **Mukacheve**

Mukacheve (city, western Ukraine) : (Russian *Mukachevo*); 1919–1938, 1944–1945 Czech *Mukačevo*; to 1918, 1938–1945 Hungarian *Munkács*; to 1867 German *Munkatsch* (The city was under German-Hungarian occupation in World War II.)

Mukachevo *see* **Mukacheve**

Mukden *see* **Shenyang**

Mukhtuya *see* **Lensk**

Mulgrave Islands *see* **Mili**

Mülhausen *see* **Mulhouse**

Mulhouse (city, northeastern France) : 1871–1918, 1940–1944 German *Mülhausen*

Mullach Íde *see* **Malahide**

Mullingar (town, central Ireland) : Irish *An Muileann gCearr*

Mulungu (town, northeastern Brazil) : 1944–1948 *Camarazal*

Mumbai (city, western India) : to 1995 *Bombay*

Mumbles (village, southern Wales) : Welsh *Y Mwmbwls* (The village is now a district of Swansea.)

Muminabad *see* **Leningrad**

Mŭ'minobod *see* **Leningrad**

München *see* **Munich**

München-Gladbach *see* **Mönchengladbach**

Münchengrätz *see* **Mnichovo Hradiště**

Mundelein (town, Illinois, east central United States) : originally *Mechanics Grove* (The village was successively named *Holcomb*, *Rockefeller*, and *Area* before gaining its present name in 1924.)

Mundo Novo *see* **Urupês**

Munich (city, southern Germany) : [German *München*]

Munkács *see* **Mukacheve**

Munkatsch *see* **Mukacheve**

Münsterberg *see* **Ziębice**

Muqui (town, southeastern Brazil) : to 1944 Portuguese *São João do Muqui*

Murang'a (town, south central Kenya) : to 1963 *Fort Hall*

Muraszerdahely *see* **Mursko Središće**

Muraszombat *see* **Murska Sobota**

Murav'yovo *see* **Mažeikiai**

Murchison (town, central New Zealand) : formerly *Hampden*

Murchison Falls *see* **Kabalega Falls**

Murewa (town, eastern Zimbabwe) : to 1982 *Mrewa*

Murgap (town, east central Tajikistan) : to *c*.1929 Russian *Pamirsky Post*

Murmansk (city, northwestern Russia) : to 1917 *Romanov-na-Murmane*

Murphy's Station *see* **Sunnyvale**

Murray Bridge (town, South Australia, southern Australia) : to 1940 *Mobilong*

Murshidabad (city, northwestern India) : to 1704 *Makhsudabad*

Murska Sobota (town, northeastern Slovenia) : to 1918, 1941–1944 Hungarian *Muraszombat*

Mursko Središće (town, northern Croatia) : to 1918, 1941–1944 Hungarian *Muraszerdahely*

Murviedro *see* **Sagunto**

Musala (mountain, southwestern Bulgaria) : 1949–1962 *Stalin Peak*

Muscat and Oman *see* **Oman**

Muscatine (city, Iowa, north central United States) : to 1850 *Bloomington*

Musketaquid *see* [2]**Concord**

Mussolinia di Sardegna *see* **Arborea**

Mustafakemalpaşa (town, northwestern Turkey) : formerly *Kirmasti*

Mustafapaşa *see* **Svilengrad**

Mŭstanli *see* Momchilgrad
Mustayevka *see* Mustayevo
Mustayevo (village, southwestern Russia) : to
  c.1940 *Mustayevka*
Mutare (town, eastern Zimbabwe) : to 1982 *Um-
  tali*
Mutina *see* Modena
Mutum (city, southeastern Brazil) : to 1939 Por-
  tuguese *São Manuel do Mutum*
Muxaluando (town, southern Angola) : to
  c.1976 Portuguese *General Freire*
Muy Vavi *see* Ayo
Muztor *see* Toktogul
Mvuma (town, central Zimbabwe) : to 1982
  Umvuma
Mwenezi (town, southern Zimbabwe) : to 1982
  Nuanetsi
Mwynglawdd *see* Minera
Myadel' *see* Myadzel
Myadzel (town, northwestern Belarus) : (Russian
  Myadel'); 1919–1939 Polish *Miadziok* to 1918
  Russian *Myadel'*
Myall Creek Station *see* Dalby
Myanmar (republic, southeastern Asia) : to 1989
  Burma (The former name is still widely current
  in the media and everyday speech, and is some-
  times preferred on political grounds by those
  who object to the country's military regime.)
Myjava (town, western Slovakia) : to 1918 Hun-
  garian *Miava*
Mykhaylo-Kotsyubyns'ke (town, northern
  Ukraine) : (Russian *Mikhaylo-Kotsyubinskoye*);
  to *c*.1935 *Kozyol*
¹Mykolayiv (city, southern Ukraine) : (Russian
  Nikolayev); to 1918 Russian *Nikolayev*
²Mykolayiv (town, western Ukraine) : (Russian
  Nikolayev); to 1919 Polish *Mikołajów* (The
  town is formally known as *Mykolayiv na
  Dnistri*, Russian *Nikolayev na Dnestre*, denot-
  ing its location on the Dniester, for distinc-
  tion from ¹Mykolayiv.)
Mykolayivka *see* Novovorontsovka
Mykolayivka-Vyrivs'ka *see* ²Zhovtneve
Mykulynci (town, western Czech Republic) :
  (Russian *Mikulintsy*); to 1939 Polish *Mikulińce*
Mykytine *see* Nikopol'
Mykytin Rih *see* Nikopol'
Mylae *see* Milazzo
Mymensingh (city, north central Bangladesh) :
  formerly *Nasirabad*
Mynydd Du *see* Black Mountains
Myrne (town, southeastern Ukraine) : (Russian
  Mirnoye); to 1958 *Karans'kyy Kam'yanyy Kar'yer*
  (Russian *Karansky Kamenny Kar'yer*)
Myrzakent (town, southern Kazakhstan) : for-
  merly Russian *Slavyanka*

Myślibórz (town, northwestern Poland) : to 1945
  German *Soldin*
Mysłowice (town, southern Poland) : to 1921,
  1939–1945 German *Myslowitz*
Myslowitz *see* Mysłowice
Mysore *see* Karnataka
Mysovka (village, western Russia) : to 1945 Ger-
  man *Karkeln*
Mysovsk *see* ²Babushkin
Mytilene (town, eastern Greece) : modern Greek
  Mitilíni; to 1913 Turkish *Midilli*
Mytilene *see* Lesbos
Naas (town, eastern Ireland) : Irish *An Nás*
Nabadwip (city, northeastern India) : formerly
  Nadia
Naberezhnyye Chelny (city, western Russia) :
  1982–1988 *Brezhnev*; to 1930 *Chelny*
Nabeul (town, northeastern Tunisia) : Roman
  Neapolis
Nāblus (town, northern West Bank) : Roman
  Neapolis (Some scholars identify Neapolis as
  the biblical city of *Shechem*, but its site is now
  usually located around a mile east.)
Naboomspruit *see* Mookgophong
Nabresina *see* Aurisina
Na Buirgh *see* Borve
Na Cealla Beaga *see* Killybegs
Nachod *see* Náchod
Náchod (town, northeastern Czech Republic) :
  to 1918, 1939–1945 German *Nachod*
Naciria (town, northern Algeria) : to *c*.1962
  French *Haussonvillers*
Na Clocha Liatha *see* Greystones
Nadezhda (town, western Bulgaria) : formerly
  Gerdima (The town is now a residential dis-
  trict of Sofia.)
Nadezhdinsk *see* Serov
Nadezhdinsky Priisk *see* Aprel'sk
Nadezhdinsky Zavod *see* Serov
Nadia *see* Nabadwip
Nadterechnaya (town, southwestern Russia) : to
  1944 *Nizhny Naur*
Nadvirna (town, western Ukraine) : (Russian
  Nadvornaya); to 1939 Polish *Nadwórna*
Nadvornaya *see* Nadvirna
Nadwórna *see* Nadvirna
Naga (city, north central Philippines) : to 1914
  Spanish *Nueva Caceres*
Nagahama *see* Ozyorsky
Nagybánya *see* Baia Mare
Nagybecskerek *see* Zrenjanin
Nagybittse *see* Bytče
Nagykanizsa (city, southwestern Hungary) : to
  1867 German *Grosskanischa*
Nagykapos *see* Vel'ké Kapušany
Nagykároly *see* Carei

Nagykikinda *see* Kikinda
Nagymárton *see* Mattersburg
Nagymegyer *see* Vel'ký Meder
Nagymihály *see* Michalovce
Nagyrőce *see* Revúca
Nagyszalonta *see* Salonta
Nagyszeben *see* Sibiu
Nagyszöllös *see* Vynohradiv
Nagyszombat *see* Trnava
Nagytapolcsány *see* Topol'čany
Nagyvárad *see* Oradea
Nahanni Butte (village, Northwest Territories, northwestern Canada) : alternate Inuit *Tthenaagoo*
Na h-Eileanan an Iar *see* Western Isles
Nahr al- ʿĀṣī *see* Orontes
Naibo *see* Dobroye
Naibuchi *see* Nayba
Naihoro *see* ¹Gornozavodsk
Nairo *see* Gastello
Naissus *see* Niš
Nakambe (river, western Africa) : to 1986 *White Volta*, formerly alternate *Volta Blanche* (The native name is mostly used in Burkina Faso.)
Nakel *see* Nakło nad Notecią
Nakhrachi *see* Kondinskoye
Nakło nad Notecią (town, north central Poland) : 1939–1945 German *Nakel*
Naldrug *see* Osmanabad
Nálepkovo *see* Vondrišel
Nalubaale Falls (south central Uganda) : to 2000 *Owen Falls*
Namaland *see* Namaqualand
Namaqualand (region, southwestern Africa) : alternate *Namaland*
Namen *see* Namur
Námestó *see* Námestovo
Námestovo (town, northern Slovakia) : to 1918 Hungarian *Námestó*
Namibe (town, southwestern Angola) : to 1982 Portuguese *Moçâmedes*
Namibia (republic, southwestern Africa) : 1915–1968 *South West Africa*; 1884–1915 *German South West Africa*
Namslau *see* Namysłów
Namur (city, south central Belgium) : Flemish *Namen*
Namysłów (town, southwestern Poland) : to 1945 German *Namslau*
Nanaimo (city, British Columbia, southwestern Canada) : to 1860 *Colville Town*
Nanhyfer *see* Nevern
Naniwa *see* Osaka
Nanjing (city, east central China) : conventional English *Nanking*; 1644–1912 *Jiangning*
Nanking *see* Nanjing

Nanning (city, southern China) : 1913–1945 *Yongning*
Nanterre (town, northern France) : Roman *Nemetodurum*
Nantes (city, northwestern France) : Breton *Naoned*; Roman *Condivincum*
Nantong (city, eastern China) : to 1724 *Tongzhou* (The city was renamed to avoid confusion with Tongzhou near Beijing.)
Nanumanga (island, northern Tuvalu) : formerly *Hudson Island*
Naoned *see* Nantes
Naples (city, southwestern Italy) : [Italian *Napoli*]; Roman *Neapolis*
Napoléon-Vendée *see* La Roche-sur-Yon
Napoléonville *see* Pontivy
Napoli *see* Naples
Naracoorte (town, South Australia, southern Australia) : to 1869 *Kincraig*
Narberth (town, southwestern Wales) : Welsh *Arberth*
Narbo Martius *see* Narbonne
Narbonne (city, southern France) : Roman *Narbo Martius* (The full title of the first Roman colony in Gaul, following its enlargement by the emperor Claudius, was *Colonia Julia paterna Claudia Narbo Martius decumanorum*.)
Narborough Island *see* Fernandina
Narda *see* Arta
Nardò (town, southern Italy) : Roman *Neretum*
Narimanov (town, southwestern Russia) : to 1984 *Nizhnevolzhsk*
Narimanova, imeni *see* Bankä
Narni (town, central Italy) : Roman *Narnia*
Narnia *see* Narni
Nartkala (town, southwestern Russia) : to 1967 *Dokshukino*
Narva-Jõesuu (town, northeastern Estonia) : to 1917 German *Hungerburg*
Nar'yan-Mar (city, northwestern Russia) : 1933–1935 *imeni Dzerzhinskogo*; to 1933 *Beloshchel'ye*
¹Naryn (administrative region, central Kyrgyzstan) : to 1990 *Tyan'-Shan'* (The region's former name derives from the *Tien Shan* mountain chain that extends east into China.)
²Naryn (town, eastern Uzbekistan) : formerly *Khakkulabad*
Naryshkino *see* Kuznetsk
Năsăud (town, north central Romania) : to 1918, 1940–1944 Hungarian *Naszód*; to 1867 German *Nussdorf*
Na Sceirí *see* Skerries
Nash (village, southeastern Wales) : Welsh *Trefonnen*
Nashua (city, New Hampshire, northeastern

United States) : to 1837 *Dunstable* (The city
was formed in the year stated by merging with
a village of its present name, itself known until
1803 as *Indian Head*.)

Nashville (city, Tennessee, east central United
States) : to 1784 *Fort Nashborough*

Nasirabad *see* **Mymensingh**

Nasrat *see* **Nawabshah**

Naszód *see* **Năsăud**

Natal *see* **KwaZulu-Natal**

Natchez (town, Mississippi, southeastern United
States) : originally *Fort Rosalie*

Natchitoches (city, Louisiana, southern United
States) : originally *Fort St. Jean Baptiste*

Natividade *see* **Natividade da Serra**

Natividade da Serra (town, southeastern Brazil)
: to 1944 *Natividade*

Naugatuck (town, Connecticut, northeastern
United States) : originally *Salem Bridge*

Naugatuck *see* **Seymour**

Naujaat *see* **Repulse Bay**

Naumburg am Queis *see* **Nowogrodziec**

Naumiestis (town, southwestern Lithuania) : to
1918 Polish *Władysławów*

Nauportus *see* **Vrhnika**

Nauru (island republic, southwestern Pacific) :
formerly *Pleasant Island*

Nauvoo (town, Illinois, north central United
States) : to 1840 *Commerce*

Navabad (town, west central Tajikistan) : (Russian *Novabad*); to 1950 *Shul'mak*

Navahrudak (town, western Belarus) : (Russian
Novogrudok); 1919–1939 Polish *Nowogródek*

Navan (town, eastern Ireland) : Irish *An Uaimh*

Navarino *see* **Pylos**

Navarra *see* **Navarre**

Navarre (region, northern Spain) : [Spanish
Navarra] (English prefers the French form of
the name for the ancient kingdom, which extended into southern France, keeping *Navarra*
for the modern Spanish province.)

Navio *see* ²**Brough**

Navoiy (city, central Uzbekistan) : to 1958 *Kermine*

Návpaktos (town, western Greece) : to 1830
Turkish *İnebahti*; formerly Italian *Lepanto*
(The Italian form of the name is preserved for
the naval battle of 1571, in a nearby strait, in
which the Turks were defeated by the Holy
League.)

Návplion (town, southern Greece) : to 1830
Turkish *Navpliya*

Navpliya *see* **Návplion**

Nawabshah (city, southern Pakistan) : originally
Nasrat

Nayba (river, eastern Russia) : 1905–1945 Japanese *Naibuchi*

Nayoshi *see* **Lesogorsk**

Nazerat *see* **Nazareth**

Nazaré (city, eastern Brazil) : formerly *Nazareth*

Nazaré *see* **Nazaré da Mata**

Nazaré da Mata (city, northeastern Brazil) : to
1944 *Nazaré*

Nazareth (town, northern Israel) : [Hebrew *Nazerat*; Arabic *An Nāşirah*] (Nazareth was the
childhood home of Jesus and Arabic *naşrānī*
means "Christian.")

Nazareth *see* **Nazaré**

Nazimovo *see* **Putyatin**

Nazran' (town, southwestern Russia) : 1944–
1967 *Kosta-Khetagurovo*; earlier *Georgiye-
Osetinskoye*

Nazyvayevsk (town, southern Russia) : *c.*1935–
1945 *Novonazyvayevka*; to *c.*1935 *Sibirsky*

N'dalatando (town, northwestern Angola) : to
1975 Portuguese *Vila Salazar*

N'Djamena (city, southwestern Chad) : to 1973
French *Fort-Lamy*

Neal's Station *see* **Parkersburg**

Neapolis *see* (1) **Nabeul**; (2) **Nāblus**; (3) **Naples**

Near East *see* **Middle East**

Neath (town, southern Wales) : Welsh *Castell-
nedd*; Roman *Nidum*

Néau *see* **Eupen**

Nebitdag (city, western Turkmenistan) : to late
1930s *Nefte-Dag*

Nedenes *see* **Aust-Agder**

Nederland *see* **Netherlands**

Nedvigovka (village, southwestern Russia) : ancient Greek and Roman *Tanais* (The village
stands at the mouth of the **Don** River, itself
known by the same classical name.)

Ñeembucú *see* ²**Pilar**

Neenah (city, Wisconsin, north central United
States) : to 1856 *Winnebago Rapids*

Neftçala (town, southeastern Azerbaijan) : (Russian *Neftechala*); formerly Russian *imeni 26
Bakinskikh Kommunarov*

Neftechala *see* **Neftçala**

Nefte-Dag *see* **Nebitdag**

Neftekamsk (city, western Russia) : formerly
Kasevo

Nefteyugansk (city, central Russia) : to 1967
Ust'-Balyk

Neftezavodsk *see* **Seydi**

Negotin (village, central Macedonia) : 1913–1941
Serbian *Sveti Djordje*

Negroponte *see* **Euboea**

Neidenburg *see* **Nidzica**

Neidín *see* **Kenmare**

Neisse *see* **Nysa**

Nejdek (town, western Czech Republic) : to
1918, 1938–1945 German *Neudeck*

Nekhayevskaya (village, southwestern Russia) :
1956–1992 *Nekhayevsky* (The village had town
status under the former name.)
Nekhayevsky *see* **Nekhayevskaya**
Nekrasovskoye (town, western Russia) : to 1938
Bol'shiye Soli
Nelepovsky Khutor *see* **Artemove**
Nelipivs'kyy Khutir *see* **Artemove**
[1]**Nelson** (city, central New Zealand) : Maori
Wakatu
[2]**Nelson** (town, British Columbia, southwestern
Canada) : to 1888 *Stanley*
Nelsonville *see* **Cowansville**
Neman (town, western Russia) : to 1945 German
Ragnit
Nemausus *see* **Nîmes**
Německý Brod *see* **Havlíčkův Brod**
Nemetacum Atrebatum *see* **Arras**
Nemetocenna *see* **Arras**
Nemetodurum *see* **Nanterre**
Németpróna *see* **Nitrianske Pravno**
Németújvár *see* **Güssing**
Nemours *see* **Ghazaouet**
Nen *see* **Nene**
Nenagh (town, south central Ireland) : Irish *An
tAaonach*
Nene (river, central and eastern England) : alter-
nate *Nen* (The alternate spelling strictly applies
to the river's upper reaches and the main name
to its lower, better-known course.)
Neocaesarea *see* **Niksar**
Neokastro *see* **Pylos**
Nepisiguit *see* **Bathurst**
Nepolocăuţii *see* **Nepolokivtsi**
Nepolokivtsi (town, western Ukraine) : (Russian
Nepolokovtsy); 1919–1940 Romanian *Nepolo-
căuţii*; to 1918 German *Nepolokoutz*
Nepolokoutz *see* **Nepolokivtsi**
Nepolokovtsy *see* **Nepolokivtsi**
Neppel *see* **Moses Lake**
Neretum *see* **Nardò**
Nerium Promontorium *see* **Finisterre, Cape**
Nero *see* **Krn**
Nesebŭr (town, eastern Bulgaria) : to 1878 Turk-
ish *Misivri*; ancient Greek *Mesembria* (The
original Greek name, or a form of it, was cur-
rent until 1934.)
Nesselsdorf *see* **Kopřivnice**
Nesterov (town, western Russia) : 1938–1945
German *Ebenrode*; to 1938 German *Stallupö-
nen*
Nesterov *see* **Zhovkva**
Nesvetevich *see* **Proletars'k**
Nesvitovych *see* **Proletars'k**
Nesvizh *see* **Nyasvizh**
Netherby (village, northern England) : Roman

Castra Exploratorum (This is the only example
in England of Latin *castra*, "camp," in a
Roman name although there are several in
continental Europe, as **Castres** in France. As a
regular word, however, it gave the modern
names of English cities such as **Manchester**,
Rochester, and **Winchester**.)
Netherlands (kingdom, western Europe) :
[Dutch *Nederland*]; conventional English *Hol-
land* (The name *Holland* strictly applies only
to the two western provinces of North Hol-
land and South Holland, Dutch *Noord-Hol-
land* and *Zuid-Holland*.)
Netherlands Antilles (island federation, south-
ern West Indies) : to 1954 *Dutch West Indies*
Netherlands East Indies *see* **Indonesia**
Netum *see* **Noto**
Neubentschen *see* **Zbąszynek**
Neubidschow *see* **Nový Bydžov**
Neuchâtel (town, western Switzerland) : German
Neuenburg
Neudamm *see* **Dębno**
Neudeck *see* **Nejdek**
Neuenburg *see* **Neuchâtel**
Neuenburg an der Elbe *see* **Nymburk**
Neufahrwasser *see* **Nowy Port**
Neugard *see* **Nowogard**
Neugradisca *see* **Nova Gradiška**
Neuhardenberg (town, eastern Germany) :
1949–1990 *Marxwalde*
Neuhaus *see* (1) **Dobrna**; (2) **Jindřichův
Hradec**
Neuhäusel *see* **Nové Zámky**
Neuhausen *see* **Gur'yevsk**
Neukirch *see* **Timiryazevo**
Neukuhren *see* **Pionersky**
Neu-Langenburg *see* **Tukuyu**
Neumagen (village, western Germany) : Roman
Noviomagus
Neumarkt *see* (1) **Nowy Targ**; (2) **Środa Śląska**
Neumarktl *see* **Tržič**
Neu-Mecklenburg *see* **New Ireland**
Neumittelwalde *see* **Międzybórz**
Neupaka *see* **Nová Paka**
Neu-Pommern *see* **New Britain**
Neurode *see* **Nowa Ruda**
Neusalz *see* **Nowa Sól**
Neusandez *see* **Nowy Sącz**
Neusatz *see* **Novi Sad**
Neuschwanenburg *see* **Gulbene**
Neusiedl am See (town, eastern Austria) : to 1919
Hungarian *Nezider*
Neusohl *see* **Banská Bystrica**
Neuss (city, western Germany) : Roman *Novae-
sium*
Neustadt *see* (1) **Eberswalde**; (2) **Prudnik**

Neustadt an der Haardt *see* Neustadt an der Weinstrasse

Neustadt an der Mettau *see* Nové Město nad Metují

Neustadt an der Weinstrasse (city, southwestern Germany) : to 1936, 1945–1950, *Neustadt an der Haardt*; Medieval Latin *Nova Civitas*

Neustadt bei Pinne *see* Lwówek

Neustädtel *see* Nowe Miasteczko

Neustadt in Westpreussen *see* Wejherowo

Neustadtl *see* Nové Město na Moravě

Neustadt-Schirwindt *see* Kudirkos Naumiestis

Neustettin *see* Szczecinek

Neuteich *see* Nowy Staw

Neutitschein *see* Nový Jičín

Neutomischl *see* Nowy Tomyšl

Neutra *see* Nitra

Neuville (village, Quebec, southeastern Canada) : to 1919 *Pointe-aux-Trembles*

Neuwarp *see* Nowe Warpno

Neuwedell *see* Drawno

Nevdubstroy *see* ²Kirovsk

Nevel'sk (town, eastern Russia) : 1905–1945 Japanese *Honto*

Never (town, eastern Russia) : formerly *Larinsky*

Nevern (village, southwestern Wales) : Welsh *Nyfer*, alternate Welsh *Nanhyfer*

Nevers (town, central France) : Roman *Noviodunum*

Neves *see* Neves Paulista

Neves Paulista (town, southeastern Brazil) : 1944–1948 *Iboti*; to 1944 *Neves*

Nevrokop *see* Gotse Delchev

Nevskoye (village, western Russia) : 1938–1945 German *Schlossbach*; to 1938 German *Pillupönen*

New Amsterdam *see* (1) Buffalo; (2) New York

New Anzac-on-Sea *see* Peacehaven

Newark (city, New Jersey, northeastern United States) : formerly *New Milford*; originally *Pesayak Towne*

Newark *see* Niagara-on-the-Lake

New Barbadoes *see* Hackensack

New Beverly *see* ²Burlington

Newborough (village, northwestern Wales) : Welsh *Niwbwrch*

Newbridge (town, southeastern Wales) : Welsh *Trecelyn*

Newbridge *see* Droichead Nua

Newbridge-on-Wye (village, eastern Wales) : Welsh *Y Bontnewydd-ar-Wy*

New Britain (island, eastern Papua New Guinea) : 1884–1920 German *Neu-Pommern*

New Britain *see* Ormond Beach

New Brookland *see* West Columbia

New Brunswick (city, New Jersey, northeastern United States) : formerly *Inian's Ferry*; originally *Prigmore's Swamp*

Newburyport *see* St. Joseph

New Butler *see* Butler

New Caledonia (island territory, southwestern Pacific) : French *Nouvelle-Calédonie* (The islands were named by the British in 1774 but annexed by France in 1853.)

New Caledonia *see* British Columbia

New Cambridge *see* Bristol

¹Newcastle (city, northeastern England) : Roman *Pons Aelii*

²Newcastle (village, southern Wales) : Welsh *Castell-newydd* (The village is now a district of Bridgend.)

³Newcastle (town, southeastern Northern Ireland) : Irish *An Caisleán Nua*

Newcastle *see* Webster City

New Castle (town, Delaware, northeastern United States) : 1655–1664 Dutch *Nieuw Amstel*; originally *Santhoeck*

Newcastle Emlyn (town, southwestern Wales) : Welsh *Castellnewydd Emlyn*

New Connecticut *see* Vermont

New Delhi *see* Delhi

New Denver (village, British Columbia, southwestern Canada) : to 1892 *Eldorado*

New Edinburgh *see* Dunedin

Newfield *see* Bridgeport

New Forest (southern England) : Medieval Latin *Nova Foresta* (As elsewhere in British place-names, *forest* here means specifically "hunting preserve" rather than just "region of trees.")

New France *see* Canada

New Harmony (town, Indiana, north central United States) : originally German *Harmonie*

Newhaven *see* Le Havre

New Haven (city, Connecticut, northeastern United States) : to 1640 *Quinnipiac*

New Hebrides *see* Vanuatu

New Helvetia *see* Sacramento

New Holland *see* Australia

New Hope (town, Pennsylvania, northeastern United States) : originally *Coryel's Ferry* (The town lies across the Delaware River from Lambertville, and the original ferry plied between the two places.)

New Inverness *see* Darien

New Ireland (island, eastern Papua New Guinea) : 1884–1914 German *Neu-Mecklenburg* (Politically, the province of New Ireland includes other islands, notably New Hanover.)

New Johnston *see* ²Cornwall

New Liskeard (town, Ontario, southeastern Canada) : originally *Thornloe*

New London (city, Connecticut, northeastern United States) : to 1658 *Pequot*

Newmarket (town, Ontario, southeastern Canada) : to *c*.1810 *Beman's Corners*

New Market (town, Virginia, eastern United States) : to 1796 *Crossroads*

New Milford *see* **Newark**

New Moat (village, southwestern Wales) : Welsh *Y Môt*

New Norfolk (town, Tasmania, southeastern Australia) : to 1827 *Elizabeth Town*

New Orleans (city, Louisiana, southern United States) : to 1803 French *Nouvelle-Orléans*

New Orleans Village *see* **Torrington**

¹Newport (city, southeastern Wales) : Welsh *Casnewydd-ar-Wysg*

²Newport (town, southwestern Wales) : Welsh *Trefdraeth*

³Newport (town, western Ireland) : Irish *Baile Uí Fhiacháin*

Newport *see* **Newport Beach**

Newport Beach (city, California, southwestern United States) : formerly *Newport*

New Quay (village, western Wales) : Welsh *Ceinewydd*

New Radnor (village, eastern Wales) : Welsh *Maesyfed* (The village was the original county town of *Radnorshire*, Welsh *Sir Faesyfed*, abolished in 1974.)

New Ross (town, southeastern Ireland) : Irish *Rhos Mhic Thriúin*

Newry (town, southeastern Northern Ireland) : Irish *An tIúr*

Newry Station *see* **Atwood**

New Sarum *see* **Salisbury**

New Siberian Islands (northeastern Russia) : [Russian *Novosibirskiye Ostrova*]

New Site *see* **²Andalusia**

New South Wales *see* **Australia**

Newstead (village, southeastern Scotland) : Roman *Trimontium*

Newton (city, Massachusetts, northeastern United States) : to 1691 *New Towne*

Newton *see* (1) **²Picton**; (2) **Ridgewood**

Newtonferry (village, Western Isles, northwestern Scotland) : Gaelic *Port nan Long*

Newton in Makerfield *see* **Newton-le-Willows**

Newton-le-Willows (town, northwestern England) : formerly *Newton in Makerfield* (The town's adoption of the current name causes potential confusion with a village of the same name in Yorkshire.)

Newton's Station *see* **Glen Ellyn**

Newtown (town, east central Wales) : Welsh *Y Drenewydd*

Newtown *see* (1) **Elmira**; (2) **Macon**

New Town *see* **²Wilmington**

Newtownards (town, eastern Northern Ireland) : Irish *Baile Nua na hArda*

Newtownbarry *see* **Bunclody**

New Towne *see* (1) **²Cambridge**; (2) **Newton**

New Tredegar (town, southern Wales) : Welsh *Tredegar Newydd*

New Westminster (city, British Columbia, southwestern Canada) : originally *Queensborough*

New Windsor *see* **¹Windsor**

New York (city, New York, northeastern United States) : to 1664 *New Amsterdam* (Dutch *Nieuw Amsterdam*) (The city's name is applied by many only to the borough of Manhattan, as coextensive with New York County, although it is properly that of the whole of New York City, or Greater New York, including the "outer boroughs" of the Bronx, Brooklyn, Queens, and **Staten Island**.)

New Zealand (independent state, southwestern Pacific) : Maori *Aotearoa*; formerly Dutch *Staaten Landt*

Ney-Val'ter *see* **Sverdlovo**

Nezametny *see* **Aldan**

Nezider *see* **Neusiedl am See**

Ngaru *see* **Port Hedland**

Nguna (island, central Vanuatu) : formerly *Montagu Island*

Ngunza *see* **Sumbe**

Nhlangano (town, southwestern Swaziland) : formerly *Goedgegun*

Niagara *see* **Niagara-on-the-Lake**

Niagara Falls (city, Ontario, southeastern Canada) : 1856–1881 *Clifton*; to 1856 *Elgin*

Niagara-on-the-Lake (town, Ontario, southeastern Canada) : to 1906 *Niagara*; earlier *Newark* (The addition to the name distinguished the town from nearby **Niagara Falls**.)

Nicaea *see* (1) **İznik**; (2) **Nice**

Nicaragua *see* **Rivas**

Nice (city, southern France) : 1814–1860 Italian *Nizza*; Roman *Nicaea*

Nicephorium *see* **Ar Raqqah**

Nicholas II Land *see* **Severnaya Zemlya**

Nicomedia *see* **İzmit**

Nico Pérez *see* **José Batlle y Ordoñez**

Nicopolis *see* **Nikopol**

Nicosia (city, north central Cyprus) : [modern Greek *Levkosía*; Turkish *Lefkoşa*]; formerly *Ledra* (In 1974 the city was divided by the Attila Line, with the southern sector in the Greek-speaking Republic of Cyprus and the northern in the Turkish Republic of Northern Cyprus. In 2008 the border checkpoint in Ledra Street, the city's main shopping street, was reopened, leading to hopes of reunification for the island as a whole.)

Nidaros *see* **Trondheim**

Nidum *see* **Neath**

Nidzica (town, northeastern Poland) : to 1945 German *Neidenburg*

Niegocin, Lake (northeastern Poland) : to 1945 German *Löwentin*

Niemcza (town, southwestern Poland) : to 1945 German *Nimptsch*

Niemodlin (town, southwestern Poland) : to 1945 German *Falkenberg*

Nieśwież *see* **Nyasvizh**

Nieuport *see* **Nieuwpoort**

Nieuw Amstel *see* **New Castle**

Nieuw Amsterdam *see* **New York**

Nieuwpoort (town, western Belgium) : French *Nieuport*

Nihon *see* **Japan**

Niitoi *see* **Novoye**

Nijmegen (city, eastern Netherlands) : 1939–1944 German *Nimwegen*; Roman *Noviomagus*

Nijvel *see* **Nivelles**

Nikel' (town, northwestern Russia) : to 1944 Finnish *Kolosjoki*

Nikitino *see* **Nikopol'**

Nikitin Rog *see* **Nikopol'**

Nikitinskiye Promysly *see* [1]**Kirovsky**

Nikitovka (village, western Russia) : to 1945 German *Marienhof*

Nikolainkaupunki *see* **Vaasa**

Nikolaistad *see* **Vaasa**

Nikolayev *see* [1,2]**Mykolayiv**

Nikolayevka *see* **Novovorontsovka**

Nikolayevka-Vyrevskaya *see* [2]**Zhovtneve**

Nikolayevsk *see* **Pugachyov**

Nikolayevskoye *see* [2]**Krasnogvardeyskoye**

Nikolsburg *see* **Mikulov**

Nikol'sk (city, western Russia) : to 1954 *Nikol'skaya Pestravka*

Nikol'sk *see* **Ussuriysk**

Nikol'skaya Pestravka *see* **Nikol'sk**

Nikol'skaya Sloboda *see* **Osa**

Nikol'skoye *see* **Sheksna**

Nikol'sk-Ussuriysky *see* **Ussuriysk**

Nikol'sky *see* **Satpayev**

Nikol'sky Khutor *see* **Sursk**

Nikopol (town, northern Bulgaria) : to 1878 Turkish *Nyebol*; Roman *Nicopolis*

Nikopol' (city, east central Ukraine) : to 1782 *Mykytyne* (Russian *Nikitino*); earlier *Mykytyn Rih* (Russian *Nikitin Rog*)

Niksar (town, north central Turkey) : Roman *Neocaesarea*

Nikšić (city, central Montenegro) : formerly *Onogošt*; Roman *Anagastum*

Nikumaroro (atoll, central Kiribati) : formerly *Gardner Island*

Nikunau (island, western Kiribati) : formerly *Byron Island*

Nile (river, eastern and northeastern Africa) : [Arabic *An Nīl*]

Niles (city, Ohio, north central United States) : 1834–1843 *Nilestown*; to 1834 *Heaton's Furnace*

Niles Center *see* **Skokie**

Nilestown *see* **Niles**

Nimburg *see* **Nymburk**

Nîmes (city, southern France) : Roman *Nemausus*

Nimptsch *see* **Niemcza**

Nimrud (ancient city, northern Iraq) : biblical *Calah*

Nimwegen *see* **Nijmegen**

Nin (village, southern Croatia) : 1941–1943 Italian *Nona*; Roman *Aenona*

Ninety Mile Beach *see* **Eighty Mile Beach**

Ningbo (city, eastern China) : 1911–1949 *Ningzian*

Ningxian *see* **Ningbo**

Niquelândia (city, east central Brazil) : to 1944 Portuguese *São José do Tocantins*

Niš (city, southeastern Serbia) : Roman *Naissus*

Nísia Floresta (town, eastern Brazil) : to 1948 *Papari*

Nisibis *see* **Nusaybin**

Niterói (city, eastern Brazil) : to 1836 Portuguese *Villa Real da Praia Grande*

Nitra (city, southwestern Slovakia) : to 1918 Hungarian *Nyitra*; to 1867 German *Neutra*

Nitrianske Pravno (village, west central Slovakia) : to 1918 Hungarian *Németpróna*; to 1867 German *Deutsch-Proben*

Niuafo'ou (island, northern Tonga) : formerly *Proby Island*

Niuatoputopu (island, northern Tonga) : formerly *Boscawen Island*

Nivelles (town, central Belgium) : Flemish *Nijvel*

Nivenskoye (village, western Russia) : to 1945 German *Wittenberg*

Niwbwrch *see* **Newborough**

Nizhnegorsky *see* **Nyzhn'ohirs'kyy**

Nizhnesaraninsky *see* **Sarana**

Nizhneserginsky Zavod *see* **Nizhniye Sergi**

Nizhnetroitsky (town, western Russia) : to 1928 *Nizhnetroitsky Zavod*

Nizhnetroitsky Zavod *see* **Nizhnetroitsky**

Nizhneturinsky Zavod *see* **Nizhnyaya Tura**

Nizhnevolzhsk *see* **Narimanov**

Nizhniye Kresty *see* **Chersky**

Nizhniye Sergi (town, west central Russia) : to 1928 *Nizhneserginsky Zavod*

Nizhniye Ustriki *see* **Ustrzyki Dolne**

Nizhny Agdzhakend *see* **Goranboy**

Nizhnyaya Dobrinka *see* **Dobrinka**

Nizhnyaya Tura (city, west central Russia) : to 1929 *Nizhneturinsky Zavod*

Nizhny Naur *see* **Nadterechnaya**

Nizhny Novgorod (city, western Russia) : 1932–1990 *Gor'ky* (The city's name, "Lower Novgorod," distinguishes it from **Veliky Novgorod**, to the north near St. Petersburg, the adjective describing its status rather than its relative geographical position.)

Nizov'ye (village, western Russia) : to 1945 German *Waldau*

Nizza *see* **Nice**

No *see* **Thebes**

Nocera Inferiore (town, southern Italy) : Roman *Nuceria Alfaterna*

Nocera Umbra (town, central Italy) : Roman *Nuceria*

Noda *see* ¹**Chekhov**

Nogales (town, Arizona, southwestern United States) : to 1882 *Isaacson*

Nogaysk *see* **Prymors'k**

Noginsk (city, western Russia) : 1781–1930 *Bogorodsk*; originally *Rogozha*

Nohays'ke *see* **Prymors'k**

Nolinsk (town, western Russia) : 1940–1957 *Molotovsk*

Nome (town, Alaska, northwestern United States) : originally *Anvil City*

Nomentum *see* **Mentana**

Nona *see* **Nin**

Nonouti (atoll, western Kiribati) : formerly *Sydenham Island*

Noph *see* **Memphis**

Norakert *see* **Baghramyan**

Norashen *see* **Şärur**

Norba *see* **Norma**

Nor-Bayazet *see* **Gavarr**

Nordenskjöld Sea *see* **Laptev Sea**

Nordkapp *see* **North Cape**

Nord-Ostsee Kanal *see* **Kiel Canal**

Norfolk (town, Nebraska, central United States) : formerly *Norfork*; originally *North Fork*

Norfolk Broads *see* **Broads, The**

Norfork *see* **Norfolk**

Norge *see* **Norway**

Norinberga *see* **Nürnberg**

Norma (village, western Italy) : Roman *Norba*

Normal (town, Illinois, north central United States) : to 1857 *North Bloomington*

Normandie *see* **Normandy**

Normandy (region, northern France) : [French *Normandie*]

Normanton *see* **Port Elgin**

Norman Wells (village, Northwest Territories, northwestern Canada) : alternate Inuit *Legohli*

Northampton *see* (1) **Allentown**; (2) **Mount Holly**

North Bloomington *see* **Normal**

North Borneo *see* **Sabah**

North Bridgewater *see* **Brockton**

North Cape (northern Norway) : [Norwegian *Nordkapp*]

North Chelsea *see* **Revere**

North East Frontier Agency *see* **Arunachal Pradesh**

Northern *see* **Limpopo**

Northern Ireland (territory, western United Kingdom) : colloquially *Ulster* (The colloquial name is properly that of the province of nine counties that existed before the 1922 division of **Ireland** into an independent state in the south and a region of the United Kingdom in the north. The present Northern Ireland has only six counties.)

Northern Rhodesia *see* **Zambia**

Northern Transvaal *see* **Limpopo**

North Fork *see* **Norfolk**

North Greenfield *see* **West Allis**

North Island (northern New Zealand) : Maori *Te Ika a Maui* (The Maori name, meaning "the fish of Maui," contrasts with those of **South Island** and **Stewart Island**.)

North Land *see* **Severnaya Zemlya**

North Little Rock (city, Arkansas, south central United States) : to 1901 *Argenta*; earlier *Huntersville*; to 1853 *De Cantillon* (Argenta was annexed by the city of Little Rock in 1890.)

Northop (village, northeastern Wales) : Welsh *Llaneurgain*

North Sea (northwestern Europe) : formerly usually *German Ocean*; Roman *Mare Germanicum*

North Tarrytown *see* **Sleepy Hollow**

Northton (village, Western Isles, northwestern Scotland) : Gaelic *Taobh Tuath*

North Uist (island, Western Isles, northwestern Scotland) : Gaelic *Uibhist a' Tuath*

North Vancouver (city, British Columbia, southwestern Canada) : 1872–1907 *Moodyville*

Northwich (town, northwestern England) : Roman *Condate*

North Yakima *see* **Yakima**

Norton de Matos *see* **Balombo**

Norusovo *see* **Kalinino**

Norwalk (city, California, southwestern United States) : originally *Corvallis*

Norway (kingdom, northwestern Europe) : [Norwegian *Norge*]

Norwood (village, Ontario, southeastern Canada) : to 1838 *Keeler's Mills*

Nossa Senhora da Conceição de Campinas de Matto Grosso *see* **Campinas**

Nossa Senhora da Conceição dos Guarulhos *see* **Guarulhos**

Nossa Senhora das Dores de Tatuibi *see* **Limeira**

Nossa Senhora do Livramento (town, northeastern Brazil) : 1944–1948 Portuguese *São José dos Cocais*; to 1944 Portuguese *Livramento*

Nossa Senhora dos Prazeres de Itapetininga *see* **Itapetininga**

Nosy Boraha (island, eastern Madagascar) : formerly French *Ste.-Marie*

Nöteborg *see* **Shlissel'burg**

Noto (town, southern Italy) : Roman *Netum*

Notre-Dame-de-Foy *see* **Ste.-Foy**

Notre-Dame-des-Hermites *see* **Einsiedeln**

Nottaway *see* **Senneterre**

Nouadhibou (town, northwestern Mauritania) : to 1960s French *Port-Étienne*

Nouméa (town, southern New Caledonia, South Pacific) : formerly French *Port-de-France*

Nouvelle Anvers *see* **Makanza**

Nouvelle-Calédonie *see* **New Caledonia**

Nouvelle-France *see* **Canada**

Nouvelle-Lambèse *see* **Batna**

Nouvelle-Orléans *see* **New Orleans**

Nouvelles-Hébrides *see* **Vanuatu**

Novabad *see* **Navabad**

Nová Baňa (town, south central Slovakia) : to 1918 Hungarian *Újbánya*

Nova Chaves *see* **Muconda**

Nova Civitas *see* **Neustadt an der Weinstrasse**

Nova Dantzig *see* **Cambé**

Nova Era (town, southeastern Brazil) : 1930–1944 Portuguese *Presidente Vargas*; to 1930 Portuguese *São José da Lagoa*

Novaesium *see* **Neuss**

Nova Freixo *see* **Cuamba**

Nova Gaia *see* **Cambundi-Catembo**

Nova Gorica (town, western Slovenia) : 1919–1947 Italian *Gorizia Montesanto* (See note for **Gorizia**.)

Nova Gradiška (town, eastern Croatia) : to 1867 German *Neugradisca*

Nova Iguaçu (city, eastern Brazil) : formerly *Maxambamba* (The city is now a suburb of Rio de Janeiro.)

Nova Khrestivka *see* ¹**Kirovs'ke**

Nova Lamego *see* **Gabú**

Nova Lisboa *see* **Huambo**

Nova Nadezhda (village, southeastern Bulgaria) : to 1948 *Knyaginya Nadezhda* (The earlier name, meaning "Princess Nadezhda," became unacceptable following the abolition of the monarchy, so the authorities shrewdly adapted it to a form meaning "New Hope.")

Novantarum Peninsula *see* **Rinns of Galloway**

Nová Paka (town, northern Czech Republic) : to 1918, 1939–1945 German *Neupaka*

Nova Prata (town, southern Brazil) : to 1944 *Prata*

Novara (city, northwestern Italy) : Roman *Novaria*

Novaria *see* **Novara**

Nova Sintra *see* **Catabola**

Nova Siri (town, southern Italy) : ancient Greek *Siris*

Nova Sofala *see* **Sofala**

Nova Vicenza *see* **Farroupilha**

Novaya Aleksandriya *see* **Puławy**

Novaya Bukhara *see* **Kogon**

Novaya Derevnya *see* **Novosibirsk**

Novaya Eushta *see* **Timiryazevsky**

Novaya Krestovka *see* ¹**Kirovs'ke**

Novaya Lyalya (town, west central Russia) : to *c.*1928 *Novolyalinsky Zavod*

Novaya Nikol'skaya *see* **Osa**

Novaya Pis'myanka *see* **Leninogorsk**

Novaya Zemlya (island group, northwestern Russia) : formerly English *Nova Zembla*

Novaya Zhizn' *see* **Kazanka**

Nova Zagora (city, east central Bulgaria) : to 1878 Turkish *Yenizağra*

Nova Zembla *see* **Novaya Zemlya**

Nové Město nad Metují (town, northern Czech Republic) : to 1918, 1939–1945 German *Neustadt an der Mettau*

Nové Mesto nad Šatorom *see* **Slovenské Nové Mesto**

Nové Mesto nad Váhom (town, western Slovakia) : to 1918 Hungarian *Vágújhely*; to 1867 German *Waag-Neustadt*

Nové Město na Moravě (town, east central Czech Republic) : to 1918, 1939–1945 German *Neustadtl*

Nové Zámky (town, southwestern Slovakia) : to 1918, 1938–1945 Hungarian *Érsekújvár*; to 1867 German *Neuhäusel*

Novgorod *see* **Veliky Novgorod**

Novgradets *see* **Suvorovo**

Novi *see* (1) **Bosanski Novi**; (2) **Sidi Ghiles**

Novi Kritsim *see* **Stamboliyski**

Noviodunum *see* (1) **Nevers**; (2) **Nyon**

Noviomagus *see* (1) **Chichester**; (2) **Crayford**; (3) **Lisieux**; (4) **Neumagen**; (5) **Nijmegen**; (6) **Noyon**; (7) **Speyer**

Noviomagus Regnorum *see* **Chichester**

¹**Novi Pazar** (town, eastern Bulgaria) : to 1878 Turkish *Yenipazar*

²**Novi Pazar** (city, southwestern Serbia) : to 1913 Turkish *Yenipazar*

Novi Sad (city, northern Serbia) : to 1918, 1941–1944 Hungarian *Újvidék*; to 1867 German *Neusatz*

Novi Travnik (town, central Bosnia-Herzegovina) : formerly *Pucarevo*

Novo-Aleksandrovka *see* **Melitopol'**

[1]Novoaleksandrovsk (city, southwestern Russia) : to 1971 *Novoaleksandrovskaya*

[2]Novoaleksandrovsk (town, eastern Russia) : 1905–1945 Japanese *Konuma*

Novoaleksandrovsk *see* **Zarasai**

Novoaleksandrovskaya *see* **[1]Novoaleksandrovsk**

Novoalekseyevka *see* **Khobda**

Novoaltaysk (town, southern Russia) : to 1962 *Chesnokovka*

Novoarkhangelsk *see* **Sitka**

Novoasbest (town, west central Russia) : to 1933 *Krasnouralsky Rudnik*

Novoazovsk *see* **Novoazovs'k**

Novoazovs'k (town, southeastern Ukraine) : (Russian *Novoazovsk*); 1959–1966 *Novoazovs'ke* (Russian *Novoazovskoye*); 1923–1959 *Bud'onnivka* (Russian *Budyonnovka*); to 1923 *Novomykolayivka* (Russian *Novonikolayevka*)

Novoazovs'ke *see* **Novoazovs'k**

Novoazovskoye *see* **Novoazovs'k**

Novobureysky (town, southeastern Russia) : formerly *Bureya-Pristan'*

Novocheremshansk (town, western Russia) : formerly *Stary Salavan*

Novodvinsk (city, northwestern Russia) : to 1977 *Pervomaysky*

Novoekonomicheskoye *see* **Dymytrov**

Novoekonomichne *see* **Dymytrov**

Novogeorgiyevsk *see* (1) **Modlin**; (2) **Svitlovods'k**

Novogordino *see* **Krasnoye Ekho**

Novograd-Volynsk *see* **Novohrad-Volyns'kyy**

Novograd-Volynsky *see* **Novohrad-Volyns'kyy**

Novogroznensky *see* **Oyskhara**

Novogrudok *see* **Navahrudak**

Novoheorhiyivs'ke *see* **Svitlovods'k**

Novohrad-Volyns'kyy (city, northwestern Ukraine) : (Russian *Novograd-Volynsky*); to 1925 Russian *Novograd-Volynsk* (The earlier Russian name was adjusted to conform with Ukrainian usage.)

Novokashirsk (town, western Russia) : c.1935–c.1957 *Kaganovich*; 1932–c.1935 *Ternovsk*; to 1932 *Ternovsky* (The town was incorporated into the city of Kashira in 1963.)

Novokaterynoslav *see* **Svatove**

Novokazalinsk *see* **Ayteke Bi**

Novokiyevskoye *see* **Kraskino**

Novokubansk (city, southwestern Russia) : to 1966 *Novokubansky*

Novokubansky *see* **Novokubansk**

Novokuznetsk (city, southern Russia) : 1932–1961 *Stalinsk*; to 1931 *Kuznetsk-Sibirsky*

Novolakskoye (village, southwestern Russia) : to 1944 *Yaryksu-Aukh*

Novolyalinsky Zavod *see* **Novaya Lyalya**

Novolyubino *see* **Lyubinsky**

Novo-Mariinsk *see* **Anadyr'**

Novo Mesto (town, southeastern Slovenia) : to 1918 German *Rudolfswerth*

Novominsk *see* **Mińsk Mazowiecki**

Novomoskovsk (city, western Russia) : 1934–1961 *Stalinogorsk*; to 1934 *Bobriki*

Novomykolayivka *see* (1) **Chkalove**; (2) **Novoazovs'k**

Novonazyvayevka *see* **Nazyvayevsk**

Novonikolayevka *see* (1) **Chkalove**; (2) **Novoazovs'k**

Novonikolayevsk *see* **Novosibirsk**

Novonikolayevsky *see* **Novosibirsk**

Novooleksandrivka *see* **Melitopol'**

Novopashiysky *see* **[2]Gornozavodsk**

Novopavlovsk (town, southwestern Russia) : to 1981 *Novopavlovskaya*

Novopavlovskaya *see* **Novopavlovsk**

Novopetrovskoye *see* **Fort-Shevchenko**

Novoradomsk *see* **Radomsko**

Novo Redondo *see* **Sumbe**

Novorossiysk *see* **Dnipropetrovs'k**

Novoselivka *see* **[2]Frunze**

Novoselivs'ke (town, southern Ukraine) : (Russian *Novosyolovskoye*); to 1944 *Fraidorf* (The town was a Jewish settlement from the mid–1920s to World War II.)

Novo Selo *see* **Dŭlgopol**

Novosel'skoye *see* **Achkhoy-Martan**

Novoseltsi *see* **Elin Pelin**

Novoshakhtinsk (city, southwestern Russia) : 1929–1939 *Komintern*; earlier *imeni III Internatsionala*

Novosibirsk (city, southern Russia) : 1903–1926 *Novonikolayevsk*; 1895–1903 *Novonikolayevsky*; 1894–1895 *Aleksandrovsky*; to 1894 *Novaya Derevnya* (The current name of the Siberian city was selected by readers of a regional newspaper. Other proposals were *Krasnograd*, *Krasnokuznetsk*, *Krasnosibirsk*, *Obgorod*, *Oktyabr'grad*, *Sibgrad*, and *Sibkraygrad*.)

Novosibirskiye Ostrova *see* **New Siberian Islands**

Novo-Starobinsk *see* **Salihorsk**

Novostroyevo (village, western Russia) : to 1945 German *Trempen*

Novosyolovka *see* **[2]Frunze**

Novosyolovskoye *see* Novoselivs'ke
Novotroitskoye *see* (1) Sokuluk; (2) Tole Bi
Novourgench *see* Urganch
Novovoronezh (city, western Russia) : to 1987
  Novovoronezhsky
Novovoronezhsky *see* Novovoronezh
Novovorontsovka (town, south central Ukraine)
  : to 1821 *Mykolayivka* (Russian *Nikolayevka*)
Novovyatsk (city, western Russia) : 1939–1955
  Lesozavodsky; to 1939 *Grukhi* (The former city
  was incorporated into Kirov in 1989.)
Novoye (village, eastern Russia) : 1905–1945
  Japanese *Niitoi*
Novoyekaterinoslav *see* Svatove
Novy Afon *see* Akhali Ap'oni
Nový Bor (town, northern Czech Republic) : to
  1946 *Bor u České Lípy*
Nový Bydžov (town, north central Czech Re-
  public) : to 1918, 1938–1945 German *Neubid-
  schow*
Novy Donbass *see* Dymytrov
Nový Jičín (city, eastern Czech Republic) : to
  1918, 1938–1945 German *Neutitschein*
Novy Margelan *see* Farg'ona
Novy Uzen' *see* Zhanaozen
Novy Yarychev *see* Novyy Yarychiv
Novyy Donbas *see* Dymytrov
Novyye Aldy *see* Chernorech'ye
Novyye Aneny *see* Anenii Noi
Novyye Kholmogory *see* Arkhangel'sk
Novyye Petushki *see* Petushki
Novyy Yarychiv (town, western Ukraine) : (Rus-
  sian *Novy Yarychev*) : 1349–1772, 1919–1939
  Polish *Jaryczów Nowy*
Novy Zay *see* Zainsk
Nowa Ruda (town, southwestern Poland) : to
  1945 German *Neurode*
Nowa Sól (town, western Poland) : to 1945 Ger-
  man *Neusalz*
Nowawes *see* Babelsberg
Nowe Miasteczko (town, western Poland) : to
  1945 German *Neustädtel*
Nowe Święciany *see* Švenčionéliai
Nowe Warpno (town, northwestern Poland) : to
  1945 German *Neuwarp*
Nowogard (town, northwestern Poland) : to
  1945 German *Neugard*
Nowogródek *see* Navahrudak
Nowogrodziec (town, southwestern Poland) : to
  1945 German *Naumburg am Queis*
Nowy Bytom *see* Ruda Śląska
Nowy Dwór Gdański (town, northern Poland) :
  1772–1945 German *Tiegenhof*
Nowy Port (suburban district, northern Poland)
  : 1793–1945 German *Neufahrwasser* (Nowy
  Port is a port area of Gdańsk.)

Nowy Sącz (city, southeastern Poland) : to 1945
  German *Neusandez*
Nowy Staw (town, northern Poland) : 1772–1945
  German *Neuteich*
Nowy Targ (town, southern Poland) : to 1918,
  1940–1945 German *Neumarkt*
Nowy Tomyśl (town, western Poland) : 1793–
  1807, 1815–1919, 1939–1945 German *Neu-
  tomischel*
Noyon (town, northern France) : Roman *Novio-
  magus*
Nozhay-Yurt (village, southwestern Russia) :
  1940s–1950s *Andalaly*
Nsanje (city, southern Malawi) : to 1964 *Port
  Herald*
Ntshingwayo Dam (eastern South Africa) : to
  2000 *Chelmsford Dam*
Nuanetsi *see* Mwenezi
Nuceria *see* Nocera Umbra
Nuceria Alfaterna *see* Nocera Inferiore
Nuestra Señora de Guadalupe de Ponce *see*
  Ponce
Nuestra Señora de la Candelaria de El Banco
  see El Banco
Nuestra Señora de la Candelaria de Mayagüez
  see Mayagüez
Nuestra Señora de la Paz *see* La Paz
Nuestra Señora del Espíritu Santo Zuñiga *see*
  Goliad
Nuestra Señora del Puerto de las Conchas *see*
  ¹San Fernando
Nueva Buenos Aires *see* Bahía Blanca
Nueva Caceres *see* Naga
Nueva Ciudad de San Salvador *see* Nueva San
  Salvador
Nueva Córdoba *see* Cumaná
Nueva Filipina *see* Pinar del Río
Nueva Isabela *see* Santo Domingo
Nueva Madrid *see* Ocaña
Nueva San Salvador (city, west central El Salva-
  dor) : originally *Nueva Ciudad de San Salvador*
Nueva Valencia del Rey *see* ²Valencia
Nueva Villa de Salamanca *see* San Germán
Nueva Zamora *see* Maracaibo
Nukha *see* Şäki
Nukulaelae (atoll, southern Tuvalu) : formerly
  Mitchell Island
Nukunonu (atoll, central Tokelau) : formerly
  Duke of Clarence Island
Numantia *see* Garray
Nunap Isua *see* Farewell, Cape
Nunnepog *see* Edgartown
Nurabad *see* Nurobod
Nuremberg *see* Nürnberg
Nuristan (region, eastern Afghanistan) : formerly
  Kafiristan

Nürnberg (city, south central Germany) : traditional English *Nuremberg*; Medieval Latin *Norinberga* (The traditional spelling became familiar from the "Nuremberg trials" of German war criminals after World War II.)

Nurobod (town, east central Uzbekistan) : (Russian *Nurabad*); to 1983 *Sovetabad*

Nusaybin (town, southeastern Turkey) : ancient Greek *Nisibis*

Nussdorf *see* **Năsăud**

Nuuk (town, southwestern Greenland) : to 1979 *Godthåb*

Nyagan' (town, west central Russia) : formerly *Nyakh*

Nyahururu (town, central Kenya) : to 1975 *Thomson's Falls*

Nyakh *see* **Nyagan'**

Nyanda *see* **Masvingo**

Nyando *see* **Rooseveltown**

Nyasa, Lake *see* **Malawi, Lake**

Nyasaland *see* **Malawi**

Nyasvizh (city, western Belarus) : (Russian *Nesvizh*); 1919–1939 Polish *Nieśwież*; to 1918 Russian *Nesvizh*

Nyebol *see* **Nikopol**

Nyfer *see* **Nevern**

Nyitra *see* **Nitra**

Nyitrabánya *see* **Handlová**

Nyland *see* **Uudenmaan**

Nylstroom *see* **Modimolle**

Nymburk (town, west central Czech Republic) : 1939–1945 German *Neuenburg an der Elbe*; to 1918 German *Nimburg*

Nyon (town, western Switzerland) : Roman *Noviodunum*

Nysa (city, southern Poland) : to 1945 German *Neisse*

Nystad *see* **Uusikaupunki**

Nyzhn'ohirs'kyy (town, southern Ukraine) : (Russian *Nizhnegorsky*); to 1944 *Seitler*

N'zeto (town, northwestern Angola) : formerly *Ambrizete*

Oak Bluffs (town, Massachusetts, northeastern United States) : to 1907 *Cottage City*

Oak Glen *see* **Glenview**

Oak Park (town, Illinois, north central United States) : originally *Oak Ridge*

Oak Ridge *see* **Oak Park**

Oban (town, southern New Zealand) : alternate *Half-Moon Bay*

Obbe *see* **Leverburgh**

Obdorsk *see* **Salekhard**

Óbecse *see* **Bečej**

Obedinenie (village, northern Bulgaria) : 1941–1978 *Knyaz Simeonovo*

Obedovo *see* [4]**Oktyabr'sky**

Oberdorf *see* **Remennikovo**

Oberglogau *see* **Głogówek**

Oberhaid *see* **Horní Dvořiště**

Oberlaibach *see* **Vrhnika**

Obernick *see* **Oborniki**

Obernigk *see* **Oborniki Śląskie**

Obernik *see* **Oborniki**

Oberpahlen *see* **Põltsamaa**

Ober-Radkersburg *see* **Gornja Radgona**

Oberwart (town, eastern Austria) : to 1919 Hungarian *Felsőőr*

Obiralovka *see* [1]**Zheleznodorozhny**

Oborniki (town, western Poland) : 1939–1945 German *Obernick*; 1815–1919 German *Obernik*

Oborniki Śląskie (town, southwestern Poland) : to 1945 German *Obernigk*

Obruchevo *see* **Dashtobod**

Obukhivka *see* [2]**Kirovs'ke**

Obukhovka *see* [2]**Kirovs'ke**

Ocaña (city, northern Colombia) : originally *Nueva Madrid*

Ocean Beach *see* **Miami Beach**

Ocean Island *see* **Banaba**

Ocean Springs (town, Mississippi, southeastern United States) : 1853–1854 *Lynchburg*; to 1853 *Fort Maurepas*

Ochiai *see* **Dolinsk**

Ocriculum *see* **Otricoli**

Ocrinum Promontorium *see* **Lizard, The**

Octapitarum Promontorium *see* **St. David's Head**

Ödenburg *see* **Sopron**

Odenpäh *see* **Otepää**

Oder (river, northeastern Czech Republic/southwestern Poland/northeastern Germany) : Czech and Polish *Odra* (For much of its course the river forms the border between Poland and Germany.)

Oderberg *see* **Bohumín**

Odertal *see* **Zdzieszowice**

Oderzo (town, northeastern Italy) : Roman *Opitergium*

Odesa *see* **Odessa**

Odessa (city, southern Ukraine) : [Ukrainian *Odesa*]; (Russian *Odessa*); to 1918 Russian *Odessa*

Odessus *see* **Varna**

Odolanów (town, western Poland) : 1793–1807, 1815–1919, 1939–1945 German *Adelnau*

Odorheiu Secuiesc (city, central Romania) : to 1918, 1940–1944 Hungarian *Székelyudvarhely*

Odra *see* **Oder**

Odrin *see* **Edirne**

Oea *see* [2]**Tripoli**

Oels *see* **Oleśnica**

Ofanto (river, southeastern Italy) : Roman *Aufidus*

Offaly (county, east central Ireland) : Irish *Uíbh Fhailí*; 1577–1920 English *King's County*

Offa's Dyke (entrenchment, eastern Wales) : Welsh *Clawdd Offa* (The linear earthwork that today approximately corresponds to the border between England and Wales was built in the 8th century by Offa, king of Mercia, to mark the western boundary of his territory.)

Offutt Air Force Base (Nebraska, central United States) : to 1924 *Fort Crook*

Ogasawara-gunto *see* **Bonin Islands**

Ogden (city, Utah, western United States) : originally *Brownsville*

Oglethorpe, Mt. (Georgia, southeastern United States) : to 1929 *Grassy Mountain*

Ogmore-by-Sea (village, southern Wales) : Welsh *Ogwr*

Ogmore Vale (village, southern Wales) : Welsh *Cwm Ogwr*

Ognyanovo (village, south central Bulgaria) : to 1948 *Maritsa*

Ogumkiqueok *see* **Liverpool**

Ogwr *see* **Ogmore-by-Sea**

Ógyalla *see* **Hurbanovo**

O'Higgins Land *see* **Antarctic Peninsula**

Ohlau *see* **Oława**

Ohri *see* **Ohrid**

Ohrid (town, southwestern Macedonia) : 1915–1918 Bulgarian *Okhrida*; to 1913 Turkish *Ohri*; ancient Greek *Lychidnos*

Okchelar *see* ²**Aleksandrovo**

Okhrida *see* **Ohrid**

Okiato *see* **Russell**

Okinawa (city, southern Japan) : formerly *Koza*

Okny *see* **Krasni Okny**

Oko *see* **Yasnomorsky**

Okonek (town, northwestern Poland) : to 1945 German *Ratzebuhr*

Okotoks (town, Alberta, southwestern Canada) : to 1897 *Dewdney*

Oktemberyan *see* **Armavir**

Oktyabr'sk *see* **Kandyagash**

Oktyabrs'ke (town, southern Ukraine) : (Russian *Oktyabr'skoye*); to 1945 *Biyuk-Onlar*

¹**Oktyabr'skoye** (village, southwestern Russia, near Vladikavkaz) : formerly *Kartsa*; to 1944 *Sholkhi*

²**Oktyabr'skoye** (village, southwestern Russia, near Meleuz) : 1923–1937 *Kashirinskoye*; to 1923 *Isayevo-Dedovo*

³**Oktyabr'skoye** (village, west central Russia, near Nyagan') : to 1963 *Kondinskoye*

⁴**Oktyabr'skoye** (village, western Russia, near Mariinsky Posad) : to 1939 *Ismeli*

Oktyabr'skoye *see* (1) **Oktyabrs'ke**; (2) ¹**Zhovtneve**

¹**Oktyabr'sky** (town, eastern Russia, near Ust'-Bol'sheretsk) : formerly *imeni Mikoyana*

²**Oktyabr'sky** (town, southwestern Russia, near Belgorod) : 1938–1960 *Mikoyanovka*; to 1938 *Voskresenovka*

³**Oktyabr'sky** (town, western Russia, near Bor) : to 1957 *imeni V.M. Molotova*

⁴**Oktyabr'sky** (town, western Russia, near Ivanovo) : to 1941 *Obedovo*

⁵**Oktyabr'sky** (town, western Russia, near Galich) : to 1939 *Brantovka*

⁶**Oktyabr'sky** (town, western Russia, near Mikhaylov) : to 1927 *Sapronovo*

⁷**Oktyabr'sky** (town, southwestern Russia, near Volgograd) : formerly *Kruglyakov*

⁸**Oktyabr'sky** (village, western Russia, near Krasnoufimsk) : formerly *Chad*

Oktyabr'sky *see* (1) **Aktsyabrski**; (2) **Takhtamukay**

Oława (city, southwestern Poland) : to 1945 German *Ohlau*

Olbia (town, northeastern Sardinia, Italy) : to 1939 *Terranova Pausania*

Olcinium *see* **Ulcinj**

Old Delhi *see* **Delhi**

Old Harry's Town *see* ²**Manchester**

Old Hickory (village, Tennessee, east central United States) : to 1923 *Jacksonville*

Old Sarum *see* **Salisbury**

Oldtown *see* **Harrodsburg**

Olecko (town, northeastern Poland) : 1938–1945 German *Treuburg*; 1928–1938 German *Oletzko*; to 1928 *Marggrabowa*

Oleksandrivka *see* **Lozno-Oleksandrivka**

Oleksandrivs'k *see* **Zaporizhzhya**

Oleksiyeve-Leonove *see* **Torez**

Oleksiyeve-Orlivka *see* **Shakhtars'k**

Oleksiyivka *see* **Torez**

Olenacum *see* **Ilkley**

Olenegorsk (town, northwestern Russia) : to 1957 *Olen'ya*

Olenivka *see* **Zoryns'k**

Olenivs'ki Kar'yery *see* **Dokuchayevs'k**

Olen'ya *see* **Olenegorsk**

Oleshky *see* **Tsyurupyns'k**

Oleśnica (town, southwestern Poland) : to 1945 German *Oels*

Olesno (town, southern Poland) : to 1945 German *Rosenberg*

Oletzko *see* **Olecko**

Ol'ginskoye *see* **Kochubeyevskoye**

Olicana *see* **Ilkley**

Olifantshoek *see* ⁴**Alexandria**

Olisipo *see* **Lisbon**

Olita *see* **Alytus**

Oliva *see* **Oliwa**

Olivença *see* **Lupilichi**

Olives, Mount of (ridge, south central West Bank) : alternate biblical *Olivet*

Olivet *see* **Olives, Mount of**

Oliwa (city district, northern Poland) : 1772–1919, 1939–1945 German *Oliva* (Oliwa is a residential distict of Gdańsk.)

Olkhivchyk *see* **Shakhtars'k**

Ol'khovchik *see* **Shakhtars'k**

Ol'khovsky *see* **Artyomovsk**

Olkusz (town, southern Poland) : 1940–1945 German *Ilkenau*

Ollila *see* **Solnechnoye**

Olmütz *see* **Olomouc**

Olomouc (city, eastern Czech Republic) : to 1918, 1938–1945 German *Olmütz*

Olonets (town, northwestern Russia) : formerly Finnish *Aunus*

Olsztyn (city, northeastern Poland) : 1772–1945 German *Allenstein*

Olsztynek (town, northeastern Poland) : to 1945 German *Hohenstein*

Ólubló *see* **Stará Ľubovňa**

Ol'viopil' *see* ²**Pervomays'k**

Ol'viopol' *see* ²**Pervomays'k**

Olympia (city, Washington, northwestern United States) : originally *Smithfield*

Olympus, Mt. *see* (1) **Troodos**; (2) **Ulu Dağ**

Ol'zheras *see* **Mezhdurechensk**

Omagh (town, west central Northern Ireland) : Irish *An Ómaigh*

Oman (sultanate, southeastern Arabia) : to 1970 *Muscat and Oman*

Omdurman (city, east central Sudan) : [Arabic *Umm Durmān*] (The English name is associated with the 1898 Anglo-Egyptian victory over the Sudanese tribesmen of the khalifah 'Abd Allah.)

Omiš (town, southern Croatia) : to 1918 Italian *Amissa*

Omurtag (town, east central Bulgaria) : to 1878 Turkish *Osmanpazar*

On *see* **Heliopolis**

Ondjiva (town, southern Angola) : formerly Portuguese *Vila Pereira de Eça*

Oneonta (town, New York, northeastern United States) : to 1832 *McDonald's Bridge*

Oneşti (city, eastern Romania) : to 1990 *Gheorge Gheorgiu-Dej*

Onogošt *see* **Nikšić**

Onslow Courthouse *see* ²**Jacksonville**

Ontario (province, southern Canada) : 1841–1867 *Canada West*; 1791–1841 *Upper Canada* (The historical names for the province were essentially interchangeable. *Cp.* **Quebec**.)

Oostende *see* **Ostend**

Ootacamund *see* **Udagamandalam**

Oothcaloga *see* **Calhoun**

Opatija (town, western Croatia) : to 1947 Italian *Abbazia*

Opava (city, eastern Czech Republic) : to 1918, 1938–1945 German *Troppau*

Ópazova *see* **Stara Pazova**

Opitergium *see* **Oderzo**

Opole (city, southern Poland) : to 1945 German *Oppeln*

Opon *see* **Lapu-Lapu**

Oporto (city, northwestern Portugal) : [Portuguese *Porto*] (English generally prefers the city's earlier Portuguese name, itself simply representing *o porto*, "the port.")

Oppeln *see* **Opole**

Optikogorsk *see* ¹**Krasnogorsk**

Oradea (city, northwestern Romania) : to 1918, 1940–1944 Hungarian *Nagyvárad*; to 1867 German *Grosswardein*

Oral (city, northwestern Kazakhstan) : to 1991 Russian *Ural'sk*

Oran (city, northwestern Algeria) : [Arabic *Wahrān*] (The city has retained the French colonial spelling of the Arabic name.)

¹**Orange** (town, southeastern France) : Roman *Arausio*

²**Orange** (city, California, southwestern United States) : to 1875 *Richland*

³**Orange** (town, Texas, southern United States) : 1852–1856 *Madison*; to 1852 *Green's Bluff*

Orange *see* **Hillsborough**

Orange Free State *see* **Free State**

Oranienbaum *see* **Lomonosov**

Orany *see* **Varėna**

Oraşul Stalin *see* **Braşov**

Orcades *see* **Orkney Islands**

Orchard Park (town, New York, northeastern United States) : to 1934 *East Hamburg*

Ordona (village, southeastern Italy) : Roman *Herdonia*

Ordzhonikidze *see* (1) **Denisovka**; (2) **Kharagauli**; (3) **Vladikavkaz**; (4) **Yenakiyeve**

Ordzhonikidzeabad *see* **Kofarnihon**

Ordzhonikidzegrad *see* **Bezhitsa**

Ordzhonikidze Kray *see* **Stavropol' Kray**

Ordzhonikidzevskaya *see* **Sleptsovskaya**

Orekhi-Vydritsa *see* **Arekhawsk**

Orekhovsk *see* **Arekhawsk**

Ore Mountains *see* **Erzgebirge**

Orenburg (city, southwestern Russia) : 1938–1957 *Chkalov* (The city, founded on the site of present-day **Orsk**, moved to its present location in 1743, keeping its original name.)

Orense (city, northwestern Spain) : Roman *Aquae Originis*

Oreshek *see* **Shlissel'burg**

Orestiada (town, northeastern Greece) : to 1913 Turkish *Emirli*

Øresund (strait, western Denmark/southern Sweden) : dated English *The Sound*

Orgeyev *see* **Orhei**

Orgtrud (town, western Russia) : 1927–*c*.1940 *Lemeshensky*

Orhanie *see* (1) **Botevgrad**; (2) **Kačanik**

Orhei (city, central Moldova) : (Russian *Orgeyev*); to 1918 Russian *Orgeyev*

Orientale (province, northeastern Democratic Republic of the Congo) : 1997 *Haut-Congo*; 1971–1997 *Haut-Zaïre*; 1947–1971 *Orientale*; 1933–1947 *Stanleyville*; to 1933 *Orientale*

Orizaba *see* **Citlaltépetl**

Orizona (city, east central Brazil) : to 1944 *Campo Formoso*

Orjonikidzeobod *see* **Kofarnihon**

Orkhaniye *see* **Botevgrad**

Orkney Islands (northern Scotland) : Roman *Orcades*

Orlando (city, Florida, southeastern United States) : to 1857 *Jernigan*

Orlau *see* **Orlová**

Orleans *see* **Orléans**

Orléans (city, north central France) : English *Orleans*; Roman *Aurelianum*; earlier Roman *Genabum* (The English form of the name is associated with the English siege of the town in 1429 relieved by Joan of Arc, the "Maid of Orleans," during the Hundred Years' War.)

Orléansville *see* **Ech Chélif**

Orlov (town, western Russia) : 1923–1992 *Khalturin*

Orlová (town, eastern Czech Republic) : 1939–1945 German *Orlau*; 1918–1919, 1938–1939 Polish *Orłowa*; to 1918 German *Orlau*

Orlovo (village, eastern Russia) : 1905–1945 Japanese *Ushiro*

Orłowa *see* **Orlová**

Orlyak (village, eastern Bulgaria) : to 1947 *Mackensen* (The former name is that of the German World War I commander August von Mackensen, with his own name of Scottish origin.)

Ormond Beach (city, Florida, southeastern United States) : to 1880 *New Britain*

Ormož (village, northeastern Slovenia) : to 1918 German *Friedau*

Orneta (town, northeastern Poland) : to 1945 German *Wormditt*

Orolaunum *see* **Arlon**

Orona (island, central Kiribati) : formerly *Hull Island*

Orono (town, Maine, northeastern United States) to 1840 *Stillwater*

Orontes (river, western Syria) : [Arabic *Nahr al-ʿĀṣī*]

Orontes *see* **Alwand**

Oroszvár *see* **Rusovce**

Orschowa *see* **Orşova**

Orsk (city, southwestern Russia) : originally *Orenburg* (The city stands on the original location of **Orenburg.**)

Orsona *see* **Osuna**

Orsova *see* **Orşova**

Orşova (town, southwestern Romania) : to 1918 Hungarian *Orsova*; to 1867 German *Orschowa*

Ortaköy *see* **Ivaylovgrad**

Ortelsburg *see* **Szczytno**

Orūmīyeh (city, northwestern Iran) : alternate dated *Urmia*; 1930s–1979 *Rezāʾīyeh* (The same names apply to the lake near which the city stands.)

Orvieto (town, central Italy) : Medieval Latin *Urbs Vetus*

Orzysz (town, northeastern Poland) : to 1945 German *Arys*

Osa (town, western Russia) : to 1737 *Osinskaya*; earlier *Novaya Nikol'skaya*; originally *Nikol'skaya Sloboda*

Osaka (city, southern Japan) : formerly *Naniwa*

Osca *see* **Huesca**

Osceola *see* **Winter Park**

Ösel *see* **Saaremaa**

Oshawa (city, Ontario, southeastern Canada) : to 1842 *Skea's Corners*

Oshkosh (city, Wisconsin, north central United States) : to 1840 *Athens*

Oshmyany *see* **Ashmyany**

Osijek (city, eastern Croatia) : to 1867 German *Esseg*

Osimo (town, central Italy) : Roman *Auximum*

Osinskaya *see* **Osa**

Osipenko *see* **Berdyans'k**

Öskemen (town, eastern Kazakhstan) : alternate Russian *Ust'-Kamenogorsk*

Oslo (city, southeastern Norway) : 1877–1924 *Kristiania*; 1624–1877 *Christiania*; Medieval Latin *Asloga* (The city's original site was east of the Aker River. After a disastrous fire in 1624, it was rebuilt on its present site at the head of Oslo Fjord.)

Osmanabad (district, south central India) : to *c*.1900 *Naldrug*

Osmanpazar *see* **Omurtag**

Osnabrück (city, northwestern Germany) : formerly English *Osnaburg*

Osnaburg *see* **Osnabrück**

Ośno Lubuskie (town, western Poland) : to 1945 German *Drossen*

Osoblaha (village, eastern Czech Republic) : to 1918, 1939–1945 German *Hotzenplotz*

Ossersee *see* **Zarasai**

Ossining (town, New York, northeastern United States) : to 1901 *Sing Sing* (The former name continued for the state prison here, renamed Ossining Correctional Facility in 1969.)

Ostenburg *see* **Pułtusk**

Ostend (town, western Belgium) : [Flemish *Oostende*; French *Ostende*] (The English form of the name is regularly used not only for the port but in a historical context for the raid in 1918 by British naval forces on the German submarine base here.)

Ostende *see* **Ostend**

Osterode *see* **Ostróda**

Österreich *see* **Austria**

Österreich-Ungarn *see* **Austria-Hungary**

Ostgeym *see* **Tel'manove**

Ostheym *see* **Tel'manove**

Ostian Way *see* **Via**

Ostrava (city, eastern Czech Republic) : to 1918, 1939–1945 German *Mährisch-Ostrau* (The Czech equivalent of the German name is *Moravská Ostrava*, "Moravian Ostrava," the city west of the Ostravice River. East of the river is *Slezská Ostrava*, "Silesian Ostrava.")

Ostróda (city, northeastern Poland) : to 1945 German *Osterode* (When in East Prussia, the city was known as *Osterode in Ostpreussen*, distinguishing it from *Osterode am Harz* in central Germany, now usually known as simply *Osterode*.)

Ostrog *see* **Ostroh**

Ostróg *see* **Ostroh**

Ostroh (town, western Ukraine) : (Russian *Ostrog*); 1919–1939 Polish *Ostróg*

Ostrołęka (city, northeastern Poland) : 1939–1945 German *Scharfenwiese*; to 1915 Russian *Ostrolenka*

Ostrolenka *see* **Ostrołęka**

Ostrov *see* **Ostrów Mazowiecka**

Ostrovo *see* **Arnissa**

Ostrovskoye (town, western Russia) : to 1956 *Semyonovskoye*

Ostrów Mazowiecka (town, east central Poland) : to 1915 Russian *Ostrov*

Ostrowo *see* **Ostrów Wielkopolski**

Ostrów Wielkopolski (city, west central Poland) : 1793–1807, 1815–1919, 1939–1945 German *Ostrowo*

Ostrzeszów (town, southwestern Poland) : 1793–1807, 1815–1919, 1939–1945 German *Schildberg*

Ostyako-Vogul'sk *see* **Khanty-Mansiysk**

Osuna (city, southwestern Spain) : Roman *Orsona*; earlier Roman *Urso*

Oświęcim (town, southeastern Poland) : 1940–1945 German *Auschwitz* (The German name continues in use, even among Poles, to refer to the World War II concentration camp here, formally *Auschwitz-Birkenau*, Polish *Oświęcim-Brzezinka*.)

Osypenko *see* **Berdyans'k**

Oszmiana *see* **Ashmyany**

Otaihape *see* **Taihape**

Otani *see* **Sokol**

Otdykh *see* **Zhukovsky**

Otegen Batyr (town, southeastern Kazakhstan) : formerly Russian *Energetichesky*

Otepää (town, southeastern Estonia) : to 1917 German *Odenpäh*

Otero *see* **La Junta**

Otmuchów (town, southern Poland) : to 1945 German *Ottmachau*

Otočac (town, western Croatia) : to 1867 German *Ottochacz*

Otomari *see* **Korsakov**

Otpor *see* **Zabaykal'sk**

Otradnoye (village, western Russia) : to 1945 German *Georgenswalde* (This Otradnoye, near Kaliningrad, should not be confused with the larger Otradnoye near St. Petersburg.)

Otradnoye *see* **Otradny**

Otradny (city, western Russia) : to 1956 *Otradnoye*

Otranto (town, southeastern Italy) : Roman *Hydruntum*

Otricoli (village, central Italy) : Roman *Ocriculum*

Otrogovo *see* **Stepnoye**

Otrokovice (town, southeastern Czech Republic) : to 1918, 1939–1945 German *Otrokowitz*

Otrokowitz *see* **Otrokovice**

¹Ottawa (city, Ontario, southeastern Canada) : to 1854 *Bytown*

²Ottawa (town, Illinois, north central United States) : originally *Carbonia*

Ottlukköy *see* **Panagyurishte**

Ottmachau *see* **Otmuchów**

Ottochacz *see* **Otočac**

Ottumwa (town, Iowa, north central United States) : to 1845 *Louisville*

Otvazhnoye *see* **Zhigulyovsk**

Otvazhny *see* **Zhigulyovsk**

Oudenaarde (town, western Belgium) : French *Audenarde*

Oudergem *see* **Auderghem**

Oudh *see* **Ayodhya**

Oued el Abtal (town, northwestern Algeria) : to c.1962 French *Uzès-le-Duc*

Oued Rhio (town, northern Algeria) : to *c.*1962 French *Inkermann*

Ouessant (island, northwestern France) : traditional English *Ushant*; Roman *Uxantis*; alternate Roman *Uxisama* (The English form of the name is associated with the naval battle of 1794 between the British and French fleets. Both sides claimed victory, but the English subsequently dubbed the encounter the "Glorious First of June.")

Oughterard (town, western Ireland) : Irish *Uachtar Ard*

Ouidah (town, southern Benin) : conventional English *Whydah*

Ouled Mimoun (town, northwestern Algeria) : to *c.*1962 French *Lamoricière*

Ouled Moussa (town, northern Algeria) : to *c.*1962 French *St.-Pierre-St.-Paul*

Oulmès (village, northwestern Morocco) : formerly *Tarmilate*

Oulu (city, western Finland) : to 1809 Swedish *Uleåborg*

Oulx (village, northwestern Italy) : 1937–1960 *Ulzio*

Ourinhos (city, southeastern Brazil) : formerly *Jacarézinho*

Ouro Prêto (city, eastern Brazil) : originally *Vila Rica*

Outer Hebrides *see* **Western Isles**

Outer Mongolia *see* **Mongolia**

Over-the-River *see* **San Angelo**

Overton (village, northeastern Wales) : Welsh *Owrtyn*

Ovetum *see* **Oviedo**

Oviedo (city, northern Spain) : Roman *Ovetum*

Ovilava *see* **Wels**

Owando (town, central Congo) : to 1977 French *Fort-Rousset*

Owen Falls *see* **Nalubaale Falls**

Owensboro (city, Kentucky, east central United States) : to 1866 *Rossborough*

Owen Sound (town, Ontario, southeastern Canada) : to 1857 *Sydenham*

Owrtyn *see* **Overton**

Oxford (city, south central England) : Medieval Latin *Oxonia*

Oxford *see* **Woodstock**

Oxonia *see* **Oxford**

Oxus *see* **Amu Darya**

Oyrot *see* **Altay**

Oyrot-Tura *see* **Gorno-Altaysk**

Oysangur *see* **Oyskhara**

Oyskhara (town, southwestern Russia) : 1944–1989 *Novogroznensky*; to 1944 *Oysangur*

Oyster Island *see* **Ellis Island**

Oyster River *see* ²**Durham**

Özalp (village, southeastern Turkey) : formerly *Karakalli*

Ozamiz (city, southern Philippines) : to late 1940s *Misamis*

Oznachennoye *see* **Sayanogorsk**

Ozurget'i (town, southwestern Georgia) : 1934–1991 *Makharadze*

Ozyorki (village, western Russia) : to 1945 German *Gross-Lindenau*

Ozyorsk (town, western Russia) : 1938–1945 German *Angerapp*; to 1938 German *Darkehmen* (The name Angerapp, from the river here, was adopted because the Nazis felt the earlier name was "not German enough.")

Ozyorsky (town, eastern Russia) : 1905–1945 Japanese *Nagahama*

Paamiut (settlement, southern Greenland) : formerly Danish *Frederikshåb*

Pabianice (city, central Poland) : 1940–1945 German *Pabianitz*

Pabianitz *see* **Pabianice**

Pabradė (town, eastern Lithuania) : 1921–1939 Polish *Podbrodzie*; to 1921 Russian *Podberez'ye*

Pacaca *see* **Ciudad Colón**

Pacajus (city, northeastern Brazil) : to 1944 *Guarani*

Pacific City *see* **Huntington Beach**

Pacific Ocean (between Arctic and Antarctic) : formerly *South Sea* (The Pacific, so named by Magellan in 1520, was earlier named *South Sea* by Balboa on sighting it in 1513.)

Paczków (town, southwestern Poland) : to 1945 German *Patschkau*

Padali *see* **Amursk**

Paderno (village, northern Italy) : to 1950 *Paderno Ossolaro*

Paderno Ossolaro *see* **Paderno**

Padilla (town, south central Bolivia) : to 1900s *La Laguna*

Padova *see* **Padua**

Padre Las Casas (town, southwestern Dominican Republic) : to 1928 *Túbano*

Padre Miguelinho *see* ¹**Santo Antônio**

Padua (city, northeastern Italy) : [Italian *Padova*]; Roman *Patavium*

Padus *see* **Po**

Paestum *see* **Pesto**

Pag (town, western Croatia) : to 1918 Italian *Pago* (The town is on the island of the same name.)

Pagalu *see* **Annobón**

Pagėgiai (town, southwestern Lithuania) : to 1945 German *Pogegen* (The Lithuanian and German names were equally valid over the period 1923–1939.)

Pago *see* **Pag**

Pago Pago (town, southern American Samoa) : formerly *Pango-Pango*

Pahlavi Dezh *see* **Aq Qaleh**

Paide (town, central Estonia) : to 1918 German *Weissenstein*

Painesville (town, Ohio, north central United States) : to 1816 *Champion*

Painscastle (village, eastern Wales) : Welsh *Castell-paen*

Paisley (village, Ontario, southeastern Canada) : to 1856 *Mud River*

País Vasco *see* ¹**Basque Country**

Paituk *see* **Vose**

Pakhtaabad *see* **Paxtaobod**

Paklay *see* **Xaignabouli**

Paknam *see* **Samut Prakan**

Palaestina *see* **Palestine**

Palánka *see* **Bačka Palanka**

Palantia *see* **Palencia**

Palárikovo (town, southern Slovakia) : 1945–1948 *Slovenský Meder*; to 1918, 1938–1945 Hungarian *Tótmegyer*

Palashi (village, eastern India) : English *Plassey* (The English name became familiar from the decisive victory of British forces over the nawab of Bengal here in 1757, so preparing the way for British dominion over eastern India.)

Palawan (island, southwestern Philippines) : formerly *Paragua*

Paldiski (city, northwestern Estonia) : formerly English *Baltic Port*; 1917–1939 German *Baltisch-Port*; 1783–1917 Russian *Baltiysky port*; 1723–1783 *Rogervik*

Palencia (city, north central Spain) : Roman *Palantia*

Palermo (city, southern Italy) : Roman *Panormus*

Palestina *see* **Jordânia**

Palestine (territory, southwestern Asia) : [Arabic *Filaṣṭīn*]; Roman *Palaestina*; biblical *Canaan*; alternate biblical *Zion* (The present name was introduced by the Roman emperor Hadrian in the 2d century A.D. as *Syria Palaestina*, from *Philistia*, a small area on the Mediterranean coast north of Gaza occupied by the Philistines in the 12th century B.C. The Jewish name of Palestine is *Eretz Yisra'el*, "land of **Israel**." *See also* **Jerusalem**.)

Palestrina (town, central Italy) : Roman *Praeneste*

Palestro *see* **Lakhdaria**

Palikao *see* **Tighenif**

Palissy *see* **Sidi Khaled**

Palma *see* (1) **Coreaú**; (2) **Paranã**

Palm Beach (town, Florida, southeastern United States) : to 1887 *Palm City*

Palm City *see* **Palm Beach**

Palmeira *see* **Palmeira das Missões**

Palmeira das Missões (city, southern Brazil) : to 1944 *Palmeira*

Palmeirais (town, northeastern Brazil) : to 1944 Portuguese *Belém*

Palmeiras *see* (1) **Palmeiras de Goiás**; (2) **Santa Cruz das Palmeiras**

Palmeiras de Goiás (town, central Brazil) : 1944–1948 *Mataúna*; to 1944 *Palmeiras*

Palmer Land *see* **Antarctic Peninsula**

Palmer Peninsula *see* **Antarctic Peninsula**

Palmerston *see* (1) **Darwin**; (2) **Palmerston North**

Palmerston North (city, north central New Zealand) : to 1873 *Palmerston* (The addition to the name obviated confusion with the existing town of *Palmerston* to the south. A change of name to *Manawatu* was proposed but this also existed as a river and district name.)

Palmnicken *see* **Yantarny**

Palm Springs (city, California, southwestern United States) : to *c*.1890 *Agua Caliente*

Palmyra *see* (1) **Santos Dumont**; (2) **Tadmur**

Palomar, Mt. (California, southwestern United States) : to 1901 *Smith Mountain*

Pamirsky Post *see* **Murgap**

Pampeluna *see* **Pamplona**

Pamplona (city, northern Spain) : Basque *Iruña*; formerly *Pampeluna*; Roman *Pompaelo*

Pamukkale (village, southwestern Turkey) : ancient Greek *Hierapolis*

Pamyati 13 Bortsov (village, southern Russia) : formerly *Znamensky*

Panagyurishte (town, west central Bulgaria) : to 1878 Turkish *Ottlukköy*

Panaji (city, western India) : to 1961 Portuguese *Nova Goa* (The former name, "New Goa," describes the city's status as capital of Portuguese India after the decline of Old Goa.)

Pančevo (city, north central Serbia) : to 1918 Hungarian *Pancsova*

Pancsova *see* **Pančevo**

Pandaklii *see* **Tenevo**

Pando (department, northwestern Bolivia) : to 1938 Spanish *Colonias*

Pándorf *see* **Parndorf**

Paneas *see* **Banias**

Panevezhis *see* **Panevėžys**

Panevėžys (city, north central Lithuania) : (Russian *Panevezhis*); to 1918 Russian *Ponevezh*

Panfilov *see* **Zharkent**

Pango-Pango *see* **Pago Pago**

Panj (town, southwestern Tajikistan) : (Russian *Pyandzh*); 1936–1963 Russian *Kirovabad*; 1931–1936 Russian *Baumanabad*; to 1931 *Saray-Komar*

Pannonhalma (village, northwestern Hungary) :
to 1965 *Győrszentmárton*
Panopolis *see* **Akhmīm**
Panormus *see* **Palermo**
Panticapaeum *see* **Kerch**
Papari *see* **Nísia Floresta**
Papcastle (village, northwestern England) :
Roman *Derventio* (The Roman name derived
from the **Derwent** River here.)
Papua (province, eastern Indonesia) : formerly
Irian Jaya; 1963–1969 *Irian Barat*; to 1963
Dutch New Guinea (Papua occupies the west-
ern part of the island of New Guinea. The
eastern part is occupied by the independent
state of Papua New Guinea. In 2003 the west-
ern part of Papua was demarcated as the prov-
ince of **West Papua**.)
Papua Barat *see* **West Papua**
Pará *see* **Belém**
Paradise Island (north central Bahamas) : for-
merly *Hog Island*
Paraetonium *see* **Marsa Matruh**
Paragua *see* **Palawan**
Paraguaçu *see* **Paraguaçu Paulista**
Paraguaçu Paulista (city, southeastern Brazil) :
1944–1948 *Araguaçu*; to 1944 *Paraguaçu*
Paraíba *see* **João Pessoa**
Paraibuna *see* **Juiz de Fora**
Paraná (city, northeastern Argentina) : originally
Bajada de Santa Fe
Paranã (town, southern Brazil) : to 1944 Portu-
guese *Palma*
Paranaíba (city, western Brazil) : to 1939 Portu-
guese *Santana do Paranaíba*
Parati *see* **Araquari**
Paratinga (city, eastern Brazil) : to 1944 Portu-
guese *Rio Branco*
Paravadı *see* **Provadiya**
Parchwitz *see* **Prochowice**
Parco *see* **Sinclair**
Pardubice (town, north central Czech Republic)
: to 1918, 1939–1945 German *Pardubitz*
Pardubitz *see* **Pardubice**
Paredón *see* **Anzaldo**
Parion *see* **Kemer**
¹**Paris** (city, northern France) : Roman *Parisii*;
earlier Roman *Lutetia*
²**Paris** (town, Kentucky, east central United
States) : to 1790 *Bourbontown*; originally *Hope-
well*
Parisii *see* ¹**Paris**
Parium *see* **Kemer**
Parizhskaya Kommuna *see* **Pereval's'k**
Párkány *see* **Štúrovo**
Park City (village, Kentucky, east central United
States) : to 1938 *Glasgow Junction*

Parkersburg (city, West Virginia, east central
United States) : originally *Neal's Station*
Park Ridge (city, Illinois, north central United
States) : to 1873 *Brickton*; originally *Pennyville*
Parma (city, Ohio, east central United States) :
to 1826 *Greenbriar* (The city is now a suburb
of Cleveland.)
Parmentier *see* **Sidi Ali Boussidi**
Parnamirim (town, northeastern Brazil) : to
1944 Portuguese *Leopoldina*
Parnarama (city, northeastern Brazil) : 1944–
1948 Portuguese *Matões*; to 1944 Portuguese
São José dos Matões
Parnassus *see* **Liakoura**
Parndorf (village, eastern Austria) : to 1918 Hun-
garian *Pándorf*
Pärnu (city, southwestern Estonia) : (Russian
Pyarnu); to 1918 Russian *Pernov*
Parral *see* **Hidalgo del Parral**
Parramatta (city, New South Wales, southeast-
ern Australia) : to 1791 *Rose Hill* (The city is
now a suburb of Sydney.)
Parreiras *see* **Caldas**
Pars *see* **Fārs**
Parsonstown *see* **Birr**
Partenit *see* **Frunzens'ke**
Partizansk (city, eastern Russia) : 1932–1972
Suchan; to 1932 *Suchansky Rudnik*
Partizánske (town, western Slovakia) : 1948–
1949 *Bat'ovany*; to 1948 *Šimonovany*
Partizanskoye (village, southern Russia) : to
1930s *Perovo*
Paryz'ka Komuna *see* **Pereval's'k**
Pasadena (city, California, southwestern United
States) : to 1875 *Indiana Colony*
Pasarofça *see* **Požarevac**
Pas de Calais *see* **Dover, Strait of**
Pasha Makhala *see* **Krumovo**
Pashiya (town, western Russia) : to 1929
Arkhangelo-Pashiysky Zavod
Pashmakli *see* **Smolyan**
Pašićevo *see* **Zmajevo**
Pasłęk (town, northeastern Poland) : to 1945
German *Preussisch-Holland*
Paso de la Fabrica *see* **Minatitlán**
Passaic (city, New Jersey, northeastern United
States) : to 1854 *Acquackanonk*
Passarowitz *see* **Požarevac**
Passau (city, southeastern Germany) : Roman
Castra Batava; Celtic *Bojodurum*
Passenheim *see* **Pasym**
Passo di Resia (village, northern Italy) : to 1918
German *Reschen-Scheideck* (The name is prop-
erly that of an Alpine pass on the border with
Austria.)
Pastor Montero *see* **Girardot**

Pasym (town, northeastern Poland) : to 1945 German *Passenheim*

Pataliputra *see* **Patna**

Patavium *see* **Padua**

Patersonia *see* **Launceston**

Patna (city, northeastern India) : to 1541 *Pataliputra*

Patos *see* **Patos de Minas**

Patos de Minas (city, southeastern Brazil) : to 1944 *Patos*

Patrae *see* **Patras**

Patras (city, central Greece) : ancient Greek and Roman *Patrae*

Patriarsheye *see* ²**Donskoye**

Patrimônio dos Inocentes *see* **Piratininga**

Patrocínio *see* **Pio IX**

Patschkau *see* **Paczków**

Patton Township *see* **Monroeville**

Pau d'Alho *see* **Ibirarema**

Pau Gigante *see* **Ibiraçu**

Paulis *see* **Isiro**

Paulista *see* **Paulistana**

Paulistana (city, northeastern Brazil) : to 1944 *Paulista*

Paulo Affonso *see* **Mata Grande**

Paulus Hook *see* **Jersey City**

Pavia (town, northern Italy) : Roman *Ticinum*

Pavlodar (city, northeastern Kazakhstan) : to 1861 Russian *Koryakovsky Forpost* (Unlike many towns in Kazakhstan, Pavlodar has retained its Russian name.)

Pavlograd *see* **Pavlohrad**

Pavlohrad (city, southeastern Ukraine) : (Russian *Pavlograd*)

Pavlovsk (town, northwestern Russia) : 1918–1944 *Slutsk*; to 1796 *Pavlovskoye*

Pavlovskoye *see* **Pavlovsk**

Pawellau *see* **Pawłów**

Pawłów (village, eastern Poland) : 1793–1919, 1939–1945 German *Pawellau*

Payne *see* **Kangirsuk**

Payo Obispo *see* **Chetumal**

Pays Basque *see* ²**Basque Country**

Payshanba (town, east central Uzbekistan) : to 1960 *Kara-Darya*

Pax Augusta *see* **Badajoz**

Pax Julia *see* **Beja**

Paxtaobod (town, central Uzbekistan) : (Russian *Pakhtaabad*); to 1975 *Kokankishlak*

Pazardzhik (town, west central Bulgaria) : 1878–1934 *Tatar-Pazardzhik*; to 1878 Turkish *Tatarpazarcik*

Pazin (town, western Croatia) : 1919–1945 Italian *Pisino*; to 1918 German *Mitterburg* (The Italian name was also in official use under Austrian rule.)

Peabody (city, Massachusetts, northeastern United States) : to 1868 *South Danvers*

Peć (city, western Kosovo) : 1941–1944 Albanian *Peja*; to 1913 Turkish *İpek*

Peacehaven (town, southeastern England) : to 1917 *New Anzac-on-Sea*

Pecan Grove *see* **Groves**

Pechenga (town, northwestern Russia) : 1920–1944 Finnish *Petsamo*

Pechory (town, western Russia) : 1919–1940 Estonian *Petseri*

Pécs (city, southwestern Hungary) : to 1867 German *Fünfkirchen*

Pedra Azul (town, southeastern Brazil) : to 1944 *Fortaleza*

Pedras Brancas *see* **Guaíba**

Pedro Avelino (town, northeastern Brazil) : to 1948 *Epitácio Pessoa*

Peiping *see* **Beijing**

Peipus, Lake (eastern Estonia/northwestern Russia) : Russian *Chudskoye* (The Russian name is adjectival and in that language followed by *ozero*, "lake.")

Peiskretscham *see* **Pyskowice**

Peja *see* **Peć**

Pejepscot *see* **Brunswick**

Pekin *see* **Dearborn**

Peking *see* **Beijing**

Peklevskaya *see* **Troitsky**

Pełczyce (town, western Poland) : to 1945 German *Bernstein*

Pelhřimov (town, south central Czech Republic) : to 1918, 1939–1945 German *Pilgrams*

Pelican Waterholes *see* **Winton**

Pelly Bay *see* **Kugaaruk**

Peloponnese (peninsula, southern Greece) : medieval *Morea*

Pelotas (city, southern Brazil) : to 1830 *São Francisco de Paula*

Pelovo (town, northern Bulgaria) : to 1950 *Makhlata*

Pelsőc *see* **Plešivec**

Pelusium *see* **Tell el-Farama**

Pemba (town, northeastern Mozambique) : to 1976 Portuguese *Porto Amélia*

Pembroke (town, southwestern Wales) : Welsh *Penfro*

Pembroke Dock (town, southwestern Wales) : Welsh *Doc Penfro*

Penacook Plantation *see* ³**Concord**

Penally (village, southwestern Wales) : Welsh *Penalun*

Penalun *see* **Penally**

Penang (island, western Malaysia) : formerly *Prince of Wales Island*

Penang *see* **George Town**

Pen-ar-Bed *see* Finistère

Penarlâg *see* Hawarden

Pendine (village, southwestern Wales) : Welsh *Pentywyn*

Penetangore *see* Kincardine

Penfro *see* Pembroke

Pengelli *see* Grovesend

Penley (village, northeastern Wales) : Welsh *Llannerch Banna*

Penmaen Dewi *see* St. David's Head

Pennocrucium *see* Water Eaton

Pennyville *see* Park Ridge

Penrith (city, New South Wales, southeastern Australia) : formerly *Castlereagh*; originally *Evan* (The city is now an outer suburb of Sydney.)

Pensky Sakharny Zavod *see* Karla Libknekhta, imeni

Penthièvre *see* Aïn Berda

Pentre-poeth *see* Morganstown

Pentywyn *see* Pendine

Pen-y-Bont ar Ogwr *see* Bridgend

Penzig *see* Pieńsk

Peoria (city, Illinois, north central United States) : 1814–1825 *Fort Clark*

Peparethos *see* Skópelos

Pepperellboro *see* Saco

Pequoiag *see* Athol

Pequot *see* New London

Peravia (province, southern Dominican Republic) : to 1961 Spanish *Trujillo Valdéz*

Perdido, Monte (northeastern Spain) : French *Mont Perdu* (The peak is on the border with France.)

Perdigão (town, southeastern Brazil) : to 1944 Portuguese *Saúde*

Perdizes *see* Videira

Perdu, Mont *see* Perdido, Monte

Peredniye Traki *see* Krasnoarmeyskoye

Peremyshl' *see* Przemyśl

Peremyshlyany (town, western Ukraine) : to 1939 Polish *Przemyślany*

Pereval'sk *see* Pereval's'k

Pereval's'k (city, eastern Ukraine) : (Russian *Pereval'sk*); 1926–1964 *Paryz'ka Komuna* (Russian *Parizhskaya Kommuna*); to 1926 *Seleznivs'kyy Rudnyk* (Russian *Seleznevsky Rudnik*) (The city is now part of Alchevs'k.)

Perevoz (town, western Russia) : to 1962 *P'yansky Perevoz*

Pereyaslav *see* Pereyaslav-Khmel'nyts'kyy

Pereyaslav-Khmel'nitsky *see* Pereyaslav-Khmel'nyts'kyy

Pereyaslav-Khmel'nyts'kyy (city, central Ukraine) : (Russian *Pereyaslav-Khmel'nitsky*); to 1953 *Pereyaslav*

Pereyaslavl', Lake *see* Pleshcheyevo, Lake

Pereyaslavl'-Ryazansky *see* Ryazan'

Pergamon *see* Bergama

Pergamum *see* Bergama

Périgotville *see* Aïn el Kebira

Périgueux (city, southwestern France) : Roman *Vesuna*

Peri Mirim (town, northeastern Brazil) : to 1944 *Macapá*

Perlepe *see* Prilep

Perm' (city, central Russia) : 1940–1957 *Molotov*

Përmeti (town, southern Albania) : 1919–1921 modern Greek *Premetì*

Pernambuco *see* Recife

Pernik (city, west central Bulgaria) : 1949–1963 *Dimitrovo*

Pernov *see* Pärnu

Perovo *see* Partizanskoye

Perovsk *see* Kyzylorda

Perrégaux *see* Mohammadia

Perry's Corners *see* Whitby

Perserin *see* Prizren

Pershotravensk *see* [1,2]Pershotravens'k

[1]Pershotravens'k (city, eastern Ukraine) : (Russian *Pershotravensk*); 1960–1966 *Pershotravneve* (Russian *Pershotravnevoye*), to 1960 *Shakhtars'ke* (Russian *Shakhtyorskoye*) (The Russian name does not translate the Ukrainian as *Oktyabr'sk* but merely transliterates it.)

[2]Pershotravens'k (town, west central Ukraine) : (Russian *Pershotravensk*); to 1934 *Tokarivka* (Russian *Tokaryovka*)

Pershotravnene (town, eastern Ukraine) : (Russian *Pershotravnevoye*); to 1946 *Manhush* (Russian *Mangush*)

Pershotravneve *see* (1) Mokvyn; (2) [1]Pershotravens'k

Pershotravnevoye *see* (1) Mokvyn; (2) [1]Pershotravens'k; (3) Pershotravnene

Persia *see* Iran

Persian Gulf (southwestern Asia) : alternate *Arabian Gulf* or *The Gulf*; Roman *Sinus Persicus* (The arm of the Arabian Sea, between Iran and Arabia, is named simply *The Gulf* by many Western writers to avoid offending Iraqis and some other Arabs.)

Persis *see* Fars

Perth Amboy (city, New Jersey, northeastern United States) : originally *Amboy*

Peru (town, Indiana, north central United States) : to 1834 *Miamisport*

Perugia (city, central Italy) : Roman *Perusia*

Perusia *see* Perugia

Pervomay (village, northern Kyrgyzstan) : formerly Russian *Pervomaysky*

Pervomaysk (town, western Russia) : to 1941 *Tashino*

Pervomaysk *see* [1,2]**Pervomays'k**

[1]**Pervomays'k** (town, eastern Ukraine) : (Russian *Pervomaysk*); to 1920 *Petromar'yivka* (Russian *Petromar'yevka*)

[2]**Pervomays'k** (town, south central Ukraine) : (Russian *Pervomaysk*); to 1920 *Ol'viopil'* (Russian *Ol'viopol'*) (The town arose on the merger of Ol'viopil' with two other villages.)

Pervomays'ke (town, southern Ukraine, near Dzhankoy) : (Russian *Pervomayskoye*); to 1944 *Dzurchi*

[1]**Pervomayskoye** (village, southwestern Russia, near Yershov) : to 1941 *Gnadenflyur* (The village lies in the former Volga German Autonomous Soviet Socialist Republic and its earlier name is a Russian transliteration of German *Gnadenflur*.)

[2]**Pervomayskoye** (village, southern Russia, near Tomsk) : formerly *Pyshkino-Troitskoye*

[3]**Pervomayskoye** (village, southern Russia, near Barnaul) : formerly *Srednekrayushkino*

[4]**Pervomayskoye** (village, western Russia, near Kanash) : to 1939 *Bol'shiye Arabuzy*

Pervomayskoye *see* **Pervomays'ke**

[1]**Pervomaysky** (town, western Russia, near Michurinsk) : formerly *Bogoyavlenskoye*

[2]**Pervomaysky** (village, western Russia) : to 1943 *Kukshik* (The village is now part of the city of Sterlitamak.)

[3]**Pervomaysky** (town, western Russia) : to 1938 *Spas* (The town is a suburb of Slobodskoy.)

Pervomaysky *see* (1) **Novodvinsk**; (2) **Pervomay**; (3) **Pervomays'kyy**

Pervomays'kyy (town, east central Ukraine) : (Russian *Pervomaysky*); formerly *Lykhachive* (Russian *Likhachyovo*)

Pervoural'sk (city, western Russia) : 1928–1933 *Pervoural'sky*; 1920–1928 *Shaytansky Zavod*; to 1920 *Vasil'yevsko-Shaytansky*

Pesaro (city, central Italy) : Roman *Pisaurum*

Pesayak Towne *see* **Newark**

Pescado *see* **Villa Serrano**

Pescara (city, eastern Italy) : Roman *Aternum*

Peschanoye *see* **Yashkul'**

Pesochnya *see* **Kirov**

Pessinus *see* **Balıhisar**

Pesterzsébet (town, north central Hungary) : 1919–1924 *Lenínváros*; to 1919 *Erzsébetfalva* (The town is now a suburb of Budapest.)

Pesto (village, southern Italy) : Roman *Paestum*; ancient Greek *Poseidonia*

Pestovo *see* **Zavolzh'ye**

Petelia *see* **Strongoli**

[1]**Peterborough** (city, Ontario, southeastern Canada) : to 1825 *Scott's Plains*

[2]**Peterborough** (town, South Australia, southern Australia) : to 1917 *Petersburg*

Petergof *see* **Petrodvorets**

Peterhof *see* **Petrodvorets**

Petersburg *see* [2]**Peterborough**

Petersdorf *see* **Piechowice**

Peterstone Wentlooge (village, southeastern Wales) : Welsh *Llanbedr Gwynllŵg*

Peterston-super-Ely (village, southern Wales) : Welsh *Llanbedr-y-fro*

Pétervárad *see* **Petrovaradin**

Peterwardein *see* **Petrovaradin**

Petitjean *see* **Sidi Kacem**

Petit-Sault *see* **Edmundston**

Petra Stuchki, imeni *see* **Aizkraukle**

Petre *see* **Wanganui**

Petrikau *see* **Piotrków Trybunalski**

Petroaleksandrovsk *see* **To'rtko'l**

Petrodvorets (town, western Russia) : to 1944 *Petergof*; former alternate German *Peterhof* (The town is administratively part of St. Petersburg.)

Petrograd *see* **St. Petersburg**

Petrokov *see* **Piotrków Trybunalski**

Petrokrepost' *see* **Shlissel'burg**

Petrolândia (city, northeastern Brazil) : 1939–1943 *Itaparica*; to 1939 *Jatobá*

Petromar'yevka *see* [1]**Pervomays'k**

Petromar'yivka *see* [1]**Pervomays'k**

Petropavlovsk *see* **Petropavlovsk-Kamchatsky**

Petropavlovsk-Kamchatsky (city, eastern Russia) : to 1924 *Petropavlovsk*

Petropavlovsky *see* **Severoural'sk**

Petroşani (city, west central Romania) : to 1918 Hungarian *Petrozsény*

Petroskoi *see* **Petrozavodsk**

Petrovaradin (town, northern Serbia) : to 1918, 1941–1944 Hungarian *Pétervárad*; to 1867 German *Peterwardein* (The town is now a suburb of Novi Sad.)

Petrove-Krasnosillya *see* **Petrovs'ke**

Petroverovka *see* [2]**Zhovten'**

Petrovgrad *see* **Zrenjanin**

Petrovice u Karviné (town, eastern Czech Republic) : 1939–1945 German *Petrowitz*; 1918–1919, 1938–1939 Polish *Piotrowice*; to 1918 German *Petrowitz bei Arnoldsdorf*

Petrovo-Krasnosel'ye *see* **Petrovs'ke**

Petrovskaya Sloboda *see* **Losino-Petrovsky**

Petrovs'ke (town, eastern Ukraine) : (Russian *Petrovskoye*); 1920–1963 *Petrove-Krasnosillya* (Russian *Petrovo-Krasnosel'ye*); to 1920 *Shterivs'ke* (Russian *Shterovskoye*)

Petrovskoye *see* (1) **Makhachkala;**
(2) **Petrovs'ke;** (3) **Svetlograd**
Petrovsk-Port *see* **Makhachkala**
Petrovsky Zavod *see* **Petrovsk-Zabaykalsky**
Petrovsk-Zabaykalsky (town, southern Russia) :
to 1926 *Petrovsky Zavod*
Petrovyrivka *see* ²**Zhovten'**
Petrowitz bei Arnoldsdorf *see* **Petrovice u
Karviné**
Petrozavodsk (city, northwestern Russia) : for-
merly local *Petroskoi* (The local name came
from *Petrovskoilinna*, from Russian *Petrovsky*,
"of Peter," and Karelian *linna*, "town.")
Petrozsény *see* **Petroşani**
Petrźalka (town, southwestern Slovakia) : 1938–
1945 German *Engerau*; to 1918 Hungarian
Pozsonyligetfalu; to 1867 German *Engerau*
(The town is now a district of Bratislava.)
Petsamo *see* **Pechenga**
Petseri *see* **Pechory**
Pettau *see* **Ptuj**
Petuaria *see* ³**Brough**
Petukhovo (town, southern Russia) : to 1944
Yudino
Petushki (town, western Russia) : to 1965 *Novyye
Petushki*
Pevensey (village, southeastern England) :
Roman *Anderitum*
Pezinok (town, western Slovakia) : to 1918 Hun-
garian *Bazin*; to 1867 German *Bösing*
Pharnacia *see* **Giresun**
Pharos *see* **Hvar**
Phasis *see* (1) **Poti;** (2) **Rioni**
Phazania *see* **Fezzan**
Phenix City (city, Alabama, southeastern United
States) : to 1889 *Brownville*
Philadelphia *see* (1) **Alaşehir;** (2) **Amman**
Philippeville *see* **Skikda**
Philippopolis *see* **Plovdiv**
Philipstown *see* **Daingean**
Phillips Landing *see* **Van Buren**
Philomelion *see* **Akşehir**
Phintias *see* **Licata**
Phocaea *see* **Foça**
Phuthaditjhaba (town, east central South
Africa) : originally *Witsieshoek*
Piacenza (city, northern Italy) : Roman *Placen-
tia*
Piatã (town, eastern Brazil) : to 1944 *Anchieta*
Pibrans *see* **Příbram**
Picardie *see* **Picardy**
Picardy (region, northern France) : [French
Picardie]
Pico (Spanish, "peak") : for names beginning
thus, *see* the next word, as **Duarte, Pico**
Picos *see* **Colinas**

¹**Picton** (town, Ontario, southeastern Canada) :
originally *Hallowell*
²**Picton** (town, central New Zealand) : to 1859
Newton
Pidhaytsi (town, western Ukraine) : (Russian
Podgaytsy); to 1939 Polish *Podhajce*
Pidvolochys'k (town, western Ukraine) : (Rus-
sian *Podvolochisk*); to 1929 Polish *Podwołoczyska*
Piechowice (town, southwestern Poland) : to
1945 German *Petersdorf*
Piedmont (region, northwestern Italy) : [Italian
Piemonte]
Piedras Negras (city, northeastern Mexico) :
1888–1911 *Ciudad Porfirio Díaz*
Piemonte *see* **Piedmont**
Pieńsk (village, western Poland) : to 1945 Ger-
man *Penzig*
Pierre (town, South Dakota, north central
United States) : originally *Mahto* (The original
name was current from June to December
1880.)
Pierre E. Trudeau, Mt. *see* **Logan, Mt.**
Piešt'any (city, western Slovakia) : to 1918 Hun-
garian *Pöstyén*; to 1867 German *Pistyan*
Pietarsaari (town, western Finland) : formerly
Swedish *Jakobstad* (The town was at one time
mainly Swedish-speaking.)
Pietas Julia *see* **Pula**
Pietersburg *see* **Polokwane**
Pignataro Interamna (village, central Italy) :
Roman *Interamna Lirenas*
Pig's Eye Landing *see* **St. Paul**
Pik 20 let VLKSM *see* **Pobeda Peak**
Pike Creek *see* **Kenosha**
Piła (city, west central Poland) : 1772–1945 Ger-
man *Schneidemühl*
¹**Pilar** (city, northeastern Brazil) : 1944–1948
Manguaba
²**Pilar** (town, southwestern Paraguay) : originally
Ñeembucú
Pilar *see* **Pilar do Sul**
Pilar do Sul (city, southeastern Brazil) : to 1944
Pilar
Pilawa (town, southwestern Poland) : to 1945
German *Bielau*
Pilenkovo *see* **Gant'iadi**
Pile O'Bones *see* **Regina**
Pilevne *see* **Pleven**
Pilgrams *see* **Pelhřimov**
Pillau *see* **Baltiysk**
Pillkallen *see* **Dobrovol'sk**
Pillupönen *see* **Nevskoye**
Pilsen *see* (1) **Pilzno;** (2) **Plzeň**
Pilten *see* **Piltene**
Piltene (town, northwestern Latvia) : to 1917
German *Pilten*

Pilzno (town, southeastern Poland) : 1939–1945 German *Pilsen*

Pinang *see* **George Town**

Pinar del Río (city, western Cuba) : formerly *Nueva Filipina*

Pinciacum *see* **Poissy**

Pine Bluff (city, Arkansas, south central United States) : to 1832 *Mount Marie*

Pines, Isle of *see* **Juventud, Isla de la**

Pine Tree Hill *see* ³**Camden**

Pinkiang *see* **Harbin**

Pinola *see* **Las Rosas**

Pinsk (city, southern Belarus) : 1919–1939 Polish *Pińsk*

Pińsk *see* **Pinsk**

Pinta, Isla (island, northern Galápagos Islands, Ecuador) : formerly *Abingdon Island*

Pioner (town, southern Russia) : to 1936 *Ishanovo* (The town is now incorporated into the city of Kemerovo.)

Pionersky (town, western Russia) : to 1945 German *Neukuhren*

Pio IX (town, eastern Brazil) : to 1944 *Patrocínio*

Piotrków Trybunalski (city, central Poland) : 1940–1945 German *Petrikau*; to 1915 Russian *Petrokov*

Piotrowice *see* **Petrovice u Karviné**

Piperno *see* **Priverno**

Piqua (city, Ohio, north central United States) : to 1816 *Washington*

Piracanjuba (town, central Brazil) : to 1944 Portuguese *Pouso Alto*

Piracicaba (city, southeastern Brazil) : formerly *Vila Nova da Constituição*; originally *Santo Antônio de Piracicaba*

Piraí *see* **Piraí do Sul**

Piraí do Sul (town, southern Brazil) : 1944–1948 *Piraí Mirim*; to 1944 *Piraí*

Piraí Mirim *see* **Piraí do Sul**

Pirajaí *see* **Cabrália Paulista**

Piran (town, southwestern Slovenia) : 1918–1947 Italian *Pirano*

Piranhas (town, northeastern Brazil) : 1939–1948 Portuguese *Marechal Floriano*

Pirano *see* **Piran**

Pirapora *see* **Pirapora do Bom Jesus**

Piraporo do Bom Jesus (town, southeastern Brazil) : to 1944 *Pirapora*

Piraquara (city, southern Brazil) : to *c.*1935 Portuguese *Deodoro*

Piratininga (town, southeastern Brazil) : formerly *Patrimônio dos Inocentes*

Pirchevan *see* **Zängilan**

Piriápolis (town, southern Uruguay) : formerly Spanish *Puerto del Inglés*

Pirineos *see* **Pyrenees**

Pirogovsky (town, western Russia) : to 1928 *Proletarskaya Pobeda*

Pirot (city, southeastern Serbia) : to 1878 Turkish *Şarköy*

Pisa (city, northwestern Italy) : Roman *Pisae*

Pisae *see* **Pisa**

Pisaurum *see* **Pesaro**

Piscataqua *see* ²**Portsmouth**

Piscataqua Plantation *see* **Kittery**

Pisek *see* **Písek**

Písek (city, southwestern Czech Republic) : to 1918, 1939–1945 German *Pisek*

Pishpek *see* **Bishkek**

Pisino *see* **Pazin**

Pisiquid *see* ²**Windsor**

Pistoia (city, north central Italy) : Roman *Pistoria*

Pistoria *see* **Pistoia**

Pistyan *see* **Piešťany**

Pisz (town, northeastern Poland) : to 1945 German *Johannisburg*

Pithecusae *see* **Ischia**

Pithion (village, northeastern Greece) : 1915–1919 Bulgarian *Kuleli-Burgas*; to 1915 Turkish *Küleliburgaz*

Pitschen *see* **Byczyna**

Pitt, Mt. *see* **McLoughlin, Mt.**

Pittsburgh (city, Pennsylvania, northeastern United States) : 1758–1764 *Fort Pitt*; to 1758 *Fort Duquesne*

Pittsfield (city, Massachusetts, northeastern United States) : to 1761 *Pontoosuc Plantation*

Pivka (village, southwestern Slovenia) : to 1945 Italian *San Pietro del Carso*; to 1918 German *St. Peter am Karst*

Placentia *see* **Piacenza**

Placerville (town, California, western United States) : formerly *Hangtown*; originally *Dry Diggings*

Plage des Contrebandiers *see* **Sidi el Abed**

Plăineşti *see* **Generalissimul Suvorov**

Plan *see* **Planá**

Planá (town, western Czech Republic) : to 1918, 1938–1945 German *Plan*

Plano (city, Texas, southern United States) : to 1851 *Fillmore*

Plaridel (town, northern Philippines) : to 1936 *Quingua*

Plasencia (city, western Spain) : to 12th century *Ambroz*

Plassey *see* **Palashi**

Plata, Río de la (estuary, southeastern South America) : conventional English *River Plate* (The English name of the estuary of the Paraná and Uruguay rivers is associated in military history with the battle of 1939 between a

British cruiser squadron and the German pocket battleship *Graf Spee*, as reenacted in the 1956 movie *The Battle of the River Plate*.)

Plate, River *see* **Plata, Río de la**

Plathe *see* **Płoty**

Pļaviņas (town, south central Latvia) : to 1917 German *Stockmannshof*

Plavsk (town, western Russia) : to *c.*1928 *Sergiyevskoye*

Pleasant, Mt. *see* **Eisenhower, Mt.**

Pleasantburg *see* ²**Greenville**

Pleasant Island *see* **Nauru**

Pleschen *see* **Pleszew**

Pleshcheyevo, Lake (western Russia) : formerly *Lake Pereyaslavl'*

Plešivec (village, southern Slovakia) : to 1918, 1938–1945 Hungarian *Pelsőc*

Pless *see* **Pszczyna**

Pleszew (town, west central Poland) : 1793–1807, 1815–1919, 1939–1945 German *Pleschen*

Pleven (city, northern Bulgaria) : alternate *Plevna*; to 1878 Turkish *Pilevne* (The alternate name is associated with the Russian victory over the Turks in 1877 during the Russo-Turkish War.)

Plevna *see* **Pleven**

Plezzo *see* **Bovec**

Pljevlja (town, northern Montenegro) : to 1913 Turkish *Taşlika*

Ploče (town, southern Croatia) : 1949–1991 *Kardeljevo*

Płock (city, east central Poland) : 1939–1945 German *Schröttersburg*

Plöhnen *see* **Płońsk**

Plokhino *see* ¹**Ul'yanovo**

Płońsk (town, east central Poland) : 1940–1945 German *Plöhnen*

Ploskiriv *see* ¹**Khmel'nyts'kyy**

Ploskirov *see* ¹**Khmel'nyts'kyy**

Ploskoye *see* **Stanovoye**

Ploskyriv *see* ¹**Khmel'nyts'kyy**

Płoty (town, northwestern Poland) : to 1945 German *Plathe*

Plovdiv (city, southern Bulgaria) : to 1878 Turkish *Filibe*; Roman *Trimontium*; ancient Greek *Philippopolis* (The original Greek settlement had a mixed population of dubious repute, earning it the nickname *Poneropolis*, "Crookville," from *poneros*, "wicked.")

Plymouth (village, Vermont, northeastern United States) : to 1797 *Saltash*

Plymouth *see* **Monett**

Plymouth Dock *see* **Devonport**

Plynlimon (mountain, western Wales) : Welsh *Pumlumon*

Plzeň (city, western Czech Republic) : to 1918, 1939–1945 German *Pilsen*

Po (river, northern Italy) : Roman *Padus*; alternate Roman *Eridanus* (The Eridanus was originally a purely mythical river but was identified by later classical authors with the Po. The mythical Eridanus had islands at its mouth, but the Po has none.)

Poage's Settlement *see* **Ashland**

Pobeda Peak (eastern Kyrgyzstan) : to 1943 Russian *Pik 20 let VLKSM* (The mountain is on the border with China, where it is known as *Jengish Chokusu*. Its earlier Russian name was given in 1938 to mark the 20th anniversary of the Komsomol.)

Pobedinsky *see* **Zarechny**

Pocasset *see* ³**Portsmouth**

Podberez'ye *see* **Pabradė**

Podbořany (town, western Czech Republic) : to 1918, 1938–1945 German *Podersam*

Podbrodzie *see* **Pabradė**

Podchinny (town, southwestern Russia) : to 1941 *Kratske*

Poděbrady (town, north central Czech Republic) : to 1918, 1939–1945 German *Podiebrad*

Podersam *see* **Podbořany**

Podgaytsy *see* **Pidhaytsi**

Podgorica (city, south central Montenegro) : 1946–1992 *Titograd*

Podhajce *see* **Pidhaytsi**

Podiebrad *see* **Poděbrady**

Podillya *see* **Podolia**

Podium *see* **Le Puy**

Podlein *see* **Podolínec**

Podlesnoye (village, southwestern Russia) : to 1941 *Untervalden* (The earlier name of the village, in the former Volga German Autonomous Soviet Socialist Republic, is a Russian form of German *Unterwalden*.)

Podlipki *see* **Korolyov**

Podmokly (town, northern Czech Republic) : to 1918, 1939–1945 German *Bodenbach* (In 1950 the town was incorporated into the city of Děčín.)

Podolia (region, western Ukraine) : (Russian *Podol'ye*) [Ukrainian *Podillya*]

Podolin *see* **Podolínec**

Podolínec (town, northern Slovakia) : to 1918 Hungarian *Podolin*; to 1867 German *Podlein*

Podol'ye *see* **Podolia**

Podvolochisk *see* **Pidvolochys'k**

Podwołoczyska *see* **Pidvolochys'k**

Poetovio *see* **Ptuj**

Pofadder (town, western South Africa) : 1917–1936 *Theronsville*

Pogegen *see* **Pagėgiai**

Pogranichny (town, southeastern Russia) : to 1958 *Grodekovo*

Pohnpei (island, eastern Micronesia) : formerly *Ascension Island*

Poictiers *see* **Poitiers**

Point de Galle *see* **Galle**

Pointe-aux-Trembles *see* **Neuville**

Point Edward (village, Ontario, southeastern Canada) : to 1860 *Huron*

Poissy (town, northern France) : Roman *Pinciacum*

Poitiers (city, south central France) : formerly *Poictiers*; Roman *Limonum* (The earlier spelling was long associated with the 1356 English victory over the French during the Hundred Years' War.)

Pokrovka *see* (1) **Engel's**; (2) **Leninskoe**

Pokrovka Druha *see* **Pryazovs'ke**

Pokrovka Vtoraya *see* **Pryazovs'ke**

Pokrovsk *see* **Engels**

Pokrovs'ke (town, south central Ukraine) : (Russian *Pokrovskoye*); formerly *imeny Karla Libknekhta* (Russian *imeni Karla Libknekhta*); to *c.*1926 *Shmakivs'kyy Rudnyk* (Russian *Shmakovsky Rudnik*) (The town is now a suburb of Kryvyy Rih.)

Pokrovs'ke *see* **Pryazovs'ke**

Pokrovskoye *see* (1) **Pokrovs'ke**; (2) **Pryazovs'ke**; (3) **Velikooktyabr'sky**

Pola *see* **Pula**

Poland (republic, central Europe) : [Polish *Polska*]

Polanica Zdrój (town, southwestern Poland) : to 1945 German *Bad Altheide*

Polanów (town, northwestern Poland) : to 1945 German *Pollnow*

Polatovo *see* **Stamboliyski**

Polaun *see* **Polubný**

Połczyn Zdrój (town, northwestern Poland) : to 1945 German *Bad Polzin*

Polessk (town, western Russia) : to 1945 German *Labiau*

Polesskoye *see* **Polis'ke**

Polevskoy (city, west central Russia) : to 1928 *Polevskoy Zavod*

Polevskoy Zavod *see* **Polevskoy**

Policastro Bussentino (village, southern Italy) : formerly *Policastro del Golfo*; Roman *Buxentum*

Policastro del Golfo *see* **Policastro Bussentino**

Police (city district, northwestern Poland) : to 1945 German *Pölitz* (Police was incorporated into Szczecin in 1939.)

Polička (town, east central Czech Republic) : to 1918, 1939–1945 German *Politschka*

Policoro (town, southern Italy) : ancient Greek *Heraclea*

Poliny Osipenko, imeni (village, eastern Russia) : to 1939 *Kerbi* (The aviatrix Polina Osipenko also gave the former name of **Berdyans'k**.)

Polis'ke (town, northern Ukraine) : (Russian *Polesskoye*); 1940–1958 Russian *Kaganovichi Pervyye*; 1935–1940 *Kaganovich*; to 1935 *Khabne* (Russian *Khabnoye*)

Politschka *see* **Polička**

Pölitz *see* **Police**

Polkowice (town, northern Poland) : 1938–1945 German *Heerwegen*; to 1938 German *Polkwitz*

Polkwitz *see* **Polkowice**

Pollentia *see* **Pollenza**

Pollenza (town, central Italy) : Roman *Pollentia*

Pollnow *see* **Polanów**

Pologi *see* **Polohy**

Polohy (town, southeastern Ukraine) : (Russian *Pologi*); 1928–1937 *Chubarivka* (Russian *Chubarovka*)

Polokwane (town, northeastern South Africa) : to 2003 *Pietersburg*

Polovinka *see* (1) **Ugleural'sky**; (2) **Umal'tinsky**

Polska *see* **Poland**

Poltavka *see* **Bashtanka**

Poltavskaya (village, southwestern Russia) : formerly *Krasnoarmeyskaya*

Poltoratsk *see* **Aşgabat**

Põltsamaa (town, central Estonia) : to *c.*1920 German *Oberpahlen*

Polubný (village, northern Czech Republic) : to 1918, 1938–1945 German *Polaun*

Polyanovgrad *see* **Karnobat**

Polyarny (town, northwestern Russia) : to 1930 *Aleksandrovsk*

Pomabamba *see* **Azurduy**

Pomachi *see* **Komsomolabad**

Pomba *see* **Rio Pomba**

Pomerania (region, northeastern Germany/northwestern Poland) : [German *Pommern*; Polish *Pomorze*]

Pomfret *see* **Pontefract**

Pommern *see* **Pomerania**

Pomona *see* **Mainland**

Pomoriye (town, eastern Bulgaria) : to 1934 *Ankhialo*; Roman *Anchialus*

Pomorze *see* **Pomerania**

Pompaelo *see* **Pamplona**

Pompano *see* **Pompano Beach**

Pompano Beach (city, Florida, southeastern United States) : to 1945 *Pompano*

Pompei (town, southern Italy) : to 1928 *Valle de Pompei* (The town is near the ancient city of *Pompeii*, destroyed by the eruption of Vesuvius in A.D. 79. Italian does not differentiate between the two names.)

Pompeii *see* Pompei

Pompeiopolis (historic city, southern Turkey) : formerly *Soli*

Ponce (city, southern Puerto Rico) : originally *Nuestra Señora de Guadalupe de Ponce*

Pond Bay *see* Pond Inlet

Ponde Town *see* Mansfield

Pond Inlet (village, Nunavut, northeastern Canada) : alternate Inuit *Mittimatalik*; to 1951 *Pond Bay*

Ponevezh *see* Panevėžys

Ponferrada (city, northwestern Spain) : Roman *Interamnium Flavium*

Ponizovkino *see* Krasny Profintern

Pons Aelii *see* ¹Newcastle

Pons Isarae *see* Pontoise

Pons Vetus *see* Pontevedra

Pontafel *see* Pontebba

Pont-du-Chéliff *see* Sidi Bel Attar

Pont-du-Fahs *see* El Fahs

Pontebba (town, northeastern Italy) : to 1918 German *Pontafel*

Pontefract (town, northern England) : formerly *Pomfret* (The present name is actually nearer its origin in Latin *ponte fracto*, "[at] the broken bridge.")

Pontevedra (city, northwestern Spain) : Roman *Pons Vetus*

Ponthierville *see* Ubundu

Pontibus *see* Staines

Pontivy (town, northwestern France) : 1805–1814, 1848–1871 *Napoléonville* (The former name was properly that of a new town built here by Napoleon I as the military headquarters for Brittany. The second use of the name honored Napoleon III.)

Pontoise (town, northern France) : Roman *Pons Isarae;* earlier Roman *Briva Isarae*

Pontoosuc Plantation *see* Pittsfield

Pontsenni *see* Sennybridge

Pontus Euxinus *see* Black Sea

Pontypool (town, southeastern Wales) : Welsh *Pont-y-pŵl*

Pont-y-pŵl *see* Pontypool

Poona *see* Pune

Popasna (city, eastern Ukraine) : (Russian *Popasnaya*); c.1935–1943 Russian *imeni L.M. Kaganovicha*

Popasnaya *see* Popasna

Popilian Way *see* Via

Popivka *see* ²Kirovs'k

Popköy *see* Popovo

Poplar Fields *see* Emmitsburg

Poplar Head *see* Dothan

Popovichskaya *see* Kalininskaya

Popovka *see* ²Kirovs'k

Popovo (town, northeastern Bulgaria) : to 1878 Turkish *Popköy*

Popovo *see* Iskra

Poprad (city, northern Slovakia) : to 1918 Hungarian *Poprád*; to 1867 German *Deutschendorf*

Poprád *see* Poprad

Pordenone (city, northeastern Italy) : Roman *Portus Naonis*

Porech'ye *see* Demidov

Pori (city, southwestern Finland) : formerly Swedish *Björneborg*

Poronaysk (town, eastern Russia) : 1905–1945 Japanese *Shikuka*

Póros (island, southeastern Greece) : ancient Greek *Calauria*

Porretta Terme (town, north central Italy) : to c.1931 *Bagni della Porretta*

Porsy *see* Boldumsaz

Porta do Sertão *see* Campina Grande

Portadown (town, south central Northern Ireland) : Irish *Port an Dúnáin*

Portalegre (town, eastern Portugal) : Roman *Amoea*

Port an Dúnáin *see* Portadown

Port Angeles (town, Washington, northwestern United States) : originally *Puerto de Nuestra Señora de los Angeles*

Portarlington (town, east central Ireland) : Irish *Cúil an tSúdaire*

Port Arthur (town, Ontario, southern Canada) : to 1882 *Prince Arthur's Landing* (In 1970 Port Arthur merged with Fort William and two other towns to form **Thunder Bay**.)

Port Arthur *see* Lüshun

Port Báros *see* Sušak

Port Brabant *see* Tuktoyaktuk

Port Burwell *see* Killiniq

Port Byron Junction *see* East Moline

Port-Cartier (town, Quebec, eastern Canada) : to 1962 *Shelter Bay*

Portchester (town, southern England) : Roman *Portus Ardaoni* (The Roman name is often spelled *Portus Adurni*, but the form given here is thought to be more accurate.)

Port Colborne (town, Ontario, southeastern Canada) : originally *Gravelly Bay*

Port Cooper *see* Lyttelton

Port-de-France *see* Nouméa

Port-des-Galets *see* Le Port

Port Dinorwic *see* Y Felinheli

Port Durnford *see* Bur Gavo

Port Einon *see* Port Eynon

Port Elgin (town, Ontario, southeastern Canada) : formerly *Normanton*

Portersville *see* Valparaiso

Port-Étienne *see* Nouadhibou

Port Eynon (village, southwestern Wales) : Welsh *Port Einon*

Port Fairy (town, Victoria, southeastern Australia) : originally *Belfast*

Port Florence *see* **Kisumu**

Port-Francqui *see* **Ilebo**

Port Gilbert *see* **Racine**

Porthaethway *see* **Menai Bridge**

Port Hawkesbury (town, Nova Scotia, eastern Canada) : to 1860 *Ship Harbour*

Port Harrison *see* **Inukjuak**

Port Hedland (town, Western Australia, northwestern Australia) : Aboriginal *Ngaru*

Port Herald *see* **Nsanje**

Porthmadog (town, northwestern Wales) : formerly *Portmadoc* (The name derives from William Akexander Madocks, owner of the land on which the town was built, but the present spelling also reflects the tale that the legendary prince Madog ab Owain Gwynedd set off from here to discover America in *c.*1170, some three centuries before Columbus. Madocks also developed and gave his name to the nearby village of *Tremadog*.)

Port Hope (town, Ontario, southeastern Canada) : to 1817 *Smith's Creek*

Porthsgiwed *see* **Portskewett**

Porth Tywyn *see* **Burry Port**

Port Hueneme (city, California, southwestern United States) : to 1940 *Hueneme*

Port Jackson *see* **Sydney**

Port Kelang (city, western Malaysia) : formerly *Port Swettenham*

Port Láirge *see* **Waterford**

Port la Joie *see* **Charlottetown**

Portland (city, Maine, northeastern United States) : to 1786 *Falmouth* (Successive names prior to *Falmouth* were *Machigonne*, *Indigreat*, *Elbow*, *The Neck*, and *Casco*.)

Port Laoise (town, east central Ireland) : to 1920 *Maryborough*

Port Louis *see* ²**Scarborough**

Port-Lyautey *see* **Kenitra**

Port Macquarie *see* **Bluff**

Portmadoc *see* **Porthmadog**

Port Mahon *see* **Mahón**

Port nan Long *see* **Newtonferry**

Port Natal *see* **Durban**

Port Nicholson *see* **Wellington**

Port Nis *see* **Port of Ness**

Port-Nouveau-Québec *see* **Kangiqsualujjuaq**

Porto *see* **Oporto**

Pôrto (town, northeastern Brazil) : 1930s–1944 *João Pessoa*; to 1930s *Marruás*

Pôrto Alegre (city, southern Brazil) : originally *Pôrto dos Casais*

Pôrto Alegre *see* **Luzilândia**

Porto Alexandre *see* **Tombua**

Porto Amélia *see* **Pemba**

Porto Azzurro (town, central Italy) : to 1949 *Porto Longone*

Portobello *see* **Portobelo**

Portobelo (town, northern Panama) : traditional English *Portobello*; originally *Puerto Bello* (The town gained its English name from its repeated sacking by English pirates, notably in 1668 and 1739. Sir Francis Drake was buried in the harbor here.)

Pôrto de Guaipacaré *see* **Lorena**

Pôrto dos Casais *see* **Pôrto Alegre**

Porto Edda *see* **Sarandë**

Porto Farina *see* **Ghar al-Milh**

Port of Ness (village, Western Isles, northwestern Scotland) : Gaelic *Port Nis*

Porto Grande *see* **Mindelo**

Porto Longone *see* **Porto Azzurro**

Porto Maurizio *see* **Imperia**

Port Omna *see* **Portumna**

Porto Rè *see* **Kraljevica**

Pôrto Real *see* **Iguatama**

Porto Rico *see* **Puerto Rico**

Porto Torres (town, northwestern Sardinia, Italy) : Roman *Turris Libisonis*

Port Perry (village, Ontario, southeastern Canada) : to 1852 *Scugog Village*

Port Phillip District *see* ¹**Victoria**

Port Radium *see* **Echo Bay**

Port Razoir *see* ²**Shelburne**

Port Rex *see* **East London**

Port Rois *see* **Portrush**

Port Roseway *see* ²**Shelburne**

Port Rossignol *see* **Liverpool**

Port Royal *see* **Annapolis Royal**

Portrush (town, northern Northern Ireland) : Irish *Port Rois*

Port St. John's (town, southeastern South Africa) : 1976–1993 *Umzimvubu*

Port St.-Louis *see* **Antsohimbondrona**

Port Sarnia *see* **Sarnia**

Port Senior *see* **Liverpool**

Portskewett (village, southeastern Wales) : Welsh *Porthsgiwed*

¹**Portsmouth** (city, southern England) : Roman *Magnus Portus* (The Roman name, meaning "great port," properly applied to the harbor here, and the present city arose at its mouth.)

²**Portsmouth** (city, New Hampshire, northeastern United States) : to 1653 *Strawbery Banke*; originally *Piscataqua*

³**Portsmouth** (town, Rhode Island, northeastern United States) : to 1640 *Pocasset*

Port Swettenham *see* **Port Kelang**
Portugal (republic, southwestern Europe) : Roman *Lusitania*
Portugália *see* **Chitato**
Portuguese East Africa *see* **Mozambique**
Portuguese Guinea *see* **Guinea-Bissau**
Portuguese Timor *see* **East Timor**
Portuguese West Africa *see* **Angola**
Portumna (town, west central Ireland) : Irish *Port Omna*
Portus Ardaoni *see* **Portchester**
Portus Gaditanus *see* **Puerto Real**
Portus Lemanis *see* **Lympne**
Portus Magnus *see* **Almería**
Portus Magonis *see* **Mahón**
Portus Naonis *see* **Pordenone**
Portus Veneris *see* **Port-Vendres**
Port-Vendres (town, southern France) : Roman *Portus Veneris*
Port Victoria *see* **Tarfaya**
Port-Vila (town, central Vanuatu) : alternate *Vila*
Port Weld *see* **Kuala Sepetang**
Porvoo (city, southern Finland) : formerly Swedish *Borgå* (Around 40% of the city's population are Swedish-speaking.)
Posadas (city, northeastern Argentina) : 1869–1879 *Trinchera de San José*; to 1869 *Trinchera de los Paraguayos*
Poscheg *see* **Požega**
Poseidonia *see* **Pesto**
Posen *see* **Poznań**
Poshekhon'ye (town, western Russia) : 1918–1992 *Poshekhon'ye-Volodarsk* (The second part of the former name is not that of a place but of the revolutionary V. Volodarsky.)
Poshekhon'ye-Volodarsk *see* **Poshekhon'ye**
Possum Town *see* ²**Columbus**
Poste-de-la-Baleine *see* **Kuujjuarapik**
Postojna (town, southwestern Slovenia) : to 1945 Italian *Postumia*; to 1918 German *Adelsberg*
Postumia *see* **Postojna**
Postumian Way *see* **Via**
Postville *see* ²**Lincoln**
Pöstyén *see* **Piešťany**
Postysheve *see* **Krasnoarmiys'k**
Postyshevo *see* **Krasnoarmiys'k**
Potentia *see* **Potenza**
Potenza (town, southern Italy) : Roman *Potentia*
Potgietersrus *see* **Mokopane**
Poti (town, western Georgia) : ancient Greek *Phasis*
Pottsgrove *see* **Pottstown**
Pottstown (town, Pennsylvania, northeastern United States) : to to 1815 *Pottsgrove*
Pouso Alto *see* **Piracanjuba**

Považská Bystrica (city, western Slovakia) : to 1918 Hungarian *Vágbeszterce*; to 1867 German *Waag-Bistritz*
Požarevac (town, east central Serbia) : to 1867 German *Passarowitz*; to 1833 Turkish *Pasarofça*
Požega (town, eastern Croatia) : formerly *Slavonska Požega*; to 1867 German *Poscheg*
Pozharskoye (village, southeastern Russia) : to 1939 *Tikhonovka*
Poznań (city, western Poland) : 1793–1807, 1815–1919, 1939–1945 German *Posen*
Pozsony *see* **Bratislava**
Pozsonyligetfalu *see* **Petržalka**
Pozzuoli (city, southwestern Italy) : Roman and biblical *Puteoli*; ancient Greek *Dicaearchia* (The name occurs in the Bible as that of the town where Paul spent seven days with Christians en route to Rome.)
Prabuty (town, northeastern Poland) : to 1945 German *Riesenburg*
Prachatice (town, southwestern Czech Republic) : to 1918, 1938–1945 German *Prachatitz*
Prachatitz *see* **Prachatice**
Praeneste *see* **Palestrina**
Praesidium Julium *see* ¹**Santarém**
Prag *see* **Prague**
Pragerhof *see* **Pragersko**
Pragersko (town, northeastern Slovenia) : to 1918, 1941–1945 German *Pragerhof*
Prague (city, north central Czech Republic) : [Czech *Praha*]; to 1918, 1939–1945 German *Prag* (English has adopted the French form of the name.)
Praha *see* **Prague**
Prainha *see* **Miracatu**
Prairie Rapids *see* **Waterloo**
Prairieville *see* **Waukesha**
Praschnitz *see* **Przasnysz**
Prassburg *see* **Mozirje**
Prata *see* **Nova Prata**
Pratica di Mare (village, western Italy) : Roman *Lavinium*
Prausnitz *see* **Prusice**
Praust *see* **Pruszcz Gdański**
Prävali *see* **Prevalje**
Pravda (town, eastern Russia) : 1905–1945 Japanese *Hirochi*
Pravdino (village, western Russia) : c.1930–1945 German *Grumbkowfelde*; to c.1930 German *Grumbkowkeiten*
Pravdinsk (town, western Russia) : to 1945 German *Friedland* (The German name is associated with the battle of 1807 during the Napoleonic Wars in which the allied Prussian and Russian forces were defeated by the French.)

Pravishta *see* Eleftheroupolis

Premetì *see* Përmeti

Preobrazhenskaya *see* Kikvidze

Prerau *see* Přerov

Přerov (city, eastern Czech Republic) : to 1918, 1939–1945 German *Prerau*

Prescelly *see* Preseli

Preseli (region, southwestern Wales) : dated English *Prescelly* (The English name is usually associated with the *Prescelly Hills* or *Prescelly Mountains*, Welsh *Mynydd Preseli*, from which bluestones were transported to build Stonehenge in southern England.)

Presidencia de la Plaza (town, southern Argentina) : to early 1940s *Presidente de la Plaza*

Presidente de la Plaza *see* Presidencia de la Plaza

Presidente Dutra (city, northeastern Brazil) : to 1948 *Curador*

Presidente Juán Perón *see* Chaco

Presidente Penna *see* ²Rondônia

Presidente Vargas *see* (1) Itabira; (2) Nova Era

Preslav *see* Veliki Preslav

Prešov (city, eastern Slovakia) : to 1918 Hungarian *Eperjes*

Presque Isle (town, Maine, northeastern United States) : to 1859 *Fairbanks*

Pressburg *see* Bratislava

Presteigne (town, eastern Wales) : Welsh *Llanandras*

Přeštice (town, western Czech Republic) : to 1918, 1939–1945 German *Pscheschtitz*

Pretoria *see* Tshwane

Pretoria-Witwatersrand-Vaal *see* Gauteng

Preussen *see* Prussia

Preussisch-Eylau *see* Bagrationovsk

Preussisch-Friedland *see* Debrzno

Preussisch-Holland *see* Pasłęk

Preussisch-Stargard *see* Starogard Gdański

Prevalje (town, northern Slovenia) : to 1918, 1941–1945 German *Prävali*

Préveza (town, northwestern Greece) : to 1913 Turkish *Preveze*; ancient Greek *Berenicia*

Preveze *see* Préveza

Priargunsk (town, southeastern Russia) : to 1962 *Tsurukhaytuy*

Priazovskoye *see* Pryazovs'ke

Příbor (town, eastern Czech Republic) : to 1919, 1939–1945 German *Freiberg*

Příbram (city, west central Czech Republic) : to 1918, 1939–1945 German *Pibrans*

Priestholm *see* Puffin Island

Priest's Mills *see* ³Alexandria

Priest's Valley *see* Vernon

Prievidza (city, west central Slovakia) : to 1918 Hungarian *Privigye*; to 1867 German *Privitz*

Prigmore's Swamp *see* New Brunswick

Prikumsk *see* Budyonnovsk

Prilep (city, south central Macedonia) : to 1913 Turkish *Perlepe*

Primkenau *see* Przemków

¹Primorsk (town, western Russia, near Kaliningrad) : to 1946 German *Fischhausen*

²Primorsk (town, western Russia, near St. Petersburg) : to 1940 Finnish *Koivisto*; to 1809 Swedish *Björkö*

³Primorsk (town, western Russia, near Volgograd) : formerly *Lugovaya Proleyka*

Primorsk *see* Prymors'k

Primorsko (town, southeastern Bulgaria) : formerly *Kyupriya*

Primorskoye *see* Sartana

Prince Arthur's Landing *see* Port Arthur

Prince Edward Island (province, eastern Canada) : locally (Algonquian) *Abegweit*; 1759–1799 *St. John's Island*; to 1759 French *Île St.-Jean* (In 1962 the local name was given to the passage between New Brunswick and Prince Edward Island plied by the car ferry MV *Abegweit*.)

Prince George (city, British Columbia, western Canada) : to 1915 *Fort George*

Prince of Wales Island *see* Penang

Princeton (town, New Jersey, northeastern United States) : to 1724 *Stony Brook*

Priozyorsk (town, western Russia) : to 1940 Finnish *Käkisalmi*; to 1809 Swedish *Kexholm*

Prishib *see* Leninsk

Pristen' (town, western Russia) : formerly *Mar'yino*

Priština (city, central Kosovo) : to 1913 Turkish *Prištine*

Prištine *see* Priština

Priverno (town, south central Italy) : to 1928 *Piperno*

Privigye *see* Prievidza

Privitz *see* Prievidza

Privolzhsk (city, western Russia) : to 1928 *Yakovlevskoye*

Privolzhskoye (village, southwestern Russia) : to 1941 *Kukkus*

Privolzhsky (town, southwestern Russia) : 1936–1944 *Kanukov*; to 1936 *Kalmytsky Bazar* (The town is now within the city of Astrakhan.)

Prizren (city, southern Kosovo) : to 1913 Turkish *Perserin*

Proby Island *see* Niuafo'ou

Prochowice (town, southwestern Poland) : to 1945 German *Parchwitz*

Profesor Ishirkovo (town, northern Bulgaria) : to 1942 *Kochina*

Prokhod na Republikata *see* Republic Pass

[1]**Proletarsk** (town, southwestern Russia) : to 1970 *Proletarskaya*

[2]**Proletarsk** (town, northwestern Tajikistan) : formerly Russian *Dragomirovo*

Proletarsk *see* **Proletars'k**

Proletars'k (town, eastern Ukraine) : (Russian *Proletarsk*); formerly *Nesvitovych* (Russian *Nesvetevich*) (The town was incorporated into the city of Lysychans'k in 1965.)

Proletarskaya *see* [1]**Proletarsk**

Proletarskaya Pobeda *see* **Pirogovsky**

[1]**Proletarsky** (town, western Russia, near Belgorod) : formerly *Gotnya*

[2]**Proletarsky** (town, western Russia, near Serpukhov) : to 1928 *Proletary*

Proletary *see* [2]**Proletarsky**

Promzino *see* **Surskoye**

Propontis *see* **Marmara, Sea of**

Propoysk *see* **Slawharad**

Proskuriv *see* [1]**Khmel'nyts'kyy**

Proskurov *see* [1]**Khmel'nyts'kyy**

Proskurów *see* [1]**Khmel'nyts'kyy**

Prospect Park *see* **Glen Ellyn**

Prossnitz *see* **Prostějov**

Prostějov (city, east central Czech Republic) : to 1918, 1939–1945 German *Prossnitz*

Provadiya (town, eastern Bulgaria) : to 1878 Turkish *Paravadı*

Provence (region, southeastern France) : Roman *Provincia*

Providence *see* (1) **Annapolis**; (2) **Fairfax**

Province Lands *see* **Provincetown**

Provincetown (town, Massachusetts, northeastern United States) : to 1727 *Province Lands*

Provincia *see* **Provence**

Provo (city, Utah, west central United States) : to 1850 *Fort Utah*

Prudhon *see* **Sidi Brahim**

Prudnik (town, southwestern Poland) : to 1945 German *Neustadt*

Prusia ad Olympum *see* **Bursa**

Prusice (town, southwestern Poland) : to 1945 German *Prausnitz*

Prussia (former state, north central Germany) : [German *Preussen*]

Pruszcz Gdański (town, northern Poland) : 1772–1945 German *Praust*

Prużana *see* **Pruzhany**

Pruzhany (town, western Belarus) : 1919–1939 Polish *Prużana*

Pryazovs'ke (town, southeastern Ukraine) : (Russian *Priazovskoye*); 1864–1935 *Pokrovka Druha* (Russian *Pokrovka Vtoraya*) or *Pokrovs'ke* (Russian *Pokrovskoye*); to 1864 *Siyut-Dzheret*

Prymors'k (town, southeastern Ukraine) : (Russian *Primorsk*); to 1967 *Nohays'ke* (Russian *Nogaysk*)

Prymors'ke *see* **Sartana**

Przasnysz (town, northeastern Poland) : 1940–1945 German *Praschnitz*

Przemków (town, western Poland) : to 1945 German *Primkenau*

Przemysl *see* **Przemyśl**

Przemyśl (city, southeastern Poland) : 1941–1944 German *Przemysl*; 1939–1941 Russian *Peremyshl'*; to 1918 German *Przemysl* (In the early years of World War II, 1939–41, the city was divided by the German-Soviet frontier.)

Przemyślany *see* **Peremyshlyany**

Przheval'sk *see* **Karakol**

Pscheschtitz *see* **Přeštice**

Psedakh *see* **Alanskoye**

Psirtskha *see* **Akhali Ap'oni**

Pszczółki (village, northern Poland) : 1772–1945 German *Hohenstein*

Pszczyna (towm, southwestern Poland) : to 1921, 1939–1945 German *Pless*

Ptolemaïs (town, north central Greece) : to 1913 Turkish *Kaylar*

Ptolemaïs *see* (1) **Acre**; (2) **Tolmeta**

Ptuj (town, northeastern Slovenia) : to 1918, 1941–1945 German *Pettau*; Roman *Poetovio*

Pucarevo *see* **Novi Travnik**

Puchó *see* **Púchov**

Púchov (town, western Slovakia) : to 1918 Hungarian *Puchó*

Puck (town, northern Poland) : 1772–1919, 1939–1945 German *Putzig*

Puebla (city, east central Mexico) : alternate *Puebla de Zaragoza*; to 1862 *Puebla de los Ángeles* (The city's full alternate name is *Heroica Puebla de Zaragoza*. It owes its "heroic" title to the battle of 1862, in which the Mexicans under General Ignacio Zaragoza were victorious over the French. A year later the city was occupied by the French but was recaptured by General Porfirio Díaz in 1867.)

Puebla de los Ángeles *see* **Puebla**

Puebla de Zaragoza *see* **Puebla**

Pueblo de la Capilla *see* **Sauce del Yí**

Pueblo de San José de Guadalupe *see* **San Jose**

Pueblo Viejo *see* **Villa Canales**

Puerto Acosta (town, western Bolivia) : to 1908 *Huaicho*

Puerto Aguirre *see* **Puerto Iguazú**

Puerto Bello *see* **Portobelo**

Puerto Caballos *see* **Puerto Cortés**

Puerto Cortés (city, northwestern Honduras) : to 1869 *Puerto Caballos*

Puerto de Cabras *see* **Puerto del Rosario**

Puerto del Inglés *see* **Piriápolis**

Puerto del Rosario (town, eastern Canary Islands, Spain) : to 1957 *Puerto de Cabras*

Puerto de Nuestra Señora de los Angeles *see* **Port Angeles**

Puerto Flor de Lis *see* **Ciudad del Este**

Puerto Francisco de Orellana *see* **Coca**

Puerto Iguazú (town, northeastern Argentina) : to 1940s *Puerto Aguirre*

Puerto México *see* **Coatzacoalcos**

Puerto Pérez (town, western Bolivia) : to 1900 *Chililaya*

Puerto Presidente Stroessner *see* **Ciudad del Este**

Puerto Princesa (city, western Philippines) : formerly *Cuyo*

Puerto Príncipe *see* **Camagüey**

Puerto Real (town, southwestern Spain) : Roman *Portus Gaditanus*

Puerto Rico (island state, central West Indies) : locally (Arawakan) *Borinquén*; formerly *Porto Rico*; originally *San Juan* (The island's original name came to give that of its capital city, [2]**San Juan**, while over time the port town's name passed to that of the state.)

Puerto Sandino (town, western Nicaragua) : to 1980 *Puerto Somoza*

Puerto Somoza *see* **Puerto Sandino**

Puerto Vallarta (city, west central Mexico) : formerly *Las Peñas*

Puffin Island (northwestern Wales) : alternate *Priestholm*; Welsh *Ynys Seiriol*

Pugachyov (town, western Russia) : to 1918 *Nikolayevsk*

Pugachyovo (village, eastern Russia) : 1905–1945 Japanese *Maguntan-hama*

Puglia (region, southeastern Italy) : alternate and Roman *Apulia*

Pula (city, western Croatia) : to 1947 Italian *Pola*; to 1918 German *Pola*; Roman *Pietas Julia*

Puławy (town, eastern Poland) : to 1915 Russian *Novaya Aleksandriya*

Pulgan *see* **Pülgön**

Pülgön (village, western Kyrgyzstan) : 1940–1991 *Frunzenskoye*; to 1940 *Pulgan*

Pulin *see* **Chervonoarmiys'k**

Pullman (city, Washington, northwestern United States) : originally *Three Forks*

Pułtusk (town, east central Poland) : 1940–1945 German *Ostenburg*

Pulyny *see* **Chervonoarmiys'k**

Pumlumon *see* **Plynlimon**

Pune (city, western India) : formerly English *Poona*

Puncheston (village, southwestern Wales) : Welsh *Cas-mael*

Pungarabato *see* **Ciudad Altamirano**

Punkapoag *see* [2]**Canton**

Puno (city, southern Peru) : originally *San Carlos de Puno*

Punta Arenas (city, southern Chile) : 1927–1937 *Magallanes*

Puntarenas (city, western Costa Rica) : originally *Bruselas*

Purdy's Mills *see* **Lindsay**

Purtuniq (village, Quebec, eastern Canada) : formerly *Asbestos Hill*

Pŭrvenets (village, south central Bulgaria) : to 1945 *Ferdinandovo*

Pŭrvomay (town, south central Bulgaria) : 1891–1945 *Borisovgrad*; 1878–1891 *Khadzhi-Eles*; to 1878 Turkish *Hacieles*

Pushkin (city, western Russia) : 1918–1937 *Detskoye Selo*; to 1918 *Tsarskoye Selo* (The city has now been incorporated into St. Petersburg.)

[1]**Pushkino** (village, western Russia, near Kaliningrad) : to 1945 German *Dosmahlen*

[2]**Pushkino** (village, western Russia, near Engel's) : to 1941 *Urbakh* (The earlier name of the village, in the former Volga German Autonomous Soviet Socialist Republic, is a Russian form of German *Urbach*.)

Pushkino *see* **Biläsuvar**

Putao (town, northern Myanmar) : formerly *Fort Hertz*

Puteoli *see* **Pozzuoli**

Putyatin (town, southeastern Russia) : formerly *Nazimovo*

Putzig *see* **Puck**

Pyandzh *see* (1) **Panj**; (2) **Dŭstí**

P'yansky Perevoz *see* **Perevoz**

P'yany Bor *see* **Krasny Bor**

Pyarnu *see* **Pärnu**

Pyatikhatka *see* **Pyatykhatky**

Pyatikhatki *see* **Pyatykhatky**

Pyatykhatka *see* **Pyatykhatky**

Pyatykhatky (town, east central Ukraine) : (Russian *Pyatikhatki*); to 1944 *Pyatykhatka* (Russian *Pyatikhatka*)

Pylos (town, southern Greece) : locally *Neokastro*; formerly Italian *Navarino* (The Italian name is associated with the naval battle of 1827 between European and Turkish fleets off the coast here during the Greek War of Independence.)

Pyramus *see* **Ceyhan**

Pyrenees (mountains, northeastern Spain/southwestern France) : [French *Pyrénées*; Spanish *Pirineos*]

Pyrénées *see* **Pyrenees**

Pyrénées-Atlantiques (department, southwestern France) : to 1969 *Basses-Pyrénées*

Pyrgi *see* **San Severa**

Pyritz *see* **Pyrzyce**

Pyrzyce (town, northwestern Poland) : to 1945 German *Pyritz*

Pyshkino-Troitskoye *see* ²**Pervomayskoye**

Pyshma *see* **Verkhnyaya Pyshma**

Pyshminsky Zavod *see* **Staropyshminsk**

Pyskowice (town, southern Poland) : to 1945 German *Peiskretscham*

Pytalovo (town, western Russia) : 1938–1945 Latvian *Abrene*; 1925–1938 Latvian *Jaunlatgale*

Qamanittuaq *see* **Baker Lake**

Qanliko'l (village, western Uzbekistan) : formerly *Leninobod* (Russian *Leninabad*)

Qaqortoq (town, southwestern Greenland) : to 1985 Danish *Julianehåb*

Qarshi (city, southern Uzbekistan) : 1926–1937 *Bek-Budi*

Qausuittuq *see* **Resolute**

Qazbegi (town, northern Georgia) : to 1921 *Stepantsminda*

Qazimämmäd (town, eastern Azerbaijan) : formerly *Kazi-Mahomed*; to 1939 *Adzhibakul*

Qena (city, eastern Egypt) : ancient Greek *Caene*

¹**Qeqertarsuaq** (island, western Greenland) : formerly *Disko*

²**Qeqertarsuaq** (town, western Greenland) : formerly Danish *Godhavn*

Qift (village, eastern Egypt) : ancient Greek *Coptos*

Qikiqtarjuaq (island, Nunavut, northeastern Canada) : to 1999 *Broughton Island*

Qingaq *see* **Bathurst Inlet**

Qomsheh (town, west central Iran) : to 1979 *Shahreza*

Quaqtaq (village, Quebec, eastern Canada) : formerly *Koartac*

Quartzsite (town, Arizona, southwestern United States) : originally *Fort Tyson*

Quatre Cantons, Lac des *see* **Lucerne, Lake**

Quattro Cantoni, Lago dei *see* **Lucerne, Lake**

Quebec (province and city, eastern Canada) : alternate French *Québec*; 1841–1867 *Canada East*; 1791–1841 *Lower Canada* (The historical names for the province were essentially interchangeable. *Cp.* **Ontario**.)

Québec *see* **Quebec**

Québec-Ouest *see* ¹**Vanier**

Quebec West *see* ¹**Vanier**

Queen Elizabeth National Park *see* **Ruwenzori National Park**

Queensborough *see* **New Westminster**

Queen's County *see* **Laois**

Queensferry (town, northeastern Wales) : 1828–1837 *King's Ferry*; 1826–1828 *Lower King's Ferry*; to 1826 *Lower Ferry*

Queenstown *see* **Cóbh**

Quelpart *see* **Chegu**

Quemoy (island, southeastern China) : alternate *Jinmen*

Que Que *see* **Kwekwe**

Quesnel (town, British Colombia, southwestern Canada) : to 1864 *Quesnelle Mouth*

Quesnelle Mouth *see* **Quesnel**

Quezon (province, northern Philippines) : to 1946 *Tayabas*

Quibdó (city, western Colombia) : originally *San Francisco de Quibdó*

Quimper (town, northwestern France) : [Breton *Kemper*]

¹**Quincy** (city, Illinois, north central United States) : to 1825 *Bluffs*

²**Quincy** (city, Massachusetts, northeastern United States) : to 1792 *Merry Mount*; originally *Mount Wollaston*

Quingua *see* **Plaridel**

Quinnipiac *see* **New Haven**

Qunghirot (town, western Uzbekistan) : 1969–1991 Russian *Kungrad*; to 1969 Russian *Zheleznodorozhny*

Qusantīnah *see* **Constantine**

Quseir (town, eastern Egypt) : formerly often *Kosseir*

Qyteti Stalin *see* **Kuçovë**

Raab *see* **Győr**

Rab (village, western Croatia) : 1941–1943 Italian *Arbe*; to 1918 German *Arbe* (The village is on the island of the same name.)

Rabbah *see* **Amman**

Rabbath-Ammon *see* **Amman**

Rača (city district, western Slovakia) : to 1946 *Račistorf*. (Rača is a northern district of Bratislava.)

Rachov *see* **Rakhiv**

Racibórz (city, south central Poland) : to 1945 German *Ratibor*

Racine (city, Wisconsin, north central United States) : to 1837 *Port Gilbert*

Račistorf *see* **Rača**

Rădăuţi (town, northern Romania) : to 1918 German *Radautz*

Radautz *see* **Rădăuţi**

Radekhiv (town, western Ukraine) : (Russian *Radekhov*); to 1939 Polish *Radziechów*

Radekhov *see* **Radekhiv**

Radili Ko *see* **Fort Good Hope**

Radimin *see* **Radzymin**

Radin *see* **Radzyń Podlaski**

Radków (town, southwestern Poland) : to 1945 German *Wünschelburg*

Radmannsdorf *see* **Radovljica**

Radnor Forest (eastern Wales) : Welsh *Fforest Clud* (As elsewhere in British placenames, *for-*

est here means specifically "hunting preserve" rather than just "region of trees.")

Radnorshire *see* **New Radnor**

Radomir (mountain, southwestern Bulgaria) : to 1967 *Kalabak*

Radomsko (town, central Poland) : to 1915 Russian *Novoradomsk*

Radovljica (town, northwestern Slovenia) : to 1918, 1941–1945 German *Radmannsdorf*

Radyvyliv (town, western Ukraine) : 1940–1991 *Chervonoarmiys'k* (Russian *Chervonoarmeysk*); 1919–1940 Polish *Radziwillów*; to 1919 Russian *Radzivilov*

Radziechów *see* **Radekhiv**

Radzivilov *see* **Radyvyliv**

Radziwillów *see* **Radyvyliv**

Radzymin (town, east central Poland) : to 1915 Russian *Radimin*

Radzyń Podlaski (town, eastern Poland) : to 1915 Russian *Radin*

Rae Lakes (village, Northwest Territories, north central Canada) : alternate Inuit *Gameti*

Raglan (village, southeastern Wales) : Welsh *Rhaglan*

Ragnit *see* **Neman**

Ragusa *see* **Dubrovnik**

Rahaeng *see* **Tak**

Rahó *see* **Rakhiv**

Rahouia (town, northern Algeria) : to *c.*1962 French *Montgolfier*

Rahuipukeko *see* **Huntly**

Rainier, Mt. (Washington, northwestern United States) : alternate *Mt. Tacoma* (The mountain's Indian name gave that of the city of **Tacoma**, 45 miles to the northwest.)

Rajasthan (state, northwestern India) : to 1948 *Rajputana* (The former name applied to a region approximating to that of the present state, which later added other small areas.)

Rajputana *see* **Rajasthan**

Rajshahi (city, western Bangladesh) : formerly *Rampur Boalia*

Rakhine (state, western Myanmar) : formerly *Arakan*

Rakhiv (town, western Ukraine) : (Russian *Rakhov*); 1944–1945 Czech *Rachov*; 1939–1944 Hungarian *Rahó*; 1919–1939 Czech *Rachov*; to 1918 Hungarian *Rahó*

Rakhmanlare *see* **Rozino**

Rakhov *see* **Rakhiv**

Rakishki *see* **Rokiškis**

Rakiura *see* **Stewart Island**

Rakonitz *see* **Rakovnik**

Rakovets *see* **Grozdyovo**

Rakovnik (town, western Czech Republic) : to 1918, 1939–1945 German *Rakonitz*

Rakovski *see* ¹**Dimitrovgrad**

Rakvere (town, northern Estonia) : to 1918 German *Wesenberg*

Ralston's Colony *see* **Rapid City**

Rampur Boalia *see* **Rajshahi**

Ramsey (island, southwestern Wales) : Welsh *Ynys Dewi*

Rancagua (city, north central Chile) : originally *Villa Santa Cruz de Triana*

Rancho Rodeo de las Aguas *see* **Beverly Hills**

Rand *see* **Des Plaines**

Rand, The *see* **Witwatersrand**

Randolph (town, Massachusetts, northeastern United States) : to 1793 *Cochato*

Ranenburg *see* **Chaplygin**

Rangitoto *see* **D'Urville Island**

Rangoon *see* **Yangôn**

Rankin Inlet (village, Nunavut, north central Canada) : alternate Inuit *Kangiqcliniq*

Rankovićevo *see* (1) **Banatski Karlovac**; (2) **Kraljevo**

Rann *see* **Brežice**

Rantomari *see* **Yablochny**

Rapa Nui *see* **Easter Island**

Raphoe (town, northwestern Ireland) : Irish *Ráth Bhoth*

Rapid City (town, Manitoba, southern Canada) : to 1877 *Ralston's Colony*

Rapids City *see* **Cedar Rapids**

Rappoltsweiler *see* **Ribeauvillé**

Raritan *see* **Edison**

Raseiniai (town, west central Lithuania) : (Russian *Raseynyay*); to 1918 Russian *Rossiyeny*

Ras el Ma (town, northwestern Algeria) : to *c.*1962 French *Bedeau*

Ras el Oued (town, northeastern Algeria) : to *c.*1962 French *Tocqueville*

Raseynyay *see* **Raseiniai**

Rashīd (city, northern Egypt) : alternate traditional *Rosetta* (The traditional name became widely known from the Rosetta stone, discovered here in 1799.)

Rasony (town, northern Belarus) : (Russian *Rossony*); to *c.*1940 *Stanislavovo*

Rastenburg *see* **Kętrzyn**

Rastorguyevo *see* **Vidnoye**

Rastyapino *see* **Dzerzhinsk**

Ratae Corieltauvorum *see* **Leicester**

Ráth Bhoth *see* **Raphoe**

Ráth Caola *see* **Rathkeale**

Rathkeale (town, southwestern Ireland) : Irish *Ráth Caola*

Ráth Luirc (town, southern Ireland) : to 1939 *Charleville* (The town's shorter Irish name is *An Ráth*.)

Ráth Mealtain *see* **Rathmelton**

Rathmelton (town, northwestern Ireland) : Irish *Ráth Mealtain*

Ratibor *see* Racibórz

Ratisbon *see* Regensburg

Ratmanov Island *see* Diomede Islands

Rat Portage *see* Kenora

Rattlesnake Station *see* Mountain Home

Ratzebuhr *see* Okonek

Raudnitz an der Elbe *see* Roudnice nad Labem

Rauschen *see* Svetlogorsk

Rautenberg *see* Uzlovoye

Rautu *see* Sosnovo

Rava-Rus'ka (town, western Ukraine) : (Russian *Rava Russkaya*); to 1939 Polish *Rawa Ruska*

Rava Russkaya *see* Rava-Rus'ka

Ravenglass (village, northwestern England) : Roman *Glannoventa*

Rawa Ruska *see* Rava-Rus'ka

Rawicz (town, west central Poland) : 1793–1807, 1815–1919, 1939–1945 German *Rawitsch*

Rawitsch *see* Rawicz

Rawlins (town, Wyoming, western United States) : originally *Rawlins Springs*

Rawlins Springs *see* Rawlins

Razdan *see* Hrazdan

Razdol'noye *see* Rozdon'ne

Razgrad (city, northeastern Bulgaria) : to 1878 Turkish *Hezargrad*

Razino (village, western Russia) : to 1945 German *Doristhal*

Razlog (town, southwestern Bulgaria) : to 1878 Turkish *Mehomie*

Reate *see* Rieti

Rechitsa *see* Rechytsa

Rechytsa (city, southeastern Belarus) : (Russian *Rechitsa*); to 1918 Russian *Rechitsa*

Recife (city, eastern Brazil) : formerly *Pernambuco*; 17th century Dutch *Mauritzstad*

Reculver (village, southeastern England) : Roman *Regulbium*

Recz (town, northwestern Poland) : to 1945 German *Reetz*

Reda (town, northern Poland) : 1772–1919, 1939–1945 German *Rheda*

Red Bluff (town, California, western United States) : originally *Leodocia*

Redding *see* Elizabeth City

Redenção *see* Redenção da Serra

Redenção da Serra (town, southeastern Brazil) : to 1944 *Redenção*

Red Jacket *see* Calumet

Redriff *see* Rotherhithe

Red River (southeastern Asia) : alternate Chinese *Yuan* or Vietnamese *Hong*

Red Sea (northeastern Africa/western Saudi Arabia) : Roman *Mare Rubrum*; alternate Roman *Sinus Arabicus* (The Red Sea lies between Arabic-speaking countries and its Arabic name is *Al Baḥr al-Aḥmar*, meaning the same as the English.)

Redwood City (city, California, western United States) : to 1858 *Embarcadero*

Reetz *see* Recz

Regar *see* Tursunzade

Regele Carol II *see* Suvorove

Regele Mihai I *see* Suvorove

Regensburg (city, southeastern Germany) : formerly *Ratisbon*; Roman *Castra Regina*

Regenwalde *see* Resko

Reggio di Calabria (city, southern Italy) : Roman *Regium Julium* (The Roman name occurs in the Bible as *Rhegium*, the town where Paul waited for a wind en route to Rome.)

Reggio nell'Emilia (city, northern Italy) : Roman *Regium Lepidum*

Reghin (town, central Romania) : to 1918, 1940–1944 Hungarian *Szászrégen*; to 1867 German *Sächsisch-Regen*

Regina (city, Saskatchewan, southern Canada) : 1857–1882 *Wascana*; originally *Pile O'Bones*

Regium Julium *see* Reggio di Calabria

Regium Lepidum *see* Reggio nell'Emilia

Regulbium *see* Reculver

Reïbell *see* Ksar Chellala

Reichenau *see* Bogatynia

Reichenau an der Knieschna *see* Rychnov nad Kněžnou

Reichenau bei Gablonz *see* Rychnov u Gablonce

Reichenbach *see* Dzierżoniów

Reichenberg *see* Liberec

Reichenstein *see* Złoty Stok

Reichshof *see* Rzeszów

Reichstadt *see* Zákupy

Reims (city, northeastern France) : conventional English *Rheims*; Roman *Durocortorum*

Reivilo (town, west central South Africa) : to 1927 *Klein Boetsap*

Remchi (town, northwestern Algeria) : to *c.*1962 French *Montagnac*

Remennikovo (village, southwestern Russia) : to 1941 *Oberdorf* (The town's earlier German name is due to its location in the former Volga German Autonomous Soviet Socialist Republic.)

Remington's Corners *see* Ilion

Renaix *see* Ronse

Renault *see* Sidi Mohammed Ben Ali

Renier *see* Aïn Makhlouf

Rennes (city, northwestern France) : Breton *Roazhan*; Roman *Condate*

Reno (city, Nevada, western United States) : to 1868 *Lake's Crossing*

Repelen-Baerl *see* Rheinkamp

Repino (town, western Russia) : to 1948 Finnish *Kuokkala*

Reppen *see* Rzepin

Republic Pass (central Bulgaria) : [Bulgarian *Prokhod na Republikata*], to 1950 *Khainboaz*

Repulse Bay (village, Nunavut, northern Canada) : alternate Inuit *Naujaat*

Rerigonius Sinus *see* Ryan, Loch

Reriutaba (town, northeastern Brazil) : to 1944 Portuguese *Santa Cruz*

Resan *see* Resen

Reschen-Scheideck *see* Passo di Resia

Resen (village, western Macedonia) : 1913–1941 Serbian *Resan*; to 1913 Turkish *Resne*

Resiczabánya *see* Reşiţa

Resina *see* Ercolano

Resistencia (city, northeastern Argentina) : to 1876 *San Fernando del Rio Negro* (The earlier name was that of a Jesuit mission abandoned in 1773 after the order was suppressed.)

Reşiţa (city, western Romania) : to 1918 Hungarian *Resiczabánya*

Resko (town, northwestern Poland) : to 1945 German *Regenwalde*

Resne *see* Resen

Resolute (village, Nunavut, northern Canada) : alternate Inuit *Qausuittuq*

Resülayn *see* Ceylanpınar

Reszel (town, northeastern Poland) : to 1945 German *Rössel*

Réunion (island, western Indian Ocean) : 1810–1848 *Bourbon*; 1801–1810 *Bonaparte*; 1793–1801 *Réunion*; 1649–1793 *Bourbon*; 1642–1649 *Isle Mascareigne*, to 1642 *Santa Apollonia* (The island has been a French possession since 1642 with the exception of the years 1810–15, when it was taken by the British, who restored the earlier name *Bourbon*.)

Reutov (city, western Rusia) : to 1940 *Reutovo*

Reutovo *see* Reutov

Reval *see* Tallinn

Revel' *see* Tallinn

Revelstoke (town, British Columbia, southwestern Canada) : formerly *Farwell*; originally *Second Crossing* (The original settlement was on a slightly different site.)

Revere (city, Massachusetts, northeastern United States) : 1846–1871 *North Chelsea*; originally *Rumney Marsh* (The settlement was part of Boston until 1739, when it became part of Chelsea.)

Revúca (town, south central Slovakia) : to 1918 Hungarian *Nagyrőce*

Rezā'īyeh *see* Orūmīyeh

Rezekne *see* Rēzekne

Rēzekne (city, eastern Latvia) : (Russian *Rezekne*); 1939–1945 German *Rositten*; 1772–1918 Russian *Rezhitsa*

Rezhitsa *see* Rēzekne

Rha *see* Volga

Rhaeadr Gwy *see* Rhayader

Rhaglan *see* Raglan

Rhayader (town, central Wales) : Welsh *Rhaeadr Gwy*

Rheda *see* Reda

Rhegium *see* Reggio di Calabria

Rheims *see* Reims

Rhein *see* Rhine

Rheinkamp (city, western Germany) : formerly *Repelen-Baerl*

Rheinschanze *see* Ludwigshafen

Rhenus *see* Rhine

Rhin *see* Rhine

Rhine (river, central and western Europe) : [German *Rhein*; French *Rhin*; Dutch *Rijn*]; Roman *Rhenus*

Rhinocolura *see* Al 'Arīsh

Rhisca *see* Risca

Rhiwabon *see* Ruabon

Rhodanus *see* Rhône

Rhode Island (Rhode Island, northeastern United States) : to 1644 *Aquidneck* (This is the past and present name of the island on which the state of Rhode Island, officially Rhode Island and Providence Plantations, was formed and ratified the U.S. Constitution in 1790.)

Rhodes (city, southeastern Greece) : [modern Greek *Rodos*]; to 1947 Italian *Rodi*; to 1912 Turkish *Rodos* (The city lies on the island of the same name, known to the Romans as *Rhodus*.)

Rhodesia *see* Zimbabwe

Rhodus *see* Rhodes

Rhône (river, southern France) : Roman *Rhodanus*

Rhoose (village, southern Wales) : Welsh *Y Rhws*

Rhos Mhic Thriúin *see* New Ross

Rhos-on-Sea (town, northern Wales) : Welsh *Llandrillo-yn-Rhos*

Rhum *see* Rum

Rhuthun *see* Ruthin

Rhydaman *see* Ammanford

Rhymney (town, southern Wales) : Welsh *Rhymni*

Rhymni *see* Rhymney

Riaba (village, northwestern Equatorial Guinea) : formerly Portuguese *La Concepción*

Riachão *see* Riachão do Dantas

Riachão do Dantas (town, northeastern Brazil) : to 1944 *Riachão*

Ribas do Rio Pardo (town, western Brazil) : to 1944 *Rio Pardo*

Ribeauvillé (town, eastern France) : alternate German *Rappoltsweiler*

Ribchester (village, northwestern England) : Roman *Bremetenacum Veteranorum*

Ribeirão *see* **Guapó**

Ribeirão Prêto (city, southeastern Brazil) : formerly *Entre Rios*; originally *São Sebastião do Ribeirão Prêto*

Richborough Port (village, southeastern England) : Roman *Rutupiae*

Richland *see* ²**Orange**

¹**Richmond** (town, southeastern England) : to 1501 *Sheen* (The full name of the town near London is *Richmond upon Thames*, distinguishing it from *Richmond*, Yorkshire, for which it is named, thanks to Henry VII, earl of Richmond, who built his palace here.)

²**Richmond** (city, Indiana, north central United States) : to 1818 *Smithville*

Richmond *see* (1) **Staten Island**; (2) ³**Windsor**

Richmond Hill (town, Ontario, southeastern Canada) : to 1819 *Mount Pleasant*

Ricomagus *see* **Riom**

Ridder (city, eastern Kazakhstan) : 1941–2002 Russian *Leninogorsk*

Ridgeville *see* **Evanston**

Ridgewood (town, New Jersey, northeastern United States) : 1829–1866 *Godwinville*; to 1829 *Newton*

Riduna *see* **Alderney**

Riedsburg *see* ²**Kent**

Riesenburg *see* **Prabuty**

Riesengebirge (mountains, southwestern Poland/northern Czech Republic) : [Polish *Karkonosze*; Czech *Krkonoše*]; alternate English *Giant Mountains* (The German name predominates because on the Polish side the mountains were formerly in Germany.)

Rieti (town, central Italy) : Roman *Reate*

Rijeka (city, northwestern Croatia) : to 1943 Italian *Fiume* (The city was successively under Austrian, Croatian, Hungarian, French, and Italian rule from 1471 to 1943, during which time the Italian name was mostly dominant. It then remained in general English use.)

Rijn *see* **Rhine**

Rijssel *see* **Lille**

Rijswijk (town, northwestern Netherlands) : English *Ryswick* (The English name is historically preserved for the two treaties of 1697 ending the War of the Grand Alliance.)

Rimaszombat *see* **Rimavská Sobota**

Rimavská Sobota (town, south central Slovakia) : to 1918, 1938–1945 Hungarian *Rimaszombat*; to 1867 German *Gross-Steffelsdorf*

Rimini (city, northern Italy) : Roman *Ariminum*

Rimmon *see* **Seymour**

Rimske Toplice (village, central Slovenia) : to 1918 German *Römerbad*

Rincón de Zárate *see* **Zárate**

Rinns of Galloway (peninsula, southwestern Scotland) : Roman *Novantarum Peninsula*

Río Benito *see* ¹**Mbini**

Rio Bonito *see* (1) **Caiapônia**; (2) **Tangará**

Río Branco (town, northeastern Uruguay) : to 1909 *Artigas*

Rio Branco *see* (1) **Arcoverde**; (2) **Paratinga**; (3) **Roraima**; (4) **Visconde do Rio Branco**

Rio Brilhante (town, western Brazil) : 1944–1948 *Caiuás*; to 1943 *Entre Rios*

Rio Claro (city, southeastern Brazil) : formerly *São João Batista do Morro Azul*; originally *São João Batista da Beira do Ribeirão Claro*

Rio da Dúvida *see* ²**Roosevelt**

Rio das Flores (town, southeastern Brazil) : to 1943 *Santa Teresa*

Rio do Sul (city, southern Brazil) : formerly *Itajahy do Sul*; earlier *Bela Aliança*

Rio Grande (city, southern Brazil) : originally *São Pedro do Rio Grande do Sul*

Riom (town, central France) : Roman *Ricomagus*

Río Martín *see* **Martil**

Río Muni *see* ²**Mbini**

Rioni (river, western Georgia) : ancient Greek *Phasis*

Rio Novo *see* **Ipiaú**

Rio Pardo *see* (1) **Iúna**; (2) **Ribas do Rio Pardo**; (2) **Rio Pardo de Minas**

Rio Pardo de Minas (city, southeastern Brazil) : to 1944 *Rio Pardo*

Rio Pomba (town, southeastern Brazil) : to 1948 *Pomba*

Rio Prêto *see* **São José do Rio Prêto**

Río Seco *see* **Villa de María**

Rippin *see* **Rypin**

Ripton *see* **Shelton**

Risca (town, southeastern Wales) : Welsh *Rhisga*

Rishtan (town, eastern Uzbekistan) : *c.*1940–1977 Russian *Kuybyshevo*; 1937–*c.*1940 Russian *imeni Kuybysheva*

Risingham (historic locality, northeastern England) : Roman *Habitancum*

Ritlyab *see* **Sayasan**

Rivas (town, southwestern Nicaragua) : originally *Nicaragua*

River Forest (town, Illinois, north central United States) : to 1870 *Thatcher* (The town is now a residential suburb of Chicago.)

River Junction *see* **Chattahoochee**

River Plate *see* Plata, Rio de la

Riverside (city, California, southwestern United States) : originally *Jurupa*

Riverton (town, Wyoming, western United States) : originally *Wadsworth*

Rivet *see* Meftah

Rivière-du-Loup (town, Quebec, eastern Canada) : to 1919 *Fraserville*

Rivne (city, western Ukraine) : (Russian *Rovno*); 1919–1939 Polish *Równe*

Rivoli *see* Hasei Nameche

Riyadh (city, east central Saudi Arabia) : [Arabic *Ar Riyāḍ*]

Rizdvyans'ke *see* Syvas'ke

Roanne (town, east central France) : Roman *Rodumna*

Roanoke (city, Virginia, eastern United States) : to 1882 *Big Lick*

Roazhon *see* Rennes

Robber's Roost *see* Ellensburg

Robertson, Lake *see* Manyame, Lake

Robertstown (town, eastern Ireland) : Irish *Baile Riobaird*

Robinson Crusoe (island, eastern Juan Fernández, South Pacific) : formerly *Más a Tierra*

Robur *see* Basel

Roburnia *see* ²Amsterdam

Roçadas *see* Xangongo

Roch (village, southwestern Wales) : Welsh *Y Garn*

¹Rochester (city, southeastern England) : Roman *Durobrivae*

²Rochester (hamlet, northern England) : Roman *Bremenium*

³Rochester (city, New York, northeastern United States) : to 1822 *Rochesterville*

Rochesterville *see* ³Rochester

Rockefeller *see* Mundelein

Rockford (city, Illinois, north central United States) : originally *Midway*

Rock Island (city, Illinois, north central United States) : to 1841 *Stephenson*

Rockland (town, Maine, northeastern United States) : to 1850 *East Thomaston*

Rockport *see* ²Lakewood

Rock Springs (village, Wisconsin, northern United States) : to 1947 *Ableman*

Rockville (city, Maryland, northeastern United States) : to 1801 *Williamsburg*; originally *Montgomery Court House*

Rockwood (village, Ontario, southeastern Canada) : to c.1848 *Brotherstown*

Rodez (town, southern France) : Roman *Segodunum*

Rodi *see* Rhodes

Rodos *see* Rhodes

Rodosto *see* Tekirdağ

Rodumna *see* Roanne

Roeselare (town, western Belgium) : French *Roulers*

Rofreit *see* Rovereto

Rogaška Slatina (town, eastern Slovenia) : to 1918 German *Rohitsch-Sauerbrunn*

Rogatin *see* Rohatyn

Roger Simpson Island *see* Abemama

Rogerstone (village, southeastern Wales) : Welsh *Tŷ-du* (The village is now an industrial suburb of Newport.)

Rogervik *see* Paldiski

Rogozha *see* Noginsk

Rohatyn (town, western Ukraine) : (Russian *Rogatin*); to 1939 Polish *Rohatyn*

Rohe Potae *see* King Country

Rohitsch-Sauerbrunn *see* Rogaška Slatina

Rokiškis (town, northeastern Lithuania) : to 1918 Russian *Rakishki*

Rokitzan *see* Rokycany

Rokycany (town, west central Czech Republic) : to 1918, 1939–1945 German *Rokitzan*

Rolândia (city, southern Brazil) : 1944–1948 *Caviúna*

Roma *see* ¹Rome

Romania (republic, southeastern Europe) : [Romanian *România*]; formerly English *Roumania* or *Rumania*

România *see* Romania

Romanov *see* ²Dzerzhyns'k

Romanov-Borisoglebsk *see* Tutayev

Romanovka *see* Basarabeasca

Romanov-na-Murmane *see* Murmansk

Romanovsky Khutor *see* ¹Kropotkin

¹Rome (city, western Italy) : [Italian *Roma*]; Roman *Roma*

²Rome (city, New York, northeastern United States) : to 1819 *Lynchville*

Römerbad *see* Rimske Toplice

Römerstadt *see* Rýmařov

Romit (village, western Tajikistan) : to c.1935 *Uramir*

Rommani (town, northwestern Morocco) : formerly French *Marchand*

Roncesvalles (village, northern Spain) : alternate French *Roncevaux*

Roncevaux *see* Roncesvalles

Rondeau *see* ²Blenheim

¹Rondônia (state, western Brazil) : to 1956 *Guaporé*

²Rondônia (town, western Brazil) : formerly *Presidente Penna*

Ronne Ice Shelf (northwestern Antarctica) : formerly *Edith Ronne Land*

Ronse (town, west central Belgium) : French *Renaix*

¹Roosevelt (village, New Jersey, northeastern United States) : formerly *Jersey Homesteads*

²Roosevelt (river, northwestern Brazil) : to 1914 *Rio da Dúvida*

Roosevelt Island (New York, northeastern United States) : 1921–1973 *Welfare Island*; to 1921 *Blackwell's Island*

Rooseveltown (village, New York, northeastern United States) : to 1934 *Nyando*

Roraima (state, northern Brazil) : to 1962 *Rio Branco*

Rosário *see* (1) **Rosário do Catete**; (2) **Rosário do Sul**

Rosário do Catete (town, northeastern Brazil) : to 1944 *Rosário*

Rosário do Sul (city, southern Brazil) : to 1944 *Rosário*

Rosarno (town, southern Italy) : ancient Greek *Medma*

Roscianum *see* **Rossano**

Ros Comáin *see* **Roscommon**

Roscommon (town, north central Ireland) : Irish *Ros Comáin*

Ros Cré *see* **Roscrea**

Roscrea (town, central Ireland) : Irish *Ros Cré*

Roseau *see* **Dominion City**

Roseburg (town, Oregon, northwestern United States) : originally *Deer Creek*

Rose Hill *see* **Parramatta**

Rosenau *see* **Rožňava**

Rosenberg *see* (1) **Olesno**; (2) **Ružomberok**; (3) **Susz**

Rosetta *see* **Rashīd**

Roshchino (town, western Russia) : to 1948 Finnish *Raivola* (The town passed from Finland to the USSR in 1940 but retained its Finnish name until 1948.)

Rositten *see* **Rēzekne**

Rossano (town, southern Italy) : Roman *Roscianum*

Rossbach *see* ²**Hranice**

Rossborough *see* **Owensboro**

Rössel *see* **Reszel**

Rossett (village, northeastern Wales) : Welsh *Yr Orsedd*

Rossiten *see* **Rybachy**

Rossiya *see* **Russia**

Rossiyeny *see* **Raseiniai**

Rossland (town, British Columbia, southwestern Canada) : to 1894 *Thompson*

Rossony *see* **Rasony**

Ross's Landing *see* **Chattanooga**

Rostovtsevo *see* **Bulung'ur**

Rota (island, southern Northern Mariana Islands) : formerly *Sarpan*

Rot-Front *see* **Dobropillya**

Rotherhithe (district of London, southeastern England) : formerly *Redriff*

Rotomagus *see* **Rouen**

Rottweil (city, southwestern Germany) : Roman *Arae Flaviae* (The rottweiler dog, named for the city, descended from the cattle dog left by the Roman legions here.)

Rotuma (island, northern Fiji) : formerly *Grenville Island*

Roudnice nad Labem (town, northwestern Czech Republic) : to 1918, 1939–1945 German *Raudnitz an der Elbe*

Rouen (city, northern France) : Roman *Rotomagus*

Roulers *see* **Roeselare**

Roumania *see* **Romania**

Rovereto (town, northern Italy) : to 1919 German *Rofreit*

Rovigno *see* **Rovinj**

Rovinj (town, western Croatia) : to 1945 Italian *Rovigno*

Rovno *see* **Rivne**

Rovnoye (town, southwestern Russia) : to 1941 *Zelman* (The town's earlier German name is due to its location in the former Volga German Autonomous Soviet Socialist Republic.)

Równe *see* **Rivne**

Roxas (city, central Philippines) : formerly *Capiz*

Roycroft *see* **Rycroft**

Różana *see* **Ruzhany**

Rozdol'ne (town, southern Ukraine) : (Russian *Razdol'noye*); to 1944 *Ak-Sheikh*

Rozenberg *see* **Rozivka**

Rozhdestvenskoye *see* (1) **Dzerzhinskoye**; (2) **Syvans'ke**

Rozino (village, central Bulgaria) : 1934–1951 *Bozhidar*; to 1934 Turkish *Rakhmanlare*

Rozivka (town, southeastern Ukraine) : (Russian *Rozovka*); c.1935–1941 *Lyuksemburg*; to c.1935 *Rozenberg* (The town was founded by German colonists as *Rosenberg*, a name that later fortuitously adapted well to that of the German socialist agitator Rosa Luxemburg.)

Rožňava (town, southern Slovakia) : to 1918, 1938–1945 Hungarian *Rozsnyó*; to 1867 German *Rosenau*

Rozovka *see* **Rozivka**

Rózsahegy *see* **Ružomberok**

Rozsnyó *see* **Rožňava**

Ruabon (town, northeastern Wales) : Welsh *Rhiwabon*

Ruanda *see* **Rwanda**

Rubezhnaya *see* **Rubizhne**

Rubezhnoye *see* **Rubizhne**

Rubizhna *see* **Rubizhne**

Rubizhne (city, eastern Ukraine) : (Russian *Rubezhnoye*) : 1930–*c*.1940 *Rubizhna* (Russian *Rubezhnaya*); 1923–1930 *Chervonyy Prapor* (Russian *Krasnoye Znamya*); to 1930 *Rus'ko-Kraska* (Russian *Russko-Kraska*)

Rückers *see* **Szczytna**

Ruda Śląska (town, southern Poland) : alternate *Nowy Bytom*; to 1945 German *Morgenroth*

Rudki *see* **Rudky**

Rudky (town, western Ukraine) : (Russian *Rudki*); to 1939 Polish *Rudki*

Rudnaya Pristan' (town, eastern Russia) : to 1972 *Tetyukhe-Pristan'* (The town, on the Sea of Japan, should not be confused with the identically named place further down the coast.)

Rudnichny (town, west central Russia) : to 1933 *Auerbakhovsky Rudnik*

Rudnik imeni Karla Libknekhta *see* **Soledar**

Rudnik imeni Shvartsa *see* **Zhovti Vody**

Rudnik-Ingichka *see* **Ingichka**

Rudny (town, eastern Russia) : to 1972 *Lifudzin*

Rudnyk imeny Karla Libknekhta *see* **Soledar**

Rudnyk imeny Shvartsa *see* **Zhovti Vody**

Rudolf, Lake *see* **Turkana, Lake**

Rudolfswerth *see* **Novo Mesto**

Rügenwalde *see* **Darłowo**

Rukhlovo *see* **Skovorodino**

Rum (island, western Scotland) : 1888–1957 popularly *Rhum*

Rumania *see* **Romania**

Rumburg *see* **Rumburk**

Rumburk (town, northern Czech Republic) : to 1918, 1938–1945 German *Rumburg*

Rummelsburg *see* **Miastko**

Rumney (village, southeastern Wales) : Welsh *Tredelerch* (The village is now a district of the city of Cardiff.)

Rumney Marsh *see* **Revere**

Rumyantseva *see* **Vladimira Il'icha Lenina, imeni**

Rupella *see* **La Rochelle**

Rusçuk *see* **Ruse**

Ruse (city, northeastern Bulgaria) : to 1878 Turkish *Rusçuk*

Ruše (town, northeastern Slovenia) : to 1918 German *Maria Rast*

Rushan *see* **Rushon**

Rushon (village, east central Tajikistan) : (Russian *Rushan*); to *c*.1935 *Kalay-Valmar*

Rus'ko-Kraska *see* **Rubizhne**

Rusovce (town, southwestern Slovakia) : to 1947 Hungarian *Oroszvár*; to 1867 German *Karlburg* (The town is now a district of Bratislava.)

Ruspina *see* **Monastir**

Russ Adir *see* **Melilla**

Russell (town, northeastern New Zealand) : originally *Okiato*

Russellville (town, Kentucky, east central United States) : to 1798 *Big Boiling Springs*

Russia (republic, eastern Europe/western Asia) : [Russian *Rossiya*]; 1922–1991 *Soviet Union* (The former name, in full *Union of Soviet Socialist Republics*, abbreviated *USSR*, was used not only for the territory of the present country, historically the *Russian Soviet Federated Socialist Republic*, abbreviated *RSFSR*, but for the larger republic that included present Armenia, Azerbaijan, Belarus, Estonia, Georgia, Kazakhstan, Kyrgyzstan, Latvia, Lithuania, Moldova, Tajikistan, Turkmenistan, Ukraine, and Uzbekistan. The name *Russia* was widely used during the Soviet period for each of these geographical entities.)

Russian America *see* **Alaska**

Russko-Kraska *see* **Rubizhne**

Rust *see* **El Cerrito**

Rutaka *see* **Aniva**

Rutek *see* **Vrútky**

Ruth (village, North Carolina, eastern United States) : to 1939 *Hampton*

Ruthenia *see* **Transcarpathian Oblast**

Rutherford (town, New Jersey, northeastern United States) : to 1875 *Boiling Springs*

Ruthin (town, northern Wales) : Welsh *Rhuthun*

Rutland Water (artificial lake, east central England) : to 1976 *Empingham Reservoir*

Ruttka *see* **Vrútky**

Rutupiae *see* **Richborough Port**

Ruwenzori National Park (southwestern Uganda) : formerly *Queen Elizabeth National Park*

Ruzhany (town, western Belarus) : to 1939 Polish *Różana*

Ružomberok (town, northern Slovakia) : to 1918 Hungarian *Rózsahegy*; to 1867 German *Rosenberg*

Rwanda (republic, east central Africa) : formerly usually *Ruanda*

Ryan, Loch (sea inlet, southwestern Scotland) : Roman *Rerigonius Sinus* (A Roman fort or camp *Rerigonium* was nearby, perhaps where the town of Stranraer now stands.)

Ryazan' (city, western Russia) : to 1778 *Pereyaslavl'-Ryazansky*

Rybachy (village, western Russia) : to 1945 German *Rossitten*

Rybach'ye *see* **Balykchy**

Rybinsk (city, western Russia) : 1984–1989 *Andropov*; 1957–1984 *Rybinsk*; 1946–1957 *Shcherbakov*

Rychnov nad Knežnou (town, northeastern Czech Republic) : to 1918, 1939–1945 German *Reichenau an der Knieschna*

Rychnov u Jablonce (village, northern Czech Republic) : to 1918, 1939–1945 German *Reichenau bei Gablonz*

Rycroft (village, Alberta, western Canada) : 1920–1933 *Roycroft*; to 1920 *Spirit River*

Rykovo *see* **Yenakiyeve**

Rýmařov (town, eastern Czech Republic) : to 1918, 1938–1945 German *Römerstadt*

Ryojun *see* **Lüshun**

Rypin (town, north central Poland) : 1940–1945 German *Rippin*

Ryswick *see* **Rijswijk**

Rzepin (town, western Poland) : to 1945 German *Reppen*

Rzeszów (city, southeastern Poland) : 1940–1945 German *Reichshof*

Saar an der Sazava *see* **Žd'ár nad Sázavou**

Saarbruck *see* **Saarbrücken**

Saarbrücken (city, western Germany) : 1793–1815 French *Sarrebruck* (A "compromise" English spelling *Saarbruck* was formerly often found. The river here rises in France as the *Sarre* then flows into Germany as the *Saar*.)

Saaremaa (island, western Estonia) : formerly Swedish and German *Ösel* (The island, originally in German hands, passed to Denmark in 1560, Sweden in 1645, and Russia in 1710, before becoming part of Estonia in 1917. All names mean basically "island.")

Saarlautern *see* **Saarlouis**

Saarlouis (city, southwestern Germany) : 1935–1945 German *Saarlautern* (The city, founded in France in 1680 but awarded to Prussia in 1815, was administered by France from 1919 to 1935 and from 1945 to 1957, after which it retained its French name.)

Saaz *see* **Žatec**

Sabaneta *see* **Santiago Rodríguez**

Sabah (state, eastern Malaysia) : to 1963 *North Borneo*

Sabaria *see* **Szombathely**

Sabinov (town, northeastern Slovakia) : to 1918 Hungarian *Kisszeben*

Sablino *see* ²**Ul'yanovka**

Sabra (town, northwestern Algeria) : to *c.*1962 French *Turenne*

Sabrina *see* **Severn**

Sachsen *see* **Saxony**

Sachs Harbour (village, Northwest Territories, northwestern Canada) : alternate Inuit *Ikaahuk*

Sächsisch-Bereg *see* **Berehove**

Sächsisch-Regen *see* **Reghin**

Saco (town, Maine, northeastern United States) : 1762–1805 *Pepperellboro;* 1718–1762 *Biddeford* (The name *Biddeford*, originally that of a single plantation either side of the Saco River, was retained by the city now so named when the two communities separated in 1762.)

Sacramento (city, California, western United States) : to 1848 *New Helvetia*

Sacramento *see* **Itatupã**

Sacred Way *see* **Via**

Sá da Bandeira *see* **Lubango**

Sadovo (town, south central Bulgaria) : formerly *Cheshnegir*

Sadovoye (village, southwestern Russia) : to 1944 *Kegulta*

Sądowa Wisznia *see* **Sudova Vyshnya**

Saepinum *see* **Altilia**

Saetabicula *see* **Alzira**

Şafãkis *see* **Sfax**

Šafárikovo *see* **Tornal'a**

Sagan *see* **Żagań**

Sagunto (town, eastern Spain) : to 1877 *Murviedro*; Roman *Saguntum* (The town's modern name is a deliberate revival of the Roman one.)

Saguntum *see* **Sagunto**

Sahiwal (city, east central Pakistan) : formerly *Montgomery*

Saida (city, southwestern Lebanon) : [Arabic *Şaydã*]; biblical *Sidon*

Saigon *see* **Ho Chi Minh City**

Sain Dunwyd *see* **St. Donats**

Sain Ffagan *see* **St. Fagans**

St. Albans (city, southeastern England) : Roman *Verulamium* (The Roman city stood on the west side of the present one, not where the cathedral now stands, as sometimes stated. Writing in A.D. 731, the Venerable Bede referred to the city by names which today would be spelled *Verulamchester* or *Watlingchester*. The Anglo-Saxons who gave the latter name also gave that of *Watling Street*, the Roman road from London to St. Albans.)

St.-André *see* **Sint-Andries**

St. Andrews *see* **Thamesford**

St.-Arnaud *see* **El Eulma**

St. Asaph (village, northern Wales) : Welsh *Llanelwy*

St. Athan (village, southern Wales) : Welsh *Sain Tathan*

Sain Tathan *see* **St. Athan**

St.-Bertrand-de-Comminges (village, southern France) : Roman *Lugdunum Convenarum*

St. Brides Major (village, southern Wales) : Welsh *Saint-y-brid* (*Major* refers to the status of the church, not the size of the village, which is half as big as **St. Brides Minor**.)

St. Brides Minor (town, southern Wales) : Welsh *Llansanffraid-ar-Ogwr*

St. Charles (city, Missouri, central United States) : 1771–1804 Spanish *San Carlos Borromeo*; to 1771 French *Les Petites Côtes*

St. Charles *see* **Denver**

St. Christopher and Nevis *see* **St. Kitts and Nevis**

St. Clair *see* **East Liverpool**

St.-Claude (town, eastern France) : Roman *Condate*

St. Clears (village, southwestern Wales) : Welsh *Sanclêr*

St.-Cloud *see* **Gdyel**

St. Croix (island, eastern West Indies) : to 1674 *Santa Cruz*

St.-Dalmas-de-Tende (village, southeastern France) : to 1947 Italian **San Dalmazzo di Tenda**

St. David's (city, southwestern Wales) : Welsh *Tyddewi*, Medieval Latin *Menevia*. (The community, a famous religious center with a cathedral, officially became a city in 1994.)

St. David's Head (peninsula, southwestern Wales) : Welsh *Penmaen Dewi*; Roman *Octapitarum Promontorium*

St.-Denis-du-Sig *see* **Sig**

St. Dogmaels (village, southwestern Wales) : Welsh *Llandudoch*

St.-Domingue *see* (1) **Haiti**; (2) **Hispaniola**; (3) **Santo Domingo**

St. Donats (village, southern Wales) : Welsh *Sain Dunwyd*

Ste.-Foy (city, Quebec, eastern Canada) : originally *Notre-Dame-de-Foy*

Sainte Genevieve (town, Missouri, central United States) : originally *Le Vieux Village*

Ste.-Marie *see* **Nosy Boraha**

Saintes (city, western France) : Roman *Mediolanum Santonum*

Ste.-Scholastique *see* **Mirabel**

St.-Eugène *see* **Bologhine**

St.-Évariste Station *see* **La Guadeloupe**

St. Fagans (village, southern Wales) : Welsh *Sain Ffagan*

St. Ferdinand *see* **Florissant**

St. Francis *see* **Helena**

St. Gall (town, northeastern Switzerland) : [French *St.-Gall*; German *Sankt-Gallen*; Italian *San Gallo*]

St.-Gall *see* **St. Gall**

St.-Gilles (town, central Belgium) : Flemish *Sint-Gillis* (The town is now a suburb of Brussels.)

St.-Gilles-lez-Termonde *see* **Sint-Gillis-bij-Dendermonde**

St.-Gilles-Waas *see* **Sint-Gillis-Waas**

St.-Jean d'Acre *see* **Acre**

St.-Jerôme (city, Quebec, southeastern Canada) : originally *Dumontville*

St. John's Island *see* **Prince Edward Island**

St. Joseph (town, north central United Sates) : to 1833 *Newburyport*; earlier *Saranac*; originally *Fort Miami*

St.-Joseph-d'Alma *see* **Alma**

St. Kitts and Nevis (island state, eastern West Indies) : alternate *St. Christopher and Nevis*

St. Leonard (city, Quebec, southeastern Canada) : to 1962 *St.-Léonard-de-Port-Maurice* (The city is now a suburb of Montreal.)

St.-Léonard-de-Port-Maurice *see* **St. Leonard**

St.-Louis *see* **Boufatis**

St. Mary's Mission *see* **Mission**

St. Michael's Town *see* ¹**Bridgetown**

St.-Moritz (town, eastern Switzerland) : German *Sankt Moritz*; locally (Romansh) *San Murezzan*

St.-Nicolas *see* **Sint-Niklaas**

St. Patrick's Plain *see* **Singleton**

St. Paul (city, Minnesota, northern United States) : to 1841 *Pig's Eye Landing*

St. Peter am Karst *see* **Pivka**

St. Peters *see* **Bathurst**

St. Petersburg (city, western Russia) : [Russian *Sankt-Peterburg*]; 1924–1991 *Leningrad*; 1914–1924 *Petrograd* (The name *Leningrad* is historically associated with the 900-day German siege of the city in World War II, when around a million persons lost their lives.)

St.-Pierre-de-la-Pointe-aux-Esquimaux *see* **Havre-St.-Pierre**

St.-Pierre-du-Lac *see* **Val-Brillant**

St.-Pierre-St.-Paul *see* **Ouled Moussa**

St.-Stanislas (village, Quebec, southeastern Canada) : to 1962 *Deux-Rivières*

St.-Sulpice *see* **La Salle**

St. Thomas (city, Ontario, southeastern Canada) : formerly *Sterling*; originally *Kettle Creek Village*

St. Thomas *see* **Charlotte Amalie**

St.-Trond *see* **Sint-Truiden**

Saint-y-brid *see* **St. Brides Major**

Sajókazinc *see* **Kazincbarcika**

Sakaehama *see* **Starodubskoye**

Sakakawea, Lake (North Dakota, northern United States) : formerly *Garrison Reservoir*

Sak'art'velo *see* **Georgia**

Sakarya (river, northwestern Turkey) : ancient Greek *Sangarius*

Sakha (republic, northeastern Russia) : to 1992 usually *Yakutia*

Sakhalin (island, eastern Russia) : formerly Japa-

nese *Karafuto* (Although the Japanese name
was sometimes applied to the whole island, it
properly denoted the part south of latitude
50°00′N, assigned to Japan in 1905 but transferred to the USSR in 1945.)

Şäki (city, northern Azerbaijan) : (Russian
Sheki); to 1968 *Nukha*

Šakiai (town, southwestern Lithuania) : (Russian
Shakyay); to 1918 Russian *Shaki*

Sakız *see* **Khíos**

Sakulka *see* **Sokółka**

Šal'a (city, southwestern Slovakia) : to 1918,
1930–1943 Hungarian *Vágsellye*

Salacgriva (town, northern Latvia) : to 1917 German *Salismünde*

Salamanca (city, western Spain) : Roman *Salmantica*

Salarian Way *see* **Via**

Salaspils (town, central Latvia) : to 1917 German
Kirchholm

Saldae *see* **Bejaïa**

Saldus (town, southwestern Latvia) : to 1918
German *Frauenburg*

Salé (city, northwestern Morocco) : formerly English *Sallee*

Salekhard (city, northern Russia) : to 1933 *Obdorsk*

Salem *see* (1) **Bardstown**; (2) **Jerusalem**

Salem Bridge *see* **Naugatuck**

Salem Village *see* **Danvers**

Salerno (city, southern Italy) : Roman *Salernum*

Salernum *see* **Salerno**

Salihorsk (city, south central Belarus) : (Russian
Soligorsk); to 1959 *Novo-Starobinsk*

Salinae *see* (1) **Droitwich**; (2) **Middlewich**

Salinas *see* **Salinópolis**

Salinópolis (city, northern Brazil) : to 1944 *Salinas*

Salisburg *see* **Mazsalaca**

Salisburgum *see* **Salzburg**

Salisbury (city, southern England) : alternate
dated *Sarum* (The city's official name is *New
Sarum*, as against *Old Sarum*, the nearby site
of the Roman town of *Sorviodunum*, which
took its own name from the Iron Age hillfort
here. *Sarum* itself is not a Roman name, but
an abbreviation of an early form of the present
name with the Latin ending -*um*.)

Salisbury *see* **Harare**

Salismünde *see* **Salacgriva**

Salla (village, northeastern Finland) : to 1940
Kursu (In 1940 the original village of Salla,
30 miles to the northeast, was transferred
to the USSR and renamed **Kuolayarvi**. The
population was then evacuated to this new
site.)

Salla *see* **Kuolayarvi**

Sallee *see* **Salé**

Salliq *see* **Coral Harbour**

Salmantica *see* **Salamanca**

Salmas (town, northwestern Iran) : 1930–1980
Shahpur

Salonica *see* **Salonika**

Salonika (city, northwestern Greece) : [modern
Greek *Thessaloniki*]; alternate English *Salonica*;
Roman and biblical *Thessalonica*

Salonta (town, western Romania) : to 1918,
1940–1945 Hungarian *Nagyszalonta*

Salop *see* **Shropshire**

Sal'sk (town, southwestern Russia) : to 1926 *Torgovaya*

Salta (city, northwestern Argentina) : originally
San Felipe de Lerma

Saltash *see* **Plymouth**

Salt Lake City (city, Utah, west central United
States) : to 1868 *Great Salt Lake City*

Saltrou *see* **Belle-Anse**

Salt Sea *see* **Dead Sea**

Saluciae *see* **Saluzzo**

Saluzzo (town, northwestern Italy) : Roman
Saluciae

Salvador (city, eastern Brazil) : formerly *Bahia*
(The former name is still that of the state of
which the city is capital.)

Salvador *see* **El Salvador**

Salyuzi *see* ²**Kotelnikovo**

Salzburg (city, western Austria) : Roman *Salisburgum*

Salzburgen *see* **Château-Salins**

Salzgitter (city, north central Germany) : to 1951
Watenstedt-Salzgitter (The city was founded in
1942 on the amalgamation of 28 villages, one
of which was Watenstedt.)

Samanala *see* **Adam's Peak**

Samara (city, southwestern Russia) : 1935–1991
Kuybyshev

Samarkand (city, southeastern Uzbekistan) : ancient Greek *Marakanda*

Samarkandsky *see* **Temirtau**

Samarobriva *see* **Amiens**

Sambir (town, western Ukraine) : (Russian *Sambor*); to 1939 Polish *Sambor*

Sambor *see* **Sambir**

Şämkir (town, western Azerbaijan) : (Russian
Shamkhor); c.1928–1937 *Annenfeld*

Samoa (island monarchy, South Pacific) : to 1997
Western Samoa

Šamorin (town, southwestern Slovakia) : to 1918,
1938–1945 Hungarian *Somorja*

Samos (town, southeastern Greece) : formerly
Limìn Vathéos (The town, on the island of the
same name, had a name meaning "harbor of

Vathy," for a nearby port, itself known by the Turkish name of *Vatı* to 1912.)

Samsun (city, northern Turkey) : ancient Greek *Amisus*

Samter *see* **Szamotuły**

Samut Prakan (town, south central Thailand) : locally *Paknam*

Samut Songkhram (town, western Thailand) : locally *Meklong*

Şan'ā' *see* **Sanaa**

Sanaa (city, western Yemen) : [Arabic *Şan'ā'*]

San Ambrosio de Linares *see* **Linares**

San Angelo (city, Texas, southern United States) : formerly *Santa Angela*; originally *Over-the-River*

San Antonio, Mt. (California, southwestern United States) : formerly *Mt. Baldy*

San Antonio de Cortés (town, west central Honduras) : to early 1930s *Talpetate*

San Antonio de Padua de Guayama *see* **Guayama**

San Bartolo *see* **General Simón Bolívar**

San Bartolomé *see* **Venustiano Carranza**

San Beise *see* **Choybalsan**

San Bernardo de la Frontera de Tarija *see* **Tarija**

San Blas Islands (northeastern Panama) : formerly *Las Mulatas*

San Buenaventura *see* **Ventura**

San Candido (town, northern Italy) : to 1918 German *Innichen*

San Carlos *see* **Luba**

San Carlos de Puno *see* **Puno**

San Carlos Borromeo *see* **St. Charles**

Sanchursk (town, western Russia) : to 1918 *Tsaryovosanchursk*

Sanclêr *see* **St. Clears**

¹San Cristóbal (province, south central Dominican Republic) : to 1961 *Trujillo*

²San Cristobal (island, eastern Galápagos Islands, Ecuador) : formerly *Chatham Island*

San Cristóbal de las Casas (city, southeastern Mexico) : 1934–1948 *Ciudad de las Casas*; 1848–1934 *San Cristóbal de las Casas*; 1829–1848 *Ciudad de San Cristóbal*; 1536–1829 *Ciudad Real de Chiapa*; 1535–1536 *San Cristóbal de los Llanos*; originally *Villarreal de Chiapa de los Españoles*

San Cristóbal de los Llanos *see* **San Cristóbal de las Casas**

San Dalmazzo di Tenda *see* **St.-Dalmas-de-Tende**

Sandalwood Island *see* **Sumba**

San Daniele del Carso *see* **Štanjel na Krasu**

Sandanski (town, southwestern Bulgaria) : to 1949 *Sveti Vrach*

Sand Hill *see* **Kitchener**

Sandhills *see* **Deniliquin**

Sandhurst *see* **Bendigo**

San Diego (city, California, southwestern United States) : formerly *San Diego de Alcalá de Henares*; to 1602 *San Miguel*

San Diego de Alcalá de Henares *see* **San Diego**

Sandomierz (town, southeastern Poland) : to 1915 Russian *Sandomir*

Sandomir *see* **Sandomierz**

Sand Point *see* **Titusville**

Sandwich Island *see* **Éfaté**

Sandwich Islands *see* **Hawaii**

Sandwick (village, Western Isles, northwestern Scotland) : Gaelic *Sanndabhaig*

Sandy Lane (village, southern England) : Roman *Verlucio*

San Eugenio *see* **Artigas**

San Felipe de Lerma *see* **Salta**

San Felipe del Rio *see* **Del Rio**

¹San Fernando (city, eastern Argentina) : formerly *San Fernando de Buena Vista*; to 1806 *Nuestra Señora del Puerto de las Conchas* (The city is now part of Greater Buenos Aires.)

²San Fernando (city, southwestern Spain) : to 1813 *Isla de León*

San Fernando de Buena Vista *see* **San Fernando**

San Fernando del Rio Negro *see* **Resistencia**

San Francisco (city, California, western United States) : to 1847 *Yerba Buena*

San Francisco de Quibdó *see* **Quibdó**

San Francisco Gotera (town, eastern El Salvador) : to 1887 *Gotera*

San Fructuoso *see* **Tacuarembó**

San Gabriel *see* **Ciudad Venustiano Carranza**

San Gallo *see* **St. Gall**

Sangarius *see* **Sakarya**

San Germán (town, western Puerto Rico) : to 1570 *Nueva Villa de Salamanca* (The present name was assumed from an earlier settlement in a different location.)

San Germano *see* **Cassino**

San Giorgio *see* **Giurgiu**

San Giovanni di Medua *see* **Shëngjin**

San Giuliano Terme (town, central Italy) : to 1935 *Bagni San Giuliano*; Roman *Aquae Calidae Pisanorum*

Sango (village, southeastern Zimbabwe) : formerly Portuguese *Vila Salazar*

Sangorodok *see* **Ust'-Vorkuta**

San Ignacio (town, western Belize) : formerly *Cayo*

San Ildefonso (town, central Spain) : alternate *La Granja*

Sanirajak *see* Hall Beach

San Isidro (city, eastern Argentina) : to 1816 *Costa de Monte Grande* (The city is now a district of Greater Buenos Aires.)

San Javier de Bella Isla *see* Linares

San Jerónimo de Buenavista *see* Montería

San Jerónimo Ixtepec *see* Ciudad Ixtepec

San Jose (city, California, western United States) : originally *Pueblo de San José de Guadalupe*

San José (city, central Costa Rica) : originally *Villa Nueva*

San José de Buena Vista de Curicó *see* Curicó

San José de Cúcuta *see* Cúcuta

San José de Guasimal *see* Cúcuta

San Jose de la Isla *see* Genaro Codina

San José de los Amoles *see* Cortazar

¹San Juan (province, west central Dominican Republic) : to 1961 *Benefactor* (The present province is smaller in area than the original.)

²San Juan (city, northern Puerto Rico) : originally *Puerto Rico* (The city's original name, Spanish for "rich port," gave that of **Puerto Rico**, the state of which it is now the capital, while the island's original name passed to that of the city.)

³San Juan (city, west central Argentina) : originally *San Juan de la Frontera*

San Juan *see* Puerto Rico

San Juan Bautista *see* Villahermosa

San Juan de la Frontera *see* ³San Juan

San Juan de la Frontera de los Chachapoyas *see* Chachapoyas

San Juan de los Esteros *see* Matamoros

San Juan de Vera de las Siete Corrientes *see* Corrientes

Sankt Gallen *see* St. Gall

Sankt Gotthard *see* Szentgotthárd

Sankt Ilgen *see* Šentilj

Sankt Joachimsthal *see* Jáchymov

Sankt Michel *see* Mikkeli

Sankt-Mikhel *see* Mikkeli

Sankt Moritz *see* St.-Moritz

Sankt-Peterburg *see* St. Petersburg

Şanlıurfa (city, southeastern Turkey) : formerly *Urfa*; to 1637 *Edessa*

San Martin Land *see* Antarctic Peninsula

San Miguel *see* (1) Diez y Ocho de Julio; (2) San Diego

San Murrezan *see* St.-Moritz

Sanndabhaig *see* Sandwich

San Nicolás de Buenos Aires (town, central Mexico) : to 1941 *Malpaís*

San Paolo di Civitate (village, south central Italy) : Roman *Teanum Apulum*

San Pablo del Monte *see* Vicente Guerrero

San Pedro Remate *see* Bella Vista

San Pietro del Carso *see* Pivka

San Rafael *see* La Estrelleta

¹San Salvador (island, eastern Bahamas, West Indies) : formerly *Watling Island* (When Columbus landed on the island in 1492 he recorded its native name as *Guanahani*.)

²San Salvador (island, central Galápagos, Ecuador) : alternate *Santiago* or *James Island*

San Salvador *see* El Salvador

San Severa (village, western Italy) : ancient Greek *Pyrgi*

San Stefano *see* Yeşilköy

Santa Angela *see* San Angelo

Santa Ana de Coriana *see* Coro

Santa Apollonia *see* Réunion

Santa Bárbara *see* Santa Bárbara d'Oeste

Santa Bárbara d'Oeste (city, southeastern Brazil) : to 1944 *Santa Bárbara*

Santa Barbara Islands (California, southwestern United States) : alternate *Channel Islands*

Santa Catalina del Saltadero del Guaso *see* Guantánamo

Santa Cruz (island, central Galápagos Islands, Ecuador) : formerly *Indefatigable Island*

Santa Cruz *see* (1) Aracruz; (2) Corumbalina; (3) Reriutaba; (4) St. Croix; (5) Santa Cruz do Sul

Santa Cruz das Palmeiras (town, southeastern Brazil) : to 1944 *Palmeiras*

Santa Cruz de Bravo *see* Felipe Carrillo Puerto

Santa Cruz de Galeana *see* Juventino Rosas

Santa Cruz do Sul (city, southern Brazil) : to 1944 *Santa Cruz*

Santa Fe (city, New Mexico, southwestern United States) : originally *Villa Real de la Santa Fé de San Francisco de Asis*

Santa Fé de Bacatá *see* Bogotá

Santa Isabel *see* (1) General Trías; (2) Malabo

Santa Luiza de Mossoró *see* Mossoró

Santa Luzia *see* Luziânia

Santa María (island, southern Galápagos, Ecuador) : alternate *Charles Island*

Santa María Asunción Tlaxiaco *see* Tlaxiaco

Santa María del Puerto del Príncipe *see* Camagüey

Santa Maria di Capua Vetere (village, southern Italy) : Roman *Capua* (The Roman city, whose modern name means "St. Mary of Old Capua," gave the name of nearby **Capua**.)

Santa Marinella (town, western Italy) : Roman *Castrum Novum*

Santa Maura *see* Levkás

Santana *see* Uruaçu

Santana do Paranaíba *see* Paranaíba

Santander *see* Cantabria

[1]Santarém (city, central Portugal) : Roman *Praesidium Julium*; earlier Roman *Scalabis*

[2]Santarém (city, northern Brazil) : originally *Tapajós*

Santarém *see* Ituberá

Santa Rita do Araguaia *see* Guiratinga

Santa Rita do Paranaíba *see* Itumbiara

Santa Rosa *see* (1) Bella Unión; (2) Ciudad Mendoza; (3) Santa Rosa do Viterbo

Santa Rosa de Copán (city, northwestern Honduras) : 1812–1869 *Los Llanos de Santa Rosa*; to 1812 *Los Llanos*

Santa Rosa do Viterbo (town, southeastern Brazil) : 1944–1948 *Icaturama*; to 1944 *Santa Rosa*

Santa Teresa *see* Rio das Flores

Santa Ursula y las Once Mil Virgines *see* Virgin Islands

Santhoeck *see* New Castle

[1]Santiago (city, central Chile) : originally *Santiago del Nuevo Extremo*

[2]Santiago (city, southern Brazil) : to 1938 *Santiago do Boqueirão*

Santiago *see* (1) [2]San Salvador; (2) Santiago de los Caballeros

Santiago de Guayaquil *see* Guayaquil

Santiago del Nuevo Extremo *see* [1]Santiago

Santiago de los Caballeros (city, northern Dominican Republic) : to 1504 *Santiago*

Santiago de los Valles de Moyobamba *see* Moyobamba

Santiago do Boqueirão *see* [2]Santiago

Santiago Rodríguez (town, northwestern Dominican Republic) : to 1936 *Sabaneta*

Santiponce (town, southwestern Spain) : Roman *Italica*

Santi Quaranta *see* Sarandë

Santiváñez (town, central Bolivia) : to 1900s *Caraza*

Santo *see* Kim

Santo Amaro *see* (1) General Câmara; (2) Santo Amaro da Imperatriz; (3) Santo Amaro das Brotas

Santo Amaro da Imperatriz (town, southern Brazil) : 1944–1948 *Cambirela*; to 1944 *Santo Amaro*

Santo Amaro das Brotas (town, northeastern Brazil) : to 1944 *Santo Amaro*

[1]Santo Antônio (town, northeastern Brazil) : 1944–1948 *Padre Miguelinho*

[2]Santo Antônio (city, southern Brazil) : to 1938 *Santo Antônio da Patrulha*

Santo Antônio *see* Santo Antônio do Leverger

Santo Antônio da Cachoeira *see* Itaguatins

Santo Antônio da Patrulha *see* [2]Santo Antônio

Santo Antônio de Balsas *see* Balsas

Santo Antônio de Piracicaba *see* Piracicaba

Santo Antônio do Campestre *see* Lins

Santo Antônio do Jaguari *see* São João da Boa Vista

Santo Antônio do Leverger (town, western Brazil) : 1944–1948 *Leverger*; 1939–1943 *Santo Antônio*; to 1939 *Santo Antônio do Rio Abaixo*

Santo Antônio do Rio Abaixo *see* Santo Antônio do Leverger

Santo Domingo (city, southern Dominican Republic) : 1936–1961 *Ciudad Trujillo*; to 1502 *Nueva Isabela* (The original city, in an adjacent location, was destroyed by a hurricane. The French form of the city's name, *St.-Domingue*, was formerly applied both to Haiti and sometimes also to the entire island of Hispaniola of which the Dominican Republic now occupies the eastern two thirds.)

Santo Domingo *see* (1) Dominican Republic; (2) Hispaniola

San Tomás de la Nueva Guayana de la Angostura *see* Ciudad Bolívar

Santorini *see* Thera

Santos Apóstoles San Simón y Judas *see* Gila Bend

Santos Fumont (city, southeastern Brazil) : to 1930s *Palmyra*

Santo Tomé de Guayana *see* Ciudad Guayana

San Vincente de la Ciénaga *see* Silver City

São Benedito *see* (1) Beneditinos; (2) São Benedito do Rio Preto

São Benedito do Rio Preto (town, northeastern Brazil) : to 1944 *São Benedito*

São Bento *see* (1) São Bento do Sul; (2) São Bento do Una

São Bento do Sul (city, southern Brazil) : 1944–1948 *Serra Alta*; to 1944 *São Bento*

São Bento do Una (city, northeastern Brazil) : to 1944 *São Bento*

São Bernardo *see* São Bernardo do Campo

São Bernardo do Campo (city, southeastern Brazil) : formerly *Borda do Campo*; originally *São Bernardo*

São Carlos (city, southeastern Brazil) : formerly *São Carlos do Pinhal*

São Carlos do Pinhal *see* São Carlos

São Felipe *see* Içana

São Francisco *see* (1) Itapagé; (2) São Francisco do Conde; (3) São Francisco do Maranhão; (4) São Francisco do Sul

São Francisco de Paula *see* Pelotas

São Francisco do Conde (town, eastern Brazil) : to 1944 *São Francisco*

São Francisco do Maranhão (town, northeast-

ern Brazil) : 1944–1948 *Iguaratinga*; to 1944
São Francisco

São Francisco do Sul (city, southern Brazil) : to
1944 *São Francisco*

São Gonçalo *see* **São Gonçalo dos Campos**

São Gonçalo dos Campos (city, eastern Brazil) :
to 1944 *São Gonçalo*

São Gonçalo dos Campos *see* **Araripina**

São João Batista da Beira do Ribeirão Claro
see **Rio Claro**

São João Batista do Morro Azul *see* **Rio Claro**

São João da Boa Vista (city, southeastern Brazil)
: formerly *São João do Jaguari*; originally *Santo
Antônio do Jaguari*

São João da Bocâina *see* **Bocâina**

São João de Camaquã *see* **Camaquã**

São João de Montenegro *see* [2]**Montenegro**

São João do Jaguari *see* **São João da Boa Vista**

São João do Muqui *see* **Muqui**

São Joaquim *see* (1) **São Joaquim da Barra**;
(2) **São Joaquim do Monte**

São Joaquim da Barra (city, southeastern Brazil)
: to 1944 *São Joaquim*

São Joaquim do Monte (town, northeastern
Brazil) : 1944–1948 *Camaratuba*; to 1944 *São
Joaquim*

São Jorge da Mina *see* **Elmina**

São José da Lagoa *see* **Nova Era**

São José das Aldeias Altas *see* **Caxias**

São José do Campestre (town, northeastern
Brazil) : to 1944 *Campestre*

São José do Rio Negrinho *see* **Manaus**

São José do Rio Prêto (city, southeastern Brazil)
: to 1944 *Rio Prêto*

São José dos Campos (city, southeastern Brazil)
: formerly *Vila de São José do Paraíba*; earlier
Vila de São José do Sul; originally *Vila Nova de
São José*

São José dos Cocais *see* **Nossa Senhora do
Livramento**

São José dos Matões *see* **Parnarama**

São José do Tocantins *see* **Niquelândia**

São Lourenço *see* (1) **São Lourenço da Mata**;
(2) **São Lourenço do Sul**

São Lourenço da Mata (city, northeastern
Brazil) : to 1944 *São Lourenço*

São Lourenço do Sul (city, southern Brazil) : to
1944 *São Lourenço*

São Luís (city, northeastern Brazil) : formerly
São Luiz do Maranhão

São Luiz de Cáceres *see* **Cáceres**

São Luiz do Maranhão *see* **São Luís**

São Manuel *see* **Eugenópolis**

São Manuel do Mutum *see* **Mutum**

São Mateus *see* (1) **Jucás**; (2) **São Mateus do
Sul**

São Mateus do Sul (city, southern Brazil) : to
1943 *São Mateus*

São Miguel *see* **São Miguel das Matas**

São Miguel das Matas (town, eastern Brazil) : to
1944 *São Miguel*

São Paulo *see* **Frei Paulo**

São Paulo de Luanda *see* **Luanda**

São Pedro *see* **São Pedro do Sul**

São Pedro do Cariry *see* **Caririaçu**

São Pedro do Rio Grande do Sul *see* **Rio
Grande**

São Pedro do Sul (town, southern Brazil) : to
1944 *São Pedro*

São Roque *see* **São Roque do Paraguaçu**

São Roque do Paraguaçu (town, eastern Brazil)
: to 1944 *São Roque*

São Salvador do Congo *see* **Mbanza-Congo**

São Sebastião *see* **São Sebastião do Passé**

São Sebastião da Grama (town, southeastern
Brazil) : to 1948 *Grama*

São Sebastião do Passé (city, eastern Brazil) : to
1944 *São Sebastião*

São Sebastião do Ribeirão Prêto *see* **Ribeirão
Prêto**

São Vicente *see* (1) **Araguatins**; (2) **General
Vargas**

Sapé *see* **Sapeaçu**

Sapeaçu (town, eastern Brazil) : to 1944 *Sapé*

Sapronovo *see* [6]**Oktyabr'sky**

Sarabuz *see* [1]**Hvardiys'ke**

Sarafand *see* **Tsrifin**

Saragossa (city, northeastern Spain) : [Spanish
Zaragoza]; Roman *Caesaraugusta*

Sarajevo (city, southeastern Bosnia-Herzegovina)
: to 1878 Turkish *Bosna-Saray*

Sarana (town, western Russia) : to 1933 *Nizhnesaraninsky*

Saranac *see* **St. Joseph**

Saranbey *see* **Septemvri**

Sarandë (town, southern Albania) : 1940–1943
Italian *Porto Edda*; 1939–1940 Italian *Santi Quaranta*; 1919–1921 modern Greek *Hagioi Saranta*

Saranŭovo *see* **Septemvri**

Saratovskaya Manufaktura *see* **Krasny Tekstil'shchik**

Saray-Komar *see* **Panj**

Sarbinowo (village, western Poland) : to 1945
German *Zorndorf*

Sardarabad *see* **Armavir**

Sardarova Karakhana, imeni *see* **Lenin**

Sardegna *see* **Sardinia**

Sardinia (island, western Mediterranean) : [Ital-
ian *Sardegna*]

Sarepta *see* (1) [3]**Krasnoarmeysk**; (2) **Tsrifin**

Sarh (city, southern Chad) : formerly French
Fort-Archambault

Sark *see* **Jersey**

Sarnia (city, Ontario, southeastern Canada) : to 1836 *Port Sarnia*; originally *The Rapids* (The city is now officially *Sarnia-Clearwater*.)

Sarnia *see* **Guernsey**

Sarpan *see* **Rota**

Sarrebruck *see* **Saarbrücken**

Sarışaban *see* **Khrisoupolis**

Şarköy *see* **Pirot**

Sars (town, western Russia) : to 1939 *Sarsinsky Zavod*

Sarsinsky Zavod *see* **Sars**

Sartana (town, southeastern Ukraine) : 1946– 1992 *Prymors'ke* (Russian *Primorskoye*)

Sarum *see* **Salisbury**

Şärur (town, southwestern Azerbaijan) : 1964– 1990 Russian *Il'ichyovsk*; to 1964 *Norashen*

Saryar *see* **Khadzhi-Dimitrovo**

Sarykemer (village, southeastern Kazakhstan) : formerly Russian *Mikhaylovka*

Sarykol' (town, northern Kazakhstan) : formerly Russian *Uritsky*; earlier *Uritskoye*; to 1923 Russian *Vsekhsvyatskoye*

Sassmacken *see* **Valdemārpils**

Sátoraljaújhely *see* **Slovenské Nové Mesto**

Satpayev (town, central Kazakhstan) : formerly Russian *Nikol'sky*

Satu Mare (city, northwestern Romania) : to 1867, 1940–1944 Hungarian *Szatmárnémeti*

Sauce *see* **Juan Lacaze**

Sauce del Yí (town, south central Uruguay) : to 1924 Spanish *Pueblo de la Capilla*

Saudakent (village, southern Kazakhstan) : formerly *Baykadam*

Saúde *see* **Perdigão**

Saudi Arabia (kingdom, southwestern Asia) : [Arabic *Al 'Arabīyah as-Sa'ūdīyah*]

Saugeen *see* **Southampton**

Saugus *see* **Lynn**

Saujbulagh *see* **Mahabad**

Saumalkol' (town, northern Kazakhstan) : formerly Russian *Volodarskoye*

Saurimo (town, northeastern Angola) : formerly Portuguese *Vila Henrique de Carvalho*

Saverne (town, northeastern France) : Roman *Tres Tabernae*

Savoie *see* **Savoy**

Savoy (region, southeastern France) : [French *Savoie*]

Saxony (region, southeastern Germany) : [German *Sachsen*]

Sayanogorsk (city, southern Russia) : to 1975 *Oznachennoye*

Sayasan (village, southwestern Russia) : 1944– c.1957 *Ritlyab*

Saybrook *see* **Deep River**

Saybusch *see* **Żywiec**

Şaydā' *see* **Saida**

Sazanovka *see* **Anan'evo**

Sazonovo (town, western Russia) : to 1947 *Belyye Kresty*

Sbeïtla (town, north central Tunisia) : Roman *Sufetula*

Scalabis *see* **¹Santarém**

Scaldis *see* **Scheldt**

Scamander *see* **²Menderes**

¹Scarborough (city, Ontario, southeastern Canada) : to 1793 *Glasgow* (The city is now a borough of Metropolitan Toronto.)

²Scarborough (town, southern Tobago, Trinidad and Tobago) : formerly *Port Louis*

Scardona *see* **Skradin**

Scarpanto *see* **Karpathos**

Schaarbeek *see* **Schaerbeek**

Schaerbeek (town, central Belgium) : Flemish *Schaarbeek* (The town is now an industrial suburb of Brussels.)

Schaffhausen (town, northern Switzerland) : French *Schaffhouse*; Italian *Sciaffusa*

Schaffhouse *see* **Schaffhausen**

Scharfenwiese *see* **Ostrołęka**

Scharnikau *see* **Czarnków**

Schässburg *see* **Sighişoara**

Schatzlar *see* **Žacléř**

Schefferville (village, Newfoundland and Labrador, eastern Canada) : to 1955 *Knob Lake*

Schelde *see* **Scheldt**

Scheldt (river, western Europe) : French *Escaut*; Flemish *Schelde*; Roman *Scaldis*

Schemnitz *see* **Banská Štiavnica**

Scherpenheuvel (town, east central Belgium) : French *Montaigu*

Schieratz *see* **Sieradz**

Schildberg *see* **Ostrzeszów**

Schippenbeil *see* **Sępolno Krajńskie**

Schirwindt *see* **Kutuzovo**

Schivelbein *see* **Świdwin**

Schlan *see* **Slaný**

Schlawa *see* **Sława**

Schlawe *see* **Sławno**

Schlesien *see* **Silesia**

Schlesiersee *see* **Sława**

Schlesisch-Schumbarg *see* **Havířov**

Schlettstadt *see* **Sélestat**

Schlichtingsheim *see* **Szlichtyngowa**

Schlochau *see* **Człuchów**

Schloppe *see* **Człopa**

Schlossbach *see* **Nevskoye**

Schlossberg *see* **Dobrovol'sk**

Schluckenau *see* **Šluknov**

Schlüsselburg *see* **Shlissel'burg**

Schmiedeberg *see* **Kowary**

Schmiegel *see* Śmigiel
Schneidemühl *see* Piła
Schömberg *see* Chełmsko Śląskie
Schönau *see* Świerzawa
Schönberg *see* Sulików
Schöneck *see* Skarszewy
Schönlanke *see* Trzcianka
Schönstein *see* Šoštanj
Schreckenstein *see* Střekov
Schreiberhau *see* Sklarska Poręba
Schrimm *see* Śrem
Schroda *see* Środa Wielkopolska
Schröttersburg *see* Płock
Schubin *see* Szubin
Schwaben *see* Swabia
Schwanenburg *see* Gulbene
Schwarzheide (town, eastern Germany) : to 1936
  Wendish *Zschornegosda* (The Wendish name,
  in modern form *Corny Hózd*, was translated
  into German in 1936 and the original village,
  which grew in the 1920s into a dormitory for
  workers at Lauchhammer and in the lignite
  mines near Senftenberg, was raised to town
  status in 1967.)
Schwarzwald *see* Black Forest
Schwarzwasser *see* Czarna Woda
Schweidnitz *see* Świdnica
Schweiz *see* Switzerland
Schwerin an der Warte *see* Skwierzyna
Schwetz *see* Świecie
Schwiebus *see* Świebodzin
Sciaffusa *see* Schaffhausen
Scilly Island *see* ²Manuae
Scilly Isles (southwestern England) : Roman
  Silina; ancient Greek *Cassiterides* (The form of
  the Roman name is conjectural, and an alter-
  nate form, *Silimnus*, recorded by Pliny, is al-
  most certainly corrupt. The Greek name,
  meaning "tin islands," from Greek *kassiteros*,
  "tin," is usually applied to the Scillies but may
  have had a more general reference to lands in
  western Europe where tin was mined.)
Ścinawa (town, southwestern Poland) : to 1945
  German *Steinau an der Oder*
Scitis *see* Skye
Scodra *see* Shkodër
Scone (town, New South Wales, southwestern
  Australia) : originally *Invermein*
Scoresbysund *see* Ittoqqortoormiit
Scotia *see* Scotland
Scotland (country, northern Great Britain) :
  Gaelic *Alba*; Medieval Latin *Scotia*; Roman
  Caledonia (The Gaelic name is related to *Al-
  bion* as an ancient name of Britain as a whole.
  The Roman name, also spelled *Calidonia*, ap-
  plied generally to Scotland north of a line

from the Firth of Forth in the east to the Firth
of Clyde in the west, although it was also
sometimes used for the whole of northern
Britain. The name is present today in the
Caledonian Canal, which extends diagonally
across northern Scotland from the Moray Firth
in the northeast to Loch Linnhe in the southwest, while traces of the classical name survive
in the town of *Dunkeld* and nearby castle *Ro-
hallion*, northwest of Perth, and the mountain
Schiehallion, near Kinloch Rannoch. *See also*
New Caledonia. The Medieval Latin name is
preserved in that of *Nova Scotia*, Canada.)
Scottish Borders (administrative region, south-
  eastern Scotland) : to 1996 *Borders*
Scott's Plains *see* ¹Peterborough
Scranton (city, Pennsylvania, northeastern
  United States) : 1850–1851 *Scrantonia*; 1845–
  1850 *Harrison*; to 1845 *Slocum Hollow*; earlier
  Unionville; originally *Deep Hollow*
Scrantonia *see* Scranton
Scratching River *see* Morris
Scugog Village *see* Port Perry
Scutari *see* (1) Shkodër; (2) Üsküdar
Scylacium *see* Squillace
Scythopolis *see* Bet She'an
Seabra *see* Tarauacá
Sea Mills (village, southwestern England) :
  Roman *Abona* (The Roman name is that of the
  Avon River here. Sea Mills is now a district of
  Bristol.)
Sea of : for names beginning thus, *see* the next
  word, as **Azov, Sea of**
Searcy (town, Arkansas, south central United
  States) : to 1835 *White Sulphur Springs*
Sebastea *see* Sivas
Sebastopol *see* Sevastopol'
Sebastopolis *see* Sokhumi
Sebenico *see* Šibenik
Sebeş (town, central Romania) : to 1918 Hungar-
  ian *Szászsebes*; to 1867 German *Mühlbach*
Sechenovo (village, western Russia) : to 1945
  Tyoply Stan
Seckenburg *see* Zapovednoye
Second Crossing *see* Revelstoke
Sedalia (town, Missouri, central United States) :
  originally *Sedville*
Sedlčany (town, west central Czech Republic) :
  to 1918, 1939–1945 German *Seltschan*
Sedlets *see* Siedlce
Sedovo *see* Syedove
Sedunum *see* Sion
Sedville *see* Sedalia
Seeburg *see* Jeziorany
Seelowitz *see* Židlochovice
Segaon *see* Sevagram

Segeberg *see* **Bad Segeberg**
Segedunum *see* **Wallsend**
Segelocum *see* **Littleborough**
Segesvár *see* **Sighişoara**
Segewold *see* **Sigulda**
Segni (town, western Italy) : Roman *Signia*
Segodunum *see* **Rodez**
Segontium *see* **Caernarfon**
Segovia *see* **Coco**
Seguntia *see* **Sigüenza**
Seibersdorf *see* **Zebrzydowice Dolne**
Seidenberg *see* **Zawidów**
Seine (river, northern France) : Roman *Sequana*
Seine-Inférieure *see* **Seine-Maritime**
Seine-Maritime (department, northern France) :
    to 1955 *Seine-Inférieure*
Seis de Septiembre *see* **Morón**
Seitenberg *see* **Stronie Śląskie**
Seitler *see* **Nyzhn'ohirs'kyy**
Sejny (town, northeastern Poland) : to 1915 Rus-
    sian *Seyny*
Seldzhikovo *see* **Kaloyanovo**
Sélestat (town, northeastern France) : 1870–1918
    German *Schlettstadt*
Seleznevsky Rudnik *see* **Pereval's'k**
Seleznivs'kyy Rudnyk *see* **Pereval's'k**
Sellafield (village, northwestern England) : to
    1971 *Windscale* (Both names are associated
    with the nuclear power station and reprocess-
    ing plant here.)
Selma (town, Alabama, southeastern United
    States) : to *c.*1819 *Moore's Bluff*
Selmecbánya *see* **Banská Štiavnica**
Seltschan *see* **Sedlčany**
Selukwe *see* **Shurugwi**
Selvi *see* **Sevlievo**
Semey (city, northeastern Kazakhstan) : to 1991
    Semipalatinsk
Semibratovo (town, western Russia) : to 1948
    Isady
Semil *see* **Semily**
Semily (town, northern Czech Republic) : to
    1918, 1939–1945 German *Semil*
Semiozyornoye *see* **Auliyekol'**
Semipalatinsk *see* **Semey**
Sem' Kolodezey *see* **Lenine**
Semlin *see* **Zemun**
Semyonovka *see* **Arsenyev**
Semyonovskoye *see* (1) **Bereznik**; (2) **Ostrov-
    skoye**
Sena Gallica *see* **Senigallia**
Sena Julia *see* **Siena**
Senaki (town, western Georgia) : 1976–1991
    Tskhakaya; 1933–1976 *Mikha Tskhakaya*
Seneca *see* **West Seneca**
Senftenberg *see* **Žamberk**

Senhor do Bonfim (city, eastern Brazil) : to 1944
    Bonfim
Senica (city, western Slovakia) : to 1918 Hungar-
    ian *Szenic*
Senigallia (city, central Italy) : Roman *Sena Gal-
    lica*
Senir *see* **Hermon, Mt.**
Senj (town, western Croatia) : to 1918 German
    Zengg
Senneterre (town, Quebec, southeastern Can-
    ada) : to 1918 *Nottaway*
Sennybridge (village, south central Wales) :
    Welsh *Pontsenni*
Sens (town, north central France) : Roman
    Agedincum
Sensburg *see* **Mrągowo**
Senta (city, northern Serbia) : to 1918, 1941–1944
    Hungarian *Zenta*
Šentilj (village, northeastern Slovenia) : to 1918,
    1941–1945 German *Sankt Ilgen*
Sentosa (island, southern Singapore) : to 1970
    Blakang Mati
Sentyanivka *see* ²**Frunze**
Sentyanovka *see* ²**Frunze**
Sępólno Krajeńskie (town, northwestern
    Poland) : 1772–1919, 1939–1945 German *Zem-
    pelburg*
Sepopol (village, northeastern Poland) : to 1945
    German *Schippenbeil*
Sepsiszentgyörgy *see* **Sfîntu Gheorghe**
Septemvri (town, west central Bulgaria) : to 1950
    Saranŭovo; to 1878 Turkish *Saranbey*
Sept-Îles (city, Quebec, eastern Canada) : alter-
    nate English *Seven Islands*
Sequana *see* **Seine**
Seradz *see* **Sieradz**
Serafimovich (town, southwestern Russia) : to
    1933 *Ust'-Medveditskaya*
Serbia (republic, southeastern Europe) : [Serbian
    Srbija]; formerly English *Servia*
Serbs, Croats, and Slovenes, Kingdom of *see*
    Yugoslavia
Serdica *see* **Sofia**
Serdobol' *see* **Sortavala**
Serebryanyye Prudy (town, western Russia) : to
    *c.*1928 *Sergiyevy Prudy*
Sereda *see* **Furmanov**
Serendip *see* **Sri Lanka**
Seres *see* **Serres**
Sereth *see* **Siret**
Serfice *see* **Servia**
Sergiopol' *see* **Ayagoz**
Sergiyev *see* **Sergiyev Posad**
Sergiyev Posad (city, western Russia) : 1930–1991
    Zagorsk; 1919–1930 *Sergiyev*; to 1918 *Sergiyevsky
    Posad*

Sergiyevskoye *see* Plavsk
Sergiyevsky *see* Fakel
Sergiyevsky Posad *see* Sergiyev Posad
Sergiyevy Prudy *see* Serebryanyye Prudy
Sergo *see* Stakhanov
Serov (city, west central Russia) : 1938–1939
   Nadezhdinsk; 1935–1939 *Kabakovsk*;
   1934–1935 *Nadezhdinsk*; to 1934 *Nadezhdinsky
   Zavod*
Serpa Pinto *see* Menongue
Serpets *see* Sierpc
Serra Alta *see* São Bento do Sul
Serra Branca (town, eastern Brazil) : 1944–1948
   Itamorotinga
Serramazzoni (village, north central Italy) : to
   1948 *Monfestino in Serra Mazzoni*
Serra Negra *see* Serra Negra do Norte
Serra Negra do Norte (town, northeastern
   Brazil) : to 1944 *Serra Negra*
Serra Talhada (city, northeastern Brazil) : to
   1939 *Villa Bella*
Serravalle Libarna *see* Serravalle Scrivia
Serravalle Scrivia (village, northern Italy) : for-
   merly *Serravalle Libarna*
Serres (city, northeastern Greece) : to 1913 Turk-
   ish *Seres*
Serrinha *see* Juripiranga
Sertânia (city, northeastern Brazil) : to 1944 Por-
   tuguese *Alagoa de Baixo*
Sertãozinho *see* Major Isidoro
Servia (town, north central Greece) : to 1913
   Turkish *Serfice*
Servia *see* Serbia
Sesana *see* Sežana
Sessa Aurunca (town, central Italy) : Roman
   Suessa Aurunca
Sessions' Settlement *see* Bountiful
Sète (town, southern France) : to 1936 *Cette*
Seti *see* Mestia
Seto-naikai *see* Inland Sea
Sevagram (town, west central India) : to 1940
   Segaon
Sevan (town, central Armenia) : to *c*.1935 Rus-
   sian *Yelenovka*
Sevastopol' (city, southern Ukraine) : formerly
   English *Sebastopol* (The English name is his-
   torically associated with the siege of the town
   in 1854–55 during the Crimean War and with
   the Soviet stand against German forces here in
   1942 during World War II.)
Seven Islands *see* Sept-Îles
Seven Sisters (village, southern Wales) : Welsh
   Blaendulais
Severn (river, southern Wales/western England) :
   Welsh *Hafren*; Roman *Sabrina*
Severnaya Zemlya (archipelago, northern Rus-

sia) : occasional alternate English *North Land*;
   to 1926 Russian *Zemlya Imperatora Nikolaya II*
   (English *Nicholas II Land*)
Severnoye (village, western Russia) : formerly
   Sok-Karmala
Severn Sea *see* Bristol Channel
Severny Rudnik *see* Kirove
Severny Suchan *see* Uglekamensk
Severodonetsk *see* Syeverodonets'k
Severodvinsk (city, northwestern Russia) :
   1938–1957 *Molotovsk*; to 1938 *Sudostroy*
Severo-Kuril'sk (town, eastern Russia) :
   1905–1945 Japanese *Kashiwabara*
Severomorsk (city, northwestern Russia) : to
   1951 *Vayenga*
Severoural'sk (town, western Russia) : to 1944
   Petropavlovsky (The mining town arose in 1944
   on the union of Petropavlovsky with *Sever-
   oural'skiye Boksitovyye Rudniki*, "Northern
   Urals Bauxite Mines," taking its name from
   the latter.)
Seversk *see* Sivers'k
Sevilla *see* Seville
Seville (city, southwestern Spain) : [Spanish
   Sevilla]; Roman *Hispalis*
Sevlievo (town, northern Bulgaria) : to 1878
   Turkish *Selvi*
Sevluš *see* Vynohradiv
Sevlyush *see* Vynohradiv
Seydi (town, northeastern Turkmenistan) : for-
   merly Russian *Neftezavodsk*
Seymour (town, Connecticut, northeastern
   United States) : 1805–1850 *Humphreyville*;
   1735–1805 *Chusetown*; 1670–1735 *Rimmon*;
   originally *Naugatuck*
Seyny *see* Sejny
Sežana (town, southwestern Slovenia) : to 1947
   Italian *Sesana*
Sfax (city, eastern Tunisia) : [Arabic *Ṣafāqis*]
Sfîntu Gheorghe (city, central Romania) : to
   1918, 1940–1945 Hungarian *Sepsiszentgyörgy*
's-Gravenbrakel *see* Braine-le-Comte
's-Gravenhage *see* Hague, The
Shaanxi (province, east central China) : alternate
   Shensi (The first syllables of this name and that
   of the neighboring province of Shanxi sound
   identical in Chinese except in tone. Hence the
   arbitrary alteration of *a* to *e* in the alternate
   spelling and the doubling of *a* in the standard
   Pinyin transliteration.)
Shaarihan *see* Shahrihon
Shaba *see* Katanga
Shabalino *see* ¹Leninskoye
Shabani *see* Zvishavani
Shabbaz *see* Beruniy
Shade's Mills *see* Galt

Shafirkan *see* Shofirkon

Shāhābād *see* Eslāmābād-e Gharb

Shaḥḥāt (village, northeastern Libya) : ancient Greek and biblical *Cyrene*

Shahi *see* Gha'em Shahr

Shahjahanabad *see* Delhi

Shahpur *see* Salmas

Shahreza *see* Qomsheh

Shahrihon (town, eastern Uzbekistan) : (Russian *Shakhrikhan*); 1961–1970 Russian *Moskovsky*; *c.*1940–1961 Russian *Stalino*; 1937–*c.*1940 Russian *imeni Stalina*; to 1937 *Shaarikhan*

Shahsavar *see* Tonekabon

Shaidan (town, northern Tajikistan) : to 1945 *Asht*

Shakhimardan *see* Hamza

Shakhrikhan *see* Shahrihon

Shakhtars'k (town, eastern Ukraine) : (Russian *Shakhtyorsk*); 1945–1953 *Katyk* (The town was formed in 1953 on the merger of *Oleksiyeve-Orlivka* [Russian *Alekseyevo-Orlovka*], *Katyk* [to 1945 Russian *Zapadno-Gruppsky*], and *Olkhivchyk* [Russian *Ol'khovchik*].)

Shakhtars'ke *see* ¹Pershotravens'k

Shakhty (city, southwestern Russia) : to 1920 *Aleksandrovsk-Grushevsky*

Shakhty *see* Gusinoozersk

Shakhtyorsk (town, eastern Russia) : 1905–1945 Japanese *Toro*

Shakhtyorsk *see* Shakhtars'k

Shakhtyorskoye *see* ¹Pershotravens'k

Shaki *see* Šakiai

Shakotan *see* Malokurilskoye

Shakyay *see* Šakiai

Shali (town, southwestern Russia) : 1944–1957 *Mezhdurech'ye*

Shamkhor *see* Şämkir

Shamo *see* Gobi

Shamva (town, northeastern Zimbabwe) : formerly *Abercorn*

Shana *see* Kurilsk

Shangdu (town, northern China) : formerly poetic *Xanadu*

Shansi *see* Shanxi

Shanxi (province, east central China) : alternate *Shansi* (See the comments for **Shaanxi**.)

Sharapkino *see* Sverdlovs'k

Sharapkyne *see* Sverdlovs'k

Sharjah *see* Ash Shāriqah

Sharypovo (town, southern Russia) : 1985–1988 *Chernenko*

Shatilki *see* Svyetlahorsk

Shatura (city, western Russia) : to 1928 *Shaturtorf*

Shaturtorf *see* Shatura

Shaumiani (town, southern Georgia) : 1925–1936 *Shaumyan*; to 1925 *Shulaveri*

Shaumyan *see* Shaumiani

Shaumyanovsk *see* Goranboy

Shavgar *see* Turkestan

Shavli *see* Šiauliai

Shawnee (city, Kansas, central United States) : originally *Gum Springs*

Shaytansky Zavod *see* Pervoural'sk

Shcheglovsk *see* Kemerovo

Shcherbakov *see* Rybinsk

Shcherbinovka *see* ¹Dzerzhyns'k

Shcherbynivka *see* ²Dzerzhyns'k

Shchors (town, northern Ukraine) : to 1935 *Snovsk*

Shchorsk *see* Shorchs'k

Shchors'k (town, east central Ukraine) : (Russian *Shchorsk*); to 1939 *Bozhedarivka* (Russian *Bozhedarovka*)

Shchuchin *see* (1) Shchuchyn; (2) Szczuczyn

Shchuchinsk (city, northern Kazakhstan) : to 1939 Russian *Shchuch'ye*

Shchuch'ye *see* Shchuchinsk

Shchuchyn (town, western Belarus) : (Russian *Shchuchin*); 1919–1939 Polish *Szczuczyn Nowogródski*; to 1918 Russian *Shchuchin*

Shchuchyn *see* Szczuczyn

Shebunino (town, eastern Russia) : 1905–1945 Japanese *Minami-nayoshi*

Shechem *see* Nāblus

Sheen *see* ¹Richmond

Sheep Mountain *see* Coolidge, Mt.

Sheki *see* Şäki

Sheksna (town, western Russia) : formerly *Nikol'skoye*

¹Shelburne (town, Ontario, southeastern Canada) : to 1865 *Jelly's Corner*

²Shelburne (town, Nova Scotia, eastern Canada) : 1713–1783 *Port Roseway*; to 1713 *Port Razoir*

Shelekhovo (village, eastern Russia) : 1905–1945 Japanese *Kakumabetsu*

Shell Beach *see* Huntington Beach

Shelter Bay *see* Port-Cartier

Shelton (town, Connecticut, northeastern United States) : to 1789 *Ripton*

Shëngjin (town, northwestern Albania) : formerly Italian *San Giovanni di Medua*

Shensi *see* Shaanxi

Shenyang (city, northeastern China) : formerly Manchu *Mukden* (The Manchu name is associated with the 1931 "Mukden Incident," when the Japanese army used an explosion on the railroad near Shenyang as an excuse to occupy the city and the rest of Manchuria.)

Shepherdstown (town, West Virginia, east central United States) : to 1798 *Mecklenburg*

Sheppard's Fall *see* Almonte

Shepparton (town, Victoria, southeastern Australia) : 1853–1855 *Sheppartown*; to 1853 *Macguire's Punt.*

Sheppartown *see* **Shepparton**

's-Hertogenbosch (city, southern Netherlands) : commonly *Den Bosch*; 1794–1814 French *Bois-le-Duc*

Shetland (island group, northern Scotland) : alternate *Zetland*

Shevchenko (town, eastern Ukraine) : to 1921 *Lysa Hora* (Russian *Lysaya Gora*)

Shevchenko *see* **Aktau**

¹Shevchenkove (town, northeastern Ukraine) : (Russian *Shevchenkovo*); to 1922 *Bulatselivka* (Russian *Bulatselovka*)

²Shevchenkove (town, central Ukraine) : (Russian *Shevchenkovo*); to 1929 *Kyrylivka* (Russian *Kirillovka*)

Shevchenkove *see* **Dolyns'ka**

Shevchenkovo *see* (1) **Dolyns'ke**; (2) **¹,²Shevchenkove**

Shexian (city, eastern China) : to 1912 *Huicheng*

Shibboleth *see* **Mason City**

Shibetoro *see* **Slavnoye**

Shikhirdany *see* **¹Chkalovskoye**

Shikhrany *see* **Kanash**

Shikirlikitai *see* **Suvorove**

Shikuka *see* **Poronaysk**

Shilute *see* **Šilute**

Shimba *see* **Dachnoye**

Ship Harbour *see* **Port Hawkesbury**

Shiraura *see* **²Vzmor'ye**

Shirenewton (village, southeastern Wales) : Welsh *Drenewedd Gelli-farch*

Shiritoru *see* **Makarov**

Shirley City *see* **Woodburn**

Shirokolanovka *see* **Shyrokolanivka**

Shkodër (city, northwestern Albania) : formerly Italian *Scutari*; to 1913 Turkish *İşkodra*; Roman *Scodra*

Shlissel'burg (town, western Russia) : 1944–1991 *Petrokrepost'*; 1702–1944 German *Schlüsselburg*; 1612–1702 Swedish *Nöteborg*; to 1612 Russian *Oreshek*

Shmakivs'kyy Rudnyk *see* **Pokrovs'ke**

Shmakovsky Rudnik *see* **Pokrovs'ke**

Shofirkon (town, central Uzbekistan) : (Russian *Shafirkan*); c.1935–1937 *Bauman*; to c.1935 *Khodzhaarif*

Sholkhi *see* **¹Oktyabr'skoye**

Shopokov (town, northern Kyrgyzstan) : to 1985 Russian *Krasnooktyabr'sky*

Shpakovskoye (village, southwestern Russia) : formerly *Mikhaylovskoye*

Shqipëri *see* **Albania**

Shropshire (county, western England) : alternate *Salop* (The alternate name was official for the county from 1974 to 1980.)

Shtefan Vode *see* **Ştefan Vodă**

Shterivs'ke *see* **Petrovs'ke**

Shterovskoye *see* **Petrovs'ke**

Shulaveri *see* **Shaumiani**

Shul'mak *see* **Navabad**

Shumanay (town, western Uzbekistan) : to 1950 *Taza-Bazar*

Shumen (city, northeastern Bulgaria) : 1950–1965 *Kolarovgrad*

Shumnu Bokhchalar *see* **Kaolinovo**

Shurugwi (town, central Zimbabwe) : to 1982 *Selukwe*

Shushan *see* **Susa**

Shvenchyonelyay *see* **Švenčionėliai**

Shvenchyonis *see* **Švenčionys**

Shwebo (town, north central Myanmar) : to c.1753 *Moksobomyo*

Shyaulyay *see* **Šiauliai**

Shykyrlykytay *see* **Suvorove**

Shymkent (town, southern Kazakhstan) : to 1991 Russian *Chimkent*

Shyrokolanivka (village, southern Ukraine) : (Russian *Shirokolanovka*); c.1935–1945 *imeny Karla Libknekhta* (Russian *imeni Karla Libknekhta*); to c.1935 *Landau*

Siam *see* **Thailand**

Sianów (town, northwestern Poland) : to 1945 German *Zanow*

Šiauliai (city, northern Lithuania) : (Russian *Shyaulyay*); to 1918 Russian *Shavli*

Siazan' *see* **Siyäzän**

Sibari (village, southern Italy) : ancient Greek *Thurii*; earlier ancient Greek *Sybaris* (The village is now part of the town of Cassano allo Ionio. Its original Greek name gave English *sybaritic*, from the wealth and luxury of the city's inhabitants.)

Šibenik (town, southern Croatia) : to 1943 Italian *Sebenico*

Siberia (region, eastern Russia) : [Russian *Sibir'*]

Sibir' *see* **Siberia**

Sibirsky *see* **Nazyvayevsk**

Sibirtsevo (town, southeastern Russia) : to 1972 *Manzovka*

Sibiu (city, central Romania) : to 1918 Hungarian *Nagyszeben*; to 1867 German *Hermannstadt*

Sicca Veneria *see* **Le Kef**

Sichelberg *see* **Sierpc**

Sichirlichitai *see* **Suvorove**

Sicilia *see* **Sicily**

Sicily (island, southern Italy) : [Italian *Sicilia*]

Sidi Akacha (village, northern Algeria) : to c.1962 French *Montenotte*

Sidi Ali (village, northwestern Algeria) : to
c.1962 French *Cassaigne*

Sidi Ali Ben Youb (village, northwestern Algeria) : to c.1962 French *Chanzy*

Sidi Ali Boussidi (village, northwestern Algeria)
: to c.1962 French *Parmentier*

Sidi Allal Bahraoui (village, northwestern Morocco) : formerly French *Monod*

Sidi Bel Attar (village, northwestern Algeria) : to
c.1962 French *Pont du Chéliff*

Sidi Ben Adda (village, northwestern Algeria) :
to c.1962 French *Trois-Marabouts*

Sidi Ben Yekba (village, northwestern Algeria) :
to c.1962 French *Kléber*

Sidi Brahim (village, northwestern Algeria) : to
c.1962 French *Prudhon*

Sidi el Abed (village, northwestern Morocco) :
formerly French *Plage des Contrebandiers*

Sidi Ghiles (village, northern Algeria) : to c.1962
French *Novi*

Sidi Hamadouche (village, northwestern Algeria) : to c.1962 French *Les Trembles*

Sidi Kacem (city, northern Morocco) : formerly
French *Petitjean*

Sidi Khaled (village, northwestern Algeria) : to
c.1962 French *Palissy*

Sidi Lahssen (village, northwestern Algeria) : to
c.1962 French *Détrie*

Sidi Lakhdar (village, northern Algeria) : to
c.1962 French *Lavarande*

Sidi Mohammed Ben Ali (village, northern Algeria) : to c.1962 French *Renault*

Sidi Rafa (village, northern Libya) : formerly
Italian *Beda Littoria*

Sidirókastro (town, northeastern Greece) : to
1913 Turkish *Demirhisar*

Sidon *see* **Saida**

Siebenbürgen *see* **Transylvania**

Siedlce (town, east central Poland) : to 1915 Russian *Sedlets*

Siemianowice Śląskie (city, southern Poland) :
1939–1945 German *Laurahütte*

Siena (city, central Italy) : Roman *Sena Julia*

Sieradz (town, central Poland) : 1949–1945 German *Schieratz*; to 1915 Russian *Seradz*

Sieraków (town, western Poland) : 1939–1945
German *Zirke*

Sierpc (town, north central Poland) : 1940–1945
German *Sichelberg*; to 1915 Russian *Serpets*

Sifton *see* **Lemberg**

Sig (town, northwestern Algeria) : to c.1962
French *St.-Denis-du-Sig*

Sighetu-Marmaţiei (city, northern Romania) :
to 1918, 1940–1944 Hungarian *Máramarossziget*; to 1867 German *Marmaroschsiget*

Sighişoara (town, central Romania) : to 1918

Hungarian *Segesvár*; to 1867 German *Schässburg*

Signia *see* **Segni**

Sigüenza (town, central Spain) : Roman *Seguntia*

Sigulda (town, north central Latvia) : to 1017
German *Segewold*

Sihanoukville (city, southern Cambodia) : formerly *Kompong Som*

Silberberg *see* **Srebrna Góra**

Silchester (village, southern England) : Roman
Calleva Atrebatum

Silesia (region, southwestern Poland/northern
Czech Republic/southeastern Germany) :
[German *Schlesien*] (Most of Silesia is today in
Poland, but the German name remains current
as the region was formerly in Germany.)

Sili *see* **Sully**

Silia Hermia *see* **Covilhã**

Silina *see* **Scilly Isles**

Silistra (city, northeastern Bulgaria) : to 1878
Turkish *Silistre*; Roman *Durostorum*

Silistre *see* **Silistra**

Sillein *see* **Žilina**

Šilutė (city, western Lithuania) : (Russian
Shilute); 1921–1939, 1939–1945 German *Heidekrug* (Both German and Lithuanian names
were in official use from 1821 to 1939.)

Silva Jardim (town, southeastern Brazil) : to
1943 *Capivari*

Silvan (town, eastern Turkey) : ancient Greek
Martyropolis; originally ancient Greek *Tigranocerta*

Silvânia (town, central Brazil) : to 1944 *Bonfim*

Silva Porto *see* **Kuito**

Silver City (town, New Mexico, southwestern
United States) : to 1876 Spanish *San Vincente
de la Ciénaga*

Sim (town, west central Russia) : to c.1928 *Simsky Zavod*

Simão Dias (city, northeastern Brazil) : to 1944
Anápolis

Simbirsk (city, western Russia) : 1924–1991
Ul'yanovsk

Simeonovgrad (town, south central Bulgaria) :
1945–1989 *Maritsa*; to 1945 *Zlaten Dol* (The
town arose in 1933 on the union of two villages either side of the Maritsa River.)

Simferopol' (city, southern Ukraine) : to 1783
Ak-Mechet'

Sim Kolodyaziv *see* **Lenine**

Šimonovany *see* **Partizánske**

Simsky Zavod *see* **Sim**

Simson's Ranges *see* **Maryborough**

Sin *see* **Tell el-Farama**

Sinai, Mt. (northeastern Egypt) : alternate *Gebel
Musa*; biblical *Mt. Horeb*

Sinclair (village, Wyoming, west central United States) : to 1943 *Parco*

Sinegorsk (town, eastern Russia) : 1905–1945 Japanese *Kawakami*

Sinel'nikovo *see* **Synel'nykove**

Sîngerai (village, north central Moldova) : formerly Russian *Lazovsk*

Singidunum *see* **Belgrade**

Singleton (town, New South Wales, southeastern Australia) : to 1822 *St. Patrick's Plain*

Sing Sing *see* **Ossining**

Sinkiang Uighur *see* **Xinjiang Uygur**

Sinop (town, northern Turkey) : ancient Greek *Sinope* (The classical name is associated with the Russian naval victory over the Turks in 1853 during the Russo-Turkish War, an event leading to the Crimean War of 1854–56.)

Sinoya *see* **Chinhoyi**

Sint-Andries (village, northwestern Belgium) : French *St.-André*

Sint-Gillis *see* **St.-Gilles**

Sint-Gillis-bij-Dendermonde (village, northern Belgium) : French *St.-Gilles-lez-Termonde*

Sint-Gillis-Waas (town, northern Belgium) : French *St.-Gilles-Waas*

Sint-Jans-Molenbeek *see* **Molenbeek-St.-Jean**

Sint-Katelijne-Waver (town, northern Belgium) : French *Wavre-Ste.-Catherine*

Sint-Niklaas (town, northern Belgium) : French *St.-Nicolas*

Sintra (city, western Portugal) : formerly mostly *Cintra*

Sint-Truiden (town, east central Belgium) : French *St.-Trond*

Sinus Arabicus *see* **Red Sea**

Sinus Gallicus *see* **Lion, Golfe du**

Sinus Persicus *see* **Persian Gulf**

Sion (town, southwestern Switzerland) : German *Sitten*; Roman *Sedunum*

Sioux City (city, Iowa, north central United States) : to 1857 *Thompsonville*

Sipolilo *see* **Guruve**

Siponzh *see* **Bartang**

Siqueira Campos (town, southern Brazil) : to c.1935 *Colonia Mineira*

Siqueira Campos *see* **Guaçuí**

Siracusa *see* **Syracuse**

Sirdaryo (town, eastern Uzbekistan) : (Russian *Syrdar'ya*); formerly Russian *Syrdar'insky*; to 1947 Russian *Syrnovorossiysk*

Siret (town, northern Romania) : to 1918 German *Sereth*

Şiria (village, western Romania) : to 1918 Hungarian *Világos*

Sirion *see* **Hermon, Mt.**

Siris *see* **Nova Siri**

Sisak (town, northern Croatia) : to 1867 German *Sissek*

Sissek *see* **Sisak**

Sisson *see* **Mount Shasta**

Sitka (city, Alaska, northwestern United States) : to 1867 *Novoarkhangelsk*

Sitniki (town, western Russia) : to 1946 *Kozlikha*

Sitten *see* **Sion**

Sittwe (city, western Myanmar) : formerly *Akyab*

Sivas (city, central Turkey) : Roman *Sebastea*

Sivashskoye *see* **Syvas'ke**

Sivers'k (town, eastern Ukraine) : (Russian *Seversk*); to 1973 *Yama*

Siyäzän (town, northeastern Azerbaijan) : (Russian *Siazan'*); to 1954 *Kyzyl-Burun*

Siyut-Dzheret *see* **Pryazovs'ke**

Sizebolu *see* **Sozopol**

Sjælland (island, eastern Denmark) : formerly English *Zealand* (The English form of the name lies behind that of **New Zealand**.)

Skalica (town, western Slovakia) : to 1918 Hungarian *Szakolca*; to 1867 German *Skalitz*

Skalitz *see* **Skalica**

Skanderoon *see* **İskenderun**

Skarszewy (town, northern Poland) : to 1945 German *Schöneck*

Skawina (town, southern Poland) : 1940–1945 German *Konradshof*

Skea's Corners *see* **Oshawa**

Skenfrith (village, southeastern Wales) : Welsh *Ynysgynwraidd*

Skernevitsy *see* **Skierniewice**

Skerries (town, eastern Ireland) : Irish *Na Sceirí*

Skerries, The (island, northwestern Wales) : Welsh *Ynysoedd y Moelrhoniaid* (The island comprises a number of interconnecting rocks. Hence its plural English and Welsh names.)

Skibbereen (town, southwestern Ireland) : Irish *An Sciobairín*

Skierniewice (town, east central Poland) : to 1915 Russian *Skernevitsy*

Skikda (city, northeastern Algeria) : to c.1962 French *Philippeville*

Skit *see* **Divnogorsk**

Skobelev *see* **Farg'ona**

Skoczów (town, southern Poland) : to 1918, 1939–1945 German *Skotschau*

Škofja Loka (town, western Slovenia) : to 1918, 1941–1945 German *Bischoflack*

Skokie (village, Illinois, east central United States) : to 1940 *Niles Center*

Skópelos (island, eastern Greece) : ancient Greek *Peparethos*

Skopje (city, northern Macedonia) : 1913–1941 Serbian *Skoplje*; to 1913 Turkish *Üsküb*

Skoplje *see* **Skopje**

Skotovataya *see* **Verkhn'otorets'ke**

Skotschau *see* **Skoczów**

Skotuvata *see* **Verkhn'otorets'ke**

Skovorodino (town, southeastern Russia) : to *c.*1940 *Rukhlovo*

Skradin (village, southern Croatia) : to 1918, 1941–1944 Italian *Scardona*

Skuratovsky (town, western Russia) : to 1948 *Yuzhny*

Skwierzyna (town, western Poland) : 1793–1807, 1815–1945 German *Schwerin an der Warte*

Skye (island, northwestern Scotland) : Roman *Scitis*

Slane (town, eastern Ireland) : Irish *Baile Shláine*

Slaný (town, west central Czech Republic) : to 1918, 1939–1945 German *Schlan*

Slaughter *see* ²**Auburn**

Slavgorod *see* **Slawharad**

Slavkov u Brna (town, eastern Czech Republic) : to 1918, 1939–1945 German *Austerlitz* (The German name is noted for the battle of 1805 in which the French defeated the combined Russian and Austrian forces.)

Slavnoye (village, eastern Russia) : 1905–1945 Japanese *Shibetoro*

Slavonia (region, northern Croatia) : [Serbo-Croat *Slavonija*]

Slavonija *see* **Slavonia**

Slavonska Požega *see* **Požega**

Slavonski Brod (city, eastern Croatia) : to 1867 German *Brod*

Slavsk (town, western Russia) : to 1945 German *Heinrichswalde*

Slavskoye (village, western Russia) : to 1945 German *Kreuzberg*

Slavyanka *see* **Myrzakent**

Slavyanogorsk *see* **Slov'yanohirs'k**

Slavyanovo (town, northern Bulgaria) : to 1934 *Turski Trŭstenik*

Slavyansk *see* **Slov'yans'k**

Slavyanskaya *see* **Slavyansk-na-Kubani**

Slavyansk-na-Kubani (city, southwestern Russia) : to 1958 *Slavyanskaya*

Sława (town, western Poland) : 1937–1945 German *Schlesiersee*; to 1937 German *Schlawa*

Slawentzitz *see* **Sławięcice**

Slawharad (town, eastern Belarus) : (Russian *Slavgorod*); to 1945 *Propoysk*

Sławięcice (village, southern Poland) : *c.*1935–1945 German *Ehrenforst*; to *c.*1935 German *Slawentzitz*

Sławno (town, northwestern Poland) : to 1945 German *Schlawe*

Sleepy Hollow (village, New York, northeastern United States) : 1874–1996 *North Tarrytown*; originally *Beekmanton*

Sleptsovskaya (village, southwestern Russia) : formerly *Ordzhonikidzevskaya*

Sligeach *see* **Sligo**

Sligo (town, northwestern Ireland) : Irish *Sligeach*

Sliven (city, east central Bulgaria) : to 1878 Turkish *İslimie*

Sloboda *see* **Ezhva**

Slobodskoye *see* **Chaplygin**

Slocum Hollow *see* **Scranton**

Slomikhino *see* **Zhalpaktal**

Slonim (city, western Belarus) : 1913–1939 Polish *Słonim*

Słonim *see* **Slonim**

Słońsk (town, western Poland) : to 1945 German *Sonnenburg*

Slovakia (republic, central Europe) : [Slovak *Slovensko*] (The country was formed in 1993 from the eastern part of **Czechoslovakia**, the western part becoming the **Czech Republic**.)

Slovenia (republic, southeastern Europe) : [Slovene *Slovenija*]

Slovenija *see* **Slovenia**

Slovenj Gradec (town, northern Slovenia) : to 1918, 1941–1945 German *Windischgrätz*

Slovenské Nové Mesto (town, southeastern Slovakia) : to 1918, 1938–1945 Hungarian *Sátoraljaújhely* (The town lies in two communities either side of the border with Hungary, here formed by the Sátor River. The Hungarian town, bearing the old Hungarian name, is known to the Slovaks as *Nové Mesto nad Šatorom*. Both of these names mean "new town on the Sátor," while the name of the Slovakian community means "Slovakian new town.")

Slovensko *see* **Slovakia**

Slovenský Meder *see* **Palárikovo**

Slov'yanohirs'k (town, eastern Ukraine) : (Russian *Slavyanogorsk*); to 1964 *Banivs'ke* (Russian *Bannovsky*)

Slov'yans'k (city, eastern Ukraine) : (Russian *Slavyansk*)

Šluknov (town, northern Czech Republic) : to 1918, 1939–1945 German *Schluckenau*

Słupca (town, west central Poland) : 1940–1945 German *Slupka*; to 1915 Russian *Sluptsy*

Slupka *see* **Słupca**

Słupsk (city, northern Poland) : to 1945 German *Stolp*

Sluptsy *see* **Słupca**

Slutsk *see* **Pavlovsk**

Smaldeel *see* **Theunissen**

Smarhon' (town, northwestern Belarus) : (Russian *Smorgon'*); 1919–1939 Polish *Smorgonie*; to 1918 Russian *Smorgon*

Smidovich (town, eastern Russia) : formerly *In*

Śmigiel (town, western Poland) : 1793–1807, 1815–1919, 1939–1945 German *Schmiegel*

Smirnenski (village, northeastern Bulgaria) : 1934–1950 *Knyazheva Polyana*; to 1934 Turkish *Bei-alan.*

Smirnovo (town, northern Kazakhstan) : to 1973 *Smirnovsky*

Smirnovsky *see* Smirnovo

Smithfield *see* Olympia

Smith Mountain *see* Palomar, Mt.

Smith's Creek *see* Port Hope

Smith's Crossroads *see* Dayton

Smithton *see* ¹Columbia

Smithville (village, Ontario, southeastern Canada) : formerly *Griffintown*

Smithville *see* ²Richmond

Smolyan (city, southern Bulgaria) : to 1934 Turkish *Pashmakli*

Smorgon' *see* Smarhon'

Smorgonie *see* Smarhon'

Smychka (town, western Russia) : to 1929 *Ivanovskoye* (The town is now part of Volokolamsk.)

Smyrna (town, Delaware, northeastern United States) : to 1806 *Duck Creek Cross Roads*

Smyrna *see* İzmir

Snare Lakes *see* Wekwetì

Snegurovka *see* Tetiyiv

Snežnik (mountain, southern Slovenia) : 1919–1947 Italian *Monte Nevoso*

Śniardwy (lake, northeastern Poland) : to 1945 German *Spirding*

Śniatyn *see* Snyatyn

Sniečkus *see* Visaginas

Snina (town, eastern Slovakia) : to 1918 Hungarian *Szinna*

Snovsk *see* Shchors

Snowdon (mountain, northwestern Wales) : Welsh *Yr Wyddfa*

Snowdonia (mountain region, northwestern Wales) : Welsh *Eryri* (The region centers on Snowdon.)

Snowdrift *see* Łutselk'e

Snyatyn (town, western Ukraine) : to 1939 Polish *Śniatyn*

Sobięcin (town, southwestern Poland) : to 1945 German *Hermsdorf*

Sobinka (town, western Russia) : early 1920s *Komavangard*

Sobótka (town, southwestern Poland) : to 1945 German *Zobten*

Sobradinho (town, southern Brazil) : to 1938 *Jacuí*

Sobrance (town, eastern Slovakia) : to 1918, 1939–1945 Hungarian *Szobránc*

Socorro *see* Fronteiras

Södertälje (town, east central Sweden) : originally *Tälje*

Sofia (city, west central Bulgaria) : [Bulgarian *Sofiya*]; to 1878 Turkish *Sofya*; to 1376 Bulgarian *Sredets*; Roman *Serdica*

Sofiya *see* Sofia

Sofiyevka *see* (1) Karlo-Marksove; (2) Vil'nyans'k

Sofiyevsky Rudnik *see* Karlo-Marksove

Sofiyivka *see* (1) Karlo-Marksove; (2) Vil'nyans'k

Sofiyivs'kyy Rudnyk *see* Karlo-Marksove

Soflu *see* Soufli

Sofulu *see* Soufli

Sofya *see* Sofia

Sohrau *see* Żory

Soignies (town, southwestern Belgium) : Flemish *Zinnik*

Soissons (city, northern France) : Roman *Suessionae*

Sokhumi (city, northwestern Georgia) : (Russian *Sukhumi*); 1848–1935 Russian *Sukhum*; 17th–19th century Turkish *Sukhum-Kale*; earlier *Tskhum*; Roman *Sebastopolis*; ancient Greek *Dioscurias*

Sok-Karmala *see* Severnoye

Sokol (town, eastern Russia) : 1905–1945 Japanese *Otani*

Sokolka *see* Sokółka

Sokółka (town, northeastern Poland) : 1939–1941 Belarussian *Sakulka*; to 1918 Russian *Sokolka*

Sokolov (town, western Czech Republic) : 1945–1948 *Falknov*; to 1918, 1938–1945 German *Falkenau* (The full former Czech and German names were *Falknov nad Ohří* and *Falkenau an der Eger*, for the river here.)

Sokuluk (town, northern Kyrgyzstan) : 1937–1957 *Kaganovich*; to 1937 Russian *Novotroitskoye*

Solda (village, northern Italy) : to 1918 German *Sulden*

Şoldăneşti (town, northeastern Moldova) : 1985–1988 *Chernenko*

Soldatsky (town, northeastern Uzbekistan) : to *c.*1930 *Yangi-Bazar*

Soldau *see* Działdowo

Soldin *see* Myślibórz

Soledade (town, northeastern Brazil) : 1944–1948 *Ibiapinópolis*

Soledade *see* Soledade de Minas

Soledade de Minas (town, southeastern Brazil) : 1944–1948 *Ibatuba*; to 1944 *Soledade*

Soledar (town, eastern Ukraine) : 1961–1991 *Karlo-Libknekhtivs'k* (Russian *Karlo-Libknekhtovsk*); 1938–1965 *imeny Karla*

Libknekhta (Russian *imeni Karla Libknekhta*); early 1920s–1938 *Rudnyk imeny Karla Libknekhta* (Russian *Rudnik imeny Karla Libknekhta*); to early 1920s *Bryantsivs'kyy Rudnyk* (Russian *Bryantsovsky Rudnik*)

Soletto *see* **Solothurn**

Soleure *see* **Solothurn**

Solfach *see* **Solva**

Soli *see* **Pompeiopolis**

Soligorsk *see* **Salihorsk**

Sol'-Iletsk (town, southwestern Russia) : to 1945 *Iletsk*; earlier *Iletskaya Zashchita*

Solnechnogorsk (city, western Russia) : to 1938 *Solnechnogorsky* (The city was formed in 1928 from the merger of the villages of *Solnechnaya Gora* and *Podsolnechnoye*.)

Solnechnoye (town, western Russia) : to 1948 Finnish *Ollila*

Solnechny *see* **Gorny**

Solntsevo (town, western Russia) : formerly *Korovino*

Solonópole (town, northeastern Brazil) : to 1944 *Cachoeira*

Solothurn (town, northwestern Switzerland) : French *Soleure*; Italian *Soletto*

Solva (village, southwestern Wales) : Welsh *Solfach*

Sombak'e *see* **Yellowknife**

Sombor (city, northwestern Serbia) : to 1918, 1941–1944 Hungarian *Zombor*

Somers Islands *see* **Bermuda**

Somersworth (town, New Hampshire, northeastern United States) : to 1893 *Great Falls*

Somerville (city, Massachusetts, northeastern United States) : originally *Cow Commons*

Sommerfeld *see* **Lubsko**

Somorja *see* **Šamorin**

Sompallón *see* **El Banco**

Son *see* **Sonsky**

Song Da *see* **Black River**

Songjin *see* **Kimch'aek**

Songnim (city, southwestern North Korea) : 1910–1945 *Kyŏmip'o*

Sonnenburg *see* **Słońsk**

Sonsky (town, southern Russia) : to 1940 *Son*

[1]**Sopot** (town, central Bulgaria) : 1950–1965 *Vazovgrad*

[2]**Sopot** (city, northern Poland) : 1772–1945 German *Zoppot*

Sopron (city, northwestern Hungary) : to 1921 German *Ödenburg*

Sorau *see* **Żary**

Sord *see* **Swords**

Sorel (town, Quebec, southeastern Canada) : 1787–1845 *William Henry*

Soroca (city, northern Moldova) : (Russian *Soroki*); 1918–1940, 1941–1944 Romanian *Soroca*; to 1918 Russian *Soroki*

Sorochinsk (town, southwestern Russia) : to *c.*1935 *Sorochinskoye*

Sorochinskoye *see* **Sorochinsk**

Soroka *see* **Belomorsk**

Soroki *see* **Soroca**

Sorokino *see* **Krasnodon**

Sorokyne *see* **Krasnodon**

Sorrento (town, southern Italy) : Roman *Surrentum*

Sorsk (town, southern Russia) : formerly *Dzerzhinsky*

Sortavala (city, northwestern Russia) : to 1918 *Serdobol'* (The present name is Finnish.)

Sorviodunum *see* **Salisbury**

Sosnogorsk (town, northwestern Russia) : to 1957 *Izhma*

Sosnove (town, northwestern Ukraine) : (Russian *Sosnovoye*); to 1946 *Lyudvypil'* (Russian *Lyudvipol'*)

Sosnovitsy *see* **Sosnowiec**

Sosnovo (village, western Russia) : to 1948 Finnish *Rautu* (The village was transferred from Finland to the USSR in 1940 but retained its Finnish name until 1948.)

Sosnovoborsk (town, western Russia) : to *c.*1940 *Litvino*

Sosnovoye *see* **Sosnove**

Sosnowiec (city, southern Poland) : 1940–1945 German *Sosnowitz*; to 1915 Russian *Sosnovitsy*

Sosnowitz *see* **Sosnowiec**

Šoštanj (village, northern Slovenia) : to 1918 German *Schönstein*

Sosva (town, west central Russia) : to 1938 *Sosvinsky Zavod*

Sosvinsky Zavod *see* **Sosva**

Sotsgorodok *see* **Hirnyk**

Sotshorodok *see* **Hirnyk**

Soudan *see* **Sudan**

Soufli (town, northeastern Greece) : to 1919 Bulgarian *Soflu*; to 1913 Turkish *Sofulu*

Souk el Arba de l'Oued Beth (village, northwestern Morocco) : formerly French *Camp-Bataille*

Souk Eltnine (village, northwestern Morocco) : formerly French *Valgravé*

Souk Jemaâ Oulad Abbou (village, northwestern Morocco) : formerly French *Foucauld*

Souk Tleta Loulad (village, northwestern Morocco) : formerly French *Venet-Ville*

Sound, The *see* **Øresund**

Soure *see* **Caucaia**

Sour el Ghozlane (town, northern Algeria) : to *c.*1962 French *Aumale*

Sousse (city, northeastern Tunisia) : [Arabic

Sūsā]; 6th century Roman *Justinianopolis*; 5th century Roman *Hunericopolis*, earlier Roman *Hadrumetum* (The modern city should not be confused with the ancient city of **Susa** in present-day Iran.)

South Abington *wee* **Whitman**

South Africa (republic, southern Africa) : [Afrikaans *Suid-Afrika*] (There are various indigenous names for South Africa, one of the best-known being *Azania*. The Dutch form of the name, *Zuid-Afrika*, gave ZA as the country's international vehicle registration.)

South African Republic *see* **Transvaal**

Southampton (town, Ontario, southeastern Canada) : to 1895 *Saugeen*

South Bend (city, Indiana, east central United States) : to 1830 *Southold*; earlier *Big St. Joseph Station*

South Danvers *see* **Peabody**

South-Eastern *see* **Cross River**

Southern Ocean *see* **Antarctic Ocean**

Southern Rhodesia *see* **Zimbabwe**

South Floral Park (village, New York, northeastern United States) : to 1931 *Jamaica Square*

South Holland (town, Illinois, north central United States) : to 1870 Dutch *De Laage Prairie* (The town is now a southern suburb of Chicago.)

South Island (central and southern New Zealand) : Maori *Te Waka a Maui*; formerly *Middle Island* (The Maori name, meaning "the canoe of Maui," contrasts with those of **North Island** and **Stewart Island**. South Island is still colloquially known as "the Middle" for its location between these two.)

South Lawn *see* **Harvey**

South Malden *see* **Everett**

South Northfield *see* **Glenview**

Southold *see* **South Bend**

Southport *see* **Kenosha**

South Riverside *see* **Corona**

South Sea *see* **Pacific Ocean**

South Shields (town, northeastern England) : Roman *Arbeia*

South Uist (island, Western Isles, northwestern Scotland) : Gaelic *Uibhist a' Deas*

South West Africa *see* **Namibia**

Sovet (village, southwestern Tajikistan) : formerly *Kzyl-Mazar*

Sovetabad *see* (1) **Ghafurov**; (2) **Nurobod**; (3) **Xonobod**

Sovetobod *see* **Ghafurov**

¹**Sovetsk** (city, western Russia, near Kaliningrad) : to 1945 German *Tilsit*

²**Sovetsk** (town, western Russia, near Vyatka) : to 1937 *Kukarka*

Sovetskaya (village, southwestern Russia) : formerly *Urupskaya*

Sovetskaya Gavan' (city, eastern Russia) : formerly *Imperatorskaya Gavan'*

¹**Sovetskoye** (town, western Russia, near Engel's) : to 1941 *Mariental*

²**Sovetskoye** (village, western Russia, near Buguruslan) : formerly *Mordovskaya Bokla*

Sovetskoye *see* (1) **Kashkatau**; (2) **Ketchenery**; (3) **Khebda**; (4) **Zelenokumsk**

Sovetsky (town, western Russia) : to 1948 Finnish *Johannes* (The town passed from Finland to the USSR in 1940 but retained its Finnish name until 1948.)

Sovetsky *see* **Sovyets'kyy**

Soviet Union *see* **Russia**

Sovyets'kyy (town, southern Ukraine) : (Russian *Sovetsky*); to 1950 *Ichki-Grammatikovo*

Sozopol (city, eastern Bulgaria) : to 1878 Turkish *Sizebolu*; ancient Greek *Apollonia* (There were many ancient cities of the Greek name, the chief being in Illyria, where it was Caesar's headquarters during his assualt on Dyrrhacium, now **Dürres**.)

Spaccaforno *see* **Ispica**

Spain (kingdom, southwestern Europe) : [Spanish *España*]; Roman *Hispania*; alternate Roman *Iberia* (The alternate Roman name survives in the name of the peninsula occupied by modern Spain and Portugal.)

Spalato *see* **Split**

Spalatum *see* **Split**

Spanish Guinea *see* **Equatorial Guinea**

Spanish Netherlands *see* **Belgium**

Spanish Sahara *see* **Western Sahara**

Sparnacum *see* **Épernay**

Sparta (historic city, southern Greece) : alternate *Lacedaemon*

Spas *see* ³**Pervomaysky**

Spassk *see* (1) **Bednodem'yanovsk**; (2) **Bolgar**; (3) **Spassk-Dal'ny**; (4) **Spassk-Ryazansky**

Spassk-Dal'ny (city, southeastern Russia) : to *c.*1930 *Spassk*

Spassk-Ryazansky (town, western Russia) : to 1929 *Spassk*

Spassk-Tatarsky *see* **Bolgar**

Speen (village, southern England) : Roman *Spinis* (The Roman settlement here was probably more exactly at Woodspeen, just west of Speen, itself now a suburb of Newbury.)

Spence Bay *see* **Taloyoak**

Speyer (city, southwestern Germany) : formerly English *Spires*; Roman *Augusta Nemetum*; earlier Roman *Noviomagus*

Spinis *see* **Speen**

Spirding *see* **Śniardwy**

Spires *see* **Speyer**

Spirit River *see* **Rycroft**

Spišská Nová Ves (city, east central Slovakia) : to 1918 Hungarian *Igló*; to 1867 German *Zipser-Neudorf*

Spišska Stara Ves (town, northern Slovakia) : to 1918 Hungarian *Szepesófalu*; to 1867 German *Altendorf*

Spišské Podhradie (town, east central Slovakia) : to 1918 Hungarian *Szepesváralja*; to 1867 German *Kirchdrauf*

Spitak (town, northwestern Armenia) : to 1948 *Amamlu*

Spitsevka (village, southwestern Russia) : to *c.*1940 *Spitsevskoye*

Spitsevskoye *see* **Spitsevka**

Split (city, western Croatia) : to 1918, 1941–1943 Italian *Spalato*; Roman *Spalatum*

Spokane (city, Washington, northwestern United States) : originally *Spokane Falls*

Spokane Falls *see* **Spokane**

Spokojna Góra *see* **Mirsk**

Spoletium *see* **Spoleto**

Spoleto (town, central Italy) : Roman *Spoletium*

Springs of Palomas *see* **Truth or Consequences**

Sprottau *see* **Szprotawa**

Squillace (village, southern Italy) : ancient Greek *Scylacium*

Srbija *see* **Serbia**

Srbobran (town, northern Serbia) : to 1918, 1941–1944 Hungarian *Szenttamás*

Srebrna Góra (town, southwestern Poland) : to 1945 German *Silberberg*

Sredets (town, southeastern Bulgaria) : 1950–1989 *Grudovo*; 1934–1950 *Sredets*; to 1934 Turkish *Karabunar*

Sredets *see* **Sofia**

Srednekrayushkino *see* ³**Pervomayskoye**

Śrem (town, western Poland) : 1793–1807, 1815–1919, 1939–1945 German *Schrimm*

Sremska Mitrovica (town, western Serbia) : to 1867 German *Mitrowitz*; Roman *Sirmium* (The first word of the name distinguishes the town from **Kosovska Mitrovica** in Kosovo.)

Sremski Karlovci (town, north central Serbia) : to 1867 German *Karlowitz*

Srikakulam (town, southeastern India) : formerly *Chicacole*

Sri Lanka (island republic, northern Indian Ocean) : to 1972 *Ceylon*; formerly literary *Serendip*; Roman *Taprobane* (*Serendip*, which gave English *serendipity*, is an Arabic corruption of a Sanskrit name.)

Środa Śląska (town, southwestern Poland) : to 1945 German *Neumarkt*

Środa Wielkopolska (town, west central Poland) : 1793–1807, 1815–1919, 1939–1945 German *Schroda*

Srpski Itebej *see* **Itebej**

Staaten Landt *see* **New Zealand**

Stabiae *see* **Castellammare di Stabia**

Stablo *see* **Stavelot**

Stabroek *see* ¹**Georgetown**

Stacy's Corners *see* **Glen Ellyn**

Stadtroda (town, west central Germany) : to 1925 *Roda* (In the year stated German *Stadt*, "town," was added to the name of the river on which the town stands.)

Stahlheim *see* **Amnéville**

Staines (town, southeastern England) : Roman *Pontibus* (The Roman name means "[at] the bridges." Staines arose by a crossing of the Thames River.)

Stakhanov (city, eastern Ukraine) : 1943–1978 *Kadiyivka* (Russian *Kadiyevka*); 1937–1943 *Sergo*; to 1937 *Kadiyivka* (Russian *Kadiyevka*)

Stakhanovo *see* **Zhukovsky**

Stalin *see* (1) **Braşov**; (2) **Varna**

Stalina, imeni *see* **Shahrihon**

Stalinabad *see* **Dushanbe**

Stalindorf *see* ³**Zhovtneve**

Stalingrad *see* **Volgograd**

Staliniri *see* **Ts'khinvali**

Stalinka *see* **Chervonozavods'ke**

Stalino *see* (1) **Donets'k**; (2) **Shahrihon**

Stalinogorsk *see* **Novomoskovsk**

Stalinogród *see* **Katowice**

Stalin Peak *see* (1) **Gerlachovský Peak**; (2) **Ismoili Somoni, Peak**; (3) **Musala**

Stalinsk *see* **Novokuznetsk**

Stalins'ke *see* ³**Zhovtneve**

Stalinskoye *see* ³**Zhovtneve**

Stalinsky *see* **Bol'shevo**

Stallupönen *see* **Nesterov**

Stamboliyski (town, southern Bulgaria) : 1969–1979 *Novi Kritsim*; 1964–1969 *Kritsim*; 1926–1964 *Gára Kritsim*; to 1926 *Polatovo* (Bulgarian *gára* means "railroad station.")

Stamboul *see* **Istanbul**

Stamora Moraviţa (village, western Romania) : to 1918 Hungarian *Temesmóra*

Stampae *see* **Étampes**

Stanbridge Falls *see* **Bedford**

Stanhope (town, New Jersey, northeastern United States) : to 1815 *Andover Forge*

Stanichno-Luganskoye *see* **Stanychno-Luhans'ke**

Stanimaka *see* **Asenovgrad**

Stanislau *see* **Ivano-Frankivs'k**

Stanislav *see* **Ivano-Frankivs'k**

Stanislaviv *see* **Ivano-Frankivs'k**

Stanislavovo *see* Rasony

Stanisławów *see* Ivano-Frankivs'k

Stanitsa Luganskaya *see* Stanychno-Luhans'ke

Štanjel na Krasu (village, western Slovenia) : to 1947 Italian *San Daniele del Carso*

Stanke Dimitrov *see* Dupnitsa

Stanley *see* [2]Nelson

Stanley Falls *see* Boyoma Falls

Stanley Pool *see* Malebo Pool

Stanleyville *see* (1) Kisangani; (2) Orientale

Stann Creek *see* Dangriga

Stanovoye (village, western Russia) : formerly *Ploskoye*

Stantsiya-Regar *see* Tursunzade

Stanwix (village, northwestern England) : Roman *Uxelodunum* (Stanwix is now a district of Carlisle.)

Stanychno-Luhans'ke (town, eastern Ukraine) : (Russian *Stanichno-Luganskoye*); 1935–1938 *Kosyorove* (Russian *Kosiorovo*); earlier *Stanytsya Luhans'ka* (Russian *Stanitsa Luganskaya*); originally *Luhans'k* (Russian *Lugansk*).

Stanytsya-Luhans'ka *see* Stanychno-Luhans'ke

Staoinebrig *see* Stoneybridge

Stará Ďala *see* Hurbanovo

Stará Ľubovňa (town, northern Slovakia) : to 1918 Hungarian *Ólubló*; to 1867 German *Altlublau*

Stara Pazova (town, northern Serbia) : to 1918, 1941–1944 Hungarian *Ópazova*

Stara Planina *see* Balkan Mountains

Staraya Barda *see* [2]Krasnogorskoye

Stara Zagora (city, central Bulgaria) : to 1878 Turkish *Eskizagra*; Roman *Augusta Trajana*

Starbuck Island (eastern Kiribati) : formerly *Volunteer Island*

Stargard in Pommern *see* Stargard Szczeciński

Stargard Szczeciński (city, northwestern Poland) : to 1945 German *Stargard in Pommern*

Stari Bečej *see* Bečej

Staritsy *see* Kirawsk

Starkenbach *see* Jilemnice

Starodubskoye (village, eastern Russia) : 1905–1945 Japanese *Sakaehama*

Starogard Gdański (town, northern Poland) : 1772–1919, 1939–1945 German *Preussisch-Stargard*

Starokonstantinov *see* Starokostyantyniv

Starokostyantyniv (city, west central Ukraine) : (Russian *Starokonstantinov*); to 1918 Russian *Starokonstantinov*

Staromar'yevka (village, southwestern Russia) : to *c*.1940 *Staromar'yevskoye*

Staromar'yevskoye *see* Staromar'yevka

Staromlinovka *see* Staromlynivka

Staromlynivka (village, eastern Ukraine) : (Russian *Staromlinovka*); to 1946 *Staryy Kermenchyk* (Russian *Stary Kermenchik*)

Staropyshminsk (town, west central Russia) : to 1943 *Pyshminsky Zavod*

Staroutkinsk (town, west central Russia) : to 1933 *Utkinsky Zavod*

Stary Dashev *see* Dashiv

Stary Kermenchik *see* Staromlynivka

Stary Sącz (town, southern Poland) : 18th–19th century, 1940–1945 German *Altsandez*

Stary Salavan *see* Novocheremshansk

Stary Sambor *see* Staryy Sambir

Stary Smokovec (town, northern Slovakia) : to 1918 Hungarian *Tátrafüred*; to 1867 German *Altschmecks* (The town was formed from the separate villages of *Dolný Smokovec*, *Horný Smokovec*, and *Starý Smokovec*, respectively Lower, Upper, and Old Smokovec.)

Staryy Dashiv *see* Dashiv

Staryy Kermenchyk *see* Staromlynivka

Staryy Sambir (town, western Ukraine) : (Russian *Stary Sambor*); to 1939 Polish *Stary Sambor*

State Line *see* Hammond

Staten Island (borough, New York, northeastern United States) : to 1975 *Richmond* (The former name of the New York City borough is still current for the county with which Staten Island is coextensive.)

Statesville (city, North Carolina, eastern United States) : to 1789 *Fourth Creek*

Stavelot (town, eastern Belgium) : Flemish *Stablo*

Stavropol' (city, southwestern Russia) : 1935–1943 *Voroshilovsk*

Stavropol' *see* Tol'yatti

Stavropol' Kray (region, southwestern Russia) : 1937–1943 *Ordzhonikidze Kray*

Stębark (village, northeastern Poland) : to 1945 German *Tannenberg* (The German name is associated with two battles. The first, between this village and Grünfelde or Grünwald, after which it is also named, was a Polish-Lithuanian victory in 1410 over the Teutonic Knights. The second led to a German victory over the Russians in 1914.)

Stefanie, Lake *see* Ch'ew Bahir

Ştefan Vodă (village, eastern Moldova) : (Russian *Shtefan Vode*); formerly *Suvorovo*; earlier *Biruintsa*

Stegman *see* Artesia

Ştei (town, western Romania) : formerly *Doctor Petru Groza*

Steiermark (state, central and southeastern Austria) : English conventional *Styria*

Stein *see* Kamnik

Steinamanger *see* Szombathely

Steinau an der Oder *see* Ścinawa

Steinbrück *see* Zidani Most

Steinschönau *see* Kamenický Šenov

Steitztown *see* ²Lebanon

Stellarton (town, Nova Scotia, eastern Canada) :
to 1889 *Albion Mines*

Steornabhagh *see* Stornoway

Stepanakert *see* Xankändi

Stepanavan (town, northern Armenia) : to 1924
Dzhalal-ogly

Stepantsminda *see* Qazbegi

Stephenson *see* Rock Island

Stepnogorsk *see* Stepnohirs'k

Stepnohirs'k (town, southeastern Ukraine) :
(Russian *Stepnogorsk*); to 1987 *Sukhoivanivs'ke*
(Russian *Sukhoivanovskoye*)

Stepnoy *see* Elista

Stepnoye (town, southwestern Russia) : formerly
Otrogovo (This Stepnoye should not be confused with the more southerly town of the
same name east of Georgiyevsk.)

Steptoeville *see* Walla Walla

Sterling *see* St. Thomas

Sternberg *see* Šternberk

Šternberk (town, eastern Czech Republic) : to
1918, 1938–1945 German *Sternberg*

Sterzing *see* Vipiteno

Stettin *see* Szczecin

Stettler (town, Alberta, west central Canada) : to
1906 *Blumenau*

Stewart Island (southern New Zealand) : Maori
Rakiura; earlier Maori *Te Punga a Maui*. (The
earlier Maori name, meaning "the anchor of
Maui," contrasts with those of North Island
and South Island.)

Stidia (village, northwestern Algeria) : to *c.*1962
French *Georges Clemenceau*

Stillwater *see* Orono

Štip (town, east central Macedonia) : to 1913
Turkish *İştip*; ancient Greek *Antibos*

Stockmannshof *see* Pļaviņas

Stockton (city, California, western United
States) : to 1850 *Tuleburg*

Stolp *see* Słupsk

Stołpce *see* Stowbtsy

Stolpmünde *see* Ustka

Stolptsy *see* Stowbtsy

Stonefort (village, Illinois, north central United
States) : to 1934 *Bolton*

Stoneybridge (village, Western Isles, northwestern Scotland) : Gaelic *Staoinebrig*

Stoney Creek *see* Melfort

Stony Brook *see* Princeton

Stony Hill *see* Ludlow

Storms, Cape of *see* Good Hope, Cape of

Stornoway (town, Western Isles, northwestern
Scotland) : Gaelic *Steornabhagh*

Storojineţ *see* Storozhynets'

Storozhinets *see* Storozhynets'

Storozhynets' (town, western Ukraine) : (Russian *Storozhinets*); 1919–1940 Romanian *Storojineţ*; to 1918 German *Storozynetz*

Storozynetz *see* Storozhynets'

Stowbtsy (town, west central Belarus) : (Russian
Stolptsy); 1919–1939 Polish *Stołpce*; to 1918 Russian *Stolptsy*

Strabane (town, northwestern Northern Ireland)
: Irish *An Srath Bán*

Stradbally (town, east central Ireland) : Irish *An
Sráidbhaile*

Strait of Dover *see* Dover, Strait of

Strakonice (town, southwestern Czech Republic)
: to 1918, 1939–1945 German *Strakonitz*

Strakonitz *see* Strakonice

Stralsund (city, northeastern Germany) : 1648–
1815 Swedish *Strålsund*

Strålsund *see* Stralsund

Strasbourg (city, northeastern France) : formerly
English *Strasburg*; 1871–1919, 1940–1944 German *Strassburg*; Roman *Argentoratum*

Strasburg *see* Strasbourg

Strasburg in Westpreussen *see* Brodnica

Strassburg *see* Strasbourg

Strass-Somerein *see* Hegyeshalom

Stratfield *see* Bridgeport

¹Stratford (city, Ontario, southeastern Canada) :
to 1835 *Little Thames*

²Stratford (town, northwestern New Zealand) :
formerly *Stratford-on-Patea*

Stratford-on-Patea *see* ²Stratford

Stratonicea *see* Eskihisar

Strato's Tower *see* Caesarea

Strawbery Banke *see* ²Portsmouth

Štrba (town, northern Slovakia) : to 1918 Hungarian *Csorba*

Streator (town, Illinois, north central United
States) : to 1872 *Unionville*; originally *Hardscrabble*

Strehlen *see* Strzelin

Střekov (town, northwestern Czech Republic) :
to 1918, 1939–1945 German *Schreckenstein*
(The town is now a district of Ústí nad
Labem.)

Strelno *see* Strzelno

Stříbro (town, western Czech Republic) : to
1918, 1939–1945 German *Miess*

Striegau *see* Strzegom

Strigonium *see* Esztergom

Strokestown (village, north central Ireland) :
Irish *Béal na mBuillí*

Stromboli (island, Lipari Islands, Italy) : ancient Greek *Strongyle*

Strongoli (village, southern Italy) : Roman *Petelia*

Strongyle *see* **Stromboli**

Stronie Śląskie (town, southwestern Poland) : to 1945 German *Seitenberg*

Stropkov (town, northeastern Slovakia) : to 1918 *Sztropkó*

Strumica (town, southeastern Macedonia) : to 1913 Turkish *Istrumca*

Stry *see* **Stryy**

Stryj *see* **Stryy**

Stryy (town, western Ukraine) : (Russian *Stry*); to 1939 Polish *Stryj*

Strzegom (city, southwestern Poland) : to 1945 German *Striegau*

Strzelce (town, southern Poland) : to 1945 German *Gross-Strehlitz*

Strzelce Krajeńskie (town, western Poland) : to 1945 German *Friedeberg*

Strzelin (town, southwestern Poland) : to 1945 German *Strehlen*

Strzelno (town, central Poland) : 1793–1807, 1815–1919, 1939–1945 German *Strelno*

Stuart *see* **Alice Springs**

Štubnianske Teplice *see* **Turčianske Teplice**

Stuchka *see* **Aizkraukle**

Stuhlweissenburg *see* **Székesfehérvár**

Stuhm *see* **Sztum**

Stupino (city, western Russia) : *c.*1935–1938 *Elektrovoz*

Štúrovo (town, southern Slovakia) : to 1918, 1938–1945 Hungarian *Párkány*

Stutthof *see* **Sztutowo**

Styria *see* **Steiermark**

Subiaco (town, central Italy) : Roman *Sublaqueum*

Sublaqueum *see* **Subiaco**

Subotica (city, northern Serbia) : to 1918, 1941–1944 Hungarian *Szabadka*; to 1867 German *Maria-Theresiopel*

Suceava (city, northeastern Romania) : to 1918 German *Suczawa* (The German name adopted its Polish form.)

Sucha Góra Orawska *see* **Suchá Hora**

Suchá Hora (town, northern Slovakia) : 1920–1924, 1938–1939 Polish *Sucha Góra Orawska*; to 1918 Hungarian *Szuchahora*

Suchan (town, northwestern Poland) : to 1945 German *Zachan*

Suchan *see* **Partizansk**

Suchansky Rudnik *see* **Partizansk**

Sucre (city, south central Bolivia) : to 1840 *Chuquisaca*; originally *La Plata*

Sudan (republic, northeastern Africa) : [Arabic *As Sūdān*]; formerly English *Soudan*; to 1956 officially *Anglo-Egyptian Sudan* (The English name, from the French, also applied to the much larger Sudan that extended across Africa from the west coast to the mountains of Ethiopia.)

Sudanese Republic *see* **Mali**

Sudauen *see* **Suwałki**

Sudest Island *see* **Tagula**

Sudostroy *see* **Severodvinsk**

Sudova Vyshnya (town, western Ukraine) : (Russian *Sudovaya Vyshnya*); to 1939 Polish *Sądowa Wisznia*

Sudovaya Vyshnya *see* **Sudova Vyshnya**

Suessa Aurunca *see* **Sessa Aurunca**

Suessionae *see* **Soissons**

Suessula *see* **Cancello**

Suez (city, northeastern Egypt) : [Arabic *As Suways*]

Sufetula *see* **Sbeïtla**

Suffolk (city, Virginia, eastern United States) : to 1742 *Constant's Warehouse*

Sufikishlak *see* **Akhunbabayev**

Sug-Aksy (village, southern Russia) : formerly *Sut-Khol'*

Şuhut (village, west central Turkey) : ancient Greek *Synnada*

Suid-Afrika *see* **South Africa**

Suisse *see* **Switzerland**

Sukarnapura *see* **Jayapura**

Sukarno, Mt. *see* **Jaya, Mt.**

Sukhoivanivs'ke *see* **Stepnohirs'k**

Sukhoivanovskoye *see* **Stepnohirs'k**

Sukhum *see* **Sokhumi**

Sukhumi *see* **Sokhumi**

Sukhum-Kale *see* **Sokhumi**

Sukkertoppen *see* **Maniitsoq**

Sulawesi (island, eastern Indonesia) : to 1945 *Celebes* (The earlier name remains current for the *Celebes Sea*, between Sulawesi and the Philippines.)

Sulden *see* **Solda**

Sulechów (town, western Poland) : to 1945 German *Züllichau*

Sulęcin (town, western Poland) : to 1945 German *Zielenzig*

Sulików (town, southwestern Poland) : to 1945 German *Schönberg*

Sulimov *see* **Cherkessk**

Sulin *see* **Krasny Sulin**

Sully (village, southern Wales) : Welsh *Sili* (The village is now a suburb of Barry.)

Sultanabad *see* **Arāk**

Sumba (island, southern Indonesia) : formerly *Sandalwood Island*

Sumbe (town, western Angola) : 1975–1981 *Ngunza*; to 1975 *Novo Redondo*

Summerside (town, Prince Edward Island, eastern Canada) : originally *Green's Shore*

Šumperk (city, eastern Czech Republic) : to 1918, 1938–1945 German *Mährisch-Schönberg*

Sumter (city, South Carolina, southeastern United States) : to 1856 *Sumterville*

Sumterville *see* **Sumter**

Sunbury *see* ²**Bangor**

Sunderland (village, Ontario, southeastern Canada) : to 1868 *Brock*

Sunnyvale (city, California, western United States) : to 1912 *Encinal*; originally *Murphy's Station*

Suomenlinna (island fortress, southern Finland) : to 1809 Swedish *Sveaborg*

Suomi *see* **Finland**

Sur (town, southern Lebanon) : biblical *Tyre* (This name, representing Arabic *Ṣūr*, should not be confused with that of *Sur*, also Arabic *Ṣūr*, eastern Oman.)

Ṣūr *see* **Sur**

Surendranagar (town, western India) : to *c.*1950 *Wadhwan*

Surinam (republic, northeastern South America) : to 1975 *Dutch Guiana*

Sūrīyah *see* **Syria**

Surrentum *see* **Sorrento**

Sursk (town, western Russia) : to 1955 *Nikol'sky Khutor*

Surskoye (town, west central Russia) : to *c.*1930 *Promzino*

Susa (ancient city, southwestern Iran) : biblical *Shushan*

Sūsā *see* **Sousse**

Sušak (town, western Croatia) : 1941–1943 Italian *Borgonovo*; to 1918 Hungarian *Port Báros* (From 1934 to 1941 Sušak was a separate port belonging to Yugoslavia, the main port being that of the Italian city of Fiume, now **Rijeka**, with which it reunited in 1947.)

Susanino (town, western Russia) : to 1938 *Molvitino*

Suschitz *see* **Sušice**

Susiana *see* **Khuzestan**

Sušice (town, southwestern Czech Republic) : to 1918, 1939–1945 German *Suschitz*

Susz (town, northeastern Poland) : to 1945 German *Rosenberg*

Sut-Khol' *see* **Sug-Aks**

Suvalki *see* **Suwałki**

Suvorove (town, southern Ukraine) : (Russian *Suvorovo*); 1941–1944 Romanian *Regele Mihai I*; *c.*1930–1940 Romanian *Regele Carol II*; to *c.*1930 Ukrainian *Shykyrlykytay* (Russian *Shikirlikitai*; Romanian *Sichirlichitai*) (The town was founded in 1815 by Bulgarian settlers

from the future Romania, and the names with Romanian *regele*, "king," are of Romanian kings.)

Suvorovo (town, eastern Bulgaria) : to 1950 *Novgradets*; earlier *Kozludzha*

Suvorovo *see* (1) **Ştefan Vodă**; (2) **Suvorove**

Suwałki (city, northeastern Poland) : 1940–1945 German *Sudauen*; to 1918 Russian *Suvalki*

Suyetikha *see* **Biryusinsk**

Svalava *see* **Svalyava**

Svalyava (town, western Ukraine) : 1944–1945 Czech *Svalava*; 1939–1944 Hungarian *Szolyva*; 1919–1939 Czech *Svalava*; to 1918 Hungarian *Szolyva*

Svatove (town, eastern Ukraine) : (Russian *Svatovo*); 1825–1923 *Novokaterynoslav* (Russian *Novoyekaterinoslav*); earlier *Svatova Luchka*

Svatovo *see* **Svatove**

Sveaborg *see* **Suomenlinna**

Švenčionėliai (town, eastern Lithuania) : (Russian *Shvenchyonelyay*); 1919–1939 Polish *Nowe Święciany*

Švenčionys (town, eastern Lithuania) : (Russian *Shvenchyonis*); 1919–1938 Polish *Święciany*; to 1918 Russian *Sventsyany*

Sventsyany *see* **Švenčionys**

Sverdlova, imeni *see* **Sverdlovs'k**

Sverdlova, imeny *see* **Sverdlovs'k**

Sverdlovo (village, southwestern Russia) : to 1941 *Ney-Val'ter* (The earlier name of the village, in the former Volga German Autonomous Soviet Socialist Republic, is a Russian transliteration of German *Neu-Walter*.)

Sverdlovo *see* **Sverdlovsky**

Sverdlovsk *see* (1) **Sverdlovs'k**; (2) **Yekaterinburg**

Sverdlovs'k (city, eastern Ukraine) : (Russian *Sverdlovsk*); 1930s–1938 *imeny Sverdlova* (Russian *imeni Sverdlova*); earlier *Sharapkyne* (Russian *Sharapkino*); originally *Dovzhykove-Orlovs'ke* (Russian *Dolzhikovo-Orlovskoye*)

Sverdlovsky (town, western Russia) : to 1928 *Sverdlovo*

Sverdlovsky Priisk *see* **Is**

Sverige *see* **Sweden**

Sveta Anastasiya (island, southeastern Bulgaria) : formerly *Bolshevik*

Sveti Djordje *see* **Negotin**

Sveti Konstantin (village, eastern Bulgaria) : formerly *Druzhba*

Sveti Vrach *see* **Sandanski**

Svetlogorsk (town, western Russia) : to 1945 German *Rauschen*

Svetlogorsk *see* **Svyetlahorsk**

Svetlograd (town, southwestern Russia) : to 1965 *Petrovskoye*

Svetlovodsk *see* Svitlovods'k

Svetloye *see* Svetly

Svetly (town, western Russia) : 1945–1955 *Svetloye*; to 1945 German *Kobbelbude*

Svetogorsk (town, northwestern Russia) : 1918–1948 Finnish *Enso* (The town passed from Finland to the USSR in 1940 but retained its Finnish name until 1948.)

Svetozarevo *see* Jagodina

Svidník (town, northeastern Slovakia) : to 1918 Hungarian *Szvidnik*

Svilengrad (town, southeastern Bulgaria) : to 1913 Turkish *Mustafapaşa*

Svishtov (town, northern Bulgaria) : to 1878 Turkish *Ziştov*

Svitavy (town, east central Czech Republic) : to 1918, 1938–1945 German *Zwittau*

Svitlovods'k (city, east central Ukraine) : (Russian *Svetlovodsk*); 1962–1969 *Kremhes* (Russian *Kremges*); 1961–1962 *Khrushchov* (Russian *Khrushchyov*); formerly *Novoheorhiyivs'ke* (Russian *Novogeorgiyevsk*) (The town was flooded by the Kremenchug reservoir from 1954 to 1960 and its residents moved to a new site near the dam. Hence the name *Kremhes*, an abbreviation meaning "Kremenchug hydroelectric power plant.")

Svizzera *see* Switzerland

Svoboda (village, western Russia) : to 1945 German *Janichen*

Svoboda *see* Liski

Svobodny (city, southeastern Russia) : to 1924 *Alekseyevsk*

Svrčinovec (town, northwestern Slovakia) : 1938–1939 Polish *Świerczynowiec*

Svyatogorovsky Rudnik *see* Dobropillya

Svyatoy Krest *see* Budyonnovsk

Svyetlahorsk (town, southeastern Belarus) : (Russian *Svetlogorsk*); to 1961 *Shatilki*

Swabia (region, southwestern Germany) : [German *Schwaben*]

Swansea (city, southern Wales) : Welsh *Abertawe*

Swaziland (kingdom, southeastern Africa) : locally *KaNgwane* (The local name was that of a South African bantustan or "homeland" for Swazi people that existed from 1977 to 1994.)

Sweden (kingdom, northwestern Europe) : [Swedish *Sverige*]

Sweetsburg (village, Quebec, southeastern Canada) : formerly *Churchville* (The village was annexed to **Cowansville** in 1964.)

Świdnica (city, southwestern Poland) : to 1945 German *Schweidnitz*

Świdwin (town, northwestern Poland) : to 1945 German *Schivelbein*

Świebodzice (town, southwestern Poland) : to 1945 German *Freiburg in Schlesien*

Świebodzin (town, western Poland) : to 1945 German *Schwiebus*

Święciany *see* Švenčionys

Świecie (town, north central Poland) : 1772–1919, 1939–1945 German *Schwetz*

Świeradów Zdrój (town, southwestern Poland) : to 1945 German *Bad Flinsberg*

Świerczynowiec *see* Svrčinovec

Świerzawa (town, southwestern Poland) : to 1945 German *Schönau*

Swindon (administrative district, southern England) : to 1997 *Thamesdown* (The present unitary authority was created from the former district council of the town of *Swindon*.)

Swinemünde *see* Świnoujście

Swinford (town, western Ireland) : Irish *Béal Átha na Muice*

Świnoujście (town, northwestern Poland) : to 1945 German *Swinemünde*

Switzerland (republic, west central Europe) : [French *Suisse*; German *Schweiz*; Italian *Svizzera*]; Roman *Helvetia*

Swords (town, eastern Ireland) : Irish *Sord*

Sybaris *see* Sibari

Syców (town, southwestern Poland) : to 1945 German *Gross-Wartenberg*

Sydenham *see* Owen Sound

Sydenham Island *see* Nonouti

Sydney (city, New South Wales, southeastern Australia) : earlier *Sydney Cove*; originally *Port Jackson* (The original name remains for the sea inlet now usually known as *Sydney Harbour*, which the city surrounds, while Sydney Cove, as part of the harbor, still exists under the name *Circular Quay*.)

Sydney Cove *see* Sydney

Sydney Island *see* Manra

Syedove (town, southeastern Ukraine) : (Russian *Sedovo*); 1938–1955 *imeny H.Ya. Syedova* (Russian *imeni G.Ya. Sedova*); to 1938 *Kryva Kosa* (Russian *Krivaya Kosa*)

Syene *see* Aswan

Syevernyy Rudnyk *see* Kirove

Syeverodonets'k (city, eastern Ukraine) : (Russian *Severodonetsk*); to 1958 Russian *Leskhimstroy*

Syktyvkar (city, western Russia) : to 1930 *Ust'-Sysol'sk*

Symnes Landing *see* [1]Aylmer

Synel'nykove (city, east central Ukraine) : (Russian *Sinel'nikovo*); mid–1930s *imeny Tovarysha Katayevycha* (Russian *imeni Tovarishcha Khatayevicha*)

Synnada *see* Şuhut

Syn'ovyds'ko-Vyzhnye *see* Verkhnye
Syn'ovydne
Synowódsko-Wyżnie *see* Verkhnye
Syn'ovydne
Syracusae *see* Syracuse
Syracuse (city, southern Italy) : [Italian *Siracusa*];
Roman *Syracusae* (The English name of the
city stems from its fame as a Greek colony and
its mention in the Bible as the port where Paul
stayed three days during his journey to Rome.)
Syrdar'insky *see* Sirdaryo
Syrdar'ya (river, southern Kazakhstan) : ancient
Greek *Jaxartes*
Syrdar'ya *see* Sirdaryo
Syria (republic, southwestern Asia) : [Arabic
Sūrīyah; alternate Arabic *Ash Shām*] (The al-
ternate Arabic name is the same as that for
Damascus.)
Syria Palaestina *see* Palestine
Syrnovorossiysk *see* Sirdaryo
Syuginsky *see* Mozhga
Syvas'ke (town, southern Ukraine) : (Russian
Sivashskoye); to 1935 *Rizdvyans'ke* (Russian
Rozhdestvenskoye)
Szabadka *see* Subotica
Szakolca *see* Skalica
Szamosújvár *see* Gherla
Szamotuły (town, western Poland) : 1793–1807,
1815–1919, 1939–1945 German *Samter*
Szászsebes *see* Sebeş
Szászrégen *see* Reghin
Szatmárnémeti *see* Satu Mare
Szczawno Zdrój (town, southwestern Poland) :
to 1945 German *Bad Salzbrunn*
Szczecin (city, northwestern Poland) : to 1945
German *Stettin*
Szczecinek (town, northwestern Poland) : to
1945 German *Neustettin*
Szczuczyn (town, northeastern Poland) :
1939–1941 Belarussian *Shchuchyn*; to 1918 Rus-
sian *Shchuchin*
Szczuczyn Nowogródski *see* Shchuchyn
Szczytna (town, southwestern Poland) : to 1945
German *Rückers*
Szczytno (town, northeastern Poland) : to 1945
German *Ortelsburg*
Szeged (city, southern Hungary) : to 1867 Ger-
man *Szegedin*
Szegedin *see* Szeged
Székelyudvarhely *see* Odorheiu Secuiesc
Székesfehérvár (city, west central Hungary) : to
1867 German *Stuhlweissenburg*; Medieval Latin
Alba Regalis
Szenic *see* Senica
Szentgotthárd (town, western Hungary) : to
1867 German *Sankt Gotthard*

Szenttamás *see* Srbobran
Szepesófalu *see* Spišská Stara Ves
Szepesváralja *see* Spišské Podhradie
Szepsi *see* Moldava nad Bodvou
Szilasbalhás *see* Mezőszilas
Szinna *see* Snina
Szklarska Poręba (town, southwestern Poland) :
to 1945 German *Schreiberhau* (The hamlets of
Szklarska Poręba Górna, *Szklarska Poręba
Dolna*, and *Szklarska Poręba Średnia* had the
German names *Ober-Schreiberhau*, *Nieder-
Schreiberhau*, and *Mittel-Schreiberhau*, respec-
tively Upper, Lower, and Middle, but nearby
Szklarska Poręba Huta, "Factory," was *Josephi-
nenhütte*.)
Szlichtyngowa (town, western Poland) : to 1945
German *Schlichtingsheim*
Szobránce *see* Sobrance
Szolyva *see* Svalyava
Szombathely (city, western Hungary) : to 1867
German *Steinamanger*; Roman *Sabaria*
Szőny (village, northern Hungary) : Roman
Brigetio
Szprotawa (town, southwestern Poland) : to
1945 German *Sprottau*
Sztálinváros *see* Dunaújváros
Sztropkó *see* Stropkov
Sztum (town, northern Poland) : 1793–1945
German *Stuhm*
Sztutowo (village, northern Poland) : 1793–1945
German *Stutthof*
Szubin (town, west central Poland) : 1793–1807,
1815–1919, 1939–1945 German *Schubin*
Szuchahora *see* Suchá Hora
Szumbark Śląski *see* Havířov
Szvidnik *see* Svidník
Taal, Lake (north central Philippines) : formerly
Lake Bombon
Tabaiana *see* Itabaiana
Table Cape *see* Wynyard
Tabor *see* Tábor
Tábor (city, south central Czech Republic) : to
1918, 1939–1945 German *Tabor*
Tabuaeran (island, northeastern Kiribati) : to
1979 *Fanning Island*
Tacape *see* Gabès
Tacarigua *see* Valencia, Lake
Tachov (town, western Czech Republic) : to
1918, 1939–1945 German *Tachow*
Tachow *see* Tachov
Tacoma (city, Washington, northwestern United
States) : originally *Commencement City*
Tacoma, Mt. *see* Rainier, Mt.
T'ačovo *see* Tyachiv
Tacuarembó (city, north central Uruguay) : for-
merly Spanish *San Fructuoso*

Tacurupucú *see* Hernandarias

Tadcaster (town, northern England) : Roman *Calcaria*

Tadmor *see* Palmyra

Tadmur (city, south central Syria) : ancient Greek and Roman *Palmyra*; biblical *Tadmor* (The Greek name is thought to have evolved from the biblical one.)

Taehan *see* Korea

Tafahi (island, northern Tonga) : formerly *Boscawen Island*

Taff's Well (village, southern Wales) : Welsh *Ffynnon Taf*

Tagdempt *see* Tiaret

Tagula (island, southeastern Papua New Guinea) : formerly *Sudest Island*

Tagus (river, central Spain and Portugal) : [Spanish *Tajo*; Portuguese *Tejo*] (English speakers generally know the river by its Roman name.)

Taiei *see* Ugol'ny

Taihape (town, north central New Zealand) : formerly *Otaihape* (The name dropped the original Maori prefix *o* meaning "place of.")

Taihei *see* Udarny

Tairbeart *see* Tarbert

Taiwan (island state, western Pacific) : formerly Portuguese *Formosa*

Tajikabad *see* Tojikobod

Taiyuan (city, northeastern China) : formerly *Yangku*

Tajo *see* Tagus

Tak (town, western Thailand) : locally *Rahaeng*

Takhtamukay (village, southwestern Russia) : formerly *Oktyabr'sky*; to 1938 *Khakurate*

Talacharn *see* Laugharne

Talas (city, northwestern Kyrgyzstan) : to 1937 Russian *Dmitriyevskoye*

Talavera de la Reina (city, central Spain) : Roman *Caesarobriga*

Taldom (town, western Russia) : 1921–1929 *Leninsk*

Taldykorgan (city, southeastern Kazakhstan) : (Russian *Taldy-Kurgan*); to 1920 *Gavrilovka*

Taldy-Kurgan *see* Taldykorgan

Talin (town, western Armenia) : to 1978 *Verin-Talin*

Talitsa (town, west central Russia) : to *c*.1928 *Talitsky Zavod*

Talitsky Zavod *see* Talitsa

Tälje *see* Södertälje

Talley (village, southwestern Wales) : Welsh *Talyllychau*

Tallin *see* Tallinn

Tallinn (city, northern Estonia) : (Russian *Tallin*); 1941–1944 German *Reval*; to 1918 Russian *Revel'*

Taloyoak (village, Nunavut, northern Canada) : to 1999 *Spence Bay*

Talpetate *see* San Antonio de Cortés

Talsen *see* Talsi

Talsi (town, northwestern Latvia) : to 1918 German *Talsen*

Talybont-on-Usk (village, east central Wales) : Welsh *Tal-y-Bont ar Wysg* (The additions to the name were made in *c*.1960 to distinguish this *Tal-y-Bont* from the many others.)

Talyllychau *see* Talley

Tamalameque *see* El Banco

Taman Negara National Park (northwestern Malaysia) : to 1957 *King George V National Park*

Tamanrasset (town, southern Algeria) : to *c*.1962 French *Fort-Laperrine*

Tamar (river, southwestern England) : Roman *Tamarus* (The modern and Roman names of the river are directly related to those of the ¹Thames.)

Tamarus *see* Tamar

Tamatave *see* Toamasina

Tamesis *see* ¹Thames

Tamil Nadu (state, southeastern India) : to 1969 *Madras*

Tamise *see* Temse

Tammerfors *see* Tampere

Tampere (city, southwestern Finland) : to 1809 Swedish *Tammerfors*

Tanais *see* (1) Don; (2) Nedvigovka

Tananarive *see* Antananarivo

Tanatis *see* Thanet, Isle of

Tangar *see* Huangyuan

Tangará (town, southern Brazil) : to 1944 *Rio Bonito*

Tangier (city, northern Morocco) : formerly (and still alternate) English *Tangiers*; Roman *Tingis*

Tangiers *see* Tangier

Tanis (ancient city, northern Egypt) : biblical *Zoan*

Tannenberg *see* Stębark

Tanner's Crossing *see* Minnedosa

Tannu-Tuva *see* Tyva

Taobh Tuath *see* Northton

Taormina (town, southern Italy) : Roman *Tauromenium*

Tapajós *see* ²Santarém

Taperoá (town, northeastern Brazil) : 1944–1948 Portuguese *Batalhão*

Tapiau *see* Gvardeysk

Tapolyvarannó *see* Vranov nad Topl'ou

Taprobane *see* Sri Lanka

Taquari *see* Taquarituba

Taquarituba (town, southeastern Brazil) : to 1944 *Taquari*

Ṭarābulus al-Gharb *see* ²Tripoli
Ṭarābulus ash-Shām *see* ¹Tripoli
Taranaki *see* Egmont, Mt.
Taranovskoye (town, northern Kazakhstan) :
  formerly *Viktorovka*
Taranto (city, southern Italy) : Roman *Tarentum*
Tarauacá (town, western Brazil) : to 1944 *Seabra*
Taraz (city, southeastern Kazakhstan) : 1991–1997
  Zhambyl; 1938–1991 Russian *Dzhambul*; 1936–
  1938 *Mirzoyan*; 1856–1936 *Aulie-Ata*
Tarbert (village, Western Isles, northwestern
  Scotland) : Gaelic *Tairbeart*
Tarentum *see* Taranto
Tarfaya (town, southwestern Morocco) : 1950–
  1958 *Villa Bens* or *Cabo Yubi*; earlier *Port Vic-
  toria*
Târgu Mureş (city, north central Romania) : to
  1918, 1940–1944 Hungarian *Marosvásárhely*
Tarifa (town, southern Spain) : Roman *Julia
  Joza*; alternate Roman *Julia Traducta*
Tarija (city, southern Bolivia) : originally *San
  Bernardo de la Frontera de Tarija*
Tarmilate *see* Oulmès
Târnăveni (town, central Romania) : to 1930
  Diciosânmartin (The earlier name transliterates
  Hungarian *Dicsőszentmárton*, "St. Martin the
  Glorious," meaning Martin of Tours, born in
  Hungary.)
Tarnopil' *see* Ternopil'
Tarnopol *see* Ternopil'
Tarnopol' *see* Ternopil'
Tărnovo *see* Veliko Tărnovo
Tarnow *see* Tarnów
Tarnów (city, southern Poland) : 1940–1945 Ger-
  man *Tarnow*
Tarnowitz *see* Tarnowskie Góry
Tarnowskie Góry (town, southern Poland) : to
  1921, 1939–1945 German *Tarnowitz*
Tarquinia (town, central Italy) : to 1922 *Corneto*;
  Roman *Tarquinii* (The town's present name is
  a deliberate revival of the Roman one.)
Tarquinii *see* Tarquinia
Tarracina *see* Terracina
Tarraco *see* Tarragona
Tarragona (city, northeastern Spain) : Roman
  Tarraco
Tarrant *see* Arun
Tarta (town, western Turkmenistan) : formerly
  Kianly
Tärtär (town, central Azerbaijan) : formerly *Mir-
  Bashir*; to 1949 *Terter*
Tartu (city, eastern Estonia) : 1893–1918 Russian
  Yur'yev; 1224–1893 German *Dorpat*; 1030–
  1224 Russian *Yur'yev*
Tarvedunum *see* Dunnet Head
Tarvis *see* Tarvisio

Tarvisio (town, northeastern Italy) : to 1918 Ger-
  man *Tarvis*
Tarvisium *see* Treviso
Tashauz *see* Daşoguz
Tashino *see* Pervomaysk
Tashir (town, northwestern Armenia) : formerly
  Kalinino; to 1935 *Vorontsovka*
Tashkent (city, eastern Uzbekistan) : [Uzbek
  Toshkent]
Tasiujaq (village, Quebec, eastern Canada) : for-
  merly *Leaf Bay*
Taşlica *see* Pljevlja
Tasmania (island state, southeastern Australia) :
  to 1856 *Van Diemen's Land*
Tata (town, northern Hungary) : to 1867 Ger-
  man *Totis*
Tatarpazarcik *see* Pazardzhik
Tatar-Pazardzhik *see* Pazardzhik
Tátrafüred *see* Stary Smokovec
Tátra-Lomnic *see* Tatranská Lomnica
Tatra-Lomnitz *see* Tatranská Lomnica
Tatranská Lomnica (village, northern Slovakia) :
  to 1918 Hungarian *Tátra-Lomnic*; to 1867 Ger-
  man *Tatra-Lomnitz*
Tatsienlu *see* Kangding
Tauragė (town, western Lithuania) : to 1918 Rus-
  sian *Tavrogi*; to 1793 German *Tauroggen*
Taurasia *see* Turin
Taurida *see* Crimea
Tauroggen *see* Tauragė
Tauromenium *see* Taormina
Taus *see* Domažlice
Tavastehus *see* Hämeenlinna
Tavau *see* Davos
Tavrida *see* Crimea
Tavrogi *see* Tauragė
Tavus *see* Tay
Tay (river, central Scotland) : Roman *Tavus*
Tayabas *see* Quezon
Tayncha *see* Tayynsha
Tayynsha (town, northern Kazakhstan) : (Rus-
  sian *Tayncha*); formerly Russian *Krasnoarmeysk*
Taza-Bazar *see* Shumanay
Taza-Kala *see* Gubadag
Tazoult-Lambèse (town, northeastern Algeria) :
  Roman *Lambaesis*
Tazovskoye *see* Tazovsky
Tazovsky (town, northern Russia) : formerly
  Tazovskoye; earlier *Khal'mer-Sede*
T'bilisi (city, east central Georgia) : to 1936 *Tiflis*
Tbilisskaya (village, southwestern Russia) : to
  1936 *Tiflisskaya*
Tchikala-Tcholohanga (town, central Angola) :
  formerly Portuguese *Vila Nova*
Tczew (town, north central Poland) : 1772–1919,
  1949–1945 German *Dirschau*

Teano (town, southern Italy) : Roman *Teanum Sidicinum*

Teanum Apulum *see* San Paolo di Civitate

Teanum Sidicinum *see* Teano

Teate *see* Chieti

Tébessa (town, eastern Algeria) : Roman *Theveste*

Tecső *see* Tyachiv

Teesville *see* Waynesboro

Teet'lit Zhen *see* Fort McPherson

Teggiano (town, southern Italy) : Roman *Tegianum*

Tegianum *see* Teggiano

Tegucigalpa *see* Francisco Morazán

Teheran *see* Tehran

Tehran (city, northern Iran) : alternate *Teheran*

Te Ika a Maui *see* North Island

Teixeira Pinto *see* Canchungo

Tejo *see* Tagus

Tejuco *see* Diamantina

Tekirdağ (city, northwestern Turkey) : to 1923 *Rodosto*; ancient Greek *Bisanthe*

Tel Aviv-Jafo *see* Jaffa

Telford (town, western England) : to 1968 *Dawley*

Telford and Wrekin (administrative district, western England) : to 1998 *The Wrekin*

Tell el-Farama (village, northeastern Egypt) : Roman *Pelusium*; biblical *Sin*

Tell es Sultan *see* Jericho

Tel'manove (town, southeastern Ukraine) : (Russian *Tel'manovo*); to 1935 *Ostheym* (Russian *Ostgeym*) (The earlier name represents German *Ostheim*.)

Tel'mansk *see* Gubadag

Tel'novsky (town, eastern Russia) : 1905–1945 Japanese *Kita-kozawa*

Telo Martius *see* Toulon

Tel'shi *see* Telšiai

Tel'shyay *see* Telšiai

Telšiai (city, northwestern Lithuania) : (Russian *Tel'shyay*); to 1918 Russian *Tel'shi*

Telukbayur (town, western Indonesia) : formerly *Emmahaven*

Tembershchina *see* Uzyn

Tembershchyna *see* Uzyn

Temeschwar-Josephstadt *see* Timişoara

Temesmóra *see* Stamora Moraviţa

Temesvár *see* Timişoara

Temir-Khan-Shura *see* Buynaksk

Temirtau (city, east central Kazakhstan) : to 1945 Russian *Samarkandsky*

Tempe (city, Arizona, southwestern United States) : to 1880 *Hayden's Ferry*

Tempelburg *see* Czaplinek

Templemore (town, south central Ireland) : Irish *An Teampall Mór*

Templeton (village, southwestern Wales) : Welsh *Tredeml*

Temse (town, northern Belgium) : French *Tamise*

Tenby (town, southwestern Wales) : Welsh *Dinbych-y-pysgod*

Tenda *see* Tende

Tende (village, southeastern France) : to 1947 Italian *Tenda*

Tenedos *see* Bozcaada

Tenevo (village, southeastern Bulgaria) : 1934–1950 *Tervel*; to 1934 *Pandaklii*

Ten Eyck *see* Dearborn

Tenge (town, southwestern Kazakhstan) : to 1977 *Uzen*

Tengi-Kharam *see* Dehqonobod

Teniente Bullaín (town, western Bolivia) : to early 1940s *Dalence*

Tenochtitlán *see* Mexico City

Tent Town *see* Douglas

Tentyra *see* Dendera

Tepelenë (town, southern Albania) : 1919–1921 modern Greek *Tepelenion*

Tepelenion *see* Tepelenë

Tepl *see* Teplá

Teplá (town, western Czech Republic) : to 1918, 1938–1945 German *Tepl*

Teplice (city, northwestern Czech Republic) : formerly *Teplice-Šanov*; to 1918, 1938–1945 German *Teplitz-Schönau*

Teplice nad Metují (town, northeastern Czech Republic) : to 1918, 1939–1945 German *Wekelsdorf*

Teplice-Šanov *see* Teplice

Teplitz-Schönau *see* Teplice

Teplogorsk *see* Teplohirs'k

Teplohirs'k (town, eastern Ukraine) : (Russian *Teplogorsk*); to 1977 *Irmine* (Russian *Irmino*); formerly *Irmins'kyy Rudnyk* (Russian *Irminsky Rudnik*)

Teploozyorsk (town, southeastern Russia) : formerly *Tyoploye Ozero*

Te Punga a Maui *see* Stewart Island

Teraina (island, northeastern Kiribati) : to 1979 *Washington Island*

Teramo (city, central Italy) : Roman *Interamnium*

Terebovlya (town, western Ukraine) : to 1939 Polish *Trembowla*

Terekty (town, eastern Kazakhstan) : formerly Russian *Alekseyevka*

Terezín (town, northern Czech Republic) : to 1918, 1939–1945 German *Theresienstadt*

Tergeste *see* Trieste

Terijoki *see* Zelenogorsk

Termini Imerese (town, southern Italy) : Roman *Thermae Himerenses*

Terminus *see* (1) **Atlanta**; (2) **Dillon**
Termonde *see* **Dendermonde**
Terni (city, central Italy) : Roman *Interamna Nahars*
Ternopil' (city, western Ukraine) : (Russian *Ternopol'*); to 1938 Polish *Tarnopol*; 1918–1919 Ukrainian *Tarnopil'*; 1914–1917 Russian *Tarnopol'* (The earlier Russian name is associated with the 1917 Austro-German victory over the Russians here during World War I.)
Ternopol' *see* **Ternopil'**
Ternovsk *see* **Novokashirsk**
Ternovskoye *see* **Trunovskoye**
Ternovsky *see* **Novokashirsk**
Terracina (town, western Italy) : Roman *Tarracina*
Terranova di Sicilia *see* **Gela**
Terranova Pausania *see* **Olbia**
Terter *see* **Tärtär**
Tervel (town, northeastern Bulgaria) : 1913–1940 Romanian *Curt-Bunar*; to 1878 Turkish *Kurt-bunar*
Tervel *see* **Tenevo**
Teschen *see* (1) **Český Těšín**; (2) **Cieszyn**
Tessin *see* **Ticino**
Tessville *see* **Lincolnwood**
Teterboro (village, New Jersey, northeastern United States) : to 1943 *Bendix*
Tetiyev *see* **Tetiyiv**
Tetiyiv (town, central Ukraine) : (Russian *Tetiyev*); formerly *Snegurovka*
Tetovo (city, northwestern Macedonia) : to 1913 Turkish *Kalkandelen*
Tetri-Tskaro (town, southern Georgia) : to *c.*1945 *Agbulakh*
Tetschen *see* **Děčín**
Tetyukhe *see* **Dal'negorsk**
Tetyukhe-Pristan' *see* **Rudnaya Pristan'**
Teuchezhsk *see* **Adygeysk**
Tevere *see* **Tiber**
Tevis Bluff *see* **Beaumont**
Te Waka a Maui *see* **South Island**
Tezebazar (town, northern Turkmenistan) : formerly Russian *Andreyevsk*
Thailand (kingdom, southeastern Asia) : to 1939, 1945–1948 *Siam*
¹Thames (river, southern England) : Roman *Tamesis* (The latter part of the Roman name gave *Isis* as an alternate name for the Thames in its course through Oxford.)
²Thames (river, Ontario, southeastern Canada) : to 1792 *La Tranche*
Thames *see* **Waihou**
Thamesdown *see* **Swindon**
Thamesford (village, Ontario, southeastern Canada) : formerly *St. Andrews*

Thamugadi *see* **Timgad**
Thanet, Isle of (peninsula, southeastern England) : Roman *Tanatis* (The peninsula was at one time a proper island.)
Thatcher *see* **River Forest**
The Aqueduct *see* **Welland**
Thebacha *see* **Fort Smith**
Thebae *see* **Thebes**
Theben *see* ²**Devín**
The Bend *see* **Moncton**
Thebes (historic city, northern Egypt) : [Arabic *Ṭībah*]; Roman *Thebae*; ancient Greek *Diospolis*; biblical *No*; ancient Egyptian *Waset*
The Camp *see* **Maitland**
The Corners *see* (1) **Clinton**; (2) **Walnut Creek**
The Crushers *see* **Katoomba**
Thedford (village, Ontario, southeastern Canada) : to 1859 *Widder Station*
The Falls *see* ¹**Trenton**
The Ferry *see* ³**Windsor**
The Forks *see* **Wallaceburg**
The Grove *see* **Glenview**
The Gulf *see* **Persian Gulf**
The Hague *see* **Hague, The**
The Lizard *see* **Lizard, The**
The Neck *see* **Portland**
Thenia (town, northern Algeria) : to *c.*1962 French *Ménerville*
Theodosia *see* **Feodosiya**
Thera (island, southeastern Greece) : alternate *Santorini*
The Rapids *see* **Sarnia**
Theresienstadt *see* **Terezín**
Therma *see* **Eagle Nest**
Thermae Himerenses *see* **Termini Imerese**
Theronsville *see* **Pofadder**
Thessalonica *see* **Salonika**
Thessaloniki *see* **Salonika**
The Swamp *see* **Toowoomba**
Thetford Mines (town, Quebec, southeastern Canada) : formerly *Kingsville*
Theunissen (town, central South Africa) : formerly *Smaldeel*
Theveste *see* **Tébessa**
The Wrekin *see* **Telford and Wrekin**
Thiersville *see* **Ghriss**
Thionville (town, northeastern France) : 1870–1919 German *Diedenhofen*
Thomastown (town, southeastern Ireland) : Irish *Baile Mhic Andáin*
Thompson *see* **Rossland**
Thompsonville *see* **Sioux City**
Thomson's Falls *see* **Nyahururu**
Thorburn (village, Nova Scotia, eastern Canada) : to 1886 *Vale Colliery*
Thorn *see* **Toruń**

Thorn Grove *see* **Chicago Heights**
Thornloe *see* **New Liskeard**
Thoune *see* **Thun**
Thourout *see* **Torhout**
Three Forks *see* **Pullman**
Three Partners' Mill *see* **¹Lakewood**
Three Rivers *see* **Trois-Rivières**
Thun (town, west central Switzerland) : French *Thoune*
Thunder Bay (city, Ontario, southern Canada) : alternate *Lakehead* (The city was created in 1970 on the amalgamation of the twin cities of Fort William and Port Arthur and adjacent townships. *Lakehead* is properly the area around the bay that gave the city's name.)
Thurgau (canton, northeastern Switzerland) : French *Thurgovie*
Thurgovie *see* **Thurgau**
Thurii *see* **Sibari**
Thüringen *see* **Thuringia**
Thuringia (region, southern Germany) : [German *Thüringen*]
Thurles (town, south central Ireland) : Irish *Durlas*
Thyatira *see* **Akhisar**
Thysdrus *see* **El Djem**
Thysville *see* **Mbanza-Ngungu**
Tiaret (city, northern Algeria) : formerly *Tagdempt*
Ṭībah *see* **Thebes**
Tiber (river, central Italy) : [Italian *Tevere*]; Roman *Tiberis*
Tiberias, Sea of *see* **Galilee, Sea of**
Tiberis *see* **Tiber**
Tibet (autonomous region, southwestern China) : [Tibetan *Bod*; Chinese *Xizang*]
Tibur *see* **Tivoli**
Ticino (canton, southern Switzerland) : French *Tessin*
Ticinum *see* **Pavia**
Ticonderoga (village, New York, northeastern United States) : to 1759 *Fort Carillon*
Tiegenhof *see* **Nowy Dwór Gdański**
Tienen (town, central Belgium) : French *Tirlemont*
Tierra de O'Higgins *see* **Antarctic Peninsula**
Tiflis *see* **T'bilisi**
Tiflisskaya *see* **Tbilisskaya**
Tigh a Ghearraidh *see* **Tigharry**
Tigharry (village, Western Isles, northwestern Scotland) : Gaelic *Tigh a Ghearraidh*
Tighenif (town, northwestern Algeria) : formerly *Palikao*
Tighina (city, southeastern Moldova) : 1940–1991 Russian *Bendery*; 1919–1940 Romanian *Tighina*; 1538–1918 Russian *Bendery* (The alternate form *Bender* was also current.)

Tigranocerta *see* **Silvan**
Tigris (river, southeastern Turkey/northern Iraq) : [Arabic *Ad Dijla*]; biblical *Hiddekel*
Tikhon'kaya *see* **Birobidzhan**
Tikhonovka *see* **Pozharskoye**
Tikhono-Zadonsky *see* **²Kropotkin**
Tikirarjuaq *see* **Whale Cove**
Tilbury (town, Ontario, southeastern Canada) : to 1895 *Tilbury Centre*
Tilbury Centre *see* **Tilbury**
Tiligulo-Berezanka *see* **Berezanka**
Tilsit *see* **¹Sovetsk**
Tiltonsville (village, Ohio, north central United States) : to 1930 *Grover*
Timashyovsk (town, southwestern Russia) : to 1966 *Timashyovskaya*
Timashyovskaya *see* **Timashyovsk**
Timbiras (town, northeastern Brazil) : to 1944 *Monte Alegre*
Timbuctoo *see* **Timbuktu**
Timbuktu (city, central Mali) : alternate French *Tombouctou*; traditional English *Timbuctoo* (The traditional form entered the English language as a generic name for a remote place.)
Timgad (town, northeastern Algeria) : Roman *Thamugadi*
Timiryazevo (village, western Russia) : to 1945 German *Neukirch*
Timiryazevsky (town, southern Russia) : to 1940 *Novaya Eushta*
Timişoara (city, western Romania) : to 1918 Hungarian *Temesvár*; to 1867 German *Temeschwar-Josephstadt*
Timon (city, northeastern Brazil) : to 1944 *Flores*
Timor Timur *see* **East Timor**
Tinea *see* **Tyne**
Tingis *see* **Tangier**
Tingvalla *see* **Karlstad**
Tintern (village, southeastern Wales) : Welsh *Tyndyrn*
Tiobraid Árann *see* **Tipperary**
Tipp City (town, Ohio, north central United States) : formerly *Tippecanoe City*
Tippecanoe City *see* **Tipp City**
Tipperary (town, south central Ireland) : Irish *Tiobraid Árann*
Tiptona *see* **¹Columbus**
Tirana *see* **Tiranë**
Tiranë (city, central Albania) : alternate *Tirana*
Tırhala *see* **Trikala**
Tirlemont *see* **Tienen**
Tırnova *see* (1) **Malko Tărnovo**; (2) **Veliko Tărnovo**
Tirol *see* **Tyrol**
Tirolo *see* **Tyrol**
Tirschtiegel *see* **Trzciel**

Tiruchchirappalli (city, southern India) : formerly (and still also alternate) *Trichinopoly*

Tischnowitz *see* **Tišnov**

Tišnov (town, southeastern Czech Republic) : to 1918, 1939–1945 German *Tischnowitz*

Tisovec (town, south central Slovakia) : to 1918 Hungarian *Tiszolc*

Tissemsilt (town, northern Algeria) : to *c.*1962 French *Vialar*

Tiszaszederkény *see* **Tiszaújváros**

Tiszaújváros (town, northeastern Hungary); 1970–1990 *Lenínváros*; to 1970 *Tiszaszederkény*

Tiszolc *see* **Tisovec**

Titicut *see* **Bridgewater**

Titograd *see* **Podgorica**

Titova Korenica (village, western Croatia) : to *c.*1945 *Korenica*

Titova Mitrovica *see* **Kosovska Mitrovica**

Titovo Užice *see* **Užice**

Titovo Velenje *see* **Velenje**

Titov Veles *see* **Veles**

Titov Vrbas *see* **Vrbas**

Titusville (city, Florida, southeastern United States) : to 1874 *Sand Point*

Tivoli (city, central Italy) : Roman *Tibur*

Tlaxiaco (town, southeastern Mexico) : alternate formal *Heroica Ciudad de Tlaxiaco*; formerly *Santa María Asunción Tlaxiaco*

Tłuste *see* **Tovste**

Tmolus *see* **Boz Dağ**

Toamasina (city, eastern Madagascar) : formerly French *Tamatave*

Tobias Barreto (city, northeastern Brazil) : to 1944 *Campos*

Toblach *see* **Dobbiaco**

Tobruk (city, northern Libya) : ancient Greek *Antipyrgos*

Tocantinópolis (city, north central Brazil) : to 1944 *Boa Vista*

Tocqueville *see* **Ras el Oued**

Todi (town, central Italy) : Roman *Tuder*

Todor Ikonomovo (village, northeastern Bulgaria) : to 1934 *Makhmuzlii*

Todos Santos *see* ¹**Concord**

Togliattigrad *see* **Tol'yatti**

Tojikobod (town, central Tajikistan) : (Russian *Tajikabad*); to 1949 *Kalay-Lyabiob*

Tokarivka *see* ²**Pershotravens'k**

Tokaryovka *see* ²**Pershotravens'k**

Tokelau (island group, central Pacific) : 1919–1946 *Union Islands*

Töketerebes *see* **Trebišov**

Tokmak (city, southeastern Ukraine) : to 1962 *Velykyy Tokmak* (Russian *Bol'shoy Tokmak*)

Toktogul (town, west central Kyrgyzstan) : formerly *Muztor*; 1940–1944 *Toktogul*; to 1940 *Akchi-Karasu*

Tokyo (city, east central Japan) : to 1868 *Edo*

Tôlanaro (town, southeastern Madagascar) : formerly French *Fort-Dauphin*

Tolbiacum *see* **Zülpich**

Tolbukhin *see* **Dobrich**

Tole Bi (village, southeastern Kazakhstan) : formerly Russian *Novotroitskoye*

Toledo (city, central Spain) : Roman *Toletum*

Tolentino (town, central Italy) : Roman *Tolentinum*

Tolentinum *see* **Tolentino**

Toletum *see* **Toledo**

Toliary (town, southwestern Madagascar) : to 1978 *Tuléar*

Tolkemit *see* **Tolkmicko**

Tolkmicko (town, northern Poland) : 1772–1945 German *Tolkemit*

Tolmeta (town, northeastern Libya) : ancient Greek *Ptolemaïs*

Tolosa *see* **Toulouse**

Tolstoye *see* **Tovste**

Tol'yatti (city, western Russia) : to 1964 *Stavropol'* (The city, named for the Italian Communist politician Palmiro Togliatti, became known to Italians as *Togliattigrad*, translating Russian *gorod Tol'yatti*, "city of Tol'yatti," following construction of the Italian-backed FIAT automobile manufacturing plant here, the largest in Russia.)

Tomanivi (mountain, western Fiji) : formerly *Mt. Victoria*

Tomari (town, eastern Russia) : 1905–1945 Japanese *Tomarioru*

Tomari *see* **Golovnino**

Tomarikishi *see* **Vakhrushev**

Tomarioru *see* **Tomari**

Tombiacum *see* **Zülpich**

Tombouctou *see* **Timbuktu**

Tombua (town, southwestern Angola) : formerly Portuguese *Porto Alexandre*

Tomesha *see* **Death Valley**

Tomi *see* **Constanţa**

Tomislavgrad (town, southwestern Bosnia-Herzegovina) : 1945–1991 *Duvno*

Tønder (town, southwestern Denmark) : 1864–1920 German *Tondern*

Tondern *see* **Tønder**

Tonekabon (town, northern Iran) : to 1980 *Shahsavar*

Tonga (island kingdom, southwestern Pacific) : formerly *Friendly Islands*

Tongeren (town, northeastern Belgium) : French *Tongres*

Tongking *see* **Hanoi**

Tongres *see* Tongeren
Tongzhou *see* Nantong
Tonkin *see* Hanoi
Tonquin *see* Hanoi
Toowoomba (city, Queensland, eastern Australia) : originally *The Swamp*
Topol'čany (city, western Slovakia) : to 1918 Hungarian *Nagytapolcsány*
Topolovgrad (town, southeastern Bulgaria) : to 1934 *Kavaklii*; to 1878 Turkish *Kavaklı*
Topolya *see* Bačka Topola
Topornino *see* Kushnarenkovo
Torda *see* Turda
Torez (city, southeastern Ukraine) : 1870s–1964 *Chystyakove* (Russian *Chistyakovo*); 1840–1870s *Oleksiyeve-Leonove* (Russian *Alekseyevo-Leonovo*); earlier *Oleksiyivka* (Russian *Alekseyevka*)
Torgovaya *see* Sal'sk
Torhout (town, western Belgium) : French *Thourout*
Torino *see* Turin
Torlak *see* Tsar Kaloyan
Tornal'a (town, southern Slovakia) : 1949–1990 *Šafárikovo*; to 1918, 1938–1945 Hungarian *Tornalja*
Tornalja *see* Tornal'a
Torneå *see* Tornio
Tornio (town, western Finland) : to 1809 Swedish *Torneå*
Toro *see* Shakhtyorsk
Toronto (city, Ontario, southeastern Canada) : 1793–1834 *York* (The earlier name remains represented in the metropolitan borough of *York*.)
Torrington (city, Connecticut, northeastern United States) : to 1732 *New Orleans Village*
To'rtko'l (town, western Uzbekistan) : (Russian *Turtkul*); to *c*.1920 Russian *Petroaleksandrovsk*
Tortona (town, northwestern Italy) : Roman *Dertona*
Toruń (city, northern Poland) : 1793–1807, 1815–1919, 1939–1945 German *Thorn*
Toscana *see* Tuscany
Toscanella *see* Tuscania
Toshkent *see* Tashkent
Totis *see* Tata
Tótmegyer *see* Palárikovo
Toul (town, northeastern France) : Roman *Tullum*
Toulon (city, southeastern France) : Roman *Telo Martius*
Toulouse (city, southern France) : Roman *Tolosa*
Tourane *see* Da Nang
Tournai (city, southwestern Belgium) : Flemish *Doornik*; Roman *Turnacum*

Tours (city, west central France) : Roman *Caesarodunum*
Tovarishcha Khatayevicha, imeni *see* Synel'nykove
Tovarkovo *see* Tovarkovsky
Tovarkovsky (town, western Russia) : 1932–1957 *Kaganovich*; to 1932 *Tovarkovo*
Tovarysha Katayevycha, imeny *see* Synel'nykove
Tovste (town, western Ukraine) : (Russian *Tolstoye*); to 1939 Polish *Tłuste*
Towcester (town, south central England) : Roman *Lactodurum*
Town of Kansas *see* [1]Kansas City
Towyn *see* Tywyn
Toyohara *see* Yuzhno-Sakhalinsk
Toyota (city, central Japan) : to 1938 *Koromo*
Trabzon (city, northeastern Turkey) : formerly *Trebizond*; ancient Greek *Trapezus* (The former name is historically valid for the Greek empire, with the city as its capital, that existed from 1204 to 1461.)
Tracadigetche *see* Carleton
Trachenberg *see* Żmigród
Tragurium *see* Trogir
Trail (town, British Columbia, southwestern Canada) : to 1897 *Trail Creek*
Trail Creek *see* Trail
Trajani Portus *see* Civitavecchia
Trajan Way *see* Via
Trajectum ad Mosam *see* Maastricht
Trajectum ad Rhenum *see* Utrecht
Trakai (town, southeastern Lithuania) : (Russian *Trakay*); to 1918 Russian *Troki*
Trakay *see* Trakai
Tralee (town, southwestern Ireland) : Irish *Trá Lí*
Trá Lí *see* Tralee
Transcarpathian Oblast (administrative region, western Ukraine) : (Russian *Zakarpatskaya Oblast*); [Ukrainian *Zakarpats'ka Oblast*]; formerly *Ruthenia*
Transilvania *see* Transylvania
Transjordan *see* Jordan
Transvaal (region, northeastern South Africa) : 1857–1877, 1884–1902 *South African Republic* (The former name should not be confused with that of the present Republic of **South Africa**.)
Transylvania (region, western and central Romania) : [Romanian *Transilvania*]; 1867–1918 Hungarian *Erdély*; earlier German *Siebenbürgen*
Trapani (city, southern Italy) : Roman *Drepanum*
Trapezus *see* Trabzon
Trau *see* Trogir
Traù *see* Trogir

Trautenau *see* Trutnov

Trbovlje (town, central Slovenia) : to 1918, 1941–1945 German *Trifail*

Treamlod *see* Ambleston

Třebechovice pod Orebem (town, east central Czech Republic) : to 1918, 1939–1945 German *Hohenbruck*

Treberfedd *see* Middletown

Třebíč (town, southern Czech Republic) : to 1918, 1939–1945 German *Trebitsch*

Trebišov (city, southeastern Slovakia) : to 1918 Hungarian *Töketerebes*

Trebitsch *see* Třebíč

Trebizond *see* Trabzon

Trebnitz *see* Trzebnica

Třeboň (town, southern Czech Republic) : to 1918, 1939–1945 German *Wittingau*

Trecelyn *see* Newbridge

Tredegar Newydd *see* New Tredegar

Tredelerch *see* Rumney

Tredeml *see* Templeton

Trefaldwyn *see* Montgomery

Trefdraeth *see* ²Newport

Treffynnon *see* Holywell

Trefonnen *see* Nash

Treforgan *see* Morganstown

Treforys *see* Morriston

Trefyclo *see* Knighton

Trefynwy *see* Monmouth

Tregatwg *see* Cadoxton

Tre-groes *see* ³Whitchurch

Tre-gŵyr *see* Gowerton

Treletert *see* Letterston

Trembowla *see* Terebovlya

Tremedal *see* Monte Azul

Tremessen *see* Trzemeszno

Trenćianske Teplice (town, western Slovakia) : to 1918 Hungarian *Trencsén-Teplic*; to 1867 German *Trentschiner Bad*

Trenčín (town, western Slovakia) : to 1918 Hungarian *Trencsén*; to 1867 German *Trentschin*

Trencsén *see* Trenčín

Trencsén-Teplic *see* Trenćianske Teplice

Trent (river, east central England) : Roman *Trisantona*

Trent *see* Trento

Trentino-Alto Adige (region, northeastern Italy) : 1919–1947 *Venezia Tridentina*

Trento (city, northern Italy) : to 1918 German *Trient*; formerly English *Trent*; Roman *Tridentum* (The English name is historically preserved for the Council of Trent, the ecumenical council of the Roman Catholic church, which met here in the 16th century.)

¹Trenton (city, New Jersey, northeastern United States) : to 1721 *The Falls*

²Trenton (city, Michigan, northern United States) : 1837–1847 *Truago*; to 1837 *Truaxton*

³Trenton (town, Ontario, southeastern Canada) : formerly *Trent Town*; originally *Trent Port*

Trent Port *see* ³Trenton

Trentschin *see* Trenčín

Trentschiner Bad *see* Trenćianske Teplice

Trent Town *see* ³Trenton

Treptow *see* Altentreptow

Treptow an der Rega *see* Trzebiatów

Três Rios (city, southeastern Brazil) : to 1943 *Entre Rios*

Tres Tabernae *see* Saverne

Tresimwn *see* Bonvilston

III Internatsionala, imeni *see* Novoshakhtinsk

Treuburg *see* Olecko

Treurfontein *see* Coligny

Treves *see* Trier

Trèves *see* Trier

Treviso (city, northeastern Italy) : Roman *Tarvisium*

Trewyddel *see* Moylgrove

Trichinopoly *see* Tiruchchirappalli

Tridentum *see* Trento

Trient *see* Trento

Trier (city, western Germany) : 1801–1815 French *Trèves*; formerly English *Treves*; Roman *Augusta Treverorum*

Triest *see* Trieste

Trieste (city, northeastern Italy) : to 1919 German *Triest*; Roman *Tergeste*

Trifail *see* Trbovlje

Trigo de Morais *see* Chókwé

Trikala (town, northern Greece) : to 1881 Turkish *Tırhala*

Trikora (mountain, western Indonesia) : to 1963 *Wilhelmina Top*

Trim (town, eastern Ireland) : Irish *Baile Átha Troim*

Trimontium *see* (1) Newstead; (2) Plovdiv

Trinchera de los Paraguayos *see* Posadas

Trinchera de San José *see* Posadas

Třinec (town, eastern Czech Republic) : 1939–1945 German *Trzynietz*; 1918–1919, 1938–1939 Polish *Trzyniec*; to 1918 German *Trzynietz*

¹Tripoli (city, northwestern Lebanon) : [Arabic *Ṭarābulus ash-Shām*]; ancient Greek *Tripolis*. (The Greek name was that of the capital of a federation of three cities: *Sidon* [now **Saida**], *Tyre* [now **Sur**], and *Aradus* [now **Arwad**]. The Arabic name, meaning "northern Tripoli," distinguishes the city from ²**Tripoli**.)

²Tripoli (city, northwestern Libya) : [Arabic *Ṭarābulus al-Gharb*]; ancient Greek *Tripolis*. (The Greek name was originally that of a federation of three cities: *Leptis Magna* (now **Lab-**

dah), *Sabrata*, and *Oea*, which last alone sur-
vived into medieval times and became identified with the present city. The Arabic name,
meaning "western Tripoli," distinguishes the
city from ¹**Tripoli**.)
Tripolis *see* ¹,²**Tripoli**
Trisantona *see* (1) **Arun**; (2) **Trent**
Trnava (city, western Slovakia) : to 1918 Hungar-
ian *Nagyszombat*; to 1867 German *Tyrnau*
Trogir (town, southern Croatia) : 1941–1943 Ital-
ian *Traù*; to 1918 German *Trau*; Roman *Tra-
gurium*
Troia *see* ¹**Troy**
Trois-Marabouts *see* **Sidi Ben Adda**
Trois-Rivières (city, Quebec, southeastern
Canada) : English *Three Rivers*
Troitskosavsk *see* **Kyakhta**
Troitsky (city, west central Russia) : to 1928
Peklevskaya
Troki *see* **Trakai**
Trondheim (city, central Norway) : 1930–1931
Nidaros; 1537–1930 *Trondhjem*; 1016–1537
Nidaros; originally *Kaupangr* (The earlier name
lives on in the city's *Nidaros* cathedral.)
Trondhjem *see* **Trondheim**
Troodos (mountain, southwestern Cyprus) : for-
merly *Mt. Olympus* (This is not the famous
Mt. Olympus, home of the Greek gods, which
is in northeastern Greece.)
Troppau *see* **Opava**
Trotsk *see* (1) **Chapayevsk**; (2) **Gatchina**
Troupsville *see* **Carrollton**
Troupville *see* **Valdosta**
¹**Troy** (historic city, western Turkey) : Roman
Troia; alternate Roman *Ilium*; ancient Greek
Ilion (The precise site of ancient Troy was
definitively identified only in the 19th century
as a large mound south of the Dardanelles
known by the Turkish name *Hisarlık*.)
²**Troy** (city, New York, northeastern United
States) : to 1789 *Vanderheyden's Ferry*
Troy *see* (1) ²**Aylmer**; (2) **Fall River**
Troyes (city, northeastern France) : Roman *Civi-
tas Tricassium*; earlier Roman *Augustobona*
Trstená (town, northern Slovakia) : to 1918 Hun-
garian *Trsztena*
Trsztena *see* **Trstená**
Truago *see* ²**Trenton**
Truaxton *see* ²**Trenton**
Trucial Oman *see* **United Arab Emirates**
Trucial States *see* **United Arab Emirates**
Trud (village, south central Bulgaria) : to 1943
Klimentina; to 1889 *Chiriplii*
Trudovaya Kommuna imeni Dzerzhinskogo
see **Dzerzhinsky**
Trujillo (town, western Spain) : Roman *Turgalium*

Trujillo *see* ¹**San Cristóbal**
Trujillo, Monte *see* **Duarte, Pico**
Trujillo Bajo *see* **Carolina**
Trujillo Valdéz *see* **Peravia**
Truk *see* **Chuuk**
Trunovskoye (village, southwestern Russia) : to
1936 *Ternovskoye*
Truth or Consequences (town, New Mexico,
southwestern United States) : 1916–1950 *Hot
Springs*; to 1916 *Springs of Palomas* (The town's
original name was that of the springs by which
it arose.)
Trutnov (town, northern Czech Republic) : to
1918, 1938–1945 German *Trautenau*
Trzcianka (town, northwestern Poland) : to 1945
German *Schönlanke*
Trzciel (town, western Poland) : to 1945 German
Tirschtiegel
Trzcińsko Zdrój (town, northwestern Poland) :
to 1925 *Bad Schönfliess in Neumark*
Trzebiatów (town, northwestern Poland) : to
1945 German *Treptow an der Rega*
Trzebnica (town, southwestern Poland) : to 1945
German *Trebnitz*
Trzemeszno (town, west central Poland) : 1793–
1807, 1815–1919, 1939–1945 German *Tremessen*
Tržič (town, northern Slovenia) : to 1918,
1941–1945 German *Neumarktl*
Trzyniec *see* **Třinec**
Trzynietz *see* **Třinec**
Tsarekonstantinovka *see* ¹**Kuybysheve**
Tsarekostyantynivka *see* ¹**Kuybysheve**
Tsarevicha Alekseya *see* **Maly Taymyr**
Tsarevo (town, southeastern Bulgaria) : 1950–
1989 *Michurin*; 1934–1950 *Tsarevo*; to 1934
Vasiliko
Tsaritsyn *see* **Volgograd**
Tsaritsyno *see* ¹**Lenino**
Tsar Kaloyan (town, northeastern Bulgaria) : to
1934 *Torlak*; earlier *Khlebarovo*
Tsarskoye Selo *see* **Pushkin**
Tsaryovokokshaysk *see* **Yoshkar-Ola**
Tsaryovosanchursk *see* **Sanchursk**
Tschaslau *see* **Čáslav**
Tschechische Teschen *see* **Česky Těšín**
Tschenstochau *see* **Częstochowa**
Tschirnau *see* **Czernina**
Tselinograd *see* **Astana**
Tsementny *see* **Fokino**
Tsentrosoyuz *see* **Komsomol's'kyy**
Tshwane (city, northeastern South Africa) : to
2007 *Pretoria* (The new name was officially
applied to the metropolitan area of Pretoria
rather than the inner city.)
Tsiigehtchic (village, Northwest Territories,
northwestern Canada) : to 1999 *Arctic Red River*

Tskhakaya *see* Senaki
Ts'khinvali (city, north central Georgia) : 1934–1961 *Staliniri*
Tskhum *see* Sokhumi
Tsulukidze *see* Khoni
Tsurukhaytuy *see* Priargunsk
Tsyurupinsk *see* Tsyurupyns'k
Tsyurupy, imeni (town, western Russia) : to 1935 *Vanilovo*
Tsyurupyns'k (town, southern Ukraine) : (Russian *Tsyurupinsk*); to 1928 *Oleshky* (Russian *Alyoshki*)
Tthedzeh Koe *see* Wrigley
Tthenaagoo *see* Nahanni Butte
Tuaim *see* Tuam
Tuam (town, western Ireland) : Irish *Tuaim*
Tuapeka *see* Lawrence
Túbano *see* Padre Las Casas
Tuchel *see* Tuchola
Tuchola (town, northern Poland) : 1772–1919, 1939–1945 German *Tuchel*
Tucuruí (city, northeastern Brazil) : to 1944 *Alcobaça*
Tuczno (town, northwestern Poland) : to 1945 German *Tütz*
Tuder *see* Todi
Tüffer *see* Laško
Tuktoyaktuk (village, Northwest Territories, northwestern Canada) : 1939–1950 *Port Brabant*
Tukum *see* Tukums
Tukums (town, northern Latvia) : to 1918 Russian *Tukum*
Tukuyu (town, southwestern Tanzania) : formerly German *Neu-Langenburg*
Tulach Mhór *see* Tullamore
Tulatovo *see* Iriston
Tulça *see* Tulcea
Tulcea (city, southeastern Romania) : to 1878 Turkish *Tulça*
Tuléar *see* Toliary
Tuleburg *see* Stockton
Tulita (village, Northwest Territories, northwestern Canada) : to 1999 *Fort Norman*
Tullamore (town, central Ireland) : Irish *Tulach Mhór*
Tullum *see* Toul
Tumanyan (town, northern Armenia) : to 1951 *Dzagidzor*
Tun *see* Ferdows
Tunes *see* Tunis
Tunis (city, northeastern Tunisia) : Roman *Tunes*
Tunis *see* Tunisia
Tunisia (republic, northern Africa) : formerly *Tunis*
Tupaciretã *see* Tupanciretã

Tupanciretã (city, southern Brazil) : to 1938 *Tupaciretã*
Tupelo (city, Mississippi, southern United States) : originally *Gum Pond*
Tura (town, central Russia) : to 1938 *Tur'inskaya Kul'tbaza*
Turanga *see* Gisborne
Turar Ryskulov (town, southern Kazakhstan) : formerly Russian *Vannovka*
Turčianske Teplice (town, west central Slovakia) : to 1945 *Štubnianske Teplice*
Turčiansky Svätý Martin *see* Martin
Turda (city, northwestern Romania) : to 1918 Hungarian *Torda*
Turdossin *see* Tvrdošín
Turenne *see* Sabra
Turgalium *see* Trujillo
Tŭrgovishte (city, east central Bulgaria) : 1878–1909 *Eski Dzhumaya*; to 1878 Turkish *Eski-cumaa* (The city should not be confused with Târgovişte, south central Romania.)
Turin (city, northeastern Italy) : [Italian *Torino*]; Roman *Augusta Taurinorum*; earlier Roman *Taurasia*
Tur'inskaya Kul'tbaza *see* Tura
Tur'inskiye Rudniki *see* Krasnotur'insk
Turkana, Lake (northern Kenya) : to 1975 (and still alternate) *Lake Rudolf*
Turkestan (city, southern Kazakhstan) : formerly *Yasi*; earlier *Shavgar*
Turkey (republic, southeastern Europe/southwestern Asia) : [Turkish *Türkiye*] (European Turkey represents only about 3 percent of the country's area. Asian Turkey is also known as **Anatolia**.)
Turkey Hill *see* Fitchburg
Türkiye *see* Turkey
Türkmenabat (city, eastern Turkmenistan) : 1940–1999 *Chardzhou*; 1927–1940 *Chardzhuy*; 1924–1927 *Leninsk-Turkmensky*
Turkmenbashi (city, northwestern Turkmenistan) : to 1994 Russian *Krasnovodsk*
Turku (city, southwestern Finland) : to 1809 Swedish *Åbo*
Turnacum *see* Tournai
Turnau *see* Turnov
Turnov (town, northern Czech Republic) : to 1918, 1939–1945 German *Turnau*
Turócszentmárton *see* Martin Turris Libisonis *see* Porto Torres
Turski Trŭstenik *see* Slavyanovo
Tursunzade (town, western Tajikistan) : 1952–1978 *Regar*; to 1952 Russian *Stantsiya-Regar*
Turtkul' *see* To'rtk'ol
Turtucaia *see* Tutrakan
Tuscania (town, central Italy) : to 1911 *Toscanella*

Tuscany (region, central Italy) : [Italian *Toscana*]

Tusket Wedge *see* **Wedgeport**

Tutayev (city, western Russia) : to 1918 *Romanov-Borisoglebsk* (The former name represents the two sections of the town, either side of the Volga.)

Tutrakan (town, northeastern Bulgaria) : 1913–1940 Romanian *Turtucaia*

Tütz *see* **Tuczno**

Tuva *see* **Tyva**

Tuvalu (island republic, southwestern Pacific) : to 1978 *Ellice Islands* (In 1916 the islands became part of the British *Gilbert and Ellice Islands* colony, with the *Gilbert Islands* giving the name of **Kiribati**.)

Tver' (city, western Russia) : 1931–1991 *Kalinin*

Tvrdošín (town, northern Slovakia) : to 1918 Hungarian *Turdossin*

Twardogóra (town, southwestern Poland) : to 1945 German *Festenberg*

Twickenham *see* **Huntsville**

Tyachev *see* **Tyachiv**

Tyachiv (town, western Ukraine) : (Russian *Tyachev*); 1944–1945 Czech *T'ačovo*; 1938–1944 Hungarian *Tecső*; 1919–1938 Czech *T'ačovo*; to 1918 Hungarian *Tecső*

Tyan'-Shan' *see* ¹**Naryn**

Tyatino (village, eastern Russia) : 1905–1945 Japanese *Chinomiji*

Tyddewi *see* **St. David's**

Tŷ-du *see* **Rogerstone**

Tylyhulo-Berezanka *see* **Berezanka**

Tymovskoye (town, eastern Russia) : to 1949 *Derbinskoye*

Tynda (city, eastern Russia) : to 1975 *Tyndinsky*

Tyndinsky *see* **Tynda**

Tyndyrn *see* **Tintern**

Tyne (river, northeastern England) : Roman *Tinea*

Tyngstown *see* ²**Manchester**

Týn nad Vltavou (town, southern Czech Republic) : to 1918, 1939–1945 German *Moldautein*

Tyoploye Ozero *see* **Teploozyorsk**

Tyoply Klyuch *see* **Klyuchevsk**

Tyoply Stan *see* **Sechenovo**

Tyras *see* (1) **Bilhorod-Dnistrovs'kyy**; (2) **Dniester**

Tyre *see* **Sur**

Tyrisevä *see* **Ushkovo**

Tyrnau *see* **Trnava**

Tyrol (region, western Austria/northern Italy) : alternate *Tirol*; [Italian *Tirolo*] (The northern part of the region is now the Austrian state of *Tirol*, with the German form of the name. In 1919 the southern part became the Italian district of *Alto Adige*, now **Trentino-Alto Adige**.)

Tyuriseva *see* **Ushkovo**

Tyva (republic, southern Russia) : (Russian *Tuva*); formerly Russian *Tannu-Tuva*; to 1921 Mongolian *Uriankhai*

Tywyn (village, western Wales) : formerly mostly *Towyn* (The present spelling distinguishes the village from *Towyn* in northern Wales. Both are seaside resorts.)

Uachtar Ard *see* **Oughterard**

Ubaíra (town, eastern Brazil) : to 1944 *Areia*

Ubaitaba (town, eastern Brazil) : to 1944 *Itapira*

Ubangi-Shari *see* **Central African Republic**

Ubirama *see* **Lençóis Paulista**

Ubundu (town, northeastern Democratic Republic of the Congo) : to 1966 French *Ponthierville*

Uccle (town, central Belgium) : Flemish *Ukkel* (The town is now a suburb of Brussels.)

Uch-Korgon (village, western Kyrgyzstan) : 1938–1957 Russian *Molotovabad*; to 1938 *Uch-Kurgan* (The village should not be confused with the town of *Uchkurgan*, eastern Uzbekistan.)

Uchkuprik (village, eastern Uzbekistan) : *c.*1940–1957 Russian *Molotovo*; 1937–*c.*1940 Russian *imeni Molotova*; to 1937 *Uchkupryuk*

Uchkupryuk *see* **Uchkuprik**

Uch-Kurgan *see* **Uch-Korgon**

Udagamandalam (town, southern India) : formerly English *Ootacamund*

Udarny (town, eastern Russia) : 1905–1945 Japanese *Taihei*

Udd *see* **Chkalov**

Udine (province, northeastern Italy) : 1923–*c.*1945 *Friuli*

Udmurt Autonomous Oblast *see* **Udmurt Republic**

Udmurt Autonomous Republic *see* **Udmurt Republic**

Udmurtia *see* **Udmurt Republic**

Udmurt Republic (western Russia) : alternate *Udmurtia*; 1934–1991 *Udmurt Autonomous Republic*; 1932–1934 *Udmurt Autonomous Oblast*; 1920–1932 *Votyak Autonomous Oblast* (The various names involve a change in political status or ethnic appellation.)

Ugernum *see* **Beaucaire**

Uggehnen *see* **Matrosovo**

Uglegorsk (town, eastern Russia) : 1905–1945 Japanese *Esutoru*

Uglegorsk *see* **Vuhlehirs'k**

Uglekamensk (village, southeastern Russia) : to 1972 *Severny Suchan*

Ugleural'sky (town, west central Russia) : to 1951 *Polovinka*

Uglezavodsk (town, eastern Russia) : 1905–1945 Japanese *Higashi-naibuchi*

Ugnev *see* Uhniv
Ugodsky Zavod *see* Zhukovo
Ugol'ny (village, eastern Russia) : 1905–1945
  Japanese *Taiei*
Ugol'ny *see* Karpinsk
Ugol'nyye Kopi *see* Kopeysk
Uherské Hradiště (city, southeastern Czech Re-
  public) : to 1918, 1939–1945 German *Un-
  garisch-Hradisch*
Uherský Brod (town, southeastern Czech Re-
  public) : to 1918, 1939–1945 German *Ungar-
  isch-Brod*
Uherský Ostroh (town, southeastern Czech Re-
  public) : to 1918, 1939–1945 German *Un-
  garisch-Ostra*
Uhniv (town, western Ukraine) : (Russian
  Ugnev); to 1939 Polish *Uhnów*
Uhnów *see* Uhniv
Uhtua *see* Kalevala
Uíbh Fhailí *see* Offaly
Uibhist a' Deas *see* South Uist
Uibhist a' Tuath *see* North Uist
Uíge (town, northwestern Angola) : formerly
  Portuguese *Vila Marechal Carmona*
Ujazd (town, southern Poland) : to 1945 German
  Bischofstal
Újbánya *see* Nová Baňa
Uji-yamada *see* Ise
Ujlak *see* Veľké Zálužie
Ujung Pandang (city, central Indonesia) : for-
  merly *Macassar*
Újverbász *see* Vrbas
Újvidék *see* Novi Sad
UK *see* United Kingdom
Ukhta (city, northwestern Russia) : to 1939
  Chibyu
Ukhta *see* Kalevala
Ukkel *see* Uccle
Ukmergė (town, east central Lithuania) : to 1918
  Russian *Vilkomir*
Ukraina *see* Ukraine
Ukraine (republic, central Europe) : (Russian
  Ukraina); [Ukrainian *Ukrayina*]
Ukrainsk *see* Ukrains'k
Ukrains'k (town eastern Ukraine) : (Russian
  Ukrainsk); to 1963 *Lisivka* (Russian *Lesovka*)
Ukrayina *see* Ukraine
Ukrepleniye Kommunizma *see* Ivanishchi
Uku (village, western Angola) : formerly Por-
  tuguese *Vila Nova do Seles*
Ulaanbaatar *see* Ulan Bator
Ulala *see* Gorno-Altaysk
Ulan Bator (city, north central Mongolia) :
  [Mongolian *Ulaanbaatar*]; to 1924 *Urga*
Ulan-Ude (city, southeastern Russia) : to 1934
  Verkhneudinsk

Ulcinj (town, southern Montenegro) : formerly
  Italian *Dulcegno*; to 1880 Turkish *Ülgün*
Uleåborg *see* Oulu
Ülgün *see* Ulcinj
Ulongue (village, northwestern Mozambique) :
  1945–1975 Portuguese *Vila Coutinho*
Ulster *see* Northern Ireland
Ulu Dağ (mountain, northwestern Turkey) : for-
  merly *Mt. Olympus.* (This is not the famous
  Mt. Olympus, home of the Greek gods, which
  is in northeastern Greece.)
Ulugbek (town, northeastern Uzbekistan) : for-
  merly *Khodzhaakhrar*
Uluqsaqtuua *see* Holman
Uluru *see* Ayers Rock
[1]Ul'yanovka (town, south central Ukraine) : to
  1924 *Hrushka* (Russian *Grushka*)
[2]Ul'yanovka (town, western Russia) : to 1923
  Sablino
[1]Ul'yanovo (village, western Russia, near
  Sukhinichi) : to 1938 *Plokhino*
[2]Ul'yanovo (village, western Russia, near Kalin-
  ingrad) : to 1945 German *Breitenstein*
Ul'yanovo *see* Dashtobod
Ul'yanovsk *see* Simbirsk
Ulzio *see* Oulx
Umal'tinsky (village, eastern Russia) : to 1942
  Polovinka
Umanskaya *see* Leningradskaya
Umba (town, northwestern Russia) : formerly
  Lesnoy
Umm Durmān *see* Omdurman
Umtali *see* Mutare
Umvuma *see* Mvuma
Umzimvubu *see* Port St. John's
Una *see* Ibiúna
Ungarisch-Altenburg *see* Magyaróvár
Ungarisch-Brod *see* Uherský Brod
Ungarisch-Hradisch *see* Uherské Hradiště
Ungarisch-Ostra *see* Uherský Ostroh
Ungarn *see* Hungary
Ungeny *see* Ungheni
Ungheni (city, western Moldova) : (Russian
  Ungeny); 1919–1940 Romanian *Ungheni*; to
  1918 Russian *Ungeny*
Ungvár *see* Uzhhorod
União *see* (1) Jaguaruana; (2) União dos Pal-
  mares
União dos Palmares (city, northeastern Brazil) :
  to 1944 *União*
[1]Union (town, New Jersey, northeastern United
  States) : originally *Connecticut Farms*
[2]Union (town, South Carolina, southeastern
  United States) : originally *Unionville*
Union Colony *see* Greeley
Union Islands *see* Tokelau

Union of Soviet Socialist Republics *see* **Russia**

Uniontown (town, Pennsylvania, northeastern United States) : originally *Beeson's Town*

Unionville *see* (1) **Scranton**; (2) **Streator**; (3) ²**Union**

United Arab Emirates (federation, southwestern Asia) : to 1971 *Trucial States* or *Trucial Oman* (Oman itself is not one of the seven emirates that comprise the federation.)

United Arab Republic *see* **Egypt**

United Kingdom (kingdom, western Europe) : formally *United Kingdom of Great Britain and Northern Ireland*; colloquially *UK* (The informal name *Britain*, more commonly applied to **Great Britain**, is also sometimes used for the United Kingdom, as also is *England*, properly the southern part of the country, but also its chief and largest part.)

United Kingdom of Great Britain and Northern Ireland *see* **United Kingdom**

United Provinces of Agra and Oudh *see* **Uttar Pradesh**

United States (federal republic, southern North America) : formally *United States of America*; colloquially *USA*; informally *America*

United States of America *see* **United States**

Unruhstadt *see* **Kargowa**

Untervalden *see* **Podlesnoye**

Upland *see* ²**Chester**

Upper Canada *see* **Ontario**

Upper Canisteo *see* **Hornell**

Upper Peru *see* **Bolivia**

Upper Volta *see* **Burkina Faso**

Uqsuqtuq *see* **Gjoa Haven**

Ur (ancient city, southern Iraq) : biblical *Ur of the Chaldees*

Uralets (town, west central Russia) : to 1933 *Krasny Ural*

Uralmedstroy *see* **Krasnoural'sk**

Ural'sk *see* **Oral**

Uramir *see* **Romit**

Urbakh *see* ²**Pushkino**

Urbino (town, central Italy) : Roman *Urbinum Hortense*

Urbinum Hortense *see* **Urbino**

Urbs Vetus *see* **Orvieto**

Urfa *see* **Şanlıurfa**

Urga *see* **Ulan Bator**

Urganch (city, southern Uzbekistan) : to 1929 Russian *Novourgench* (The city, formerly *Urgench*, should not be confused with *Keneurgench*, Turkmenistan, 85 miles to the northwest.)

Urgench *see* **Urganch**

Uriankhai *see* **Tyva**

Uriconium *see* **Wroxeter**

Uritsk (town, western Russia) : to 1925 *Ligovo* (The town is now part of St. Petersburg.)

Uritskoye *see* **Sarykol'**

Uritsky *see* **Sarykol'**

Urmia *see* **Orūmīyeh**

Ur of the Chaldees *see* **Ur**

Uroševac (village, southern Kosovo) : to 1913 Turkish *Firusbey*

Ursat'yevskaya *see* **Xovos**

Urso *see* **Osuna**

Uruaçu (city, central Brazil) : to 1944 Portuguese *Santana*

Urumyenikoy *see* **Bŭlgarevo**

Urundi *see* **Burundi**

Urupês (town, southeastern Brazil) : to 1944 Portuguese *Mundo Novo*

Urupskaya *see* **Sovetskaya**

Urus-Martan (city, southwestern Russia) : 1944–1957 *Krasnoarmeyskoye*

Uryu *see* **Kirillovo**

USA *see* **United States**

Uściług *see* **Ustyluh**

Ushant *see* **Ouessant**

Ushiro *see* **Orlovo**

Ushkovo (village, northwestern Russia) : to 1948 Finnish *Tyrisevä* (The village passed to the USSR in 1940, but retained its Finnish name, in russianized form *Tyuriseva*, until 1948.)

Usk (town, southeastern Wales) : Welsh *Brynbuga*; Roman *Burrium* (The river on which the town stands, and from which it takes its present name, was known to the Romans as *Isca*. The same river flows through **Caerleon**.)

Üsküb *see* **Skopje**

Üsküdar (town, northwestern Turkey) : formerly *Scutari*; ancient Greek *Chrysopolis* (The town is now a district of Istanbul.)

Usol'ye *see* **Usol'ye-Sibirskoye**

Usol'ye-Sibirskoye (city, southern Russia) : to 1940 *Usol'ye*

Usol'ye-Solikamskoye *see* **Berezniki**

Uspenka *see* ²**Kirovsky**

USSR *see* **Russia**

Ussuriysk (city, eastern Russia) : 1935–1957 *Voroshilov*; 1926–1935 *Nikol'sk-Ussuriysky*; to 1926 *Nikol'sk*

Ust'-Abakanskoye *see* **Abakan**

Ust'-Balyk *see* **Nefteyugansk**

Ust'-Belokalitvenskaya *see* **Belaya Kalitva**

Ust'-Borovaya *see* **Borovsk**

Ust'-Dvinsk *see* **Daugavgrīva**

Ustilug *see* **Ustyluh**

Ústí nad Labem (city, northwestern Czech Republic) : to 1918, 1948–1945 German *Aussig an der Elbe*

Ústí nad Orlicí (town, northeastern Czech Republic) : to 1918, 1939–1945 German *Wilden-schwert*

Ustinov *see* **Izhevsk**

Ustka (town, northwestern Poland) : to 1945 German *Stolpmünde*

Ust'-Katav (city, western Russia) : to 1943 *Ust'-Katavsky Zavod*

Ust'-Katavsky Zavod *see* **Ust'-Katav**

Ust'-Kamenogorsk *see* **Öskemen**

Ust'-Medveditskaya *see* **Serafimovich**

Ust'-Orda *see* **Ust'-Ordynsky**

Ust'-Ordynsky (town, eastern Russia) : to 1941 *Ust'-Orda*

Ust'-Penzhino *see* **Kamenskoye**

Ustronie Morskie (village, northern Poland) : to 1945 German *Henkenhagen*

Ustrzyki Dolne (town, southeastern Poland) : 1939–1951 Russian *Nizhniye Ustriki*

Ust'-Sysol'sk *see* **Syktyvkar**

Ust'-Vorkuta (town, northwestern Russia) : formerly *Sangorodok*

Ustyluh (town, western Ukraine) : (Russian *Ustilug*); to 1939 Polish *Uściług*

Usumbura *see* **Bujumbura**

Uszor *see* **Hviezdoslavov**

Utah (state, western United States) : to 1850 *Deseret* (The original name was given in 1849 to the state proclaimed by Mormon settlers in Salt Lake City. The U.S. government did not recognize it, and in 1850 instead legislated the *Utah Territory*, which in 1896 took its present name, applied to a much reduced area.)

Utena (city, eastern Lithuania) : to 1918 Russian *Utsyany*

Utkinsky Zavod *see* **Staroutkinsk**

Utrecht (city, central Netherlands) : Roman *Trajectum ad Rhenum* (The Roman name locates the city at a crossing of the **Rhine**, just as **Maastricht** arose by a crossing of the **Meuse**.)

Utsyany *see* **Utena**

Uttar Pradesh (state, northern India) : 1902–1950 *United Provinces of Agra and Oudh*

Uudenmaan (province, southern Finland) : formerly *Uusimaa*; to 1809 Swedish *Nyland*

Uuras *see* **Vysotsk**

Uusikaupunki (town, southwestern Finland) : to 1809 Swedish *Nystad* (The Swedish name is preserved historically for the 1721 treaty between Russia and Sweden.)

Uusimaa *see* **Uudenmaan**

Uvalde (town, Texas, southern United States) : to 1856 *Encina*

Uxantis *see* **Ouessant**

Uxelodunum *see* **Stanwix**

Uxisama *see* **Ouessant**

Uzen *see* **Tenge**

Uzenitsa *see* **Uzyn**

Uzenytsa *see* **Uzyn**

Uzès-le-Duc *see* **Oued el Abtal**

Uzhgorod *see* **Uzhhorod**

Uzhhorod (city, western Ukraine) : (Russian *Uzhgorod*); 1944–1945 Czech *Užhorod*; 1938–1944 Hungarian *Ungvár*; 1919–1938 Czech *Užhorod*; to 1918 Hungarian *Ungvár* (The city was under Hungarian control from the late 11th century to 1918 and was under Hungarian occupation during World War II.)

Užhorod *see* **Uzhhorod**

Užice (city, western Serbia) : 1947–1992 *Titovo Užice*

Uzin *see* **Uzyn**

Uzlovoye (village, western Russia) : to 1945 German *Rautenberg*

Uzunköprü (town, northwestern Turkey) : 1920–1922 modern Greek *Maura Gefura*

Uzyn (town, central Ukraine) : (Russian *Uzin*); 1773–*c*.1800 *Tembershchyna* (Russian *Tembershchina*); originally *Uzenytsa* (Russian *Uzenitsa*)

Uzynkol' (village, northern Kazakhstan) : formerly Russian *Leninskoye*; earlier Russian *Dem'yanovka*

Vaasa (city, southwestern Finland) : 1855–1917 *Nikolainkaupunki*; to 1809 Swedish *Vasa* (The Swedish equivalent of the earlier Finnish name was *Nikolaistad*.)

Vác (city, northern Hungary) : to 1867 German *Waitzen*

Vacca *see* **Béja**

Vadinsk (village, western Russia) : to *c*.1940 *Kerensk*

Vadodara (city, western India) : formerly *Baroda* (This Baroda, in Gujarat state, should not be confused with the cities of the same name in Madhya Pradesh and Rajasthan states.)

Vagarshapat *see* **Ejmiatsin**

Vágbeszterce *see* **Považská Bystrica**

Vágsellye *see* **Šal'a**

Vágújhely *see* **Nové Mesto nad Váhom**

Vajdahunyad *see* **Hunedoara**

Vakhrushev (town, eastern Russia) : 1905–1945 Japanese *Tomarikishi*

Vakhsh (town, southeastern Tajikistan) : to 1950s Russian *Vakhstroy*

Vakhstroy *see* **Vakhsh**

Valahia *see* **Wallachia**

Valašské Meziříčí (town, eastern Czech Republic) : to 1918, 1939–1945 German *Wallachisch-Meseritsch*

Val-Brillant (village, Quebec, southeastern Canada) : 1913–1916 *St.-Pierre-du-Lac*; to 1913 *Cedar Hall*

Valdemārpils (town, northwestern Latvia) : to
1917 German *Sassmacken*

Valdez (town, Alaska, northwestern United
States) : to 1898 *Copper City*

Val'dgeym *see* Dobropillya

Valdosta (city, Georgia, southeastern United
States) : to 1859 *Troupville*; originally *Franklinville* (The original town was renamed when
moved east to its present site.)

Vale Colliery *see* Thorburn

Valegotsulovo *see* Dolyns'ke

Valença *see* (1) Marquês de Valença;
(2) Valença do Piauí

Valença do Piauí (town, northeastern Brazil) :
1944–1948 Portuguese *Berlengas*; to 1944 Portuguese *Valença*

Valence (town, southeastern France) : Roman
Valentia

¹Valencia (city, eastern Spain) : Roman *Valentia*

²Valencia (city, northwestern Venezuela) : originally *Nueva Valencia del Rey*

³Valencia (island, southern Ireland) : alternate
Valentia; Irish *Dairbhre* (*Valencia* is a corruption of Irish *Béal Inse*, the name of the sound
between the island and the mainland.)

Valentia *see* (1) Valence; (2) ¹,³Valencia

Vale of Glamorgan (county, southern Wales) :
Welsh *Bro Morgannwg* (The county was
formed in 1996 in the historic region of Glamorgan. Welsh *bro*, "vale," is the opposite of
bryn, "hill.")

Valerian Way *see* Via

Valga (town, southern Estonia) : alternate Latvian *Valka*; to 1918 Russian *Valk* (The town lies
on the border with Latvia.)

Valgravé *see* Souk Eltnine

Valinhos *see* Guaraúna

Valk *see* Valga

Valka *see* Valga

Valladolid *see* Morelia

Valladolid de Santa María de Comayagua *see*
Comayagua

Valle di Pompei *see* Pompei

Valley (village, northwestern Wales) : Welsh *Y
Fali*

Valley City (town, North Dakota, northern
United States) : to 1881 *Worthington*

Valley Junction *see* West Des Moines

Valmiera (town, northern Latvia) : to 1917 German *Wolmar*

Valozhyn (town, northwestern Belarus) : (Russian *Volozhin*); 1919–1939 Polish *Wołożyn*; to
1918 Russian *Volozhin*

Valparaíba *see* Cachoeira Paulista

Valparaiso (city, Indiana, north central United
States) : originally *Portersville*

Valverde *see* Mao

Vanadzor (city, northern Armenia) : 1935–1992
Kirovakan; to 1935 *Karaklis*

Van Buren (town, Arkansas, south central
United States) : to 1838 *Phillips Landing*

Van Buren *see* Kettering

Vancouver (city, British Columbia, southwestern Canada) : to 1886 *Granville*

Vanderheyden's Ferry *see* ²Troy

Van Diemen's Land *see* Tasmania

Vandsburg *see* Więcbork

¹Vanier (town, Quebec, eastern Canada) : to
1966 *Quebec West* or French *Québec-Ouest*

²Vanier (town, Ontario, southeastern Canada) :
to 1969 *Eastview*

Vanilovo *see* Tsyurupy, imeni

Vannes (town, northwestern France) : Breton
Guened

Vannovka *see* Turar Ryskulov

Vannovsky *see* Hamza

Vanuatu (island republic, southwestern Pacific) :
to 1980 *New Hebrides*; alternate former French
Nouvelles-Hébrides (The island territory was
named by the British in 1774 but gained its
joint French name in 1906 when a condo-
minium was set up.)

Vapincum *see* Gap

Varanasi (city, northeastern India) : formerly
Benares

Varapayeva (town, northwestern Belarus) : (Russian *Voropayevo*); 1919–1939 Polish
Woropajewo; to 1918 Russian *Voropayevo*

Varaždin (city, central Croatia) : to 1867 German
Warasdin

Varcar Vakuf *see* Mrkonjić-Grad

Varėna (town, southern Lithuania) : to 1920
Russian *Orany* (From 1920 to 1939 the town
itself remained in Lithuania but its railroad
station, named *Orany*, was in Poland.)

Vardenis (town, eastern Armenia) : to 1969
Basargechar

Varna (city, northeastern Bulgaria) : 1949–1956
Stalin; ancient Greek *Odessus*

Varnsdorf (town, northern Czech Republic) : to
1918, 1938–1945 German *Warnsdorf*

Varttirayiruppu *see* Watrap

Vasa *see* Vaasa

Vasconia *see* (1) ¹Basque Country; (2) Gascony

Vasiliko *see* Tsarevo

Vasil Levski (village, south central Bulgaria) : to
1934 *Mitizirovo*

Vasil'yevsko-Shaytansky *see* Pervoural'sk

Vasilyova Sloboda *see* Chkalovsk

Vasilyovo *see* Chkalovsk

Vasto (town, eastern Italy) : Roman *Histonium*

Vasvár (town, western Hungary) : formerly German *Eisenburg*

Vathy *see* **Samos**

Vatı *see* **Samos**

Vatican (papal state, western Italy) : [Italian *Vaticano*]

Vaticano *see* **Vatican**

Vatra Dornei (town, northern Romania) : to 1918 German *Dorna Watra*

Vaud (canton, western Switzerland) : German *Waadt*

Vawkavysk (town, western Belarus) : (Russian *Volkovysk*); 1919–1939 Polish *Wołkowysk*; to 1918 Russian *Volkovysk*

Vayenga *see* **Severomorsk**

Vazovgrad *see* ¹**Sopot**

Vealtown *see* **Bernardsville**

Vectis *see* **Wight, Isle of**

Vedi (town, southern Armenia) : to *c.*1935 *Beyuk-Vedi*

Vedra *see* **Wear**

Veedersburg *see* ¹**Amsterdam**

Veglia *see* **Krk**

Veii *see* **Isola Farnese**

Vejprty (town, northwestern Czech Republic) : to 1918, 1938–1945 German *Weipert*

Veldes *see* **Bled**

Velenje (town, northern Slovenia) : formerly *Titovo Velenje*

Veles (town, central Macedonia) : 1946–1991 *Titov Veles*; 1913–1946 *Veles*; to 1913 Turkish *Köprülü*

Velia *see* **Castellammare**

Velika Kikinda *see* **Kikinda**

Velikaya Bagachka *see* **Velyka Bahachka**

Velikaya Mikhaylovka *see* **Velyka Mykhaylivka**

Velikaya Novosyolka *see* **Velyka Novosilka**

Veliki Bečkerek *see* **Zrenjanin**

Veliki Preslav (town, eastern Bulgaria) : formerly *Preslav*; earlier Turkish *Eski Stambul*

Velikiye Mosty *see* **Velyki Mosty**

Velikoalekseyevsky *see* **Baxt**

Velikooktyabr'sky (town, western Russia) : to 1941 *Pokrovskoye*

Veliko Tărnovo (city, north central Bulgaria) : to 1965 *Tărnovo*; to 1878 Turkish *Tırnova*

Veliky Novgorod (city, western Russia) : to 1998 *Novgorod*; originally Scandinavian *Holmgard* (The city's current name, distinguishing it from **Nizhny Novgorod**, derives from its medieval title *Gospodin Veliky Novgorod,* "Lord Great Novgorod.")

Velingrad (city, southwestern Bulgaria) : to 1949 *Kamenitsa* (The city was formed on the amalgamation of Kamenitsa with two other villages.)

Velitrae *see* **Velletri**

Velká Bíteš (town, east central Czech Republic) : to 1918, 1939–1945 German *Gross-Bitesch*

Velká Deštná (mountain, northeastern Czech Republic) : to 1918, 1939–1945 German *Deschnaer Kuppe*

Velké Březno (village, northern Czech Republic) : to 1918, 1939–1945 German *Gross-Priesen*

Velké Hamry (town, northern Czech Republic) : to 1918, 1939–1945 German *Grosshammer*

Velké Karlovice (village, eastern Czech Republic) : to 1918, 1939–1945 German *Gross-Karlowitz*

Veľké Kapušany (town, eastern Slovakia) : to 1938–1945 Hungarian *Nagykapos*

Velké Losiny (village, northeastern Czech Republic) : to 1918, 1939–1945 German *Gross-Ullersdorf*

Velké Meziříčí (town, south central Czech Republic) : to 1918, 1939–1945 German *Gross-Meseritsch*

Velké Opatovice (town, east central Czech Republic) : to 1918, 1939–1945 German *Gross-Opatowitz*

Velké Pavlovice (town, southeastern Czech Republic) : to 1918, 1939–1945 German *Gross-Pawlowitz*

Velké Popovice (village, central Czech Republic) : to 1918, 1939–1945 German *Gross-Popowitz*

Veľké Zálužie (village, southwestern Slovakia) : to 1948 *Ujlak*

Veľký Meder (town, southwestern Slovakia) : 1948–1990 *Čalovo*; to 1918, 1938–1945 Hungarian *Nagymegyer*

Velký Šenov (town, northern Czech Republic) : to 1918, 1939–1945 German *Gross-Schönau*

Velletri (town, central Italy) : Roman *Velitrae*

Velunia *see* **Carriden**

Velvary (town, northwestern Czech Republic) : to 1918, 1939–1945 German *Welwarn*

Velyka Bahachka (town, west central Ukraine) : (Russian *Velikaya Bagachka*); to 1925 *Bahachka* (Russian *Bagachka*)

Velyka Mykhaylivka (town, southern Ukraine) : (Russian *Velikaya Mikhaylovka*); to 1945 *Hrosulove* (Russian *Grosulovo*)

Velyka Novosilka (town, southeastern Ukraine) : (Russian *Velikaya Novosyolka*); to 1946 *Velykyy Yanysol'* (Russian *Bol'shoy Yanisol'*)

Velyka Seydemynukha *see* **Kalinins'ke**

Velyki Mosty (town, western Ukraine) : (Russian *Velikiye Mosty*); 1919–1939 Polish *Mosty Wielkie*

Velykyy Tokmak *see* **Tokmak**

Velykyy Yanysol' *see* **Velyka Novosilka**

Venedig *see* **Venice**

Venetia *see* (1) **Venezia**; (2) **Venice**

Venet-Ville *see* **Souk Tleta Loulad**

Venezia (historical region, northern Italy) : Roman *Venetia* (The Italian name is now both that of a province of the autonomous region of Veneto and of its capital, the city of **Venice**.)

Venezia *see* **Venice**

Venezia Tridentina *see* **Trentino-Alto Adige**

Vengrov *see* **Węgrów**

Venice (city, northeastern Italy) : [Italian *Venezia*]; 1815–1866 German *Venedig*; 1805–1815 French *Venise*; 1797–1805 German *Venedig*; Roman *Venetia*

Venise *see* **Venice**

Venosa (town, southern Italy) : Roman *Venusia*

Venta Belgarum *see* [1]**Winchester**

Venta Icenorum *see* **Caistor St. Edmund**

Venta Silurum *see* **Caerwent**

Ventspils (city, western Latvia) : 1939–1945 German *Windau*; to 1918 Russian *Vindava*

Ventura (city, California, southwestern United States) : officially *San Buenaventura*

Venusia *see* **Venosa**

Venustiano Carranza (town, southern Mexico) : to 1934 *San Bartolomé*

Veracruz (city, east central Mexico) : originally *Villa Rica de la Vera Cruz*

Veranópolis (town, southern Brazil) : to 1944 *Alfredo Chaves*

Verbeia *see* **Wharfe**

Verblyud *see* **Zernograd**

Vercovicium *see* **Housesteads**

Verebély *see* **Vráble**

Vergel *see* **Bom Jardim**

Verin-Talin *see* **Talin**

Verkhneavzyano-Petrovsk *see* **Verkhny Avzyan**

Verkhnedvinsk *see* **Vyerkhnyadzvinsk**

Verkhnesaldinsky Zavod *see* **Verkhnyaya Salda**

Verkhneserginsky Zavod *see* **Verkhniye Sergi**

Verkhnetoretskoye *see* **Verkhn'otorets'ke**

Verkhneturinsky Zavod *see* **Verkhnyaya Tura**

Verkhneudinsk *see* **Ulan-Ude**

Verkhneufaleysky Zavod *see* **Verkhny Ufaley**

Verkhneye Sinevidnoye *see* **Verkhnye Syn'ovydne**

Verkhniye Sergi (town, west central Russia) : to 1938 *Verkhneserginsky Zavod*

Verkhn'otorets'ke (town, eastern Ukraine) : (Russian *Verkhnetoretskoye*); to 1978 *Skotuvata* (Russian *Skotovataya*)

Verkhnya Khortytsya (town, southeastern Ukraine) : (Russian *Verkhnyaya Khortitsa*); to 1930s *Khortytsya* (Russian *Khortitsa*) (The town is now a suburb of Zaporizhzhya.)

Verkhny Avzyan (town, west central Russia) : to 1942 *Verkhneavzyano-Petrovsk*

Verkhnyaya Kortitsa *see* **Verkhnya Khortytsya**

Verkhnyaya Pyshma (city, west central Russia) : to 1946 *Pyshma*

Verkhnyaya Salda (city, west central Russia) : to 1928 *Verkhnesaldinsky Zavod*

Verkhnyaya Tura (town, west central Russia) : to to *c*.1928 *Verkhneturinsky Zavod*

Verkhny Dashkesan *see* **Daşkäsän**

Verkhnye Syn'ovydne (town, western Ukraine) : (Russian *Verkhneye Sinevidnoye*); to 1946 *Syn-o'vyds'ko Vyzhnye* (Polish *Synowódsko-Wyżnie*)

Verkhny Ufaley (city, west central Russia) : to 1940 *Verkhneufaleysky Zavod*

Verkhovina *see* **Verkhovyna**

Verkhovyna (town, southwestern Ukraine) : (Russian *Verkhovina*); to 1962 *Zhab'ye*; 1919–1939 Polish *Żabie*

Verlucio *see* **Sandy Lane**

Vermilion (town, Alberta, west central Canada) : to 1906 *Breage*

Vermilionville *see* **Lafayette**

Vermont (state, northeastern United States) : originally *New Connecticut*

Vernal (town, Utah, west central United States) : to 1893 *Ashley Center*

Vernon (city, British Columbia, southwestern Canada) : 1885–1887 *Centreville*; originally *Priest's Valley*

Verny *see* **Almaty**

Véroia (town, northeastern Greece) : to 1913 Turkish *Karaferya*; biblical *Berea*

Verro *see* **Võru**

Vershino-Darasunsky (town, eastern Russia) : formerly *Darasun*

Verteris *see* [4]**Brough**

Vertis *see* **Worcester**

Verulamium *see* **St. Albans**

Verwoerdburg *see* **Centurion**

Verzhbolovo *see* **Virbalis**

Veselí nad Lužnicí (town, southern Czech Republic) : to 1918, 1939–1945 German *Wesseli an der Lainsitz*; earlier *Frohenbruck an der Lainsitz*

Veselí nad Moravou (town, southeastern Czech Republic) : to 1918, 1939–1945 German *Wesseli an der March*

Vesnovo (village, western Russia) : to 1945 German *Kussen*

Vesontio *see* **Besançon**

Vesuna *see* **Périgueux**

Vesuvio *see* **Vesuvius**

Vesuvius (volcano, southwestern Italy) : [Italian *Vesuvio*]

Veszprém (city, western Hungary) : to 1867 German *Wesprim*

Vetluzhsky (town, western Russia) : to 1960

Golyshi (This Vetluzhsky, northwest of Sharya, should not be confused with the one further south, just north of Krasnyye Baki.)

Veurne (town, northwestern Belgium) : French *Furnes*

Vevey (town, western Switzerland) : Roman *Vibiscum*

Via : For ease of reference, Italy's main Roman roads are grouped together here. The roads were built to link Rome with the Roman provinces, so that "All roads lead to Rome." The English equivalent name usually adds *n* to the Latin name followed by *Way* to translate *Via*, so that the first great road, the *Via Appia*, is the *Appian Way*. (Exceptions are the *Via Latina*, or *Latin Way*, *Via Ostiensis*, or *Ostian Way*, and the *Via Trajana*, or *Trajan Way*.) Rome itself had the *Via Sacra*, or *Sacred Way*. For road routes, *see* either a map of Roman Italy, as in *Muir's Historical Atlas: Ancient and Classical*, plates 12–13, or a written description, as in Hornblower and Spawforth, pp. 1594–6 (see Bibliography, p. 255).
    Via Aemilia, Via Annia, Via Appia, Via Aurelia, Via Cassia, Via Clodia, Via Domitia, Via Flaminia, Via Julia, Via Labicana, Via Latina, Via Ostiensis, Via Popilia, Via Postumia, Via Salaria, Via Trajana, Via Valeria

Vialar *see* **Tissemsilt**

Vibiscum *see* **Vevey**

Viborg *see* **Vyborg**

Vibo Valentia (town, southern Italy) : to 1928 *Monteleone di Calabria*; Roman *Vibo Valentia*; earlier Roman *Hipponium* (The town's present name is a deliberate revival of the Roman name.)

Vicente Guerrero (town, central Mexico) : to 1940 *San Pablo del Monte*

Vicente Noble (town, southwestern Dominican Republic) : to 1943 *Alpargatal*

Vicentia *see* **Vicenza**

Vicenza (city, northeastern Italy) : Roman *Vicentia*

Vich (town, northeastern Spain) : Roman *Vicus Ausonensis*; earlier Roman *Ausa*

Vichy (town, central France) : Roman *Vicus Calidus*

Victor Hugo *see* **Hamadia**

[1]**Victoria** (state, southeastern Australia) : to 1851 *Port Phillip District*

[2]**Victoria** (city, British Columbia, southwestern Canada) : formerly *Fort Victoria*; originally *Fort Camosun*

Victoria *see* (1) **Labuan**; (2) **Limbe**

Victoria, Lake (east central Africa) : alternate *Victoria Nyanza*

Victoria, Mt. *see* **Tomanivi**

Victoriacum *see* **Vitoria**

Victoria Falls (southern Zambia/northwestern Zimbabwe) : locally *Mosi-oa-Tunya* (The local name applies only to the falls, not to the town of *Victoria Falls*, Zimbabwe.)

Victoria Nyanza *see* **Victoria, Lake**

Victoriaville (town, Quebec, southeastern Canada) : to 1861 *Demersville*

Vicus Ausonensis *see* **Vich**

Vicus Calidus *see* **Vichy**

Vicus Elbii *see* **Viterbo**

Vicus Julii *see* **Aire-sur-l'Adour**

Videira (city, southern Brazil) : to 1944 *Perdizes*

Vidin (city, northwestern Bulgaria) : Roman *Bononia*

Vidnoye (city, western Russia) : to 1965 *Rastorguyevo*

Vienna (city, eastern Austria) : to 1918 Hungarian *Bécs*; 1806–1867 German *Wien*; Roman *Vindobona* (English has adopted the Italian form of the city's name, although Vienna was never part of Italy. The distinctive Hungarian name is of Turkish origin.)

Vienna *see* **Vienne**

Vienne (town, southeastern France) : Roman *Vienna*

Vierwaldstätter See *see* **Lucerne, Lake**

Viesīte (town, southern Latvia) : to 1917 German *Eckengraf*

Vievis (town, southeastern Lithuania) : 1919–1930 Polish *Jewie*; to 1918 Russian *Yev'ye*

Vigia *see* **Almanara**

Viipuri *see* **Vyborg**

Vijniţa *see* **Vyzhnytsya**

Viktorovka *see* **Taranovskoye**

Vila *see* **Port-Vila**

Vila Adolfo *see* **Catanduva**

Vila Alferes Chamusca *see* (1) **Chókwé**; (2) **Guijá**

Vila Arriaga *see* **Bibala**

Vila Bugaço *see* **Camanongue**

Vila Cabral *see* **Lichinga**

Vila Coutinho *see* **Ulongue**

Vila da Ponte *see* **Kuvango**

Vila de Albuquerque *see* **Mariana**

Vila de Aljustrel *see* **Cangamba**

Vila de Almoster *see* **Chiange**

Vila de João Belo *see* **Xai-Xai**

Vila de São José do Paraíba *see* **São José dos Campos**

Vila de São José do Sul *see* **São José dos Campos**

Vila Fontes *see* **Caia**

Vila Formosa de Nossa Senhora do Destêrro de Jundiaí *see* **Jundiaí**

Vila General Machado *see* Camacupa

Világos *see* Şiria

Vila Gouveia *see* Catandica

Vila Henrique de Carvalho *see* Saurimo

Viļaka (town, eastern Latvia) : to 1917 German *Marienhausen*

Vila Luísa *see* Marracuene

Vila Marechal Carmona *see* Uíge

Vila Mariano Machado *see* Ganda

Vila Nova *see* Tchikala-Tcholohanga

Vila Nova da Constituição *see* Piracicaba

Vila Nova de Gaza *see* Xai-Xai

Vila Nova de São José *see* São José dos Campos

Vila Nova do Seles *see* Uku

Vila Paiva de Andrada *see* Gorongosa

Vila Pereira de Eça *see* Ondjiva

Vila Pery *see* (1) Chimoio; (2) Manica

Vila Rica *see* Ouro Prêto

Vila Rica de Oropesa *see* Huancavelica

Vila Robert Williams *see* Caála

Vila Salazar *see* (1) N'dalatando; (2) Sango

Vila Teixeira da Silva *see* Bailundo

Vila Teixeira de Sousa *see* Luau

Vila Trigo de Morais *see* Chókwé

Vileyka (town, northwestern Belarus) : 1919–1939 Polish *Wilejka*

Viljandi (town, southern Estonia) : (Russian *Vil'yandi*); to 1918 German *Fellin*

Vilkavishkis *see* Vilkaviškis

Vilkaviškis (town, southwestern Lithuania) : (Russian *Vilkavishkis*); to 1918 Russian *Volkovyshki*

Vilkomir *see* Ukmergė

Villa Alba *see* General San Martín

Villa Americana *see* Americana

Villa Bella *see* (1) Ilhabela; (2) Serra Talhada

Villa Bens *see* Tarfaya

Villa Canales (town, south central Guatemala) : to 1921 *Pueblo Viejo* (The town is now part of Guatemala City metropolitan area.)

Villa Cisneros *see* Dakhla

Villa Corregidora *see* El Pueblito

Villa da Barra *see* Manaus

Villa de Carrión *see* Atlixco

Villa de Cecilia *see* Ciudad Madero

Villa de María (town, central Argentina) : to *c.*1945 *Río Seco*

Villa de Oropeza *see* Cochabamba

Villa de San Antonio del Camino *see* Merlo

Villa de Santa Catalina del Guadalcázar del Valle de Moquegua *see* Moquegua

Villa do Forte da Assumpção *see* Fortaleza

Villa Felipe II *see* Villahermosa

Villa General Pérez (town, western Bolivia) : to 1930s *Charazani*

Villaggio Mussolini *see* Arborea

Villahermosa (city, southeastern Mexico) : to 1915 *San Juan Bautista*; originally *Villa Felipe II*

Villa Hidalgo *see* Ciudad Hidalgo

Villa Juárez *see* Ciudad Mante

Villa Nueva *see* San José

Villa Real da Praia Grande *see* Niterói

Villa Real de la Santa Fé de San Francisco de Asis *see* Santa Fe

Villa Rica de la Vera Cruz *see* Veracruz

Villarreal de Chiapa de los Españoles *see* San Cristóbal de las Casas

Villa Sanjurjo *see* Al Hoceima

Villa Santa Cruz de Triana *see* Rancagua

Villa Serrano (town, southern Bolivia) : to 1940s *Pescado*

Villavieja *see* Heredia

Vilebois *see* Villebois-Lavalette

Villebois-Lavalette (town, western France) : to 1622 *Villebois* (In the year stated the town added the name of a famous admiral.)

Ville-Marie-de-Montréal *see* Montreal

Villmanstrand *see* Lappeenranta

Vil'na *see* Vilnius

Vilnius (city, southeastern Lithuania) : (Russian *Vil'nyus*); 1919–1939 Polish *Wilno*; to 1918 Russian *Vil'na*

Vil'nyans'k (town, east central Ukraine) : (Russian *Vol'nyansk*); 1935–1966 *Chervonoarmiys'ke* (Russian *Chervonoarmeyskoye*); to 1935 *Sofiyivka* (Russian *Sofiyevka*) (The Russian equivalent of the Ukrainian name, *Krasnoarmeyskoye*, was used from 1935 to 1944.)

Vil'nyus *see* Vilnius

Vilvoorde (town, northern Belgium) : French *Vilvorde*

Vilvorde *see* Vilvoorde

Vil'yandi *see* Viljandi

Viminacium *see* Kostolac

Vindava *see* Ventspils

Vindobona *see* Vienna

Vindomora *see* Ebchester

Vindonissa *see* Windisch

Vinegaroon *see* Langtry

Vinkovci (city, eastern Croatia) : to 1867 German *Winkowcze*

Vinnitsa *see* Vinnytsya

Vinnytsya (city, west central Ukraine) : (Russian *Vinnitsa*); to 1918 Russian *Vinnitsa*

Vinodel'noye *see* Ipatovo

Vinogradnoye (village, southwestern Russia) : to 1944 German *Gnadenburg* (The village was in the former Volga German Autonomous Soviet Socialist Republic.)

Vinogradov *see* Vynohradiv

Vipiteno (town, northeastern Italy) : to 1918 German *Sterzing*

Viranteke *see* **Kapitan Andreevo**

Virbalis (town, southwestern Lithuania) : to 1918 Russian *Verzhbolovo*

Virden (town, Manitoba, southern Canada) : formerly *Manchester*; to 1882 *Gopher Creek*

Virgilio (town, northern Italy) : Roman *Andes*

Virginia (town, northern Ireland) : Irish *Achadh an Iúir*

Virgin Islands (northeastern West Indies) : originally Spanish *Santa Ursula y las Once Mil Virgines* (The islands are now politically divided into the *British Virgin Islands* and the **Virgin Islands of the United States.**)

Virgin Islands of the United States (northeastern West Indies) : to 1917 *Danish West Indies*

Viroconium *see* **Wroxeter**

Virovitica (town, central Croatia) : to 1867 German *Wirowititz*

Virunga (mountain range, east central Africa) : alternate *M'fumbiro* (The range, mainly in the Democratic Republic of the Congo, but extending east into Rwanda, Burundi, and Uganda, is usually known in the latter country by the alternate name.)

Virunga National Park (eastern Democratic Republic of the Congo) : to 1972 *Albert National Park* (The formal French name is *Parc National des Virunga*.)

Vis (island, southwestern Croatia) : to 1918 Italian *Lissa*

Visaginas (city, eastern Lithuania) : to 1992 *Sniečkus*

Visconde do Rio Branco (town, southeastern Brazil) : to 1944 *Rio Branco*

Visé (town, eastern Belgium) : Flemish *Wezet*

Vishnyovka *see* **Arshaly**

Vishnyovoye *see* **Vyshneve**

Vislinsky Zaliv *see* **Vistula Lagoon**

Vistula (river, central Poland) : [Polish *Wisła*]; to 1918, 1939–1945 German *Weichsel*

Vistula Lagoon (northern Poland/western Russia) : [Polish *Zalew Wiślany*, Russian *Vislinsky Zaliv*]; to 1945 German *Frisches Haff*

Vitebsk *see* **Vitsyebsk**

Viterbo (city, central Italy) : Roman *Vicus Elbii*

Vitkovice (town, northeastern Czech Republic) : to 1918 German *Witkowitz* (The town is now a district of Ostrava.)

Vitodurum *see* **Winterthur**

Vitoria (city, northeastern Spain) : Medieval Latin *Victoriacum*

Vitória *see* **Vitória de Santo Antão**

Vitória da Conquista (city, northeastern Brazil) : to 1891 *Conquista*

Vitória de Santo Antão (city, northeastern Brazil) : to 1944 *Vitória*

Vitória do Alto Parnaíba *see* **Alto Parnaíba**

Vitória do Baixo Mearim *see* **Vitória do Mearim**

Vitória do Mearim (city, northeastern Brazil) : 1944–1948 *Baixo Mearim*; to 1944 *Vitória do Baixo Mearim*

Vitsyebsk (city, northeastern Belarus) : (Russian *Vitebsk*); to 1918 Russian *Vitebsk*

Vittorio *see* **Vittorio Veneto**

Vittoriosa (town, eastern Malta) : formerly *Birgu*

Vittorio Veneto (town, northeastern Italy) : to 1923 *Vittorio*

Vizcaya (province, northern Spain) : formerly English *Biscay* (The former English name is still current for the great bay that is named for the province. *See* **Biscay, Bay of.**)

Vizhnitsa *see* **Vyzhnytsya**

Vlaanderen *see* **Flanders**

Vladikavkaz (city, southwestern Russia) : 1954–1990 *Ordzhonikidze*; 1944–1954 *Dzaudzhikau*; 1931–1944 *Ordzhonikidze*

Vladimira Il'icha Lenina, imeni (town, western Russia) : to c.1938 *Rumyantsevo*

Vladimirovka *see* **Yuzhno-Sakhalinsk**

Vladimir-Volynsky *see* **Volodymyr-Volyns'kyy**

Vladislavovas *see* **Kudirkos Naumiestis**

Vlaším (town, central Czech Republic) : to 1918, 1939–1945 German *Wlaschim*

Vlasovo-Ayuta *see* **Ayutinsky**

Vlissingen (town, southwestern Netherlands) : dated English *Flushing* (The English name is associated with the seaport's strategic location and the many battles there.)

Vlorë (city, southwestern Albania) : to 1913 Turkish *Avlonya*; ancient Greek *Aulon*

Vlotslavek *see* **Włocławek**

Vltava (river, west central Czech Republic) : to 1918 German *Moldau*

V.M. Molotova, imeni *see* **³Oktyabr'sky**

Vodena *see* **Edessa**

Vodnjan (town, western Croatia) : 1918–1945 Italian *Dignano d'Istria*; Roman *Attinianum*

Vodop'yanovo *see* **²Donskoye**

Vogelkop *see* **Doberai**

Volaterrae *see* **Volterra**

Volcei *see* **Buccino**

Volga (river, western Russia) : ancient Greek *Rha*

Volga-Baltic Waterway (western Russia) : to 1964 *Mariinsk Water System* (The network of rivers and canals linking the Volga River with the Baltic Sea was officially renamed *Volgo-Baltiysky Vodny Put' imeni V.I. Lenina*.)

Volgograd (city, southwestern Russia) : 1925–1961 *Stalingrad*; to 1925 *Tsaritsyn* (The former

Russian name is preserved in history for the long and bloody battle of 1942–43 which finally brought Soviet victory over the German occupying army.)

Volhynia (region, eastern Europe) : [Ukrainian and Russian *Volyn'*; Polish *Wołyń*] (The name of the historical region is now that of a western province of Ukraine.)

Volkhov (city, western Russia) : 1936–1940 *Volkhovstroy*; 1927–1936 *Zvanka*; 1923–1927 *Volkhov*; to 1923 *Gostinopolye*

Volkhovstroy *see* **Volkhov**

Volkovyshki *see* **Vilkaviškis**

Volkovysk *see* **Vawkavysk**

Volney *see* **Fulton**

Vol'nyansk *see* **Vil'nyans'k**

Volodarskoye *see* **Saumalkol'**

Volodymyr-Volyns'kyy (town, northwestern Ukraine) : (Russian *Vladimir-Volynsky*); 1919–1939 Polish *Włodzimierz*

Volos (city, eastern Greece) : ancient Greek *Iolcus*

Volozhin *see* **Valozhyn**

Volsinii *see* **Bolsena**

Volta Blanche *see* **Nakambe**

Volterra (town, western Italy) : Roman *Volaterrae*

Volunteer Island *see* **Starbuck Island**

Volyn' *see* **Volhynia**

Volzhsk (city, western Russia) : to 1940 *Lopatino*

Vondrišel (village, east central Slovakia) : 1948–1990 *Nálepkovo*; to 1918 Hungarian *Merény*; to 1867 German *Wagendrüssel*

Vorontsovka *see* **Tashir**

Vorontsovo-Aleksandrovskoye *see* **Zelenokumsk**

Voropayevo *see* **Varapayeva**

Voroshilov *see* **Ussuriysk**

Voroshilovabad *see* **Kalinin**

Voroshilovgrad *see* **Luhans'k**

Voroshilovsk *see* (1) **Alchevs'k**; (2) **Stavropol'**

Voroshylovhrad *see* **Luhans'k**

Voroshylovs'k *see* **Alchevs'k**

Vorovskogo, imeni (town, western Russia) : to 1941 *Khrapunovo* (The town should not be confused with the identically named smaller town near Gus'-Khrustal'ny, to the east.)

Vorst *see* **Forest**

Võru (town, southeastern Estonia) : (Russian *Vyru*); to 1918 Russian *Verro*

Vose (town, southwestern Tajikistan) : c.1935–c.1960 *Kolkhozobod* (Russian *Kolkhozabad*); to c.1935 *Paituk*

Voskresenovka *see* ²**Oktyabr'sky**

Voskresensk *see* **Istra**

Voskresenskoye *see* **Kirovo**

Vostochny (village, eastern Russia) : 1905–1945 Japanese *Motodomari*

Votyak Autonomous Oblast *see* **Udmurt Republic**

Voznesenskaya Manufaktura *see* ¹**Krasnoarmeysk**

Voznesensky *see* **Krasny Oktyabr'**

Vráble (town, southwestern Slovakia) : to 1918, 1938–1945 Hungarian *Verebély*

Vraça *see* **Vratsa**

Vrakhóri *see* **Agrínion**

Vranov nad Topl'ou (city, eastern Slovakia) : to 1918 Hungarian *Tapolyvarannó*

Vratsa (city, northwestern Bulgaria) : to 1878 Turkish *Vraça*

Vrbas (town, northern Serbia) : formerly *Titov Vrbas*; to 1918, 1941–1944 Hungarian *Újverbász* (The Hungarian name properly applies to *Novi Vrbas*, "New Vrbas," not *Stari Vrbas*, Hungarian *Overbász*, "Old Vrbas," across the Danube-Risza canal.)

Vrbno pod Pradědem (town, eastern Czech Republic) : to 1918, 1939–1945 German *Würbenthal*

Vrchlabí (town, northern Czech Republic) : to 1918, 1938–1945 German *Hohenelbe*

Vrchnika (town, western Slovenia) : to 1918 German *Oberlaibach*; Roman *Nauportus*

Vršac (city, northeastern Serbia) : to 1918 German *Werschetz*

Vrútky (town, northwestern Slovakia) : to 1918 Hungarian *Ruttka*; to 1867 German *Ruttek* (The town is now a district of the city of Martin.)

Vsekhsvyatskoye *see* **Sarykol'**

Vsetín (city, eastern Czech Republic) : to 1918, 1939–1945 German *Wsetin*

Vuhlehirs'k (town, eastern Ukraine) : (Russian *Uglegorsk*); to 1958 *Khatsapetivka* (Russian *Khatsapetovka*)

Vukovar (city, eastern Croatia) : to 1867 German *Wukowar*

Vŭlkova Slatina *see* **Doktor Yosifovo**

Vyatka (city, western Russia) : 1934–1991 *Kirov*; to 1780 *Khlynov*

Vyborg (city, northwestern Russia) : 1918–1940 Finnish *Viipuri*; originally Swedish *Viborg*

Vyerkhnyadzvinsk (town, northern Belarus) : (Russian *Verkhnedvinsk*); to 1962 *Drissa*

Vygoda *see* **Vyhoda**

Vyhoda (town, western Ukraine) : (Russian *Vygoda*); to 1939 Polish *Wygoda*

Vynohradiv (town, western Ukraine) : (Russian *Vinogradov*); 1944–1945 Czech *Sevluš* (Russian *Sevlyush*); 1939–1944 Hungarian *Nagyszöllös*; 1919–1938 Czech *Sevluš*; to 1918 Hungarian *Nagyszöllös*

Vyru *see* **Võru**

Vyshneve (town, east central Ukraine) : (Russian *Vishnyovoye*); to 1961 *Erastivka* (Russian *Erastovka*)

Vyškov (town, southeastern Czech Republic) : to 1918, 1939–1945 German *Wischau*

Vysokaye (town, southwestern Belarus) : (Russian *Vysokoye*); 1919–1939 Polish *Wysokie Litewskie*; to 1918 Russian *Vysoko-Litovsk*

Vysoké Mýto (town, central Czech Republic) : to 1918, 1939–1945 German *Hohenmauth*

Vysoké nad Jizerou (town, northern Czech Republic) : to 1918, 1939–1945 German *Hochstadt*

Vysoko-Litovsk *see* **Vysokaye**

Vysokoye *see* **Vysokaye**

Vysotsk (town, northwestern Russia) : to 1948 Finnish *Uuras* (The town passed from Finland to the USSR in 1940 but retained its Finnish name until 1948.)

Vyšší Brod (village, southern Czech Republic) : to 1918, 1939–1945 German *Hohenfurth*

Vyzhnytsya (town, western Ukraine) : (Russian *Vizhnitsa*), 1919–1940 Romanian *Vijniţa*; to 1918 German *Wiznitz*

¹Vzmor'ye (village, western Russia) : to 1945 German *Grossheidekrug*

²Vzmor'ye (village, eastern Russia) : 1905–1945 Japanese *Shiraura*

Waadt *see* **Vaud**

Waag-Bistritz *see* **Považská Bystrica**

Waag-Neustadt *see* **Nové Mesto nad Váhom**

Wąbrzeźno (town, northern Poland) : 1772–1919, 1939–1945 German *Briesen*

Wadhwan *see* **Surendranagar**

Wadowice (town, southern Poland) : 1940–1945 German *Frauenstadt*; 18th–19th century, 1939–1940 German *Wadowitz*

Wadowitz *see* **Wadowice**

Wadsworth *see* **Riverton**

Wagendrüssel *see* **Vondrišel**

Wągrowiec (town, west central Poland) : 1793–1807, 1815–1919, 1939–1945 German *Wongrowitz*

Wagstadt *see* **Bílovec**

Wahlstatt *see* **Legnickie Pole**

Waihou (river, northern New Zealand) : formerly *Thames* (The earlier name is preserved in the town of *Thames* at the river's mouth.)

Wainwright (town, Alberta, west central Canada) : to 1909 *Denwood*

Wairoa (town, northeastern New Zealand) : formerly *Clyde*

Wairoa *see* **Waverley**

Waitzen *see* **Vác**

Wakatu *see* **¹Nelson**

Wakeham *see* **Kangiqsujuaq**

Wałbrzych (city, southwestern Poland) : to 1945 German *Waldenburg*

Wałcz (town, northwestern Poland) : 1772–1919, 1939–1945 German *Deutsch-Krone*

Waldau *see* **Nizovye**

Waldenburg *see* **Wałbrzych**

Wales (principality, western Great Britain) : Welsh *Cymru*; Roman *Cambria*

Walker Town *see* **Walkerville**

Walkerville (town, Ontario, southeastern Canada) : to 1858 *Walker Town* (In 1935 the town was annexed to the city of Windsor.)

Wall (village, central England) : Roman *Letocetum*. (The nearby town of *Lichfield* took the *Lich-* of its name from the Roman name, itself from Celtic words meaning "gray wood," adding Old English *feld*, modern *-field*, to mean "open land.")

Wallaceburg (town, Ontario, southeastern Canada) : originally *The Forks*

Wallachia (region, southern Romania) : [Romanian *Valahia*]

Wallachisch-Meseritsch *see* **Valašské Meziříčí**

Walla Walla (city, Washington, northwestern United States) : to 1862 *Steptoeville*

Wallingford (town, Connecticut, northeastern United States) : to 1670 *East River*

Wallis Plains *see* **Maitland**

Wallonia (region, southern Belgium) : [French *Wallonie*]

Wallonie *see* **Wallonia**

Wallsend (town, northeastern England) : Roman *Segedunum* (The town lies at the eastern end of the Roman wall known as *Hadrian's Wall*.)

Walnut City *see* **Arkansas City**

Walnut Creek (city, California, western United States) : to 1860 *The Corners*

Wanganui (city, north central New Zealand) : to 1845 *Petre*

Wangerin *see* **Węgorzyno**

Wangkü *see* **Chang'an**

Wankie *see* **Hwange**

Wansen *see* **Wiązów**

Wantland's Ferry *see* **²Jacksonville**

Warasdin *see* **Varaždin**

Wardsesson *see* **²Bloomfield**

Waremme (town, east central Belgium) : Flemish *Borgworm*

Warmbad *see* **Bela-Bela**

Warmbaths *see* **Bela-Bela**

Warner Robins (city, Georgia, southeastern United States) : formerly *Wellston* (The original village was renamed when Robins Air Force base was established nearby in 1943.)

Warnsdorf *see* **Varnsdorf**

¹Warren (city, Michigan, north central United

States) : 1838–1839 *Alba*; originally *Hickory*
(The city is now a suburb of Detroit.)

²**Warren** (town, Massachusetts, northeastern
United States) : to 1834 *Western*

Warsaw (city, east central Poland) : [Polish
Warszawa]; 1795–1807, 1939–1945 German
Warschau

Warschau *see* **Warsaw**

Warszawa *see* **Warsaw**

Wartenburg *see* **Barczewo**

Wartha *see* **Bardo**

Warthbrücken *see* **Koło**

Warthenau *see* **Zawiercie**

Wascana *see* **Regina**

Waset *see* **Thebes**

¹**Washington** (town, North Carolina, eastern
United States) : to 1776 *Forks of Tar River*

²**Washington** (town, Pennsylvania, northeastern
United States) : to 1781 *Bassett-town*; originally
Catfish's Camp

Washington *see* (1) **Macomb**; (2) **Piqua**

Washington Court House *see* **Fayetteville**

Washington Island *see* **Teraina**

Washington's Furnace *see* ¹**Lakewood**

Waskaganish (village, Quebec, eastern Canada) :
formerly *Fort-Rupert*; earlier *Fort-St.-Jacques*;
originally *Fort-Charles*

Wąsosz (town, western Poland) : to 1945 German *Herrnstadt*

Watenstedt-Salzgitter *see* **Salzgitter**

Water Eaton (village, central England) : Roman
Pennocrucium (This Water Eaton, near Penk-
ridge, should not be confused with two other
villages of the same name, the first now part of
the town of Bletchley, the other near Oxford.)

Waterford (town, southeastern Ireland) : Irish
Port Láirge

Waterloo (city, Iowa, north central United
States) : to 1851 *Prairie Rapids*

Waterloo *see* **Austin**

Waterman Junction *see* **Barstow**

Watertown (town, Connecticut, northeastern
United States) : to 1780 *Westbury*

Watertown *see* **Wethersfield**

Waterville (town, southwestern Ireland) : Irish
An Coireán

Watkins Glen (village, New York, northeastern
United States) : to 1852 *Jefferson*

Watling Island *see* ¹**San Salvador**

Watrap (town, southeastern India) : to early
1920s *Varttirayiruppu*

Watts (town, California, southwestern United
States) : to 1900 *Mud Town* (The town is now
a district of Los Angeles.)

Waukegan (city, Illinois, north central United
States) : to 1849 *Little Fort*

Waukesha (city, Wisconsin, north central United
States) : originally *Prairieville*

Wausau (city, Wisconsin, north central United
States) : to 1872 *Big Bull Falls*

Waver *see* **Wavre**

Waverley (town, north central New Zealand) :
formerly *Wairoa* (The earlier Maori name was
changed as it already existed for **Wairoa**,
among other places.)

Wavre (town, central Belgium) : Flemish *Waver*

Wavre-Ste.-Catherine *see* **Sint-Katelijne-
Waver**

Wayne (village, Ohio, north central United
States) : to 1931 *Freeport*

Waynesboro (town, Virginia, eastern United
States) : to 1801 *Teesville*

Wear (river, northeastern England) : Roman
Vedra

Webster City (town, Iowa, north central United
States) : to 1856 *Newcastle*

Wedgeport (town, Nova Scotia, eastern Canada)
: to 1909 *Tusket Wedge*

Węgliniec (town, southwestern Poland) : to 1945
German *Kohlfurt*

Węgorzewo (town, northern Poland) : to 1945
German *Angerburg*

Węgorzyno (town, northwestern Poland) : to
1945 German *Wangerin*

Węgrów (town, eastern Poland) : to 1915 Russian
Vengrov

Wehlau *see* **Znamensk**

Weichsel *see* **Vistula**

Weipert *see* **Vejprty**

Weissenburg *see* **Alba Iulia**

Weissenfels *see* **Fusine in Valromana**

Weissenstein *see* **Paide**

Weisskirchen *see* **Bela Crkva**

Weiss-stein *see* **Biały Kamień**

Weisswasser *see* **Bělá pod Bezdězem**

Weistritz *see* **Bystrzyca**

Wejherowo (town, northern Poland) : 1772–1919,
1939–1945 German *Neustadt in Westpreussen*

Wekelsdorf *see* **Teplice nad Metují**

Wekweti (village, Northwest Territories, northern Canada) : to 1999 *Snare Lakes*

Welfare Island *see* **Roosevelt Island**

Welland (city, Ontario, southeastern Canada) :
1842–1856 *Merrittsville*; to 1842 *The Aqueduct*

Wellington (city, central New Zealand) : originally *Port Nicholson* (The original name is preserved for the harbor here, also known as
Wellington Harbour, much as **Sydney,** Australia, surrounds Port Jackson, itself alternately
known as Sydney Harbour.)

Wellsburg (town, West Virginia, east central
United States) : to 1816 *Charles Town*

Wellsford (village, northern New Zealand) : Maori *Whakapirau*

Wellston *see* **Warner Robins**

Wels (city, north central Austria) : Roman *Ovilava*

Welshpool (town, eastern Wales) : Welsh *Y Trallwng*

Welsh St. Donats (village, southern Wales) : Welsh *Llanddunwyd* (The first word of the name distinguishes this village, historically in a manor subject to Welsh law, from **St. Donats**, some 8 miles to the southwest.)

Welungen *see* **Wieluń**

Welwarn *see* **Velvary**

Welwitschia *see* **Khorixas**

Wenden *see* **Cēsis**

Wenvoe (village, southern Wales) : Welsh *Gwenfô*

Werschetz *see* **Vršac**

Wesenberg *see* **Rakvere**

Weseritz *see* **Bezdružice**

Wesermünde *see* **Bremerhaven**

Wesleyville (village, Newfoundland and Labrador, eastern Canada) : to 1884 *Coal Harbour*

Wesprim *see* **Veszprém**

Wesseli an der Lainsitz *see* **Veselí nad Lužnicí**

Wesseli an der March *see* **Veselí nad Moravou**

West Allis (city, Wisconsin, north central United States) : 1880–1902 *North Greenfield*; originally *Honey Creek* (The city is now a suburb of Milwaukee.)

Westbourne *see* **Zanesville**

Westbury *see* **Watertown**

West Cambridge *see* [2]**Arlington**

West Columbia (town, South Carolina, southeastern United States) : to 1938 *New Brookland*

West Des Moines (city, Iowa, north central United States) : to 1938 *Valley Junction*

Western (province, western Zambia) : to 1969 *Barotseland* (The province's present name was held earlier by **Copperbelt** province, to the north.)

Western *see* [2]**Warren**

Western Isles (northwestern Scotland) : Gaelic *Eilean Siar*; alternate *Outer Hebrides* (The islands, part of the **Hebrides**, bear the full formal Gaelic name *Na h-Eileanan an Iar*.)

Western Sahara (territory, northwestern Africa) : 1958–1976 *Spanish Sahara*

Western Samoa *see* **Samoa**

Westfalen *see* **Westphalia**

West Hammond *see* **Calumet City**

West Hanover *see* **Morristown**

West Hartford (town, Connecticut, northeastern United States) : to 1806 *West Society*

West Hoosac *see* **Williamstown**

West Irian Jaya *see* **West Papua**

West Lafayette (city, Indiana, north central United States) : 1866–1888 *Chauncey*; to 1866 *Kingston*

West Lake *see* **Kagera**

West Lothian (administrative region, southeastern Scotland) : formerly *Linlithgowshire*

West Maitland *see* **Maitland**

Westmeath (county, north central Ireland) : Irish *An Iarmhí*

West Memphis (city, Arkansas, south central United States) : to 1927 *Bragg's Spur*

Weston under Penyard (village, west central England) : Roman *Ariconium*

West Orange (town, New Jersey, northeastern United States) : originally *Fairmount*

West Papua (province, eastern Indonesia) : to 2007 *West Irian Jaya* (In 2003 the western part of the province of **Papua** was demarcated as the new province of *Irian Jaya Barat*, or *West Irian Jaya*. In 2007 it was renamed *Papua Barat*, or *West Papua*.)

Westphalia (region, western Germany) : [German *Westfalen*]

West Point *see* **Apalachicola**

Westport (town, western Ireland) : Irish *Cathair na Mart*

Westport Landing *see* [1]**Kansas City**

West's Corner *see* **Milverton**

West Seekonk *see* **East Providence**

West Seneca (town, New York, northeastern United States) : to 1852 *Seneca*

West Shefford *see* **Bromont**

West Society *see* **West Hartford**

West Wyalong (town, New South Wales, southeastern Australia) : originally *Main Camp*

Wethersfield (town, Connecticut, northeastern United States) : to 1637 *Watertown*

Wexford (town, southeastern Ireland) : Irish *Loch Garman*

Whakapirau *see* **Wellsford**

Whale Cove (village, Nunavut, north central Canada) : alternate Inuit *Tikirarjuaq*

Whapmagoostui *see* **Kuujjuarapik**

Wharfe (river, northern England) : Roman *Verbeia* (The Roman name may also have been that of the fort at **Ilkley**, on this river.)

Whatcom *see* **Bellingham**

Wha Ti (village, Northwest Territories, northern Canada) : to 1999 *Lac la Martre*

Whitby (town, Ontario, southeastern Canada) : to 1855 *Perry's Corners*

[1]**Whitchurch** (town, western England) : Roman *Mediolanum*

[2]**Whitchurch** (village, southeastern Wales) : Welsh *Yr Eglwys Newydd* (The village is now a district of the city of Cardiff.)

[3]**Whitchurch** (village, southwestern Wales) :
Welsh *Tre-groes*

White Nile (river, southern Sudan) : [Arabic
Baḥr al-Abyaḍ]

White Russia *see* **Belarus**

White's Fort *see* **Knoxville**

White Sulphur Springs *see* **Searcy**

White Valley *see* **Lumby**

White Volta *see* **Nakambe**

Whitford (village, northeastern Wales) : Welsh
Chwitffordd

Whitland (village, southwestern Wales) : Welsh
Hendy-gwyn

Whitman (town, Massachusetts, northeastern
United States) : to 1886 *South Abington*

Whyalla (city, South Australia, southern Australia) : to 1920 *Hummock Hill*

Whydah *see* **Ouidah**

Wiązów (town, southwestern Poland) : to 1945
German *Wansen*

Wick (village, southern Wales) : Welsh *Y Wig*

Wicklow (town, eastern Ireland) : Irish *Cill
Mhantáin*

Widder Station *see* **Thedford**

Więcbork (town, northwestern Poland) : to 1945
German *Vandsburg*

Wielbark (town, northeastern Poland) : to 1945
German *Willenberg*

Wieleń (town, western Poland) : 1793–1807,
1815–1919, 1939–1945 German *Filehne*

Wieliczka (town, southern Poland) : 1940–1945
German *Gross-Salze*

Wielka Wieś (town, southern Poland) : 1772–
1919, 1939–1945 German *Grossendorf bei
Putzig* (The district of *Władisławowo* was
named *Hallerowo* from 1919 to 1939.)

Wieluń (town, south central Poland) : 1940–
1945 German *Welungen*

Wien *see* **Vienna**

Wierzchowo (village, northern Poland) : 1772–
1807, 1815–1945 German *Firchau*

Wiesbaden (city, western Germany) : Roman
Aquae Mattiacae

Wieselburg *see* **Moson**

Wiesengrund *see* **Dobřany**

Wietstock *see* **Wysoka**

Wietz *see* **Witnica**

Wight, Isle of (southern England) : Roman *Vectis*

Wildenschwert *see* **Ústi nad Orlicí**

Wildersburgh *see* **Barre**

Wilds *see* [2]**Florence**

Wilejka *see* **Vileyka**

Wilhelmina Top *see* **Trikora**

Wilhelm-Pieck-Stadt *see* **Guben**

Willenberg *see* **Wielbark**

William Henry *see* **Sorel**

Williamsburg (town, Virginia, eastern United
States) : to 1699 *Middle Plantation*

Williamsburg *see* **Rockville**

Williams Landing *see* **Greenwood**

Wiliamstown (town, Massachusetts, northeastern United States) : to 1765 *West Hoosac*

Willingboro (town, New Jersey, northeastern
United States) : 1959–1963 *Levittown*

[1]**Williston** (town, North Dakota, northern
United States) : originally *Little Muddy*

[2]**Williston** (town, southwestern South Africa) :
to 1919 *Amandelboom*

Willmore City *see* **Long Beach**

Will's Creek *see* **Cumberland**

Willyama *see* **Broken Hill**

[1]**Wilmington** (city, Delaware, northeastern
United States) : 1655–1739 *Altena*; earlier *Fort
Christina*

[2]**Wilmington** (city, North Carolina, eastern
United States) : originally *New Town*

Wilno *see* **Vilnius**

Wiltwyck *see* [1]**Kingston**

[1]**Winchester** (city, southern England) : Roman
Venta Belgarum

[2]**Winchester** (city, Virginia, eastern United
States) : to 1752 *Fredericktown*

Windau *see* **Ventspils**

Windisch (town, northern Switzerland) : Roman
Vindonissa

Windisch-Feistritz *see* **Ilirska Bistrica**

Windischgrätz *see* **Slovenj Gradec**

Windscale *see* **Sellafield**

[1]**Windsor** (town, south central England) :
officially *New Windsor* (The town grew up by
Windsor Castle, built near the original Windsor, now contrastingly named *Old Windsor*.)

[2]**Windsor** (town, Nova Scotia, eastern Canada) :
to 1764 *Pisiquid*

[3]**Windsor** (city, Ontario, southeastern Canada) :
to 1836 *Richmond*; originally *The Ferry*

Wing's Falls *see* **Glens Falls**

Winkowcze *see* **Vinkovci**

Winnebago Rapids *see* **Neenah**

Winnipeg (city, Manitoba, southern Canada) :
to 1835 *Fort Garry* (This and earlier forts on
the site formed the nucleus of the new city, incorporated in 1873.)

Winona (city, Minnesota, north central United
States) : originally *Montezuma*

Wińsko (town, southwestern Poland) : to 1945
German *Winzig*

Winter Haven (city, Florida, southeastern
United States) : to 1884 *Harris' Corner*

Winter Park (city, Florida, southeastern United
States) : 1870–1881 *Osceola*; originally *Lakeview*

Winterthur (city, northern Switzerland) : Roman *Vitodurum*

Winton (town, Queensland, east central Australia) : originally *Pelican Waterholes*

Wintonbury *see* ¹**Bloomfield**

Winzig *see* **Wińsko**

Wirbeln *see* **Zhavoronkovo**

Wirowititz *see* **Virovitica**

Wirsitz *see* **Wyrzysk**

Wischau *see* **Vyškov**

Wisconsin Dells (town, Wisconsin, northern United States) : to 1931 *Kilbourn*

Wisconsin Rapids (city, Wisconsin, northern United States) : to 1920 *Grand Rapids* (Grand Rapids and Centralia, either side of the Wisconsin River, were consolidated in 1900.)

Wise (town, Virginia, eastern United States) : to 1924 *Gladville*; originally *Big Glades*

Wisła *see* **Vistula**

Wiston (village, southwestern Wales) : Welsh *Cas-wis*

Witkowitz *see* **Vitkovice**

Witkowo (town, west central Poland) : 1939–1945 German *Wittingen*

Witnica (town, western Poland) : to 1945 German *Wietz*

Witsieshoek *see* **Phuthaditjhaba**

Wittenberg *see* **Nivenskoye**

Wittingau *see* **Třeboň**

Wittingen *see* **Witkowo**

Witwatersrand (rocky ridge, northeastern South Africa) : popularly *The Rand*

Wiznitz *see* **Vyzhnytsya**

Władysławów *see* **Naumiestis**

Władisławowo *see* **Wielka Wieś**

Wlaschim *see* **Vlaším**

Wleń (town, southwestern Poland) : to 1945 German *Lähn*

Włocławek (city, north central Poland) : 1939–1945 German *Leslau*; 1815–1915 Russian *Vlotslavek*

Włodzimierz *see* **Volodymyr-Volyns'kyy**

Wodzisław Śląski (city, southern Poland) : 1939–1945 German *Loslau*

Wohlau *see* **Wołów**

Wołczyn (town, southern Poland) : to 1945 German *Konstadt*

Woldenberg *see* **Dobiegniew**

Wolframs-Eschenbach (town, southwestern Germany) : to 1917 *Eschenbach* (The present name does not derive from a merger with another town but from the addition of the name of the medieval poet Wolfram von Eschenbach, who was born here.)

Wolf's Castle (village, southwestern Wales) : Welsh *Cas-blaidd*

Wolin (town, northwestern Poland) : to 1945 German *Wollin*

Wołkowysk *see* **Vawkavysk**

Wollin *see* **Wolin**

Wollstein *see* **Wolsztyn**

Wolmar *see* **Valmiera**

Wolów (town, southwestern Poland) : to 1945 German *Wohlau*

Wołożyn *see* **Valozhyn**

Wolsztyn (town, western Poland) : 1793–1807, 1815–1919, 1939–1945 German *Wollstein*

Wołyń *see* **Volhynia**

Wongrowitz *see* **Wągrowiec**

Woodbridge (town, Ontario, southeastern Canada) : to 1854 *Burwick* (In 1971 Woodbridge merged with the town of Vaughan.)

Woodburn (town, Indiana, north central United States) : to 1936 *Shirley City*

Woodland (city, California, western United States) : to 1859 *Yolo City*

Woodland Hills (town, California, southwestern United States) : to 1941 *Girard* (The town is now a suburban section of Los Angeles.)

Woodstock (city, Ontario, southeastern Canada) : originally *Oxford*

Worcester (city, west central England) : Roman *Vertis* (The precise name of the original Roman town is tentative, as in fact is its identification with the modern city.)

Worcester *see* **Marquette**

Wormditt *see* **Orneta**

Worms (city, southwestern Germany) : Roman *Augusta Vangionum*; Celtic *Borbetomagus*

Woropajewo *see* **Varapayeva**

Worthington *see* **Valley City**

Wrecsam *see* **Wrexham**

Wrekin, The *see* **Telford and Wrekin**

Wreschen *see* **Września**

Wrexham (town, northeastern Wales) : Welsh *Wrecsam*

Wright's Ferry *see* ²**Columbia**

Wrightstown *see* ²**Hull**

Wrigley (village, Northwest Territories, northwestern Canada) : alternate Inuit *Tthedzeh Koe*

Wrocław (city, southwestern Poland) : to 1945 German *Breslau*

Wroxeter (village, western England) : Roman *Viroconium*; alternate Roman *Uriconium* (The Roman name may have originally been that of the fort on the Wrekin, a nearby hill.)

Września (town, west central Poland) : 1793–1807, 1815–1919, 1939–1945 German *Wreschen*

Wrzeszcz (town, northern Poland) : 1793–1945 German *Langfuhr* (Wrzeszcz is now a district of the city of Gdańsk.)

Wschowa (town, western Poland) : 1793–1807, 1815–1945 German *Fraustadt*

Wsetin *see* **Vsetín**

Wukowar *see* **Vukovar**

Wünschelburg *see* **Radków**

Wuppertal (city, western Germany) : to 1930 *Barmen-Elberfeld* (The city was formed in 1929 from the merger of Barmen and Elberfeld with other towns.)

Würbenthal *see* **Vrbno pod Pradědem**

Wutsin *see* **Changzhou**

Wyandotte *see* ²**Kansas City**

Wye (river, southern Wales/western England) : Welsh *Gwy*

Wygoda *see* **Vyhoda**

Wynyard (town, Tasmania, southeastern Australia) : to 1861 *Table Cape*

Wyrzysk (town, northwestern Poland) : 1793–1807, 1815–1919, 1939–1945 German *Wirsitz*

Wysoka (town, northwestern Poland) : 1793–1807, 1815–1919, 1939–1945 German *Wietstock*

Wysokie Litewskie *see* **Vysokaye**

Wysokie Mazowieckie (town, northeastern Poland) : to 1915 Russian *Mazovetsk*

Xaignabouli (town, northwestern Laos) : to 1946 *Paklay* (Xaignabouli was in Thailand from 1941 to 1946.)

Xai-Xai (town, southern Mozambique) : 1928–1976 Portuguese *Vila de João Belo*; 1922–1928 Portuguese *Vila Nova de Gaza*

Xá-Muteba (village, northern Angola) : formerly Portuguese *Cinco de Outubro*

Xanadu *see* **Shangdu**

Xangongo (town, southern Angola) : formerly Portuguese *Roçadas*

Xankändi (city, southwestern Azerbaijan) : 1923–1991 *Stepanakert*; to 1923 *Khankendy*

Xanlar (town, western Azerbaijan) : to 1938 *Yelenendorf*

Xánthi (city, northeastern Greece) : to 1913 Turkish *Eskice*

Xatl'o Dehe *see* **Hay Beach**

Xhora *see* **Elliotdale**

Xiaguan *see* ¹**Dali**

Xiamen (city, southeastern China) : alternate dated *Amoy*

Xianggang *see* **Hong Kong**

Xinjiang Uygur (region, western China) : alternate *Sinkiang Uighur*; to 1878 *Chinese Turkestan* (Both forms of the Chinese name are often shortened, respectively as *Xinjiang* and *Sinkiang*, omitting the ethnic name.)

Xinjing *see* **Changchun**

Xions *see* **Książ Wielkopolski**

Xiririca *see* **Eldorado**

Xizang *see* **Tibet**

Xonobod (town, eastern Uzbekistan) : (Russian *Khanabad*); formerly Russian *Sovetabad*; to 1972 *Karabagish*

Xovos (town, eastern Uzbekistan) : (Russian *Khavast*); to 1963 Russian *Ursat'yevskaya*

Yablochny (town, eastern Russia) : 1905–1945 Japanese *Rantomari*

Yafo *see* **Jaffa**

Yakima (city, Washington, northwestern United States) : to 1918 *North Yakima*

Yakova *see* **Djakovica**

Yakovlevskoye *see* **Privolzhsk**

Yakunchikov *see* **Krasny Mayak**

Yakutia *see* **Sakha**

Yaloven' *see* **Ialoveni**

Yama *see* **Sivers'k**

Yambol (city, southeastern Bulgaria) : to 1878 Turkish *Yambolu*

Yambolu *see* **Yambol**

Yamburg *see* **Kingisepp**

Yanaw *see* **Ivanava**

Yangi-Bazar *see* (1) **Kofarnihon**; (2) **Soldatsky**

Yangiyer (town, eastern Uzbekistan) : formerly Russian *Chernyayevo*

Yangiyul (city, eastern Uzbekistan) : to *c*.1935 *Kaunchi*

Yangku *see* **Taiyuan**

Yangôn (city, south central Myanmar) : to 1989 *Rangoon*; to 1756 *Dagon* (The present form of the city's name more accurately reflects its Burmese pronunciation.)

Yangtze (river, China) : alternate *Chang* (The name was formerly familiar in the expanded form *Yangtze Kiang*, where the second word, more correctly *Jiang*, means simply "river." The alternate name may similarly appear on maps as *Chang Jiang*.)

Yaniv *see* **Ivano-Frankove**

Yanivka *see* **Ivanivka**

Yanov *see* (1) **Ivanava**; (2) **Ivano-Frankove**

Yanovka *see* **Ivanivka**

Yantarny (town, western Russia) : to 1945 German *Palmnicken*

Yantsivs'kyy Kar'yer *see* ²**Kam'yane**

Yantsovsky Kar'yer *see* ²**Kam'yane**

Yanushpil' *see* **Ivanopol'**

Yanushpol *see* **Ivanopil'**

Yanya *see* **Ioannina**

Yaryksu-Aukh *see* **Novolakskoye**

Yasenivs'kyy (town, eastern Ukraine) : (Russian *Yasenovsky*); to 1954 *Lobivka* (Russian *Lobovka*)

Yasenovsky *see* **Yasenivs'kyy**

Yashkul' (town, western Russia) : 1943–1957 *Peschanoye*

Yasi *see* **Turkestan**

Yasinya (town, western Ukraine) : 1944–1945

Czech *Jasina*; 1939–1944 Hungarian *Körömező*; 1919–1939 Czech *Jasina*; to 1918 Hungarian *Körömező*

Yaski *see* **Lesogorsky**

Yasnogorsk (town, western Russia) : to 1965 *Laptevo*

Yasnomorsky (village, eastern Russia) : 1905–1945 Japanese *Oko*

Yasnoye (village, western Russia) : 1938–1945 German *Kuckerneese*; to 1938 *Kaukehmen*

Yassıhüyük (village, northwestern Turkey) : Roman *Gordium*; ancient Greek *Gordion*

Yathrib *see* **Medina**

Yavoriv (town, western Ukraine) : (Russian *Yavorov*); to 1919 Polish *Jaworów*

Yavorov *see* **Yavoriv**

Yazoo City (town, Mississippi, southeastern United States) : 1830–1839 *Manchester*; originally *Hanan's Bluff*

Y Bala *see* **Bala**

Y Barri *see* **Barry**

Y Bermo *see* **Barmouth**

Y Bont-faen *see* **Cowbridge**

Y Bontnewydd-ar-Wy *see* **Newbridge-on-Wye**

Y Clas-ar-Wy *see* **Glasbury**

Y Drenewydd *see* **Newtown**

Yeghegnadzor (town, south central Armenia) : *c*.1935–1957 *Mikoyan*; to *c*.1935 *Keshishkend*

Yegindykol' (village, north central Kazakhstan) : formerly Russian *Krasnoznamenskoye*

Yegorshino *see* **Artyomovsky**

Yekabpils *see* **Jēkabpils**

Yekaterinburg (city, western Russia) : 1924–1991 *Sverdlovsk*

Yekaterinenshtadt *see* **Marks**

Yekaterinodar *see* **Krasnodar**

Yekaterinofeld *see* **Bolnisi**

Yekaterinoslav *see* **Dnipropetrovs'k**

Yekaterinovskaya *see* **Krylovskaya**

Yelenendorf *see* **Xanlar**

Yelenovka *see* (1) **Sevan**; (2) **Zoryns'k**

Yelenovskiye Kar'yery *see* **Dokuchayevs'k**

Yelgava *see* **Jelgava**

Yelizavetgrad *see* **Kirovohrad**

Yelizavetpol *see* **Gäncä**

Yelizovo (city, eastern Russia) : to 1924 *Zavoyko*

Yellowknife (town, Northwest Territories, west central Canada) : alternate Inuit *Sombak'e*

Yellow River *see* **Huang Ho**

Yellow Sea (western Pacific) : [Chinese *Huang Hai*; alternate Chinese *Hwang Hai*] (The **Huang Ho** flows into the Yellow Sea through the Bo Hai or Gulf of Chihli.)

Yelyzavethrad *see* **Kirovohrad**

Yemen (republic, southwestern Asia) : [Arabic *Al Yaman*]

Yemva (town, western Russia) : to 1985 *Zheleznodorozhny*

Yen *see* **Beijing**

Yenakiyeve (city, eastern Ukraine) : (Russian *Yenakiyevo*); 1935–1943 *Ordzhonikidze*; *c*.1928–1935 *Rykovo*

Yenakiyevo *see* **Yenakiyeve**

Yenice *see* **Giannitsa**

Yeni Derbent *see* **Dŭlgopol**

Yenipazar *see* [1,2]**Novi Pazar**

Yenišehir *see* **Lárissa**

Yenizağra *see* **Nova Zagora**

Yenukidze *see* **Ambrolauri**

Yeraliyev *see* **Kuryk**

Yerba Buena *see* **San Francisco**

Yerevan (city, central Armenia) : to 1936 Russian *Erivan*

Yermak *see* [1]**Aksu**

Yermalner *see* **Melville Island**

Yermolovsk *see* **Gyachrypsh**

Yerushalayim *see* **Jerusalem**

Yerzhar *see* [2]**Gagarin**

Yeşilköy (village, northwestern Turkey) : formerly Italian *San Stefano* (The Italian name is historically preserved for the treaty between Russia and Turkey signed here in 1878.)

Yesman *see* [1]**Chervone**

Yevdokimovskoye *see* [3]**Krasnogvardeyskoye**

Yev'ye *see* **Vievis**

Yezhovo-Cherkessk *see* **Cherkessk**

Yezo *see* **Hokkaido**

Yezupil' *see* [1]**Zhovten'**

Yezupol' *see* [1]**Zhovten'**

Y Fali *see* **Valley**

Y Felinheli (town, northwestern Wales) : formerly *Port Dinorwic* (The port town originally exported slate from the nearby *Dinorwic* quarry.)

Y Fenai *see* **Menai Strait**

Y Fenni *see* **Abergavenny**

Y Fflint *see* **Flint**

Y Garn *see* **Roch**

Y Gelli Gandryll *see* **Hay-on-Wye**

Y Grysmwnt *see* **Grosmont**

Yirga Alem (town, southern Ethiopia) : 1936–1941 Italian *Dalle*

Yisra'el *see* **Israel**

Y Môt *see* **New Moat**

Y Mwmbwls *see* **Mumbles**

Y Mynydd Du *see* **Black Mountain**

Y Mynyddoedd Duon *see* **Black Mountains**

Ynys Bŷr *see* **Caldey**

Ynys Dewi *see* **Ramsey**

Ynys Echni *see* **Flatholm**

Ynys Enlli *see* **Bardsey**

Ynys Gybi *see* **Holy Island**

Ynysgynwraidd *see* Skenfrith
Ynysoedd y Moelrhoniaid *see* Skerries, The
Ynysowen *see* Merthyr Vale
Ynys Seiriol *see* Puffin Island
Yokuntown *see* Lenox
Yolo City *see* Woodland
Yongning *see* Nanning
¹York (city, northern England) : Roman *Ebo-racum* (The 2d-century A.D. geographer Ptol-emy recorded the name as *Eborakon*. Under the Anglo-Saxons the city was known as *Eofor-wic* and then under the Vikings *Jórvik*, the lat-ter eventually giving the present name.)
²York (town, Maine, northeastern United States) : to 1652 *Gorgeana*
York *see* Toronto
York River *see* Bancroft
Yoshkar-Ola (city, western Russia) : 1919–1927 *Krasnokokshaysk*; to 1919 *Tsaryovokokshaysk*
Youghal (town, southern Ireland) : Irish *Eochaill*
Youssoufia (town, west central Morocco) : for-merly French *Louis-Gentil*
Youth, Isle of *see* Juventud, Isla de la
Ypres (town, western Belgium) : Flemish *Ieper* (Although in the Flemish-speaking half of Bel-gium, the town is usually referred to by its French name. It was held by France from 1678 to 1716 and 1792 to 1814 and became widely known under this name as the scene of major battles in World War I, when English-speaking combatants dubbed it "Wipers.")
Yr Eglwys Lwyd *see* Ludchurch
Yr Eglwys Newydd *see* ²Whitchurch
Yr Hôb *see* Hope
Y Rhws *see* Rhoose
Yr Orsedd *see* Rossett
Yr Wyddfa *see* Snowdon
Yr Wyddgrug *see* Mold
Y Trallwng *see* Welshpool
Yuan *see* Red River
Yudino *see* Petukhovo
Yug (town, western Russia) : to 1943 *Yugovskoy Zavod*
Yugo-Kamsky (town, western Russia) : to 1929 *Yugokamsky Zavod*
Yugokamsky Zavod *see* Yugo-Kamsky
Yugorsk (town, west central Russia) : formerly *Komsomol'sky*
Yugoslavia (historic republic, southeastern Eu-rope) : [Serbian *Jugoslavija*]; to 1929 *Kingdom of Serbs, Croats, and Slovenes* (Serbo-Croat *Kraljevina Serba, Hrvata i Slovenaca*) (In 1945 the kingdom became a federation of **Bosnia-Herzegovia**, **Croatia**, **Macedonia**, **Montene-gro**, **Serbia**, and **Slovenia**. In 1991 four of these declared their independence, leaving just

Serbia and Montenegro to form a rump *Fed-eral Republic of Yugoslavia*. In 2006 they also became independent, and the name Yugoslavia disappeared from the map.)
Yugovskoy Zavod *see* Yug
Yuma (city, Arizona, southwestern United States) : 1862–1873 *Arizona City*; to 1862 *Colorado City*
Yumrukchal *see* Botev Peak
Yunnanfu *see* Kunming
Yunokommunarovsk *see* Yunokomunarivs'k
Yunokomunarivs'k (town, eastern Ukraine) : (Russian *Yunokommunarovsk*); 1924–1965 *imeny Yunykh Komunariv* (Russian *imeni Yun-ykh Kommunarov*); to 1924 *Bunge Rudnyk* (Russian *Bunge Rudnik*)
Yunykh Kommunarov, imeni *see* Yunokomu-narivs'k
Yunykh Komunariv, imeny *see* Yunokomuna-rivs'k
Yur'yev *see* (1) Bila Cerkva; (2) Tartu
Yuryuzan' (town, western Russia) : to 1943 *Yuryuzansy Zavod*
Yuryuzansky Zavod *see* Yuryuzan'
Yutian *see* Changning
Yuzhno-Kuril'sk (town, eastern Russia) : 1905–1945 Japanese *Furukamappu*
Yuzhno-Sakhalinsk (town, eastern Russia) : 1905–1945 Japanese *Toyohara*; to 1905 Russian *Vladimirovka*
Yuzhnoukrainsk *see* Yuzhnoukrayins'k
Yuzhnoukrayins'k (town, south central Ukraine) : (Russian *Yuzhnoukrainsk*); to 1987 *Kostyanty-nivka* (Russian *Konstantinovka*)
Yuzhny *see* Skuratovsky
Yuzivka *see* Donets'k
Yuzovka *see* Donets'k
Yverdon (city, western Switzerland) : German *Iferten*; Roman *Eburodunum*
Y Waun *see* Chirk
Y Wig *see* Wick
Zabaykal'sk (town, southern Russia) : formerly *Otpor*
Żabie *see* Verkhovyna
Ząbkowice Śląskie (town, southwestern Poland) : to 1945 German *Frankenstein*
Zaboyshchik *see* Kurganovka
Zábřeh (town, east central Czech Republic) : to 1918, 1938–1945 German *Hohenstadt*
Zabrze (city, southern Poland) : 1915–1945 Ger-man *Hindenburg*
Zachan *see* Suchan
Žacléř (town, northeastern Czech Republic) : to 1918, 1939–1945 German *Schatzlar*
Zadar (city, southern Croatia) : 1919–1945 Italian *Zara*; Roman *Jadera*

Żagań (city, southwestern Poland) : to 1945 German *Sagan*

Zagorsk *see* **Sergiyev Posad**

Zagorsky *see* **Krasnozavodsk**

Zagreb (city, central Croatia) : to 1867 German *Agram*

Zahirabad (town, south central India) : formerly *Ekeli*

Zainsk (city, western Russia) : to 1978 *Novy Zay*

Zaire *see* **Congo**

Zaïre *see* **Congo, Democratic Republic of the**

Zakamensk (town, southern Russia) : to 1959 *Gorodok*

Zakarpats'ka Oblast' *see* **Transcarpathian Oblast**

Zakarpatskaya Oblast' *see* **Transcarpathian Oblast**

Zakharivka *see* **Frunzivka**

Zakharovka *see* **Frunzivka**

Zákupy (town, northern Czech Republic) : to 1918, 1938–1945 German *Reichstadt*

Zakynthos (island, western Greece) : alternate *Zante*

Zalău (city, northwestern Romania) : to 1918, 1940–1944 Hungarian *Zilah*

Zaleshchiki *see* **Zalishchyky**

Zales'ye (village, western Russia) : 1938–1945 German *Liebenfelde*; to 1938 German *Mehlauken*

Zaleszczyki *see* **Zalishchyky**

Zalew Wiślany *see* **Vistula Lagoon**

Zalishchyky (town, western Ukraine) : (Russian *Zaleshchiki*); to 1939 Polish *Zaleszczyki*

Žamberk (town, northeastern Czech Republic) : to 1918, 1938–1945 German *Senftenberg*

Zambia (republic, south central Africa) : to 1964 *Northern Rhodesia*

Zamość (city, east central Poland) : to 1915 Russian *Zamost'ye*

Zamost'ye *see* **Zamość**

Zancle *see* **Messina**

Zanesville (city, Ohio, north central United States) : to 1801 *Westbourne*

Zängilan (town, southern Azerbaijan) : to 1957 *Pirchevan*

Zanow *see* **Sianów**

Zante *see* **Zakynthos**

Zapadno-Gruppsky *see* **Shakhtars'k**

Zapaluta *see* **La Trinitaria**

Zaporizhzhya (city, southeastern Ukraine) : (Russian *Zaporozh'ye*); to 1921 *Oleksandriv'sk* (Russian *Aleksandrovsk*)

Zaporozh'ye *see* **Zaporizhzhya**

Zapotlán el Grande *see* **Ciudad Guzmán**

Zapovednoye (village, western Russia) : to 1945 German *Seckenburg*

Zara *see* **Zadar**

Zaragoza *see* **Saragossa**

Zarasai (town, northeastern Lithuania) : 1941–1944 German *Ossersee*; to 1918 Russian *Novo-aleksandrovsk*

Zárate (city, eastern Argentina) : 1932–1946 Spanish *General Uriburu*; earlier *Rincón de Zárate*

Zaravecchia *see* **Biograd na Moru**

Zarechny (town, western Russia) : formerly *Pobedinsky*

Zaria (city, north central Nigeria) : to late 16th century *Zazzau*

Żary (city, western Poland) : to 1945 German *Sorau*

Zasieki (village, western Poland) : to 1945 German *Forst* (The village, originally a suburb of the city of Forst, eastern Germany, was transferred to Poland in 1945.)

Zaslav *see* **Zaslawye**

Zaslavl' *see* **Zaslawye**

Zaslawye (town, west central Belarus) : (Russian *Zaslavl'*); to *c.*1935 Russian *Zaslav*; earlier Russian *Izyaslavl'*

Žatec (town, northwestern Czech Republic) : to 1918, 1938–1945 German *Saaz*

Zatish'ye *see* **Elektrostal'**

Zavitaya *see* **Zavitinsk**

Zavitinsk (town, eastern Russia) : to 1954 *Zavitaya*

Zavodoukovsk (town, west central Russia) : to 1960 *Zavodoukovsky*

Zavodoukovsky *see* **Zavodoukovsk**

Zavodskoy *see* ²**Komsomol'sky**

Zavolzhsk (town, western Russia) : to 1954 *Zavolzh'ye*

Zavolzh'ye (city, western Russia) : to 1960 *Pestovo*

Zavolzh'ye *see* **Zavolzhsk**

Zavoyko *see* **Yelizovo**

Zawidów (town, southwestern Poland) : to 1945 German *Seidenberg*

Zawiercie (city, southern Poland) : 1940–1945 German *Warthenau*

Zazzau *see* **Zaria**

Zbąszyń (town, western Poland) : 1793–1807, 1815–1919, 1939–1945 German *Bentschen*

Zbąszynek (town, western Poland) : to 1945 German *Neubentschen*

Žd'ár nad Sázavou (city, east central Czech Republic) : to 1918, 1939–1945 German *Saar an der Sazava*

Zdolbuniv (town, western Ukraine) : (Russian *Zdolbunov*); 1919–1939 Polish *Zdołbunów*; to 1918 Russian *Zdolbunov*

Zdolbunov *see* **Zdolbuniv**

Zdołbunów *see* **Zdolbuniv**

Zdzieszowice (village, southwestern Poland) : to 1945 German *Odertal*

Zealand *see* **Sjælland**

Zebrzydowice Dolne (town, southern Poland) : to 1918, 1939–1945 German *Seibersdorf*

Zeebrugge (town, northwestern Belgium) : French *Bruges-sur-Mer* (The town is the port for **Bruges**.)

Zehden *see* **Cedynia**

Zelaya (department, eastern Nicaragua) : formerly *Bluefields*

Zelena *see* ²**Druzhba**

Zelenodol'sk (town, western Russia) : to 1932 *Zelyony Dol*

Zelenogorsk (town, western Russia) : to 1948 Finnish *Terijoki* (The town passed to the USSR in 1940 but retained its Finnish name until 1948.)

Zelenogradsk (town, western Russia) : to 1945 German *Kranz* (The town should not be confused with the much larger *Zelenograd*, now a satellite suburb of Moscow.)

Zelenokumsk (city, southwestern Russia) : 1963–1965 *Sovetskoye*; to 1963 *Vorontsovo-Aleksandrovskoye*

Zelensk *see* ¹**Asaka**

Železná Ruda (village, southwestern Czech Republic) : to 1918, 1938–1945 German *Eisenstein* (The village lies on the German border opposite Bayerisch Eisenstein.)

Železný Brod (town, northern Czech Republic) : to 1918, 1939–1945 German *Eisenbrod*

Želiezovce (town, southern Slovakia) : to 1918 Hungarian *Zseliz*

Zelman *see* **Rovnoye**

Zelyony Dol *see* **Zelenodol'sk**

Zemen (town, western Bulgaria) : formerly *Belovo*

Zemlya Imperatora Nikolaya II *see* **Severnaya Zemlya**

Zempelburg *see* **Sępólno Krajeńskie**

Zemun (town, north central Serbia) : to 1867 German *Semlin* (Zemun is now incorporated into Belgrade.)

Zengg *see* **Senj**

Zenkovka *see* ²**Chkalovskoye**

Zenta *see* **Senta**

Zernograd (city, southwestern Russia) : 1933–1960 *Zernovoy*; to 1933 *Verblyud*

Zernovoy *see* **Zernograd**

Zestap'oni (town, west central Georgia) : to 1924 *Kvirily*; formerly alternate *Dzhugeli*

Zetland *see* **Shetland**

Zeugma *see* **Balkis**

Zeytun *see* **Lamía**

Zgorzelec (town, western Poland) : to 1945 German *Görlitz-Moys* (The town was originally a section of the city of Görlitz, eastern Germany, on the right bank of the Neisse River. In 1945 it passed to Poland as a separate entity under the equivalent Polish name.)

Zhab'ye *see* **Verkhovyna**

Zhahti Koe *see* **Fort Providence**

Zhalpaktal (town, western Kazakhstan) : formerly Russian *Furmanovo*; to 1935 Russian *Slomikhino*

Zhambyl *see* **Taraz**

Zhanaozen (town, southwestern Kazakhstan) : formerly Russian *Novy Uzen'*

Zhangaqazaly *see* **Ayteke Bi**

Zhangde *see* **Anyang**

Zhangjiakou (city, northeastern China) : alternate Mongolian *Kalgan*

Zhanjiang (city, southeastern China) : 1898–1945 French *Fort-Bayard*

Zharkent (city, southeastern Kazakhstan) : 1942–1991 Russian *Panfilov*; to 1942 Russian *Dzharkent*

Zhavoronkovo (village, western Russia) : to 1945 German *Wirbeln*

Zhdanov *see* **Mariupol'**

Zhdanovsk *see* **Beyläqan**

Zhelaniya, Cape (northwestern Russia) : formerly *Cape Mauritius*

¹**Zheleznodorozhny** (city, western Russia, near Moscow) : to 1939 *Obiralovka*

²**Zheleznodorozhny** (town, western Russia, near Kaliningrad) : to 1945 German *Gerdauen*

Zheleznodorozhny *see* (1) **Qunghirot**; (2) **Yemva**

Zheleznogorsk *see* **Zheleznogorsk-Ilimsky**

Zheleznogorsk-Ilimsky (city, southern Russia) : to 1965 *Zheleznogorsk*

Zhelyu Voivoda (village, eastern Bulgaria) : formerly *Mikhaylovo*

Zhengxian *see* **Zhengzhou**

Zhengzhou (city, east central China) : 1913–1949 *Zhengxian*

Zherdevka (town, western Russia) : to 1954 *Chibizovka*

Zhezdy (town, central Kazakhstan) : to 1962 *Marganets*, earlier *Kotabaru*

Zhidachov *see* **Zhydachiv**

Zhigulyovsk (city, western Russia) : 1949–1952 *Otvazhny*; 1946–1949 *Otvazhnoye*

Zhilyanka *see* **Kargalinskoye**

Zhirnovsk (town, southwestern Russia) : 1954–1958 *Zhirnovsky*; to 1954 *Zhirnoye*

Zhirnovsky *see* **Zhirnovsk**

Zhirnoye *see* **Zhirnovsk**

Zhitomir *see* **Zhytomyr**

Zhivkovo (village, west central Bulgaria) : to 1878 Turkish *Avliköy*

Zhob (town, southwestern Pakistan) : 1889–
1970s *Fort Sandeman*
Zholkva *see* **Zhovkva**
Zhovkva (town, western Ukraine) : (Russian
Zholkva); 1951–1991 Russian *Nesterov*; 1941–
1944 German *Zolkiew*; to 1939 Polish *Żółkiew*
Zhovta Richka *see* **Zhovti Vody**
[1]Zhovten' (town, western Ukraine) : to 1940
Yezupil' (Polish *Jezupol*, Russian *Yezupol'*)
[2]Zhovten' (village, southern Ukraine) : to *c.*1938
Petrovyrivka (Russian *Petroverovka*)
Zhovti Vody (city, eastern Ukraine) : (Russian
Zhyoltyye Vody); 1939–1957 *Zhovta Richka*
(Russian *Zhyoltaya Reka*); to 1939 *Rudnyk imeny
Shvartsa* (Russian *Rudnik imeni Shvartsa*)
[1]Zhovtneve (town, southern Ukraine) : (Russian
Zhovtnevoye); 1938–1961 Russian *Oktyabr'skoye*;
to 1938 Ukrainian *Bohoyavlens'ke* (Russian *Bo-
goyavlensk*) (The town became part of the city
of Mykolayiv in 1973.)
[2]Zhovtneve (town, northern Ukraine) : (Russian
Zhovtnevoye); to 1957 *Mykolayivka-Vyrivs'ka*
(Russian *Nikolayevka-Vyrevskaya*)
[3]Zhovtneve (village, eastern Ukraine) : (Russian
Zhovtnevoye); 1944–1961 *Stalins'ke* (Russian
Stalinskoye); *c.*1928–1944 *Stalindorf*; to *c.*1928
Russian *Izluchistaya*
Zhovtnevoye *see* [1,2,3]**Zhovtneve**
Zhukovo (village, western Russia) : to 1974
Ugodsky Zavod
Zhukovsky (town, western Russia) : 1938–1947
Stakhanovo; to 1938 *Otdykh*
Zhydachiv (town, western Ukraine) : (Russian
Zhidachov); to 1939 Polish *Żydaczów*
Zhyoltaya Reka *see* **Zhovti Vody**
Zhyoltyye Vody *see* **Zhovti Vody**
Zhytomyr (city, west central Ukraine) : (Russian
Zhitomir); to 1939 Polish *Żytomierz*; to 1918
Russian *Zhitomir*
Zichenau *see* **Ciechanów**
Zidani Most (village, central Slovenia) : to 1918,
1941–1945 German *Steinbrück*
Židlochovice (town, southeastern Czech Repub-
lic) : to 1918, 1939–1945 German *Seelowitz*
Ziębice (town, southwestern Poland) : to 1945
German *Münsterberg*
Ziebingen *see* **Cybinka**
Ziegenhals *see* **Głuchołazy**
Zielenzig *see* **Sulęcin**
Zielona Góra (city, western Poland) : to 1945
German *Grünberg*
Zighoud Youcef (town, northeastern Algeria) :
to *c.*1962 French *Condé-Smendou*
Zilah *see* **Zalău**
Žilina (city, northwestern Slovakia) : 1939–1945
German *Sillein*; 1867–1918 Hungarian *Zsolna*

Zimbabwe (republic, south central Africa) :
1964–1980 *Rhodesia*; to 1964 *Southern Rhodesia*
Zimnitsa (village, eastern Bulgaria) : to 1878
Turkish *Kashlaköy*
Zimogor'ye *see* **Zymohir'ya**
Zinnik *see* **Soignies**
Zinov'yevsk *see* **Kirovohrad**
Zinov'yevs'k *see* **Kirovohrad**
Zinten *see* **Kornevo**
Zion *see* (1) **Israel**; (2) **Jerusalem**; (2) **Palestine**
Zipser-Neudorf *see* **Spišská Nová Ves**
Zirke *see* **Sieraków**
Ziştov *see* **Svishtov**
Ziwa Magharibi *see* **Kagera**
Zlaté Hory (town, northeastern Czech Republic)
: to 1919, 1939–1945 German *Zuckmantel*
Zlaté Moravce (town, southwestern Slovakia) :
to 1918 Hungarian *Aranyoszmarót*
Zlaten Dol *see* **Simeonovgrad**
Zlatna (town, central Romania) : to 1920 Ger-
man *Klein-Schlattern*
Zlatograd town, southern Bulgaria) : to 1934
Dara Dere; to 1878 Turkish *Darıdere*
Zlín (city, southeastern Czech Republic) : 1948–
1990 *Gottwaldov*
Złocieniec (town, northwestern Poland) : to
1945 German *Falkenberg*
Złoczów *see* **Zolochiv**
Zlokuchen *see* **Ivanski**
Złotoryja (town, southwestern Poland) : to 1945
German *Goldberg*
Złotów (town, northwestern Poland) : to 1945
German *Flatow*
Złoty Stok (town, southwestern Poland) : to
1945 German *Reichenstein*
Žlutice (town, western Czech Republic) : to
1918, 1938–1945 German *Luditz*
Zmajevo (village, northern Serbia) : to 1947
Pašićevo
Żmigród (town, southwestern Poland) : 1793–
1807, 1815–1919, 1939–1945 German *Trachen-
berg*
Zmiyiv (town, northeastern Ukraine) : (Russian
Zmiyov); 1976–1990 *Hotval'd* (Russian *Got-
val'd*) (The earlier name represents that of the
Austrian-born Czech president Kliment Gott-
wald, who also gave the former name of **Zlín**.)
Zmiyov *see* **Zmiyiv**
Znaim *see* **Znojmo**
Znamensk (town, western Russia) : to 1945 Ger-
man *Wehlau*
Znamensky *see* **Pamyati 13 Bortsov**
Znin *see* **Żnin**
Żnin (town, west central Poland) : 1940–1945
German *Diefurt*; 1793–1807, 1815–1919 Ger-
man *Znin*

Znojmo (city, southern Czech Republic) : to 1918, 1948–1945 German *Znaim*

Zoan *see* **Tanis**

Zobten *see* **Sobótka**

Zolkiew *see* **Zhovkva**

Żółkiew *see* **Zhovkva**

Zolochev *see* **Zolochiv**

Zolochiv (town, western Ukraine) : (Russian *Zolochev*); to 1939 Polish *Złoczów*

Zolotushino *see* **Gornyak**

Zólyom *see* **Zvolen**

Zombor *see* **Sombor**

Zoppot *see* ²**Sopot**

Zorinsk *see* **Zoryns'k**

Zorndorf *see* **Sarbinowo**

Żory (town, southern Poland) : to 1945 German *Sohrau*

Zoryns'k (town, eastern Ukraine) : (Russian *Zorinsk*); to 1963 *Olenivka* (Russian *Yelenovka*)

Zoug *see* **Zug**

Zrenjanin (city, northern Serbia) : 1930s–1947 *Petrovgrad*; 1918–1930s *Veliki Bečkerek*; to 1918 Hungarian *Nagybecskerek*

Zschornegosda *see* **Schwarzheide**

Zselizs *see* **Želiezovce**

Zsolna *see* **Žilina**

Zsombolya *see* **Jimbolia**

Zuckmantel *see* **Zlaté Hory**

Zug (town, north central Switzerland) : French *Zoug*

Zuider Zee *see* **IJsselmeer**

Zula la Vieja *see* **La Piedad Cavadas**

Züllichau *see* **Sulechów**

Zülpich (town, western Germany) : Roman *Tolbiacum*

Zülz *see* **Biała**

Zurich (city, northern Switzerland) : German *Zürich*; Italian *Zurigo*

Zürich *see* **Zurich**

Zurigo *see* **Zurich**

Zvanka *see* **Volkhov**

Zvenigovo (town, western Russia) : to *c.*1940 *Zvenigovsky Zaton*

Zvenigovsky Zaton *see* **Zvenigovo**

Zvishavane (town, south central Zimbabwe) : formerly *Shabani*

Zvolen (town, central Slovakia) : 1939–1945 German *Altsohl*; 1867–1918 Hungarian *Zólyom*

Zvornik (town, eastern Bosnia-Herzegovina) : to 1878 Turkish *İzvornik*

Zwaanendael *see* **Lewes**

Zweibrücken (city, southwestern Germany) : 1801–1815 French *Deux-Ponts*; Medieval Latin *Bipontium*

Zwischenwässern *see* **Medvode**

Zwittau *see* **Svitavy**

Żydaczów *see* **Zhydachiv**

Zymohir'ya (town, eastern Ukraine) : (Russian *Zimogor'ye*); to 1961 *Cherkas'ke* (Russian *Cherkasskoye*)

Żytomierz *see* **Zhytomir**

Żywiec (town, southern Poland) : 1939–1945 German *Saybusch*

Appendix I:
Names of Places
in Non-English Languages

Below is a selection of well-known placenames in their non–English forms, represented by members of seven different language families: French (Romance), German (Germanic); Turkish (Turkic), Finnish (Finno-Ugric), Polish (Slavic), Welsh (Celtic), and Chinese (Sino-Tibetan). French has the fullest representation, with the names arranged by categories. The Chinese names have their own preamble.

1. *French*

I. CONTINENTS

Africa : Afrique
America : Amérique
Antarctica : Antarctique
Asia : Asie
Europe : Europe

II. COUNTRIES

Afghanistan : Afghanistan
Albania : Albanie
Algeria : Algérie
Andorra : Andorre
Angola : Angola
Argentina : Argentine
Armenia : Arménie
Australia : Australie
Austria : Autriche
Azerbaijan : Azerbaïdjan
Bahrain : Bahreïn
Bangladesh : Bangladesh
Belarus : Belarus
Belgium : Belgique
Belize : Belize
Benin : Bénin
Bhutan : Bhoutan
Bolivia : Bolivie
Bosnia-Herzegovina : Bosnie-Herzégovine
Botswana : Botswana
Brazil : Brésil
Brunei : Brunei

Bulgaria : Bulgarie
Burkina Faso : Burkina
Burundi : Burundi
Cambodia : Cambodge
Cameroon : Cameroun
Canada : Canada
Cape Verde : Cap-Vert
Central African Republic : République Centrafricaine
Chad : Tchad
Chile : Chili
China : Chine
Colombia : Colombie
Congo, Democratic Republic of the : République Démocratique du Congo
Congo, Republic of the : République du Congo
Costa Rica : Costa Rica
Côte d'Ivoire : Côte d'Ivoire
Croatia : Croatie
Cuba : Cuba
Cyprus : Chypre
Czech Republic : République Tchèque
Denmark : Danemark
Djibouti : Djibouti
Dominica : Dominique
Dominican Republic : République Dominicaine
Ecuador : Équateur
Egypt : Égypte
El Salvador : Salvador

England : Angleterre
Equatorial Guinea : Guinée Équatoriale
Eritrea : Érythrée
Estonia : Estonie
Ethiopia : Éthiopie
Fiji : Fiji
Finland : Finlande
France : France
French Guiana : Guyane Française
Gabon : Gabon
Gambia : Gambie
Georgia : Géorgie
Germany : Allemagne
Ghana : Ghana
Great Britain : Grande-Bretagne
Greece : Grèce
Grenada : Grenade
Guadeloupe : Guadeloupe
Guatemala : Guatemala
Guinea : Guinée
Guinea-Bissau : Guinée-Bissau
Guyana : Guyane
Haiti : Haïti
Honduras : Honduras
Hungary : Hongrie
Iceland : Islande
India : Inde
Indonesia : Indonésie
Iran : Iran
Iraq : Iraq
Ireland : Irlande

Israel : Israël
Italy : Italie
Japan : Japon
Jordan : Jordanie
Kazakhstan : Kazakhstan
Kenya : Kenya
Kiribati : Kiribati
Kosovo : Kosovo
Kuwait : Koweït
Kyrgyzstan : Kirghizstan
Laos : Laos
Latvia : Lettonie
Lebanon : Liban
Lesotho : Lesotho
Liberia : Liberia
Libya : Libye
Liechtenstein : Liechtenstein
Lithuania : Lituanie
Livorno : Livourne
Luxembourg : Luxembourg
Macedonia : Macédoine
Madagascar : Madagascar
Malawi : Malawi
Malaysia : Malaisie
Maldives : Maldives
Mali : Mali
Malta : Malte
Mauritania : Mauritanie
Mauritius : Maurice
Mexico : Mexique
Moldova : Moldova
Monaco : Monaco
Mongolia : Mongolie
Montenegro : Monténégro
Morocco : Maroc
Mozambique : Mozambique
Myanmar : Myanmar
Namibia : Namibie
Nepal : Népal
Netherlands : Pays-Bas
New Zealand : Nouvelle-Zélande
Nicaragua : Nicaragua
Niger : Niger
Nigeria : Nigeria
Northern Ireland: Irlande du
    Nord
North Korea : Corée du Nord
Norway : Norvège
Oman : Oman
Padua : Padoue
Pakistan : Pakistan
Palestine : Palestine
Panama : Panamá
Papua New Guinea : Papouasie-
    Nouvelle-Guinée
Paraguay : Paraguay
Peru : Pérou
Philippines : Philippines
Poland : Pologne

Polynesia : Polynésie
Portugal : Portugal
Qatar : Qatar
Réunion : Réunion
Romania : Roumanie
Russia : Russie
Rwanda : Rwanda
San Marino : Saint-Marin
São Tomé and Príncipe : São
    Tomé et Príncipe
Saudi Arabia : Arabie Saoudite
Scotland : Écosse
Senegal : Sénégal
Serbia : Serbie
Sierra Leone : Sierra Leone
Singapore : Singapour
Slovakia : Slovaquie
Slovenia : Slovénie
Somalia : Somalie
South Africa : Afrique du Sud
South Korea : Corée du Sud
Spain : Espagne
Sri Lanka : Sri Lanka
Sudan : Soudan
Surinam : Suriname
Swaziland : Swaziland
Sweden : Suède
Switzerland : Suisse
Syria : Syrie
Taiwan : Taïwan
Tajikistan : Tadjikistan
Tanzania : Tanzanie
Thailand : Thaïlande
Togo : Togo
Tunisia : Tunisie
Turin : Turin
Turkey : Turquie
Turkmenistan : Turkménistan
Tuvalu : Tuvalu
Uganda : Ouganda
Ukraine : Ukraine
United Arab Emirates : Émirats
    Arabes Unis
United Kingdom : Royaume-
    Uni
United States : États-Unis
Uruguay : Uruguay
Uzbekistan : Ouzbékistan
Vanuatu : Vanuatu
Vatican : Vatican
Venezuela : Venezuela
Vietnam : Viêt Nam
Wales : Pays de Galles
Western Sahara : Sahara Occi-
    dental
Yemen : Yémen
Zambia : Zambie
Zimbabwe : Zimbabwe

III. REGIONS AND DISTRICTS

Algarve : Algarve
Anatolia : Anatolie
Andalusia : Andalousie
Aragon : Aragon
Asturias : Asturies
Basque Country : Pays Basque
Bavaria : Bavière
Black Forest : Forêt-Noire
Bohemia : Bohème
British Columbia : Colombie-
    Brittanique
Brittany : Bretagne
Burgundy : Bourgogne
Calabria : Calabre
California : Californie
Campania : Campanie
Cantabria : Cantabrique
Carinthia : Carinthie
Carolina : Caroline
Castile : Castille
Catalonia : Catalogne
Cornwall : Cornouailles
Crimea : Crimée
Dalmatia : Dalmatie
Extremadura : Estrémadure
Flanders : Flandre
Florida : Floride
Franconia : Franconie
Free State : État Libre
Friesland : Frise
Galicia : Galice
Gascony : Gascogne
Georgia : Géorgie
Goa : Goa
Holland : Hollande
Jutland : Jylland
Karelia : Carélie
Labrador : Labrador
La Mancha : La Manche
Lapland : Laponie
Liguria : Ligurie
Lombardy : Lombardie
Louisiana : Louisiane
Marches : Marches
Moldavia : Moldavie
Moravia : Moravie
New Brunswick : Nouveau-
    Brunswick
New England : Nouvelle-
    Angleterre
New Mexico : Nouveau-
    Mexique
New South Wales : Nouvelle-
    Galles du Sud
Newfoundland : Terre-Neuve
Normandy : Normandie

Northern Territory : Territoire-du-Nord
Northwest Territories : Territoires du Nord-Ouest
Nova Scotia : Nouvelle-Écosse
Patagonia : Patagonie
Pennsylvania : Pennsylvanie
Picardy : Picardie
Piedmont : Piémont
Pomerania : Poméranie
Prince Edward Island : Île du Prince-Édouard
Prussia : Prusse
Puglia : Pouille
Punjab : Pendjab
Rhineland : Rhénanie
Ruthenia : Ruthénie
Savoy : Savoie
Saxony : Saxe
Siberia : Sibérie
Silesia : Silésie
South Australia : Australie-Méridionale
Swabia : Souabe
Thuringia : Thuringe
Transylvania : Transylvanie
Tuscany : Toscane
Tyrol : Tyrol
Umbria : Ombrie
Virginia : Virginie
Wallachia : Valachie
Wallonia : Wallonie
Western Australia : Australie-Occidentale
Westphalia : Westphalie
Zeeland : Zélande

IV. TOWNS AND CITIES

Aachen : Aix-la-Chapelle
Acre : Acre
Adelaide : Adélaïde
Agrigento : Agrigente
Aleppo : Alep
Alessandria : Alexandrie
Alexandria : Alexandrie
Algeciras : Algéciras
Algiers : Alger
Ancona : Ancône
Andorra la Vella : Andorre-la-Vieille
Antwerp : Anvers
Aosta : Aoste
Assisi : Assise
Athens : Athènes
Baghdad : Bagdad
Barcelona : Barcelone
Basel : Bâle
Beijing : Pékin
Beirut : Beyrouth

Belgrade : Belgrade
Benevento : Bénévent
Bergamo : Bergame
Berlin : Berlin
Bern : Berne
Biel : Bienne
Bologna : Bologne
Bragança : Bragance
Bremen : Brême
Brig : Brigue
Bruges : Bruges
Brussels : Bruxelles
Bucharest : Bucarest
Budapest : Budapest
Buenos Aires : Buenos Aires
Cádiz : Cadix
Cairo : Le Caire
Canterbury : Cantorbéry
Cape Town : Le Cap
Cartagena : Carthagène
Caserta : Caserte
Catania : Catane
Cologne : Cologne
Como : Côme
Copenhagen : Copenhague
Córdoba : Cordoue
Cremona : Crémone
Damascus : Damas
Den Helder : Le Helder
Dover : Douvres
Dresden : Dresde
Dublin : Dublin
Dunkirk : Dunkerque
Edinburgh : Édimbourg
Ferrara : Ferrare
Florence : Florence
Frankfurt : Francfort
Freiburg : Fribourg
Gaeta : Gaète
Geneva : Genève
Genoa : Gênes
Gerona : Gérone
Ghent : Gand
Granada : Grenade
Groningen : Groningue
Hague, The : La Haye
Hamburg : Hambourg
Hanover : Hanovre
Havana : La Havane
Helsinki : Helsinki
Istanbul : Istanbul
Jerusalem : Jérusalem
Kabul : Kaboul
Koblenz : Coblence
Kraków : Cracovie
La Coruña : La Corogne
Latakia : Lattaquie
Leiden : Leyde
Lisbon : Lisbonne

London : Londres
Lucca : Lucques
Madrid : Madrid
Mainz : Mayence
Manila : Manille
Mantua : Mantoue
Mecca : La Mecque
Messina : Messine
Mexico City : Mexico
Milan : Milan
Modena : Modène
Montreal : Montréal
Moscow : Moscou
Munich : Munich
Murcia : Murcie
Naples : Naples
New Orleans : La Nouvelle-Orléans
New York : New York
Nice : Nice
Nicosia : Nicosie
Nijmegen : Nimègue
Novara : Novare
Nuremberg : Nuremberg
Oporto : Porto
Ostend : Ostende
Ostia : Ostie
Ourense : Orense
Palermo : Palerme
Pamplona : Pampelune
Paris : Paris
Parma : Parme
Pavia : Pavie
Philadelphia : Philadelphie
Piacenza : Plaisance
Pisa : Pise
Prague : Prague
Quebec : Québec
Ragusa : Raguse
Ravenna : Ravenne
Regensburg : Ratisbonne
Rome : Rome
Saarbrücken : Sarrebruck
Saarlouis : Sarrelouis
St. Petersburg : Saint-Pétersbourg
Salamanca : Salamanque
Salerno : Salerne
Salonika : Thessalonique
Salzburg : Salzbourg
San Francisco : San Francisco
San Sebastián : Saint-Sébastien
Santiago de Compostela : Saint-Jacques-de-Compostelle
Santo Domingo : Saint-Domingue
São Paolo : São Paolo
Saragossa : Saragosse
Savona : Savone

Schaffhausen : Schaffhouse
Segovia : Ségovie
Seoul : Séoul
Seville : Séville
's-Hertogenbosch : Bois-le-Duc
Siena : Sienne
Sofia : Sofia
Solothurn : Soleure
Sparta : Sparte
Speyer : Spire
Split : Split
Spoleto : Spolète
Stockholm : Stockholm
Tangier : Tanger
Taranto : Tarente
Tarragona : Tarragone
Thun : Thoune
Timbuktu : Tombouktou
Tokyo : Tokyo
Toledo : Tolède
Trento : Trente
Treviso : Trévise
Trier : Trèves
Tunis : Tunis
Valencia : Valence
Venice : Venise
Ventimiglia : Vintimille
Verona : Vérone
Vicenza: Vicence
Vienna : Vienne
Viterbo : Viterbe
Vlissingen : Flessingue
Warsaw : Varsovie
Zurich : Zurich

V. Oceans

Arctic : Arctique
Atlantic : Atlantique
Indian : Indien
Pacific : Pacifique

VI. Seas, Lakes, Bays, Gulfs, Inlets, and Channels

Adriatic Sea : Mer Adriatique
Aegean Sea : Mer Égée
Albert, Lake : Lac Albert
Baltic Sea : Mer Baltique
Barents Sea : Mer de Barents
Bering Sea : Mer de Béring
Biscay, Bay of : Golfe de
    Gascogne
Black Sea : Mer Noire
Bothnia, Gulf of : Golfe de Bot-
    nie
Caribbean Sea : Mer des Antilles
Carpentaria, Gulf of : Golfe de
    Carpentarie
Caspian Sea : Mer Caspienne

Constance, Lake : Lac de Con-
    stance
Coral Sea : Mer de Corail
Dead Sea : Mer Morte
Dover, Strait of : Pas de Calais
Edward, Lake : Lac Édouard
English Channel : Manche
Erie, Lake : Lac Érié
Garda, Lake : Lac de Garde
Golden Horn : Corne d'Or
Great Australian Bight : Grande
    Baie Australienne
Great Bear Lake : Grand Lac de
    l'Ours
Great Lakes Grands Lacs
Great Salt Lake : Grand Lac Salé
Great Slave Lake : Grand Lac des
    Esclaves
Huron, Lake : Lac Huron
Irish Sea : Mer d'Irlande
Lion, Gulf of : Golfe du Lion
Lucerne, Lake : Lac des Quatre-
    Cantons
Maggiore, Lake : Lac Majeur
Mediterranean Sea : Mer
    Méditerranée
Mexico, Gulf of : Golfe du Mex-
    ique
North Sea : Mer du Nord
Ontario, Lac : Lac Ontario
Persian Gulf : Golfe Persique
Pigs, Bay of : Baie des Cochons
Red Sea : Mer Rouge
Reindeer Lake : Lac Caribou
Superior, Lake : Lac Supérieur
Tiberias, Lake : Lac de Tibériade
Tyrrhenian Sea : Mer Tyrrhéni-
    enne
White Sea : Mer Blanche
Yellow Sea : Mer Jaune

VII. Rivers

Amazon : Amazone
Congo : Zaïre
Danube : Danube
Ebro : Èbre
Euphrates : Euphrate
Ganges : Gange
Indus : Indus
Jordan : Jourdain
Nile : Nil
Po : Pô
Rhine : Rhin
Rhône : Rhône
St. Lawrence : Saint-Laurent
Tagus : Tage
Thames : Tamise
Tiber : Tibre
Ticino : Tessin

Tigris : Tigre
Vistula : Vistule
Volga : Volga

VIII. Islands

Admiralty Islands : Îles de l'Ami-
    rauté
Aeolian Islands : Îles Éoliennes
Alderney : Aurigny
Amirante Islands : Îles Amirantes
Antigua : Antiqua
Antilles : Antilles
Ascension : Ascension
Azores : Açores
Bahamas : Bahamas
Balearic Islands : Baléares
Barbados : Barbade
Bermuda : Bermudes
Bismarck Archipelago : Archipel
    Bismarck
Borneo : Bornéo
British Isles : Îles Brittaniques
Canary Islands : Îles Canaries
Cape Breton Island : Île du Cap
    Breton
Capri : Capri
Channel Islands : Îles Anglo-
    Normandes
Christmas Island : Île Christmas
Comoros : Comores
Cook Islands : Îles Cook
Corsica : Corse
Crete : Crète
Curaçao : Curaçao
Cyclades : Cyclades
Dodecanese : Dodécanèse
Easter Island : Île de Pâques
Estados, Isla de los : Île des États
Falkland Islands : Îles Malouines
Faroes : Îles Féroé
Frisian Islands : Îles de la Frise
Galápagos Islands : Îles Galápa-
    gos
Gran Canaria : Grande Canarie
Greenland : Groenland
Grenada : Grenade
Grenadines : Îles Grenadines
Guernsey : Guernesey
Hebrides : Îles Hébrides
Hispaniola : Hispaniola
Ionian Islands : Îles Ioniennes
Jamaica : Jamaïque
Java : Java
Jersey : Jersey
Kuril Islands : Îles Kouriles
Leeward Islands : Îles Sous-le-
    Vent
Loyalty Islands : Îles Loyauté
Madeira : Madère

Majorca : Majorque
Mariana Islands : Îles Mariannes
Marquesas Islands : Îles Marquises
Marshall Islands : Îles Marshall
Martinique : Martinique
Mascarene Islands : Îles Mascareignes
Micronesia : Micronésie
Minorca : Minorque
Moluccas : Îles Moluques
New Britain : Nouvelle-Bretagne
New Caledonia : Nouvelle-Calédonie
New Guinea : Nouvelle-Guinée
New Ireland : Nouvelle-Irlande
New Siberian Islands : Nouvelle-Sibérie
Nicobar Islands : Îles Nicobar
Novaya Zemlya : Nouvelle-Zemble
Oceania : Océanie
Orkney : Orcades
Puerto Rico : Porto Rico
St. Helena : Sainte-Hélène
St. Kitts : Saint-Kitts
St. Lucia : Sainte-Lucie
St. Vincent : Saint-Vincent
Samoa : Samoa
Sardinia : Sardaigne
Sark : Sercq
Scilly Isles : Sorlingues
Severnaya Zemlya : Terre du Nord
Shetland : Shetland
Sicily : Sicile
Society Islands : Îles de la Société
Staten Island *see* Estados, Isla de los
Sumatra : Sumatra
Tasmania : Tasmanie
Tierra del Fuego : Terre de Feu
Tortuga : Île de la Tortue
Trinidad and Tobago : Trinité-et-Tobago
Tristan da Cunha : Tristan da Cunha
Ushant : Ouessant
Virgin Islands : Îles Vierges
West Indies : Indes Occidentales
Windward Islands : Îles du Vent
Zanzibar : Zanzibar

IX. Mountains

Alps : Alpes
Andes : Andes
Apennines : Apennin
Appalachian Mountains : Appalaches

Ardennes : Ardennes
Atlas : Atlas
Carpathian Mountains : Carpates
Cascade Range : Chaîne des Cascades
Caucasus : Caucase
Coast Mountains : Chaîne Côtière
Dolomites : Dolomites
Himalaya : Himalaya
Matterhorn : Mont Cervin
Olympus : Olympe
Pindus Mountains : Pinde
Pyrenees : Pyrénées
Rocky Mountains : Montagnes Rocheuses
Table Mountain : Montagne de la Table
Urals : Oural

X. Capes, Promontories, and Peninsulas

Agulhas, Cape : Cap des Aiguilles
Cod, Cape : Cap Cod
Giant's Causeway : Chaussée des Géants
Good Hope, Cape of : Cap de Bonne-Espérance
Horn, Cape : Cap Horn
Horn of Africa : Corne de l'Afrique
Land's End : Land's End
Palmas, Cape : Cap des Palmes
York, Cape : Cap York

2. *German*

Adriatic Sea : Adriatisches Meer
Aegean Sea : Ägäisches Meer
Afghanistan : Afghanistan
Africa : Afrika
Albania : Albanien
Algeria : Algerien
Algiers : Algier
Alps : Alpen
Alsace-Lorraine : Elsaß-Lothringen
Amazon : Amazonas
America : Amerika
Andes : Andes
Andorra : Andorra
Angola : Angola
Antarctica : Antarktis
Antwerp : Antwerpen
Appalachian Mountains : Appalachen
Aragon : Aragon
Arctic : Arktis
Argentina : Argentinien

Armenia : Armenien
Asia : Asien
Athens : Athen
Atlantic : Atlantik
Atlas : Atlas
Australia : Australien
Austria : Österreich
Azores : Azoren
Baghdad : Bagdad
Bahamas : Bahamas
Bahrain : Bahraïn
Balearic Islands : Balearen
Baltic Sea : Ostsee
Bangladesh : Bangladesh
Barbados : Barbados
Barents Sea : Barentssee
Basel : Basel
Bavaria : Bayern
Beirut : Beirut
Belgium : Belgiem
Belgrade : Belgrad
Belize : Belize
Bering Sea : Beringmeer
Berlin : Berlin
Bermuda : Bermuda
Bern : Bern
Biscay, Bay of : Golf von Biskaya
Black Forest : Schwarzwald
Black Sea : Schwarzes Meer
Bohemia : Böhmen
Bolivia : Bolivien
Borneo : Borneo
Bosnia-Herzegovina : Bosnien-Herzegowina
Bothnia, Gulf of : Bottnischer Meerbusen
Botswana : Botswana
Brazil : Brasilien
British Isles : Britische Inseln
Brittany : Bretagne
Bruges : Brügge
Brunei : Brunei
Brussels : Brüssel
Bucharest : Bukarest
Budapest : Budapest
Buenos Aires : Buenos Aires
Bulgaria : Bulgarien
Burgundy : Burgund
Cairo : Kairo
California : Kalifornien
Cambodia : Kambodscha
Cameroon : Kamerun
Canada : Kanada
Canary Islands : Kanarische Inseln
Cape Town : Kapstadt
Cape Verde : Kapverden
Capri : Capri
Caribbean Sea : Karibisches Meer

Carinthia : Kärnten
Carpathian Mountains : Karpaten
Carthage : Karthago
Caspian Sea : Kaspisches Meer
Castile : Kastilien
Caucasus : Kaukasus
Central African Republic : Zentralafrikanische Republik
Chad : Tschad
Channel Islands : Kanalinseln
Chile : Chile
China : China
Christmas Island : Weihnachtsinsel
Cologne : Köln
Congo : Kongo
Copenhagen : Kopenhagen
Coral Sea : Korallenmeer
Cornwall : Cornwall
Corsica : Korsika
Costa Rica : Costa Rica
Côte d'Ivoire : Elfenbeinküste
Crete : Kreta
Crimea : Krim
Croatia : Kroatien
Cuba : Kuba
Curaçao : Curaçao
Cyprus : Zypern
Czech Republic : Tschechien
Dalmatia : Dalmatien
Damascus : Damaskus
Danube : Donau
Dead Sea : Totes Meer
Denmark : Dänemark
Dolomites : Dolomiten
Dominica : Dominika
Dominican Republic : Dominikanische Republik
Dunkirk : Dünkirchen
Easter Island : Osterinsel
Egypt : Ägypten
England : England
English Channel : Ärmelkanal
Equatorial Guinea : Äquatorial-Guinea
Estonia : Estland
Ethiopia : Äthiopen
Euphrates : Euphrat
Europe : Europa
Falkland Islands : Falklandinseln
Faroes : Färöer
Fiji : Fidschiinseln
Finland : Finnland
Flanders : Flandern
Florence : Florenz
France : Frankreich
Franconia : Franken
French Guiana : Französisch-Guayana

Friesland : Friesland
Frisian Islands : Friesische Inseln
[1]Galicia (in eastern Europe) : Galizien
[2]Galicia (in Spain) : Galicien
Gambia : Gambia
Ganges : Ganges
Geneva : Genf
Genoa : Genua
[1]Georgia (in USA) : Georgia
[2]Georgia (in Europe) : Georgien
Germany : Deutschland
Ghana : Ghana
Ghent : Gent
Gibraltar : Gibraltar
Good Hope, Cape of : Kap der guten Hoffnung
Gran Canaria : Gran Canaria
Great Australian Bight : Große Australische Bucht
Great Britain : Großbritannien
Great Lakes : Große Seen
Greece : Griechenland
Greenland : Grönland
Grenada : Grenada
Guadeloupe : Guadelupe
Guatemala : Guatemala
Guernsey : Guernsey
Guinea : Guinea
Guyana : Guyana
Hague, The : Den Haag
Haiti : Haiti
Hanover : Hannover
Havana : Havanna
Hebrides : Hebriden
Himalaya : Himalaya
Holland : Holland
Honduras : Honduras
Horn, Cape : Kap Hoorn
Hungary : Ungarn
Iceland : Island
India : Indien
Indian Ocean : Indischer Ozean
Indonesia : Indonesien
Ionian Sea : Ionisches Meer
Iran : Iran
Iraq : Irak
Ireland : Irland
Irish Sea : Irische See
Israel : Israel
Istanbul : Istanbul
Italy : Italien
Jamaica : Jamaika
Japan : Japan
Java : Java
Jersey : Jersey
Jerusalem : Jerusalem
[1]Jordan (country) : Jordanien
[2]Jordan (river) : Jordan

Jutland : Jütland
Kenya : Kenia
Korea : Korea
Kosovo : Kosovo
Kraków : Krakau
Kuwait : Kuwair
Kyrgyzstan : Kirgistan
Labrador : Labrador
Laos : Laos
Lapland : Lappland
Latvia : Lettland
Lebanon : Libanon
Leeward Islands : Inseln über dem Winde
Lesotho : Lesotho
Liberia : Liberia
Libya : Libyen
Liechtenstein : Liechtenstein
Liguria : Ligurie
Lisbon : Lissabon
Lithuania : Litauen
Ljubljana : Laibach
Lombardy : Lombardei
London : London
Lucerne, Lake : Vierwaldstätter See
Luxembourg : Luxemburg
Macedonia : Makedonien
Madagascar : Madagaskar
Madeira : Madeira
Madrid : Madrid
Majorca : Mallorca
Malawi : Malawi
Malaysia : Malaysia
Maldives : Malediven
Malta : Malta
Martinique : Martinique
Mauritius : Mauritius
Mecca : Mekka
Mediterranean Sea : Mittelmeer
Mexico : Mexiko
Mexico City : Mexiko City
Milan : Mailand
Minorca : Menorca
Moldova : Moldawien
Moluccas : Molukken
Monaco : Monaco
Mongolia : Mongolei
Montenegro : Montenegro
Moravia : Mähren
Morocco : Marokko
Moscow : Moskau
Mozambique : Mosambik
Munich : München
Myanmar : Myanmar
Namibia : Namibia
Naples : Neapel
Nepal : Nepal
Netherlands : Niederlande

Neu Delhi : Neu-Delhi
New England : Neuengland
Newfoundland : Neufundland
New Guinea : Neuguinea
New Mexico : New Mexico
New Orleans : New Orleans
New South Wales : Neusüdwales
New York : New York
New Zealand : Neuseeland
Nicaragua : Nicaragua
Nice : Nizza
Niger : Niger
Nigeria : Nigeria
Nile : Nil
Normandy : Normandie
Northern Ireland : Nordirland
North Korea : Nordkorea
North Sea : Nordsee
Norway : Norwegen
Nova Scotia : Neuschottland
Nuremberg : Nürnberg
Oceania : Ozeanien
Olympus : Olymp
Oman : Oman
Orkney : Orkneyinseln
Ostend : Ostende
Pacific : Pazifik
Pakistan : Pakistan
Palestine : Palästina
Panama : Panama
Papua New Guinea : Papua-
   Neuguinea
Paraguay : Paraguay
Paris : Paris
Patagonia : Patagonien
Pennsylvania : Pennsylvania
Persian Gulf : Persischer Golf
Peru : Peru
Philippines : Philippinen
Poland : Polen
Polynesia : Polynesien
Pomerania : Pommern
Portugal : Portugal
Prague : Prag
Prussia : Preußen
Puerto Rico : Puerto Rico
Punjab : Pandschab
Pyrenees : Pyrenäen
Qatar : Katar
Red Sea : Rotes Meer
Rhine : Rhein
Rhineland : Rheinland
Rhodes : Rhodos
Rocky Mountains : Rocky
   Mountains
Romania : Rumänien
Rome : Rom
Russia : Russland
Rwanda : Ruanda

Samoa : Samoa
San Marino : San Marino
Sardinia : Sardinien
Saudi Arabia : Saudi-Arabien
Saxony : Sachsen
Scilly Isles : Scillyinseln
Scotland : Schottland
Senegal : Senegal
Serbia : Serbien
Seville : Sevilla
's-Hertogenbosch : Herzogen-
   busch
Shetland : Shetlandinseln
Siberia : Sibirien
Sicily : Sizilien
Sierra Leone : Sierra Leone
Silesia : Schlesien
Singapore : Singapur
Slovakia : Slowakei
Slovenia : Slowenien
Somalia : Somalia
South Africa : Südafrika
South Australia : Südaustralien
South Korea : Südkorea
Spain : Spanien
Sparta : Sparta
Sri Lanka : Sri Lanka
Sudan : Sudan
Sumatra : Sumatra
Swabia : Schwaben
Sweden : Schweden
Switzerland : Schweiz
Syria : Syrien
Table Mountain : Tafelberg
Taiwan : Taïwan
Tajikistan : Tadschikistan
Tangier : Tanger
Tanzania : Tansania
Tasmania : Tasmanien
Thailand : Thaïland
Thames : Themse
Tiber : Tiber
Tibet : Tibet
Tierra del Fuego : Feuerland
Togo : Togo
Tokyo : Tokio
Transylvania : Siebenbürgen
Tunis : Tunes
Tunisia : Tunesien
Turkey : Türkei
Turkmenistan : Turkmenistan
Tuscany : Toskana
Tyrol : Tirol
Tyrrhenian Sea : Tyrrhenisches
   Meer
Uganda : Uganda
Ukraine : Ukraine
United Arab Emirates : Vere-
   inigte Arabische Emirate

United Kingdom : Vereinigtes
   Königreich
United States : Vereinigte Staaten
Urals : Ural
Uruguay : Uruguay
Uzbekistan : Usbekistan
Vatican : Vatikan
Venezuela : Venezuela
Venice : Venedig
Vienna : Wien
Vietnam : Vietname
Virgin Islands : Jungferninseln
Virginia : Virginia
Vistula : Weichsel
Volga : Wolga
Wales : Wales
Warsaw : Warschau
West Indies : Westindische Inseln
Westphalia : Westfalen
White Sea : Weißes Meer
Windward Islands : Inseln über
   dem Winde
Yellow Sea : Gelbes Meer
Yemen : Jemen
Zambia : Sambia
Zanzibar : Sansibar
Zimbabwe : Simbabwe
Zurich : Zürich

3. *Turkish*

Africa : Afrika
Albania : Arnavutluk
Algeria : Cezayir
America : Amerika
Asia : Asya
Australia : Avustralya
Austria : Avusturya
Belgium : Belçika
Black Sea : Karadeniz
Brazil : Brezilya
Bulgaria : Bulgaristan
Canada : Kanada
China : Çin
Crete : Girit
Cyprus : Kıbrıs
Denmark : Danimarka
Egypt : Mısır
England : İngiltere
Ethiopia : Habeşistan
Europe : Avrupa
Finland : Finlandiya
France : Fransa
Georgia : Gürcistan
Germany : Almanya
Greece : Yunanistan
Hungary : Macaristan
Iceland : İzlanda
India : Hindistan

Israel : İsrail
Italy : İtalya
Japan : Japonya
Lebanon : Lübnan
Mediterranean Sea : Akdeniz
Morocco : Fas
Norway : Norveç
Pacific Ocean : Büyük Okyanus
Palestine : Filistin
Poland : Lehistan
Portugal : Portekiz
Romania : Romanya
Russia : Rusya
Scotland : İskoçya
Spain : İspanya
Sweden : İsveç
Switzerland : İsviçre
Syria : Suriye
Turkey : Türkiye
United States : Birleşik Devletler

4. Finnish

Africa : Afrikka
America : Amerikka
Asia : Aasia
Athens : Ateena
Austria : Itävalta
Belgium : Belgia
Brazil : Brasilia
Britain : Britannia
Canada : Kanada
China : Kiina
Copenhagen : Köopenhamina
Cyprus : Kypros
Denmark : Tanska
Egypt : Egypti
England : Englanti
Europe : Eurooppa
Finland : Suomi
France : Ranska
Germany : Saksa
Greece : Kreikka
Hungary : Unkari
Iceland : Islanti
India : Intia
Ireland : Irlanti
Israel : Israel
Italy : Italia
Japan : Japani
Lebanon : Libanon
London : Lontoo
Mediterranean Sea : Välimeri
Netherlands : Alankomaat
Norway : Norja
Pacific Ocean : Tyyni Valtameri
Palestine : Palestiina
Poland : Puola
Romania : Romania

Rome : Rooma
Russia : Venäjä
Scotland : Skotlanti
Spain : Espanja
Sweden : Ruotsi
Switzerland : Sveitsi
Turkey : Turkki
United States : Yhdysvallat

5. Polish

Africa : Afryka
America : Ameryka
Asia : Azja
Athens : Ateny
Belgium : Belgia
Brussels : Bruksela
Cairo : Kair
Canada : Kanada
China : Chiny
Denmark : Dania
Egypt : Egipt
England : Anglia
Europe : Europa
Finland : Finlandia
France : Francja
Germany : Niemiec
Greece : Grecja
Hungary : Węgry
India : Indie
Ireland : Irlandia
Israel : Izrael
Italy : Włochy
Japan : Japonia
Lebanon : Liban
Lisbon : Lisbona
London : Londyn
Madrid : Madryt
Mediterranean Sea : Morze
    Śródziemne
Mexico : Meksyk
Moscow : Moskwa
Munich : Monachium
Newfoundland : Nowa Fundlan-
    dia
New Mexico : Nowy Meksyk
New Orleans : Nowy Orlean
New York : : Nowy Jork
New Zealand : Nowa Zelandia
Nova Scotia : Nowa Szkocja
Pacific Ocean : Ocean Spokoyny
Paris : Paryż
Pennsylvania : Pensylwania
Philadelphia : Filadelfia
Poland : Polska
Red Sea : Morze Czerwone
Rhine : Ren
Rome : Rzym
Spain : Hiszpania

Sweden : Szwecja
Switzerland : Szwajcaria
Texas : Teksas
Turkey : Turcja
United States : Stany Zjednoc-
    zone
Vienna : Wiedeń
Wales : Walia
Warsaw : Warszawa

6. Welsh

Africa : Affrica
Alps : Yr Alpau
America : Yr Amerig
Argentina : Ariannin
Athens : Athen
Atlantic Ocean : Môr Iwerydd
Australia : Awstralia
Austria : Awstria
Baltic Sea : Môr Llychlyn
Bath : Caerfaddon
Belgium : Gwlad Belg
Bristol : Bryste
Bristol Channel : Môr Hafren
Britain : Prydain
Brittany : Llydaw
Burgundy : Bwrgwyn
Cambridge : Caergrawnt
Canterbury : Caergaint
Carlisle : Caerliwelydd
Chester : Caer
Cornwall : Cernyw
Danube : Donaw
Dead Sea : Y Môr Marw
Devon : Dyfnaint
Dublin : Dulyn
Edinburgh : Caeredin
Egypt : Yr Aifft
England : Lloegr
English Channel : Môr Udd
Europe : Ewrop
France : Ffrainc
Germany : Yr Almaen
Glastonbury : Ynys Afallon
Gloucester : Caerloyw
Greece : Groeg
Hebrides : Ynysoedd Heledd
Hereford : Henffordd
Iceland : Ynys-yr-iâ
Ireland : Iwerddon
Isle of Man : Ynys Manaw
Isle of Wight : Ynys Wyth
Istanbul : Caergystennin
Italy : Yr Eidal
Jerusalem : Caersalem
Jordan : Iorddonen
Kent : Caint
Lancashire : Sir Gaerhirfryn

Lebanon : Libanus
Leicester : Caerlŷr
Leominster : Llanllieni
Liverpool : Lerpwyl
London : Llundain
Ludlow : Llwydlo
Manchester : Manceinion
Mediterranean Sea : Y Môr
 Canoldir
Netherlands : Yr Iseldiroedd
Newcastle : Castellnewydd
New York : Efrog Newydd
Nile : Nil
Norway : Norwy
Orkney Islands : Ynysoedd Erch
Oswestry : Croesoswallt
Oxford : Rhydychen
Pacific Ocean : Y Môr Tawel
Poland : Gwlad Pŵyl
Pyrenees : Pyrenau
Red Sea : Y Môr Coch
Rhine : Rhein
Rome : Rhufain
Russia : Rwsia
Salisbury : Caersallog
Scandinavia : Llychlyn
Scotland : Yr Alban
Severn : Hafren
Shrewsbury : Amwythig
Somerset : Gwlad-yr-haf
Spain : Yr Ysbaen
Switzerland : Y Swistir
Thames : Tafwys
Turkey : Twrci
United States : Yr Unol
 Dalaethiau
West Indies : India'r Gorllewin
Winchester : Caer-wynt
Worcester : Caerwrangon
York : Efrog

7. Chinese

Most Chinese names of non-Chinese places are phonetic renderings, given here in their romanized forms. Some are recognisably close to the original, as *dákǎ* for *Dhaka*, *lìmǎ* for *Lima*. Others are approximations, allowing for the particularities of the Chinese language. Any name with *r*, for example, will usually have this letter rendered as *l*, as *ānkǎlā* for *Ankara*, *luōmǎ* for *Rome*. This results from the so-called "flied lice" phenomenon, occasioned by the absence of *r* in Chinese. In other

cases, consonants are simply omitted, as *dānmài* for *Denmark*, *āijí* for *Egypt*. In some instances the name consists of a shortened form of the non–Chinese placename, usually that of the accented syllable, followed by a Chinese word. A well-known example is *měizhōu* for *America*, where *měi* is the stressed syllable of the name followed by Chinese *zhōu*, "continent." By contrast, the name of the *United States of America* is *měiguó*, with *měi* followed by *guó*, "country," "nation." Chinese *guó* is found in other names, such as *yīngguó* for *England*, *fǎguó* for *France* (note the omitted *r*.) Other "continent" names on the lines of *měizhōu* are *fēizhōu* for *Africa*, *yàzhōu* for *Asia*, and *ōuzhōu* for *Europe*.

The Chinese ideograms used for transliteration purposes usually have a meaning of their own, although this is not understood in the placename. Thus, the *měi* of *America* happens to mean "beautiful," and the *fēi* of *Africa* means "wrong." In *niǔyuē*, the Chinese rendering of *New York*, *niǔ* properly means "button," while *yuē* is "to make an appointment," and in *bālí*, the transliteration of *Paris* (with *l* for *r*), *bā* properly means "to hope earnestly," while *lí* is "multitude." If taken literally, some of the Chinese meanings are hardly complimentary. *America* can be literally interpreted as "beautiful continent," but by the same token *Asia* could be understood as "inferior continent," since Chinese *yà* means "inferior," "second." On the other hand, some names are descriptively meaningful, as for *Antarctica*, referring to its location at the South Pole, or directly translate a generic word, as for the *Pacific Ocean*, with its calm ("pacific") waters.

Certain Chinese names do not transliterate an international name but an indigenous one. The Chinese name of *Korea*, for example, represents the Korean name, while that of *Belgium*

phonetically represents the country's native French name.

The transliterations below, with parenthetical glosses where appropriate, are printed lower case to reflect the original, while diacritics denote the four Chinese tones: (a) level (*ā*), (b) rising (*á*), (c) falling-rising (*ǎ*), and (d) falling (*à*).

Accra : ākèlā
Addis Ababa : yàdìsǐyàbèibā
Aden : yàdīngchéng
Afghanistan : āfùhán (Persian
 stan, "country," omitted)
Africa : fēizhōu (*zhōu*, "continent")
Alaska : ālāsījiā
Albania : a'ěrbāníyà
Algeria : a'ěrjíliyà
Algiers : a'ěrjí'ěr
America : měizhōu (*zhōu*, "continent")
Amsterdam : āmǔsītèdān
Angola : āngēlā
Ankara : ānkǎlā
Antarctica : nánjízhōu (*nán*,
 "south," *jí*, "pole," *zhōu*, "continent")
Antarctic Regions : nánjídài
 (*nán*, "south," *jí*, "pole," *dài*,
 "belt")
Arctic Ocean : běibīngyáng (*běi*,
 "north," *bīng*, "ice," *yáng*,
 "ocean")
Arctic Regions : běijídìdài (*běi*,
 "north," *jí*, "extreme," *dì*,
 "land," *dài*, "belt")
Argentina : āgēntíng
Asia : yàzhōu (*zhōu*, "continent")
Asunción : yàsōngsēn
Athens : yǎdiǎn
Atlantic Ocean : dàxīyáng (*dà*,
 "great," *xī*, "west," *yáng*,
 "ocean")
Australia : àodàlìyà
Austria : àodìlì
Baghdad : bāgédá
Balkan Mountains :
 bā'ěrgānshān (*shān*, "mountains")
Baltic Sea : bōluódìhǎi (*hǎi*, "sea")
Bamako : bāmǎkē
Bangkok : màngǔ
Bangladesh : mèngjiālā (Bengali
 desh, "country," omitted)
Bangui : bānjí
Beirut : bèilǔtè

Belgium : bǐlìshí (representing French *Belgique*)
Belgrade : bèi'ěrgéláidé
Benghazi : bānjiāxī
Berlin : bólín
Berne : bó'ěrní
Bhutan : bùdān
Black Sea : hēihǎi (*hēi*, "black," *hǎi*, "sea")
Bogotá: bōgēdà
Bolivia : bōlìwéiyà
Bonn : bō'ēn
Brasília : bāxīlìyà
Brazil : bāxī
Brazzaville : bùlāchāiwéi'ěr
Brussels : bùlǔsài'ěr (representing French *Bruxelles*)
Bucharest : bùjiālèsītè
Budapest : bùdápèisī
Buenos Aires : bùyínuòsī àilìsī
Bujumbura : bùqióngbùlā
Bulgaria : bǎojiālìyà
Burundi : bùlóngdí
Cairo : kāiluó
Cambodia: jiǎnpǔzhài
Cameroon : kāmàilóng
Canada : jiānádà
Canberra : kānpéilā
Caracas : jiālājiāsī
Caucasus : gāojiāsuǒ
Central African Republic : zhōng fēi gònghéguó (*zhōng*, "middle," *fēi*, "Africa," *gònghéguó*, "republic," from *gòng* "common," *hé*, "peace," *guó*, "country")
Chad : zhàdé
Chile : zhìlì
China : zhōngguó (*zhōng*, "middle," *guó*, "country")
Colombia : gēlúnbǐyà
Colombo : kēlúnpō
Conakry : kēnàkèlǐ
Congo : gāngguǒ
Copenhagen : gēběnhāgēn
Costa Rica : gēsīdálíjiā
Crimea : kèlǐmǐyà
Cuba : gǔbā
Cyprus : sàipǔlùsī
Czech Republic: jiékè gònghéguó (*gònghéguó*, "republic")
Dakar : dákǎ'ěr
Damascus : dámǎshìgē
Danube : duōnǎohé (representing German *Donau* plus *hé*, "river")
Dar es Salaam : dálèisī sàlāmǔ
Delhi : délǐ
Denmark : dānmài

Dhaka : dákǎ
Dominican Republic : duōmǐníjiā gònghéguó (*gònghéguó*, "republic")
Dublin : dūbǎilín
Ecuador : èguāduō'ěr
Egypt : āijí
England : yīngguó (*guó*, "country")
English Channel : yīngjílì hǎixiá (*hǎixiá*, "channel," from *hǎi*, "sea," *xiá*, "strait")
Ethiopia :āisàiébǐyà
Europe : ōuzhōu (*zhōu*, "continent")
Finland : fēnlán
France : fǎguó (*guó*, "country")
Gabon : jiāpéng
Gambia : gāngbǐyà
Ganges : hénghé (*hé*, "river")
Geneva : rìnèiwǎ
Germany : déyìzhì (representing German *Deutschland* but without -*land*)
Ghana : jiānà
Gibraltar : zhíbùluótuó
Great Britain : dàbùlièdiān (*dà*, "great")
Greece : xīlà (representing Greek *Hellas*)
Guatemala : wēidìmǎlā
Guinea : jǐnèiyà
Hague, The : hǎiyá (representing French *La Haye* but without *La*)
Haiti : hǎidì
Havana : hāwǎnà
Helsinki : hè'ěrxīnjī
Himalayas : xǐmǎlāyǎshān (*shān*, "mountains")
Hiroshima : guǎngdǎo (*guǎng*, "broad," *dǎo*, "island," translating the Japanese)
Honduras : hóngdūlāsī
Hong Kong : xiānggǎng (*Hong Kong* is a corruption of Chinese *xiāng*, "fragrant," *gǎng*, "harbor")
Hungary : xiōngyálì
Iceland : bīngdǎo (*bīng*, "ice," *dǎo*, "island")
India : yìndù (representing *Hindu*)
Indonesia : yìndùníxīyà
Iran : yīlǎng
Iraq : yīlākè
Ireland : àiěrlán
Islamabad : yīsīlánbǎo
Israel : yǐsèliè

Italy : yìdàlì
Jakarta : yǎjiādá
Japan : rìběn (*rì*, "sun," *běn*, "origin," translating the Japanese)
Jordan : yuēdàn
Kabul : kābù'ěr
Kampala : kǎnpàlā
Karachi : kǎlāqí
Kashmir : kèshímǐ'ěr
Kathmandu : jiādémǎndū
Kenya : kěnníyà
Khartoum : kātǔmù
Kigali : jījiālǐ
Kinshasa : jīnshāsà
Kolkata (Calcutta) : jiā'ěrgèdá
Korea : cháoxiǎn (representing Korean *Chosŏn*)
Kuala Lumpur : jílóngpō
Kuril Islands : qiāndǎo (*qiān*, "thousand," *dǎo*, "island," translating Japanese name, from *chi*, "thousand," *shima*, "island")
Kuwait (country) : kēwēitè
Kuwait (city) : kēwēitèchéng (*chéng*, "city")
Lagos : lāgèsī
Laos : lǎowō
La Paz : lābāsī
Lebanon : líbānùn
Lhasa : lāsàshì
Liberia : lìbǐlǐyà
Libreville : lìbówéi'ěr
Libya : lìbǐyà
Lima : lìmǎ
Lisbon : lǐsīběn
Lomé : luòměi
London : lúndùn
Luanda : luó'āndá
Lusaka : lúsàkǎ
Luxembourg : lúsēnbǎo
Madrid : mǎdélǐ
Mali : mǎlǐ
Malaysia : mǎláixīyà
Malta : mǎ'ěrtā
Managua : mǎnàguā
Manila : mǎnílā
Mediterranean Sea : dìzhōnghǎi (*dì*, "land," *zhōng*, "middle," *hǎi*, "sea")
Mexico : mòxīgē
Mexico City : mòxīgēchéng (*chéng*, "city")
Mogadishu : mójiādíshā
Mongolia : měnggǔ
Monrovia : měngluówéiyà
Montevideo : měngdéwéidìyà
Morocco : móluògē
Moscow : mòsīkē

Mozambique : mòsānbígěi
Mumbai (Bombay) : mèngmǎi
Myanmar (Burma) : miǎndiàn
Nairobi : nèiluóbì
Nepal : níbó'ěr
Netherlands : hélán (representing
  Dutch *Holland*)
New York : niǔyuē
New Zealand : xīnxīlán (*xīn*,
  "new")
Niamey : níyàměi
Nicaragua : níjiālāguā
Nicosia : níkēxīyà
Niger : nírì'ěr
Nigeria : nírìlìyà
Norway : nuówēi
Oceania : dàyángzhōu (*dà*,
  "great," *yáng*, "ocean," *zhōu*,
  "continent")
Oslo : àosīlù
Ottawa : wòtàihuā
Pacific Ocean : tàipíngyáng (*tài*,
  "great," *píng*, "smooth," *yáng*,
  "ocean")
Pakistan : bājīsītǎn
Palestine : bālēsītǎn
Panama : bānámǎ
Panama Canal : bānámǎ yùnhé
  (*yùnhé*, "canal," from *yùn*,
  "transport," *hé*, "river")
Panama City : bānámǎchéng
  (*chéng*, "city")
Paraguay : bālāguī
Paris : bālí
Peru : mìlǔ
Philippines : fēilǜbīn
Phnom Penh : jīnbiān
Port-au-Prince : tàizǐgǎng (*tàizǐ*,
  "crown prince," from *tài*,
  "greatest," *zǐ*, "son," *gǎng*,
  "port")

Porto-Novo : bōduōnuòfú
Portugal : pútǎoyá
Prague : bùlāgé
Puerto Rico : bōduōlígè
Quito : jīduō
Rabat : lābātè
Reykjavík : léikèyǎwèikè
Riyadh : lìyǎdé
Rome : luōmǎ
Russia : éluósī
Rwanda : lúwàngdá
Sana : sànà
San José : shèngyuēsè
San Juan : shènghú'ān
San Salvador : shèngsà'ěrwǎduō
Santiago : shèngdìyàgē
Santo Domingo : shèng-
  duōmínggè
Saudi Arabia : shātè ālābó
Senegal : sàinèijiā'ěr
Seoul : hànchéng (*hán*, "Han
  [River]," *chéng*, "city")
Siberia : xībólìyà
Singapore : xīnjiāpō
Slovakia : sīluòfákè
Sofia : suǒfēiyà
Somalia : suǒmǎlǐ
South Africa : nánfēi (*nán*,
  "south," *fēi*, "Africa")
Spain : xībānyá (representing
  Spanish *España*)
Sri Lanka : sīlǐ lánkǎ
Stockholm : sīdégē'ěrmó
Sudan : sūdān
Suez Canal : sūyīshì yùnhé
  (*yùnhé*, "canal")
Sweden : ruìdiǎn
Switzerland : ruìshì (representing
  French *Suisse*)
Syria : xùlìyà
Taiwan : táiwān

Tanzania : tǎnsāngníyà
Tegucigalpa : tègǔxījiā'ěrbā
Tehran : déhēilán
Tel-Aviv : táilāwéifū
Thailand : tàiguó (*guó*, "land")
Tibet : xīzàng (*xī*, "west," *zàng*,
  "storehouse")
Tiranë : dìlānà
Togo : duōgē
Tokyo : dōngjīng (*dōng*, "east,"
  jīng, "capital," translating the
  Japanese)
Tunis : tūnísī
Tunisia : tūnísī
Turkey : tǔ'ěrqí
Uganda : wūgàndá
Ulan Bator: wūlánbātuō
United States of America :
  měiguó (*měi*, "America," *guó*,
  "country")
Ural Mountains : wūlā'ěr shān-
  mài (*shānmài*, "range," from
  shān, "mountain," *mài*,
  "veins")
Uruguay : wūlāguī
Valetta : wǎláitǎ
Venezuela : wěinèiruìlā
Vienna : wéiyěnà
Vientiane : wànxiàng
Vietnam : yuènán
Vladivostok : fúlādíwòsītuōkè
Volga : fú'ěrjiāhé
Warsaw : huáshā
Washington : huáshèngdùn
Wellington : huìlíngdùn
Yangon (Rangoon) : yǎngguāng
Yaoundé : yǎwēndé
Yemen : yěmén
Zambia : zànbǐyà

Appendix II:
Fictional Names of Places

A number of places, some well known, others less so, appear under alternate names in works of fiction. The following is a selection, based largely on the sources listed at the end.

Real names with identities and locations are given first, with their fictional names and the author in whose works they occur. Different names for one and the same place are numbered for distinction, as the three names for *Birmingham*, but where such names occur in the works of a single author, the author's name appears only once, following the enumeration, as the five different names for *Eastwood*, all in the writings of D.H. Lawrence.

Some fictional places, such as Mark Twain's Pikesville and Pokeville, cannot be precisely or even partially identified with a real place, so cannot justifiably be included below.

A cross-referenced listing of fictional names to real names follows the main listing.

Abbotsbury (village, southern England) : Abbotsea (Thomas Hardy)

Abingdon (town, southern England) : Babington (Dorothy Richardson)

Adelboden (town, southwestern Switzerland) : Oberland (Dorothy Richardson)

Affpuddle (village, southern England) : East Egdon (Thomas Hardy

Aldershot (town, southern England) : Quartershot (Thomas Hardy)

Alton (town, southern England): Galton (Compton Mackenzie)

Ampthill (town, east central England) : Cowfold (Mark Rutherford)

Anoka (town, Minnesota, United States) : Lake Wobegon (Garrison Keillor)

Arbroath (town, eastern Scotland) : (1) Fairport (Walter Scott); (2) Redlintie (J.M. Barrie)

Arbuthnott (village, eastern Scotland) : Kinraddie (Lewis Grassic Gibbon)

Ashbourne (town, central England) : Oakbourne (George Eliot)

Asheville (city, North Carolina, eastern United States) : (1) Altamont; (2) Libya Hill (Thomas Wolfe)

Astley (village, central England) : Knebley (George Eliot)

Auburn *see* [3]**Auburn** in main entries.

Baltimore (city, Maryland, northeastern United States) : Bridgepoint (Gertrude Stein)

Banbury (town, south central England) : Candleford (Flora Thompson)

Barnstaple (town, southwestern England) : Downstable (Thomas Hardy)

Basingstoke (town, southern England) : Stoke-Barehills (Thomas Hardy)

Bay Roberts (town, Newfoundland, eastern Canada) : Peterport (R.T.S. Lowell)

Beaminster (town, southern England) : Emminster (Thomas Hardy)

Bedford (town, east central England) : Eastthorpe (Mark Rutherford)

Benicia (city, California, southwestern United States) : San Spirito (Sinclair Lewis)

Berau (village, northwestern New Guinea) : Sambir (Joseph Conrad)

Bere Regis (village, southern England) : Kingsbere (Thomas Hardy)

Berkshire (county, south central England) : North Wessex (Thomas Hardy)

Birmingham (city, central England) : (1) Birchester (W.H. Mallock); (2) North Bromwich (Francis Brett Young); (3) Rummidge (David Lodge)

Birstall (village, northern England) : Briarfield (Charlotte Brontë)

Blandford Forum (town, southern England) : Shottsford Forum (Thomas Hardy)

Blundeston (village, eastern

England) : Blunderstone (Charles Dickens)

Boscastle (village, southwestern England) : Castle Boterel (Thomas Hardy)

Bournemouth (city, southern England) : Sandbourne (Thomas Hardy)

Bradenham (village, south central England) : Hurstley (Benjamin Disraeli)

Bradford (city, northern England) : (1) Bruddersford (J.B. Priestley); (2) Stradhoughton (Keith Waterhouse); (3) Warley (John Braine)

Bridlington (town, northeastern England) : Bretton (Charlotte Brontë)

Bridport (town, southern England) : Port-Bredy (Thomas Hardy)

Bromley (town, southeastern England) : (1) Boystone (V.S. Pritchett); (2) Bromstead (H.G. Wells)

Brussels (city, central Belgium) : Villette (Charlotte Brontë)

Bude (town, southwestern England) : Stratleigh (Thomas Hardy)

Bulkington (village, central England) : Raveloe (George Eliot)

Burford (town, south central England) : Wychford (Compton Mackenzie)

Burslem (town, central England) : Bursley (Arnold Bennett)

Cairo (town, Illinois, north central United States) : Eden (Charles Dickens)

Camelford (town, southwestern England) : Camelton (Thomas Hardy)

Canterbury (city, southeastern England) : (1) Cambry (Russell Hoban); (2) Tercanbury (W. Somerset Maugham)

Capri (island, southwestern Italy) : (1) Nepenthe (Norman Douglas); (2) Sirene (Compton Mackenzie)

Cerne Abbas (village, southern England) : Abbot's Cernel (Thomas Hardy)

Chapala (city, central Mexico) : Sayula (D.H. Lawrence)

Chapel Hill (town, North Car-

olina, eastern United States) : Pulpit Hill (Thomas Wolfe)

Charminster (village, southern England) : Charmley (Thomas Hardy)

Chatham (town, southeastern England) : (1) Dullborough; (2) Mudfog (Charles Dickens)

Chilvers Cotton (village, central England) : Shepperton (George Eliot)

Chipping Camden (town, south central England) : Northbridge (Angela Thirkell)

Church Stretton (town, west central England) : Shepwardine (Mary Webb)

Clovelly (village, southwestern England) : (1) Aberalva (Charles Kingsley); (2) Steepways (Charles Dickens)

Clun (village, west central England) : Dysgwlfas-on-the-Wild Moors (Mary Webb)

Combray *see* **Illiers-Combray** in main entries.

Corfe Castle (village, southern England) : Corvsgate Castle (Thomas Hardy)

Cornwall (county, southwestern England) : Nether Wessex (Thomas Hardy)

Cortland (city, New York, northeastern United States) : Lycurgus (Theodore Dreiser)

Cossall (village, central England) : Cossethay (D.H. Lawrence)

Cottisford (village, south central England) : Forflow (Flora Thompson)

Coventry (city, central England) : (1) Middlemarch (George Eliot); (2) Treby Magna (George Eliot)

Coyoacán (city, central Mexico) : Tlacolula (D.H. Lawrence)

Cranborne (village, southern England) : Chaseborough (Thomas Hardy)

Cullen (village, northeastern Scotland) : Portlossie (George Macdonald)

Cumnor (village, south central England) : Lumsdon (Thomas Hardy)

Darlington (town, northeastern England) : Stuffington (W.M. Thackeray)

Dartington (village, southwestern

England) : Darling (James Anthony Froude)

Dent (town, northwestern England) : Millfield (Ivy Compton-Burnett)

Derby (city, central England) : Stoniton (George Eliot)

Derbyshire (county, central England) : Loamshire (George Eliot)

Devon (county, southwestern England) : Lower Wessex (Thomas Hardy)

Dewsbury (town, northern England) : Cressley (Stan Barstow)

Diss (town, eastern England) : Deerbrook (Harriet Martineau)

Dorchester (town, southern England) : Casterbridge (Thomas Hardy)

Dorset (county, southern England) : South Wessex (Thomas Hardy)

Dovedale (valley, north central England) : Eagledale (George Eliot)

Dunbeath (village, northeastern Scotland) : Dunster (Neil Gunn)

Dunster (village, southwestern England) : Markton (Thomas Hardy)

Eastbourne (town, southeastern England) : Westbourne (Susan Hill)

East Chaldon (village, southern England) : Folly Down (T.F. Powys)

Eastwood (town, central England) : (1) Beldover; (2) Bestwood; (3) Eberwich; (4) Tevershall; (5) Woodhouse (D.H. Lawrence)

Eaton Socon (village, eastern England) : Eton Slocomb (Charles Dickens)

Ecclefechan (town, southern Scotland) : Entepfuhl (Thomas Carlyle)

Ellastone (village, central England) : Hayslope (George Eliot)

Ethiopia (country, northeastern Africa) : (1) Azania; (2) Ishmaelia (Evelyn Waugh)

Evershot (village, southern England) : Evershead (Thomas Hardy)

Exeter (city, southwestern England) : (1) Chatteris (W.M. Thackeray); (2) Exonbury (Thomas Hardy)

Faroe Islands (northern Atlantic) : Norlands (John Buchan)

Fawley (village, southern England) : Marygreen (Thomas Hardy)

Fleet (hamlet, southern England) : Moonfleet (J. Meade Falkner)

Fleetwood (town, northwestern England) : Sandyshore (Mary Louisa Molesworth)

Florida (village, Missouri, central United States) : Hawkeye (Mark Twain)

Folkestone (town, southeastern England) : (1) Fork Stoan (Russell Hoban); (2) Pavilionstone (Charles Dickens)

Fordington (suburb of Dorchester, southern England) : Durnover (Thomas Hardy)

Fortuneswell (town, southern England) : Street of Wells (Thomas Hardy)

Fowey (town, southwestern England) : Troy Town (Arthur Quiller-Couch)

Frampton (village, southern England) : Scrimpton (Thomas Hardy)

Fredonia (town, New York, northeastern United States) : Hadleyburg (Mark Twain)

Gainsborough (town, east central England) : St. Ogg's (George Eliot)

Glasgow (city, south central Scotland) : Unthank (Alasdair Gray)

Gloucester (city, western England) : Aldminster (Joanna Trollope)

Gloucestershire (county, western England) : Rutshire (Jilly Cooper)

Grayshott (village, southern England) : Heatherley (Flora Thompson)

Great Bookham (village, southeastern England) : Highbury (Jane Austen)

Great Clacton (town, eastern England) : Millfield (Ivy Compton-Burnett)

Greenville (city, South Carolina, southeastern United States) : Blackstone (Thomas Wolfe)

Halifax (town, northern England) : Annotsfield (Phyllis Bentley)

Hampshire (county, southern England) : (1) Barset or Barsetshire (Anthony Trollope); (2) Upper Wessex (Thomas Hardy)

Hanley (town, central England) : Hanbridge (Arnold Bennett)

Hannibal (city, Missouri, central United States) : (1) Dawson's Landing; (2) St. Petersburg (Mark Twain)

Harrisburg (city, Pennsylvania, northeastern United States) : Fort Penn (John O'Hara)

Harrogate (town, northern England) : Brawton (James Herriot)

Hartlepool (town, northeastern England) : Cockleton (W.M. Thackeray)

Hartshead (village, northern England) : Nunnelly (Charlotte Bronte)

Hastings (town, southeastern England) : Mugsborough (Robert Tressell)

Hathersage (village, north central England) : Morton (Charlotte Brontë)

Hazelbury Bryan (village, southern England) : Nuttlebury (Thomas Hardy)

Henley-on-Thames (town, south central England) : (1) Lower Binfield (George Orwell); (2) Thames Lockenden (Patrick Hamilton)

Herkimer County (New York, northeastern United States) : Cataraqui County (Theodore Dreiser)

Higham on the Hill (village, central England) : Tripplegate (George Eliot)

Holmbury St. Mary (village, southeastern England) : Summer Street (E.M. Forster)

Huddersfield (town, northern England) : Annotsfield (Phyllis Bentley)

Hugh Town (town, Isles of Scilly, southwestern England) : Giant's Town (Thomas Hardy)

Illiers (town, north central France) : Combray (Marcel Proust)

Irvine (town, west central Scotland) : Gudetown (John Galt)

Isle of Portland (peninsula, southern England) : Isle of Slingers (Thomas Hardy)

Isles of Scilly (southwestern England) : Isles of Lyonesse (Thomas Hardy)

Jamestown (town, Tennessee, east central United States) : Obedstown (Mark Twain)

Jersey City (city, New Jersey, northeastern United States) : Packer City (Francis T. Field)

Juniper Hill (hamlet, south central England) : Lark Rise (Flora Thompson)

Katha (town, north central Myanmar) : Kyautada (George Orwell)

Kelmscott (village, south central England) : Hurstcote (Theodore Watts-Dunton)

Kendal (town, northwestern England) : Pencaster (John Cunliffe)

Kilbarrack (suburb of Dublin, eastern Ireland) : Barrytown (Roddy Doyle)

Kirkby Lonsdale (town, northwestern England) : Lowton (Charlotte Brontë)

Kirriemuir (town, east central Scotland) : Thrums (J.M. Barrie)

Knoxville (city, Tennessee, east central United States) : Delisleville (Frances Hodgson Burnett)

Knutsford (town, northwestern England) : (1) Cranford; (2) Hollingford (Elizabeth Gaskell); (3) Mallingford (Mary Louisa Molesworth)

Lafayette County (Mississippi, southern United States) : Yoknapatawpha County (William Faulkner)

Langar (village, central England) : Battersby (Samuel Butler)

Laugharne (village, southern Wales) : Llareggub (Dylan Thomas)

Launceston (town, southwestern England) : St. Launce's (Thomas Hardy)

Leek (town, central England) : (1)

Axe; (2) Manefold (Arnold Bennett)

Letcombe Bassett (village, south central England) : Cresscombe (Thomas Hardy)

Little Easton (village, eastern England) : Matchings Easy (H.G. Wells)

Longton (town, central England) : Longshaw (Arnold Bennett)

Lykens (town, Pennsylvania, northeastern United States) : Lyons (John O'Hara)

Lyme Regis (town, southern England) : Buddlecombe (Henry Handel Richardson)

Lytchett Minster (village, southern England) : Flychett (Thomas Hardy)

Maiden Newton (village, southern England) : Chalk Newton (Thomas Hardy)

Maidstone (town, southeastern England) : Muggleton (Charles Dickens)

Manchester (city, north central England) : (1) Doomington (Louis Golding); (2) Drumble; (3) Milton (Elizabeth Gaskell)

Marion (town, Massachusetts, northeastern United States) : Marmion (Henry James)

Marion City (village, Missouri, central United States) : Goshen (Mark Twain)

Marlborough (town, southern England) : Marlbury (Thomas Hardy)

Marnhull (village, southern England) : Marlott (Thomas Hardy)

Martin (village, southern England) : Winterbourne Bishop (W.H. Hudson)

Melbury Osmond (village, southern England) : Great Hintock (Thomas Hardy)

Midhurst (town, southern England) : Wimblehurst (H.G. Wells)

Milborne Port (town, southern England) : Millpool (Thomas Hardy)

Milton Abbas (village, southern England) : Middleton Abbey (Thomas Hardy)

Minneapolis (city, Minnesota, northern United States) : Zenith (Sinclair Lewis)

Montacute (village, southwestern England) : Nevilton (John Cowper Powys)

Moorgreen Reservoir (central England) : (1) Nethermere; (2) Willey Water (D.H. Lawrence)

Napoleon (town, Arkansas, south central United States) : Bricksville (Mark Twain)

Neuwied (city, western Germany) : Sarkeld (George Meredith)

New Brunswick (city, New Jersey, northeastern United States) : New Boynton (Francis T. Field)

Newbury (town, southern England) : Kennetbridge (Thomas Hardy)

Newcastle-under-Lyme (town, central England) : Oldcastle (Arnold Bennett)

Newchurch (village, northern England) : Goldshaw (Harrison Ainsworth)

Norbury (village, central England) : Norburne (George Eliot)

Nottingham (city, central England) : (1) Knarborough (D.H. Lawrence); (2) Nottwich (Grahame Greene)

Nuneaton (town, central England) : Milby (George Eliot)

Oban (town, western Scotland) : Port (Alan Warner)

Ochiltree (village, western Scotland) : Barbie (George Douglas Brown)

Ottery St. Mary (town, southwestern England) : Clavering St. Mary (W.M. Thackeray)

Owermoigne (village, southern England) : Nether Moynton (Thomas Hardy)

[1]Oxford (city, south central England) : Christminster (Thomas Hardy)

[2]Oxford (city, Mississippi, southern United States) : Jefferson (William Faulkner)

Palmyra (town, Missouri, central United States) : Constantinople (Mark Twain)

Peebles (town, southern Scotland) : Priorsford (O. Douglas)

Pentridge (village, southern England) : Trantridge (Thomas Hardy)

Penzance (town, southwestern England) : Pen-Zephyr (Thomas Hardy)

Perth Amboy (city, New Jersey, northeastern United States) : Port Alby (Francis T. Field)

Piddletrenthide (village, southern England) : Longpuddle (Thomas Hardy)

Poole (town, southern England) : Havenpool (Thomas Hardy)

Port Jervis (town, New York, northeastern United States) : Whilomville (Stephen Crane)

Portofino (village, northwestern Italy) : Castagneto ("Elizabeth" [Elizabeth von Arnim])

[1]Portsmouth (city, southern England) : Lymport (George Meredith)

[2]Portsmouth (city, New Hampshire, northeastern United States) : Rivermouth (T.B. Aldrich)

Pottsville (city, Pennsylvania, northeastern United States) : (1) Gibbsville (John O'Hara); (2) Vermissa (Arthur Conan Doyle)

[1]Preston (town, northwestern England) : Coketown (Charles Dickens)

[2]Preston (village, southern England) : Creston (Thomas Hardy)

Puddletown (village, southern England) : Weatherbury (Thomas Hardy)

Ramsgate (town, southeastern England) : Ram (Russell Hoban)

Reading (town, south central England) : (1) Aldbrickham (Thomas Hardy); (2) Belford Regis (Mary Russell Mitford)

Redruth (town, southwestern England) : Redrutin (Thomas Hardy)

Ringwood (town, southern England) : Oozewood (Thomas Hardy)

Robin Hood's Bay (village, northeastern England) : Bramblewick (Leo Walmsley)

Rocester (village, central England) : Rosseter (George Eliot)

Rochester (city, southeastern England) : (1) Cloisterham; (2) Dullborough (Charles Dickens)

Roston (village, central England) : Broxton (George Eliot)

Rye (town, southeastern England) : Tilling (E.F. Benson)

St. Ives (town, southwestern England) : Porthkerris (Rosamund Pilcher)

St. Juliot (village, southwestern England) : Endelstow (Thomas Hardy)

Salisbury (city, southern England) : (1) Barchester (Anthony Trollope); (2) Melchester (Thomas Hardy)

Salisbury Plain (plateau, southern England) : Great Plain (Thomas Hardy)

Sandaig (hamlet, western Scotland) : Camusfearna (Gavin Maxwell)

Sandgate (village, southeastern England) : Bonnycliff (Dorothy Richardson)

Sandwich (town, southeastern England) : Sunwich Port (W.W. Jacobs)

Sauk Centre (town, Minnesota, northern United States) : (1) Gopher Prairie; (2) Joralemon (Sinclair Lewis)

Saverton (town, Missouri, central United States) : Hookerville (Mark Twain)

Shaftesbury (town, southwestern England) : Shaston (Thomas Hardy)

Sheffield (city, northern England) : Hillsborough (Charles Reade)

Sherborne (town, southwestern England) : (1) Ramsgard (John Cowper Powys); (2) Sherton Abbas (Thomas Hardy)

Shifnal (town, west central England) : Market Blandings (P.G. Wodehouse)

Shrewsbury (town, west central England) : Silverton (Mary Webb)

Shropham (village, eastern England) : Dulditch (Mary Mann)

Sidmouth (town, southwestern England) : (1) Baymouth (W.M. Thackeray); (2) Sanditon (Jane Austen)

Silverdale (village, northwestern England) : Abermouth (Elizabeth Gaskell)

Silverton (village, southwestern England) : Silverthorn (Thomas Hardy)

Sint-Truiden (town, east central Belgium) : Longres (Aldous Huxley)

Sligo (town, northwestern Ireland) : Ballah (W.B. Yeats)

Somerset (county, southwestern England) : Outer Wessex (Thomas Hardy)

Southampton (city, southern England) : Bevishampton (George Meredith)

South Harting (village, southern England) : Siddermorton (H.G. Wells)

Southsea (town, southern England) : Solentsea (Thomas Hardy)

Southwold (town, eastern England) : Hardborough (Penelope Fitzgerald)

Staffordshire (county, central England) : Stonyshire (George Eliot)

Stinsford (village, southern England) : (1) Mellstock; (2) Tollamore (Thomas Hardy)

Stockingford (village, central England) : (1) Paddiford; (2) Whittlecombe (George Eliot)

Stoke-on-Trent (town, central England) : Knype (Arnold Bennett)

Stromness (town, northern Scotland) : Hamnavoe (George Mackay Brown)

Sturminster Newton (town, southern England) : Stourcastle (Thomas Hardy)

Sudbury (town, eastern England) : Eatanswill (Charles Dickens)

Swanage (town, southern England) : Knollsea (Thomas Hardy)

Syston (village, east central England) : Willingham (Walter Scott)

Tarbert (village, western Scotland) : Brieston (John MacDougall Hay)

Tarrant Hinton (village, southern England) : Trantridge (Thomas Hardy)

Taunton (town, southwestern England) : Toneborough (Thomas Hardy)

Tewkesbury (town, western England) : Nortonbury (Dinah Craik)

Theale (village, south central England) : Gaymead (Thomas Hardy)

Thirsk (town, northern England) : Darrowby (James Herriot)

Tincleton (village, southern England) : Stickleford (Thomas Hardy)

Tiverton (town, southwestern England) : Tivworthy (Thomas Hardy)

Tolpuddle (village, southern England) : Tolchurch (Thomas Hardy)

Tonbridge (town, southeastern England) : Sawston (E.M. Forster)

Torquay (town, southwestern England) : Tor-upon-Sea (Thomas Hardy)

Trent (river, central England) : Floss (George Eliot)

Troy Town (hamlet, southern England) : Roy-Town (Thomas Hardy)

Truro (town, southwestern England) : (1) Polchester (Hugh Walpole); (2) Trufal (Thomas Hardy)

[1]Tunstall (town, central England) : Turnhill (Arnold Bennett)

[2]Tunstall (village, northwestern England) : Brocklebridge (Charlotte Brontë)

Turville Heath (village, southeastern England) : Rapstone (John Mortimer)

Underwood (village, central England) : Nuttall (D.H. Lawrence)

Valencia (city, northern Venezuela) : Sulaco (Joseph Conrad)

Wakefield (city, northern England) : (1) Dunfield (George Gissing); (2) Highfield (David Storey); (3) Mirefields (Morley Roberts)

Wantage (town, south central England) : Alfredston (Thomas Hardy)

Wareham (town, southern England) : Anglebury (Thomas Hardy)

Weimar (city, southern Germany) : (1) Kalbsbraten; (2) Pumpernickel (W.M. Thackeray)

Wells (town, southwestern England) : Fountall (Thomas Hardy)

Weston under Lizard (village, west central England) : Blandings Parva (P.G. Wodehouse)

West Stafford (village, southern England) : Lew Everard (Thomas Hardy)

Weyhill (village, southern England) : Weydon Priors (Thomas Hardy)

Weymouth (town, southern England) : (1) Budmouth Regis; (2) Melport (Thomas Hardy)

Whitby (town, northeastern England) : (1) Burnharbour (Leo Walmsley); (2) Monkshaven (Elizabeth Gaskell)

Whitstable (town, southeastern England) : Blackstable (W. Somerset Maugham)

Wiesbaden (city, western Germany) : Roulettenburg (Fyodor Dostoevsky)

Willenhall (town, central England) : Wodgate (Benjamin Disraeli)

Wiltshire (county, southern England) : (1) Barset or Barsetshire (Anthony Trollope); (2) Mid Wessex (Thomas Hardy)

Wimborne Minster (town, southern England) : Warborne (Thomas Hardy)

Winchester (city, southern England) : (1) Barchester (Anthony Trollope); (2) Hillstone (Florence Marryat); (3) Thurchester (Charles Palliser); (4) Wintoncester (Thomas Hardy)

Wirksworth (town, central England) : Snowfield (George Eliot)

Wool (village, southern England) : Wellbridge (Thomas Hardy)

Wychwood Forest (south central England) : Witch Wood (John Buchan)

Yeovil (town, south western England) : Ivel (Thomas Hardy)

Zell am Zee (town, west central Austria) : Kaprun (D.H. Lawrence)

Cross References — Fictional Names to Real Names

Abbot's Cernel : Cerne Abbas
Abbotsea : Abbotsbury
Aberalva : Clovelly
Abermouth : Silverdale
Aldbrickham : Reading
Aldminster : Gloucester
Alfredston : Wantage
Altamont : Asheville
Anglebury : Wareham
Annotsfield : (1) Halifax; (2) Huddersfield
Axe : Leek
Azania : Ethiopia
Babington : Abingdon
Ballah : Sligo
Barbie : Ochiltree
Barchester : (1) Salisbury; (2) Winchester
Barrytown : Kilbarrack
Barset : (1) Hampshire; (2) Wiltshire
Barsetshire : (1) Hampshire; (2) Wiltshire
Battersby : Langar
Baymouth : Sidmouth
Beldover : Eastwood
Belford Regis : Reading
Bestwood : Eastwood
Bevishampton : Southampton
Birchester : Birmingham
Blackstable : Whitstable
Blackstone : Greenville
Blandings Parva : Weston under Lizard
Blunderstone : Blundeston
Bonnycliff : Sandgate
Boystone : Bromley
Bramblewick : Robin Hood's Bay
Brawton : Harrogate
Bretton : Bridlington
Briarfield : Birstall
Bricksville : Napoleon
Bridgepoint : Baltimore
Brieston : Tarbert
Brocklebridge : [2]Tunstall
Bromstead : Bromley
Broxton : Roston
Bruddersford : Bradford
Buddlecombe : Lyme Regis
Budmouth Regis : Weymouth
Burnharbour : Whitby
Bursley : Burslem
Cambry : Canterbury
Camelton : Camelford

Camusfearna : Sandaig
Candleford : Banbury
Castagneto : Portofino
Casterbridge : Dorchester
Castle Boterel : Boscastle
Cataraqui County : Herkimer County
Chalk Newton : Maiden Newton
Charmley : Charminster
Chaseborough : Cranborne
Chatteris : Exeter
Christminster : [1]Oxford
Clavering St. Mary : Ottery St. Mary
Cloisterham : Rochester
Cockleton : Hartlepool
Coketown : [1]Preston
Combray : Illiers
Constantinople : Palmyra
Corvsgate Castle : Corfe Castle
Cossethay : Cossall
Cowfold : Ampthill
Cranford : Knutsford
Cresscombe : Letcombe Bassett
Cressley : Dewsbury
Creston : [2]Preston
Darling : Dartington
Darrowby : Thirsk
Dawson's Landing: Hannibal
Deerbrook : Diss
Delisleville : Knoxville
Doomington : Manchester
Downstable : Barnstaple
Drumble : Manchester
Dulditch : Shropham
Dullborough : Chatham
Dunfield : Wakefield
Dunster : Dunbeath
Durnover : Fordington
Dysgwlfas-on-the-Wild-Moors : Clun
Eagledale : Dovedale
East Egdon : Affpuddle
Eastthorpe : Bedford
Eatanswill : Sudbury
Eberwich : Eastwood
Eden : Cairo
Emminster : Beaminster
Endelstow : St. Juliot
Entepfuhl : Ecclefechan
Eton Slocomb : Eaton Socon
Evershead : Evershot
Exonbury : Exeter
Fairport : Arbroath
Floss : Trent
Flychett : Lytchett Minster
Folly Down : East Chaldon
Fordlow : Cottisford
Fork Stoan : Folkestone

Fort Penn : Harrisburg
Fountall : Wells
Fredonia : Hadleyburg
Galton : Alton
Gaymead : Theale
Giant's Town : Hugh Town
Gibbsville : Pottsville
Goldshaw : Newchurch
Gopher Prairie : Sauk Centre
Goshen : Marion City
Great Hintock : Melbury
    Osmond
Great Plain : Salisbury Plain
Gudetown : Irvine
Hamnavoe : Stromness
Hanbridge : Hanley
Hardborough : Southwold
Havenpool : Poole
Hawkeye : Florida
Hayslope : Ellastone
Heatherley : Grayshott
Highbury : Great Bookham
Highfield : Wakefield
Hillsborough : Sheffield
Hillstone : Winchester
Hollingford : Knutsford
Hookerville : Saverton
Hutscote : Kelmscott
Hurstley : Bradenham
Ishmaelia : Ethiopia
Isle of Slingers : Isle of Portland
Isles of Lyonesse : Isles of Scilly
Ivel : Yeovil
Jefferson : [2]Oxford
Joralemon : Sauk Centre
Kalbsbraten : Weimar
Kaprun : Zell am See
Kennetbridge : Newbury
Kingsbere : Bere Regis
King's Hintock : Melbury
    Osmond
Knarborough : Nottingham
Knebley : Astley
Knollsea : Swanage
Knype : Stoke-on-Trent
Kyautada : Katha
Lake Wobegon : Anoka
Lark Rise : Juniper Hill
Lew Everard : West Stafford
Libya Hill : Asheville
Llareggub : Laugharne
Loamshire : Derbyshire
Longpuddle : Piddletrenthide
Longres : Sint-Truiden
Longshaw : Longton
Lower Binfield : Henley-on-
    Thames
Lower Wessex : Devon
Lowton : Kirkby Lonsdale

Lumsdon : Cumnor
Lycurgus : Cortland
Lymport : [1]Portsmouth
Lyons : Lykens
Mallingford : Knutsford
Manefold : Leek
Market Blandings : Shifnal
Markton : Dunster
Marlbury : Marlborough
Marlott : Marnhull
Marmion : Marion
Marygreen : Fawley
Matchings Easy : Little Easton
Melbury Osmond : Great Hin-
    tock
Melchester : Salisbury
Mellstock : Stinsford
Melport : Weymouth
Middlemarch : Coventry
Middleton Abbey : Milton Abbas
Mid Wessex : Wiltshire
Milby : Nuneaton
Millfield : (1) Dent; (2) Great
    Clacton
Millpool : Milborne Port
Milton : Manchester
Mirefields : Wakefield
Monkshaven : Whitby
Moonfleet : Fleet
Morton : Hathersage
Mudfog : Chatham
Muggleton : Maidstone
Mugsborough : Hastings
Nepenthe : Capri
Nethermere : Moorgreen Reser-
    voir
Nether Moynton : Owermoigne
Nether Wessex : Cornwall
Nevilton : Montacute
New Boynton : New Brunswick
Norburne : Norbury
Norlands : Faroe Islands
Northbridge : Chipping Camp-
    den
North Bromwich : Birmingham
North Wessex : Berkshire
Nortonbury : Tewkesbury
Nottwich : Nottingham
Nunnelly : Hartshead
Nuttall : Underwood
Nuttlebury : Hazelbury Bryan
Oakbourne : Ashbourne
Obedstown : Jamestown
Oberland : Adelboden
Oozewood : Ringwood
Outer Wessex : Somerset
Packer City : Jersey City
Paddiford : Stockingford
Pavilionstone : Folkestone

Pencaster : Kendal
Pen-Zephyr : Penzance
Peterport : Bay Roberts
Polchester : Truro
Port : Oban
Port Alby : Perth Amboy
Port-Bredy : Bridport
Porth Kerris : St. Ives
Portlossie : Cullen
Priorsford : Peebles
Pulpit Hill : Chapel Hill
Pumpernickel : Weimar
Quartershot : Aldershot
Ram : Ramsgate
Ramsgard : Sherborne
Rapstone : Turville Heath
Raveloe : Bulkington
Redlintie : Arbroath
Redrutin : Redruth
Rivermouth : [2]Portsmouth
Roulettenburg : Wiesbaden
Roy-Town : Troy Town
Rummidge : Birmingham
Rutshire : Gloucestershire
St. Launce's : Launceston
St. Ogg's : Gainsborough
St. Petersburg : Hannibal
Sambir : Berau
Sanditon : Sidmouth
San Spirito : Benicia
Sandbourne : Bournemouth
Sandyshore : Fleetwood
Sarkeld : Neuwied
Sawston : Tonbridge
Sayula : Chapala
Scrimpton : Frampton
Shaston : Shaftesbury
Shepperton : Chilvers Cotton
Shepwardine : Church Stretton
Sherton Abbas : Sherborne
Shottsford Forum : Blandford
    Forum
Siddermorton : South Harting
Silverthorn : Silverton
Silverton : Shrewsbury
Sirene : Capri
Snowfield : Wirksworth
Solentsea : Southsea
South Wessex : Dorset
Steepways : Clovelly
Stickleford : Tincleton
Stoke-Barehills : Basingstoke
Stoniton : Derby
Stonyshire : Staffordshire
Stourcastle : Sturminster Newton
Stradhoughton : Bradford
Stratleigh : Bude
Street of Wells : Fortuneswell
Stuffington : Darlington

Sulaco : Valencia
Summer Street : Holmbury St. Mary
Sunwich Port : Sandwich
Tercanbury : Canterbury
Tevershall : Eastwood
Thames Lockenden : Henley-on-Thames
Thrums : Kirriemuir
Thurchester : Winchester
Tilling : Rye
Tivworthy : Tiverton
Tlacolula : Coyoacán
Tolchurch : Tolpuddle
Tollamore : Stinsford
Toneborough : Taunton
Tor-upon-Sea : Torquay
Trantridge : Pentridge
Trantridge : Tarrant Hinton
Treby Magna : Coventry
Tripplegate : Higham on the Hill
Troy Town : Fowey
Trufal : Truro
Turnhill : ᶦTunstall
Unthank : Glasgow
Upper Wessex : Hampshire
Vermissa : Pottsville
Villette : Brussels
Warborne : Wimborne Minster
Warley : Bradford
Weatherbury : Puddletown
Wellbridge : Wool
Westbourne : Eastbourne
Weydon Priors : Weyhill
Whilomville : Port Jervis
Whittlecombe : Stockingford

Willey Water : Moorgreen Reservoir
Willingham : Syston
Wimblehurst : Midhurst
Winterbourne Bishop : Martin
Wintoncester : Winchester
Witch Wood : Wychwood Forest
Wodgate : Willenhall
Woodhouse : Eastwood
Wychford : Burford
Yoknapatawpha : Lafayette
Zenith : Minneapolis

Sources

Bentley, Nicolas, Michael Slater, and Nina Burgis. *The Dickens Index*. Oxford: Oxford University Press, 1988.

Bradbury, Malcolm, gen. ed. *The Atlas of Literature*. London: De Agostini Editions, 1996.

Cowan, Robert. *The Dictionary of Urbanism*. Tisbury: Streetwise Press, 2005.

Hahn, Daniel, and Nicholas Robins. *The Oxford Guide to Literary Britain and Ireland*. 3d ed. Oxford: Oxford University Press, 2008.

Hardwick, Michael. *A Literary Atlas and Gazetteer of the British Isles*. Newton Abbot: David & Charles, 1973.

_____, and Mollie Hardwick.

The Charles Dickens Encyclopedia. Ware: Wordsworth Editions, 1992 [1973].

Harper, Charles G. *The Hardy Country*. 3d ed. London: A. & C. Black, 1925.

Hayward, Arthur L. *The Dickens Encyclopædia*. London: George Routledge, 1924.

Ousby, Ian. *Blue Guide Literary Britain*. 2d ed. London: A. & C. Black, 1990.

Philip, Alex J., and Laurence Gadd. *A Dickens Dictionary*. London: Simpkin Marshall, 1928.

Pinion, F.B. *A Thomas Hardy Dictionary*. Basingstoke: Macmillan, 1989.

Rasmussen, R. Kent. *Mark Twain A to Z*. New York: Facts on File, 1955.

Rintoul, M.C. *Dictionary of Real People and Places in Fiction*. London: Routledge, 1993.

Room, Adrian. "The Case for Casterbridge: Thomas Hardy as Placename Creator," in *Names* (Journal of the American Name Society), Vol. 37, No. 1, March 1989, pp. 4–5.

Varlow, Sally. *A Reader's Guide to Writers' Britain*. London: Prion, 1996.

Select Bibliography

The titles below were consulted during the compilation of the present work. Foreign titles are supplied with an English translation, and some titles have an added descriptive note.

Appleton, Richard and Barbara. *The Cambridge Dictionary of Australian Places.* Cambridge: Cambridge University Press, 1992.

Aurousseau, M. *The Rendering of Geographical Names.* London: Hutchinson University Library, 1957. ["Whether we like it or not, geographical names have to be considered from two opposed positions, that of our own language, and that of the rest of the world."]

Austin, Tim, comp. *The Times Style and Usage Guide.* London: Times Books, 2003.

Bahn, Paul (ed.). *The Penguin Archaeology Guide.* London: Penguin Books, 2001.

Barnes, Victor S., gen. ed. *The Modern Encyclopædia of Australia and New Zealand.* Sydney: Horwitz-Grahame, 1964.

Batowski, Henryk. *Słownik Nazw Miejscowych Europy Środkowej i Wschodniej XIX i XX Wieku* (Placename dictionary of Central and Eastern Europe in the 19th and 20th centuries). Warsaw: Państwowe Wydawnictwo Naukowe, 1964. [A slim, 86-page volume listing renamings in Albania, Belorussia, Bulgaria, Czechoslovakia, Estonia, Finland, Greece, Hungary, Latvia, Lithuania, Moldavia, Poland, Romania, Russia in Europe (as part of the former RSFSR), Turkey in Europe, Ukraine, Yugoslavia, and the border regions of Austria, Germany, and Italy, as well as the island of Cyprus.]

Bursa, G.R.F. "Creating a political landscape: The art of geographical name changing in Bulgaria," in *Diplomacy & Statecraft*, Vol. 5, No. 3, November 1994, pp. 534–568.

_____. "Political changes of names of Soviet towns," in *Slavonic and East European Review*, No. 63, 1985, pp. 161–193.

Butler, Audrey. *Collins Dictionary of Dates.* 8th ed. Glasgow: HarperCollins, 1996.

Campbell, Harry. *Whatever Happened to Tanganyika? The Place Names That History Left Behind.* London: Portico, 2007.

Cherpillot, André. *Dictionnaire étymologique des noms géographiques* (Etymological dictionary of geographical names). Paris: Masson, 1991.

Coates, Richard, and Andrew Breeze. *Celtic Voices, English Places.* Stamford: Shaun Tyas, 2000.

Cohen, Saul B, ed. *The Columbia Gazetteer of the World.* 3 vols. New York, NY: Columbia University Press, 1998.

Collins Latin Dictionary. Glasgow: HarperCollins, 1997. [A bilingual dictionary with a "Roman life and culture" section listing over 400 ancient and medieval Latin placenames with their modern equivalents.]

Davies, John, Nigel Jenkins, Menna Baines, and Peredur I. Lynch. *The Welsh Academy Encyclopaedia of Wales.* Cardiff: University of Wales Press, 2008.

Delamarre, Xavier. *Dictionnaire de la langue gauloise* (Dictionary of the Gaulish language). 2d ed. Paris: Editions Errance, 2003. [Contains an index of Gallo-Roman placenames in both France and elsewhere in Europe.]

Downing, David. *An Atlas of Territorial and Border Disputes.* London: New English Library, 1980.

Everett-Heath, John. *The Concise Dictionary of World Place-Names.* Oxford: Oxford University Press, 2005.

Freedman, David Noel, ed.-in-chief. *Eerdmans Dictionary of the Bible.* Grand Rapids, MI: Wm. B Eerdmans, 2000.

Gazetteer of Ireland. Dublin: The Placenames Branch of the Ordnance Survey, 1989.

Gorskaya, M.V. *English-Russian and Russian-English Geographical Dictionary.* Moscow: Russky Yazyk, 1994. [Valuable not only for its Russian equivalents of English placenames but also as a worldwide gazetteer of the English names themselves.]

Graesse, Johann Gustav Theodor. *Orbis latinus: oder Verzeichnis der wichtigsten lateinischen Orts- und Ländernamen* (The Latin world, or Register of the most important Latin names of places and countries). Revised by Friedrich Benedict. Berlin: Transpress VEB Verlag für Verkehrswesen, 1980. [Reprint of 2d ed., 1909]

Groom, Nigel. *A Dictionary of Arabic Topography and Placenames.* Beirut: Librairie du Liban/London: Longman, 1983.

Hamilton, William B. *The Macmillan Book of Canadian Place Names.* Toronto: Macmillan, 1978.

Hazlitt, William. *The Classical Gazetteer.* London: Studio Editions, 1995. [Reprint of 1st ed., 1851]

Hobson, Archie, ed. *The Cambridge Gazetteer of the United States and Canada.* Cambridge: Cambridge University Press, 1995.

Hogg, Ian V. *The Hutchinson Dictionary of Battles.* Oxford: Helicon, 1995.

Hornblower, Simon, and Antony Spawforth, eds. *The Oxford Classical Dictionary.* 3d ed. Oxford: Oxford University Press, 1996.

Jones, Barri, and David Mattingly. *An Atlas of Roman Britain.* Oxford: Blackwell, 1990.

Kalesnik, S.V., ed.-in-chief. *Entsiklopedicheskiy slovar' geograficheskikh nazvaniy* (Encyclopedic dictionary of placenames). Moscow: Sovetskaya Entsiklopediya, 1973. [Worldwide coverage, and good for the many renamings in the former Soviet Union.]

Kirchherr, Eugene C. *Place Names of Africa 1935–1986: A Political Gazetteer.* Metuchen, NJ: Scarecrow Press, 1987.

Komkov, A.M. ed.-in-chief. *Slovar' geograficheskikh nazvaniy zarubezhnykh stran* (Dictionary of foreign placenames). 3d ed. Moscow: Nedra, 1986. [A gazetteer of world placeames outside the former Soviet Union.]

_____, et al. *Nazvaniya SSSR, soyuznykh respublik i zarubezhnykh stran na 20 yazykakh* (Names of the USSR, union republics and foreign countries in 20 languages). Moscow: VINITI, 1974.

Mason, Oliver, comp. *Bartholomew Gazetteer of Places in Britain.* 2d ed. Edinburgh: John Bartholomew, 1986.

Matthews, C.M. *Place-Names of the English-Speaking World.* London: Weidenfeld and Nicolson, 1972.

Merriam-Webster's New Geographical Dictionary. 3d ed. Springfield, MA: Merriam-Webster, 1997.

Nelson, Derek. *Off the Map: The Curious History of Place-Names.* New York: Kodansha America, 1997. [Pertinent for the present book is Chapter 8: "Multiple Names Mean Confusion and Contention," pp. 137–154.]

The New Encyclopædia Britannica. 30 vols. 15th ed. Chicago, IL: Encyclopædia Britannica, 2002.

Owen, Hywel Wyn, and Richard Morgan. *Dictionary of the Place-Names of Wales.* Llandysul: Gomer, 2007.

Peterson, Charles B. "The Nature of Soviet Place-Names." *Names* (Journal of the American Name Society). Vol. 25, No. 1, March 1977, pp. 15–24.

Raper, Peter E. *New Dictionary of South African Place Names.* Johannesburg: Jonathan Ball, 2004.

Reed, A.W. *Place Names of Australia.* Sydney: Reed Books, 1973. [Includes lists of Aboriginal names and of renamed places.]

_____. *The Story of New Zealand Place Names.* Wellington: A.H & A.W. Reed, 1952.

Ritter, R.M. ed. and comp. *The Oxford Dictionary for Writers and Editors.* 2d ed. Oxford: Oxford University Press, 2000.

Rivet, A.L.F., and Colin Smith. *The Place-Names of Roman Britain.* London: Batsford, 1979.

Room, Adrian. *African Placenames.* 2d ed. Jefferson, NC: McFarland, 2008.

_____. *A Dictionary of Irish Place-Names.* Rev. ed. Belfast: Appletree Press, 1994.

_____. *Dictionary of Translated Names and Titles.* London: Routledge & Kegan Paul, 1986.

_____. *Nicknames of Places.* Jefferson, NC: McFarland, 2006.

_____, comp. *Place-Name Changes 1900–1991.* Metuchen, NJ: Scarecrow Press, 1993.

_____. *Placenames of France.* Jefferson, NC: McFarland, 2004.

_____. *Placenames of Russia and the Former Soviet Union.* Jefferson, NC: McFarland, 1996.

_____. *Placenames of the World.* Jefferson, NC. McFarland, 2005.

Rosenthal, Eric. *Encyclopaedia of Southern Africa.* 7th ed. Cape Town: Juta, 1978.

Share, Bernard. *Naming Names.* Dublin: Gill & Macmillan, 2001. [A dictionary of Irish proper names of all types, with an Introduction that includes a discussion of placenames, past and present, and the anglicization of indigenous names.]

Sivin, Nathan, Frances Wood, Penny Brooke, and Colin Ronan (eds.). *The Contemporary Atlas of China.* London: Weidenfeld & Nicolson, 1988.

Slovar' geograficheskikh nazvaniy SSSR (Dictionary of placenames of the USSR). 2d ed. Moscow: Nedra, 1983.

Spaull, Hebe. *New Place Names of the World.* London: Ward Lock, 1970. [A slim volume marred by many misprints but still of value if consulted with care.]

Stewart, George R. *American Place-Names.* New York: Oxford University Press, 1970. [Coverage is confined to the continental United States and accordingly omits Hawaii.]

_____. *Names on the Globe.* New York: Oxford University Press, 1975. [A worldwide survey of the naming of places, although with little on alternate or changed placenames.]

_____. *Names on the Land: A Historical Account of Place-Naming in the United States.* Boston, MA: Houghton Mifflin, 1967

Stewart, John. *African States and Rulers: An Encyclopedia of Native, Colonial and Independent States and Rulers Past and Present.* 3d ed. Jefferson, NC: McFarland, 2006.

Stielers Handatlas. 10th ed. Gotha: Justus Perthes, 1920–25. [A major German atlas with a supplementary index, pp. 317–336, listing places renamed after World War I in Finland, the Baltic States, Poland, Czechoslovakia, Romania, Hungary, Yugoslavia, South Tirol (now Alto Adige, Italy), Alsace-Lorraine (now in France), Eupen-Malmédy (now in Belgium), and Nord Slesvig (now South Jutland, Denmark).]

Sturmfels, Wilhelm, and Heinz Bischof. *Unsere Ortsnamen* (Our placenames). 3d ed. Bonn: Dümmler, 1961. [A dictionary of world placename origins, with due recognition of alternate and former names in European countries.]

The Times Comprehensive Atlas of the World. 12th ed. London: Times Books, 2007. [The index to this atlas gives alternate names of various types, including placenames in use within the previous 50 years, with an emphasis on particularly prominent earlier names.]

Treharne. R.F., and Harold Fullard. *Muir's Historical Atlas: Ancient and Classical.* 6th ed. London: George Philip, 1963.

_____, and _____. *Muir's Historical Atlas: Medieval and Modern.* 11th ed. London: George Philip, 1969. [This title and that above were published in a single volume by Book Club Associates, London, in 1973.]

Warrington, John. *Everyman's Classical Dictionary.* 3d ed. London: J.M. Dent, 1969.

Where's Where: A Descriptive Gazetteer. London: Eyre Methuen, 1974. [An anonymous so-called "*Who's Who* of places" that includes former and fictional placenames.]